CRITICAL AND EXEGETICAL HANDBOOK
TO THE EPISTLES OF ST. PAUL
TO TIMOTHY AND TITUS

CRITICAL AND EXEGETICAL
HANDBOOK

TO THE

EPISTLES OF ST. PAUL

TO

TIMOTHY AND TITUS.

BY

JOH. ED. HUTHER, Th.D.,

PASTOR AT WITTENFORDEN BEI SCHWERIN

TRANSLATED FROM THE FOURTH IMPROVED AND ENLARGED
EDITION OF THE GERMAN BY

DAVID HUNTER, B.D.,

LATE SCHOLAR IN HEBREW AND BIBLICAL CRITICISM IN THE UNIVERSITY OF GLASGOW

WIPF & STOCK · Eugene, Oregon

Wipf and Stock Publishers
199 W 8th Ave, Suite 3
Eugene, OR 97401

Critical and Exegetical Handbook to the Epistles of St. Paul to Timothy and Titus
By Huther, Johann Eduard and Hunter, David
Softcover ISBN-13: 978-1-6667-0430-3
Hardcover ISBN-13: 978-1-6667-0431-0
eBook ISBN-13: 978-1-6667-0432-7
Publication date 3/3/2021
Previously published by T. & T. Clark, 1881

This edition is a scanned facsimile of the original edition published in 1881.

AUTHOR'S PREFACE.

IN publishing the fourth edition of my Commentary on the Pastoral Epistles, I recall with painful feeling the man who began and conducted the work in which I count it a special honour to take part. When the third edition of my Commentary on the Epistle of James appeared in the year 1870, he was still busy with undiminished mental vigour in conducting his work nearer to that goal of completion, which he had kept before him from the first. At that time I did not anticipate that in a few years he would be called away from his work. Through his death Science has sustained a heavy loss, but she has this comfort, that if he himself has departed from her, the work to which he devoted the labour of a lifetime still remains, a brilliant example of the most thorough and unbiassed exegesis, of an exegesis which, holding itself free from all subjective caprice, " devotes itself soberly, faithfully, submissively, to the service of the Divine Word." The works of Meyer testify that he himself adhered to the law which he set down for the expositors of the holy Word, viz. that " they must interpret its pure contents as historical facts in a manner *simple, true,* and *clear, without bias* and independent of dogmatic prejudice, neither adding nor taking away anything, and abstaining from all conjectures of their own " (Preface to the fifth edition of the Commentary on 1 Cor.). — Since he invited me to take part in the work, it has been my constant endeavour to imitate his example; and it shall always be so with me, so long as I am spared to go on with it. Of what use is it, either to theological science or to the Church, if the expounder of the holy Scriptures uses his acuteness in endeavouring to confirm from them his own preconceived opinions, instead of faithfully interpreting and presenting the thoughts actually contained in them?—The same endeavour has guided me in this new revision, as will be shown, I hope, by the revision itself. In addition to the scrutiny to which I have subjected my earlier work, I have also carefully considered and examined the writings on the Pastoral Epistles, published since 1866, when the third edition of this Commentary appeared. Above all, I have examined the third edition of van Oosterzee's Commentary, the practical exposition by Plitt, and Hofmann's Commentary. While fully acknowledging the acuteness displayed in Hofmann's exposition, I have but seldom been able to agree with it; for the most part, I have felt myself bound to refute it. However convincing it may frequently appear at the first glance, as frequently it will not bear an unbiassed, scrutinizing consideration. While it certainly does not yield itself to exuberant fancies, it still follows a mode of exegesis, in which the chief purpose is to put forth new and striking explanations, and then to support them with all kinds of ingenious arguments— Nevertheless I feel myself bound to express my thanks to it, because it has incited me to examine the thought of the holy text all the more carefully and thoroughly.

The disfavour with which the Pastoral Epistles used often to be regarded has gradually disappeared, and rightly; for the more deeply we enter into the spirit of their contents, the more they appear worthy of the apostle whose name they bear. Excellent service in presenting their fulness of thought has been done by Stirm, a deacon in Reutlingen, in his treatise published in the *Jahrbuch für deutsche Theologie* (vol. xviii. No. 1, 1872), and called "Hints for Pastoral

Theology contained in the Pastoral Epistles." The more they who are entrusted with the clerical office make use of the contents of these epistles as their guiding star, the richer in blessing will their labours be. — To that same end may the Lord of the Church bless this my new work!

JOH. ED. HUTHER.

WITTENFÖRDEN, *November* 1875.

THE PASTORAL EPISTLES.

INTRODUCTION.

SECTION 1.—TIMOTHY AND TITUS.

1. TIMOTHY.—He was the son of a Christian Jewess (γυναικὸς Ἰουδαίας πιστῆς, Acts xvi. 1) named Eunice (2 Tim. i. 5), and of a Greek. We cannot determine for certain his place of birth. The passage in Acts xx. 4 does not prove that he was born in Derbe, since the position of καί forbids the connection of Τιμόθεος with Δερβαῖος.[1] From Acts xvi 1, we might possibly take Lystra to be his birthplace. If this be right, we may from it explain why in Acts xx. 4, Τιμόθεος, without more precise description, is named along with Caius of Derbe, since Lystra lies in the neighbourhood of Derbe.[2] From his mother and his grandmother, called Lois, he had enjoyed a pious education; and he had early been made acquainted with the holy scriptures of the Jews (2 Tim. i. 5, iii. 14, 15). When Paul on his second missionary journey came into closer connection with him, he was already a Christian (μαθητής), and possessed a good reputation among the believers in Lystra and Iconium. Paul calls him his τέκνον (1 Tim. i. 2, 18 ; 2 Tim. i. 2 ; 1 Cor.

---

[1] Wieseler (*Chronol. des apost. Zeitalters*, p 25) argues that Δερβαῖος should go with Τιμόθεος. He points out that in xix. 29, Γάιος is called a *Macedonian* along with Aristarchus, and that xx. 4 would agree with this if καὶ Γάιος were joined to Θεσσαλονικέων. But in this construction καί before Σεκοῦνδος is superfluous The Gaius here named is not to be held identical with the one mentioned in xix. 29 ; see Meyer on Acts xx. 4.

[2] According to Otto, the ἦν does not denote Timothy's *abode*, but only his temporary *sojourn* occasioned by the presence of Paul—an assertion which the context flatly contradicts.

iv. 17), from which it would appear that he had been converted by the preaching of the apostle, probably during the apostle's first stay in Lystra (Acts xiv. 6, 7); and, according to the reading: παρὰ τίνων, in the passage 2 Tim. iii. 14, by means of his mother and grandmother. Paul, after circumcising him, because his father was known in the district to be a Gentile,[1] adopted him as his assistant in the apostleship. From that time forward, Timothy was one of those who served the apostle (εἶς τῶν διακονούντων αὐτῷ, Acts xix. 22), his συνεργός. The service (διακονία) consisted in helping the apostle in the duties of his office, and was therefore not identical with the office of those called evangelists (this against Wiesinger). See on 2 Tim. iv. 5 —Timothy accompanied the apostle through Asia Minor to Philippi; but when Paul and Silas left that city (Acts xvi. 40), he seems to have remained behind there for some time, along with some other companions of the apostle. At Berea they were again together. When Paul afterwards travelled to Athens, Timothy remained behind (with Silas) at Berea; but Paul sent a message for him to come soon (Acts xvii. 14, 15).[2] From Athens, Paul sent him to Thessalonica, to inquire into the condition of the church there and to strengthen it (1 Thess. iii. 1–5). After completing this task, Timothy joined Paul again in Corinth (Acts xviii. 5; 1 Thess. iii. 6). The two epistles which Paul wrote from that place to the Thessalonians were written in Timothy's name also (1 Thess. i. 1; 2 Thess. i. 1).[3] When Paul on his third missionary journey remained for some considerable time in Ephesus, Timothy was with him; where he was in the interval is unknown. Before the tumult

---

[1] From the expression: ὅτι Ἕλλην ὑπῆρχεν (Acts xvi 3), Otto wishes to infer that the father was "*properly* a Hellene, but that not much of a Gentile nature was to be seen in him," because ὑπάρχειν, in contrast to φαίνεσθαι, is = "to be fundamentally" (¹).

[2] There is no tenable ground for Otto's assertion that Silas remained at Berea, and that Timothy, after completing the apostle's commission in Thessalonica, joined Silas again at Berea on the return journey, from which place the two travelled together to Corinth.

[3] Otto asserts that in Corinth Timothy made "his *first* attempts at the κήρυγμα τοῦ λόγου (2 Cor. i. 19)," which is in manifest contradiction with 1 Thess. iii. 1–5. Στηρίζειν and παρακαλεῖν περὶ τῆς πίστεως necessarily include the κηρύσσειν τὸν λόγον, and are not to be regarded merely as the fulfilment of a "*messenger's duty*, demanding no particular experience nor ability."

occasioned by Demetrius, Paul sent him from Ephesus to Macedonia (Acts xix. 22). Immediately afterwards the apostle wrote what is called the First Epistle to the Corinthians, from which it would appear that Timothy had been commissioned to go to Corinth, but that the apostle expected him to arrive there after the epistle (1 Cor. iv. 17, xvi. 10, 11). Matthies asserts without proof that Timothy did not carry out this journey. — When Paul wrote from Macedonia the Second Epistle to the Corinthians, Timothy was again with him;[1] for Paul composed that epistle also in Timothy's name, a very natural act if Timothy had shortly before been in Corinth.— He next travelled with the apostle to Corinth; his presence there is proved by the greeting which Paul sent from him to the church in Rome (Rom. xvi. 21).—When Paul after three months left Greece, Timothy, besides others of the apostle's assistants, was in his company. He travelled with him ἄχρι τῆς 'Ασίας, i.e as far as Philippi, from which the passage across to Asia Minor was usually made. From there Timothy and some others went before the apostle to Troas, where they remained till the apostle also arrived (Acts xx. 3-6). At this point there is a considerable blank in Timothy's history, since he is not mentioned again until the apostle's imprisonment in Rome.[2] He was with the apostle at that time, because Paul put his name also to the Epistles to the Colossians, to Philemon, and to the Philippians. This fact is at the same time a proof that no other of his assistants in the apostleship stood in such close relations with him as Timothy.—When Paul wrote the last epistle, he intended to send him as soon as possible to Philippi, in order to obtain by him exact intelligence regarding the circumstances of the churches there (Phil. ii. 19 ff.).

From our two Epistles to Timothy we learn also the following facts regarding the circumstances of his life :—

According to 1 Tim. i. 3, Paul on a journey to Macedonia left him behind in Ephesus, that he might counteract the false

---

[1] Wieseler assumes that Timothy joined Paul again while still in Ephesus (l c. pp. 57 f), but his proofs are not decisive.

[2] In this it is presupposed that the two Epistles to the Colossians and to the Ephesians, and the Epistle to Philemon, were written in Rome, and not, as Meyer assumes, in Cæsarea.

doctrine which was spreading there more and more. Perhaps on this occasion—if not even earlier—Timothy was solemnly ordained to his office by the laying on of hands on the part of the apostle and the presbytery. At this ordination the fairest hopes of him were expressed in prophetic language (comp. 1 Tim. i. 18, iv. 14; 2 Tim. i. 6), and he made a good confession (1 Tim. vi. 12).—Paul at that time, however, hoped soon to come to him again.—As to the period of Paul's apostolic labours into which this falls, see § 3.—Later on, Paul was a prisoner in Rome. When he was expecting his death as near at hand, he wrote to Timothy to come to him soon, before the approach of winter, and to bring him Mark, together with certain belongings left behind in Troas (2 Tim. iv. 9, 11, 13, 21).—Regarding this imprisonment of Paul, see § 3.

Timothy is only once mentioned elsewhere in the N. T., and that is in Heb. xiii. 23. It is very improbable that the Timothy there mentioned is another person; and from the passage we learn that when the epistle was written, he was again freed from an imprisonment, and that its author, as soon as he came, wished, along with him, to visit those to whom the epistle was directed.

According to the tradition of the church, Timothy was the first bishop of Ephesus. Chrysostom, indeed, merely says: δῆλον, ὅτι ἐκκλησίαν λοιπὸν ἦν πεπιστευμενος ὁ Τιμόθεος, ἢ καὶ ἔθνος ὁλόκληρον τὸ τῆς 'Ασίας (Homil. 15, on 1 Tim.); but Eusebius (Hist. Eccles iii. 4), says directly: Τιμόθεος τῆς ἐν 'Εφέσῳ παροικίας ἱστορεῖται πρῶτος τὴν ἐπισκοπὴν εἰληφέναι. Comp. also Const. Apost. i. 7, ch. 46; Photii Bibl. 254.—From the First Epistle only this much is clear, that the apostle gave to him a right of superintending the church at Ephesus, similar to that which the apostles exercised over the churches. It was a position from which afterwards the specially episcopal office might spring, but it cannot be considered as identical with the latter.

2. *Titus.*—Regarding the circumstances of his life, we possess still less information than regarding those of Timothy. He was also one of Paul's assistants, and is first mentioned as such in Gal. ii. 1, where Paul tells us that he took Titus with him to Jerusalem on the journey undertaken fourteen

years after his conversion or after his first stay in Jerusalem. Though Titus was of Gentile origin, Paul did not circumcise him, that there might be no yielding to his opponents.— When Paul wrote the First Epistle to the Corinthians, he sent Titus to Corinth, that a report might be brought to him of the state of matters there. Paul was disappointed in his hope of finding him again at Troas (2 Cor. ii. 13), but afterwards joined him in Macedonia (2 Cor. vii. 6). The news brought by Titus led him to compose the Second Epistle. With this he sent Titus a second time to Corinth, where he was at the same time to complete the collection for the poor of the church in Jerusalem, which he had already on a previous occasion begun (2 Cor. viii. 6, 16, 23).—When Paul, from his imprisonment in Rome, wrote the Second Epistle to Timothy, Titus was not with him, but had gone to Dalmatia (2 Tim. iv. 10). On this point we do not possess more exact information.

From the Epistle to Titus itself, we learn that he had assisted the apostle in his missionary labours in Crete, and had been left behind there in order to make the further arrangements necessary for forming a church (Tit. i. 5). By the epistle he is summoned to come to Nicopolis, where Paul wished to spend the winter (Tit. iii. 12) —Paul calls him his γνήσιον τέκνον κατὰ κοινὴν πίστιν, from which it appears that he had been converted to Christianity by Paul.

According to the tradition of the church, Titus was installed by Paul as the first bishop of Crete Eusebius (*Hist. Eccles.* iii. 4): Τιμόθεός γε μὴν τῆς ἐν Ἐφέσῳ παροικίας ἱστορεῖται πρῶτος τὴν ἐπισκοπὴν εἰληχέναι· ὡς καὶ Τίτος τῶν ἐπὶ Κρήτης ἐκκλησιῶν; comp. Jerome, *Catal. Script. Eccles;* Theodoret on 1 Tim. iii.; Theophylact, *Proem. ad Tit ; Const. Apost.* vii. 46. He is said to have died and been buried in Crete in his ninety-fourth year.

SECTION 2.—CONTENTS OF THE PASTORAL EPISTLES.

First Epistle to Timothy. — The epistle begins with a reminder that the apostle had left Timothy behind in Ephesus in order to counteract the heresies of certain teachers. These heresies are described in detail, and the evangelic principle of life is placed in opposition to them (i. 3-10) by directing attention to the gospel as it had been entrusted to the apostle. This furnishes an opportunity for expressing his thanks for the grace shown to him in it (11-17), to which is added an exhortation to Timothy to act rightly in regard to it (18-20). Then follow particular directions, first as to public intercessions and the behaviour of the men and women in the meetings of the church (ii. 1-15), and then as to the qualities necessary in a bishop and a deacon (iii. 1-13). After briefly pointing out the essential truth of the gospel (14-16), the apostle goes on to speak further regarding the heretics, and confutes their arbitrary rules (iv. 1-6). After this we have further exhortations to Timothy,—first as to his behaviour towards the heresy (7-11), then as to his official labours (12-16), and lastly in reference to his attitude towards the individual members of the church. Under this last head are given more detailed instructions about widows and presbyters (v 1-25), to which are added some special remarks regarding slaves (vi. 1, 2).—After another attack on the heretics (3-10), there follow again exhortations to Timothy to be true to his calling, which are interrupted by an allusion to the rich (11-22).

Second Epistle to Timothy.—The epistle begins with the apostle's assurance to Timothy that, full of desire to see him again, he remembered him always in prayer, and was convinced of his unfeigned faith (i 3-5). This is followed by an exhortation to stir up the gift of the Spirit imparted to him, and not be ashamed of the gospel, but to be ready to suffer for it (6-8); his attention also is directed to the grace of God revealed in the gospel, and to the apostle's example (9-12). Then follow further exhortations to Timothy to hold fast the doctrine he had received, and to preserve the good thing entrusted to him, the apostle also reminding him of the conduct of the Asiatics who had turned away from him, and of the fidelity of Onesiphorus (13-18).—The doctrine received from the apostle he is to deliver to other tried men, but he himself is to suffer as a good soldier of Jesus Christ, and to remember the Risen One; just as he, the apostle, suffers for Christ's sake, that the elect may become partakers of blessedness (ii. 1–13). Then follow warnings against the heresy, which may exercise on many a corrupting influence, but cannot destroy the building founded by God (14–19). Instructions are also given how Timothy is to conduct himself towards this heresy, and towards those who give themselves up to it (20–26). With prophetic spirit the apostle points next to the moral ruin which threatens to appear in the future in the most varied forms. He pictures the conduct of the heretics, and exhorts Timothy on the contrary—in faithful imitation of his exemplar as before — to hold fast by that which he knows to be the truth (iii. 1–17). In reference to the threatening general apostasy from the pure doctrine of the gospel, the apostle exhorts Timothy to perform faithfully the evangelic duties of his office, especially as he himself was already at the end of his apostolic career (iv. 1–8). Then follow various special commissions, items of news, greetings, the repeated summons to come to him soon before the approach of winter, and finally the Christian benediction with which the epistle closes.

The Epistle to Titus.—After a somewhat elaborate preface, Paul reminds Titus that he had left him behind in Crete for the purpose of ordaining presbyters in the churches there. The qualities are named which the presbyter ought to possess, and Paul points out the upholding of the pure gospel as the most important requisite of all, that the presbyter may be able to withstand the continually growing influence of the heretics. The mention of the heretics in Crete gives the apostle an opportunity of quoting a saying of Epimenides, which describes the character of the Cretans, while at the same time he sketches the heretics, with their arbitrary commands and their hypocritical life, and vindicates against them the principle of life in the gospel (i. 5–16). Then follow rules of conduct for the various members of the church, for old and young, men and women, together with an exhortation to Titus to show a good example in work and doctrine, and especially to call upon the slaves to be faithful to their masters. These exhortations are supported by pointing to the moral character of God's grace (ii. 1–15).—Then follows the injunction that Titus is to urge the Christians to obedience towards the higher powers, and to a peaceful behaviour towards all men. The latter point is enforced by pointing to the undeserved grace of God which has been bestowed on Christians (iii. 1–7). To this are added warnings against heresy, and directions how Titus is to deal with a heretic (8–11). The epistle closes with an injunction to come to the apostle at Nicopolis, some commissions, greetings, and the benediction.

The First Epistle to Timothy and the Epistle to Titus are letters on business, both occasioned by the apostle's desire to impart to his colleagues definite instructions for their work in Ephesus and in Crete respectively. The Epistle to Titus has at the same time the purpose of enjoining him, after the arrival of Artemas or Tychicus, to come to Paul at Nicopolis. —The Second Epistle to Timothy is a letter "purely personal" (Wiesinger), occasioned by the wish of the apostle to see him as soon as possible in Rome. It was written, too, for the purpose of encouraging him to faithfulness in his calling as a Christian, and particularly in his official labours. The apostle felt all the greater need for writing, that he perceived in his colleague a certain shrinking from suffering.—The instructions in the First Epistle to Timothy refer to the meetings of the church, to prayer and the behaviour of the women in the meetings, to the qualifications of bishops and deacons, to widows, to the relation of slaves to their masters, but at the same time also to Timothy's conduct in general as well as in special cases.—In the Epistle to Titus the apostle instructs him regarding the ordination of bishops, the conduct of individual members of the church, both in particular according to their age, sex, and position, and also in their general relation to the higher powers and to non-Christians. In all three epistles, besides the more general exhortations to faithfulness in word and act, there is a conspicuous reference to *heretics* who threaten to disturb the church. The apostle exhorts his fellow-workers not only to hold themselves free from the influence of such men, but also to counteract the heresy by preaching the pure doctrine of the gospel, and to warn the church against the temptations of such heresy. He imparts also rules for proper conduct towards the heretics.

The three epistles are closely related in contents, and also in the expression and the form in which the thoughts are developed. They have thus received a definite impress, which distinguishes them from the apostle's other epistles. All Paul's epistles contain expressions peculiar to him alone, and this is certainly the case with every one of these three. But there is also in them a not inconsiderable number of expressions peculiar to them all, or even to two of them, and often repeated in them, but occurring only seldom or not at all in the other epistles of the N. T. The nature of the Christian life is denoted specially by εὐσέβεια, 1 Tim. ii. 2, iii. 16, etc.; 2 Tim. iii 5, Tit. i. 1 (εὐσεβέω, 1 Tim. v. 4; εὐσεβῶς, 2 Tim. iii. 12; Tit. ii 12). The following virtues are specially extolled as Christian:—σεμνότης, 1 Tim. ii. 2, iii. 4; Tit. ii. 7 (σεμνός, 1 Tim. iii. 8, 11; Tit. ii 2), σωφροσύνη, 1 Tim. ii. 9, 15 (σώφρων, 1 Tim. iii. 2; Tit. i. 8, ii. 2, 5; σωφρόνως, Tit. ii. 12; σωφρονέω, Tit. ii. 6; σωφρονίζειν, Tit. ii. 4; σωφρονισμός, 2 Tim. i. 7). The same or very similar words, which occur seldom or nowhere else, are used to denote the doctrine of the gospel; e.g. the word διδασκαλία, especially in connection with ὑγιαινοῦσα, 1 Tim. i. 10; 2 Tim. iv. 3; Tit. i. 9, ii. 1. The use of ὑγιαίνω and ὑγιής in general is peculiar to the Pastoral Epistles: λόγοι ὑγιαίνοντες, 1 Tim. vi. 3; 2 Tim. i. 13; λόγος ὑγιής, Tit. ii. 8. We may also note: ἡ κατ' εὐσέβειαν διδασκαλία, 1 Tim. vi. 3, and ἡ ἀλήθεια ἡ κατ' εὐσέβειαν, Tit. i. 1; ἡ καλὴ διδασκαλία, 1 Tim. iv. 6 (καλός is also a word which occurs very often in all three epistles). Even in describing the heresy there is a great agreement in all three. Its substance is denoted in a more general way by μῦθοι, 1 Tim. i. 4; 2 Tim. iv. 4; Tit. i. 14; more specially by γενεαλογίαι, 1 Tim. i 4; Tit. iii. 9. Frequently it is reproached with occasioning foolish investigations (μωραί ζητήσεις), as in 1 Tim. vi. 4; 2 Tim. ii. 23; Tit. iii. 9. In 1 Tim. i. 6 it is on this account called ματαιολογία, and in accordance with this the heretics are called in Tit. i. 10 ματαιολόγοι. In 1 Tim. vi. 4 the blame of λογομαχίαι is given to it, and in 2 Tim. ii. 14 there is a warning against λογομαχεῖν. The same reproach is contained in αἱ βέβηλοι κενοφωνίαι, which is found in 1 Tim. vi. 20, and 2 Tim. ii. 16.—But also in other respects there is a striking agreement in these epistles. Among the points of agreement are the formula, πιστὸς ὁ λόγος, 1 Tim i. 15, iii. 1, iv. 9; 2 Tim. ii. 11; Tit. iii. 8; the word ἀρνέομαι, 1 Tim. v. 8; 2 Tim. ii. 12, 13, iii. 5; Tit. i. 16, ii. 12; the formula of assurance, διαμαρτύρεσθαι ἐνώπιον (τοῦ θεοῦ καὶ κυρίου 'I. Χρ.), 1 Tim. v. 21; 2 Tim. ii. 14, iv. 1; the figurative expression, ἡ παγὶς τοῦ διαβόλου, 1 Tim. iii. 7; 2 Tim. ii. 26; the phrase, φυλάσσειν τὴν παραθήκην, 1 Tim. vi. 20; 2 Tim. ι 12, 14; further, the words, κατ' ἐπιταγήν, 1 Tim. i. 1; Tit. i. 3; ὑπομιμνήσκειν, 2 Tim ii. 14, Tit. iii. 1; δι' ἣν αἰτίαν, 2 Tim. i. 6, 12; Tit i. 13; ἡ ἐπιφάνεια (τοῦ κυρίου), used of the future return of Christ, 1 Tim. vi 14, 2 Tim. iv. 1, 8; Tit. ii. 13; δεσπότης (instead of κύριος, Eph. vi. 5; Col iii. 22), 1 Tim. vi 1; 2 Tim. ii. 21; Tit. ii. 9; παραιτεῖσθαι, 1 Tim iv. 7, v. 11; 2 Tim. ii. 23; Tit. iii. 10, διαβεβαιοῦσθαι περί τινος, 1 Tim. i. 7; Tit. iii 8, etc.—Wherever in the three epistles the same subject is spoken of, substantially the same expressions and turns of expression are used, though with some modifications Thus the benedictions in the inscription agree: χάρις, ἔλεος, εἰρήνη (Tit. i. 4 should, however, perhaps have the reading: χάρις καὶ εἰρήνη). In reference to the redemption by Christ we have in 1 Tim. ii. 6. ὁ δοὺς ἑαυτὸν ἀντίλυτρον ὑπὲρ πάντων; and Tit. ii. 14. ὃς ἔδωκεν ἑαυτὸν ὑπὲρ ἡμῶν, ἵνα λυτρώσηται ἡμᾶς; in reference to his office Paul says in 1 Tim. ii. 7: εἰς ὃ (τὸ μαρτύριον) ἐτέθην ἐγὼ κῆρυξ καὶ ἀπόστολος ... διδάσκαλος ἐθνῶν; and so also in 2 Tim. i 11. The necessary qualities of the bishop are mentioned in the same way in 1 Tim. iii. 2 ff. and Tit. i. 6: μιᾶς γυναικὸς ἀνήρ, σώφρων, φιλόξενος, μὴ πάροινος, μὴ πλήκτης The general exhortations to Timothy in 1 Tim. vi. 11 and 2 Tim. ii. 22 agree with each other almost to the very letter.

In the other Pauline epistles the fulness of the apostle's thought struggles with the expression, and causes peculiar difficulties in exposition. The thoughts slide into one another, and are so intertwined in many forms that not seldom the new thought begins before a correct expression has been given to the thought that preceded. Of this confusion there is no example in the Pastoral Epistles. Even in such passages as come nearest to this confused style, such as the beginning of the First and Second Epistles to Timothy (Tit. ii. 11 ff., iii. 4 ff.), the connection of ideas is still, on the whole, simple. It is peculiar that, as De Wette has shown, the transition from the special to a general truth is often made suddenly— thus 1 Tim. i. 15, ii. 4–6, iv. 8–10; 2 Tim. i. 9 ff, ii. 11–13, iii. 12; Tit ii. 11–14, iii. 4–7; and that after such general thoughts a resting-point is often sought in an exhortation or instruction addressed to the receivers of the epistle, as in 1 Tim. iv. 6, 11, vi. 2; 2 Tim. ii. 14, iii. 5; Tit. ii. 15, iii. 8.

SECTION 3.—TIME AND PLACE OF THE COMPOSITION OF THE PASTORAL EPISTLES.

1. *First Epistle to Timothy.*—Regarding the *time of the composition of this epistle,* different views from an early period have been put forward, since the indications contained in the epistle itself leave a difficulty in assigning to it its proper place in the events of the apostle's life. According to these indications, Paul had been for some time with Timothy in Ephesus, and had travelled from there to Macedonia, leaving Timothy behind in Ephesus to take his place. Probably the epistle was written by Paul from Macedonia, to remind Timothy of his charge, and to give him suitable instructions; for, although Paul hoped to return to Ephesus soon, still a delay was regarded as possible (chap. iii. 14, 15)—According to Acts, Paul was twice in Ephesus. The first occasion was on his second missionary journey from Antioch, when he was returning from Corinth to Antioch (Acts xviii. 19). On this first occasion he stayed there only a short time, as he wished to be in Jerusalem in time for the near-approaching festival. The composition cannot be assigned to that occasion, since there was at that time no Christian church in Ephesus, and Paul was not travelling to Macedonia.—On his third missionary journey Paul was in Ephesus a second time. This time he stayed

for two or three years, and then, after the riot caused by Demetrius, travelled to Macedonia and Greece (Acts xx. 1, 2). Theodoret, and after him many other expositors, assume that Paul wrote the epistle on this journey to Macedonia, or in Macedonia. But to this the following circumstances are opposed:—(1) According to Acts xix. 22, Paul, before his own departure from Ephesus, had already sent Timothy to Macedonia; we are not told that Timothy, after being commissioned to go to Corinth (1 Cor. iv. 17), returned *to Ephesus* again before the apostle's departure, as the apostle certainly had expected (according to 1 Cor. xvi. 11). (2) When Paul undertook that journey, he did not intend to return soon to Ephesus (1 Cor. xvi. 6, 7), which decidedly was his intention at the time of the composition of the epistle (1 Tim. iii 14); and on his return journey from Greece he sailed from Troas past Ephesus for the express purpose of avoiding any stay there (Acts xx. 16). (3) According to 2 Cor. i 1, Timothy was in Macedonia with Paul when he wrote the Second Epistle to the Corinthians, and, according to Acts xx. 4, he accompanied the apostle on his journey from Corinth to Philippi. Timothy therefore must also have left Ephesus after the apostle's departure, although the apostle had charged him to remain there till his own return (1 Tim. iv. 13), and this we can hardly suppose to have been the case. All these reasons prove that the apostle's journey from Ephesus to Macedonia, mentioned in Acts xx. 1, cannot be the same with that of which he speaks in 1 Tim. i. 3.

Some expositors (Bertholdt, Matthies), alluding to Acts xx. 3-5, suppose that Timothy set out from Corinth before the apostle, and then went to Ephesus, where he received the epistle. The supposition is, however, contradicted by πορευόμενος εἰς Μακεδονίαν. This objection Bertholdt can get rid of only by the most arbitrary combinations, Matthies only by most unwarrantably explaining πορευόμενος to be equivalent to πορευόμενον. Besides, Luke's historical narrative is against the whole hypothesis, unless, as Bertholdt actually does, we charge it with an inaccuracy which distorts the facts of the case.—If the composition of the epistle is to be inserted among the incidents in the apostle's life known to us, the only hypothesis left is, that the apostle's journey from Ephesus to Macedonia, which is mentioned in 1 Tim. i 3, and during which Timothy was left behind by him in Ephesus, falls into the period of his sojourn for two or three years in Ephesus, but is not mentioned by Luke. This is the supposition of Wieseler (*Chronologie des apostol. Zeitalters*), who follows Mosheim and Schrader. It is not only admitted, on the whole, that the apostle may possibly have made a journey which Luke leaves unnoticed, but there are also several passages in the Epistles to the Corinthians (1 Cor. xvi. 17; 2 Cor. ii. 1, xii. 14, 21, xiii. 1, 2) which put it beyond doubt that Paul had been in Corinth not *once* but *twice* before their composition, but that the second time he had stayed there only a short time. For this journey, of which Luke tells us nothing, we can find no place in the apostle's history, unless during his stay at Ephesus ; see Wieseler, *l.c.* pp. 232 ff. It is natural, therefore, to identify this journey with the one to Macedonia mentioned in 1 Tim. i. 3, and to suppose that the epistle was written on this journey from Macedonia. There are still, however, several considerations against this view. One is that both the church organization presupposed in the epistle, and the requirement that the ἐπίσκοπος should not be νεόφυτος, indicate that the church had already been some time in existence. To this Wieseler, indeed, replies that the journey was undertaken shortly before the end of the apostle's stay in Corinth, so that the church had then been long enough in existence to justify the presupposition and the requirement But still there is against this hypothesis the consideration that it supposes the apostle to have been in Corinth *himself, shortly* before the composition of the First Epistle to the Corinthians, so that he could not therefore have any sufficient occasion for *writing* to the church there. Besides, the passage in Acts xx. 29, 30 is against Wieseler's view. According to the epistle, the heresy had already made its way into the church at Ephesus, but, according to that passage, Paul mentions the heresy as something to be expected in the future. Supposing even that the words ἐξ ὑμῶν αὐτῶν do not refer to the church, but only to the presbyters assembled at Miletus, still εἰς ὑμᾶς in ver. 29 must be taken to refer generally to the Christians in Ephesus. Surely Paul, in his address to the presbyters, would not have passed over the presence of heretics in Ephesus, if he knew the church to be so much threatened by the danger that he thought it necessary, even before this, to give Timothy solemn instructions regarding it, as he does in his epistle.—Further, the view implies that Paul had only *for a short time* been separated from Timothy, and that he must have sent him away *immediately* after his own return. But how does the whole character of the epistle agree with this? The instructions which Paul gives to Timothy indicate that the latter was to labour in the church for some time; and the greater the danger threatened it by the heresy, the more inconsistent it seems that Paul, after giving these instructions, should have taken Timothy away so soon from his labours in the church.—The views mentioned hitherto proceed from a presupposed interpretation of 1 Tim. i. 3, viz. that Paul commissioned Timothy to remain in Ephesus, and that the commission was given when Paul departed from Ephesus to Macedonia. This presupposition, however, has been declared erroneous by several expositors, who refer πορευόμενος εἰς Μακεδονίαν not to the apostle, but to Timothy. Paulus explains προσμεῖναι as = "abide by a thing," joins πορευόμενος εἰς Μακεδ. to ἵνα παραγγείλῃς, and takes the latter imperatively, so that the sense is: "As I have exhorted thee to abide in Ephesus, and warn them against false doctrine, so do thou travel now to Macedonia, and exhort certain people there to abstain from false doctrine." The opinion of Paulus is therefore that Paul wrote the epistle during his imprisonment at Cæsarea.— Schneckenburger and Bottger try to help the matter by conjecture, wishing both to read, instead of προσμεῖναι, the participle προσμείνας. The former then assumes that the epistle was composed at the time denoted in Acts xxi. 26; the latter, that it was written in Patara (Acts xxi. 1), or in Miletus (Acts xx. 17). These obviously are arbitrary suppositions. If the journey to Macedonia, mentioned in 1 Tim. i. 3, is not to be understood as one made by the apostle, but as made by Timothy, then it is much more natural to suppose with Otto that this is the journey of Timothy which is mentioned in Acts xix. 22, and that Paul wrote the epistle in Ephesus. This is the view which Otto has sought to establish in the first book of his work of research, *Die geschichtlichen Verhaltnisse der Pastoralbriefe.* But this, too, is wrecked on the right explanation of 1 Tim. i. 3, which refers πορευόμενος εἰς Μακ. to the subject contained in παρεκάλεσα; see on this point the exposition of the passage.

The Epistle to Titus. — The following are the historical circumstances to which this epistle itself points. After Paul had laboured in Crete, he left Titus behind there. Then he wrote to the latter this epistle, instructing him, so soon as Artemas and Tychicus had been sent to him, to come with all haste to Nicopolis, where the apostle had resolved to pass the winter.—The epistle, indeed, contains nothing definite regarding the first beginning of Christianity in Crete, nothing regarding the duration and extent of the apostle's labours there, nothing regarding the length of time which intervened between the apostle's departure from Crete and the composition of the epistle; but it is probable that when Paul came to Crete he found Christianity already existing there, and that he himself remained there only a short time; for on the one hand there were already Christian churches there in the chief places, at least in several towns of the island, at the time of composing the epistle, while on the other hand they were still unorganized. It is probable that the epistle was written by Paul not long after his departure, for it is not to be supposed that Paul would leave his substitute in the apostleship long without written instructions. It is probable also that Paul gave Titus these instructions some time before the beginning of winter, for it would have been meaningless to give instructions, unless Paul intended Titus to labour in Crete for some considerable time.

If we set out with the presupposition that the composition of the epistle is to be placed in that period of the Apostle Paul's life which is described in Acts, we may thus state more definitely the question regarding the apostle's stay in Crete, and the composition of the epistle. Did both take place *before,* or *after,* or *during* the two or three years' stay in Ephesus (Acts xix)? Each of these suppositions has its supporters among expositors and critics. Those who place the two events in the period *before* the stay at Ephesus, assume as a fixed date *either* the time during which Paul was first in Corinth (Acts xviii. 1–18) (Michaelis), *or* the time during which he was travelling from Corinth to Ephesus (Acts xviii. 18, 19) (Hug, Hemsen), *or, lastly*, the time after he had passed through Galatia and Phrygia in the beginning of his third missionary journey, and before he went from there to Ephesus (Acts xviii. 23) (Credner, Neudecker). To all these views alike, however, there is this objection, that Apollos could not be the apostle's assistant before the (second) arrival in Corinth (Acts xviii. 24–xix. 1), whereas he is so named in this epistle. We would then have to suppose that another Apollos was meant here—which would be altogether arbitrary. There are, besides, special objections to these three views. Against the *first*, according to which Paul had made the journey from Corinth to Crete, and from there to Nicopolis in Epirus (iii. 12), and had then returned to Corinth, it may be urged that the apostle's second stay in Corinth, alluded to in 1 Cor. xvi. 7, 2 Cor. ii. 1, etc., did not take place *then*, but *later*. Against the *second*, we might object not only that the journey from Corinth to Jerusalem was undertaken with some haste, so as to leave no room for labours in Crete, but also that it takes Nicopolis to be the town in Cilicia, without giving any reason why Paul should pass the winter there and not in Antioch. As to the *third* view, which is, that Paul for this third missionary journey had chosen Ephesus mainly as his goal (Acts xviii. 21), and that his labours, therefore, on the journey thither consisted only in confirming those who already believed (Acts xviii. 23: ἐπιστηρίζων πάντας τοὺς μαθητάς), how are we to reconcile with it the facts that Paul, instead of going at once to Ephesus from Phrygia, went to Crete and Corinth, that he there resolved to pass the winter in Nicopolis (by which Credner in his *Einl. in d. N. T.* understands the town in Cilicia), and that then only did he go to Ephesus?—There is still less justification for the opinion of some expositors, that Paul travelled to Crete at the date defined by Acts xv. 41, and wrote the epistle later during his two or three years' stay in Ephesus. The former part of this is contradicted by the route (comp xv. 41 and xvi. 1) furnished by the apostle himself; the latter, by the circumstance that almost the whole of the apostle's second, and a part of his third, missionary journey lay between the beginning of Titus' independent labours in Crete and the despatch of the epistle to him

The *second* supposition is, that both events are to be placed in the time *after* the apostle's stay at Ephesus, *i.e.* in the period mentioned in Acts xx 1-3. Its representatives, as before, differ as to the details. *Some* suppose that Paul, on the journey from Ephesus to Greece, went from Macedonia (vv. 1, 2) to Crete; *others*, that he undertook this journey during his three months' stay in Greece (ver. 3). According to the *former* opinion, we should have to suppose that Titus, after completing his second mission to Corinth, returned again to the apostle in Macedonia; that Paul then made the journey with him to Crete, and from there returned to Macedonia alone; that he then wrote the epistle from Macedonia, and afterwards went to Corinth. In this way, therefore, Paul after composing the Second Epistle to the Corinthians would have twice journeyed past Greece, whereas it must have been of great importance to him, after the last news he had received from Corinth, not to put off his journey thither —The *latter* opinion, supported particularly by Matthies, refutes itself, in so far as the three months which Paul spent in Hellas were winter months, in which travelling to and fro to Crete was hardly possible. Besides, it was when Paul returned from Crete that he formed his plan of passing the winter at Nicopolis. He then informed Titus of it, with the remark that he was to come to him in that place, after he had first waited for the arrival of Artemas or Tychicus. Wiesinger is right in saying: " Unless we exercise ingenuity, we must take the κέκρικα παραχειμάσαι (chap. iii. 12) to have been written before the approach of winter."

The *third* supposition is, that Paul undertook the journey to Crete from Ephesus before his departure to Macedonia, and also wrote the Epistle to Titus from there. Wieseler defends it with great acuteness It puts the case in this way. After Paul had stayed over two years in Ephesus, he made by way of Macedonia (1 Tim. i. 3) a journey (the second, not mentioned in Acts) to Corinth. On this journey, which was but *short*, he was accompanied by Titus, who also went with him to Crete. On departing from Crete, he left Titus behind there, returned to Ephesus, and from Ephesus wrote the Epistle to Titus. Then he sent Timothy to Macedonia, instructing him to go to Corinth, and wrote afterwards our First Epistle to the Corinthians He next sent Tychicus and Artemas to Crete, and bade Titus return to him. Titus was sent afterwards to Corinth. Paul went on the journey to Macedonia, hoping to meet Titus at Troas. They did not meet, however, at Troas, but in Macedonia, when Titus was a second time sent away to Corinth. After the apostle had written our Second Epistle to the Corinthians, he went through Macedonia to Nicopolis in Epirus, where he spent the first months of winter, going afterwards to Corinth. —However well all this seems to go together, there are still the following reasons against the hypothesis :—(1) If Paul made the second journey to Corinth at the time here mentioned, he can have employed only a short time in it. How, then, can we conceive that he used this short time for missionary labours in Crete ? (2) Paul wrote to Titus that he was to remain in Crete till Tychicus and Artemas were sent to him, and that then he was to come to Nicopolis. This hypothesis would make out that he had changed his mind, for according to it he bade Titus come to him at *Ephesus*. Besides, we cannot think that, just after he had assigned to Titus an important task in Crete, he should take him so quickly away from it again. (3) It is improbable also that Paul should have chosen for his winter residence a town in which he had not been before, and where, therefore, he could not know how he would be received. His resolution seems rather to presuppose that he had laboured before in Nicopolis.[1] (4) In 1 Cor. xvi. 6 Paul

---

[1] Otto objects to this, that Paul might very well spend a winter in a town in which he had not before preached , but that is not the point The point is that Paul should have formed a resolution to remain for the winter in a town, even before he knew whether his preaching would be received there or not.

writes to the Corinthians: πρὸς ὑμᾶς δὲ τυχὸν παραμενῶ, ἢ καὶ παραχειμάσω. According to Wieseler, this πρὸς ὑμᾶς is not to be referred to the Corinthians alone, but generally to the Christians in Achaia, to whom (according to i. 2) the epistle is addressed. As Nicopolis in Epirus, on the authority of Tacitus,[1] was counted as belonging to Achaia, Wieseler is of opinion that by spending the winter in Nicopolis the apostle kept the promise given in that passage. But although the epistle was not directed merely to the church in Corinth, it has a special reference to that church, so that its readers could surely understand the words only of an intended stay in Corinth, and not in a place so far distant from Corinth. Paul could not possibly be thinking then of Nicopolis, as is obvious from the fact that at that time, as Wieseler himself maintains, he had not been there; he did not preach the gospel in Nicopolis till later. Paul, however, in the epistle regarded his readers as *Christians* only, not as those who were afterwards to be converted to Christianity. Lastly, although Augustus extended the name of Achaia to Epirus, it does not follow that in common life Nicopolis was considered to be in Achaia. It should be added, too, that Paul, in Wieseler's representation, had not at all fulfilled the promise given in Tit iii. 13, for he supposes that the apostle remained in Nicopolis only two months of winter, and therefore went to Corinth in the middle of winter. —There may be, too, some accessory circumstances which are favourable to Wieseler's view, and give it an air of probability; such circumstances as the following:—that Apollos was along with Paul in Ephesus (1 Cor xvi. 12; Tit iii. 13); that Tychicus as an Asiatic (Acts xx. 4) probably became acquainted with Paul in Ephesus, and that the mention of him in Tit. iii. 13 agrees with the composition of the epistle

---

[1] Tacitus, *Ann.* ii. 53 "Sed eum honorem Germanicus iniit apud urbem Achajae Nicopolim." Pliny also, *Nat Hist* iv. 2, assigns Nicopolis to Acarnania, while Strabo, xvii p. 840, describes, according to the arrangement of the Emperor Augustus, the province in these words · 'Εβδόμην δ' 'Αχαίαν μέχρι Θιτταλίας καὶ Αἰτωλῶν καὶ 'Ακαρνάνων καί τινων 'Ηπειρωτίκων ἐθνῶν, ὅσα τῇ Μακεδονίᾳ προσώριστο " (Wieseler, l.c p. 353) In opposition to Wieseler's assertion, Otto (pp 362–366) seeks to prove that Nicopolis itself was not counted in Achaia, but only the suburb of the town situated on the Acarnanian side.

in Ephesus; that by the two brothers who accompanied Titus to Corinth we may understand Tychicus and Trophimus —make the theory probable, but cannot completely establish its correctness. Like Wieseler, Reuss (*Gesch. d. heil. Schriften d. N. T.*, 2d ed. 1853, § 87, pp. 73 f.) connects the apostle's journey to Crete with his *second* (see Meyer on 2 *Cor*, Introd. § 2, Rem) journey to Corinth during the three years' stay at Ephesus; but he differs from Wieseler in supposing that Paul journeyed first to Crete and then to Corinth, that from the latter place he wrote the epistle, that he then went farther to the north to Illyricum, where trace of him is lost, and returned to Ephesus towards the end of winter. To all this we must say that not only is it inconceivable that Paul should have interrupted his three years' stay by various missionary journeys, occupying so much time, and to districts so remote, but also that Acts xx. 31 contradicts such a theory. Otto, too, refutes the theory of the apostle's journey to Crete, and the composition of the epistle during the three years' stay at Ephesus. In his opinion, Paul made from Ephesus an excursion to Crete,—not mentioned in Acts by Luke, — and on that occasion visited Corinth ἐν παρόδῳ (1 Cor. xvi 7 ; 2 Cor. ii 1, xii. 14, 21, xiii. 1, 2). Then in Ephesus, after he had written the lost epistle to the Corinthians (1 Cor. v. 9), he addressed a letter to Titus whom he had left in Crete.—The passages quoted put it beyond doubt that Paul from Ephesus made a visit to Corinth ἐν παρόδῳ before composing what is called his First Epistle to the Corinthians. Not only, however, is there no indication that Crete was at that time the goal of his journey, but it is also improbable The theory makes the journey in any case a short one, and Paul could not well choose for its goal a country in which he could not beforehand determine the length of his stay, as he had not been there before. Otto recognises fully the objections arising from the contents of the epistle, which are against placing the date of composition in the three years' stay; but he thinks to overcome them by supposing that the dates in it rest on a plan of the journey, afterwards altered by the apostle. It is certainly clear from 2 Cor. i. 15, 16, 23, that Paul, on account of circumstances in Corinth, did indeed alter the plan of the journey he had previously formed; but that he ever intended to go to Nicopolis in order to spend the winter there, is a fiction contradicted by what he says himself in the passages quoted. According to these, his original plan was to come from Ephesus direct to Corinth, to pass from there to Macedonia, and to return from Macedonia to Corinth again in order to set out for Judea. There is no trace in the apostle's plans of a journey to Epirus and a winter residence in Nicopolis. The latter he could not even think of, for the reason quoted above.

2. *Second Epistle to Timothy.*—The historical circumstances alluded to in the epistle prove that it was written by the apostle in imprisonment in Rome; comp. i. 8, 12, 16, 17, etc.—This imprisonment has been held to be the same as that mentioned by Luke in the Acts, and a different date has therefore been assigned to the composition of the epistle. Wieseler, following Hemsen, Kling, and others, supposes that the epistle belongs to the time following the διετία, mentioned in Acts xxviii. 30, and was therefore composed after the Epistle to the Philippians. He rests his supposition on two grounds—(1) That while in his Epistle to the Philippians the apostle was still able to cherish the hope of being soon set free, in this epistle he expresses definite anticipations of death. (2) That in Phil. ii. 19-24 the apostle expresses his intention of sending Timothy to Philippi, and that at the time of composing this epistle Timothy was actually in those regions, viz. at Ephesus. Against this second ground Otto rightly maintains that "Timothy would not have served the apostle as a child his father," if after being expected to bring (Phil. ii. 19) comfort to the imprisoned apostle by the news from Philippi, he did not return at once to Rome, but proceeded instead to Ephesus, and there remained till the apostle "by a solemn apostolic message compelled him to return." Besides, Otto insists that, as Wieseler's interpretation of 2 Tim. iv. 16 is that "the apostle is telling Timothy of his first ἀπολογία," the latter according to this was sent away *before* the first judicial hearing, *i.e.* before he could know how the case would end; whereas according to Phil. ii. 23, 24, "he makes the despatch

of Timothy depend on his expectation of a favourable conclusion of the trial."—On these grounds Otto rejects Wieseler's hypothesis, but at the same time he himself—agreeing with Schrader, Matthies, and others—supposes that the epistle was written in the beginning of the διετία mentioned, and therefore *before* the composition of the Epistle to the Philippians. But, as Wieseler and Wiesinger rightly observe, " the whole position of the apostle as represented in the epistle " is against this view. According to the apostle's utterances in the Epistle to the Philippians, he was uncertain about the fate hanging over him, but circumstances had so shaped themselves that the expectation of being freed from imprisonment decidedly prevailed with him, and hence he wrote: πέποιθα ἐν κυρίῳ, ὅτι . . . ταχέως ἐλεύσομαι. In *this* epistle there is no trace of any such expectation. The apostle rather sees his end close approaching, chap. iv. 6–8; and although in the first ἀπολογία he had been rescued, as he says, ἐκ στόματος λέοντος, and now expresses the hope that the Lord would rescue him ἀπὸ παντὸς ἔργου πονηροῦ, he is thinking not of a release from imprisonment, but of a rescue εἰς τὴν βασιλείαν αὐτοῦ τὴν ἐπουράνιον Otto indeed maintains that the apostle's expressions in chap. iv. 6–8 do not refer to the end of his life, but to the end appointed to him of his missionary labours in the apostleship, and that in the Second Epistle to Timothy there is no trace whatever of anticipations or expectations of death; but this assertion is based on an exposition which, however acute, is anything but tenable. See on this the commentary on the passages in question.—Besides, several of the special notices made by the apostle weigh against the composition of the epistle during the imprisonment mentioned by Luke. Of special weight are the remarks regarding Erastus and Trophimus. Of the former Paul says that he remained in Corinth; of the latter, that he was left behind in Miletus sick. This presupposes a journey made by the apostle to Rome by way of Corinth and Miletus. But on the voyage which Paul made from Caesarea to Rome as a prisoner, he did not touch at these places. Hence we cannot but suppose that the reference in both cases is to the apostle's previous journey to Jerusalem; but against this there is the inconceivability of his still mentioning those circumstances after a lapse of several years. Besides, according to Acts xxi. 29, Trophimus was with the apostle in Jerusalem. Wieseler can only get over this by the following artificial combination: "The ship in which Paul as a prisoner embarked at Caesarea in order to be brought to Rome, went to Adramyttium in the neighbourhood of Troas. With it Paul went as far as Myra in Lycia. There he embarked in another ship which sailed direct for Italy. Trophimus accompanied the apostle to Myra; there he stayed behind on account of his illness, in order to go on with the ship from Adramyttium as far as Miletus, which was probably his place of residence, and where he wished to stay." This arrangement, artificial to begin with, is contradicted by the apostle's expression in chap. iv. 20. Besides, all this could not but have been long known to Timothy, who was with Paul in the interval, known all the more if, as Wieseler thinks, the apostle had intended to take Trophimus with him to Rome as a witness against his Jewish accusers. It is an unsatisfactory device to maintain that the emphasis is laid on $Τρόφιμον\ δέ$ and on $ἀσθενοῦντα$, and that Paul by this remark wished to remind Timothy only of the *feeble health* of Trophimus, which might even prevent him from coming to Rome. The sentence has anything but the form of such a reminder.—Otto attacks the point in a different way, by questioning the presence of Trophimus in Jerusalem at the time when the apostle was put in prison. He asserts that $ἦσαν\ προεωρακότες$ in Acts xxi. 29 must be referred to the apostle's presence in Jerusalem four years previously, since according to Acts xx. 4 Trophimus accompanied the apostle on his return from his third missionary journey only into Asia and no farther. Against this, however, it is to be noted that the apostle's companions there named did really go farther, as is plain from Acts xxi. 12; for by the $ἡμεῖς$ Luke cannot have meant himself alone, but himself and the companions who had accompanied the apostle on his journey to Macedonia. $Ἄχρι\ τῆς\ Ἀσίας$ in Acts xx. 4 simply means that these companions of the apostle remained with him till he had come to the place where the passage across to Asia was made. There they left him, crossing over to Troas without him; but later on, Paul again came to them here, and then they continued their journey in company. No hint is given by Luke that they remained at Miletus after the apostle's departure. There is therefore no ground for assuming that Trophimus was not in Jerusalem when the apostle was put in prison. Rather the opposite. It is inconceivable that the Asiatic Jews should after so long a time have used a suspicion formed four years before as a ground of complaint against the apostle. We do not see why they should not have brought it forward when it was formed. Besides, according to Otto's hypothesis, these same Asiatic Jews must be regarded as having been present in Jerusalem on both occasions.—In regard to the mention of Erastus, Wieseler is of opinion that he too was important to the apostle as a witness, and that the apostle had summoned him to Rome either through Timothy himself or through Onesiphorus, but that he stayed on nevertheless at Corinth, and that this is what Paul now communicates to Timothy. But there is nowhere the slightest trace of such a summons. Further, the order in which ver. 20 occurs, by no means makes it probable that it referred to judicial matters. Something was said of these in vv 16 and 17, and these verses could not but have been connected with ver 20 if the reference in them had been the same; they are, however, separated from it by the greetings in ver. 19. On the other hand, they are immediately attached to the apostle's summons to Timothy to come to him $\pi\rho\grave{o}$ $\chi\epsilon\iota\mu\hat{\omega}\nu o\varsigma$. It is more than probable that vv. 20 and 21 stand in a similar relation to each other as do vv 9 and 10. In the latter, Timothy knew that Demas, Crescens, and Titus were with Paul in Rome, and so Paul announces that they had left him; in the former, Timothy was in the belief that Erastus and Trophimus had accompanied Paul to Rome, and so Paul now announces that this was not the case. In this way everything stands in a simple, natural connection.— Otto's explanation, too, is unsatisfactory. According to Acts xix. 22, Paul during his stay in Ephesus sent Erastus along with Timothy to Macedonia. Otto now supposes that both were to make this journey by way of Corinth, and there await the apostle. But afterwards Paul changed the plan of his journey; he himself proceeding to Macedonia without touching at Corinth, and sending for Timothy to come thither, while Erastus remained at that time in Corinth, to which fact allusion is now made in Ἔραστος ἔμεινεν ἐν Κορίνθῳ. This, however, is inconceivable. If the case were as Otto thinks, Timothy himself could not but know very well that Erastus, with whom he had made the journey to Corinth, had been left behind in Corinth. And what purpose was the allusion to serve, since the stay of Erastus in Corinth some years before could in no way furnish a reason for his not being with Paul in Rome after the lapse of these years?— Further, if we suppose that the epistle was composed during the apostle's imprisonment in Rome, which is known to us, the charge given to Timothy in chap. iv. 13 is very strange. According to Otto, Paul left behind the articles here mentioned when he set out from Troas, as is mentioned in Acts xx. 13, because they were a hindrance to his journeying on foot, and he intended to return into those parts later. But according to Acts xx. 22–25, the apostle at that time cherished no such intention; and if those articles were a hindrance to his journeying on foot, his companions might have taken them on board ship.—Finally, it is worth noting that in the epistle no mention whatever is made of Aristarchus, who had accompanied the apostle to Rome. Otto tries to explain this by saying that Paul had only to mention his actual fellow-labourers in the gospel, and that Aristarchus was not one of these, but simply looked after the apostle's bodily maintenance. This, however, is one of Otto's many assertions, which are only too deficient in actual as well as apparent foundation. The result of unbiassed investigation is that the imprisonment of the Apostle Paul in Rome, during which he wrote the Second Epistle to Timothy, is not the imprisonment mentioned by Luke, during which he wrote the Epistle to the Philippians, to the Ephesians, and to Philemon.

REMARK.—Otto has attempted, not only to weaken the strength of the arguments against the composition of the epistle during that imprisonment, but also to give some as positive proofs that the epistle could have been written *only at that time*. One such argument is that, if the epistle is to belong to a second imprisonment of the apostle in Rome, the situation of the apostle during it must have been the same as during the first imprisonment. He argues that this is altogether incredible, since the apostle's favourable situation during the former had its ground only in an ἄνεσις quite unusual and produced by peculiar circumstances, an ἄνεσις which was much more considerable than that granted to him in Caesarea. The latter consisted only in this, that it was permitted to him to be attended by his own followers—whether kinsmen or servants; it was not permitted to have personal intercourse with his helpers in the apostleship, as was granted to him in Rome. This assertion rests, however, on an unjustifiable interpretation of the passage in Acts xxiv. 23, where Otto leaves the concluding words: ἢ προσέρχεσθαι αὐτῷ, altogether out of consideration. Certainly the apostle's *custodia militaris* in Rome had a mild form; but there is no proof that it may not have been so during his second imprisonment, all the less that its occasion and special circumstances are wholly unknown to us. Otto further asserts that about 63 there prevailed at the imperial court, through the influence of Poppaea, a feeling favourable to the Jews, that this feeling caused the apostle's confinement to be made more severe after lasting two years, and that this is even clearly indicated by Luke in the word ἀκωλύτως, Acts xxviii. 31. But Otto himself makes this friendly disposition to the Jews active even in 61: how then is it credible that not till 63 had it any influence in aggravating the apostle's situation? The assertion is erroneous that Luke's ἀκωλύτως indicates any such thing.—If it were the case that Nero was influenced by Poppaea's favourable inclination to the Jews to cast the blame of the fire in 64 on the Christians, it does not follow from this that Paul was not set free in the spring of 63, though this favourable disposition of the court towards the Jews might explain his condemnation in 64 after a brief imprisonment.—Wieseler thinks that "the chief judicial process against Paul and his πρώτη ἀπολογία before the emperor and his council took place only *after* the two first years of his imprisonment in Rome;" against which Otto maintains that by the πρώτη ἀπολογία in 2 Tim. iv. 16 we are to understand the process before Festus, mentioned in Acts xxv. 6–12. If Otto were right in this assertion, the Second Epistle to Timothy must have been written during the first imprisonment at Rome. But in order to confirm this assertion, Otto sees himself compelled not only to give an unwarrantable interpretation of the expressions in 2 Tim. iv. 16, 17 (see on this the exposition of the passage), but also to assume that Acts xxiv. 1–21 mentions only the preliminary process—the *nominis delatio*, not the *actio*. For the proof of this, Otto appeals to the use of ἀπεκρίθη τε ὁ Παῦλος instead of ἀπελογήσατο in Acts xxiv. 10. This, however, manifestly proves nothing, since Paul himself distinctly called his speech an ἀπολογία (ver. 10. τὸ περὶ ἐμαυτοῦ ἀπολογοῦμαι). The whole process before Felix wears so decidedly, from beginning to end, the character of the *actio*, that it cannot in any sense be considered simply a *nominis delatio*. Otto, too, falls into contradiction with himself by saying elsewhere that the *nominis delatio* took place in Jerusalem when Festus went there after entering on his office —In defence of his opinion that the epistle was written in the beginning of the first Roman imprisonment, Otto appeals further to the peculiarities which are already apparent in the first seven verses, and insists that these peculiarities can only be explained from the circumstances of that period of the apostle's life. As peculiarities of this nature, Otto mentions: (1) The emphasis laid on holding fast by the promise and faith of the fathers, both on the part of the apostle and on that of Timothy; (2) The apostle's allusion to the earliest circumstances of Timothy's life and ministry; (3) Timothy's irresolution in regard to ministering as a missionary; and (4) the repeated mention and discussion of imprisonment on the apostle's part. Taking up these points in succession, we may note the following:—(1) Not only at the time indicated, but from the very beginning of his apostolic labours, the apostle "had to consider, regarding the gospel, whether it was compatible with the faith inherited from the fathers, or involved a departure therefrom." It would be strange if the apostle had first been led to such consideration by the accusations of the Jews before Felix and Festus. (2) It is quite natural that the apostle should make less mention of the circumstances of Timothy's previous life and ministry in the First Epistle than in the Second. The former is more official in character, the latter more personal. If that allusion to Timothy's earliest circumstances is to be inexplicable after Timothy had already given proof of himself in the apostle's imprisonment in Rome, then it must be quite as inexplicable that Paul, in the beginning of his imprisonment, says not a syllable to Timothy to remind him of the fidelity which he had shown to the apostle on his third missionary journey. (3) The Second Epistle does, indeed, presuppose that Timothy had slackened in his zeal to labour and suffer for the gospel; but this might have happened later quite as much as earlier. Besides, the decline of zeal was not to such an extent as Otto in exaggeration says, "that he had almost abandoned his office through anxiety and timidity" (4) In the other epistles, written during his imprisonment, the apostle makes mention of it not less than in this. There is, however, no reason for saying that in this one he designedly explains the significance of his imprisonment in a way which suits only the beginning of the imprisonment in Rome.

From the survey we have made, it is clear that the composition of all three epistles does not fall into that period of Paul's life described in Acts, and that there is nothing in the same period to account for their origin. In spite of these opposing difficulties, it might be held as not absolutely impossible that one or other of them was written some time during that period; but there are two considerations of special weight against this—(1) There is the same difficulty *with all three* in finding a place in the period specified for the epistle, and in each case combinations more or less improbable, and of a very ingenious nature, have to be used. (2) *The very* events and circumstances in the life of the apostle which are presupposed in *these* epistles must be regarded as omitted in Acts, which is not the case to the same extent with any other of the Pauline Epistles. And even apart from all this, there are other weighty reasons against assigning their composition to that period—reasons contained in the structure of the epistles themselves. As to their contents, there runs alike through the three Epistles, as before remarked, a polemic against certain heretics. These heretics are of quite another kind than those with whom Paul has to do in the Epistles to the Galatians and to the Romans. They are similar to those against whom he contended in the Epistle to the Colossians —heretics, of such a nature as could only have arisen at a later time, and whose appearance in the church is indicated as something future in Paul's address to the Ephesian presbyters at Miletus. Christianity must have already become an aggressive power, before such a mixture of Christian with heathen - Jewish speculation could be formed as we find in these heretics.—Then as to the form of the epistles, *i.e.* the diction peculiar to them, it has manifestly another colouring than in the other Pauline Epistles, so much so that we cannot explain the difference from the fact "that these epistles were written to the apostle's pupils and assistants, the others to churches and members of churches" (Otto). It is inconceivable that the First Epistle to Timothy and the Epistle to Titus should have been written almost at the same time with the First Epistle to the Corinthians, in the period between the composition of the Epistle to the Galatians and that of the Epistle to the Romans; and it is equally inconceivable that the Second Epistle to Timothy should have been written at a time so much later than those two with which it stands in every way so closely connected. The hypothesis brings together things different in kind, and sunders those that are like one another.

REMARK — Otto's attempt to prove the close relationship between the First Epistle to Timothy and the First Epistle to the Corinthians—both of which he refers to the same church and assigns to the same period—must be considered entirely unsuccessful. The contrasts of the epistles compel Otto himself to take some precautions in order to blunt the edge of certain objections to his assertion His precautionary remarks are—(1) That the image of the condition of the Corinthian church, which was in his mind when writing the Epistle to Timothy, had become different when he wrote the First Epistle to the Corinthians; and (2) that the apostle "had to write in one fashion to the church, and in another fashion to his deputies." There are, indeed, in the epistles some points of agreement, which, however, may be satisfactorily explained by their common authorship; in both, attention is directed to heretics, and both refer more specially to the inner circumstances of the church than the apostle's other epistles. Otto has only succeeded in making it probable that the heretics in the two epistles were the same. He arbitrarily constructs for himself, out of the apostle's theses in the Epistles to the Corinthians, an image of the antitheses of the heretics, and unjustifiably refers to the latter trains of thought which are quite unsuitable. Nevertheless, he has not succeeded in proving that the heresy spoken of in the Pastoral Epistles, the nature of which may be gathered from the expressions: μῦθοι, γενεαλογίαι, etc., was also the doctrine of the heretics in Corinth.

The result of an unbiassed investigation is—(1) That all

three epistles belong to one and the same period of the apostle's life, and (2) that this period does not fall into that portion of the apostle's life with which we are more closely acquainted through Acts and the other Pauline Epistles. Their composition must accordingly belong to a later time in the apostle's life; and this is possible only if Paul was released from the imprisonment at Rome mentioned by Luke, and was afterwards a second time imprisoned there.

The narrative in Acts cannot be used to disprove the historical truth of such a release and renewed imprisonment on the apostle's part,[1] since, so far as it is concerned, the apostle's martyrdom at the close of the imprisonment there described is as much an hypothesis as the release. It depends on the notices of the elder Fathers. In this respect, however, we must not overlook the fact that in general their communications regarding the apostle are only scanty. In their writings they are not so much concerned for historical truth as for exhortation and dogma, their writings serve the present, and cast only an occasional glance on the facts of the past. Hence we are not surprised that they give but little information regarding the events of Paul's life, and that little only by allusions — The first clear and distinct notice of Paul's release from the imprisonment mentioned by Luke is found in Eusebius (*Hist. Eccles.* ii. 22): τότε μὲν (*i.e.* after the lapse of the two years, Acts xxviii 30) οὖν ἀπολογησάμενον αὖθις ἐπὶ τὴν τοῦ κηρύγματος διακονίαν λόγος ἔχει στείλασθαι τὸν ἀπόστολον, δεύτερον δ' ἐπιβάντα τῇ αὐτῇ πόλει τῷ κατ' αὐτὸν (*i.e* Nero) τελειωθῆναι μαρτυρίῳ· ἐν ᾧ δεσμοῖς ἐχόμενος τὴν πρὸς Τιμόθεον δευτέραν ἐπιστολὴν συντάττει, ὁμοῦ σημαίνων τήν τε προτέραν αὐτῷ γενομένην ἀπολογίαν καὶ τὴν παραπόδας τελείωσιν. This testimony of Eusebius has, however, not been left unquestioned. It has been declared invalid, (1) because Eusebius himself does not appeal to reliable authorities, but only to tradition (λόγος); and (2) because his conviction of the accuracy of this tradition rests only on the Second Epistle to Timothy itself, and particularly

---

[1] Otto came forward in 1860 as a decided opponent of this conjecture, and in the same year there appeared in its defence the work, *Saint Paul, sa double captivité à Rome, étude historique*, par L. Ruffet.

on his explanation of 2 Tim. iv. 16, 17. But, on the other hand, it is to be observed that the formula λόγος ἔχει (for which there also occur the expressions: λόγος κατέχει, παρειλήφαμεν, ἱστορεῖται, ἔγνωμεν, ἐμανθάνομεν, ἡ παράδοσις περιέχει) does not, in the mouth of Eusebius, quite mean "as the story goes" (Otto), but is used by him when he wishes to quote tradition as such, without intending[1] to mark it as erroneous. Hence his testimony proves this, if nothing more, that in his time the opinion prevailed that Paul was released again from that imprisonment. Then it is to be noted that Eusebius does indeed explain the quoted passage incorrectly, by understanding the words: ἐρρύσθην ἐκ στόματος λέοντος, of the release from the first imprisonment, but that this incorrect explanation arose from his conviction agreeing with the tradition, and not the tradition from the explanation, as Rudow thinks (in his prize treatise, *De argumentis histor., quibus . . . epistolarum pastoral. origo Paulina impugnata est,* Gottingen 1852): in illam sententiam adductus est interpretatione falsa . . . verborum ἐρρύσθην κ τ.λ., quae quum ad Neronem referret, putavit, apostolum jam semel saevo . . . Neronis judicio evasisse.— Though it may seem strange that Eusebius quotes no definite testimony from an older writer in support of the correctness of the tradition, still this proves nothing against it, all the less that he mentions no testimony which contradicts it. For the truth of that tradition some earlier documents seem also to speak. In the first place, the passage in Clemens Rom., 1 *Epist. ad Corinth.* chap v. The Codex Alex. is the only MS. of it preserved,[2] and its text, as amended by the conjectures of the editor Junius, runs thus: διὰ ζῆλον [ὁ] Παῦλος ὑπομονῆς βραβεῖον [ἔπεσχ]εν . . . κῆρυξ [γενό]μενος ἐν τῇ ἀνατολῇ

---

[1] It is clear that Eusebius by this formula does not mean to denote simply a vague report, for he not only directly recognises the accuracy of the λόγος under discussion, but also confirms it by his interpretation

[2] *Translator's Note.*—Another MS , fortunately unmutilated, was discovered in the library of the Holy Sepulchre, at Fanari in Constantinople, and was published in 1875 by Bryennius, metropolitan of Serrae Later still, a Syriac MS., purchased for the University of Cambridge, has been found to contain a translation of Clement's two epistles.—See *Smith's Dictionary of Christian Biography,* vol. I. p 557.

καὶ ἐν [τῇ] δύσει, τὸν γενναῖον τῆς πίστεως αὐτοῦ κλέος ἔλαβεν· δικαιοσύνην διδάξας ὅλον τὸν κόσμον κ[αὶ ἐπὶ] τὸ τέρμα τῆς δύσεως ελθὼν καὶ μαρτυρήσας ἐπὶ τῶν ἡγουμένων, οὕτως ἀπηλλάγη τοῦ κόσμου.[1] If the expression. τὸ τέρμα τῆς δύσεως, means the limits of the west, we can only understand it to be Spain, and in that case this passage favours the theory that the apostle was released from the first Roman imprisonment. The reasons urged against this by Meyer, in the fifth edition of his *Epistle to the Romans*, are not sufficient. Meyer makes appeal to the following facts.—(1) That Clement's words in general bear a strong impress of oratorical hyperbole, but this is seen at most in the expression: ὅλον τὸν κόσμον, which, however, is sufficiently explained by the previous: ἐν τῇ ἀνατολῇ κ. ἐν τ. δύσει. (2) That Clement speaks from Paul's point of view, but ἀνατολή and δύσις are simple geographical designations, just like our expressions east and west. (3) That, if Spain were meant, the μαρτυρήσας ἐπὶ τῶν ἡγουμ. would transport us to the scene of a trial in Spain; but that is not the case, since οἱ ἡγούμενοι (note the defin. article) can only be understood as denoting the highest officials of the empire, and besides, in Clement's time it was known generally that Paul had suffered martyrdom in Rome. (4) That Clement otherwise would indicate by the οὕτως that Paul's death took place in Spain; but οὕτως does nothing but bring together the preceding facts.[2] The meaning is: *in this way*, viz after he had taught righteousness to the whole world, and come to the limits of the west and "borne testimony before those in power" . . . ; οὕτως is used in the very same way here as shortly before in the passage about Peter: οὐχ ἕνα, οὐδὲ δύο, ἀλλὰ πλείονας ὑπήνεγκεν πόνους, καὶ οὕτω μαρτυρήσας ἐπορεύθη εἰς τὸν ὀφειλόμενον τόπον τῆς δόξης.—That Clement did not mean Rome by this expression, is shown by the fact that he was himself in Rome, and would therefore hardly

---

[1] The text, according to Dressel and others, runs somewhat differently. See on this point Meyer's *Comment. uber den Brief an die Romer*, 5th ed. p. 15 Meyer remarks "Still the various readings of the different revisions of the . . text make no material difference in regard to this question."

[2] Hofmann (*D. heil Schr Thl.* V. p 8) wrongly refers οὕτως only to διὰ ζῆλον; but the wide interval between οὕτως and διὰ ζῆλον is decisive against this.

speak of that city as the τέρμα τ. δύσεως, and also by the very emphatic position of those words. If Clement had not wished to point to some place beyond Rome, he would have been content with the expressions previously used, since they would have been perfectly sufficient to denote the apostle's labours in the west, and therefore in Rome. Several expositors, however, deny the proposed interpretation of the word τέρμα as equivalent to *limits*. The explanation given by Schrader and Hilgenfeld: "*the boundary limits*," and that by Matthies: "*the centre of the west*," are altogether arbitrary. Otto's explanation seems to have more justification. Following Baur and Schenkel, Otto seeks to prove, on "philological grounds which they have not supplied," that by τὸ τέρμα τῆς δύσεως we are to understand "the goal in the west appointed to the apostle." He wishes, in the secondary use of the word, to maintain the original meaning, according to which τὸ τέρμα denotes "the goal-point, the goal-pillar, in the hippodrome and the stadium." He supplies with τὸ τέρμα the genitive of the τρέχων, who in this place is Paul, and takes the genitive τῆς δύσεως as the genitive of the stadium. But the very last quotations which Otto brings forward from the classics to support his assertion, show his error. In the passage, Eurip. *Alc.* 646 · ἐπὶ τέρμ' ἥκων βίου, the pronoun is not to be supplied with τέρμα, but with βίου; it does not mean "come to *his* goal of life," but "come to the goal of *his* life." So also with the passage in *Suppl.* 369, where we have: ἐπὶ τέρμα ἐμῶν κακῶν ἱκόμενος, and not ἐπὶ τέρμα ἐμὸν κακῶν. Accordingly, in the present passage, if the third personal pronoun were to be supplied, it should be with δύσεως and not with τέρμα; but that would be meaningless. But, further, it is arbitrary here, where there is no hint of a figure taken from running a race, to supply with τὸ τέρμα the notion of the apostolic ministry, separating τῆς δύσεως from its *close* connection with τὸ τέρμα, and taking it as equivalent to ἐν τῇ δύσει; all the more that, when so understood, the words are a somewhat superfluous addition. Besides, it is improper to consider τῆς δύσεως as the stadium, and then to place the τέρμα not at the end of it, but somewhere in the middle. If τέρμα in the secondary application is to retain its original meaning, τὸ τέρμα τῆς δύσεως is either to be explained: "the goal to which the δύσις extends," or, more naturally: "the goal which is reached by passing through the δύσις." This may be the ocean which bounds the δύσις, but quite as well the extreme land of the west If the text is rightly restored by Junius, appeal may also be made to this passage for the apostle's journey to Spain, but certainly not for successful *labours* there, which rather appears to be excluded by the use of the simple ἐλθών. Wieseler, however, has his doubts about the correctness of the restoration, as he believes that the original text was not καὶ ἐπὶ τὸ τέρμα κ.τ.λ, but καὶ ὑπὸ τὸ τέρμα. This he translates: "after he had taught righteousness to the whole world, and *had appeared before the highest power of the west*, and had borne witness before the first," etc. His explanation, however, is contrary to the meaning of the word, for τέρμα does sometimes occur—only in connection with ἔχειν—in the sense of "*the highest power or decision*," but it never denotes "the supreme government." Besides, this conjecture and its explanation would designate the supreme imperial government simply as that of the west, while its authority extended equally over the east. Least of all would Clement, who, according to Wieseler's own expression, "is obviously tuning a panegyric on Paul," have used any limited description for that supreme authority. If he had understood τὸ τέρμα in that sense, he would surely have added to the word not simply τῆς δύσεως, but—as was the actual fact— τῆς ἀνατολῆς καὶ τῆς δύσεως.[1] Still less can Rudow's opinion (in the work quoted, p. 7) be justified, that we should not read ἐπί, but ὡς, and explain it as equivalent to "*paene ad finem imperii occidentalis*;" for on the one hand this gives to ὡς an impossible signification, and on the other it attributes to Clement a very commonplace thought.[2]

The second passage is found in the Muratorian Canon,

[1] Wieseler's other opinion is arbitrary, that in the words "μαρτυρήσας ἐπὶ τῶν ἡγουμένων" the ἡγούμενοι are the *principes* who composed the *concilium* which the emperor was wont to consult in his judgments.

[2] It is strange that Rudow, in his conjecture and its explanation, does not understand Spain by τέρμα τ. δυσ., but Rome (τὸ τέρμα τ. δυσ., non ad Hispaniam sed ad Romam referendum puto), which would make the meaning to be that Paul had come *almost* to Rome.

composed about A.D 170. It runs thus: Acta autem omnium apostolorum sub uno libro scribta sunt. Lucas obtime Theophile comprindit, quia sub praesentia ejus singula gerebantur, sicuti et semote passionem Petri evidenter declarat, sed profectionem Pauli ab urbe ad Spaniam proficiscentis From these words, in themselves unintelligible, this much at least is clear, that Paul's journey to Spain was the subject of tradition in the author's time. Even if, as Wieseler thinks, the word "*omittit*" has been dropped after *proficiscentis*, the words do not say that the journey did not take place, or that it was doubtful and disputed, but only that Luke did not mention it. —Otto conjectures that in the author's time some began, for ecclesiastical purposes, to maintain the journey into Spain to be an historical fact This conjecture, as well as the other, that the original text of the Canon afterwards received many interpolatory additions, is a mere makeshift in order to confirm, against the testimony of the Canon, the hypothesis that Paul did not make the journey to Spain [1]

From this passage it follows that tradition preserved the report of a journey made to Spain by the apostle, but not of successful *labours* there [2] This (confirmed by the formula in Eusebius λόγος ἔχει) agrees with the release of the apostle from the imprisonment in Rome, mentioned by Luke, since the journey could only have taken place if Paul were again at liberty.—As nothing can be shown to be decidedly inaccurate in this tradition so as to prove its impossibility, or even its improbability,[3] we are justified in using this result in

[1] It will be sufficient here to quote some of the conjectures proposed. Otto thinks that for *sicuti* and *sed, sic uti* and *sic et* should be read Laurent (*Neutest. Studien*, p 109) makes the conjecture sicuti et semota passione Petri evidenter declarat et profectione Pauli ab Urbe Spaniam proficiscentis. Many have tried to make the passage clear by retranslating it into Greek. Schott (*Der erste Brief Petri*, p. 353) translates it. καθὼς καὶ, παρτὶς μαρτυρίαν μὲν τὴν τοῦ Πέτρου φανερῶς ἀποσημαίνει, πορείαν δὲ τὴν τοῦ Παύλου ἀπὸ τῆς πόλεως εἰς τὴν Σπανίαν πορευομένου. Hofmann (*D h Schr* pp. 9 f): καθὼς καὶ παρτὶς τὸ τοῦ Πέτρου πάθος σαφῶς δηλοῖ, Παύλου δὲ τὴν πορείαν εἰς τὴν Σπανίαν πορευομένου. Comp Meyer's *Romerbrief*, 5th ed. pp. 17 f.

[2] When this is observed, it may be explained also how Innocent I. (A D. 416) could write manifestum in omnem Italiam, Gallias, Hispanias, Africam atque Siciliam . . . nullum instituisse ecclesias, nisi eas, quas venerabilis ap. Petrus aut ejus successores constituerint sacerdotes.

[3] The words of Origen in Euseb. iii 1 τί δεῖ περὶ Παύλου λέγειν ἀπὸ Ἱερουσαλὴμ

determining the date at which our epistles were composed. If we can find no suitable date for any one of them in the apostle's life, down to his first imprisonment in Rome; if, at the same time, the composition of all three necessarily belongs to one and the same period of the apostle's life, and the contents of the epistles point to a later period,—then we are surely justified in assuming that they were written after the imprisonment recorded in Acts, the First Epistle to Timothy and the Epistle to Titus in the period between this first and a second imprisonment at Rome, and the Second Epistle to Timothy during the second. This view—if we take for granted the genuineness of the epistles—is the only one tenable after the investigation we have made, and hence also more recently it has been accepted by the defenders of their authenticity (even by Bleek, who, however, disputes the authenticity of the First Epistle to Timothy), with the exception of Matthies, Wieseler, and Otto.[1]—The answer to the question, What date is to be assigned to the second imprisonment? depends on the date fixed for the first; and for this the year of Festus' entry on office furnishes a fixed point, since Paul arrived at Rome in the spring of the following year.—If, with Anger, Wieseler, Hofmann, we suppose that Festus entered on office in the year ·60, then Paul was released from the first imprisonment in 63, and the second imprisonment took place either *after* or *before* the burning of Rome and the consequent persecution of the Christians (in the summer of 64). The first supposition seems to be opposed by the fact that in the Pastoral Epistles there is not the slightest allusion to this persecution, while the second gives, from the spring of 63 to the summer of 64, too

μέχρι τοῦ 'Ιλλυρικοῦ πεπληρωκότος· τὸ εὐαγγέλιον τοῦ Χριστοῦ καὶ ὕστερον ἐν τῇ 'Ρώμῃ ἐπὶ Νέρωνος μεμαρτυρηκότος, do not exclude the *journey* to Spain (against Meyer), but any apostolic *labours* there. On the whole, however, too much should not be inferred from these brief summaries, for otherwise it might be concluded from these words that Paul had preached only from Jerusalem to Illyria, and not in Rome —It is of still less importance that there is no mention of any release of the apostle in the *Hist apostolica* of pseudo-Abdias

[1] Kolbe, too (in a review of Hofmann's commentary, *Zeitschr. f die luth. Theol u K* 1875, No. 3), will acknowledge no second imprisonment of the apostle, which he holds to be an unnecessary hypothesis, " not necessary after Wieseler in so natural a manner (!) had assigned to the Pastoral Epistles their proper place in the apostle's life."

short time for the events to which the Pastoral Epistles bear witness. It is true that the objection to the first supposition may be weakened by dating the apostle's martyrdom as late as possible, say in 67 or 68. For this we have the support of the old tradition; but on the one hand the tradition is very uncertain,[1] and on the other we would have the apostle labouring for so many years after his first imprisonment, that it would be inexplicable why not a scrap of information has been preserved regarding it. The objection to the second supposition is of less importance, for, even if the time allowed be short, it is not too short. The events would be placed in the following order:—In the spring of 63, Paul leaves Rome; he lands at Crete, where he spends a short time only, and, leaving Titus behind, proceeds to Ephesus, where he meets Timothy. Soon after he crosses to Macedonia, and from there writes the Epistle to Timothy; then somewhat later, after resolving to pass the winter in Nicopolis in Epirus, he writes the Epistle to Titus. Towards the end of winter he returns to Ephesus by way of Troas, and then proceeds, without halting there, by Miletus, where he leaves Trophimus behind sick, and by Corinth, where Erastus does not join him as he wished, to Spain; and from there (perhaps as a prisoner) to Rome. In this way he might still arrive at Rome some time before the burning, and undergo his first trial, after which he wrote the Second Epistle to Timothy.[2] Shortly before the burning, or in the persecution occasioned by it, the apostle suffered martyrdom, and by the sword, according to the testimony of tradition. Wiesinger grants, indeed, that in this view the favourable treatment of the imprisoned apostle is more natural than by

---

[1] In Jerome (*Catal* c. 15) it runs: Decimo quarto Neronis anno eodem die quo Petrus Romae pro Christo capite truncatus sepultusque est in via Ostiensi.

[2] Against this reckoning, Otto raises two points in particular—(1) the shortness of the period indicated, and (2) the apostle's summons in 2 Tim iv. 9 and 21. As to the first point, Otto grants that about five months might be sufficient for the journeys from Rome to Nicopolis, but thinks that the time from March to the middle of July 64 is too short for the journey to Spain and Rome, since the apostle " must have preached in Spain, been taken prisoner, undergone a process before the provincial court, and again made appeal to Caesar " But these presuppositions are not to be considered as at all necessary, since the actual course of events may have been quite different. As to the second point, Otto maintains that Timothy could get from Ephesus to Rome in one month, and that if the

supposing that he was imprisoned after the burning; but still he thinks that he cannot agree to it. His chief grounds against it are—(1) that the Second Epistle to Timothy is brought too close to the first; (2) that the apostle, according to 1 Tim. iii. 14 ff., did not stay so short a time in Ephesus; (3) that it is inconceivable how the Asiatics (2 Tim. i. 15–18) should be still in Rome during the time of the apostle's imprisonment, and how Timothy had already been informed of their conduct. But, on the other hand, it is to be observed (1) that there is no hint of the Second Epistle being written a long time after the First, the agreement between them rather testifying against this, (2) that from 1 Tim. iii. 14 ff. no conclusion can be drawn of a long stay made by the apostle in Ephesus; (3) that the verb ἀπεστράφησαν in 2 Tim. i. 15 does not imply the presence of the Asiatics in Rome. Ruffet agrees in the representation here given, but remarks Huther fait mourir Paul en 64, pendant la grande persécution. Il est difficile, dans ce cas, d'expliquer le procès de Paul. He gives 66 as the year of the apostle's death Against him it must be maintained that there is no ground for assuming that the process was carried out formally, and that it is arbitrary to assign 66 as the year of the apostle's death.

REMARK—Meyer (*Apgesch* 3d ed 1861, Introd. sect. 4) has sought on two grounds to prove, against Wieseler, that the retirement of Felix from office did not take place in the year 60, but in 61. His first ground is, that it follows from Josephus, *Vita*, § 3, that in the year 63 Josephus went to Rome in order to obtain the release of some priests who had been imprisoned by Felix, and sent thither. Now, if Felix retired from office in 60, Josephus would have put off his journey too long But, on the other hand, before undertaking this journey, Josephus had to await the result of the complaint (*Antiq* xx. 8. 10) made to the emperor against Felix by the Jews, and when

same time is to be given for forwarding the Epistle, Paul could not write in the beginning of July, but only in the middle or end of August, that Timothy was to make haste to come to him before winter! But even this assertion has only an apparent justification, since it rests on the unproved presupposition that Paul forwarded the letter by the shortest route, and supposed that Timothy would and could choose the shortest route for his journey. Besides, it is to be observed that ταχίως and πρὸ χειμῶνος are not immediately connected with one another.

Felix was acquitted, it could only appear to Josephus to be unfavourable to his purpose. He would hardly, therefore, undertake his journey immediately after he had received news of it. Meyer's second ground is, that from Josephus, *Antiq.* xx 8 11, it is clear that Poppaea was already Nero's wife at the time when Festus entered on office, and she became so in May 62 But the passage in question does not at all prove that. What Josephus says is this. About the time when a great impostor was destroyed with his followers by the troops which Festus, on entering office, sent against him, Agrippa built in Jerusalem the great house from which he could see into the temple The Jews built a wall to prevent his looking into the temple, and, after vainly negotiating on the matter with Festus, they brought the case before Nero by means of ambassadors. Nero gave them a favourable answer, τῇ γυναικὶ Ποππηΐᾳ ὑπὲρ τῶν Ἰουδαίων δεηθείσῃ χαριζόμενος. Josephus does not say how much time was taken up in building the house, in erecting the wall, in negotiating with Festus, in sending the ambassadors, in awaiting Nero's answer; but it is more than probable that some years must have passed while these things were going on Besides, it is at least questionable whether the use of γυνή implies that Poppaea was then Nero's wife — If Meyer's reckoning were still to be correct, the apostle's release would have taken place shortly before the fire The fact that there is no allusion to Nero's persecution in the epistles would have to be explained in this way, that the apostle was already made acquainted with it when he was with Timothy in Ephesus — Dr. H. Lehmann (*Chronologische Bestimmung der in der Apgesch Kap 13–28, erzählten Begebenheiten,* in the *Stud. u Krit* 1858, No 2, pp 312–319) gives the date of Festus' entry on office quite differently from Wieseler and Meyer. According to Lehmann's investigation, the year 58 is both the earliest and the latest possible date for the recall of Felix. He believes that Felix was not recalled *after* the year 58, because Felix was acquitted from the charge raised against him by the Jews through the intercession of his brother Pallas, *who,* according to the express statement of Josephus, *was then in high favour with Nero* But Pallas was in favour with Nero only till 59; his influence was very closely connected with that of Nero's mother, Agrippina, so that her downfall and murder in 59 would necessarily deprive Pallas of Nero's favour, just as some years later (in 62) he was poisoned by Nero, who coveted his treasures — Lehmann is of opinion also that Felix was not recalled *before* 58, because the revolt of the Egyptians (Acts xxi. 38) cannot have taken place before 56 — According to this, Paul would therefore be at liberty again in the spring of 61, which certainly would be a result very favourable to dating the composition of the Pastoral Epistles before Nero's persecution.

As to the *place of composition*, Paul wrote the First Epistle to Timothy after his departure from Ephesus, probably in Macedonia, or at least in the neighbourhood of that country, while Timothy was in Ephesus. In accordance with this, the subscription in *Auct. Synops.* runs: ἀπὸ μακεδονίας, while in the Coptic and Erpenian versions Athens is set down quite arbitrarily as the place of composition. In several MSS., on the other hand, we find the subscription which has passed into the Received Text: ἀπὸ Λαοδικείας, ἥτις ἐστὶ μητρόπολις Φρυγίας τῆς Πακατιανῆς; in Cod. A simply ἀπὸ Λαοδικείας. This place is assigned to it also in the Peschito, the Aethiopic version, in Oecumenius, Theophylact, etc. The addition τῆς Πακατιανῆς points to a division which arose in the fourth century. The opinion that the epistle was written in Laodicea is probably grounded on the fact that this epistle was regarded as identical with the ἐπιστολὴ ἐκ Λαοδικείας mentioned in Col. iv. 16. Theophylact says · τίς δὲ ἦν ἡ ἐκ Λαοδικείας; ἡ πρὸς Τιμόθεον πρώτη, αὕτη γὰρ ἐκ Λαοδικείας ἐγράφη.

The place in which the Epistle to Titus was written can only be so far determined, that it was on the apostle's journey from Crete to Nicopolis. The subscription in the Received Text runs: πρὸς Τίτον τῆς Κρητῶν ἐκκλησίας πρῶτον ἐπίσκοπον χειροτονηθέντα ἐγράφη ἀπὸ Νικοπόλεως τῆς Μακεδονίας. This has, however, arisen out of a misconception of chap. iii. 12, where the word ἐκεῖ proves that Paul, at the time of composing the epistle, was not yet in Nicopolis.—If the epistle was written on the apostle's journey, between the first and second imprisonment at Rome, we cannot, with Guericke, assume that it was composed in Ephesus; for if Paul had already in Ephesus the intention of passing the winter at Nicopolis, he could not, after leaving Ephesus and arriving in Macedonia, write to Timothy that he thought of coming again to him soon, 1 Tim. iii. 14. The Epistle to Titus can therefore have been written only after the First Epistle to Timothy.

While composing the latter, he was, indeed, thinking of a speedy return to Ephesus, but he considered it possible then that his return might be delayed (1 Tim. iii. 15) This actually took place when he resolved to pass the winter at Nicopolis, after which resolution he wrote to Titus. As to the Second Epistle to Timothy, there can be no doubt that it was written in Rome, as many subscriptions say. Only Bottger (*Beitrage*, etc., part 2) supposes that Paul wrote it in his imprisonment at Caesarea—which, however, rests on the utterly incorrect presupposition that Paul was only five days a prisoner in Rome.

SECTION 4 —THE HERETICS IN THE PASTORAL EPISTLES.

All three epistles contain warnings against heretics. These are described as follows.—

First Epistle to Timothy.—They have left the path of faith and of a good conscience (i. 5 : ὧν (*i.e.* καθαρᾶς καρδίας καὶ συνειδήσεως ἀγαθῆς καὶ πίστεως ἀνυποκρίτου) ἀστοχήσαντες ; i. 19 : ἥν (*i.e.* ἀγαθὴν συνείδησιν) τινες ἀπωσάμενοι περὶ τὴν πίστιν ἐναυάγησαν; vi. 21 : περὶ τὴν πίστιν ἠστόχησαν). They are estranged from the truth (vi. 5 : ἀπεστερημένοι τῆς ἀληθείας), and do not abide by the sound doctrine of the gospel (vi. 3). Morally corrupt (vi. 5 : διεφθαρμένοι τὸν νοῦν), they have an evil conscience (iv. 3 : κεκαυτηριασμένοι τὴν ἰδίαν συνείδησιν). Beclouded with self-conceit (vi. 4 : τετύφωται), they boast of a special knowledge (vi. 20 : τῆς ψευδωνύμου γνώσεως), which they seek to spread by teaching (i. 3 : ἑτεροδιδασκαλεῖν). Their doctrine is a meaningless, empty, profane babble (i. 6 : ματαιολογία ; vi. 20 : βέβηλοι κενοφονίαι), a doctrine of the devil (iv. 2 : διδασκαλίαι δαιμονίων). Its contents are made up of profane and silly myths (i. 4, iv. 7 : βέβηλοι καὶ γραώδεις μῦθοι) and genealogies (i. 4 : γενεαλογίαι ἀπέραντοι), which only furnish points of controversy and arouse contests of words (i. 4, vi. 4), in which they take a special delight (vi. 4 : νοσῶν περὶ ζητήσεις καὶ λογομαχίας). Without knowing the meaning of the law, they wish to be teachers of it (i. 7 : θέλοντες εἶναι νομοδιδάσκαλοί), and add to it arbitrary commands forbidding marriage and the enjoyment of many kinds of food (iv 3. κωλύοντες γαμεῖν, ἀπέχεσθαι βρωμάτων); by their ascetic life they seek to gain the reputation of piety in order to make worldly gain by it (vi. 5 : νομίζοντες, πορισμὸν εἶναι τὴν εὐσέβειαν) The *Epistle to Titus*—The heretics (i. 9 : οἱ ἀντιλέγοντες) belong especially to Judaism (i 10 : μάλιστα οἱ ἐκ περιτομῆς) While boasting of their special knowledge of God, they lead a godless life (i. 16), condemned by their own conscience (iii 11 : αὐτοκατάκριτος). What they bring forward are Jewish myths (i 14. προσέχοντες Ἰουδαικοῖς μύθοις), genealogies, points of controversy about the law (iii 9), and mere commands of men (i 14 ἐντολαὶ ἀνθρώπων ἀποστρεφομένων ἀλήθειαν) They are idle babblers (i. 10. ματαιόλογοι), who with their shameful doctrine (i 11 · διδάσκοντες ἃ μὴ δεῖ) seduce hearts (i. 10 φρεναπάται), cause divisions in the church (iii 10 · αἱρετικοὶ ἄνθρωποι), and draw whole families into destruction (i 11 ὅλους οἴκους ἀνατρέπουσι); and all this—for the sake of shameful gain (i 11 : αἰσχροῦ κέρδους χάριν).

Second Epistle to Timothy.—Here, just as in the First Epistle, the heretics are denoted as people who have fallen away from the faith, who are striving against the truth (ii. 18 : περὶ τὴν ἀλήθειαν ἠστόχησαν; iii 8 : ἀνθίστανται τῇ ἀληθείᾳ .. ἀδόκιμοι περὶ τὴν πίστιν; ii 25 : οἱ ἀντιδιατιθέμενοι), who are morally corrupt (iii 8 ἄνθρωποι κατεφθαρμένοι τὸν νοῦν; iii 13 : πονηροὶ ἄνθρωποι), who are in the snare of the devil (ii. 25), so that there already exist among them that godlessness and hypocrisy which, the Spirit declares, will characterize mankind in the last days. They seek to extend their doctrine, which is nothing but an unholy babble of empty myths, and contains nothing but points of controversy ; and this they do by sneaking into houses, and by knowing especially how to befool women (iii. 6), just like the Egyptian sorcerers who were opposed to the truth (iii. 8). — Contrary to the truth, they teach that the resurrection has already taken place (ii 18. λέγοντες τὴν ἀνάστασιν ἤδη γεγονέναι).

Have the Pastoral Epistles to do with *one* or with several

different classes of heretics? Credner (*Einleitung in d N. T.*) assumes four different classes. He takes the heretics of the Epistle to Titus to be non-Christians, and those of the two Epistles to Timothy to be apostatized Christians, while he divides the *former*—in consequence of the μάλιστα, chap. i. 10—into Jews, more precisely Essenes, and into Gentiles who are not further described, the *latter* into heretics of the present and heretics of the future (1 Tim. iv. 1 ff.; 2 Tim. iii. 2 ff.) — These distinctions are, however, not justifiable, for the expression οἱ ἐκ περιτομῆς does not necessarily denote Jews who are not Christians (comp Acts xi. 2; Gal. ii. 12). Further, μάλιστα does not establish a difference in regard to the heretics, but only indicates that some were added who were not ἐκ περιτομῆς. Lastly, in 1 Tim. iv. 1 ff. and 2 Tim. iii. 2 ff the future is certainly spoken of; but there is no hint in either of the passages that a heresy would appear different from the present one — Thiersch (*Versuch zur Herstellung*, etc, pp. 236 f. and 273 f.) divides the heretics into three groups—(1) Judaists, *i.e.* Judaizing teachers of the law to whom there still clung the spirit of Pharisaism; (2) some spiritualistic Gnostics who had suffered shipwreck in the faith; (3) impostors He supposes that the first are mentioned in the Epistle to Titus and in some passages of the First Epistle to Timothy, the second in the First and Second Epistles to Timothy, the last in 2 Tim. iii. But apostasy from the faith is charged not only against those mentioned in 1 Tim i. 19, but also against those in 1 Tim. i 3 ff., and in the Second Epistle to Timothy the same characteristics are attributed to the heretics as in the Epistle to Titus, comp. 2 Tim. ii. 23 and Tit. iii. 9. As to the impostors, they are not at all distinguished from the other heretics as a special class. — Wiesinger confesses, indeed, that the errors placed before us in the three epistles are substantially the same, but he thinks that on the one hand "more general errors" are to be distinguished from those of individuals, and on the other hand phenomena of the present from those which are designated as future. Hofmann's view is allied to this. He thinks also that those against whom Paul had a special polemic (Tit. i. 9, 10, iii. 9; 1 Tim. i. 3 ff., etc.) are distinct from those to whom Hymenaeus and Philetus belonged (2 Tim. ii. 17), and from those mentioned in 2 Tim. iii. 6 ff, and further, that those characterized in 1 Tim. iv. 1–4 are to be regarded as people of the future, and not of the present. Against this, however, it is to be maintained that such a distinction of different classes is not marked in any way by the apostle, and that the men of the future mentioned by him are characterized in substantially the same way as the men of the present against whom he directs his polemic. Mangold (*Die Irrlehrer der Pastoralbriefe*) rightly maintains that the polemic of the Pastoral Epistles is not directed against different forms of heresy, but against one and the same heresy; but he agrees with Credner in thinking that the heretics mentioned in the Epistle to Titus stood quite outside of the Christian church, since it is not said of them that they had fallen away from the faith. But against this it is to be observed that the polemic in the N. T. is everywhere directed only against those who, as members of the church, sought to disturb the true faith, and not against non-Christians who assailed the Christian faith from without[1] It is arbitrary also to distinguish the αἱρετικοί mentioned in chap. iii 10 as corrupted Christians from those named in chap. i. 10 as non-Christians.

The second question is, Of what nature was the heretical

[1] Otto decides quite differently by roundly calling the heretics *Jews*, and remarking · "I have found no passage in the two epistles, not even in *all* the Pauline Epistles, which compelled me to suppose that the heretics were members of the church." But should not this assertion be at once refuted by the fact that Paul, when speaking of non-Christians, always denotes them as such, Gentiles as Gentiles, Jews as Jews, whereas of the heretics, against whom he contends, he nowhere says that they stand outside of the Christian church? And would not both his polemic and his warnings have quite another character if the heretics did not belong externally to the church?—Otto grants that many members of the church had been led astray by those non-Christian heretics, but would not those betrayed have sought to spread their opinions among their fellow-members, and thus become false teachers themselves? Besides, Otto can support his opinion only by an artificial interpretation of the single passages in question, as is the case among others with 1 Tim 1 3 (see the exposition of the passage) and with 2 Cor xi. 13, 23. 1 Cor iii. 15 alone causes him some scruples; but he overcomes them by referring the pronoun αὐτός to ὁ θεμέλιος, altogether omitting to observe that Paul in this passage is not thinking of heretics at all. — Whether the τινὲς in Acts xv 1 were also Jews—and not Christians—Otto does not say; if he were consistent in his opinions, he would be bound to maintain the former.

tendency against which the Pastoral Epistles contend? The views on this point differ widely from one another. The heretics have been held to be—(1) *Gnostics*, either "forerunners of the Gnostics of the second century" (so most expositors), or "Cerinthians" (Mayerhoff in his work, *der Brief an die Colosser*, 1838, Neander in the first edition of his *apostol. Zeitalters*), or Gnostics of the second century, in particular Marcionites (Baur), (2) *Cabbalists* (Grotius, Baumgarten), (3) *Pharisaic Judaists* (Chrysostom, Jerome, partly also Thiersch), (4) *Essenes* (Michaelis, Heinrichs, Wegscheider, Mangold, partly also Credner), or *Therapeutae* (Ritschl); and lastly, (5) *Jewish Christians*. These last either had a preference for allegorical interpretations of the Jewish genealogies (pedigrees), which in itself was innocent and not delusive, but which might easily lead to apostasy from the faith (Wiesinger, who, however, remarks that in some are found the germs of the later gnosis), or they were busying themselves with investigations regarding the legal and historical contents of the Thora, to which they ascribed a special importance for the religious life (Hofmann). The *second* and third views have already received a sufficient refutation. The words: θέλοντες εἶναι νομοδιδάσκαλοι (1 Tim. i. 7), are the only argument in favour of the opinion that these opponents resembled those against whom Paul contended in the Epistle to the Galatians and in the first part of the Epistle to the Romans. From 1 Tim. iv. 3, Tit. i. 14, it is clear that their zeal for the law did not all agree with the pharisaically-inclined Jewish-Christians, as they did not maintain the necessity for circumcision.—*Cabbalists* they cannot be called, although there existed earlier among the orthodox Jews many elements from which was developed the cabbalistic system afterwards imprinted on the books of Jezira and Sohar; these were secret doctrines, and it cannot be proved that *these* heretics had the same views. For that matter, there are even some points here, such as forbidding to marry, the spiritualistic doctrine of the resurrection, which are foreign to Cabbala. There is only one kindred point in the phenomena of the two: they both consisted in combination of revealed religion, with speculation originally heathen.

The view that the heretics were Essenes has found in

Mangold a defender both thoroughgoing and acute; but he has been able to prove the identity of the two only by a somewhat bold assertion. Proceeding from the opinion "that Essenism was only an attempt to carry out practically the Alexandrine-Jewish philosophy in the definite arrangements of a sect," he deduces from this the unjustifiable canon: " If, therefore, any trait in the picture of the heretics should find a direct parallel, though only in such a passage of Philo as gives quite general characteristics of the Jewish-Alexandrine philosophy, we ought not to hesitate in explaining this trait to be Essenic, provided only it does not stand in contradiction with the definite information given by Philo and Josephus regarding this sect"— Mangold tries to trace back to Essenism not only the γενεαλογίαι, but also the other traits in the picture of the heretics, especially the μῦθοι, the ζητήσεις, the γνῶσις ψευδώνυμος, the asceticism, the doctrine of the resurrection, the view of the person and work of Christ, not indeed expressed, but indicated, the greed, the hypocrisy, the comparison with the Egyptian sorcerers, etc. But if he had not the aid of the canon quoted, and of an interpretation sometimes very forced, the result would simply be this, that in the heretics of the epistles there existed some traits which belonged also to Essenism. On the other hand, the heretics had many peculiarities not found among the Essenes, and the Essenes again had distinct characteristics of which there is no mention here (comp. Uhlhorn's criticism of Mangold's book in the *Gött. gel Anz.* 1857, No 179).—The fact that Mangold could only justify his assertion that the heretics were Essenes by identifying the general Jewish-Alexandrine speculation with Philonism and Essenism, is a sufficient proof that his assertion has no firm and sure ground.—Against Ritschl's view that the heretics were *Therapeutae*, Uhlhorn's remarks (in the criticism quoted) are sufficient: " They have no hesitation in assuming a quite close connection with the Jewish-Alexandrine philosophy, nor would they make any difficulty of importing into it the principles of Philo. But then new difficulties appear. If it is already hazardous to imagine Essenes in Ephesus and Crete, it might become much harder to suppose that there were Therapeutae in those regions. Their whole nature is so thoroughly

Egyptian, that we can hardly venture on the hypothesis of the sect being transplanted and extended into Asia Minor and Crete. Yet that would be the smallest difficulty The main point is that the picture of the heretics applies to the Therapeutae much less than to the Essenes; not only because the most striking characteristics of the Therapeutae are wanting, but also because there are features which do not suit the Therapeutae at all. Thus, *e g.*, the busy activity mentioned in 2 Tim. iii. 6 stands in glaring contrast with their habits of contemplation "

The view which is by far the most prevalent is, that the heresy was *Gnosticism,* either "a rough elementary form of gnosis," or one of the cultivated systems. Baur, as is well known, declares himself for the latter with great decision His judgment (*Die sog Pastoralbriefe des Ap. Paulus,* 1835, p 10) runs thus: " We have before us in the heretics of the Pastoral Epistles the Gnostics of the second century, especially the Marcionites " For the Marcionitism Baur appeals—(1) to the Antinomianism denoted in 1 Tim. i 6-11; (2) to the ascetic ἀπέχεσθαι βρωμάτων, 1 Tim. iv 3, which was founded on a certain opposition and dislike to God's creation—as to something unclean, and therefore on a decidedly dualistic view of the universe (such as Marcion in particular held); (3) to the doctrine of the resurrection, mentioned in 2 Tim. ii. 18; (4) to the express mention of the Marcionite antithesis, 1 Tim. vi. 20.—Of these reasons we must at once strike out the first and the last, as resting on an arbitrary and quite unjustifiable interpretation. As to the second, the opposition made to the asceticism of the heretics in Tit. i. 15 and 1 Tim. iv 3, 4, by no means points to a decided form of dualism; and with regard to the third ground, it is to be observed that the doctrine of the resurrection had no more connection with Gnosticism than with other speculative systems.—For the Gnosticism of the heretics, Baur produces the following grounds :—(1) The myths and genealogies by which the Valentinian series of aeons and the whole fantastic history of the pleroma were denoted. This, he says, is apparent from the adjective γραώδης, which was chosen because the Sophia-Achamoth was denoted as an old mother. (2) The emphasis laid in the epistles on the universality of the divine grace, by which is expressed the opposition to the Gnostic distinction between pneumatic and other men. But even these grounds furnish no proof that the heresy belonged to the second century, for series of emanations and particularism were not phenomena of cultivated Gnosticism alone. The interpretation of the word γραώδης, however, certainly needs no serious refutation. Baur further declares that even the author of the epistles was infected with the Marcionitism, as appears especially from the opposition in which the ἄνθρωπος of 1 Tim. ii 5 stands to ἐφανερώθη ἐν σαρκί in 1 Tim. iii. 16, also from the passage in 1 Tim. iii. 16, where two sets of clauses are opposed, the one more Gnostic, the other more anti-Gnostic; lastly, from the use of doxologies that have a Gnostic sound. But apart altogether from single pieces of arbitrary conjecture, of which Baur is guilty in his proof, how curious in itself the opinion is, that the assailant of Marcionitism should himself have been half a Marcionite, without having any suspicion of his self-contradiction! In his work, *Paulus, der Apostel Jesu Christi*, 1845, Baur brought forward yet another new and peculiar proof of his assertion that the Gnosticism of the heretics belonged to the second century. He finds it in the express statement of Hegesippus (Eusebius, *H. E* iii. 32), that the ψευδώνυμος γνῶσις did not appear openly till there were none of the apostolic circle left From this Baur draws two inferences—(1) that Gnosticism belonged only to the post-apostolic age; and (2) that the author of the Pastoral Epistles borrowed the expression ἡ ψευδώνυμος γνῶσις from Hegesippus. But against the first inference it is to be noted that in this passage it is not only not denied, but it is even expressly stated that there had existed earlier such as "corrupt the sound rule of wholesome preaching," and that it is simply remarked that the ἑτεροδιδάσκαλοι ventured only after the death of the apostles to preach their heresy quite openly and freely. Against the second inference we must maintain that the passage in Eusebius (as Thiersch in his *Versuch zur Herstellung*, etc., pp. 301 ff, and following him Wiesinger and Mangold, have proved) is not a simple quotation from Hegesippus, but that the thought only was expressed by Hegesippus, while its elaboration and form are due to Eusebius; and that

INTRODUCTION. 49

"although the Ebionite Hegesippus would hardly have used the Pastoral Epistles for expressing his own views, yet there is no reason why these expressions in Eusebius should not be traced back to the Pastoral Epistles as their source" (comp. Mangold, pp. 108-112)[1] Thus the theory that the heretics in question were Marcionites, or other Gnostics of the second century, has no real foundation; for which reason, as Mangold says, "all exegetes and writers on Introduction who have studied the question are unanimous against Baur's view" (Mangold, p. 14)—Quite as little support has been given also to the theory that the heretics were *Cerinthians;* and rightly so, since it cannot be proved that they held the doctrine of Cerinthus regarding the Demiurge, or his Docetism or the Chiliasm ascribed to him by Caius and Dionysius.—The answer to the question whether Paul's opponents were Gnostics (so far, of course, only followers of a gnosis still undeveloped) or not, depends to a large extent, if not wholly, on the meaning to be given to γενεαλογίαι Irenaeus and Tertullian, whom many later expositors have followed, understood by it, "Gnostic series of emanations." In more recent times an attempt has been made to maintain that we are to understand by it actual genealogies. Dahne (*Stud. u. Krit.* 1833, No. 4), supported by Mangold and Otto, makes it more definite, and says that by it are meant the genealogies of the Pentateuch, along with its historical sections, the former of which Philo interprets in his τρόποι τῆς ψυχῆς. But there is not the slightest indication in the Pastoral Epistles that the heretics here mentioned made any such interpretation themselves. Wiesinger has let this more definite statement drop, and explains the γενεαλογίαι to be simply Jewish genealogies. Hofmann, on the contrary, going back again to Philo, considers them to be not genealogies proper, but "the whole historical contents of the Thora."[2] Both these

---

[1] If Hegesippus did use the expression ἡ ψευδώνυμος γνῶσις, it is in any case more probable that he should have borrowed it from the First Epistle to Timothy, than that the author of the epistle should have taken it from Hegesippus

[2] This explanation Hofmann justifies by referring to Philo's division of the historical contents of the Thora into two parts τὸ περὶ τῆς τοῦ κόσμου γενέσεως and τὸ γενεαλογικόν. But though Philo uses the name τὸ γενεαλογικόν for the part after

expositors do not wish to regard Paul's opponents here as heretics in the proper sense. Wiesinger, as he developes this point, contradicts himself. For, when he grants that they cultivated an arbitrary asceticism,—that they strove after a higher holiness as well as a higher knowledge than the gospel presents, and that they sought to attain this by an allegorical interpretation of the genealogies,[1]—he is manifestly describing them as heretics in the proper sense of the term. Hofmann does not indeed fall into this contradiction, but with his view it remains wholly unexplained how they could give to the study of the historical contents of the Thora a special importance for the religious life, if they still did not seek to get from it knowledge transcending the gospel. The following points are against both these explanations:—(1) The sentence of condemnation pronounced in the epistles is so sharp, that it points to something quite different from mere unprofitable speculation Although Paul, as these argue, calls their reasonings $\mu\alpha\tau\alpha\iota o\lambda o\gamma\iota\alpha$ and $\kappa\epsilon\nu o\phi\omega\nu\iota\alpha$, he describes this empty babble of theirs not merely as a useless, foolish, old woman's chatter, but also as something unholy, *i.e.* profane ($\beta\epsilon\beta\eta\lambda o\varsigma$, comp. Heb. xii. 16), and the reasoners as those who, fallen away from the faith, contradict the truth, and are morally corrupt in thought. (2) Paul defines the $\gamma\epsilon\nu\epsilon\alpha\lambda o\gamma\iota\alpha\iota$ more precisely by the adjective $\dot{\alpha}\pi\epsilon\rho\alpha\nu\tau o\iota$, which gives, not, as it has been wrongly explained, the nature of the investigations regarding the $\gamma\epsilon\nu\epsilon\alpha\lambda o\gamma\iota\alpha\iota$ (as those "which spin on *ad infinitum*," Wiesinger, or "the end of which is never reached," Hofmann), but the nature of the $\gamma\epsilon\nu\epsilon\alpha\lambda o\gamma\iota\alpha\iota$ *themselves*. Since neither the Jewish genealogies nor the facts given in the Thora are unlimited, we can hardly understand the $\gamma\epsilon\nu\epsilon\alpha\lambda o\gamma\iota\alpha\iota$ to be anything else than "Gnostic series of emanations," which have no necessary termination in themselves, and can therefore be regarded as unlimited.—Beside the expression

the history of the creation, because it begins with a genealogy, it does not follow, as a matter of fact, that the single historical events are designated by the word γενεαλογίαι

[1] Wiesinger has not observed that allegorical interpretation is not to be regarded as the source of any special knowledge, but that knowledge obtained in other ways makes use of allegorical interpretation for its own confirmation.

γενεαλογίαι ἀπέραντοι, there are other features in the apostle's polemic pointing to the Gnostic tendencies of his adversaries here, who boasted of a special knowledge, called by Paul γνῶσις ψευδώνυμος; still their Gnosticism is quite distinct from Gnosticism proper, i.e from the Gnosticism which spread so widely in the church in the second century. The soil of the *latter* was Gentile Christianity; the soil of the *former* was Judaism, or Jewish Christianity mingled with Gentile speculation. An appeal to the Mosaic law was quite out of place in Gnosticism proper, but these heretics wished to be νομοδιδάσκαλοι. The asceticism of the Gnostics was based on dualism; the ascetic precepts of these heretics proceeded from the distinction—contained also in the law of Moses—between clean and unclean; and although they inconsistently spiritualized the contrast between spirit and matter, there is 'nothing to show that they adopted dualism proper, though we may take it for granted that they were so inclined. Gnosticism distinguishes between the Demiurge and the highest God—a distinction not known to these heretics. Finally, while Gnosticism is substantially Docetic in its view of the Redeemer's person, it is nowhere said that these heretics were Docetic; it rather appears on the whole as if the idea of redemption had not with them the central importance which it had in Gnosticism —All these details prove that, although the heresy in question was in many respects akin to Gnosticism, its nature was still distinct Peculiar to both is the mingling of revealed religion with Gentile speculation; but in the one case — in Gnosticism — Christianity itself was invaded and penetrated by heathen philosophy, while here, on the other hand, Judaism first underwent that process. This Judaism, modified by speculation and united with Christianity, assumed, indeed, new elements, and suffered thereby many alterations. Still there was no *substantial* change of form, the Christian element in *this* form of Jewish Christianity being always overpowered by the Jewish. From it there arose such phenomena as are presented in the Ebionite, the Clementine, the Elkesaitic, and other heresies which are distinguished from systems strictly Gnostic, by preserving as much as possible a monotheistic character. To this speculative Jewish Christianity belongs also the heresy mentioned and combated in the Pastoral Epistles. It does not follow, however, that it was one single system definitely developed; the apostle rather keeps in view the general tendency which embraced manifold distinctions, so that all the individual features dwelt on by him were not necessarily characteristic of all these heretics. The general judgment refers to all. All who have yielded to this tendency stand opposed both to the doctrine of the gospel as well as to Christian morality; but all did not give direct utterance to the principle that the resurrection had already taken place, or that marriage was to be avoided, and we are not bound to regard them all as impostors, or as men who put on the appearance of piety only from motives of greed. One point might be more prominent in one, another in another; they are all, however, governed by one spirit, which could only exercise a disturbing influence on true Christianity.—This tendency is substantially the same as that combated in the Epistle to the Colossians. The distinction is simply this, that at the time of composing the Pastoral Epistles the same heresy was found in a stage of higher development. The doctrine of angels had already assumed the form of an emanation theory; the contrast between spirit and matter had been made wider, and the self-seeking motives in its followers had become more distinct.[1]

SECTION 5.—AUTHENTICITY OF THE PASTORAL EPISTLES.

Eusebius reckons the Pastoral Epistles among the homologumena, as there existed not the smallest doubt of their genuineness in the catholic church. They not only stand as Pauline Epistles in the Muratorian Canon and the Peschito, but they are also repeatedly quoted as such by Irenaeus, Tertullian, and Clemens Alex. Though they are not specially quoted by earlier ecclesiastical writers, yet many expressions and sentences occur showing that they were not less known than the other Pauline Epistles, such expressions appear-

[1] To the view expressed here, Zockler (in Vilmar's *Past.-theol. Blatter*, 1865, p. 67) has given his adherence.

ing as quotations, or at least as reminiscences.[1] Clemens Rom. not only makes use of the expression εὐσέβεια, so often used in the Pastoral Epistles to denote Christian piety, but also in *Ep. I. ad Corinth.* chap. 2, we have a phrase almost agreeing with Tit. iii. 1 : ἕτοιμοι εἰς πᾶν ἔργον ἀγαθόν, and in chap. 29 there is an echo of the words in 1 Tim. ii. 8 which can hardly be denied : προσελθῶμεν αὐτῷ ἐν ὁσιότητι ψυχῆς, ἄγνας καὶ ἀμιάντους χεῖρας αἴροντες πρὸς αὐτόν —In the Epistles of Ignatius, the passage in the *Ep. ad Magnes.* chap 8 : μὴ πλανᾶσθε ταῖς ἑτεροδοξίαις, μηδὲ μυθεύμασι τοῖς παλαιοῖς, ἀνωφελέσιν οὖσιν, reminds one of 1 Tim. i. 4 and Tit. iii. 9.—Still more striking is the agreement between some passages of the Epistle of Polycarp and corresponding passages in the Pastoral Epistles. Thus in particular chap. 4 : ἀρχὴ πάντων χαλεπῶν φιλαργυρία· εἰδότες οὖν, ὅτι οὐδὲν εἰσηνέγκαμεν εἰς τὸν κόσμον, ἀλλ᾽ οὐδὲ ἐξενεγκεῖν τι ἔχομεν, ὁπλισώμεθα τοῖς ὅπλοις τῆς δικαιοσύνης, with 1 Tim. vi. 7, 10,—an agreement which even de Wette can only explain by supposing Polycarp to have been acquainted with this epistle. — In Justin Martyr the expressions θεοσέβεια and εὐσέβεια frequently occur. In his *Dialog. c Tryph.* chap 47, we have : ἡ χρηστότης καὶ ἡ φιλανθρωπία τοῦ Θεοῦ, as in Tit. iii. 4[2] In the *Ep. ad Diogn.* chap. 4, there is the expression : αὐτῶν θεοσεβείας μυστήριον μὴ προσδοκήσῃς κ τ λ, which, compared with 1 Tim. iii. 16, is not to be overlooked —Hegesippus (Euseb *H E.* iii 32), in agreement with 1 Tim vi 20, calls the heresies γνῶσις ψευδώνυμος, provided that Eusebius is quoting him verbally, and not simply giving the substance of his thought ; see p. 48.—Theophilus of Antioch says, *ad Autolyc.* iii. 14, clearly alluding to 1 Tim. ii. 1, 2 · ἔτι μὲν καὶ περὶ τοῦ ὑποτάσσεσθαι ἀρχαῖς καὶ ἐξουσίαις, καὶ εὔχεσθαι ὑπὲρ αὐτῶν, κελεύει ὑμῖν θεῖος λόγος, ὅπως ἤρεμον καὶ ἡσύχιον βίον διάγωμεν[3] In Athenagoras, also, there are several allusions

---

[1] Comp especially Otto's thorough investigation in the excursus, "The External Testimonies to the Authenticity of the Pastoral Epistles," appended to his work, *Ueber die geschichtl. Verhaltnisse der Pastoralbriefe*

[2] The appeal to Euseb *H. E.* iii. 26, who quotes words from a work of Justin's, is out of place, since the expression : τὸ μέγα τῆς θεοσεβείας μυστήριον, occurring there, does not belong to the quoted passage

[3] We should also note Theoph Ant *ad Aut.* i. 2 ὅπως ᾖ καὶ τοῦτο εἰς δεῖγμα,

to passages in our epistles; thus, *Leg. pro Christ* pp. 37, 39, etc.—It might indeed be thought strange, that when the older ecclesiastical writers are dealing with the same subjects as occur in the Pastoral Epistles, or subjects akin to them, there is not some more definite allusion to these epistles, but this is quite natural, when we take into account their relative independence.—According to the testimonies quoted, it is a point beyond dispute that the Pastoral Epistles from an early time were regarded in the catholic church as genuine Pauline Epistles. It is different, indeed, with the Gnostic heretics.[1] In Marcion's Canon all three are wanting, and Tatian acknowledged only the Epistle to Titus as genuine. We cannot infer, from the absence of the epistles in his Canon, that Marcion did not know them Jerome, in his introduction to the *Commentary on the Epistle to Titus*,[2] reproaches him as well as other heretics with rejecting the epistles wilfully. It is well known what liberties Marcion ventured to take with many N. T. writings recognised by himself as genuine; and it is quite in keeping with his usual method, that he should without further ado omit from the Canon epistles containing so decided a polemic against Gnostic tendencies. The striking fact, however, that Tatian acknowledges the Epistle to Titus as genuine, may arise from his being more easily reconciled to it than to

τοῦ μέλλειν λαμβάνειν τοὺς ἀνθρώπους μετάνοιαν καὶ ἄφεσιν ἁμαρτιῶν δι' ὕδατος καὶ λουτροῦ παλιγγενεσίας πάντας τοὺς προσιόντας τῇ ἀληθείᾳ καὶ ἀναγιννωμένους, comp. with Tit iii 5

[1] Nevertheless, in the fragments of some Gnostics, preserved to us by the Fathers, there are some passages which point back to the Pastoral Epistles Thus in Herakleon (Clem. Al. *Strom* Book iv p. 502) the phrase ἀρνήσασθαι ἑαυτὸν οὐ δύναται, is to be compared with 2 Tim ii. 13, and in the extracts from Valentinian sources which are contained in the work. Ἐκ τῶν Θεοδότου καὶ τῆς ἀνατολικῆς καλουμένης διδασκαλίας κατὰ ~οὺς Οὐαλεντίνου χρόνους ἐπιτομαί, usually appended to the writings of Clem Al, we have the expression φῶς ἀπρόσιτον, with which comp 1 Tim vi. 16. See on this, Otto, *l c*

[2] Licet non sint digni fide, qui fidem primam irritam fecerunt, Marcionem loquor et Basilidem et omnes haereticos, qui V. laniant Test, tamen eos aliqua ex parte ferremus, si saltem in Novo continerent manus suas. . . . Ut enim de ceteris epistolis taceam, de quibus quidquid contrarium suo dogmati viderant eraserunt, nonnullas integras repudiandas crediderunt, ad Timotheum videlicet utramque, ad Hebraeos et ad Titum . . . Sed Tatianus, qui et ipse nonnullas Pauli epistolas repudiavit, hanc vel maxime, h. e ad Titum, Apostoli pronuntiandam credidit, parvipendens Marcionis et aliorum qui cum eo in hac parte consentiunt, assertionem.

the Epistles to Timothy, because in it the heretics are more distinctly called *Jewish* heretics than in the latter; comp. i. 10, 14, iii 9 But however that may be, the opposition of these heretics, when the genuineness of the epistles is recognised by the Fathers, can furnish no reason for doubt, all the less that Tertullian even expresses his wonder how Marcion could have left them out of his Canon.—After Tatian, their genuineness remained uncontested till the beginning of this century, only the more recent criticism has attempted to make it doubtful At first the assault was directed against the First Epistle to Timothy After J. E. C Schmidt, in his Introduction, had expressed some doubts, its authenticity was disputed in the most decided manner by Schleiermacher in his letter to Gass, 1807 Schleiermacher acknowledged the authenticity of the two other epistles, and tried to explain the origin of the First by saying that the others had been used and imitated He was at once opposed by Planck, Wegscheider, Beckhaus, who stoutly defended the epistle attacked by him, but the controversy was by no means settled by them Criticism went farther on the way once opened, directing its weapons against the presupposition from which Schleiermacher set out in his polemic. From the inner relationship of all three epistles, it was impossible to deny that many grounds which Schleiermacher urged against the authenticity of the one epistle were not less strong against that of the others Eichhorn therefore attacked the authenticity of all three, and was followed by de Wette (in his *Einleitung ins N. T* 1826), but with some uncertainty. For although de Wette declared them to be historically inconceivable, and combined Schleiermacher's view, that the First Epistle to Timothy arose from a compilation of the other two, with Eichhorn's theory, that not one of the three was Pauline, he still confessed that the critical doubts were not sufficient to overturn the opinion cherished for centuries regarding these epistles, which did indeed contain much Pauline matter, and that the doubts therefore only affected their historical interpretation. — De Wette's theory, so wavering in itself, was besides only of a negative character. Eichhorn, on the other hand, had already tried to reach some positive result, by expressing the opinion that the epistles were written by a pupil of Paul in order to give a summary of his verbal instructions regarding the organization of churches. In this he was supported by Schott (*Isagoge*, 1830), who, in a very arbitrary fashion, ascribed the authorship to Luke.—Again, there was no lack of defenders of the epistles assailed. Hug, Bertholdt, Veilmoser, Guericke, Bohl, Curtius, Kling, and others [1] took up the defence, partly in writings of a general character, partly in special treatises. Heydenreich and Mack also made a point of refuting the charges in their commentaries on the Pastoral Epistles.—Eichhorn's positive result had remained very uncertain, a mere suggestion without any tenable grounds. So long as no firmer and better supported theory was brought forward, the defence also had no sure basis. Baur was right (*Die sog. Pastoralbriefe des Ap. P. aufs neue kritisch untersucht*, 1835) in saying that "there was no sufficient basis for a critical judgment so long as it was known only that the epistles could not be Pauline; that some positive data must also be established by which they could be transferred from the time of the apostle to some other." The theory which Baur had formed of the relations of Christian antiquity, together with the peculiar character of the Pastoral Epistles, led him to believe that they had been written while Marcionite errors were current, and written by an author who, without being able to get rid of Gnostic views himself, had in the interests of the Pauline party put his polemic against Gnostic doctrines in the mouth of the Apostle Paul. In this way Baur thought he had found a firm positive foundation for criticism, and thereby brought it to a conclusion. But his opinion did not stand uncontested. Baumgarten, Bottger, and Matthies, in particular, appeared against it, and it is only the later Tubingen school that has given adherence to it. Even de Wette, in his commentary, 1844 (though he was more decided than ever in disputing the authenticity), declared himself against it, though in a somewhat uncertain fashion. His words are: " Since the references

[1] Neander, also, in his *Gesch. der Pflanzung* . . . *der Kirche*, 1832; confessing, however, that he had not the same confident conviction of the genuineness of the First Epistle to Timothy as of the direct Pauline origin of all the other Pauline Epistles.

to Marcion are not at all certain, and the testimonies to the existence of the Pastoral Epistles cannot be got over, we must apparently assume an earlier date for their composition, say at the end of the first century."—Credner, in his *Einleitung ins N. T.* 1836, advanced a peculiar hypothesis, viz, that, of the three epistles, only the one to Titus is genuinely Pauline, with the exception of the first four verses; that the Second Epistle to Timothy is made up of two Pauline Epistles, the one written during the first, the other during the second imprisonment at Rome, and is interwoven with some pieces of the forger's own; lastly, that the First Epistle to Timothy is a pure invention As a matter of course this ingenious hypothesis found no adherents, and, later, Credner himself (*das N. T. nach Zweck, Ursprung, Inhalt fur denkende Leser der Bibel*, 1841–1843, chap. ii pp. 98 f) withdrew it, and declared all three letters to be not genuine.—Soon after the appearance of this commentary, Wiesinger, in his commentary, 1850, declared himself for the genuineness of all three epistles, and made a thorough-going defence of them. Later, however, Schleiermacher's hypothesis found a supporter in Rudow (in the work already quoted, 1850) —Reuss, in the second edition of his *Gesch. der heil. Schriften,* 1853, is not quite certain of the genuineness of the Epistle to Titus and of the First Epistle to Timothy, but is quite confident that the Second Epistle to Timothy is genuine On the other hand, Meyer, after declaring in the first edition of his *Commentary on the Epistle to the Romans,* 1836, the genuineness of the Second Epistle to Timothy to be beyond doubt, in the second edition of the same commentary, 1854, acknowledges that the three epistles stand or fall with each other; and that if they were written by Paul, it could only have been after the first imprisonment in Rome, the one mentioned by Luke. At the same time, he disputes the reality of a release and a second imprisonment, and therefore cannot admit the genuineness of all three epistles. His remarks amount to this, that the more precarious the proof of the second imprisonment, the greater justification there is for the doubts of the genuineness, doubts arising from the epistles themselves.—About the same time, Guericke, in his *Neutest. Isagogik,* 1854, re-stated his conviction of the genuineness of all three epistles. Mangold (in his work, *Die Irrlehrer der Pastoralbriefe*, 1856) admits, on the contrary, that neither the heresy mentioned in the epistles, nor the precepts contained in them regarding church matters, militate against their origin in the time of Paul. At the same time, he remarks that their authenticity is dependent on the solution of a whole series of other questions, and that the weight of these compels him to take the side of the exegetes who do not acknowledge their Pauline origin.—Bleek (*Einleitung ins N. T.* 1866) defends the genuineness of the Epistle to Titus and of the Second Epistle to Timothy. Regarding the First Epistle to Timothy, he thinks that it presents difficulties so considerable that we may suppose it to have been written in Paul's name by an author somewhat later, but within the orthodox church. Hausrath (*Der Apostel Paulus*, 1872) considers the epistles to be not genuine, but conjectures that the Second Epistle to Timothy is based " on a short letter addressed to Timothy by the apostle from his imprisonment in Rome." Plitt thinks them Pauline in contents, but supposes that " they have been worked up afterwards by the addition of one or two utterances from oral tradition, which has given a somewhat different colour to them." As the latest decided defenders of the genuineness besides Otto (1860), we may name specially, L Ruffet (1860), van Oosterzee (1861, '74), and Hofmann (1874).

The reasons which chiefly awaken doubt regarding the genuineness of the epistles are the following three.—(1) the difficulty of conceiving historically that Paul composed them ; (2) allusions and discussions which point to a later time than that of the apostles , and (3) their peculiarity in development of thought and mode of expression, departing in many respects from the epistles which are recognised to be genuine

As to the *first* reason, the difficulty exists only when we presuppose that the apostle was not released from the Roman imprisonment mentioned in Acts, and that therefore the First Epistle to Timothy and the Epistle to Titus must have been composed before, the Second Epistle to Timothy during that imprisonment, if they are to be considered genuine at all. But this presupposition, as already shown, has no sufficient grounds, and with it disappears one reason for disputing the authenticity of the epistles

In regard to the *second* reason, there are especially three points to be considered—(1) the heretics against whom all the three epistles contend; (2) the church-organization presupposed in the First Epistle to Timothy and in the Epistle to Titus; and (3) the institution of widows, mentioned in the First Epistle to Timothy.

1 In regard to the *heretics,* comp § 4. Only by taking a false view of their nature can these be adduced as testifying against the authenticity of the epistles. In what the author says of them, there is nothing which compels us to assign them to the post-apostolic age.

2. *The church - organization.* — Those who dispute the genuineness of the Pastoral Epistles, especially Baur and de Wette, reproach their author with hierarchical tendencies, and maintain that the establishment and improvement of the hierarchy, as intended by the hints given in these epistles, could not have been to Paul's advantage. While de Wette contents himself with this general remark, Baur goes more into detail. In the earlier work on the Pastoral Epistles, he remarks that in the genuine Pauline Epistles there is no trace of distinct officers for superintending churches (comp. on the contrary, Rom xii. 8. ὁ προιστάμενος; 1 Cor xii. 28: κυβερνήσεις), whereas, according to these epistles, the churches were already so organized that ἐπίσκοποι, πρεσβύτεροι, and διάκονοι have a significant prominence In this he assumes that the plural πρεσβύτεροι denotes collectively the presidents who, each with the name of ἐπίσκοπος, superintended the individual churches In the later work on Paul, Baur asserts that the Gnostics, as the first heretics proper, gave the first impulse to the establishment of the episcopal system. Granted that such was the case, that very fact would be a reason for dating the composition of the epistles earlier than the time of Gnosticism, since there is no trace in them of a regular episcopal system. Even if Baur's view regarding the relation of the expressions πρεσβύτεροι and ἐπίσκοπος were correct, the meaning of ἐπίσκοπος here would be substantially different from that which it had later in the true episcopal system. — In

our epistles we still find the simplest form of church-organization The institution of the deacons had already arisen in the beginning of the apostolic age, and although tradition does not record at what time the presbytery began or how it was introduced, it must, apart from all the evidence in Acts, have arisen very early, as we cannot conceive a church without some superintendence. But all the instructions given in our epistles regarding the presbyters and deacons have clearly no other purpose than to say that only such men should be taken as are worthy of the confidence of the church, and are likely to have a blessed influence. — Where in this is there anything hierarchical ? How different the Epistles of Ignatius are on this point ! Had the Pastoral Epistles arisen at a later time, whether at the end of the first or in the middle of the second century, the ecclesiastical offices would have been spoken of in quite another way. Wiesinger is right in insisting on the identity between bishop and presbyter which prevails in the epistles, on the entire want of any special distinctions given to individuals, and also on the absence of the diaconate in the Epistle to Titus "On the whole," says Wiesinger, "there is clearly revealed the primitive character of the apostolic church-organization" (comp. also Zockler, *l c* p. 68) Wiesinger is also right when he points to ὀρέγεσθαι ἐπισκοπῆς, to the νεόφυτος, and to the διδακτικός as signs that the epistles were composed in the later period of Paul's labours. It may be thought strange, however, that while such indications are not contained in the epistles recognised to be genuine, they are given here, but it must, on the other hand, be observed that it must have been the apostle's chief concern in the later period of his life, all the more that he saw the church threatened by heretics, to instruct the men who had to take his place in setting up and maintaining the arrangements for the life of the church.[1] There

---

[1] The charge, that the system is insisted on *too* strongly, is in any case exaggerated In the Second Epistle to Timothy nothing is said of it at all, and in the two others it is discussed only in a few single passages, and in such simple fashion that nothing more is said than is absolutely necessary In particular, the divine origin of the episcopal office is nowhere named, much less emphasized. Even Clement of Rome insists on the significance of the office quite differently from what is done here

is no ground whatever for asserting that Paul had not the least interest in ecclesiastical institutions, and that this want had its deep ground in the spirit and character of the Pauline Christianity. Besides, all this is in most striking contrast with the information given us in Acts regarding the nature of the apostle's labours.[1]

3. *The institution of widows*—Schleiermacher quoted what is said in 1 Tim. v. 9 ff. regarding the χήρα, as a proof of the later origin of this epistle. At the same time, he did not, like many other expositors, understand ver. 9 to refer to their being placed on the list of those whom the church supported, but to their admission as deaconesses; and he thinks that such a regulation, ordaining that deaconesses shall promise perpetual widowhood, that they shall not marry a second time, and that their children shall be grown up, is not conceivable in the apostolic age (*Ueber den* 1 *Br. an Tim.* pp. 215–218). While Schleiermacher thus takes χήρα to be a name for the deaconesses, Baur gives a different explanation of the word as used in ver. 9. He thinks that this expression denoted, in the ecclesiastical language of the second century, those women who devoted themselves to an ascetic mode of life, and who in this capacity formed an ecclesiastical grade very closely connected with the grade of ἐπίσκοποι, πρεσβύτεροι, and διάκονοι, on which account the name of deaconesses was given to them. It seems, says Baur further, that they were not real widows, but bore that name. As a proof of this, Baur quotes in particular the passage of Ignatius, *Ep. ad Smyrn.* chap. 13, where he greets τοὺς οἴκους τῶν ἀδελφῶν σὺν γυναιξὶ καὶ τέκνοις, καὶ τὰς παρθένους, τὰς λεγομένας χήρας. But that passage only proves that in the second century there were virgins who, of course for ascetic reasons, remained in that condition, lead a retired life, and, as solitaries, were named χῆραι.[2] It cannot, however, be in the least

---

[1] Only this much is correct, that Paul in his apostolic labours could not begin with regulations for the church, and could not expect salvation from church-organization. But later, when there had developed a manifold life in the churches, he kept organization more in mind—a fact which does not conflict with his peculiar spirit. Luther's conduct in this respect forms an interesting parallel

[2] It is incorrect to interpret, as do Bottger and Wiesinger, παρθένους of real widows, and to take the addition τὰς λεγομίνας χήρας as a more precise explana-

inferred from this that the χῆραι named in the First Epistle of Timothy were such παρθένοι; on the contrary, everything here said of the χῆραι shows that *actual widows* are meant. It is true that in ver. 9 only those widows are spoken of who can be called *church-widows;* but Baur's assertion, that at the time of the composition of the epistle, according to ver. 11, virgins also were received into the number, is an erroneous opinion, which can only be supported by a wrong interpretation of the verse. On the whole, however, it is very questionable whether we should think of deaconesses at all in the passage This view was disputed formerly by Mosheim and recently by de Wette. Mosheim supposes that the χῆραι, as ecclesiastical personages, are to be kept distinct from the deaconesses, and that Tertullian, *de vel. virg* chap. ix., speaks of those who are also called πρεσβύτιδες, presbyterae, presbyterissae (The other proof-passages to which Mosheim appeals are : Palladii *vita Chrysostomi,* p. 47 ; Hermae, *Pastor,* Vision II. p 791, ed. Fabricii.—Lucianus, *de morte Peregrini, Works,* vol iii. p. 335, ed. Reitzian ; particularly also the eleventh canon of the Council of Laodicea, which in the translation of Dionysius Exiguus runs thus . mulieres, quae apud Graecos presbyterae appellantur, apud nos autem *viduae seniores, univirae* et *matriculariae* nominantur, in ecclesia tanquam ordinatas constitui non debere) The distinction, according to Mosheim, lay in this, that the deaconesses acted as attendants, observed what went on among the women, and did not venture to sit down among the clergy ; while the *spiritual widows* occupied an honourable place in the congregation, had a kind of superintendence over other women, and were employed in instructing and educating the orphans who were maintained by the love of the churches. If Mosheim's view is correct (see on this the exposition of 1 Tim. v 9 ff), we can see no reason why such a grade of widows should not have arisen in the apostolic age. Even de Wette thinks it probable that, from the very first, pious widows had an ecclesiastical position, and his only objection is that in this place it is presupposed to be a position defined by law and resting on a formal election.

tion of the expression παρθένους In that case Ignatius could not but have said : τὰς χήρας, τὰς λεγομένας παρθένους.

But καταλεγέσθω in ver. 9 by no means presupposes an election in the proper sense. The demand that the widow should be ἑνὸς ἀνδρὸς γυνή has caused much difficulty, this difficulty, however, vanishes when the expression is rightly explained (see the exposition). Besides the points mentioned, many others are quoted in proof by the opponents of the authenticity; all these, however, fall to the ground when the passages are explained. There is no doubt that the attacks often proceed from nothing but a groundless view of the relations of the apostolic age, and not seldom rest on the wrong presupposition that usages and views met with in authors of the second century were formed only in their time, and were not rather propagated from the preceding age. We can only discuss one more point here, and that is the assumed νεότης of Timothy. It has been thought strange that in both Epistles to Timothy he should be spoken of as still a young man; that, as de Wette says, the author " places him on a low footing, reminding him, as a beginner whose faith is weak and doctrine hesitating, of his pious education, of the instruction received from Paul, of the use of the Holy Scriptures, questioning his ability to understand a parable, and exhorting him, as a coward, to brave devotion to the cause of the gospel." We need hardly remark how much exaggeration there is in this description. But as to Timothy's youth, de Wette assumes that at the time of the apostle's Roman imprisonment he had already been about ten years in the ministry of the gospel, and was then at least thirty-five years of age. This reckoning, however, is very uncertain. The manner in which he is spoken of in Acts xvi. 1 ff, on his first acquaintance with the apostle, would rather suggest that he was then a good deal younger than twenty-five. It is to be observed that Paul, in the First Epistle to the Corinthians, also feels himself compelled to remark regarding Timothy: μή τις αὐτὸν ἐξουθενήσῃ, which remark was certainly caused by his youth, see Meyer on the passage. —Besides, we must take into consideration both the difference between his age and that of the apostle, and also the relation of his age to the position which the apostle had assigned to him shortly before the composition of the epistle, and which gave him the superintendence over the church with the oldest in it, etc.[1] Further, we do not see what should have moved a forger to represent Timothy as younger than he could have been according to historical facts.—It is not right to say that the pressing exhortations imparted to him in the epistles place him on too low a footing, since Paul had had many sad experiences in the last period of his life, and he is far from refusing to put any confidence in his pupil.

As to the *third* reason, we have already remarked that the Pastoral Epistles have much that is peculiar in expression and in development of thought. The only question is, whether the peculiarity is great enough to be an argument against their apostolic origin. The number of ἅπαξ λεγόμενα occurring in them is obviously not decisive, since every one of Paul's epistles contains less or more of such expressions peculiar to itself; thus the Epistle to the Galatians has over fifty; the Epistles to the Ephesians and the Colossians have together over 140.—The use of some of these expressions in later authors (*e.g.* ἄνθρωπος τοῦ Θεοῦ in Ignatius, *Ep. ad Rom.* chap 6, διδασκαλίας δαιμονίων in Tertullian, *De praescr. haer.* chap. 7) is clearly no proof that they belong *only* to post-apostolic times. It would be otherwise if such expressions could be shown to have arisen from some view or custom which was formed only in a later age; but that is not the case. The statements that the expression μιᾶς γυναικὸς ἀνήρ presupposes an unapostolic view of marriage, that the plural βασιλεῖς points to a period when, in consequence of the custom of adoption, introduced since Hadrian, there were co-emperors besides the emperor proper, and other similar statements, made by Baur, are arbitrary and without proof. On the other hand, the peculiar circumstances of these epistles made peculiar expressions necessary. Apart from the reference to the circumstances of the church here discussed, and to the position of the receivers of the epistles as assisting the apostle

---

[1] Bleek takes objection to μηδείς σου τῆς νεότητος καταφρονείτω, because "though Timothy was not yet at the time exactly old, he had been Paul's trusted helper for many years, and had received the most weighty commissions." It is, however, to be observed, that Paul in the epistle is giving him a position in the church such as he had never before occupied.

INTRODUCTION. 65

in his ministry, there is especially the heretical tendency, which could not but exercise a distinct influence on the expression. This would happen not merely in passages directly polemical, but also in the sections containing more general exhortations connected by the author in any way with the heretical errors. Wiesinger is right in remarking: "Considering all the circumstances, that the epistles are aimed at new phenomena, that they are addressed to fellow-teachers, that they are kindred in contents, and were composed at the same time, the peculiar vocabulary is conceivable, and, in comparison with Paul's other epistles, presents no special difficulty."—The epistles are peculiar, not only in individual expressions, but also in the entire manner of their thought and composition, and from this some have tried to prove that they are not genuine. But even this phenomenon is sufficiently explained by the peculiar circumstances, in so far as they are in some sort business letters, for the express purpose of conveying to their receivers short and simple directions on certain points. In this way the lack of the dialectic, which elsewhere is so characteristic of Paul, is not surprising. Nothing is proved against their authenticity, when de Wette notes the peculiarity that "there is an inclination to turn away from the proper subject of the epistle to general truths, and then commonly a return is made, or a conclusion and resting-point found, in some exhortation or direction to the readers." Such rapid transitions to general sentences are found often enough in Paul; comp. Rom. xiii. 10, xiv. 9, 17; 1 Cor. iv. 20, vii. 10, etc. Apart from the form of presenting the subject, the mental attitude indicated in the epistles is said to testify against the Pauline authorship. De Wette directs attention to the following points as un-Pauline:—the prevailing moral view of life, the frequent injunction and commendation of good works, of the domestic virtues among others, the advocacy of moral desert which almost (?) contradicts the Pauline doctrine of grace, the defence of the law in which a moral use of it is granted. But, on the one hand, emphasis is laid most strongly on the ethical character of Christianity in all Paul's epistles; and, on the other, there is nothing in these epistles to advocate moral desert to the prejudice of divine grace. De Wette acknowledges the univeralism in 1 Tim. ii. 4, iv. 10, Tit. ii. 11, to be Pauline, but he thinks that it has a different polemical bearing from that usual with Paul. The natural reason for this is, that Paul has not to do with Judaizing opposition here, as in his other Epistles.—De Wette's chief complaint is, that the injunctions given to Titus and Timothy are too general and brief. But why could the apostle not have contented himself with giving the chief points of view from which they were to deal with the various cases? Besides, if they are really so brief, how comes it that the church has always found in them a rich treasure of pointed and pregnant instruction? Nor has the church erred in this respect, as may be seen from Stirm's excellent treatise among others: "Die pastoraltheologischen Winke der Pastoralbriefe," in the *Jahrb fur deutsche Theologie*, 1872, No 1.

It would certainly awaken justifiable scruples, if it could be proved that other Pauline epistles had been used in composing these three The passages on which this charge is founded are as follow :—From the First Epistle to Timothy, i. 12-14 compared with 1 Cor. xv. 9, 10 ; ii. 11, 12, with 1 Cor. xiv. 34, 35. From the Second Epistle to Timothy, i. 3-5 compared with Rom. i. 8 ff.; ii. 5 with 1 Cor. ix. 24 ; ii 6 with 1 Cor. ix 7 ff. ; ii. 8 with Rom. i 3 ; ii. 11 with Rom vi. 8 ; ii. 20 with Rom. ix. 21 ; iii. 2 ff. with Rom. i. 29 ff.; iv. 6 with Phil. ii. 17. From the Epistle to Titus, i. 1-4 compared with Rom. i. 1 ff. Certainly the partial agreement is too great to be considered purely accidental. But it is as natural to suppose that the same author, when led to deal with the same thoughts, employed a similar form of expression, as that a forger made use of some passages in the genuine epistles of Paul in order to give his work a Pauline colouring.

As a whole, therefore, the diction and thought peculiar to the Pastoral Epistles cannot be regarded as testifying against their genuineness. But as each of the epistles may bear special traces of non-Pauline origin, we must further consider the criticisms made against them singly.

The First Epistle to Timothy.—According to Schleiermacher, it arose out of a compilation of the two other epistles. As proof of this, Schleiermacher mentions several facts, viz., that many expressions standing in a right connection in them, are here used unsuitably, that resemblances and agreements are found which amount to an appearance of plagiarism; and that this appearance is made an undeniable truth by misunderstandings and by difficulties, only to be explained by the hypothesis of their being imported from the one epistle into the other The expressions to which Schleiermacher thus directs attention are as follow:—i 1 : σωτήρ and κατ' ἐπιταγήν (Tit. i 3); ver. 2. γνησίῳ τέκνῳ ἐν πίστει (Tit. i. 4); ver. 4. μῦθοι (Tit. i 14), προσέχειν, γενεαλογίαι (Tit. iii. 9); ζητήσεις (*idem*), ver. 6: ἀστοχήσαντες (2 Tim. ii. 18); ver. 7: διαβεβαιοῦσθαι (Tit iii. 8), ver. 10: ὑγιαίνουσα διδασκαλία, ver. 16. ὑποτύπωσις; ii. 7 compared with 2 Tim. i. 11; iii. 2: νηφάλιον (Tit ii. 2); ver. 3: ἄμαχον (Tit iii. 2); ver. 4: σεμνότης (Tit. ii. 7); ver 9 ἐν καθαρᾷ συνειδήσει (2 Tim. i. 3), ver 11: μὴ διαβόλους (Tit ii 3), iv 6: παρηκολούθηκας (2 Tim iii. 10), ver. 7 βεθήλους (2 Tim. ii. 16); ver. 9: πιστὸς ὁ λόγος (2 Tim. ii. 11, Tit. iii. 8). But when considered impartially, these expressions are by no means unsuitably used in the First Epistle to Timothy; it cannot therefore be proved that they are borrowed, and borrowed unskilfully. The agreement of the Pastoral Epistles in their mode of expression is sufficiently explained by the fact that they were written with no long interval between them Comp with this the general agreement between the Epistles to the Colossians and to the Ephesians.—Besides this, however, Schleiermacher charges the epistle not only with want of internal connection, launching out often from one subject to another, but also with containing many thoughts foreign to Paul (i 8, ii. 14, 15, ii. 5, etc.). But on the *former* point it is to be noted that the epistle is not a work on doctrine, but a business letter, in which subjects of various kinds are treated according to circumstances; and on the *latter* point, that the thoughts mentioned are not at all in contradiction with Paul's views.—De Wette, too, has no grounds for asserting that the execution does not correspond with the aims proposed in the epistle. The passage in i. 3, for example, does not justify any one in expecting an elaborate polemic against the heretics, it is sufficient for the purpose to give some of their characteristics. As a rule, Paul enters on a thorough polemic only against those opponents who disputed his gospel from presuppositions recognised by himself; this, however, was not the case with these heretics. — The charges, that the directions for managing the church are too general and insignificant, and that the exhortations given to Timothy (1. 18 f., iv. 7 ff., 12 ff., v. 23, vi. 11 ff.) are not suitable to his character and position, are not to the point; and the same may be said of the assertion, that a business letter addressed to Timothy ought to discuss the apostle's special relations with the church at Ephesus, which was so dear to him. As to other points, de Wette holds that Schleiermacher goes too far in his unfavourable judgment, and does not agree with the theory of a compilation. Still he, too, places this epistle after the other two, and considers it the last written, though he assigns all three to the same author. All this makes it inconceivable how the forger did not express in *one* epistle what he wished to write in the apostle's name.—Mangold agrees with de Wette in regarding the First Epistle to Timothy as the last written. The chief ground for this view is the advanced stage of heresy shown in the epistle. When the Epistle to Titus was written, the heretics, according to this theory, still stood outside the church as purely Jewish Essenes, and had had some trifling success only in Crete. When the Second Epistle to Timothy was composed, they had found a more favourable soil in Ephesus; by fusing their dogmas with Christian ideas they had won over notable members of the church, so that there was a danger of this heresy eating into it like a cancer. The author was not deceived in this respect, but saw "the introduction of Essene dogmas into Christianity completed," and the heretical transformation of the fundamental ideas of Christianity into Essenism carried out to its ultimate consequences; hence he wrote another Third Epistle. In the earlier epistle, however, "he had chosen the situation in Paul's imprisonment just before his death," and thus "he had now to select some earlier period in the apostle's life for writing anew." The hypothesis is clever enough, but on the one hand there is no ground for presupposing that the heresy is more advanced in the First Epistle than in the Second, and on the other hand the forger would have acted most foolishly in placing the *later* stage of the heresy in an *earlier* period. Altogether, apart from the necessary explanation which these hypotheses give of some points, they leave many other points quite untouched. Mangold, in agreement with de Wette, gives one more proof for this theory of later composition—viz. that the Hymenaeus, mentioned in the Second Epistle as a member of the church, had already been excommunicated in the First But, granting the identity of the persons, why could Paul not bring forward later as a heretic a man who had been excommunicated for his heresy? Besides, in the manner in which the man is mentioned in 2 Tim. ii. 17, there is no indication that Timothy had known anything of him before. Bleek (*Einleitung in das N. T.*) has anew sought to prove the correctness of Schleiermacher's view, that the First Epistle to Timothy is the *only* one not genuine. The chief ground on which he relies is the entire want of allusion to personal relations in the church; but this want is sufficiently explained by the motive of the epistle. Bleek thinks it strange that in the instructions regarding the bishopric no mention is made of any particular person in Ephesus fitted for the office; but we must remember that those instructions were given to Timothy not for the Ephesian Church alone. Stress is laid on the absence of any greetings from Paul to the church or to individual members of it, and from the Macedonian Christians to Timothy; but greetings were not at all necessary, and there are other epistles in which they are altogether wanting or very subordinate. All the other reasons advanced by Bleek, he himself declares to be secondary. When impartially considered, they are seen to have no weight—especially for one who, like Bleek, acknowledges that the epistle contains nothing un-Pauline.

The Epistle to Titus.—The criticisms made on this epistle by de Wette are, that it neither agrees with the state of things mentioned in it, nor corresponds with its purpose and the relation of the writer to the reader. As to the first point, it rests chiefly on the erroneous theory, that the epistle was written soon after the gospel was first preached in Crete. If Christianity had already spread to Crete and in the island before the apostle arrived there, there would be nothing strange in mentioning the multitude of heretics, nor in the blame given to the Cretans in spite of their readiness to receive Christianity, nor in the instructions which presuppose that Christianity had been some time in existence there. With regard to the second and third charge, we must note, *on the one hand*, that de Wette arbitrarily defines the purpose of the epistle to be, "to give to Titus instructions about the choice of presbyters, and about contending with heretics," which certainly makes the greatest part of the epistle appear to be a digression from its purpose; and, *on the other hand*, that the weight and importance of the general instructions and exhortations for the development of the Christian life have received too little recognition—Reuss (*Gesch. d heiligen Schriften des N. T.*, 2nd ed 1853) shows greater caution than de Wette in his opinion: "The somewhat solemn tone may excite surprise, not less so that Paul apparently found it necessary in a special letter to say things to Titus which were self-evident. This surprise may, however, give way before the consideration that Paul did not consider it necessary to deliver to his substitute a kind of official instruction and authorization as his certificate in the churches. More simply and surely it may give way, when it is remembered that the apostle wrote for special reasons and that an important matter could never appear to him to be too strongly enjoined." —As to other points, even de Wette acknowledges that the epistle, "though not written with the Pauline power, liveliness, and fulness of thought, has still the apostle's clearness, good connection, and vocabulary."

The Second Epistle to Timothy.— In this epistle, apart from the historical inconceivability which it seems to him to share with the other two, de Wette takes exception to the following points, viz.: that, as already remarked, Timothy is not treated in a proper fashion, and that many exhortations (especially ii 2, 14–16, iii. 14–iv. 2), as well as the prophetic outbursts (iii. 1–5, iv. 3) and the polemic attacks (ii. 16–21, 23, iii. 6–9, 13), do

not accord with the purpose of inviting him to come to Rome.
—But as to the first accusation, the apostle's exhortations do
not by any means presuppose *such* a feebleness of faith and
faintness of heart in Timothy, as de Wette in too harsh
a fashion represents; besides, a forger would hardly have
sketched a picture of Timothy in contradiction with the
reality. The second accusation is based solely on de Wette's
inability to distinguish between the occasion and purpose of
an epistle. De Wette further finds fault with the epistle,
that here and there it is written with no good grammatical
and logical connection, and without proper tact (for which he
appeals to iii. 11, iv. 8!); but these are subjective judgments
which decide nothing—Schleiermacher declared the process
of thought both in this epistle and in that to Titus to be
faultless; and Reuss pronounces the following judgment on
them: "Among all the Pauline Epistles assailed by criticism,
no one (except the one to Philemon) bears so clearly the
stamp of genuineness as this epistle, unless it be considered
without any perception of the state of things presented in it.
The personal references are almost more numerous than anywhere else, always natural, for the most part new, in part
extremely insignificant, the tone is at once paternal, loving,
and confidential, as to a colleague, the doctrine brief and
hastily repeated, not as to one ignorant and weak, but as from
one dying who writes for his own peace.—The reference to
the apostolic office is the chief point from beginning to end,
and there is no trace of hierarchical ambition or any other later
tendencies." Bleek is decided in maintaining the authenticity both of the Epistle to Titus and of this epistle.

The following are the results of an investigation which takes
the actual circumstances into careful consideration:—1. The
external testimonies are decidedly in favour of the authenticity
of the epistles. 2. The difficulty of bringing them into any
period of the apostle's life disappears when we assume a second
imprisonment at Rome 3 The internal peculiarity of the
epistles, both in regard to the matter discussed in them and
in regard to the process of thought and mode of expression,
presents much that is strange, but nothing to testify against

the authenticity. 4. "There is no sufficient resting-place for the critical judgment of rejection, so long as we only know that the epistles cannot be Pauline; everything depends on proving positively that they arose at a later date." Such is Baur's opinion. But this positive proof entirely breaks down. Baur's attempt has no evidence to support it; de Wette makes an uncertain conjecture; and Mangold, who sees Essenism in the heresy, himself admits that this is no reason for assigning the epistles to the post-apostolic age. If there are difficulties in vindicating the Pauline authorship, it is still more difficult to prove in whole or in part how a forger could manufacture three such epistles as these are, in form and contents, and foist them on the Apostle Paul.—Since, therefore, there is no sufficient proof of the *post-apostolic* origin of the epistles, we may further (as Wiesinger also has completely shown) maintain their right to a place in the Canon as Pauline writings, all the more that the Pauline spirit is not contradicted in them, and that, in comparison with the writings of the Apostolic Fathers, they show a decided superiority in their whole tenor.[1]

---

[1] Guericke · "The Pastoral Epistles are certainly not written in so fresh and lively a manner, nor do they enter as thoroughly into details, as do Paul's earlier epistles. They show us the great apostle as a grey-haired man, bent with age, with persecution, with anxiety (?) His hate is especially sharpened against the enemies of the kingdom of God; but he is at the same time filled with a sadness all the more deep, as he beholds the kingdom of Antichrist develop now and threaten the future. Thus the fragile (?) covering reveals all the more nobly the spirit of faith and love which dwelt within him."

Παύλου πρὸς Τιμόθεον ἐπιστολὴ πρώτη.

A, al. have the shorter inscription πρὸς Τιμόθεον ἅ, which in D E F G is preceded by the word ἄρχεται.

CHAPTER I.

Ver. 1. ἐπιταγήν] ℵ reads instead ἐπαγγελίαν, a reading not found elsewhere, and not confirmed by its meaning; it may have arisen inadvertently from 2 Tim. i. 1. — Θεοῦ σωτῆρος ἡμῶν] In the later MSS. there is great variety in the reading, partly by arranging the words differently, partly by adding the article to one or other of them, partly by inserting the word πατρός, τοῦ σωτῆρος ἡμῶν Θεοῦ, 73, 80, 116, 213, al, Arm. — τοῦ σωτῆρος Θεοῦ ἡμῶν, 37. — Θεοῦ πατρὸς καὶ σωτῆρος ἡμῶν, 38, 48, 72, al., codd. — καὶ κυρίου Ἰησοῦ Χριστοῦ] καί is omitted by various cursives, or placed before σωτῆρος; the latter in the MSS. just named, as well as in Ambros., who has Θεοῦ καὶ σωτῆρος ἡμῶν; the former in Ar. pol., which has Θεοῦ σωτῆρος ἡμῶν, κυρίου. In many cursives καί is omitted along with κυρίου following it, Θεοῦ σωτῆρος ἡμῶν, in 17, 31, al; τοῦ σωτῆρος ἡμῶν, 43, and in those above mentioned, 38, 48, 72, and in Ambros. — Cod 118 has τοῦ σωτῆρος ἡμῶν Ἰ X. καὶ κυρίου Ἰ. X — κυρίου is wanting in the most important authorities, A D* F G, many cursives and translations (Syr both, Copt. Sahid. Aeth., etc); hence it is omitted by Griesb. Scholz, Lachm. Buttm. Tisch., while Matthaei has retained it with the remark: ita omnes omnino mei. — Instead of Ἰησοῦ Χριστοῦ, the most important MSS., etc., have the reading Χριστοῦ Ἰησοῦ, which is therefore adopted by Griesb. ℵ has the same reading as the *Rec.*: καὶ κυρίου Ἰησ Χρ. — Ver. 2. ἡμῶν after πατρός is wanting in A B D* F G 17, 23, al., Copt. (not Sahid) Arm. Slav., etc., and is therefore to be deleted; the interpolation is easily explained from a comparison with the other Pauline Epistles. — Ver. 4. For γενεαλογίαις, κενολογίαις occurs as a conjecture. — Instead of ζητήσεις, ℵ, A and some cursives have ἐκζητήσεις, which is adopted by Tisch. 8. This reading may be the original one, which as a ἅπαξ λεγομ. in the N. T. was changed into the usual ζητήσεις; the meaning is the same. — Οἰκοδομίαν (*Rec.*) is found perhaps in

74   THE FIRST EPISTLE TO TIMOTHY.

no Greek MS. According to Tisch., D*** has it; but this is denied by Reiche (*Comment. crit. in N. T.* II. p. 356). It is, according to Reiche: "nil nisi error typothetarum Erasmi, aut conjectura Erasmi ipsius;" the latter he considers more probable By far the most have οἰκονομίαν, only D* and Iren. gr. ap. Epiph have οἰκοδομήν (aedificationem: Lyr. Erp. Syr. p. in m. Vulg Ambr Aug. Ambrosiast). The reading οἰκονομίαν is supported by authorities so important, that we cannot doubt its correctness. Matthaei says: οἰκονομίαν ita omnes omnino mei, ac ii quidem, qui scholia habent, etiam in scholiis, uti quoque interpretes editi, οἰκοδομίαν nihil nisi error est typothetarum Erasmi, ὁ cum ν confuso, nisi Erasmus deliberato ita correxerit ad Latinum *aedificationem* — Ver. 8 Instead of χρῆται, Lachm. reads χρήσηται, after A 73, Clem The common reading is more natural, and is to be considered right, as the other has not sufficient testimony. — Ver. 9. Instead of the regular forms πατραλῴαις and μητραλῴαις, A D F G 48, 72, 93, *al* have πατρολῴαις and μητρολῴαις, which Lachm and Tisch. have adopted; several cursives have πατραλοίαις and μητραλοίαις — Ver 11. In D* and several versions there stands before κατά the art. τῇ, a manifest interpolation in order to connect κατὰ κ τ λ. with the foregoing διδασκαλίᾳ. — Ver 12 καὶ χάριν ἔχω] The most important authorities, A F G 17, 31, 67** 71, *al.*, Copt. Aeth. Arm. Vulg, etc., also א, are against καί, which seems to have been added in order to join this verse more closely with the previous one In Matthaei καί stands without dispute. Lachm. and Tisch. 8 left it out, Tisch 7, with Wiesinger, had retained it, following D K L, several versions, and Fathers. — ἐνδυναμώσαντί με] א has the pres ἐνδυναμοῦντι, and omits με; a reading supported by no other authority. — Ver. 13. τὸν πρότερον ὄντα] A D* F G א 17, 67*** 71, 80, *al.*, Dial c Marc. have τό instead of τόν. The latter is a correction in order to join the partic. and the following subst. more closely with the previous με. Lachm. and Tisch. adopted τό. Matthaei, on the other hand, reads τόν, with the remark: τὸ πρ. in nullo meorum inveni, nisi in uno Chrysostomi α qui fortasse voluit, τὸν τὸ πρότερον. Muralto likewise reads τόν. — After ὄντα, A 73 have με, which is also adopted by Lachm. It disturbs, however, the natural connection, and the authorities for it are not sufficient; hence it is not adopted by Tisch. — Ver. 15. א omits τόν before κόσμον. — Ver 16. Lachm. and Tisch. 7, following A D, etc, read Χρ. Ἰησ., Tisch 8, following א K L P, reads Ἰησ. Χρ. — Instead of πᾶσαν, according to D K L, Tisch, rightly adopted ἅπασαν from A F G, etc. — Ver. 17 Instead of ἀφθάρτῳ, D* has the reading ἀθανάτῳ, and F G have this word

CHAP. I. 1, 2. 75

inserted after μόνῳ — The word σοφῷ is rightly rejected by Griesb. Knapp, Lachm. Tisch Buttm. and others, since A D* F G ℵ 37, 179, 73, the Syr. Copt. Arm and other versions testify against it. It was probably an interpolation from Rom. xvi 27; Matthaei retained it, remarking: Vulgatum habet et repetit Chrys. xi. 569, 570; item i. 464, c v. 393, e Ath. ii 425, 433. Attamen σοφῷ abest ap. Cyrill. v., a. 295, haud dubie casu ac per errorem Ex omnibus omnino Codd omittunt soli A D F G 37. Reiche (*Comment. crit in N. T* II. pp 360–363) maintains that σοφῷ cannot be an interpolation from Rom xvi 27, because the doxology there is not genuine See, on the other hand, Meyer in his critical remarks on the passage, he holds σοφῷ to be genuine, on internal grounds, viz.. (1) Because Paul had no reason for emphasizing the unity of God against the heretics; and (2) because the reading μόνῳ σοφῷ Θεῷ is the more difficult one But these internal grounds are insufficient against the weight of the authorities. — Ver. 18 Instead of στρατεύῃ, ℵ has στρατεύσῃ.

Vv. 1, 2. As in most of his other epistles, Paul here calls himself an apostle of Jesus Christ in the narrower sense of the term, according to which it was applied only to those immediately called by Christ to the ministry of the gospel. He directs attention to the immediate nature of the call by adding the words κατ' ἐπιταγὴν Θεοῦ σωτῆρος ἡμῶν κ τ λ In 1 Cor., 2 Cor, Eph., Col, 2 Tim, διὰ θελήματος Θεοῦ is used for a like purpose The expression κατ' ἐπιταγὴν κ.τ.λ. is found elsewhere in the inscription only in Tit. i 3, where, however, it is not placed in such close connection with ἀπόστολος as here (comp besides Rom. xvi. 26, also 1 Cor vii. 6; 2 Cor. viii 8). The θέλημα is the source of the ἐπιταγή, by which we are to understand the commission given to the apostle. By this addition the apostle expresses his "assured consciousness of the divine origin and worth of his apostleship" (Matthies). It is not, however, an "*involuntary*" expression. The apostle deliberately insists on his apostolic authority, for the very sufficient reason that he was laying down in his epistle rules for church life. Heydenreich's suggestion, that Paul meant at the same time to confirm Timothy's position, is very far-fetched. — Θεοῦ σωτῆρος ἡμῶν] This collocation of the words is only found elsewhere in the N. T. in Jude 25; in all passages of the Pastoral

Epistles it usually runs: ὁ σωτὴρ ἡμῶν Θεός. In this passage σωτὴρ ἡμῶν is added as in adjectival apposition to Θεοῦ; while in Luke i. 47 it is marked as a substantive by the article. In the Pastoral Epistles σωτήρ is used both of God (so frequently in O. T.; comp. LXX. Ps. xxiv. 5; Isa. xii. 2, xlv. 15, 21, Wisd. Sol xvi. 7; Ecclus. li. 1) and of Christ; in the other Pauline Epistles (e.g. Eph. v. 23; Phil. iii. 20), as well as in John iv 42, Acts v. 31, etc, it serves to denote Christ. Heydenreich is right in remarking that God does not bear this name as preserver and benefactor of men in general, but on account of the means He has instituted for saving and blessing us through Christ. — καὶ Χριστοῦ Ἰησοῦ] These words are added on account of the apostle's Christology; so also in Gal. i. 1. — τῆς ἐλπίδος ἡμῶν] Christ is so named because He is both "the ground of our hope" (Wiesinger) and the object of it He is hoped for, because by Him the σωτηρία is brought to completion (Calvin: in eo solo residet tota salutis nostrae materia), comp. the expression in Col. i. 27: ἡ ἐλπὶς τῆς δόξης. — Τιμοθέῳ γνησίῳ τέκνῳ ἐν πίστει] Paul calls Timothy his child; he was not so κατὰ σάρκα but ἐν πίστει, since he was converted to the faith by Paul, as we learn from 1 Cor. iv. 14–17. Paul usually calls himself the father of those who had been led to the faith by him (comp. Gal iv 19). The idea of τέκνον is strengthened by γνήσιος, perhaps by way of contrast with the heretics. The opposite of γνήσιος is νόθος or οὐκ ὄντως ὤν (comp. Plato, Rep. 293) This addition also gives prominence to the fact that Timothy was his son in the faith, not in appearance but in truth, hence Paul calls him also in 1 Cor. iv. 17 his τέκνον ἀγαπητὸν καὶ πιστὸν ἐν κυρίῳ. — ἐν πίστει] "in the sphere of faith," is not to be connected with γνησίῳ but with τέκνῳ, as defined more closely by γνησίῳ; comp. Tit. i. 4, and see Winer, p. 130 [E. T. p. 171] — χάρις, ἔλεος, εἰρήνη] This collocation occurs only in the Pastoral Epistles and in 2 John 3; in the other Pauline Epistles it runs: χάρις ὑμῖν καὶ εἰρήνη. In Gal. vi. 16, however, εἰρήνη and ἔλεος are connected with one another. In Jude 2 we have: ἔλεος ὑμῖν καὶ εἰρήνη καὶ ἀγάπη. The three expressions manifestly do not indicate three different gifts of grace, but only *one*. The

CHAP. I 3, 4. 77

distinction is, that χάρις points more to the soil from which the gift comes, and εἰρήνη denotes its nature, while the ἔλεος (standing between the two others in the Pastoral Epistles) lays stress on the element of compassionate love in χάρις[1] Otto arbitrarily finds in ἔλεος "a reference to the official position," appealing to such passages as 1 Tim i. 13, 16, 1 Cor. vii. 25, 2 Cor. iv. 1. Paul does also acknowledge that his call to the ministry of the word came from God's ἔλεος; but it does not follow from this that the word ἔλεος is used only in reference to the official position; comp. Gal. vi. 16 ; 2 Tim. i. 16, 18. — ἀπὸ Θεοῦ πατρὸς καὶ κ.τ λ.] Even with the reading ἡμῶν the genitive Χριστοῦ Ἰησοῦ cannot be made to depend on Θεοῦ. Next to the Father, Paul names Christ as the source from which the blessing comes, because all the Father's gifts of blessing come through the Son.

Vv. 3, 4. The apostle reminds Timothy, in the first place, of a previous exhortation, obviously for the purpose of impressing it more deeply on him—The most natural construction of the sentence appears to be, to take it as an anacolouthon, to connect ἐν Ἐφέσῳ with προσμεῖναι, to refer πορευόμενος to the subject of παρεκάλεσα, and to make ἵνα dependent on παρεκαλεσά σε κ.τ.λ. This construction is held by most expositors to be the only admissible one. The missing apodosis cannot, however, be supplied before ἵνα, because ἵνα is closely connected with what precedes; we may insert with Erasmus "ita facito," or with Beza "vide," or with most expositors " οὕτω καὶ νῦν παρακαλῶ" (Winer, p. 530 [E T. p. 592]). The peculiarity in such an involuntary (Buttm. p. 331) anacolouthon is, that the grammatical connection is not established by inserting the omitted apodosis. The most

---

[1] Wiesinger is right in not agreeing with Olshausen, who wishes to see in the expressions σωτήρ, ἐλπίς, ἔλεος, a special reference to the apostle's position as a prisoner Van Oosterzee aptly remarks "Grace may be called the greatest benefaction for the guilty, compassion for the suffering, peace for the contending (?) disciple of the Lord." Hofmann is right in his remark on 1 Tim. i 1, that χάρις with ἀπό does not denote God's thoughts, but "that in which His thoughts are shown, the grace which man receives." In his explanation of 1 Tim. i. 2 · " χάρις is that which is imparted to man by God, *who wishes him well*," the idea of χάρις is made far too general.

simple course is to suppose that the apostle had "οὕτω καὶ νῦν παρακαλῶ" or "οὕτω ποίει" in mind, but the place for it was lost in the abundance of the thoughts that streamed in on him.—Several expositors depart from the construction commonly accepted. Matthies takes προσμεῖναι as "stay," not as "remain behind," refers πορευόμενος not to the subject of παρεκάλεσα, but to σε (making an unjustifiable appeal to Eph iii. 17, 18, iv i. 2 ; Col. iii. 16[1]), and explains the whole thus : When Timothy was intending to travel to Macedonia, Paul had charged him to stop at Ephesus and remain there. Schneckenburger (see his *Beitrage z. Einl.* pp. 182 ff.) arbitrarily changes the infin. προσμεῖναι into the partic. προσμείνας, and refers πορευόμενος to the following clause: ἵνα παραγγείλῃς Otto treats πορευόμενος in the same way, at the same time connecting ἐν Ἐφέσῳ with παρεκάλεσα, taking προσμεῖναι in an absolute sense, making the apodosis begin with ἵνα, and translating . " Just as I exhorted you to stand firm in Ephesus, so shalt thou on the journey to Macedonia command the people not to give attention to strange teachers, nor to hold them in esteem," etc This construction is, however, so artificial, that it is obviously incorrect to every one who is not blinded by the desire of placing the date of the composition of the epistle in a period of the apostle's life known to us.

REMARK —In order to justify his view of the sentence, Otto tries to prove the incorrectness of the usual construction, and to get rid of the objections to his own. The hypothesis of an ellipsis he rejects on account of the rule that the emphatic word can never be omitted, and that if we supply the apodosis by " οὕτω καὶ νῦν παρακαλῶ," the emphatic words are καὶ νῦν But these words are not by any means the most emphatic. The apostle might be using them not specially of the contrast between past and present, but only to give point to his former exhortation , hence he might easily omit the apodosis Otto further maintains, that in the usual construction καθώς, which always denotes a material,

[1] In the passages quoted, Paul adds the participles to the previous clauses in the nom , and these participial clauses thus acquire the independence due to them according to the context. But in these passages the relation of the participial clause to the preceding main clause is quite different from what it is here, where there is no reason whatever for departing from the regular construction.

actual correspondence, even to identity of motives, and further, of material contents, does not get its full force. On this point we indeed grant that the peculiar meaning of καθώς (as distinguished from ὡς) is not distinctly marked by the expositors; but it is not at all necessary in the usual interpretation to weaken arbitrarily the force of καθώς, since the apostle's former exhortation could not but be his guide in the present one. Still less difficulty, however, is presented by καθώς, if we choose to supply οὕτω ποίει (as Hofmann does), since the meaning then is, that Timothy's conduct is to be conformed to the exhortation already given by the apostle. — Otto tries further to show that in the usual explanation the participle πορευόμενος is not in its proper place. The rules which Otto lays down on the subject of participial clauses in order to support his assertion are, on the whole, not incorrect. The passages he quotes from the N. T. certainly show that the participle following a finite verb mostly defines it more precisely; that it either explains more precisely the verbal notion, or gives the accompanying circumstances of the verb But Otto has overlooked the departures from this rule which occur in the N. T.; comp. Luke iv. 40 with Mark i. 31; Matt. xii. 49 with Acts xxvi. 1; Matt. xxii. 15 with Matt. xii. 14, further, Luke xxiv. 17.[1] It cannot be denied that the participle following sometimes gives simply the time in which the action of the finite verb takes place, that here, therefore, the πορευόμενος may simply denote the time of the former exhortation.[2] Otto quotes the passage in Acts xii. 25 as supporting the rule that the participle following should serve to explain the verbal notion, and justifies this by saying that the participle πληρώσαντες τὴν διακονίαν gives the motive of the return. But to give the motive is no explanation. In this passage, however, the position of the participle after the finite verb is justified in this way, that it gives the motive for the action expressed by the finite verb. So, too, in the passage here there is nothing to be said against the connection of πορευόμενος with παρεκάλεσα, so soon as we suppose that the journey was the

---

[1] Otto tries to weaken the force of this passage against him by assuming a rhetorical inversion, because, he says, it is declared "that taking a walk and holding solemn dispute are inconsistent with one another" (!).
[2] In his groundless denial of this, Otto thinks that if πορευόμενος be joined to παρεκάλεσα it must be assumed to be a circumstance accompanying the παρεκάλεσα, but that this assumption is impossible, since a continuing fact (part. pres) cannot be regarded as the accompanying circumstance of a concluded fact (part. aor) But Otto overlooks the fact that πορευόμενος in this connection is not to be understood in the sense of continuing a journey, but in the sense of beginning one, of setting out.

occasion for Paul giving Timothy the exhortation in question. Lastly, Otto attacks the usual construction from the notion of προσμεῖναι, because this word is explained in the construction to be equivalent to "remain, stay;" whereas, when not connected with a dative (or with a participial clause representing a dative), but standing absolutely, it has the meaning: "to maintain the position hitherto possessed, to stand firm." Hence, if any definition of place is added, it is not as a completion of the verbal notion, but only indicates where the standing firm takes place. Otto infers from this: "accordingly ἐν Ἐφέσῳ here does not complete προσμεῖναι, but rather προσμεῖναι is absolute, and ἐν Ἐφέσῳ gives the place at which the whole sentence, viz. παρεκάλεσά σε προσμεῖναι, took place." This inference is obviously incorrect, since from Otto's premises it only follows that, if ἐν Ἐφέσῳ belongs to προσμεῖναι, the place is thus given where Timothy is to stand fast, —in particular against the heretics,—it does not follow that ἐν Ἐφέσῳ may be connected with προσμεῖναι. Besides, from Acts xviii. 18, it is clear beyond dispute that προσμένειν does occur in the N T. in the weakened sense of "remain, stay"[1] Otto does not disguise the objections to his view, but he thinks that when thoroughly weighed they are more apparent than real. In this, too, he is wrong. It is indeed right to say that in the N. T. a sentence often begins with ἵνα without any verb preceding on which it depends,—and this not only in cases where the governing verbal notion is easily supplied from what precedes, as in John i 8, ix 3, xiii. 18, 2 Cor. viii. 7, but also when that is not the case, so that the clause beginning with ἵνα stands as an imperative clause, as in Eph v 33, Mark v. 23 (comp. Buttm. pp. 207 f) But in all passages where ἵνα is used elliptically, this is shown clearly and distinctly by the form of the sentence, which is not the case here It is right also to say that emphatic parts of the clause construed with ἵνα are often placed before ἵνα, so that πορευόμενος, therefore, might very well be connected with

---

[1] In this passage, also, Otto claims for προσμένειν, as a vox militaris, the meaning "keep one's ground," remarking, "for the circumstances in Corinth were such that they might well have induced Paul to cease his labours and depart." But this assertion is in contradiction with Luke's statement, that the attack attempted by the Jews through Gallio was decisively warded off. Otto's explanation, too, becomes all the more unsuitable, since, according to it, Luke would charge the apostle with not holding his ground more, and with abandoning his post.—Further, Otto seems to hesitate whether to take προσμεῖναι in the present passage as really absolute, or whether to supply with it the dative ἐμοί. After finally deciding for the former, he then explains προσμεῖναι as "keeping ground along with the leader appointed by God in the struggle against all the attacks of the heretic," and thus in self-contradiction returns to the latter, since this leader is the Apostle Paul.

the clause following ἵνα; but this, too, is always indicated clearly by the form of the sentence. Wherever words standing before ἵνα are to be referred to what follows ἵνα, these words cannot possibly be connected with what precedes them, and the part of the sentence following ἵνα is incomplete in itself, so that it has to be taken along with the part before ἵνα. It is wrong to maintain that the participial clause πορευόμενος εἰς Μακεδ. becomes emphatic by contrast with ἐν Ἐφέσῳ, inasmuch as what took place in *Ephesus* is now to take place also *on the journey to Macedonia;* for—the two things are not at all the same. In Ephesus (according to Otto's view), Paul exhorted Timothy to stand firm, but on the journey to Macedonia, Timothy is to encounter those who had been led astray. Lastly, it is right to assume that the sender of a letter, if he has anything to say of the place from which the letter is sent, may speak of it by name, comp. 1 Cor. xv. 32, xvi. 8, so that ἐν Ἐφέσῳ might convey to us that Paul was himself in Ephesus while writing; but we must take into consideration the special circumstances of the case. According to Otto, our epistle is a paper of instructions which the apostle put into Timothy's hands in Ephesus, where he wrote it before setting out for Macedonia. In that case it was improper to mention the place by name. We cannot understand, then, why Paul in such a paper of instructions should have laid special stress on the exhortation he had imparted to Timothy *in the very place* where he put that paper into his hands

Some expositors take the whole section vv. 5–17 to be a parenthesis, and ver. 18 to be the apodosis corresponding to καθώς. The awkwardness of this construction is obvious; but Plitt thinks that, though it is not without its difficulties, most may be said for it. He is wrong, however, since ταύτην τὴν παραγγελίαν, in ver. 18, does not resume the παρεκάλεσά σε. — If we avoid all subtleties, we cannot but explain it: *Even as I exhorted thee to remain in Ephesus when I set out for Macedonia, that thou mightst command certain men not to teach false doctrine . . . even so do* (or: *even so I exhort thee also now*).[1] Regarding the meaning of καθώς and προσμεῖναι, see the above remark. — παρεκάλεσα] Chrys : ἄκουε τὸ προσηνές, πῶς οὐ διδασκάλου κέχρηται ῥωμῇ, ἀλλ' οἰκέτου σχεδόν· οὐ γὰρ εἶπεν ἐπέταξα, οὐδὲ ἐκέλευσα, οὐδὲ παρῄνεσα, ἀλλὰ τί; παρεκάλεσά

---

[1] Hofmann is wrong in asserting that Paul, when he wrote καθώς (not ὡς), could not have had in mind "any expression of which the writer was the subject, but only an exhortation as to what Timothy was to do."

σε. Towards Titus, however, Paul uses the expression διεταξάμην (Tit. i. 5), although he was not less friendly towards him than towards Timothy. — πορευόμενος εἰς Μακεδονίαν] "when I went away, from Ephesus to Macedonia;" πορεύεσθαι has in itself the general meaning of going, but it is also used of going away from a place, both absolutely (Matt. xi. 7) and connected with ἀπό (Matt. xxiv. 1, xxv. 41, xix. 15: ἐκεῖθεν; Luke xiii. 31: ἐντεῦθεν). Otto explains it: "on the way to Macedonia," which is grammatically correct, but opposed to the connection of ideas. There is no ground whatever for thinking that Paul, in this expression, had in mind one particular place on the way to Macedonia, viz. Corinth. We can see no reason why Paul should have expressed himself indefinitely. Otto, indeed, is of opinion that Timothy could not have been uncertain about the meaning of the expression, and that the apostle chose it in order to spare the feelings of the Corinthians, and that he might not confess to the heretics how they had provoked his apostolic opposition to an exceptional degree. But the first reason proves too much, since Paul, if he refrained from the definite expression because Timothy knew his wishes without it, would also have refrained from the indefinite expression. The other two reasons are weak, because if Timothy was to labour successfully against the heretics, he must necessarily appeal to the authority of the apostle in whose name he was to labour Besides, such playing at hide-and-seek as Otto imputes to the apostle, is in entire contradiction with Paul's frank character — ἵνα παραγγείλῃς κ τ.λ] gives the purpose for which Timothy was to remain in Ephesus. The theory that this gives at the same time the purpose of the whole epistle (Matthies), which opinion de Wette brings forward as proving the epistle not to be genuine, is wrong. — παραγγείλῃς] does not necessarily involve the suggestion of publicity which Matthies finds in it. — τισί] The same indefinite term is used for the heretics also in vv 6, 19, iv. 1, v. 15, etc.: "certain people whom the apostle is unwilling to designate further, Timothy already knows them" (Wiesinger). — μὴ ἑτεροδιδασκαλεῖν] The word, which is not made up of ἕτερος and διδασκάλειν (= διδάσκειν), but is derived from ἑτεροδιδάσκαλος, occurs in the N. T. only here and in

vi. 3 (comp. ἑτεροζυγεῖν in 2 Cor. vi. 14). In ἕτερος there is not seldom the notion of *different in kind, strange*, something not agreeing with something else, but opposed to it. Accordingly, in the apostle's use of the word, a ἑτεροδιδάσκαλος is a teacher who teaches other things than he should teach, who puts forward doctrines in opposition to the gospel; and ἑτεροδιδασκαλεῖν here means nothing else than to teach something opposed to the gospel (Heb. xiii. 9: διδαχαῖς ποικίλαις καὶ ξέναις μὴ παραφέρεσθε); comp. 2 Cor. xi. 4; Gal. i. 6: εὐαγγέλιον ἕτερον. Wiesinger, in order to favour his theory that heresy proper is not spoken of, weakens the meaning into "teach otherwise," so that according to him it signifies "teaching things which he apart from ἡ κατ᾽ εὐσέβειαν διδασκαλία." This is incorrect, for in that case some more precise definition would have been given. — Even in classic Greek, ἕτερος, in composition, often has the meaning alleged by us; thus ἑτεροδοξεῖν = diversae opinionis esse, comp. Plato, *Theaet.* p. 190 E: δόξαν εἶναι ψευδῆ τὸ ἑτεροδοξεῖν. According to Otto, ἑτεροδιδασκαλεῖν means: "to have another teacher, to follow another teacher." Otto wrongly appeals for this to Euseb. *Hist. Eccles.* iii. 32, where ἑτεροδιδάσκαλοι does not mean false teachers, but "such members of the church as had abandoned the teaching of the apostles and become attached to strange teachers," and also to Ignat. *ad Polycarp* chap. 3, where ἑτεροδιδασκαλοῦντες has the same meaning.[1] Otto also makes appeal to the Greek usage, according to which, in composite nouns, the concluding word, if it be a noun, does not contain the subject of the fundamental thought in such composite words, but the nearer or more distant object. But this rule is only valid with *adjectival* forms. In composite *substantives*, on the contrary, the concluding word (if it be an unaltered substantive) may also denote the subject, which is only defined

[1] The first passage runs · τηνικαῦτα (viz. after the apostle's death) τῆς ἀθέου πλάνης ἀρχὴν ἐλάμβανεν ἡ σύστασις διὰ τῆς τῶν ἑτεροδιδασκάλων ἀπάτης, οἱ καὶ . . γυμνῇ λοιπὸν ἤδη κεφαλῇ τῷ τῆς ἀληθείας κηρύγματι τὴν ψευδώνυμον γνῶσιν ἀντικηρύττειν ἐπιχείρουν The relative clause shows most clearly that the word ἑτεροδιδάσκαλοι means nothing else than false teachers — The second passage is . οἱ δοκοῦντες ἀξιόπιστοι εἶναι καὶ ἑτεροδιδασκαλοῦντες μή σε καταπληττέτωσαν; in which, also, false teachers, heretics, are meant, as is evident from the injunction μή σε κ. τ. λ., as well as from the exhortation that follows.

more precisely by the word that precedes.[1]— There is no ground whatever for Schleiermacher's opinion, that the verb suggests the idea of a hierarchy. — To μὴ ἑτεροδιδασκαλεῖν there is added a second point: μηδὲ προσέχειν κ.τ λ., which Timothy is to forbid to τινές.[2] Except in the Pastoral Epistles, προσέχειν does not occur in Paul. Here, as in Tit. i. 14, it includes the notion of agreement, so also in Acts viii. 6. — μύθοις καὶ γενεαλογίαις] The καί is to be taken epexegetically; we can neither join the two expressions as an hendiadys (fabulosae genealogiae, Heumann), nor regard them as denoting different things The notion of μῦθοι has been limited too narrowly by many expositors,—as by Theodoret, who understands by it the traditional supplements to the law; or by others, who take it as denoting the allegorical system of interpretation, or the Jewish stories of miracles (such as occur in the pseudo-epigrapha or the Apocrypha), or even the Gentile mythologies. Leo is wrong in agreeing with Theodoret's exposition, appealing to Ignatius (*Ep. ad Magnes.* chap. 8), and alluding to ver. 7. From that verse it is certainly clear that heretics had peculiar views regarding the law, which were in contradiction with the gospel; but it is a mere assertion to say that μῦθοι here refers to these views, all the more that the word stands closely connected with γενεαλογίαι. De Wette limits the meaning of the word in another fashion, inferring from 2 Pet. i. 16: σεσοφισμένοι μῦθοι, that the μῦθοι here meant, formed the definite element in an *artificial* system; the notion of something artificial is obviously imported. Other expositors take the expression quite generally in the sense of "false doctrine," as Suidas explains the word. μῦθος· λόγος ψευδής, εἰκονίζων τὴν ἀλήθειαν; this is too indefinite. Paul rather employs it because it was used to denote false ideas regarding the nature

---

[1] The adj ἑτερόπους certainly does not denote "a halting foot," but "one who has a halting foot " On the contrary, κακόδουλος is not "one who has a bad slave," but "a bad slave." Comp. also μικροβασιλεύς, ψευδόμαντις, and others; in the N T., especially the expressions: ψευδοδιδάσκαλος (ψευδοπροφήτης, ψευδόμαρτυρ, ψευδαπόστολος), 2 Pet. ii 1, and καλοδιδάσκαλος, Tit. ii 3. It is to be noted, also, that in Sextus Empiricus, *Adv. Rhet.* 42, κακοδιδασκαλεῖν does not mean "to have a bad teacher," but "to teach what is bad."

[2] Without grounds in usage or in fact, Hofmann asserts that "προσέχειν τινί is not an expression applicable to a teacher, and that therefore the ἑτεροδ. was to be applied to some, and the προσέχειν κ.τ.λ. to others."

of the Godhead. The word that follows defines the nature of these μῦθοι more precisely. — On the γενεαλογίαι ἀπέραντοι, see Introd. sect. 4. Wiesinger's view, that they denote the genealogies in the O. T., as well as that of Hofmann, that they are the historical facts in the Thora, are both to be rejected. Credner's view, that the genealogies of Christ are meant, is quite arbitrary. So, too, with Chrysostom's explanation: οἶμαι καὶ "Ελληνας αὐτὸν ἐνταῦθα αἰνίττεσθαι, ὅταν λέγῃ μύθοις καὶ γενεαλογίαις, ὡς τοὺς θεοὺς αὐτῶν καταλεγόντων. It is very far-fetched to refer to the Kabbalistic Sephiroth. The application of the expression to the Essenic doctrine of angels (Michaelis), is contradicted by the fact that theories of emanations cannot be proved to have existed among the Essenes. The view upheld by most expositors, that the apostle was thinking of the series of emanations in the speculation of the heretics, must be considered the right one. It is confirmed by the addition of the adjective ἀπέραντοι. The genealogies are "unlimited," since there was no necessity for them to stop at any point whatever. The conclusion was altogether arbitrary: hence, in the various systems, the genealogies of the aeons differ from one another in all sorts of ways. — αἵτινες] is not simply an attributive relative, it gives at the same time the reason of the foregoing exhortation μὴ προσέχειν "as those which" (comp. Soph. *Oed. R* 1184, Pape, *Handworterbuch der griech. Spr.* See the word ὅστις). — Ζητήσεις παρέχουσι μᾶλλον ἢ οἰκονομίαν Θεοῦ] Both notions ζητήσεις and οἰκονομ. Θεοῦ, may be taken either *subjectively* or *objectively*. If ζητήσεις be taken *objectively*, it is "points of controversy, questions of dispute," if *subjectively*, it is "investigations, controversies, disputations" ("each one trying to maintain his arbitrary fictions," Matthies). If οἰκονομία Θεοῦ is taken *objectively*, it is "the salvation of God" ("the salvation grounded historically in Christ and publicly preached by means of His apostles," Matthies; or according to others, "the ministry of the gospel;" or, lastly, "the divine gift of grace," *i.e.* the divine influence on individuals by which they are brought to the faith). If it is taken *subjectively*, it is "the work of man as an οἰκόνομος Θεοῦ;" de Wette: "the work of a steward of God in the faith (to be awakened or to be furthered)." This latter may be taken, in a general sense, as meaning, " the Christian activity, the Christian exercise of the divine gifts of grace,"[1] or, more narrowly : " the maintaining, the strengthening in Christianity, the nourishment in the faith by the spiritual food of Christianity, which the *teachers as stewards of God* distribute," Zachariae. The meaning of παρέχουσι is also modified according to the interpretation of these two notions. If they are interpreted objectively, παρέχειν is " reach forth, present ; " if subjectively, it is " cause, bring about " (so Gal. vi. 17; also frequently in classic Greek and in the Apocrypha of the O. T.; comp. Wahl, *Clav. libr. V. T. apocryph.*, under the word). Ζήτησις is not identical with ζήτημα ; οἰκονομία is indeed used in the sense of " office of steward," but οἰκονομία Θεοῦ denotes " the preparation, the arrangement made by God " (comp. Eph. i. 10, iii. 9), and never "the divine salvation." Hence the subjective interpretation (Hofmann) is to be preferred to the objective (as formerly in this commentary ; also Wiesinger, Plitt, Oosterzee). In any case, Matthies is wrong in taking ζητήσεις subjectively and οἰκονομία Θεοῦ objectively, and then assuming that παρέχειν is used in a zeugma. Otto's explanation is purely arbitrary. He explains ζητήσεις by " speculations," and οἰκονομίαν Θεοῦ τὴν ἐν πίστει by " a system of divine order in the universe (*sc* creation and government), resting on faith, grounded in faith,—the cosmogony and physics of the Jewish gnosis " Of the latter phrase, he says that Paul " adopts the hypocritical name which the νομοδιδάσκαλοι claimed for their system, so that the ζητήσεις form the *real*, the οἶκον. ἡ ἐν πίστει, on the contrary, the *pretended* contents of the μῦθοι and γενεαλογίαι." By the addition of τὴν ἐν πίστει, the labour of the οἰκόνομος Θεοῦ is defined more precisely as one in the sphere of faith (not " causing faith," Hofmann). — μᾶλλον ἤ] as in several passages of the N. T., John iii. 19, Acts xxvii. 11, 2 Tim. iii. 4, stands here in the sense of denying the thought contained in the following member, so that (with Suidas) it is equivalent to καὶ οὔ.[2] — With

---

[1] Thus Reiche ista commenta . . non exhibent, praebent, efficiunt dispensationem (distributionem) bonorum quae Deus Christo misso in nos contulit

[2] Hofmann wrongly applies this form of expression in order to dispute the reference of γινεαλογίαι to the series of aeons, saying "How could it occur to

the reading οἰκοδομία (or οἰκοδομή) Θεοῦ, we must interpret, "the edifying in the faith as decreed by God" (Luther, inaccurately. " the improvement towards God in the faith"). Ver. 5. Τὸ δὲ τέλος τῆς παραγγελίας ἐστὶν κ τ.λ] It cannot be denied that in παραγγελίας we have an echo of παραγγείλῃς in ver. 3 ; but it does not follow that we are to understand by it the command which the apostle gave to Timothy not to teach falsely (so Bengel: praecepti quod Ephesi urgere debes). It rather stands here in contrast with the ἑτεροδιδασκαλία just mentioned, and denotes the command which is serviceable to the οἰκονομία Θεοῦ (ver. 4). It is equivalent to the ἐντολή in vi. 14, the evangelic law which forms the external rule for the conduct of Christians (Hofmann) The apostle alludes to this because he is about to pass to the doctrine of the heretics regarding the law.— It is wrong to understand by παραγγελία the *Mosaic* law (Calvin, Beza, and others), from which there would arise a thought foreign to the context, and it is unsatisfactory to take it in a general sense as "practical exhortation" (de Wette, Wiesinger, Plitt, Oosterzee), for in that case the imperative should have been used instead of ἐστιν. It is a peculiarity of the N T. usage to take expressions which of themselves have a more general signification, and to mark them off with the definite article as ideas specifically Christian; thus τὸ εὐαγγέλιον, ἡ ὁδός (often in Acts), τὸ κήρυγμα, and others — τέλος] is neither "fulfilment" nor "chief sum" (Luther, Erasmus. quod universam legis mosaicae vim compendio complectitur ac praestat est caritas), but "goal, scopus ad quem tendit παραγγελία" (Koppe, Wegscheider, de Wette, Wiesinger, and others [1]) — While the ἑτεροδιδασκαλία only causes ζητήσεις, which serve to engender divisions (γεννῶσι μάχας, 2 Tim ii. 23), the aim of the command of the gospel is love.— ἀγάπη ἐκ καθαρᾶς καρδίας κ τ.λ] The gospel proclaims to the believer *one* divine act, the reconciliation through Christ grounded in God's love, and it demands also

the apostle to treat the question only as a possible one, whether these follies of their own invention could not in some measure be useful to what he calls οἰκονομίαν Θιοῦ ? Such a possibility is not indicated by μᾶλλον ἤ

[1] Arriani *dissertt. Epict* Book I. chap. 20 . τέλος ἐστὶ τὸ ἔπεσθαι θιοῖς.

one human act, viz. love, for πλήρωμα νόμου ή αγάπη (Rom. xiii. 10). Leo and Matthies wrongly explain αγάπη here of love to God and to one's neighbour. Here and elsewhere in the N. T, where no other genitive of the object is added, we should understand by it love to one's neighbour. The words following declare of what nature this love should be. — ἐκ καθαράς καρδίας] καρδία denotes the inward centre of human life, especially as the seat of emotions and desires Hence in regard to love it is often remarked that it must come from the καρδία (comp. Matt. xii. 37), and from a heart that is pure, *i.e.* free from all self-seeking; 1 Pet. i. 22: ἐκ καθαράς καρδίας ἀλλήλους ἀγαπήσατε ἐκτενῶς; comp 1 Cor. xiii. 5: ἡ ἀγάπη . . . οὐ ζητεῖ τὰ ἑαυτῆς.—The two additions that follow: καὶ συνειδήσεως ἀγαθῆς καὶ πίστεως ἀνυποκρίτου (as is clear from 1 Tim. i. 19, iii. 9, iv. 2), are added with special reference to the heretics, who are reproached with having both an evil conscience and a pretended faith. — συνείδησις ἀγαθή (ver. 19; 1 Pet. iii. 16, καλή, Heb. xiii. 18; καθαρά, 1 Tim iii. 9; 2 Tim. i. 3) is not " the conscience pure from the guilt of sin " (de Wette), nor "the conscience reconciled with God" (van Oosterzee, Plitt), nor "the consciousness of peace with God" (Hofmann). Although "a conscience not reconciled with God and one's neighbours cannot love purely," there is no hint here of the element of reconciliation. It is simply the consciousness of cherishing no impure, wicked purposes.[1]
— πίστις] is not confidence towards one's neighbour, as it might be here when placed in connection with the idea of love, but, in accordance with the contents of the epistle, is "faith," which in Gal. v. 6 also is denoted as the ground of love.— ἀνυπόκριτος (also in Rom. xii. 9; 2 Cor. vi 6, 1 Pet. i. 22, connected with the idea of love) denotes truth and uprightness in opposition to all flattery. It is used here not without allusion to the heretics who conducted themselves as believers in order to gain a more easy admission for their heresies.

---

[1] Otto on 2 Tim. i 3 (pp 302 f) explains the expression καθαρὰ συνείδησις rightly (following Matthies) as "the self-consciousness of pure thoughts and endeavours ," but, on the other hand, he is wrong in regard to 1 Tim i 19, where he interprets ἀγαθη συνιδ. as "the conscience innocent and expectant of all salvation," "the consciousness of divine grace supporting itself by daily putting to death the old nature."

Vv. 6, 7. At ver. 6 the apostle passes to the heretics. — ων] refers to the ideas immediately preceding: ἐκ καθαρᾶς καρδίας κτλ., not—as Wiesinger rightly remarks—to ἀγάπη direct, "since εἰς ματαιολογίαν manifestly denotes a false goal in contrast with the true goal, which is ἀγάπη."[1] — ἀστοχήσαντες] This verb occurs only in the Pastoral Epistles, in this passage and also in 1 Tim. vi. 21 and 2 Tim. ii. 18 (where it is joined with περί and the accusative). Here it stands in its original sense: a scopo sive meta aberrare (comp. Plut de Defect Oracul. chap 10), which corresponds to the τέλος mentioned in ver. 5, and gives us to understand that the heretics had at first been on the way which leads to the goal, but had not remained in it. In this way Schleiermacher's criticism (p. 90), that the word here is far from clear, loses its force. — ἐξετράπησαν] ἐξ has its full force (Josephus, Antiq. xiii. 18 : ἐκτρέπεσθαι τῆς ὁδοῦ δικαίας) in this verb, which, except in Heb. xii. 13, only occurs in the Epistles to Timothy. The goal to which they have come after turning from the τέλος τῆς παραγγελίας is ματαιολογία. This word (only found here ; Tit. i. 10 : ματαιολόγοι) characterizes the heresy as empty in nature, contributing nothing to the furtherance of the Christian life. It consists on the one hand of μύθοις καὶ γενεαλογίαις, on the other of such definitions regarding the law as were opposed to evangelic doctrine. This latter reference is proved by the close connection of the verse with what follows —θέλοντες] The participle does not express contrast: "although," it gives rather a more precise definition of the previous verb ἐξετράπησαν. Some expositors (de Wette : *wish to be*, without being so in reality ; Bengel has *temere ;* so also Plitt) rightly urge that θέλειν expresses an allegation of their own ; Hofmann, on the other hand, wrongly takes it in the sense of "arbitrary assumption."[2] — νομοδιδάσκαλοι] Luther's translation is, " masters of the Scripture" (and similar explana-

---

[1] Hofmann is wrong in disputing the reason given by Wiesinger, and maintaining that παραγγελία and not τέλος τῆς παραγγελίας is opposed to ματαιολογία. There is no ground also for his assertion that ἀστοχεῖν has here the general sense of "to leave uncared for " The ἐξιτράπησαν clearly shows that ἀστοχεῖν is to be taken in its own proper sense.

[2] Hofmann's reason for this explanation is, that " νομοδιδάσκαλοι, who make the law of Israel the subject of their instruction, have no business in the church of

tions are given; Heinrichs has "teachers"); but this does not give the full force of νόμος By νόμος we must of course understand the Mosaic law, though it does not follow that the heretics here were Judaizers such as those against whom Paul contends in the Epistles to the Romans and to the Galatians: they might rather be men who acquired the name by laying down arbitrary commands in their interpretations of the law, and calling these the right knowledge of the law. Baur's theory, that Paul gave this name to the heretics because of their antinomianism, is quite arbitrary, and contrary to the natural meaning of the words. De Wette rightly disproves this by referring to Tit. i 14, from which it is abundantly clear that the heretics made it their business to lay down arbitrary commands. Baur's appeal to ver. 8, according to which he thinks the heretics must have declared that the law was not good, must decidedly be rejected, since the idea is only an arbitrary importation into ver. 8 [1] — μὴ νοοῦντες] This participle expresses contrast (Leo: quamquam ignorant), "without, however, understanding." The object of νοοῦντες is given in a sentence of two clauses· μήτε ... μήτε. The first: μήτε ἃ λέγουσι, is clear in itself, the second: μήτε περὶ τίνων διαβεβαιοῦνται, has been variously explained. Most find the difference between the clauses to lie in this, that the one refers to the utterances themselves, the other to things of which the utterance was made, i.e. to the subject-matter of the doctrine (so Raphelius, Leo, Matthies, Wiesinger, Plitt, Oosterzee, Hofmann). De Wette, again, thinks that this explanation rests on a grammatical error, and that "περὶ τίνων does not refer to the things of which corroboratory assertions were made, but to these assertions themselves" (Luther: *what they say or what they suppose*). In support of this opinion de Wette wrongly appeals to Tit. iii 8.[2] He is

the gospel" This is altogether wrong, as may be seen when, further on, Paul appears as a νομοδιδάσκαλος.

[1] Contrary to the train of thought, van Oosterzee remarks on νομοδιδάσκαλοι: "not in a good, rather in a bad, non-evangelical meaning of this word, men who mixed up law and gospel." In this explanation he overlooks the θέλοντες εἶναι

[2] The classical usage is against de Wette's explanation, comp Plutarch, *Fabii Vita*, chap 14 διαβεβαιούμενος περὶ τῶν πραγμάτων; Polyb. xii 12 6: διοριζόμενος καὶ διαβεβαιούμενος περὶ τούτων.

wrong, too, in translating διαβεβ by "corroborate;" it means rather: "give full assurance." Hofmann says, "to express oneself with confidence regarding anything." The expression is quite general, and Mack seems to be arbitrary in limiting the thought by explaining how ἃ λεγ. refers to expressions in the law brought forward as proofs of assertions with which they had no real connection, and περὶ τίν. βεβ. to those assertions for which proofs out of the law were given, and which in themselves had no meaning Paul merely says that the νομοδιδάσκαλοι possessed no insight into the nature of the law, and hence they made assertions regarding it which were not understood even by themselves[1]

Ver. 8 In contrast with the heretics' advocacy of the law, the apostle, in what follows, states its real value. — Οἴδαμεν δὲ, ὅτι κτλ] Baur wrongly infers from these words that the heretics, as Antinomians, had no desire to vindicate the law as good. It is not these first words, but the words ἐάν τις κ.τ.λ, that are directed against the heretics. In spite of Hofmann's denial, οἴδαμεν δέ stands in a concessive sense, (Wiesinger), as in Rom. vii. 14, 1 Cor viii 1, the apostle making an acknowledgment which is restricted by ἐάν τις κ.τ λ; still we cannot translate it simply by *concedimus*, as Heinrichs does. — καλὸς ὁ νόμος] By νόμος we must understand, neither the Christian moral law, nor a single part of the Mosaic law, but the latter as a whole. It is of the entire Mosaic law in its existing form as a revelation of the divine will given in a system of written commands—it is of this that Paul uses καλός as a suitable epithet. It is not enough to take καλός as equivalent to ὠφέλιμος (Theodoret), though the idea of usefulness is included in it; καλός denotes generally the internal excellence of the law, just as the same is set forth in still more significant expressions in Rom vii. 12, 14 But the good and excellent qualities of the law depend on its being applied according to its nature and signification: when applied otherwise, it ceases to be καλός. Hence Paul, in opposition to the heretics, adds: ἐάν τις αὐτῷ νομίμως χρῆται. The νομίμως, which is clearly a play on words with νόμος,

---

[1] On the conjunction of the relative and interrogative pronouns ἃ ... τίνων, see Winer, p. 159 [E. T. p 211].

only expresses the formal relation; we can only infer from the thoughts that follow what is meant by the *lawful* use of law.[1] De Wette rightly remarks: "There is in this passage nothing but what the words really say, that the Christian teacher must not uphold the law as binding on the δίκαιος." While nearly all expositors understand by τις the Christian as such, Bengel remarks: Paulus hoc loco non de auditore legis, sed de doctore loquitur, in this he is right, as is acknowledged also by de Wette, Wiesinger, van Oosterzee, Hofmann. Paul says nothing here as to how the law is to be obeyed, but rather he tells us how it is to be made use of by Christian teachers.

Vv. 9, 10 Εἰδὼς τοῦτο] is not to be referred to οἴδαμεν, but to τις, *i.e.* to the teacher of the church. The use of the same verb is against the construction with οἴδαμεν. As to the meaning of the word, it is to be observed that here, as in many other passages of the N. T., it expresses not only the idea of knowing, but also that of "weighing, considering." De Wette says, "as he knows and considers." The law is rightly used only when it is considered that, etc — ὅτι δικαίῳ νόμος οὐ κεῖται] We may, with Hofmann, take this sentence quite generally, so as to understand by νόμος not any special law, but law in general, and by δίκαιος any one who does rightly, φύσει, and not for the law's sake (Theophylact: ὃς δι' αὐτὸ τὸ καλὸν τήν τε πονηρίαν μισεῖ καὶ τὴν ἀρετὴν περιπτύσσεται) In that case we would have the same thought here as in *Antiph. ad Stobaeum,* 9 ὁ μηδὲν ἀδικῶν οὐδενὸς δεῖται νόμου (comp. also the expression of Socrates in Clemens Alex. *Stromata,* IV. 678 · νόμον ἕνεκεν ἀγαθῶν οὐκ ἂν γενέσθαι) — The sentence, however, may also be taken in such a way as to make νόμος the Mosaic law (notwithstanding the omission of the article, comp. Rom ii. 12, 14, 23, *al*), and δίκαιος the righteous man in the specially Christian sense, *i.e.* the man who, in faith as a child of God, fulfils the divine will in the free obedience of the spirit. In that case we have here

---

[1] Most expositors have on this passage told us wherein consisted the material advantage of the law; but however correct their statements in themselves may be, they are out of place, since there is no ground for them in the apostle's words.

the thought which forms the fundamental idea of Paul's view regarding the relations of the Christian to the law (comp. Rom. vi. 14; Gal. v. 18, al.). As Paul in ver. 11 appeals to the gospel entrusted to him for confirmation of the thought expressed in this verse, the connection of ideas decidedly favours the latter view, which is adopted also by Matthies, de Wette, Wiesinger, Van Oosterzee, et al. — κεῖται] has not, as Heydenreich thinks probable, the additional notion of an oppressive burden; νόμος κεῖται simply means, according to a usage current even in profane writings: "the law is given, exists." Otto rightly remarks: "the νόμος κείμενος is one which has not only been given, but is still valid." The collocation does not occur elsewhere in the N. T., comp, however, Luke ii 34 (Phil. i. 16); 1 Thess. iii. 3; especially also 2 Macc. iv. 11.— If the law was not given for the δίκαιος (as the heretics falsely maintained), then it is valid only for the ἄδικος This thought Paul emphasizes by pointing out the nature of the ἄδικος in various aspects, mentioning them at first in pairs. — ἀνόμοις δὲ καὶ ἀνυποτάκτοις] These two ideas, which express the most decided contrast, are rightly placed first. Ἄνομοι, in 1 Cor. ix 21, means the heathen (Rom. ii. 14: ἔθνη τὰ μὴ νόμον ἔχοντα); but here it means those who withstand the law, who do not serve the law, but their own pleasure; comp. Mark xv. 28.—To this corresponds the following ἀνυπότακτοι (only here and in Tit. i. 6, 10; comp. Heb. ii. 8), as a designation of those who submit themselves to no higher will, no higher order. It is quite arbitrary, with Tittmann and Leo, to refer ἀνομ to divine, and ἀνυπ. to human ordinances. — ἀσεβέσι καὶ ἁμαρτωλοῖς] These ideas (found together also in 1 Pet. iv. 18 and in Wisd. xli. 5) are distinguished from the foregoing by a more definite reference to God; ἀσεβής (used by Paul only here and in Rom. iv. 5, v. 6) is the man who does not stand in awe, who has no holy awe of God in his heart. — ἀνοσίοις καὶ βεβήλοις] give prominence to the opposition to what is holy. Ἀνόσιος (again in 2 Tim. iii. 2), when joined with ἀσεβής in the classical usage, refers to the injury of human rights (Xenophon, Cyrop. viii. 8. 13. ἀσεβεστέρους περὶ θεοὺς, καὶ ἀνοσιωτέρους περὶ συγγενεῖς). This distinction, however, cannot here be pressed. βέβηλος, which occurs only in the Epistles to Timothy and in Heb. xii. 16 (the verb βεβηλόω in Matt. xii. 5; Acts xxiv. 6), is synonymous with ἀνόσιος. In these first three pairs the ἄδικοι are characterized as those who stand opposed to what is divine, recognising no divine law, and having no awe of God, and whose life is not consecrated by communion with God—The ideas that follow refer, on the other hand, to our relations with our neighbour.— πατραλῴαις καὶ μητραλῴαις] only here in N. T.: *parricides and matricides*. Hesychius explains them: ὁ τὸν πατέρα ἀτιμάζων, τύπτων, ἢ κτείνων; and similarly Matthies: "those who actually assault father and mother." As the word occurs in this wider sense in Demosth. 732, 14; Lys. 348, ult.; Plato, *Phaed.* chap. 62, it may be so taken here. At least we cannot, with de Wette, quote the following ἀνδροφόνοις as a cogent reason against it. — ἀνδροφόνοις] 2 Macc. ix. 28; ἅπαξ λεγόμ in N T.; the compound is selected to correspond with the previous words. — πόρνοις, ἀρσενοκοίταις] refer to unchastity, the one towards the female, the other towards the male sex, for this latter, comp. Rom. i. 27; 1 Cor. vi. 9.— ἀνδραποδισταῖς] The Scholiast on Aristoph. *Plut.* v. 521, says: εἴρηται ἀνδραποδιστὴς παρὰ τὸ ἄνδρα ἀποδίδοσθαι, τουτέστι πωλεῖν. This crime is often mentioned in Greek authors; but also in Ex. xxi. 16, Deut. xxiv 7. — ψεύσταις, ἐπιόρκοις] stand both in opposition to truthfulness; ἐπίορκος is one who wantonly breaks an oath, as well as one who swears something false —We cannot help seeing that in enumerating these various classes of the ἄδικοι, the apostle has had the Decalogue in mind, not adhering to it strictly, but partly extending, partly limiting it, still without departing from its order.—In order to describe the ἀδικία as a whole, the apostle adds: καὶ εἴ τι ἕτερον τῇ ὑγιαινούσῃ διδασκαλίᾳ ἀντίκειται.— The expression ἡ ὑγιαίν. διδασκ. is one of those which only occur in the Pastoral Epistles, and help to give them a peculiar impress; comp. 2 Tim. iv. 3; Tit. ii. 1, i. 9.—In 1 Tim. vi. 3 and in 2 Tim. i. 13, we have ὑγιαίνοντες λόγοι; in Tit. ii. 8, λόγος ὑγιής. In these epistles ὑγιαίνειν is even used figuratively in another connection; thus Tit. i. 13, ii. 2 (νοσεῖν in opposite sense, 1 Tim. vi. 4); elsewhere in the N. T. it occurs only in its proper meaning. The expression διδασκαλία is particularly frequent in these epistles, sometimes denoting "the doctrine" (so here) in the objective sense, sometimes subjectively, "the teaching" (comp. chap. iv. 1, 6, 13, 16, *al*; 2 Tim iii. 10, iv. 3; Tit. i. 9 ff.).—He lays emphasis on *sound* doctrine, as opposed to the ματαιολογία of the heretics. Luther translates ὑγιαίνουσα inaccurately by "wholesome;" the wholesomeness is only the result of the soundness. By ἡ ὑγιαίν. διδ. is here meant the pure gospel, free from all foreign admixture, having nothing unclean or sickly in it. The apostle here is certainly thinking chiefly of the ethical side of the διδασκ.; still Leo is wrong in translating it "sound morality." By the form εἴ . . ἀντίκειται Paul gives us to understand that there are indeed other forms and shapes of unrighteousness, incompatible with the pure doctrine of the gospel. The neuter form τὶ ἕτερον is strange In explanation, we might appeal to passages like 1 Cor. i. 17, Heb. vii. 7, and others, where the neuter denotes persons; but the use of the verb ἀντίκειται is against this. It is better to regard it as a transition from persons to things.[1]

Ver. 11 Κατὰ τὸ εὐαγγέλιον κ.τ.λ] may be joined with ἀντίκειται, so far as the grammar goes; but the thought is against this, since the ὑγιαίν. διδασκ is simply the doctrine of the gospel, and the whole of the added clause would be very slipshod There is as little ground for joining it with διδασκαλία, as was done by Theophylact (τῇ ὑγ. διδ, τῇ οὔσῃ κατὰ τὸ εὐαγγ), and approved by many later expositors. The only right construction is to refer this addition to the whole of the preceding thought (Wiesinger, Plitt, van Oosterzee, Hofmann), so as to bring the thought to a concluding point. Similarly in Rom. ii. 16, κατὰ τὸ εὐαγγ. is joined with what precedes. The apostle asserts thereby that his doctrine regarding the law is not founded on his own private opinion, but on the gospel entrusted *to him* In order to make its authority plainer as a rule of life, he describes it as τὸ εὐαγγέλιον τῆς δόξης τοῦ μακαρίου Θεοῦ (de Wette, Matthies).—The genitive τῆς δόξης is not to be interpreted by the adjective ἔνδοξος, and then joined with τὸ εὐαγγ. (= τὸ εὐαγγ. ἔνδοξον; Luther: "according to the glorious

[1] As Wiesinger rightly remarks, vv. 9 and 10 show that the apostle is not contending here against actual Judaizers, but "against such as consider the law a means of attaining to a still higher moral perfection."

gospel"), or even with Θεοῦ (Heinrichs: = τοῦ μακαρίου καὶ ἐνδόξου Θεοῦ); the genitive should rather be allowed to retain its special meaning. Ἡ δόξα τοῦ Θεοῦ may be *the glory of the Christians*, which is given them by God (comp. Rom. v. 2. Wegscheider: "according to the gladdening doctrine of the salvation which the blessed God imparts to us;" Theodoret: εὐαγγ. δόξης τὸ κήρυγμα κέκληκεν, ἐπειδὰν τὴν μέλλουσαν δόξαν ἐπαγγέλλεται τοῖς πιστεύουσι, and Theophylact). It is more natural, however, to understand the expression here, as in 2 Cor. iv. 4, 6, Rom. ix 23, etc., of the glory dwelling in God, peculiar to Him, "revealed to the world in Jesus Christ" (Wiesinger). The relation of the genitive τῆς δόξης to τὸ εὐαγγέλιον is not to be taken to mean that the δόξα was declared to be the ground of the gospel (the gospel proceeding from the glory of God); the δόξα is rather contained in the gospel (Wiesinger, van Oosterzee, Plitt), so that it is thereby revealed and communicated to men. — God's nature is here described more precisely by the adjective μακαρίου, by which still greater emphasis is laid on God's δόξα, manifesting itself in the gospel in its peculiar power. Though the word is not foreign to the N. T., it is used only here and in vi. 15 as an attribute of God. It is not improbable that the apostle uses it with some reference to the heretics. If, in ver. 4, we are to understand by the genealogies, series of aeons emanating from God, he might readily use μακάριος of God in order to mark the divine unity, for holiness excludes all division of nature. Theodore of Mopsuestia thinks that God is here called μακάριος, not only because He has τὸ μακάριον in His nature διὰ τῆς ἀτρεπτότητος, but also because out of His grace He imparts it to us.[1] The words that follow declare that the gospel was

[1] Otto takes the reference otherwise He refers the word to the heretics, inasmuch as they taught the eternal continuance of the law: "The eternal continuance of the law presupposes a godlessness that cannot be amended. And these νομοδιδάσκαλοι teach a *blessed* God? God is not blessed if He is for ever afflicted with those opposed to Himself, with the ἀνόμοις κ τ λ. I teach that God got rid of this opposition by reconciling the world to Himself, and that we have indeed a *blessed* God." Hofmann refers μακαρίου to this, that the heretics "make the law the subject of their instruction in the place where there should only be preached the things by which God has glorified His blessedness." In any case, Paul chose the attribute, because the heresy stood in contradiction to God's blessedness.

CHAP. I. 12. 97

entrusted to the apostle: ὃ ἐπιστεύθην ἐγώ (Tit. i. 3). Regarding the construction of these words, cf Buttmann, *Gr. Gram.* § 121. 7; Winer, p. 244 [E. T. p. 287]. The same construction is found in Rom. iii. 2 ; Gal. ii. 7; 1 Thess. ii. 4; 1 Cor. ix. 17. It is to be observed that this construction of the verb πιστεύεσθαι, apart from the Pastoral Epistles, occurs only in the epistles of Paul, and only where he speaks of the gospel, or the office given him to hold [1]

Ver. 12. After pointing in these last words to his personal relation to the gospel, the apostle, down to ver. 17, describes the grace experienced by him, not merely "to let it be seen what assurance he had for his gospel" (Wiesinger), but also to prove by his own example (πρὸς ὑποτύπωσιν κ.τ.λ , ver. 16) the glory of the gospel entrusted to him as the εὐαγγ τῆς δόξης τοῦ μακαρίου Θεοῦ There is therefore no ground for de Wette's criticism, "that the self-styled apostle lets fall here the thread of his meaning, that he may not have to take it up again" This section is in the closest connection with the preceding one, since it shows how deep is the contrast between the heresy and the gospel. The heresy, on the one hand, takes up unfruitful speculations, and, whenever it wishes to become practical, it places the Christian in bondage to the law. The one thing which is all-important, the forgiveness of sins, it does not assure, and hence it does not know the compassion of the Lord On the contrary, it is of the very essence of the gospel to reveal this compassion ; and in proof of this, Paul appeals to his own experience. — χάριν ἔχω] We have the same expression in 2 Tim. i. 3 (comp also Luke xvii. 9 ; Heb. xii 28); and in the other Pauline Epistles we have instead : εὐχαριστῶ — τῷ ἐνδυναμώσαντί με] must not be limited to the strength granted for enduring afflictions and sufferings ; it is rather to be applied to his whole work as an apostle. The proper reason of thanksgiving is only furnished by the clause that follows ὅτι κ.τ λ., but an additional reason is

---

[1] We need not be surprised that here, and somewhat frequently in the Pastoral Epistles, Paul directs attention to himself and his office, if only we reflect that the apostle was fully conscious of his position towards the development of God's kingdom, and that he was bound, therefore, to vindicate fully the principle of the Christian life which he had enounced.

given in this participle.[1] — Χριστῷ Ἰησοῦ κ.τ λ.] is not to be explained, according to some older expositors: "qui me potentem reddidit Christo," *for* Christ, but as a dative closely belonging to the verb. — ὅτι πιστόν με ἡγήσατο] πιστός corresponds with the following διακονία. The reason of his thanksgiving is Christ's confidence in him that he would become a faithful διάκονος.[2] This confidence the Lord has shown by committing to him the ministry of the gospel, hence he adds: θέμενος εἰς διακονίαν, which is either "placing me in the ministry" (Heydenreich, van Oosterzee, Hofmann), or "setting me apart for the ministry" (de Wette, Plitt, Winer). The latter seems to be more in accordance with the usage of the N. T.; comp. 1 Thess. v. 9. De Wette rightly remarks that the participle does not stand for ὡς τίθεσθαί με, nor is it to be taken as a pluperfect; it is simply the proof of πιστόν με ἡγ.; see also Winer, p. 326 [E. T. p. 365]. — If the apostle's thanks are due to the Lord on the general ground of His confidence, they are all the more due that he had been before an opponent of the gospel; to this the next verse points.

Ver. 13 Τὸ πρότερον ὄντα βλάσφημον κ τ λ] τὸ πρότερον is equivalent to the adverb πρότερον, just as, in Matt. xxvi. 45, τὸ λοιπόν is equivalent to λοιπόν. The participle stands here in the relation of contrast to what precedes: "though I was before," or "I who was *nevertheless.*" — βλάσφημον] only here as a substantive; comp. on this Acts xxvi. 11. For the most part, the idea of βλασφημία is used in reference to what is divine (Suidas: ἡ εἰς Θεὸν ὕβρις). — καὶ διώκτην] Leo says: "Paulus non dictis tantum sed etiam factis furuerat in Christianos;" the word occurs only here in the N. T.; on the subject-matter, comp. Acts xxii. 4; Gal. i. 13. — καὶ ὑβριστήν] also in Rom. i. 30. Luther translates "reviler," but Wegscheider: "one who does violence." Neither translation expresses the full meaning as it is given in Tittmann's (*Syn.* p. 74) explanation: "qui prae superbia non solum con-

---

[1] According to the reading of ℵ ἐνδυναμοῦντι without μι is to be taken as a simple attribute: "Christ Jesus who bestows strength."
[2] Cf. 1 Cor. vii. 25 γνώμην δὲ δίδωμι ὡς ἠλεημένος ὑπὸ κυρίου πιστὸς εἶναι. Paul gives the nature of this διακονία in Acts xx. 24: ἡ διακονία ἣν ἔλαβον παρὰ τοῦ κυρίου Ἰησοῦ, διαμαρτύρασθαι τὸ εὐαγγέλιον τῆς χάριτος τοῦ Θεοῦ.

temnit alios, sed etiam contumeliose tractat, et injuriis afficit." Ὑβρίζειν denotes the arrogant conduct of another, whether in words or in actions. — The context leads us to think of Christ's work, or Christ Himself, as the object of the apostle's blasphemy. — Having judged his former conduct in straightforward fashion, Paul goes on to contrast with it the grace of the Lord: ἀλλ' ἠλεήθην, adding, however, by way of explanation: ὅτι ἀγνοῶν ἐποίησα ἐν ἀπιστίᾳ. De Wette is not correct in supposing that the intended aim of these words is to furnish some excuse for himself.[1] — ἠλεήθην] (Luther: "to my lot did compassion fall") is not to be limited to the pardon of his persecuting fury (Matthies: "to me was my mad eagerness in persecution most graciously forgiven"), but should be taken more generally of the grace imparted to the apostle.[2] — ἀγνοῶν] (comp. Rom. x. 2: Ζῆλον Θεοῦ ἔχων, ἀλλ' οὐ κατ' ἐπίγνωσιν), i.e. without knowing how grievously I sinned therein. The reason of this unconsciousness was ἐν ἀπιστίᾳ. Mack is wrong in inverting the relation, as if the apostle added ἐν ἀπιστίᾳ to explain his ἄγνοια. How far the ἀπιστία was one to be blamed, Paul does not here say. the idea is to be taken in its purely negative form. It was not this, but the ἄγνοια grounded on it, which lessened his guilt.[3]

Ver. 14. The last words might be so explained as to weaken seemingly the divine grace; and therefore the apostle feels bound to set forth its abundant riches. — ὑπερεπλεόνασε δὲ ἡ χάρις κ.τ.λ.] The verb ὑπερπλεονάζειν only occurs here in the N. T., and is not current in classical Greek. The simple πλεονάζειν, with the classic writers, means: "to be more, i.e. than the measure demands, therefore to go beyond the measure," but in several passages of the N. T. it has clearly

[1] Wiesinger "The words are not intended to exculpate his acts, but to explain wherein the power of divine grace began to work on him." Similarly Plitt, van Oosterzee, and others.

[2] Otto wrongly finds in ἠλεήθην a special reference to the fact that Paul "was entrusted with the ministry of the word."—What precedes in ver. 12 might seem to support this, but what follows is entirely against such a limitation of the thought.

[3] Hofmann wrongly takes ἐν ἀπιστίᾳ as in pure apposition to the participle ἀγνοῶν, and maintains that ἀγνοεῖν is not always an ignorance which simply does not even know, but a misconception of something which it should have known. But this more precise reference is clearly not contained in the words themselves

the meaning : " *become* more, therefore increase, grow larger." Comp. 2 Thess. i. 3 (synon. with ὑπεραυξάνειν); Rom. v. 20, vi. 1 (Meyer: accumulate); so also Phil. iv. 17 and 2 Cor iv. 15 (Meyer has there: "*become* abundant ... increase," and here · " be increased "). The prefix ὑπέρ serves, with Paul, to strengthen the idea with which it is joined; thus ὑπεραυξάνει, 2 Thess. i. 3, ὑπερεκπερισσοῦ, Eph. iii. 20, ὑπερλίαν, 2 Cor. xi. 5, al. In Rom. v. 20, ὑπερεπερίσσευσεν seems to mean that the ἐπλεόνασεν ἡ ἁμαρτία was surpassed by the χάρις (so Meyer, Hofmann differs). If we assume here this reference of surpassing, we cannot regard ἠλεήθην as the thing surpassed. For χάρις cannot be regarded as something surpassing ἔλεος,[1] but ὑπέρ in that case would have to be referred to τὸ πρότερον ὄντα βλάσφημον κ τ λ. Hence the apostle's meaning in ὑπερεπλεόνασεν would be that grace was manifested to him in abundant measure, far surpassing his enmity (so in a former edition of this commentary), but in that case ἀλλὰ ἠλεήθην κ.τ λ. would be parenthetical. It is more correct not to assume such a reference here, but to explain ὑπερπλεονάζειν: " to go (abundantly) beyond the measure " (Plitt, van Oosterzee, Hofmann) The apostle added ὑπερεπλ. ἡ χάρις to ἠλεήθην, because the latter expression did not seem enough to his mind, which was penetrated by the unbounded greatness of the grace he had experienced. " It is as though he wrestles with speech in order to find some sufficient expression for the feeling which quite overpowers him " (van Oosterzee). The particle δέ belongs to the relation of climax existing between the two clauses, as in Heb. xii. 6, it corresponds to the English *yea* or *aye* in a climax.[2] — μετὰ πίστεως καὶ ἀγάπης] The preposition μετά with the genitive serves to connect the fact with the points that accompany it Πίστις and ἀγάπη therefore are, properly speaking, not men-

---

[1] Chrysostom οὐκ ἐτιμωρήθην ἠλεήθην γάρ, ἆρ' οὖν τοῦτο μόνον, καὶ μέχρι τούτου ὁ ἔλεος, τοῦ μὴ δοῦναι τιμωρίαν, οὐδαμῶς ἀλλὰ καὶ ἕτερα πολλὰ καὶ μεγάλα, διὰ τοῦτο φησίν ὑπερεπλ ἡ χάρις, δηλῶν, ὅτι ὑπερέβη καὶ τὸν ἔλεον τὰ δῶρα· ταῦτα γὰρ οὐκ ἐλεοῦντός ἐστιν, ἀλλὰ φιλοῦντος καὶ σφόδρα ἀγαπῶντος Similarly Leo In this view the force of ἠλεήθην is arbitrarily weakened

[2] Hofmann explains δέ as ranking another fact with the one already mentioned; but in ἠλεήθην and ὑπερεπλ. ἡ χάρις we have not two different facts, but one and the same fact—though expressed in two different ways.

tioned as results of the χάρις, but as blessings immediately connected with χάρις. They form, as de Wette says, the subjective side of the condition of grace. Leo is right, therefore, in saying: "verbis μετὰ κ τ.λ. indicatur, π. κ ἀγ. quasi comites fuisse illius χάριτος" (so also Plitt and van Oosterzee); but he is wrong, if he means that Paul added these words to tell in what the grace was manifested as ὑπερπλεονάζουσα. — By πίστις κ ἀγ. ἡ ἐν Χρ 'Ι we are not to understand God's faithfulness and love in Christ, nor the apostle's endeavour to bring others to faith and love, nor, again, is ἐν to be explained by διά or by εἰς The words τῆς ἐν Χρ 'Ι are added to τῆς ἀγάπης, and mark the love as one " that has its ground and middle-point in Christ" (Matthies); cf 2 Tim i. 13. It is doubtful whether the addition is to be referred also to πίστεως (for this Matthies, Plitt, van Oosterzee, against it, Hofmann); since πίστεως does not properly require it, it might be better to limit the reference to ἀγάπης [1] "In contrasting his former ἀπιστία with his present increasing πίστις κ ἀγ" (Heydenreich), Paul does not lose sight of the heresy which did not effect οἰκονομία Θεοῦ ἐν πίστει (ver. 4), and had not the ἀγάπη (ver. 5) as its goal.

Ver. 15. Πιστὸς ὁ λόγος κτλ] With this formula, which is peculiar to the Pastoral Epistles (found besides here in iii. 1, iv. 9; 2 Tim. ii. 11, Tit. iii 8, only in Rev is there a similar formula: οὗτοι οἱ λόγοι πιστοὶ καὶ ἀληθινοί εἰσι, xxi. 5, xxii. 6), the apostle introduces the general thought whose truth he had himself experienced. — καὶ πάσης ἀποδοχῆς ἄξιος] This addition is also in iv. 9; the word ἀποδοχή occurs nowhere else in the N T. (comp. ἀπόδεκτος, ii. 3, v. 4) As Raphelius has shown by many proofs from Polybius, it is synonymous in later Greek with πίστις : the verb ἀποδέχεσθαι (" receive believing ") is used in the same sense in Acts ii. 41. The adjective πάσης describes the ἀποδοχή of which the word is worthy, as one complete and excluding all doubt. — ὅτι Χρ. Ἰησ. ἦλθεν εἰς τὸν κόσμον]

[1] Hofmann alleges against the connection with πίστεως, that "ἐν would have a different meaning when joined with πίστεως, according to Eph. i 15 ; Col i. 4;" but his reason is without force, as this other reference is here cut off by the intervening ἀγάπης.

This expression, found especially in John, may be explained from the saying of Christ. ἐξῆλθον παρὰ τοῦ πατρὸς καὶ ἐλήλυθα εἰς τὸν κόσμον, John xvi. 28, κόσμος having here a physical, not an ethical meaning: "the earthly world."— Ἁμαρτωλοί stands here in a general sense, and is not with Stolz to be limited to the opponents of Christianity, nor with Michaelis to the heathen. As little can the idea of σῶσαι be limited in the one direction or the other. After this general thought, that the aim of Christ's coming is none other than the σωτηρία of sinners, the apostle returns to his own case, adding, in consciousness of his guilt (ver. 13): ὧν πρῶτός εἰμι ἐγώ, "of whom I am first." Paul says this, conscious of his former determined hostility to Christ when he was a βλάσφημος κ.τ.λ. (ver. 13), and considering himself at the same time as standing at the head of sinners It is inaccurate to translate πρῶτος without qualification by "the foremost" (in opposition to Wiesinger and others). Even in Mark xii. 28, 29, πρώτη πάντων ἐντολή is the commandment which stands at the head of all, is first in the list, and δευτέρα is the one following. In order to qualify the thought, Flatt wishes to translate πρῶτος by "one of the foremost," which he thinks he can justify by the absence of the article. Wegscheider, again, wishes not to refer ὧν to ἁμαρτωλούς, but to supply σωζομένων or σεσωσμένων, and similarly Mack explains ὧν by "of which saved sinners." All these expositions are, however, to be rejected as pieces of ingenuity. The thought needs no qualification—at least not for any one who can sympathize with the apostle's *strong* feeling. The apostle does not overstep the bounds of humility in what he says in 1 Cor. xv. 9 and Eph iii. 8; neither does he overstep them here.

Ver. 16. After calling *himself* the first of sinners, Paul gives the reason why *he*, this foremost sinner, found grace. He begins with ἀλλά, since it must appear strange that grace was imparted to him. — διὰ τοῦτο ἠλεήθην] De Wette says: "therefor (to this end) did I receive grace." — ἵνα ἐν ἐμοὶ πρώτῳ ἐνδείξηται Χρ. Ἰ. τὴν ἅπασαν μακροθυμίαν. — ἐν ἐμ. πρ.] stands first for the sake of emphasis; ἐν is not equivalent to "by means of," but to "*in the case of*" (comp. Rom. vii. 19).

To supply ἁμαρτωλῷ with πρώτῳ (first ed. of this commentary, Wiesinger, van Oosterzee, and others) is arbitrary There is no need to supply anything The thought is: "in my case, Christ first showed His entire μακροθυμία."[1] Paul says this, meaning that the entire fulness of Christ's μακροθυμία (Buttmann, p. 105) could not be shown to those who before had received grace, because they had not cherished such decided enmity to Christ as he. The πρώτῳ therefore has ἅπασαν corresponding with it; the greater the guilt, the greater the manifestation of μακροθυμία. Bengel says: "cunctam longanimitatem: quum minores peccatores etiam mensura quasi minor possit restituere." It is not necessary to give the word μακροθυμία the meaning here of "magnanimity" (Heydenreich, Matthies: "long-suffering or magnanimity"). The apostle here regards the love of the Lord as not causing judgment to follow straight on condemnation, but as patient, and granting space for conversion. In this Paul has given the purpose of his pardon; but he states it still more definitely in the words that follow: πρὸς ὑποτύπωσιν τῶν μελλόντων πιστεύειν ἐπ' αὐτῷ. The expression ὑποτύπωσις, "likeness, image," occurs elsewhere only in 2 Tim. i. 13; it is synonymous with ὑπόδειγμα in 2 Pet. ii. 6, and other passages. Elsewhere in the Pauline Epistles we find τύπος (Rom. v 14, 1 Cor. x. 6, 11, Phil. iii. 17). Leo, without sufficient grounds, explains the word by *institutio* The idea of *type* is not contained in the word itself, but is here transferred to it from the μελλόντων. — πιστεύειν ἐπ' αὐτῷ] This construction of the word πιστεύειν is found in the N. T. only here and in Rom. ix 33, x. 11, 1 Pet. ii. 6, but in all these passages it occurs in words quoted from Isa xxviii. 16, where the LXX. has simply ὁ πιστεύων It may be explained in this way, that faith has confidence as its substance and basis. Matthies rightly says: "ἐπ' αὐτῷ, not so much *in Him* as the object of faith, but rather *trusting in faith on Him* as the absolute basis of our salvation." — εἰς ζωὴν αἰώνιον] These words are not to be joined to the distant ὑποτύπωσιν (Bengel), but to the

---

[1] Hofmann "If πρῶτος before had the meaning of locality, here πρώτῳ has the meaning of time as opposed to τῶν μελλόντων πιστεύειν."

πιστεύειν immediately preceding. They present the goal towards which the πιστεύειν ἐπ' αὐτῷ is directed (Wiesinger). As Paul usually sets forth his conduct to others as a type, so here he gives to his experience a typical meaning for future believers.[1] This may be explained from the peculiar and important position which he held for the development of God's kingdom on earth, and of which he was distinctly conscious.

Ver. 17. "Ex sensu gratiae fluit doxologia" (Bengel). With this doxology the apostle closes the digression begun in ver. 11, and returns again to the proper epistolary style. — τῷ δὲ βασιλεῖ τῶν αἰώνων] This designation for God is not found elsewhere in the N. T. (even the use of βασιλεύς of God only occurs elsewhere in chap. vi. 15 and Matt. v. 35), but it is found in the Apocrypha of the O T. in Tob. xiii. 6, 10. (Ecclesiasticus xxxvi. 19 : ὁ Θεὸς τῶν αἰώνων.) Οἱ αἰῶνες means either "the world," as in Heb. i. 2, xi. 3 (see Delitzsch and Lunemann on this passage), or "the times." The former meaning is adopted by Chrysostom, Leo, etc. (Leo appealing to Eusebius, de Laud. Constant. chap. vi. p 431, ed. Heinrichs: τὸν μέγαν τοῦ σύμπαντος αἰῶνος βασιλέα) ; the latter, by Matthies: "the ruler of all times, so that all generations are at the same time concretely included." In a similar way, Heydenreich has "the supreme ruler of time, and of all that takes place in its course." This latter explanation is supported as correct both by the preceding μελλόντων (van Oosterzee), and also by the ἀφθάρτῳ following, and by εἰς τοὺς αἰῶνας τῶν αἰώνων farther on.[2] It is incorrect to take αἰῶνες as equivalent to "eternity," and translate : "to the king eternal" (de Wette, but tentatively ; Hofmann : "the king who is for ever and without end "),[3] for αἰῶνες never has that meaning in itself. Only in the

---

[1] Hofmann, without grounds, disputes this view, and gives the apostle's thought in this way "The aim is to give a type, not to them, but of them ; they were to know that they had to expect such conversions as his, the conversions of revilers and persecutors." But there is no hint whatever of revilers and persecutors only in οἱ μέλλοντες πιστεύειν

[2] Comp. Ps cxlv. 13, LXX. . ἡ βασιλεία σου βασιλεία πάντων τῶν αἰώνων καὶ ἡ δεσποτεία σου ἐν πάσῃ γενεᾷ καὶ γενεᾷ.

[3] Wiesinger explains it "He is a king of the aeons, which together give the idea of eternity, just as His kingdom is an everlasting kingdom."

formulas ἀπὸ τῶν αἰώνων and εἰς τοὺς αἰῶνας does the meaning of the word approach that idea. Besides, the apostle would surely have expressed that adjectival idea by an adjective. It is quite erroneous to take the word here in the Gnostic sense of series of emanations, synonymous with γενεαλογίαι in ver. 4; for, on the one hand, no proof is given that this expression had been already used by the heretics alluded to in this epistle; and, on the other, the apostle considered the whole theory of genealogies as belonging to the sphere of myths. It was impossible, therefore, for him in his doxology to speak of God as the king of things which were to Him nothing but the inventions of fancy. — ἀφθάρτῳ] is only used of God elsewhere in Rom. i. 23 (Plut. *adv. St.* 31; Wisd. of Sol. xii. 1). Matthies · " God is the Imperishable One, because His nature is unchanging and based on itself," equivalent to ὁ μόνος ἔχων ἀθανασίαν, chap vi 16. — ἀοράτῳ] comp Heb xi. 27 (without Θεός), Rom i. 20, and Col. i. 15 (with Θεός), equivalent to ὃν εἶδεν οὐδεὶς ἀνθρώπων, οὐδὲ ἰδεῖν δύναται, chap. vi. 16; comp also John i. 18 — μόνῳ Θεῷ] chap. vi. 15 μόνος δυναστής; comp. also John v 44, xvii 3; Rom. xvi. 27: μόνῳ σοφῷ Θεῷ. The words ἀφθάρτῳ. . Θεῷ are to be taken as in apposition to τῷ βασιλεῖ. But it is doubtful whether Θεῷ is to be joined with μόνῳ only, or also with ἀφθάρτῳ and ἀοράτῳ, as is commonly done De Wette is wrong in asserting that all these predicates are used of God superfluously : they manifestly express the absolute exaltation of God above all conditioned finite being, and are occasioned naturally (which Hofmann disputes) by the contrast with the heresy which denied the absoluteness of the divine existence. — τιμὴ καὶ δόξα] The two words are united also in Rom. ii. 7, 10 ; Heb. ii. 7 ; but only here and in the Apocalypse do they occur in doxologies. Paul elsewhere uses only δόξα, and always with the article. — εἰς τοὺς αἰῶνας τῶν αἰώνων] a very common conclusion in doxologies, and found in Paul's other epistles. It is not to be overlooked that this doxology has a peculiar character distinct from those usually occurring in Paul, both in the mode of connection (elsewhere a pronoun connects them with what precedes) and also in the designation for God and the expressions used.

Ver. 18. Paul again addresses himself to Timothy direct. — ταύτην τὴν παραγγελίαν] cannot be referred back to ἵνα παραγγείλῃς in ver. 3 (Otto), because there he was speaking of a παραγγελία which Timothy was to receive, here he is speaking of a παραγγελία to which Timothy was to give heed. Nor can it be referred to καθὼς παρεκάλεσά σε (Plitt), since that denotes only a special commission, to which there is here no allusion. Some have therefore joined ταύτην immediately with the following ἵνα, and taken ἵνα as introducing the object (so Chrysostom and Theophylact, Matthies, de Wette, Wiesinger, van Oosterzee; also in this commentary; comp Winer, pp. 314 f. [E. T. p. 422]). This construction, however, is opposed by the order of the words; after the verb and the parenthesis κατὰ τὰς κ.τ.λ., we no longer expect an expansion of the thought contained in ταύτην τ παρ.[1] The only course remaining is to agree with Hofmann in referring ταύτ. τ παραγγ back to τῆς παραγγελίας in ver 5; not, however, agreeing with him in interpreting the word here, "the Christian teaching," but taking it in the same sense in both places. — παρατίθεμαί σοι] comp. 2 Tim. ii. 2. The verb is here explained by most expositors, against usage, as equivalent to "lay to heart" (Luther . " order," in the sense of "recommend to"). Otto, and following him Hofmann, took it in the sense of "give something into one's *charge*," which meaning is *possible*, but not imperative. In itself the word means "bring something before one," and is defined more precisely by its context, *i.e.* the purpose of *bringing before* is not contained in the word itself. Παρατίθεσθαι παραγγελίαν may therefore quite well mean: *propose a command to one*, viz that he may act in accordance with it.[2] — τέκνον Τιμ.] see ver. 1. — κατὰ τὰς προαγούσας ἐπὶ σὲ προφητείας] Before

---

[1] Hofmann wrongly maintains that this construction is impossible in point of language and in point of fact "in point of language, because παρατίθεσθαι does not mean *lay to heart*, but *propose*, and a command is not proposed (why not?); in point of fact, because what he calls τὰς προαγούσας ἐπί σε cannot furnish any standard for the apostle's injunction to Timothy to discharge his office well" (why not?).

[2] In Matt. xiii 24, 31, it is joined with παραβολήν, it is used of setting forth a doctrine in Acts xvii 3, it is chiefly used of setting forth food, as in the N. T. Mark viii 7, Luke ix. 16, x 8, xi 6, it has the sense of "committing to the care of" in Luke xii 48.

giving the command itself, Paul inserts these words to add force to his exhortation; for they are not (as some expositors, Oecumenius, Heumann, Flatt, wish) to be placed after ἵνα in sense, but to be joined with παρατίθεμαι. — κατά, "*in conformity with*," not "justified and occasioned by." — προαγούσας stands here quite absolutely, with the same meaning as in Heb. vii. 18 : ἀθέτησις . . γίνεται προαγούσης ἐντολῆς, "the law that preceded;"[1] the προαγ. προφητ. are accordingly "*the promises that preceded*." Matthies is wrong in explaining προάγουσα in connection with ἐπὶ σέ, as equivalent to "leading towards thee," *i.e.* "pointing or aiming towards thee." This meaning προάγειν never has, as a transitive verb it certainly means: "lead forward to any one," but this is manifestly a different idea from that which Matthies ascribes to it. Otto explains it: "the prophecies *that guide* to thee," making appeal to Xenophon, *Memorab.* iv. 1, in which passage Kuhner paraphrases προάγειν by *viam monstrare*. In this case we should have to understand it: those among the prophecies that showed others the way leading to Timothy, a statement clearly without meaning. It is, however, altogether arbitrary when Otto defines the prophecies more precisely as those that led to Timothy's ordination, or occasioned it. — ἐπὶ σέ] is not to be connected with προαγούσας, but with προφητείας, as Luther rightly translates it: "according to the former prophecies regarding thee;" or de Wette. "in accordance with the preceding prophecies on thee" (so, too, Wiesinger, van Oosterzee, Plitt, Hofmann). On the other hand, the translation: "vaticinia olim de te praenuntiata" (Heydenreich), is inaccurate. Αἱ ἐπὶ σὲ προφ. are : the prophecies (expressed) over thee (the peculiar meaning of ἐπί as descending to something should not be overlooked), while προαγ. describes these as preceding Timothy's apostleship.[2] — προφητείας] Chrysostom : τὸ τῆς διδασκαλίας

---

[1] Comp. Lunemann and Delitzsch on the passage Otto is wrong in asserting that προάγειν is never used of priority of time. While it occurs more frequently in the sense of "precede some one," it has in other passages of the N. T. (*e.g.* Matt. xxvi 32 ; Mark vi. 45) the meaning practically of "go before some one in any direction whatever," the notion of space manifestly passing into that of time. In the passage in Hebrews, Otto thinks that προάγουσα ought to mean "driving forward from one election of high priest to another" (!).

[2] In taking the words thus αἱ ἐπὶ σὲ προφητεῖαι, there is not, as Otto main-

καὶ ἱερωσύνης ἀξίωμα, μέγα ὄν, τῆς τοῦ Θεοῦ δεῖται ψήφου ... διὰ τὸ παλαιὸν ἀπὸ τῆς προφητείας γίνονται οἱ ἱερεῖς, τουτέστι ἀπό πνεύματος ἁγίου Οὕτως ὁ Τιμ ἡρέθη. This is wrong, simply because Timothy's office was not a priestly one. It is quite arbitrary to translate προφητεῖαι by: " doctrines, exhortations," or " hopes," or " good testimonies" (Heinrichs " by means of the good hope and expectation which every one cherished regarding thee "). Προφητεῖαι here, as always, are utterances proceeding from the Holy Spirit, whatever be their contents or their occasion, here it is most natural to think of prophecies made when the ἐπίθεσις τῶν χειρῶν τοῦ πρεσβυτερίου (chap. iv. 14) was imparted to Timothy and made regarding his worthy discharge of the office (Wiesinger).[1]— ἵνα στρατεύῃ ἐν αὐταῖς τὴν καλὴν στρατείαν] Purpose of the παρατίθεμαί σοι. Στρατεία (elsewhere only in 2 Cor. x. 4) is frequently translated inaccurately by " fight ," Luther is more correct: " that thou mayest exercise in it a good *knighthood.*" Στρατεία denotes the entire warfare, the only thing wrong in Luther's translation is the indefinite article. Though the Christian calling is not seldom described as a warfare, yet here the word is used specially of Timothy's office, in which he had to contend against the ἑτεροδιδασκαλοῦντες (vv 3 ff).[2] De Wette inaccurately explains it: "that thou conduct thyself worthily and bravely in the discharge of thy evangelic duty," as if the words were. ἵνα καλῶς στρατ. τὴν στρατείαν The chief accent rests on ἐν αὐταῖς, not on καλήν; the στρατεία assigned to Timothy is in itself καλή, quite apart from his behaviour in it. — ἐν αὐταῖς] According to Matthies, Winer (p. 362 [E. T. p. 484]), Wiesinger, Otto, and others, Paul conceives the προφητεῖαι as an armour round Timothy : " as though equipped

tains, a change of order not occurring in Greek; comp 2 Cor viii 2 · ἡ κατὰ βάθους πτωχεία αὐτῶν. It is also wrong to say that the prepositional clause must flow from the substantive, and that περί, therefore, should stand here for ἐπί. In the passage quoted, κατά manifestly does not flow from the idea of the substantive πτωχεία.

[1] According to Hofmann, they were prophecies " which had promised to Paul that Timothy would be a true servant of the gospel, and had confirmed him in his choice when he assumed Timothy as his colleague in the apostleship "

[2] Manifestly Paul here returns to vv. 3 ff, and so far gives reason for saying that here "we have not in form but in substance" the apodosis which was wanting before (Wiesinger).

with them;" it might, however, be more natural to translate: "*within* them," *i e.* in their limits, not exceeding them. The interpretation. *in accordance with them* (van Oosterzee, Hofmann: "the prophecies are to be regarded as a rule of conduct"), is against the usage of the N. T.

Ver. 19 The manner in which Timothy is to discharge his office, is given still more precisely in the words ἔχων πίστιν καὶ ἀγαθὴν συνείδησιν. It is difficult to bring ἔχων into direct connection with the preceding figure στρατεία (Matthies: "hold fast the faith which elsewhere, in Eph. vi 16, is called a shield, a weapon of defence in our warfare," Otto thinks that Paul conceives πίστις and ἀγ συνείδησις as "the contending power which the general commands, *i.e.* as his troops!"). It is simply "holding, maintaining" (de Wette), *i e* not denying. The reason for the collocation peculiar to this epistle of πίστις and ἀγαθὴ συνείδησις, and for the strong emphasis laid on the latter idea (comp. ver. 5, iv 2, etc.), is, that the apostle regards the denial of the ἀγ συνείδ as the source of the heresy. This is proved by the words that follow, in which Paul returns to the mention of the heretics. ἥν (viz. ἀγαθὴν συνείδησιν) τινες (comp. ver. 6). — ἀπωσάμενοι] This expression, not *strange* (de Wette) but suitable, denotes the "wantonness" (de Wette) with which the heretics sacrificed the good conscience to their selfish purposes [1] — περὶ τὴν πίστιν ἐναυάγησαν] ναυαγεῖν occurs only here in a figurative sense. Περί gives the matter in which they had made shipwreck, *i e* suffered loss Περί with the accusative, equivalent to *quod attinet ad,* is found in the N T. only in the Pastoral Epistles, comp 1 Tim vi 4, 21, 2 Tim. ii 18, iii. 8; Tit. ii. 7, see Winer, p. 379 [E T. p 506]

Ver. 20 Ὧν ἐστὶν Ὑμέναιος καὶ Ἀλέξανδρος] In 2 Tim ii. 17, the apostle names two false teachers whose words eat like a cancer—Hymenaeus and Philetus There is no ground for distinguishing between the Hymenaeus there and the one

---

[1] Van Oosterzee remarks on ἀγαθὴν συνείδησιν "as a troublesome reminder," which is not appropriate, because ἀγ συνειδ is not the conscience exhorting to good and punishing evil, but of willing and doing good —Hofmann's opinion, that the good conscience is compared to "the ballast which gives the necessary stability to a ship," is wrong, since ἀπωθεῖσθαι does not mean "to cast overboard."

here mentioned. No difficulty is caused even by the fact that " the one here is mentioned as a man cast out from the church, and the other merely as an example of error " (de Wette); for Hymenaeus and Philetus are not so *tenderly* dealt with in the other passages as de Wette seems to think. As to Alexander, we must leave it unsettled whether he is the same as the one mentioned in 2 Tim. iv. 14. The reasons are not decisive which seem to tell against the identity, viz. that in the other passage the surname ὁ χαλκεύς is added, and that " he is mentioned there not as excommunicated, but rather as still coming in contact with the apostle ; not as a heretic, but as an opponent" (de Wette). It is, however, quite arbitrary to regard the Alexander (Acts xix. 33) who took part in the uproar at Ephesus as identical with the one mentioned here (see Meyer on the passage).[1] — οὓς παρέδωκα τῷ σατανᾷ] the same excommunication of which the apostle speaks in 1 Cor. v. 5 (comp. Meyer on the passage). It is not simply excommunication from the church, but with the purpose of ensuring, through Satan's means, ὄλεθρος τῆς σαρκός to the one excommunicated. This is shown not only by the formula itself, but also by the solemnity with which Paul there expresses himself. The added clause, ἵνα παιδευθῶσιν κ.τ.λ., makes it clear that here also the apostle had in mind εἰς ὄλεθρον τ. σαρκ., for that clause at the same time gives the purpose of the παρέδωκα, which is the reformation (ἵνα τὸ πνεῦμα σωθῇ, 1 Cor. v. 5), or at least the preservation, of the excommunicated man from βλασφημεῖν.[2] — παιδεύειν] in classical Greek equivalent to "educate, especially by instruction," so

---

[1] Otto (pp 98-112) gives a very vivid and detailed picture of the tumult at Ephesus in which a certain Alexander took part, in order to prove the identity of the two Alexanders, and confirm his view regarding the date of the composition of this epistle. But even if the course of that tumult was as Otto describes it, with the aid of many arbitrary suppositions, still we can by no means infer the identity he maintains In order to prove it, Otto does not despise many strange assumptions, such as, that the designation χαλκιύς (2 Tim. iv. 14) was given to Alexander because he was one of those who manufactured the miniature silver temples , further, that he, deceived by the soothsayers, had made no objection to the union of the worship of Jehovah with heathen idolatry.

[2] In opposition to Hofmann's opinion, that neither here nor in the passage of Corinthians we are to think of an excommunication from the church, comp. Meyer on 1 Cor. v. 5.

also Acts vii. 22, xxii. 3, has elsewhere in the N. T. the meaning of "punish in order to reform," *i e.* chastise ; comp. 2 Tim. ii. 25 , 1 Cor xi 32 ; 2 Cor. vi. 9, especially Heb. xii. 5–11. In Rev. iii. 19 it stands connected with ἐλέγχειν (in Luke xxiii. 16, 22, the purpose of reformation falls quite into the background). — The ὄλεθρος τῆς σαρκός is intended by the apostle to be a chastisement to the one named, that he may be kept from further reviling The expression βλασφημεῖν shows that they had not only suffered shipwreck in faith, but in their unbelief were on the point of proceeding actually to revile the Lord.

CHAPTER II.

VER. 1 παρακαλῶ] Instead of this, D* F G, Sahid. Clar. Boern. Hilar Ambrosiast. ed Cassiod. (alicubi) Or (ter ut Rec) have the imperative παρακάλει, which is manifestly a conjecture for the purpose of giving to the words the form of a commission to Timothy — πάντων] is omitted in some codd. (G, G, Boern Or [semel]); it might easily be overlooked as merely strengthening the πρῶτον — Ver 3. In A 17, 67** ℵ, Cop Sahid. γάρ is wanting, and is therefore omitted by Lachm Buttm and Tisch 8; it is retained in Matthaei and Tisch. 7. — Ver 6 τὸ μαρτύριον καιροῖς ἰδίοις] Some codd. have the reading οὗ τὸ μαρτ. κ. ἰδ ἐδόθη (D* F G, Clar. Boern. Harl* Ambrosiast, while some cursives have the reading οὗ, but without ἐδόθη) This reading has only arisen out of a desire to connect the words more closely with what precedes The omission of the words τὸ μαρτύριον in A is to be considered merely an error in copying Lachm in his large edition (so also Buttm) left them out, in the small edition he retained them ℵ has the reading καί for τό. — Ver 7. The words ἐν Χριστῷ were rejected from the text even by Griesb. (so also Scholz, Lachm, and others), because they are wanting in the most important authorities, in A D* F G 3, 6, 23* 31, *al*., Syr. utr Arr Copt. etc , on the other hand, they are found in ℵ. Matthaei, however, has retained them with the remark: adhuc maneo in ea sententia, ut credam, ab Praxapostolis et Euchologiis exclusum esse in fine lectionis If they are compared with Rom ix 1, it is easy to explain how they came into the text — Instead of ἐν πίστει, ℵ has ἐν γνώσει. Buttm, following A, reads ἐν πνεύματι — Ver 8 Instead of the singular διαλογισμοῦ, F G 17, 47, 67** *al*, Syr utr. Boern. Or (ter sed ter ut Rec) Eus, etc., have the plural διαλογισμῶν (Tisch. 7); Matthaei remarks on this. hujusmodi lectiones plerumque placent viris graece doctis; verum in N. T. contraria ferenda est sententia. Most authorities, including ℵ, have the singular (Lachm. Buttm Tisch 8) The plural is with Reiche to be considered a mere correction, all the more that the singular of the word does not occur elsewhere in the N. T (except in Luke ix. 46, 47), comp. especially Phil. ii. 14.—Ver. 9. καὶ τάς] are

CHAP. II. 1. 113

wanting in A 71; καί alone is wanting in ℵ, and τάς alone is wanting in D* F G 67** 73, al., Or. Lachm. and Buttm. omitted both words, Tisch. only τάς. — ἢ χρυσῷ] Instead of the *Rec.* ἤ (in D*** K L, etc.), Lachm. Buttm. Tisch. rightly adopted καί, following A D* F G, etc. Tisch. retained the *Rec.* χρυσῷ, following D K L, etc.; Lachm. and Buttm, on the other hand, read χρυσίῳ, following A F G, etc. As both forms are used in the N. T, we can hardly decide which is right here.—Ver. 10. The reading ὡς instead of ὅ, found in some cursives, Arm. and Cypr., is manifestly a correction to facilitate the interpretation. — Ver. 12. Instead of γυναικὶ δὲ διδάσκειν (Tisch 7), we should follow A D F G ℵ, al., Arm. Vulg. It. Cypr Jer. Ambrosiast., and read διδάσκειν δὲ γυναικί, which has been received into the text by Lachm. Buttm. Tisch. 8. Hofm., for the sake of his exposition, prefers the *Rec.* — Ver. 14. Instead of the *Rec* ἀπατηθεῖσα, Lachm. Buttm. Tisch read the compound ἐξαπατηθεῖσα, on the testimony of A D* F G 17 28, al., Mt. K., Bas. Chrys. If the compound had not such weighty authorities in its favour, we should be inclined to account for it out of Rom. vii. 11 and 2 Cor. xi. 3. — Ver. 15. On the reading γάρ for δέ, found in some codd., Matthaei rightly remarks: ita centies istae particulae . . . praesertim in principio pro arbitrio mutantur.

Ver. 1. After directing Timothy's attention generally to the στρατεία to which he had been appointed, Paul proceeds to mention in detail the things for which, in his office, he had to care. This connection of thought is marked by the particle of transition οὖν (Wiesinger), which therefore does not stand (as de Wette, following Schleiermacher, thinks) without any logical connection.[1] — πρῶτον πάντων] is not to be taken with ποιεῖσθαι, as Luther does: "to do before everything else," but with παρακαλῶ (Heydenreich, Matthies, de Wette, Wiesinger, van Oosterzee). — ποιεῖσθαι δεήσεις κ.τ.λ.] The apostle herewith begins to give "instructions regarding public prayer" (Wiesinger). The idea of prayer is here expressed by four words Δέησις and προσευχή are connected in other passages as

[1] Hofmann's reference of οὖν to i. 15 and the conclusion of ver. 16 is far-fetched: "If Christ came into the world to save sinners, and if the long-suffering of God towards the man whom He made His apostle from being a reviler, was to be a prophecy regarding the conversion of those who were afterwards made to believe on Him, it becomes Christians not, in sectarian fashion, to limit its command to its sphere at that time, but to extend it to all men."

PASTORAL EPISTLES. H

synonyms—in Eph. vi. 18, Phil. iv. 6 ; the difference between them is this, that δέησις can be used only of petitionary prayer, προσευχή of every kind of prayer. Not less general in meaning is ἔντευξις, from ἐντυγχάνειν τινί incidere in aliquem, adire aliquem, and in reference to God : *pray* (Wisd. viii 21, xvi. 28). The reference to another is not contained in the word itself, but in the preposition connected with it, as in Rom. xi. 2 : κατά τινος ; and Rom viii. 34 ; Heb. vii. 25 : ὑπέρ τινος. Accordingly, the substantive ἔντευξις, which occurs only here and in chap iv. 5, does not in itself possess the meaning of intercession for others, but denotes simply prayer as an address to God (Wiesinger) ; comp. Plutarch, *Vita Numae*, chap. 14 : μὴ ποιεῖσθαι τὰς πρὸς τὸ θεῖον ἐντεύξεις ἐν ἀσχολίᾳ καὶ παρέργως. The three words, accordingly, are thus distinguished : in the first, the element of insufficiency is prominent ; in the second, that of devotion ; and in the third, that of child-like confidence (prayer—the heart's converse with God). Calvin is right in his remark, that Paul joined these three words together here " ut precandi studium et assiduitatem magis commendet ac vehementius urgeat."[1] — εὐχαριστίας] " prayers of thanksgiving," the apostle adds, because in Christian prayer the giving of thanks should never be wanting ; comp. Phil. iv. 6 : ἐν παντὶ τῇ προσευχῇ καὶ τῇ δεήσει μετὰ εὐχαριστίας τὰ αἰτήματα ὑμῶν γνωρίζεσθαι πρὸς τὸν Θεόν — ὑπὲρ πάντων ἀνθρώπων] is not to be referred merely to εὐχαριστία, but also to

[1] In regard to the more precise definition of the word, there is much that is arbitrary in expositors older and more recent. Thus δέησις is understood to be prayer for averting the punishment of sin ; προσευχή, prayer for the bestowal of benefits, ἔντευξις, prayer for the punishment of the unrighteous (Theodoret δέησίς ἐστιν, ὑπὲρ ἀπαλλαγῆς τινῶν λυπηρῶν ἱκετία προσφερομένη· προσευχή ἐστιν αἴτησις ἀγαθῶν ἔντευξίς ἐστι κατηγορία τῶν ἀδικούντων, so, too, Theophylact and Oecumenius). Photius (*ad Amphil.* qu. 193) explains ἐντυχία in the same way ἐντυχία (ὅταν τις κατὰ τῶν ἀδικούντων ἐντυγχάνῃ τῷ Θεῷ, προσκαλούμενος αὐτὸν εἰς ἐκδίκησιν), but the other two words differently δέησις μὲν λέγεται, ὅταν τις Θεὸν ἀξιοῖ εἰς πρᾶγμα· προσευχὴ δὲ, ὅταν ὑμνῇ τὸν Θεόν Origen (περὶ εὐχῆς, § 44) finds a climax in the succession of the words, and distinguishes προσευχαί from δεήσεις in this way, that the former are prayers joined with a δοξολογία, made for greater things and μεγαλοφυέστερον, while ἐντεύξεις are the prayers of one who has παρρησίαν τινὰ πλείονα —Still more arbitrary is Kling's explanation, that δεήσεις are prayers in reference to the circumstances of all mankind ; προσευχαί, prayers for some benefit ; ἐντεύξεις, prayers for the aversion of evil Matthies is partly right, partly wrong when he says δέησις is the prayer made with a feeling of the need of God, so

the preceding words (Wiesinger). The prayer of the Christian community (for this and not private prayer is here spoken of) is—in petition and thanksgiving—to embrace all mankind. Ver. 2. Ὑπὲρ βασιλέων] βασιλεῖς are not merely the Roman emperors, the apostle using the plural because of the emperor's colleagues (Baur); the word is to be taken, in a more general sense, as denoting the *highest* authorities in the state. — καὶ πάντων τῶν ἐν ὑπεροχῇ ὄντων] not only denoting the governors in the provinces, but all who hold the office of magistrate anywhere. The expression is synonymous with ἐξουσίαι ὑπερέχουσαι in Rom. xiii. 1 ; comp. 2 Macc. iii. 11 : ἀνὴρ ἐν ὑπεροχῇ κείμενος. Josephus calls the magistrates simply αἱ ὑπεροχαί (*Antiq.* vi. 4. 3). In the old liturgies we find, in express accordance with this passage, the δέησις ὑπὲρ βασιλέων καὶ τῶν ἐν ὑπεροχῇ, ὑπὲρ τῆς εἰρήνης τοῦ σύμπαντος κόσμου. The purpose for which intercession is specially to be made for all men in authority is given in the words that follow : ἵνα ἤρεμον καὶ ἡσύχιον βίον διάγωμεν, which, as de Wette rightly remarks, denotes the objective and not the subjective purpose. Paul does not mean here to direct attention to the value which intercession has for our own inner life, and by means of this for outward peace, as Heydenreich (" Christians are to pray also for heathen rulers, that by this prayer they may keep alive within themselves the quiet submissive spirit of citizens "), Matthies (" animated with loving thoughts towards the representatives of the government, they

that the inner side of the need *and of uprightness* (?) is particularly prominent , προσευχή, prayer, in the act of devotional address to the Godhead, *therefore with reference to the outward exercise* (?) , ἐντεύξεις, intercession, made not so much for ourselves as on behalf of others (?) —There is no ground whatever for the opinion of Heydenreich, that the first two expressions are used of prayer (δέησις = petition , προσευχή = thanksgiving) for the whole Christian community, while the other two (ἔντευξις = petition ; εὐχαριστία = thanksgiving) are used of prayer for the whole of mankind Lastly, we may note the peculiar view of Augustine (*Ep.* 59), according to which the four expressions are to be understood of prayers used at the celebration of the Lord's Supper, δεήσεις being the *precationes* before consecration , προσευχαί, the *orationes* at the benediction, consecration, and breaking of bread , ἐντεύξεις, the *interpellationes* at the benediction of the congregation , and εὐχαριστία, the *gratiarum actio* at the close of the communion. Plitt so far agrees with this view of Augustine, that he thinks the apostle's various expressions denote the various liturgical prayers, as they were defined even in ancient times at the celebration of the Eucharist (?).

are to be blameless in their walk, and to strive after the undisturbed enjoyment of outward peace"), and others think, but the apostle is speaking of the still, quiet life as a blessing which the church obtains by prayer to God for the rulers.[1] The prayer is directed, as Wiesinger rightly remarks, not for the conversion of the heathen rulers, but for the divine blessing necessary to them in the discharge of their office (Rom. xiii. 14). — The adj. ἤρεμος occurs only here[2] in the N. T., and ἡσύχιος only here and in 1 Pet. iii. 4 (synonymous with πραΰς). The expression βίον διάγειν also occurs only here; in Tit. iii. 3, διάγειν is used without βίον. — No exact distinction can be established between ἤρεμος and ἡσύχιος. Olshausen (in Wiesinger) says, without reason, that the former means: "not disquieted from without;" the latter, "from within." Ἡρέμα denotes, in classic Greek at any rate, "still, tranquil existence," but ἡσύχιος (ἥσυχος) has the same meaning, and also denotes that there is no disturbance from without. The collocation of the two words serves to give more force to the thought; a ἤρ. κ. ἡσύχ. βίος is a life led without disturbance from without, with no excitement of fear, etc. — βίον διάγειν] "spend life, more than ἄγειν" (Wiesinger); the same expression is often found in classical writers. — ἐν πάσῃ εὐσεβείᾳ καὶ σεμνότητι] Not on this, but on ἤρ. καὶ ἡσύχ. is the chief emphasis of the sentence laid (Plitt); the words only add a more precise definition. Εὐσέβεια, a word foreign to the other Pauline Epistles, and (with εὐσεβής, εὐσεβῶς, εὐσεβέω) occurring only in the Pastoral Epistles, in Acts, and in 2 Pet., denotes the godliness of the heart; σεμνότης, also peculiar to the Pastoral Epistles (σεμνός, only here and in Phil. iv. 8), denotes the becoming conduct of the Christian in all the relations of life. Hofmann is arbitrary in separating this addition from what immediately precedes, and joining it with

---

[1] Hofmann maintains, without grounds, that ἵνα κ.τ.λ. does not give the purpose of the prayer for all men and for rulers, but "the purpose for which rulers exist" (!).

[2] Nor is the positive ἤριμος used in the Greek classics As yet it has been found only in the *Inscript. Olbiopol.* n. 2059, v. 24, by Lobeck, see Winer, p. 68 [E T. p. 82]; Buttmann, p. 24 —The substantives ἡσυχία and ἠρεμία are frequently found together in the classics; *e.g.* Demosth. *de Contributione*, § 8; Bekk. s. Dorville, *On Chariton.* p. 411.

ποιεῖσθαι δεήσεις κ.τ.λ., as " denoting the manner in which the prayer commended is to be made."

Ver. 3. This verse points back to what was said in ver. 1; not, however, in such a way as to make ver. 2 a parenthesis (so in a former edition of this commentary), but rather so as to include the points mentioned in it. — τοῦτο] does not refer to the thoughts immediately preceding, but to the ποιεῖσθαι δεήσεις . . . ὑπὲρ πάντων ἀνθρώπων κ.τ.λ — The highest motive of the Christian to such prayer is the good pleasure of God. — καλὸν καὶ ἀπόδεκτον] ἀπόδεκτος (like ἀποδοχή) occurs only in this First Epistle to Timothy, it is synonymous with εὐάρεστος in Col. iii. 20 (τοῦτο γὰρ εὐάρεστόν ἐστιν ἐν κυρίῳ). — ἐνώπιον τοῦ σωτῆρος ἡμῶν Θεοῦ] is referred only to ἀπόδεκτον by several expositors, who either take καλόν absolutely (de Wette : " good in itself;" so also van Oosterzee, Matthies : " καλ. denotes the endeavour recommended in its inner worth and contents "), or, as Leo, supply with it ἐνώπιον τῶν ἀνθρώπων: " which is praiseworthy, sc. before men." The latter is clearly quite arbitrary; but even for the former there is not sufficient ground, all the more when we compare 2 Cor. viii. 21: προνοοῦμεν γὰρ καλὰ οὐ μόνον ἐνώπιον κυρίου, ἀλλὰ καὶ ἐνώπιον ἀνθρώπων[1] On σωτήρ, see i. 1. — Paul uses this name for God here because he has already in mind the thought that follows (Wiesinger).

Ver. 4. Ground of the previous thought. The general intercession is καλ. κ ἀπόδ. before God, because He, etc. It is not unusual to give in a relative clause the grounds of a previous statement. Ὅς πάντας ἀνθρώπους θέλει σωθῆναι (comp. Tit. ii. 11)] The chief accent is laid on πάντας (corresponding with ὑπὲρ πάντων, ver. 1), which is therefore placed first. God's purpose of salvation extends to all, and therefore the prayer of Christians must include all. Wiesinger, however, is right in remarking that " the apostle in ὅς κ.τ.λ. does not mean specially to give a reason for prayer for the conversion of all men, but for prayer generally as a duty of universal love to men." Chrysostom puts it differently: μιμοῦ τὸν

[1] Heydenreich's opinion is utterly erroneous, that Paul calls prayer for all καλόν, because it is not only right and good, but "brings a benefit to the Christians, by recommending them to their rulers."

Θεόν· εἰ πάντας ἀνθρώπους θέλει σωθῆναι, θέλε καὶ σύ· εἰ δὲ θέλεις, εὔχου· τῶν γὰρ τοιούτων (τῶν θελόντων) ἐστὶ τὸ εὔχεσθαι. — The true connection of thought is obscured if we supply the intermediate thought, that prayer for all, and specially for kings, serves to maintain the peace without which the spread of Christianity would be hindered.[1] — καὶ εἰς ἐπίγνωσιν ἀληθείας ἐλθεῖν] The same connection of words is found elsewhere only in 2 Tim. iii. 7; on the meaning of ἐπίγνωσις, see my *Commentary on Colossians*, pp. 74 f., Remark. — The connection of the two expressions σωθῆναι and εἰς ἐπίγν. ἀλ. ἐλθεῖν may be regarded differently. Hofmann takes them to be in substance identical; Heydenreich takes the latter as an explanation of the former, " showing how and by what means God wishes to effect the salvation of all;" he therefore regards the ἐπίγνωσις τ ἀλ. as the *means* of the σωτηρία. So, too, Winer (p 514 [E. T. p 692]): " at first the general purpose is mentioned (καί, and in pursuance of this), then the immediate purpose (as a means of attaining the other)" It is explained in the same way by Wiesinger, van Oosterzee, and others But it seems more natural to regard the ἐπίγνωσις τῆς ἀληθείας as the goal to which the rescue (σωθῆναι) leads (so, too, Plitt).[2]

Ver. 5. Εἷς γὰρ Θεός] The particle γάρ connects this verse with the thought immediately preceding (Wiesinger), and not, as Leo and Mack think, with the exhortation to pray for all[3] The apostle wishes by it to confirm the idea of the universality of the divine purpose of salvation as true and necessary : he does this first by pointing to the unity of God. There is a

---

[1] Mosheim (*Instit. Hist Eccles* maj I 36) Id sanctus homo tradit: nisi pax in orbe terrarum vigeat, fieri nullo modo posse, ut voluntati divinae, quae omnium hominum salutem cupit, satisfiat, bellis nimirum flagrantibus haud licuisset legatis Jesu Christi, secure ad omnes populos proficisci

[2] In this verse the idea of the universality of God's purpose of salvation is clearly and distinctly expressed. Calvin, in order to save his theory of predestination, has to take refuge in an exposition more than ingenious de hominum generibus, non singulis personis, sermo est, nihil enim aliud intendit, quam principes et extraneos, populos in hoc numero includere.

[3] Van Oosterzee confuses the two references. "God's universal purpose of salvation is here established in such a way that at the same time there is *to a certain extent* (!) an indication of a third motive for performing Christian intercessions."

quite similar connection of ideas in Rom. iii. 30 (emphasis is laid on God's unity in another connection in 1 Cor. viii. 6, and, in a third connection, in Eph. iv. 6). From the unity of God, it necessarily follows that there is only one purpose regarding all; for if there were various purposes for various individuals, the Godhead would be divided in its nature. As there is one God, however, so also there is one Mediator — εἷς καὶ μεσίτης Θεοῦ καὶ ἀνθρώπων] The word μεσίτης[1] occurs elsewhere in the Pauline Epistles only in Gal. iii. 19, 20, where the name is given to Moses, because through him God revealed the law to the people. Elsewhere in the N. T. the word is found only in Heb. viii. 6, ix. 15, xii 24, and in connection with διαθήκης, from which, however, it cannot (with Schleiermacher and de Wette) be concluded that the idea *mediator* refers necessarily to the *corresponding* idea *covenant*. Christ is here named the μεσίτης Θεοῦ καὶ ἀνθρώπων, because He is inter Deum et homines constitutus (Tertullian). He is the Mediator for both, in so far as only through Him does God accomplish His purpose of salvation (His θέλειν) regarding men, and in so far as only through Him can men reach the goal appointed them by God (σωθῆναι καὶ εἰς ἐπίγν. ἀλ. ἐλθεῖν). Hofmann says: "He is the means of bringing about the relation in which God wishes to stand towards men, and in which men ought to stand towards God." As with the unity of God, so also is the unity of the Mediator a surety for the truth of the thought expressed in ver. 4, that God's θέλειν refers to all men. — To define it more precisely, Paul adds. ἄνθρωπος Χριστὸς Ἰησοῦς This addition may not, as Otto and others assume, have been occasioned by opposition to the docetism of the heretics. In other epistles of the N. T. special emphasis is laid on Christ's humanity, with no such opposition to suggest it; thus Rom. v. 15; 1 Cor. xv. 21; Phil. ii. 7; Heb. ii. 16, 17. In this passage the reason for it is contained first in the designation of Christ as the μεσίτης (Theodoret: ἄνθρωπον δὲ τὸν Χριστὸν ὠνόμασεν, ἐπειδὴ μεσίτην ἐκάλεσεν· ἐνανθρωπήσας γὰρ ἐμεσίτευσεν); and

---

[1] Regarding the use of the word in classical Greek, comp. Cremer, s v. — There is no necessity for Cremer's opinion, that μεσίτης in the passages of Hebrews does not so much mean "mediator" as "surety."

further, in the manner in which Christ carried out His work of mediation, *i.e.*, as the next verse informs us, by giving Himself up to death.[1]

Ver 6. Ὁ δοὺς ἑαυτὸν ἀντίλυτρον ὑπὲρ πάντων] The word ἀντίλυτρον, which occurs only here, is synonymous with ἀντάλλαγμα in Matt. xvi. 26; it is distinguished from the simple λύτρον, as Matthies rightly remarks, only in this, that the preposition makes the idea of exchange still more emphatic According to the usage of the N. T., there can be no doubt that the apostle here alludes to Christ's reconciling death; comp., besides Tit. ii. 14, Matt. xx. 28, etc, especially 1 Pet i 18, 19, where the τίμιον αἷμα is mentioned as the means by which we are redeemed. The expression δοὺς ἑαυτόν has here—where ἀντίλυτρον is added by way of apposition to ἑαυτόν (as in Matt xx. 28, λύτρον is in apposition to τὴν ψυχὴν αὐτοῦ)—the emphatic meaning of self-surrender to death, as in Tit. ii. 14, Gal. i. 4 (comp. also in John vi 51, ἦν [τὴν σάρκα μου] δώσω, which, indeed, is uncertain critically), where δοὺς ἑαυτόν has the same meaning as παραδοὺς ἑαυτόν in Gal. ii. 20; Eph. v. 25 (comp, too, Rom. viii. 32) He gave Himself as a ransom by giving Himself up to death The thought on which it is based is this: men were held ἐν τῇ ἐξουσίᾳ τοῦ σκότους (Col. i. 13); from this they could not free themselves (τί δώσει ἄνθρωπος ἀντάλλαγμα τῆς ψυχῆς αὐτοῦ, Matt. xvi. 26); Christ therefore gave the ἀντίλυτρον necessary to free them; this ransom is *Himself* (δοὺς ἑαυτόν), *i.e.* His life · τὴν ψυχὴν αὐτοῦ, Matt. xx 28, so that by this, σωτηρία is purchased for them. This, however, was done for the benefit not of some, but of *all*. Hence Paul adds expressly ὑπέρ (equivalent to: in commodum[2]) πάντων, which is emphatic,

---

[1] The ἀνθρώπων suggested the ἄνθρωπος all the more naturally, that in the apostle's consciousness the σωτηρία of *men* could be wrought only by a man Only a *man* could reconcile *men* with God; only, indeed, the man of whom it was said ὃς ἐφανερώθη ἐν σαρκί (chap iii 16) Hofmann supposes that Christ Jesus is here called ἄνθρωπος, "in order to say that, as He became man to be mediator, He is therefore the mediator and saviour not of this or of that man, but of all men without distinction." This thought, however, is more the ground of the εἷς, for even the mediator "of this or that man" might also be a *man*.

[2] Van Oosterzee asserts, without reason, that ὑπέρ here is to be taken in the sense of substitution.

and with which he returns to the beginning of ver. 4. In this, as at i. 15, the apostle revealed the substance of the ὑγιαίνουσα διδασκαλία, only that here he defines his former expression more precisely. — In order, however, that this act of love on the Lord's part may bring forth its fruit, it must be proclaimed to the world; this is indicated in the words that follow. — τὸ μαρτύριον καιροῖς ἰδίοις] τὸ μαρτύριον is not to be taken as in apposition to ἀντίλυτρον, and explained of the death of Christ (Chrysostom: μαρτύριον τὸ πάθος); it is to be regarded as in apposition to the thought contained in the previous words of this verse (not "to the *whole* of what was previously said," Hofmann). This does not mean, however, that τὸ μαρτύριον denotes Christ's gift of Himself as a ransom (or "Christ's sacrifice"), to be "the witness of salvation set forth at the appointed time, the historical fact that the divine purpose of salvation is realized" (Matthies),[1] for μαρτύριον is not the deed itself, but the attestation, the proclamation of the deed; comp. 1 Cor i. 6, ii. 1. Nor does it mean that by μαρτύριον we are to understand the testimonium, quod Deus per Christi vitam, doctrinam et mortem protulit, vera esse ea omnia et rata, quae V. T. prophetae fore divinaverant (Heinrichs), for there is nothing to indicate an allusion to O. T. prophecy. The act of Christ already mentioned is called τὸ μαρτύριον, in so far as this was its meaning and purpose. Bengel: τὸ μαρτύριον acc. absol. ut ἔνδειγμα, 2 Thess. i. 5, innuitur testimonium redemtionis universalis[2] The reason why the preaching of the gospel is called μαρτύριον, is that its subject is an historical fact, the importance of which becomes known only by individual experience. — καιροῖς ἰδίοις] "is to be connected with τὸ μαρτύριον, just as if it were connected with τὸ μαρτυρούμενον" (Hofmann); the same expression is

---

[1] Leo's explanation is substantially the same as this Quae Christus, inquit apostolus, ad homines servandos fecit, ea sunt ipsius Dei testimonium. Quid vero testatus est Deus eo, quod Jesum Christum mori passus est? Quid aliud, quam amorem suum in genus humanum plane incomparabilem?

[2] Van Oosterzee believes that μαρτύριον here must be taken as in apposition to ἀντίλυτρον, the apostle calling the Lord's surrender of Himself the great μαρτύριον, with special reference to *the* truth mentioned in ver. 4. But against this it is to be remarked, that this explanation does not give a right definition of the relation of apposition, nor of the meaning and purpose of the μαρτύριον.

found in vi. 15; Tit. i. 3; also Gal vi. 9 (Acts xvii 26: καιροὶ προτεταγμένοι); Chrysostom: τοῖς προσήκουσι καιροῖς.

Ver. 7. This verse defines more precisely the previous μαρτύριον; it was for proclaiming the μαρτύριον that the apostle received the office entrusted to him. The chief emphasis rests on the universality; the subject of the μαρτύριον is the fact that Christ gave Himself a ransom for all. — εἰς ὃ ἐτέθην ἐγὼ κῆρυξ καὶ ἀπόστολος] Comp. on this, Eph. iii. 1–12; Col i. 25–28; 2 Tim. i 9–11. — εἰς ὅ for which (μαρτύριον), viz. "for proclaiming which." ἐτέθην is to be taken in close connection with κῆρυξ κ.τ.λ — κῆρυξ, it is true, only occurs here and in 2 Tim. i. 11 as a name for the preacher of the gospel (in 2 Pet. ii. 5, Noah is called a κῆρυξ δικαιοσύνης); but κηρύσσειν is used very frequently of the preaching of the gospel. In 1 Cor. i. 21, κήρυγμα is identical with εὐαγγέλιον. In order to direct attention to his peculiar apostolic authority, Paul adds to the general idea of κῆρυξ, the more specific expression ἀπόστολος. By the addition of ἀλήθειαν λέγω, οὐ ψεύδομαι, the truth of the εἰς ὅ is confirmed;[1] he explains himself sufficiently on account of the heretics who wished that Paul should not be considered an apostle by the appointment of God. — The further definition: διδάσκαλος ἐθνῶν, is to be taken in apposition to κῆρυξ κ. ἀπόστολος. It was added to make clearer the reference to the heathen already indicated in εἰς ὅ, not, as Hofmann thinks, to form an apposition to the subject of ἀλήθειαν λέγω; had that been so, we should have had an emphatic ἐγώ. The connected words ἐν πίστει καὶ ἀληθείᾳ do not form the object of διδ. (Heydenreich takes it as "equivalent to ἐν τῇ πίστει τῇ ἀληθινῇ, a teacher of the Gentiles who is to instruct them

[1] Wiesinger less suitably refers the addition to the διὸ ἐθνῶν, which in that case should have been preceded by a καί. Otto (p 117) unjustifiably uses this asseveration of the apostle to confirm his assertion that the epistle was written during the apostle's stay at Ephesus, insisting that Paul, after he was put in prison in Jerusalem, was acknowledged an apostle in all Christian churches, and from that time, therefore, had no occasion for this asseveration. Apart from other points, Otto errs in referring the words ἀλήθειαν κ τ λ only to the expression ἀπόστολος, whereas they apply to the entire thought in εἰς ὃ κ.τ.λ. Paul does not make asseveration that he was appointed an apostle, but that he was appointed an apostle of the μαρτύριον, the subject of which he had already mentioned. Comp. on this the passages quoted above.

in the true religion"); they are loosely added, according to a common usage of the N. T., and denote here the sphere in which he was appointed to discharge his office as teacher of the Gentiles. The peculiar point of view must not be lost by arbitrarily changing the words into ἐν τῇ πίστει τ. ἀληθινῇ, or, as Leo does, into πιστὸς καὶ ἀληθινός. It is wrong also to render πίστις here by "faithfulness," and ἀλήθ by "verity" (Hofmann: ἐν πίστει, equivalent to "faithfully," and ἐν ἀληθείᾳ to "in verity"). Πίστις is faith, the subjective relation, and ἀλήθεια is truth, the objective benefit, appropriated in faith (so also Plitt and van Oosterzee).[1]

Ver. 8. After giving, in the digression of vv. 3–7, the grounds of his exhortation to prayer for all, Paul returns to the exhortation itself in such a way as to define it more precisely in regard to those who are to offer the prayer. — βούλομαι οὖν προσεύχεσθαι τοὺς ἄνδρας ἐν παντὶ τόπῳ] "Hoc verbo (βούλομαι) exprimitur auctoritas apostolica," Bengel; comp. v. 14; Tit. iii. 18: "*I ordain*." — οὖν] Bengel's explanation: "particula *ergo* reassumit versum 1," is not quite accurate; the particle connects with ver. 1 in order to carry on the thought there expressed. — προσεύχεσθαι] Bengel: "sermo de precibus publicis, ubi sermonem orantis subsequitur multitudinis cor." Matthies wrongly disputes the opinion that προσεύχεσθαι here is used of "prayer in the congregations." The whole context shows beyond doubt that the apostle is here speaking of congregations. — τοὺς ἄνδρας] opposed to τὰς γυναῖκας, ver. 9. Paul assigns to each part its proper share in the assemblies for worship; "he has something different to say to the men and to the women" (Wiesinger). — ἐν παντὶ τόπῳ] does not stand here in opposition to the Jewish limitation to the temple (Chrysostom and others): "not once found" (de Wette), nor to the synagogue

---

[1] Bengel seems to take the words in a sense corresponding to the formula of asseveration, ἀληθ. λέγω κ.τ λ He says in regard to this formula · "pertinet haec affirmatio ad comma praecedens; nam subsequenti additur parallela ἐν π. καὶ ἀληθ ," a view for which there is no justification — Matthies expresses himself somewhat obscurely, for while he in the first place mentions faith and truth not only as the elements, but also as the aims of the teaching, he says at the end of the discussion: "The apostle is teacher of the Gentiles in such a way that he knows himself to be impregnably established thereby in faith and truth."

(Wolf), nor in reference to the various places of Christian worship in Ephesus (van Oosterzee), nor to the neighbouring congregations belonging to Timothy's diocese (Heydenreich); it is to be taken generally, not in the sense of *every* place, "where the religious *mood*, custom, or duty cherishes it" (Matthies), but to all places where Christian congregations assemble (Wiesinger). — As to the construction, ἐν παντὶ τόπῳ does not belong to προσεύχεσθαι alone, but "to the whole clause" (Wiesinger, Matthies, van Oosterzee, Hofmann). The apostle means to lay stress not on this, that men are to pray, but on *how* they are to pray; the chief emphasis, therefore, rests on ἐπαίροντας κ.τ.λ. — ἐπαίροντας ὁσίους χεῖρας] The Jews lifted up their hands not only in swearing an oath, Gen. xiv. 22 (Rev. x. 5), and in blessing, Lev. ix. 22 (Luke xxiv. 50), but also in prayer, Ps. xxviii. 2, xliv. 21, lxiii. 5, etc This passage is a proof that the same custom was observed in the Christian church. It is true that in the N T it is nowhere else mentioned, but in Clement's First Epistle to the Corinthians we have at chap. xxix. an evident allusion to this passage· προσέλθωμεν αὐτῷ ἐν ὁσιότητι ψυχῆς, ἁγνὰς καὶ ἀμιάντους χεῖρας αἴροντες πρὸς αὐτόν. — Regarding the form ὁσίους for ὁσίας, see Winer, p. 67 [E. T. p 81].[1] — The hands are holy which have not been given over to the deeds of wicked lust; the opposite is given by μιαραί, βέβηλοι χεῖρες, 2 Macc. v. 16, comp. on the expression, Job xvii. 9, Ps xxiv. 4, and in the N. T Jas. iv. 8 especially: καθαρίσατε χεῖρας καὶ ἁγνίσατε καρδίας. Hofmann is ingenious in defining ὁσίους χεῖρες more precisely by what follows: "The hands of the one praying are ὅσιοι only when he is inwardly saturated with the consecration without which his praying does not deserve the name of prayer." — χωρὶς ὀργῆς καὶ διαλογισμοῦ] Bengel is more pregnant than exact when he says: "ira, quae contraria amori et mater dubitationis; dubitatio, quae adversatur fidei. Fide et amore constat christianismus, gratiam et veritatem amplectens. Gratia fidem alit; veritas amorem Eph. iv. 5;" for διαλογισμός is not to be rendered by "doubt" (so Bengel, with Chrysostom, Theophy-

---

[1] It would be very forced to connect ὁσίους with ἐπαίροντας as a masculine, which Winer considers at least possible.

lact, Theodoret, Luther, and many others), which never is its signification. The rendering "contention" is also inaccurate; διαλογισμός is equivalent to consideration, deliberation, *cogitatio*. In the N. T. the singular occurs only here and in Luke ix. 46, 47 ; it is usually in the plural. The word is in itself a *vox media*, but it is mostly used where evil or perverted thoughts are spoken of; comp. Matt. xv. 19; Mark vii. 21 ; Luke v. 22, vi. 8, xxiv. 38. That it is to be taken here *malo sensu*, is shown by the close connection with ὀργή, which indicates that it is applied to deliberation towards one's neighbour, comp. Meyer on Phil. ii. 14, and especially Reiche, *Comment. Crit. in N. T.*, on this passage. In the Pastoral Epistles, special stress is laid on peaceableness as a Christian virtue, iii. 3 ; Tit iii. 2 ; 2 Tim. ii. 24.

Vv. 9, 10. Ὡσαύτως γυναῖκας κ.τ.λ.] After speaking of the men, Paul turns to the women, and gives some precepts regarding their behaviour in church assemblies.—As to the construction, it is obvious that the verse depends on βούλομαι in ver. 8. Several expositors, however, connect it not only with βούλομαι, but also with βούλομαι προσεύχεσθαι · " I will that the men pray . . . so also the women ;" they then take what follows : ἐν καταστολῇ κοσμίῳ κ.τ.λ, as corresponding to ἐπαίροντας κ.τ.λ., ver. 8, and as defining more precisely the manner in which the women are to pray. The infinitive κοσμεῖν, however, is against this construction. De Wette, indeed, thinks that it is added to the infinitive προσεύχεσθαι by asyndeton ; but although the connection of *several* infinitives with one another asyndetically frequently occurs (v. 14, vi. 18 ; Tit. iii. 1, 2), there is no example of *two* infinitives being thus connected.[1] Hofmann is forced to assume that κοσμεῖν " is a consequence dependent on μετὰ αἰδοῦς καὶ σωφροσύνης;" but how can self-adorning be considered a consequence of " modesty and good sense "? Though sometimes the infinitive does stand connected in such loose fashion with what precedes,

---

[1] Wiesinger unites the κοσμεῖν with the προσεύχεσθαι, and defends it with the remark, that if instead of the asyndeton of the infinitive κοσμεῖν we had the participle, there could have been no doubt regarding it. Then he asks : "Have we not elsewhere examples enough of a similar change of construction?" To this we must answer, "No," unless "similar" be taken in too wide a sense.

it would be difficult to find an instance of such a connection as Hofmann here assumes.—Against that construction there is also this point: since in ver. 8 προσεύχεσθαι means prayer made by the men aloud in the church, here in ver. 9 it would have to be taken in a weakened sense; and it is so rendered by de Wette and Hofmann: "taking part in prayer."— According to this, the verse cannot be dependent on βούλομαι προσεύχεσθαι, but on βούλομαι alone, so that ἐν καταστολῇ κ.τ λ. merely states how the women are to adorn themselves (so, too, Plitt) De Wette, indeed, thinks that objection may be made to this construction because the affirmative ἐν κατ. κ.τ.λ. is followed not only by a negative μὴ ἐν πλ. κ.τ.λ., but also by a second affirmative in ver. 10. This accumulation of clauses, however, cannot be urged, since we have a similar accumulation in vv. 11, 12. Nor is the particle ὡσαύτως an argument against us, since it stands in other places where the same predicates are not used (comp iii. 8; Tit. ii. 3). Ὡσαύτως may be used wherever the members to be connected contain something not exactly alike, but of a kindred nature, as is the case here with ὁσίους ... διαλογισμοῦ and ἐν καταστολῇ ... σωφροσύνης[1] Nothing is to take place in the church, neither among the men nor among the women, which can hurt its spiritual dignity.— ἐν καταστολῇ κοσμίῳ] καταστολή may, according to Greek usage, denote "sedateness of nature."[2] Hence it is that some expositors (de Wette among others) take it here as equivalent to *habitus*, κατάστημα (Tit. ii. 3); but it never occurs in that sense. The words that follow: μὴ ἐν πλέγμασιν ... ἱματισμῷ πολυτελεῖ, show that the word is to be understood of clothing. True, it does not originally mean this, but the letting down, *e.g.*, of the περιβολή (Plutarch, *Pericl.* 5). This meaning, however, might easily pass into

---

[1] It is necessary therefore to do, as van Oosterzee does, supply the participle προσευχομένας with γυναῖκας because of the ὡσαύτως

[2] In this sense the word is found, *e.g* in Arrian (*Epict.* ii. 10), joined with αἰδώς and ἡμερότης —In the passage of Josephus, *B J* ii 8. 4 · καταστολῆ δὲ καὶ σχῆμα σώματος ὅμοιον τοῖς μετὰ φόβου παιδαγωγουμένοις παισίν, which is commonly quoted as a proof of the meaning "clothing," the meaning is doubtful. Salmasius explains it · sedatus animus et remissus, elato et superbo tumentique oppositus, in contrast with ὀργῆς, ver. 8; but in that case the added adjective κόσμιος is superfluous.

that of "the garment hanging down," and then further, into that of "clothing in general." This is the explanation given here by most expositors (also by Plitt and Hofmann; van Oosterzee translates it: "bearing," but explains it afterwards: "καταστολή = ἔνδυμα"). Some take it quite generally; others, again, understand it of the garment enveloping the whole body (Chrysostom: ἡ ἀμπεχόνη πάντοθεν περιστέλλουσα καλῶς, μὴ περιέργως) This last explanation has no sufficient support in the etymology, nor in the ordinary usage. — κόσμιος] does not mean "delicately" (Luther), but "*modestly, honourably*" (comp. iii 2); beyond these passages, it is not found in the N. T.— μετὰ αἰδοῦς καὶ σωφροσύνης] The outward modesty which makes itself known in the dress, is to be accompanied by inward purity and chastity, since the former would otherwise be of no account. While αἰδώς denotes the inward shrinking from everything immodest, σωφροσύνη expresses the control of the desires; τὸ κρατεῖν ἡδονῶν καὶ ἐπιθυμιῶν (Luther): "with modesty and propriety."[1]—It is to be noted that σωφροσύνη (apart from Acts xxvi. 25: σωφροσύνης ῥήματα ἀποφθέγγομαι, in opposition to μαίνομαι) occurs only here and in ver. 15, and that all words kindred to it (except σωφρονεῖν in Rom. xii. 3, opposed to ὑπερφρονεῖν in 2 Cor. v. 13, denoting the opposite of the ecstatic state, also in Mark v. 15; Luke viii. 35; 1 Pet. iv. 7), such as σωφρονίζειν, σωφρονισμός, σώφρων, σωφρόνως, are found only in the Pastoral Epistles — μὴ ἐν πλέγμασιν κ.τ.λ.] Instead of πλέγματα, we have ἐμπλοκή [τριχῶν] (Isa. iii. 24: מקשה) in 1 Pet. iii. 3, which is particularly to be compared with this passage; it denotes "the artificial plaits of hair" (Clemens Alex. *Paedag.* iii. 11: περίπλοκαι ἑταιρικαὶ τῶν τριχῶν). — καὶ χρυσίῳ] The καί divides the ornament into

---

[1] The two words are also placed together elsewhere as feminine virtues. See Raphelius, who quotes, among others, the passage from Epictetus (*Enchir* chap. 62) mulieres in ornatu spem collocant omnem; quare operae pretium est, dare operam, ut sentiant, sibi non ob aliud honorem haberi, ἢ τῷ κοσμίαι φαίνεσθαι, καὶ αἰδήμονες ἐν σωφροσύνῃ Although in the *Cyropaedia* (Book viii) the two words are thus distinguished. διήρει (sc Cyrus) δὲ αἰδὼ καὶ σωφροσύνην τῇδε, ὡς τοὺς μὲν αἰδουμένους, τὰ ἐν τῷ φανερῷ αἰσχρὰ φεύγοντας, τοὺς δὲ σώφρονας, καὶ τὰ ἐν τῷ ἀφανεῖ, the distinction cannot be regarded as always valid.—Aristotle (*Rhet.* 1 9) explains σωφροσύνη in the following fashion . σωφροσύνη ἀρετή, δι' ἣν πρὸς τὰς ἡδονὰς τοῦ σώματος οὕτως ἔχουσιν, ὡς ὁ νόμος κελεύει.

two parts, πλέγματα belonging to the body itself, and what follows being the things put on the body. In 1 Pet iii. 3, we have περίθεσις χρυσίων (comp. Rev. xvii. 4) —It is wrong to connect χρυσίῳ with the previous πλέγμ. as a hendiadys for πλέγμα χρύσιον (Heinrichs). — ἢ μαργαρίταις] The gems are not named in Peter, and instead of ἱματισμὸς πολυτελής we have there ἔνδυσις ἱματίων; the adjective πολυτελής (Matt.: μαλακὰ ἱμάτια) is contrasted with κόσμιος — ἀλλ' ὃ πρέπει κ τ.λ] Most expositors (among them Wegscheider, Flatt, Heydenreich, Leo, de Wette, Wiesinger, van Oosterzee, also Winer, p 149, note 1 [E T. p. 171]) refer δι' ἔργων ἀγαθῶν to κοσμεῖν, and take ἃ πρέπει ... θεοσέβειαν as a parenthesis.[1] But there are three points against this, viz, that the ornament of the women is already named in ἐν καταστολῇ κ.τ.λ., that the preposition διά does not suit with κοσμεῖν (which is construed previously with ἐν), and that " good works " would be unsuitably described as ornament here, where he is speaking of the conduct of the women in the assemblies of the church, unless we arbitrarily limit the general idea to offerings for the poor, as is done by Heydenreich and van Oosterzee. Theodoret rightly joins δι' ἐργ. ἀγ. with the immediately preceding ἐπαγγελλ. θεοσεβ. (" εὐσέβειαν ἐπαγγέλλεσθε, καὶ τὴν δι' ἔργων ἀρετήν "); so, too, Oecumenius, Luther, Calvin, etc.; and among more recent names, Mack, Matthies, and Plitt. The comma before διά, which is found in the editions, must therefore be deleted. Hofmann connects the words with what follows, taking διά in the sense of accompanying; but διά never has such a simple copulative meaning.[2] — The relative ὅ stands here either for ἐν τούτῳ ὅ, for which Matthies appeals, but wrongly, to Rom. vi. 21 and x. 14; or more probably for καθ' ὅ. So far as the meaning goes, the various reading ὡς (καθώς, Eph. v. 3) is correct. Hofmann wishes to refer ὅ to κοσμεῖν ἑαυτάς in such a way that " the latter is mentioned as a thing

---

[1] Van Oosterzee explains it as "a causal periphrasis to show why precisely *this* ornament is extolled by the apostle."

[2] Hofmann thus paraphrases the thought "They are to do what is good, and to learn in still seclusion. The former is that which is to be accompanied by the latter." He appeals to 2 Cor. ii. 4. He does not prove, however, that that passage justifies such a paraphrase The relation between writing and tears is obviously quite different from that between learning in stillness and good works.

... seemly for women." The intervening ἀλλά, however, manifestly makes this construction impossible. — ἐπαγγελλομέναις θεοσέβειαν] ἐπαγγέλλεσθαι usually means in the N. T. "promise." Matthies accordingly renders the word here by "give information, show;" so, too, Luther: "who therein manifest blessedness." But it is more correct here to take the word in the sense in which *profiteri artem* is used, so that θεοσέβεια is regarded as an art or a handicraft. De Wette rightly says. "who make profession of blessedness;" so, too, vi. 21; comp. Xenophon, *Memor.* i 2. 7 : ἀρετὴν ἐπαγγελλόμενος (Ignatius, *ad Ephes.* chap. 14 : οὐδεὶς πίστιν ἐπαγγελλόμενος ἁμαρτάνει). — θεοσέβεια] only here in the N. T. (LXX. Gen. xx. 11 ; more frequently in the Apocrypha ; θεοσεβής, John ix. 31 ; LXX. Ex. xviii. 21), is equivalent to εὐσέβεια. — δι᾽ ἔργων ἀγαθῶν] must not be limited to works of benevolence alone. The addition of these words is fully explained by a comparison with 2 Tim iii 5. Calvin gives the connection with the preceding words rightly : si operibus testanda est pietas, in vestitu etiam casto apparere haec professio debet.

Vv. 11, 12. Further injunctions for women. — γυνὴ ἐν ἡσυχίᾳ μανθανέτω] ἐν ἡσυχίᾳ, "without speaking herself;" μανθάνειν denotes here, as in 1 Cor. xiv. 31, attention to the word in order to learn from it what is necessary for advancing and building up the Christian life. — ἐν πάσῃ ὑποταγῇ] "*in complete subordination,*" i.e. without contradiction. — The thought here expressed is to be filled up by what Paul says in 1 Cor. xiv. 35 (which passage should be particularly compared with this[1]) : εἰ δέ τι μαθεῖν θέλουσιν, ἐν οἴκῳ τοὺς ἰδίους ἄνδρας ἐπερωτάτωσιν. — " Spiritual receptivity and activity in domestic life were recognised as the appropriate destiny of women, and therefore the female sex was excluded from the public discussion of religious subjects " (Neander, *Geschichte der Pflanzung der Kirche durch die Aposteln*, Part I. p. 125). Though in Christ there is no distinction, yet

[1] Otto quotes the agreement of these passages with one another as a proof that the letters are contemporaneous. It is, however, to be observed that Paul himself, in the words : ὡς ἐν πάσαις ταῖς ἐκκλησίαις τῶν ἁγίων (1 Cor. xi. 33), describes the maxim as one which he was seeking to establish in all the churches. Hence there is nothing strange in his urging it on Timothy's attention at a later period, just as he had urged it before on the Corinthians.

Christianity does not put an end to the natural distinctions ordained by God ; it recognises them in order to inform them with its higher life. — διδάσκειν δὲ γυναικὶ οὐκ ἐπιτρέπω] Διδ. stands first in emphatic opposition to μανθάνειν, in the parallel passage (1 Cor. xiv.) διδ. stands instead of the more general word λαλεῖν. — οὐδὲ αὐθεντεῖν ἀνδρός] Leo: "αὐθεντεῖν et αὐθέντης apud seriores tantum scriptores ita occurrit, ut domini notionem involvat, melioribus scriptoribus est αὐθέντης idem quod αὐτόχειρ" (see Valckenaer, Diatr. in Eurip. rell. chap. xviii. pp. 188 ff ; Lobeck, ad Phryn. p. 120). Luther has rightly: "that she be master of her husband;" whereas in the translation. "to assume to herself respect or mastery" (Heydenreich, de Wette, van Oosterzee), the notion of assumption is imported. Hofmann, too, is wrong when he says that αὐθεντεῖν in conjunction with the genitive of the person should mean : " to act independently of this person, i.e. as one's own master"(!).—Many expositors (Matthies, and earlier, Estius, Calovius, and others) assume in this word a reference to domestic relations ; whereas Heydenreich, de Wette, Wiesinger, and others, limit even this command to behaviour in the assemblies for divine worship.[1] This last is correct, as is shown by ἀλλ᾽ εἶναι ἐν ἡσυχίᾳ, corresponding to ἐν ἡσυχίᾳ in ver. 11. Yet οὐδὲ αὐθεντεῖν τ. ἀνδρ puts the prohibition to teach under a more general point of view, and at the same time confirms it Nor can it be denied that women are not αὐθεντεῖν τ. ἀνδρ. in the assemblies, because in the apostle's opinion that does not beseem them at any time. The reason why not, is given in the verses that follow. — It is to be observed, further, that ver. 12 corresponds exactly with ver. 11 . γυνὴ . . γυναικί ; μανθανέτω . . . διδάσκειν οὐκ ἐπιτρέπω ; ἐν πάσῃ ὑποταγῇ . . . οὐδὲ αὐθεντεῖν τοῦ ἀνδρ. ; ἐν ἡσυχίᾳ . . . ἀλλ᾽ εἶναι ἐν ἡσυχίᾳ This parallelism is clear proof that the same thing is spoken of in ver. 12 as in ver. 11, which Hofmann denies. Still ver. 12 is not therefore superfluous, since it both emphasizes and more precisely defines the particular ideas in ver. 11. — ἀλλ᾽ εἶναι ἐν ἡσυχίᾳ]

---

[1] Hofmann, in opposition to these two views, maintains that the apostle here speaks of the "Christian life in general," "of all action for which there was occasion in ordinary life ; " but the context gives no ground for his assertion.

The same construction is found in 1 Cor. xiv. 34. The infinitive is dependent on a βούλομαι to be supplied from οὐκ ἐπιτρέπω—an abbreviated construction which occurs also in classic Greek.—De Wette rightly directs attention to these points, that we must not by arbitrary interpretations take away the clear definite meaning from the commands here laid down, in order to make them universal in application; and, on the other hand, that they are not to be considered as local and temporal ordinances: they are rather injunctions to be still held valid as applying to public assemblies [1]

Ver. 13. First reason for the previous prohibition, taken from the history of the creation —Ver. 14. The second reason, taken from the history of the fall. Elsewhere in the Pauline Epistles we find proofs that the historical facts of the O. T. are to the apostle full of meaning as symbols of higher, universal truths. So here, the facts that Adam was first created, and that Eve, not Adam, was tempted by the serpent, are to him prototypes and proofs that it is becoming for the wife not αὐθεντεῖν ἀνδρός, but to be meekly subordinate to the husband. Hence he says: 'Ἀδὰμ γὰρ πρῶτος ἐπλάσθη, εἶτα Εὔα. The verb πλάσσειν occurs in the N. T. only here and in Rom. ix. 20, both times in its original meaning. The meaning "*create*," here appropriate to the word, is, however, found in the LXX. Gen. ii. 7, from which passage the apostle here has drawn (comp. also 2 Macc. vii. 23 : ὁ πλάσας ἀνθρώπου γένεσιν) Compare 1 Cor. xi. 2 ff., where

---

[1] Compare with this apostolic expression, *Const. Apost* III 6   οὐκ ἐπιτρέπομεν γυναῖκας διδάσκειν ἐν ἐκκλησίᾳ, ἀλλὰ μόνον προσεύχεσθαι καὶ τῶν διδασκάλων ἐπακούειν Tertull. *De Virg Vel.* non permittitur mulieri in ecclesia loqui, sed nec docere, nec tinguere, nec ullius virilis muneris, nedum sacerdotalis officii sortem sibi vindicare. It is curious that in the *Apost. Const* it is permitted to women προσεύχεσθαι in church, while here it is granted only to men to do so. But, on the one hand, προσεύχεσθαι in the *Constitutions* does not mean exactly prayer *aloud;* and, on the other hand, this passage here does not plainly and directly forbid προσεύχεσθαι to women , it only forbids distinctly διδάσκειν on their part — There is the same apparent contradiction between 1 Cor. xiv. 34, 35, and 1 Cor. xi 5, 13. While in the former passage λαλεῖν is forbidden to women, in the latter προσεύχεσθαι and even προφητεύειν are presupposed as things done by women, and the apostle does not rebuke it.—The solution is, that Paul wishes everything in church to be done εὐσχημόνως καὶ κατὰ τάξιν; while, on the other hand, he holds by the principle · "τὸ πνεῦμα μὴ σβέννυτε" (1 Thess. v. 19). Meyer on 1 Cor. xi. 5 differs.

the apostle says that the husband is εἴκων καὶ δόξα Θεοῦ, and the wife δόξα ἀνδρός, because the husband is not ἐκ γυναικός, but the wife ἐξ ἀνδρός. De Wette, without reason, thinks that the author of this Epistle to Timothy had that passage in mind.

Ver. 14. καὶ 'Αδὰμ οὐκ ἠπατήθη] In order to justify this expression, the expositors have sought to define it more precisely, mostly by supplying πρῶτος. So Theodoret; Tertullian, too (De Hab. Mul.), says, perhaps alluding to this passage: tu divinae legis prima es desertrix. Others, again, supply ὑπὸ τοῦ ὄφεως (Matthies: "As the apostle remembers the O. T. story of the fall, there comes into his thoughts the cunning serpent by which Eve, not Adam, let herself be ensnared"). De Wette thinks that the author is insisting on the notion *be charmed, betrayed* (by sinful desire), as opposed to some other motive to sin. Hofmann arbitrarily supplies with 'Αδὰμ οὐκ ἠπατήθη the thought: "so long as he was alone." —The apparent difficulty is solved when we remember the peculiarity of allegorical interpretation, which lays stress on the definite expression as such. This here is the word ἀπατᾶν (or ἐξαπατᾶν). On this word the whole emphasis is laid, as is clearly shown by the very repetition of it. This word, however, in the Mosaic account of the fall, is used only of the woman, not of the man, for in Gen. iii. 13 the woman expressly says: ὁ ὄφις ἠπάτησέ με; the man, however, uses no such expression. And in the story there is no indication that as the woman was deceived or betrayed through the promises of the serpent, so was the man through the woman. —Adam did certainly also transgress the command, but not, as the woman, influenced by ἀπάτη. Paul, remembering this, says: 'Αδὰμ οὐκ ἠπατήθη, ἡ δὲ γυνὴ ἐξαπατηθεῖσα. Bengel. serpens mulierem decepit, mulier virum non decepit, sed ei persuasit. To supply anything whatever, only serves therefore to conceal the apostle's real meaning. — ἡ δὲ γυνὴ ἐξαπατηθεῖσα ἐν παραβάσει γέγονε] This betrayal of the woman by the serpent is mentioned by Paul also in 2 Cor. xi. 3, where he employs the same word: ἐξαπατᾶν.—The emphasis, as is apparent from what precedes, is not on the last words, but on ἐξαπατηθεῖσα; hence it is not right to supply πρώτη with ἐν παρ. γεγ. Παράβασις here, as elsewhere (οὗ οὐκ ἔστι νόμος, οὐδὲ παράβασις, Rom. iv. 15), is used in regard to a definite law.—The construction γεγονέναι ἐν occurs frequently in the N. T. in order to denote the entrance into a certain condition, a certain existence. De Wette: "fell into transgression." Luther wrongly: "and brought in transgression."—As to the thought itself, expositors find the force of this second reason to lie in the fact that in the fall the weakness of the woman, her proneness to temptation, was manifested, and that consequently it is not seemly for the woman to have mastery over the man. But did the man resist the temptation more stoutly than the woman? Paul nowhere gives any hint of that. The significant part of the Mosaic narrative to him is rather this, that the judgment of God was passed upon the woman because she had let herself be *betrayed* by the serpent, and it is in accordance with this judgment that the husband is made lord over the wife.[1]

Ver. 15. Σωθήσεται δὲ διὰ τῆς τεκνογονίας] σωθήσεται δέ is in opposition to the previous ἐν παραβάσει γέγονε. Still this sentence is not intended merely to moderate the judgment pronounced in ver. 14 (Matthies), after the apostle has forbidden to the woman any activity in church assemblies as unbecoming to her, he now points to the destiny assigned her by God, the fulfilment of which brings salvation to her. The subject of σωθήσεται is ἡ γυνή, to be supplied from the preceding words; but, of course, it applies collectively to the whole sex, while referring specially to Eve.[2] — σωθήσεται is to be taken here in the sense which it continually has in the N. T. (not then equivalent to "she will win for herself merit and reward," de Wette). Every reason to the contrary falls to the ground, if only we consider that τεκνογονία is regarded as the destiny assigned to the woman by God, and that to the woman σωτηρία is assured by it under the condition given in

[1] The right interpretation of this passage does not even in appearance contradict Rom. v. 12 In the latter, Paul does not mention the woman, but the man, as the origin of sin, but then he is thinking of the man as the image of God, of the woman as the image of the man.

[2] Even Theophylact declared against the curious view, that Mary is to be taken here as subject. Clearly also *Eve* cannot here be meant.

the words following: ἐὰν κ.τ.λ It is to be noted also, that though faith is the only source of salvation, the believer must not fail in fulfilling his duties in faith, if he is to partake in the σωτηρία. — διά is taken by several expositors (also Wiesinger) in the sense of "in;"[1] but this is wrong, for either this signification "in" passes over into the signification "by means of," or it has much the same force as "notwithstanding, in spite of" (Rom. ii. 27 ; see Meyer on the passage); διά, however, cannot be used in this sense, since τεκνογονία would in that case have been regarded as a hindrance to the attainment of the σωτηρία. This militates also against Hofmann's view, " that σώζεσθαι διά τινος has the same meaning here as in 1 Cor. iii 15, to be saved as through something;" this explanation also makes the τεκνογονία appear to be something through which the woman's σώζεσθαι is endangered.[2] — τεκνογονία, a word which occurs only here in the N. T. (as also τεκνογονέω only in chap. v. 14, and τεκνοτροφέω only in chap. v 10), can have here nothing but its etymological meaning. Some, quite wrongly, have taken it as a term for the marriage state, and others have made it synonymous with τεκνοτροφία. This latter view is found in the oldest expositors ; thus Theophylact remarks, not without wit: οὐ γεννῆσαι μόνον δεῖ, ἀλλὰ καὶ παιδεῦσαι· τοῦτο γὰρ ὄντως τεκνογονία, εἰ δὲ οὔ, οὐκ ἐστὶ τεκνογονία, ἀλλὰ τεκνοφθορία ἔσται ταῖς γυναιξί.—The question, how the τεκνογονία contributes to the σωτηρία, is answered by most by supplying[3] with the one or the other something of which there is no hint

---

[1] Van Oosterzee translates διά by "by means of," and then says: "it simply indicates a *condition* in which the woman becomes a partaker of blessedness," leaving it uncertain in what relation the apostle places τεκνογονία to σώζεσθαι

[2] Hofmann says in explanation "If it is appointed to the woman to bear children in pain, she might succumb under such a burden of life ;," but, in reply, it is to be observed that τεκνογονία does not mean "to bear children *with pain.*"

[3] Most think of the faithful fulfilment of maternal duty in the education of children. Chrysostom· τεκνογονίαν, φησι, τὸ μὴ μόνον τικεῖν, ἀλλὰ καὶ κατὰ Θεὸν ἀναγαγεῖν.—According to Heinrichs, Paul means here to say : mulier jam hoc in mundo peccatorum poenas luit, διὰ τῆς τεκνογ. eo, quod cum dolore parturit, adeoque haec τεκνογ eam quasi σώζειν putanda est, et ipsa σώζεσθαι διὰ τῆς τεκνογονίας. The passage quoted by Heinrichs, Gen iii. 16, does not denote the τεκνογονία as such, but the pains connected with it as a punishment of trans-

in the words of the apostle, and by which the thought is more or less altered. This much may be granted, that Paul, by laying stress on the τεκνογονία (the occasion for which was probably the κωλύων γαμεῖν on the part of the heretics, chap. iv. 3), assigns to the woman, who has to conduct herself as passive in the assemblies, the domestic life as the sphere in which—especially in regard to the children—she has to exercise her activity (comp. v. 14).—In order not to be misunderstood, as if he had said that the τεκνογονία as a purely external fact affects σωτηρία, he adds the following words: ἐὰν μείνωσιν ἐν πίστει κ.τ.λ. The subject of μείνωσιν is the collective idea γυνή (see Winer, pp. 481, 586 [E T. pp. 648, 787]), and not, as many older (Chrysostom and others) and later (Schleiermacher, Mack, Leo, Plitt) expositors think. "the children." This latter might indeed be supplied from τεκνογονία, but it would give a wrong idea.—It is quite arbitrary, with Heydenreich, to supply "man and wife."—Paul uses the expressions ἐν πίστει κ.τ.λ. to denote the Christian life in its various aspects. They are not to be limited to the relation of married life, πίστις denoting conjugal fidelity, ἀγάπη, conjugal love; ἁγιασμός, conjugal chastity; and σωφροσύνη, living in regular marriage. Σωφροσύνη is named along with the preceding cardinal virtues of the Christian life, because it peculiarly becomes the thoughts of a woman (comp ver 9), not because "a woman is apt to lose control of herself through her excitable temperament" (Hofmann). There is in the context no hint of a reference to female weakness.[1]

gression According to Plitt, the τεκνογ serves to further the woman's σωτηρία; on the one hand, because by the fulfilment of her wish gratitude is aroused within her, on the other hand, because of her care for her children she is preserved from many frivolities

[1] De Wette asserts too much when he says that this passage is in contradiction with 1 Cor vii. 7 ff., 25 ff., 38 ff. The truth is rather that the matter is regarded from various points of view In 1 Corinthians the apostle is delivering his judgment, while he considers the difficult position of Christians amid the hostility of the world, without for a moment denying that τεκνογονία is an ordinance of God Here, however, he is considering only the latter point, without entering into every detail.

136   THE FIRST EPISTLE TO TIMOTHY.

CHAPTER III.

VER. 1. πιστός] Instead of this, D has ἀνθρώπινος, and some Latin Fathers have humanus. "Haec lectio vetustior est Hieronymo. Quod si vero vetustior Hieronymo, vetustior quoque est nostris codicibus omnibus. Nemo tamen ita temerarius est, ut eam probaret," Matthaei. — Ver. 2. Instead of νηφάλεον, Griesb., following the weightiest authorities, accepted the form νηφάλιον; so, too, Scholz, Matthaei, Lachm. Buttm Tisch. — Ver. 3. The words μὴ αἰσχροκερδῆ are left out in A D F G 5, 6, 17, *al*, Syr. Arr Copt. etc. Griesb. is right, therefore, in striking them out; they were probably interpolated from Tit. i. 7. De Wette's suggestion, that they may have been omitted intentionally as superfluous, since ἀφιλάργυρον follows, is very improbable; comp Reiche, *Comment. crit.* on this passage. — Ver 4. For προϊστάμενον, ℵ has the form προϊστανόμενον, occurring only in later authors — Ver. 6. Several cursives have the reading καὶ παγίδα after διαβόλου, which, however, is manifestly taken from the next verse. — Ver. 7. δεῖ δὲ αὐτόν] So Griesb and Scholz, following the *Rec.*; Lachm. Buttm. and Tisch. left out αὐτόν, because it is not found in A F G H 17, Copt. Boern.; in Matthaei it stands without dispute. The insertion is more easily explained than the omission. — Ver. 9. For ἐν καθαρᾷ συνειδήσει, ℵ has the singular reading: καὶ καθαρᾶς συνειδήσεως — which can only be explained from an oversight occasioned by the genitive before — Ver 14. τάχιον] Lachm. and Buttm. read ἐν τάχει, following A C D* 17, 71, 73, *al*. (ταχεῖον and ταχέως are also found). The *Rec*, which has the testimony of D*** F G K L, *al*., Chr. Theodoret, *al*, and is retained by Tisch., is the more difficult reading; besides, in the other passages of the N. T. where the word occurs, the comparative form can be easily explained; ἐν τάχει seems to be an explanatory correction. — In ver. 15, D* Arm. Vulg. Clar Or. Ambrosiast. have σε inserted after δεῖ — Ver. 16 For the *Rec.* Θεός, the most important authorities have the reading ὅς, as A C F G[1] ℵ 17, 73, 181. Further, the Copt. Sahid. and Gothic versions, also

---

[1] On the point that in A and C there was originally written not ΘΣ but ΟΣ, comp Griesb in *Symb. crit* vol. I pp. viii.–liv, and vol. II pp 56–76; further, Tisch. *Prolegg. ad Cod. Ephr.* sec. vii. p. 39, excursus on 1 Tim iii. 16.

the Syr. Erp. Aeth. Arm., have the relative. Orig , Theod. Mops., Epiph., Cyr. Al., Jerome, Eutherius, beyond doubt, found the latter reading in their MSS ; with several others it is at least probable. The *Rec.* Θεός is found, on the other hand, in D*** K L, in nearly all cursives, in the edd. Arab. p. Slav MS., and besides, in Greg. Nyss. (who seems once, however, to have read ὅς) Chrys Theodoret, Didym. (*De Trinitate,* p. 83) Damasc. Oecum Theophyl. In Ignatius (*Ep. ad Ephes.* § 19) we find Θεὸς ἀνθρωπίνως φανερούμενος; in the *Apost. constitt.:* Θεὸς κύριε ὁ ἐπιφανεὶς ἡμῖν ἐν σαρκί; in Hippol : Θεὸς ἐν σώματι ἐφανερώθη, in Gregor. Thaum. (see pot. Apollin. in Photius): Θεὸς ἐν σαρκὶ φανερωθείς—all which passages seem to testify in favour of Θεός. —In the MS. gr. D* is found the reading ὅ. The It. and Vulg. have : mysterium s. sacramentum, quod manifestatum est, and in this they are followed by the Latin Fathers, excepting Jerome himself This translation does not, however, point necessarily to the reading ὅ; it might also be taken from ὅς, which was referred to μυστήριον. Till Wetstein, the reading ὅς was generally held to be the right one,—later also by Matthaei, Tittm. Scholz, Hahn, Heydenr. Linck, Mack ; the reading ὅ is specially defended by Wetstein and Schulthess. Almost all later critics and expositors, both on external and internal grounds, have rightly preferred the reading ὅς, which is accepted also by Lachm Buttm. Tisch. Comp the thorough investigation by Reiche, *Comment. crit.* ii., on the passage.

Ver 1. After speaking of the behaviour of men and women in the church-assemblies, Paul goes on to give instructions regarding the proper qualifications of office-bearers in the church. He begins emphatically with the introductory words: πιστὸς ὁ λόγος, which here, as in i. 15, do not refer to what precedes (Chrysostom, Erasmus, and others), but to what follows. — εἴ τις ἐπισκοπῆς ὀρέγεται] Since ἐπισκοπή corresponds with ἐπίσκοπος in ver. 2, the word does not denote here generally " the office of one who is set over others " (Hofmann), but specially "*the office of a bishop;*" for only in this way can the inferences in vv. 2 f. be drawn from what is said here. Why the previous words πιστὸς ὁ λόγος should not be in agreement with this, we cannot understand. — Ἐπισκοπή has a similar meaning in Acts i. 20, where it denotes the office of apostle ; comp. Meyer on the passage. In the N. T. the word usually means "the visitation."— ὀρέγεται does not necessarily imply here, as de Wette thinks, the notion of ambitious striving; comp. Heb. xi 16. — The ground of the ὀρέγεσθαι may indeed be ambition, but it may also be the zeal of faith and love. The apostle does not blame the ὀρέγεσθαι in itself, he merely asks us to consider that the ἐπισκοπή is a καλὸν ἔργον, and that not every one therefore may assume it. — καλοῦ ἔργου ἐπιθυμεῖ] Leo and others take ἔργον here in the sense of τί; but it seems more correct to hold by the meaning: "work, business" (Luther, Matthies, de Wette, Wiesinger, Hofmann, and others); comp. 2 Tim. iv 5: ἔργον ποίησον εὐαγγελιστοῦ; 1 Thess. v. 13, where the church is exhorted διὰ τὸ ἔργον αὐτῶν to the love of the προισταμενοι. It is, however, very doubtful, to say the least, that the word is chosen to lay stress on the thought that the ἐπισκοπή is an office of *work* and not of enjoyment (Jerome: "opus, non dignitatem, non delicias;" Bengel. "negotium, non otium"). — καλοῦ, see i. 18; 2 Tim. iv. 7.

Ver. 2. Δεῖ οὖν τὸν ἐπίσκοπον ἀνεπίληπτον εἶναι κ.τ.λ.] τὸν ἐπίσκοπον, as a name for the superintendent of the congregation, only occurs in the Pastoral Epistles (here and at Tit. i 7), and in Acts xx 28, Phil i. 1 (the verb ἐπισκοπεῖν is found in 1 Pet. v. 2). There can be no doubt that in the N. T. the ἐπίσκοποι and the πρεσβύτεροι denote the same persons. The question why these different names should be given to the same persons has been differently answered.

REMARK — Baur supposes that every single town had originally *one* superintendent, who in his relation to the congregation was called ἐπίσκοπος, but that when several ἐπίσκοποι over single congregations were taken together, they were for the most part designated by the co-ordinate name of πρεσβύτεροι He finds the chief support for his opinion in the passages, Tit. i. 5: ἵνα καταστήσῃς κατὰ πόλιν πρεσβυτέρους, and Acts xiv 23: χειροτονήσαντες . . . πρεσβυτέρους κατ' ἐκκλησίαν; but the form of expression here used does not necessarily imply that every single town (or congregation) received or was to receive only *one* presbyter. Since κατὰ πόλιν (ἐκκλησίαν) means: by cities, *i.e.* in every city, and the plural (πρεσβυτέρους) is herewith joined with it, it *may* be taken in Baur's sense, but it may also be as well taken to mean that the plural refers to each single city. The passage in Acts xv. 21, to which Baur appeals, proves nothing for his view, since it is well known that there were several synagogues in each city of the Jewish country.—According to the view of Kist (Illgen's *Zeitschrift f. hist Theol.* II. 2, pp. 47 ff.), the Christians in any one place formed originally several house-congregations, each of which had its particular superintendent. The college of presbyters then consisted of the superintendents of those house-congregations in one city, which, taken together, were regarded as *a* congregation. The passage in Epiphanius, *Haer.* lxix. 1,[1] shows that in later times such an arrangement did exist; but there is no passage in the N. T. to prove that that was the original arrangement. In the N. T. the presbyters are always named as the superintendents of one congregation, and there is nowhere any hint that each house-congregation had its special superintendent Even when James (v. 14) enjoins that a sick man is to summon τοὺς πρεσβυτέρους τῆς ἐκκλησίας, — and not the presbyter of the house-congregation of which he was a member,—his words are clearly against Kist's view. — The most probable theory is, that originally the superintendents of the single congregations—according to the analogy of Jewish custom—bore the name of πρεσβύτεροι, but that, in so far as they were ἐπισκοποῦντες in reference to the congregation, they were called ἐπίσκοποι; comp. Acts xx. 17 and 28.— There are, however, two striking facts to be noticed. In the first place, Paul in his epistles (the Pastoral Epistles excepted) makes use of the word ἐπίσκοπος *only* in Phil. i. 1, and of the word πρεσβύτεροι not at all Nay, he almost never mentions the superintendent of the congregation except in Eph. iv. 11, where he calls them ποιμένες καὶ διδάσκαλοι, and 1 Thess. v. 12, where he mentions them as προιστάμενοι ὑμῶν (comp. also Rom. xii. 8 : ὁ προιστάμενος); comp., however, the passages quoted above from Acts. From this it is clear that at first his attention was directed to the congregation only in its indivisible unity, and only by degrees does he give more prominence to its leaders. We cannot,

---

[1] "Ὅσαι ἐκκλησίαι τῆς καθολικῆς ἐκκλησίας ἐν Ἀλεξανδρείᾳ ὑπὸ ἕνα ἀρχιεπίσκοπον οὖσαι, καὶ κατ᾽ ἰδίαν ταύταις ἐπιτεταγμένοι εἰσὶ πρεσβύτεροι διὰ τὰς ἐκκλησιαστικὰς χρείας τῶν οἰκητόρων.

however, conclude from this, either that the congregations in the earlier period had no leaders, for it lay in the very nature of a congregation to have some kind of leading; or that the Pastoral Epistles were not written by Paul, for why in the later period of his career should circumstances not so have shaped themselves that he thought it necessary to give the leaders more prominence?—The second striking fact is, that both in this passage and in Tit. i. 7 the singular ἐπίσκοπος and not the plural ἐπίσκοποι is used, though in the latter passage the plural πρεσβύτεροι immediately precedes, and here at ver. 8 we have the plural διάκονοι (comp. also v. 17: οἱ καλῶς προεστῶτες πρεσβύτεροι). Is there any reason for this in the nature of the episcopate? The fact certainly might be interpreted to favour Kist's view; but it may more simply and naturally be thus explained. Both times a τις precedes, and this almost by necessity compels the use of the plural after it.

Οὖν] is not simply a particle of transition. From the fact that the ἐπισκοπή is a καλὸν ἔργον, the apostle deduces the necessity of a blameless character on the part of the ἐπίσκοπος; Bengel: bonum negotium bonis committendum — ἀνεπίληπτον εἶναι] In enumerating the qualities which an ἐπίσκοπος must possess, the apostle begins appropriately with a general idea; so also Tit. i. 7: ἀνεπίληπτος, equivalent to μὴ παρέχων κατηγορίας ἀφορμήν, Schol Thucyd. v. 17. It is important that they who stand at the head of the church should lead an irreproachable life in the opinion both of Christians and of non-Christians. — μιᾶς γυναικὸς ἄνδρα] This expression cannot here be properly referred to polygamy; for, although polygamy might at that time be still found among the civilised heathen, and even among the Jews (comp. Justin Martyr, *Dialog. c. Tryph.*; Chrysostom on the passage; Josephus, *Antiq.* vii. 2), it was as a rare exception. Besides, there is an argument against such an interpretation in the phrase ἑνὸς ἀνδρὸς γυνή, v. 9; for similarly such a phrase ought to refer to polyandry, which absolutely never occurred — Most recent expositors (Leo, Mack, de Wette, Heydenreich, Wiesinger, van Oosterzee, Plitt) take the expression as referring to a second marriage after the death of the first wife. Heydenreich quotes many testimonies from the earlier Fathers to justify this view. The results which these give are the following: —*Firstly*, Many held marriage after the death of the first wife to be something immoral. Athenagoras (*Leg pro Christo*, p. 37, edit. Colon.) calls second marriage a εὐπρεπὴς μοιχεία; and Tertullian repudiates it utterly, as do the Montanists. *Secondly*, This was, however, by no means the view that generally prevailed. It had many decided opponents, but even opponents of the view regard[1] abstinence from a second marriage as something praiseworthy, nay, meritorious. Hermas (*Past mandat.* iv. chap. 4: dic, Domine, si vir vel mulier alicujus discesserit et nupserit aliquis eorum, num quid peccat? Qui nubit, non peccat; sed si per se manserit, magnum sibi conquirit honorem apud Dominum) and the later Fathers, as Chrysostom, Epiphanius, Cyril, all write in this strain.—Clement of Alexandria (*Stromata*, iii. p 461) says, that he who marries a second time does not commit sin: οὐ γὰρ κεκώλυται πρὸς τοῦ νόμου· οὐ πληροῖ δὲ τῆς κατὰ τὸ εὐαγγέλιον πολιτείας τὴν κατ' ἐπίτασιν τελειότητα. *Thirdly*, As to those who held office in the church, it was a general principle that they should not marry a second time. The proof of this is the objection which Tertullian puts in the mouth of his opponents against his condemnation of second marriages : adeo, inquiunt, permisit Apostolus iterare connubium, ut solos qui sunt in Clero, monogamiae jugo adstrinxerit (*de Monogamia*, chap. 12). Origen's words are in complete accordance with this: ab ecclesiasticis dignitatibus non solum fornicatio, sed et nuptiae repellunt; neque enim episcopus, nec presbyter, nec diaconus, nec vidua possunt esse digami.—On the other hand, there is a weighty counter-argument in the fact that the earlier expositors of the Pastoral Epistles (Theodoret, Theophylact, Jerome, Oecumenius) do not share in this view,[2] though the practice prevailing in their day must have made the interpretation to

---

[1] Still there are exceptions, such as Theodore of Mopsuestia, who shows his freedom of thought in arguing most decidedly against this view, see Theodori ep. Mops. in N. T. commentarium, quae reperiri potuerunt; ed. O. F. Fritzsche, pp. 150–152.

[2] Chrysostom places the two views together: οὐ νομοθετῶν τοῦτο φησίν, ὡς μὴ εἶναι ἐξὸν ἄνευ τούτου (γυναικός) γίνεσθαι· ἀλλὰ τὴν ἀμετρίαν κωλύων, ἐπειδὴ ἐπὶ τῶν Ἰουδαίων ἐξῆν, καὶ δευτέροις ὁμιλεῖν γάμοις, καὶ δύο ἔχειν κατὰ ταυτὸν γυναῖκας.

them an obvious one Besides, nowhere else in the N. T. is there the slightest trace of any ordinance against second marriages, nay, in Rom. vii 2, 3, and also in 1 Cor. vii. 39, Paul declares widows to be perfectly free to marry again; in 1 Cor. vii 8, he even places widows and virgins on the same level; and in this epistle, v. 14, he says: βούλομαι νεωτέρας (χήρας) γαμεῖν. It would certainly be more than strange if the apostle should *urge* the younger widows to a step which would hinder them later in life from being received into the class of church-widows (see on chap. v. 9).—Appeal has been made to the facts that the *nuptiae secundae* were held to be unseemly for women even among the heathen (comp. Rein, *Das romische Privatrecht*, pp 211, 212, and the Latin word *univira*); but it is to be observed, on the other hand, that it was considered in no way objectionable for a *man* to marry again *after the death of his wife*, and that there exists no trace of the opposite principle (There is no ground for Heydenreich's opinion, that the priests highest in rank, *e.g.* the Pontifex Maximus, could only be married once.) Hence, neither Christians nor non-Christians could be offended if the presbyters of the churches were married a second time, and Paul would have laid down a maxim which in his day had never been heard of The undecided opposition to second marriages appeared among the Christians only in the post-apostolic age, when asceticism was already taking a non-Pauline direction, and was therefore inclined to give its own interpretation to the apostle's words. Besides, the expression here, as also in Tit. i. 6, stands in the midst of others, which denote qualities to be possessed not only by the bishop, but also by every Christian as such. Accordingly, there is good ground for taking the disputed expression simply as opposed to an immoral life, especially to concubinage. What he says then is, that a bishop is to be a man who neither lives nor has lived in sexual intercourse with any other woman than the one to whom he is married (Matthies, Hofmann [1]). Thus

---

[1] Hofmann (*Schriftbew* II. 2, p 421) says. "The injunction is, that the husband have no other wives in addition to his own wife, and the widow (chap. v. 9) no other husbands in addition to her own husband." So also in his comment. on Tit. i. 6.

interpreted, the apostle's injunction is amply justified, not only in itself, but also in regard to the extraordinary laxness of living in his day, and it is in full harmony with the other injunctions. The expression under discussion might also be possibly referred to successive polygamy, *i e.* to the re-marriage of *divorced* persons, but its terms are too general to make such a reference certain.[1]— νηφάλιον] only here and in ver. 11 (Tit. ii. 2). In its proper meaning it is equivalent to μὴ οἴνῳ πολλῷ προσέχοντα, ver 8, but it is also used in a kindred sense (like the Latin *sobrius*) to denote one who is not enchanted nor intoxicated by any fleshly passion It is used, therefore, of sobriety of spirit This is the meaning of the word here, where it is joined immediately with σώφρονα, and where the original sense follows in the word πάροινος, ver 3. Even the root-word νήφω occurs in the N T. only in the figurative sense, as in 1 Thess v 6, 8, where it is joined with γρηγορεῖν, and stands in opposition to the spiritual καθεύδειν and μεθύειν; and in 1 Pet iv. 7, where it is also connected with σωφρονεῖν —σώφρονα, κόσμιον] see ii 9.—Bengel: quod σώφρων est intus, id κόσμιος est extra Theodoret κόσμιος· καὶ φθέγματι καὶ σχήματι καὶ βλέμματι καὶ βαδίσματι ὥστε καὶ διὰ τοῦ σώματος φαίνεσθαι τὴν τῆς ψυχῆς σωφροσύνην. — φιλόξενον] in special reference to strangers who were Christian brethren, comp. 1 Pet. iv 9; Heb xiii 2; Rom. xii. 13 — διδακτικόν] " able to teach " (Luther), "*good at teaching*" (van Oosterzee). Διδακτικός is one who possesses everything that fits him for teaching, including also the inclination (Plitt. "inclined to teach") or the "willingness" (Hofmann) Hofmann is wrong in specializing it into "a *moral* quality." That is justified neither by the etymology of the word (comp. the similarly-formed πρακτικός, γραφικός, etc.), nor by the position in which

---

[1] As a matter of course, Paul did not, as Carlstadt thought, mean in these words to command the bishop to marry; but, on the other hand, there is at bottom a presupposition that it is better for a bishop to be married than to be unmarried (see vv 4, 5) —We should note also as an exegetical curiosity, that some Catholic expositors, in the interests of celibacy, have explained the word γυνή of the church —The strange opinion of Bretschneider, that μιᾶς is here the indefinite article, and that Paul meant a bishop should be married, hardly needed the elaborate refutation which is accorded to it by Winer, pp. 111 f. [E. T. p. 146]

it stands here or in 2 Tim. ii. 24. The word is found elsewhere only in Philo, *De Praem. et Virt.* 4, not in classic Greek. Though the public address in the congregation (both that of the διδασκαλία and that of the προφητεία, 1 Cor. xii.–xiv.) was permitted to every one to whom the Holy Spirit had imparted the χάρισμα, still the ἐπίσκοπος in particular had to know how to handle doctrine, in instructing the catechumens, in building up the faith of the church, and in refuting heretics (see Tit. i 9); hence Paul, in Eph. iv. 11, calls the ποίμενες of the church, διδάσκαλοι.

Ver. 3. The positive characteristics are now followed by two that are negative (or three, according to the *Rec.*): μὴ πάροινον] This word occurs only here and in Tit. i. 7. Though it is used (comp. παροινέω, LXX. Isa. xli. 12) also in the wider sense, as equivalent to *contumeliosus* (Josephus, *Antiq.* vi. 10, where it stands opposed to the word σωφρονεῖν), yet there is here no sufficient ground for departing from its original sense It is true that, as Bengel indicates, the ἀλλ' ἐπιεικῆ afterwards seems to be in favour of the wider meaning here, without special reference to drunkenness, but the contrast is the same in the other case, if we only remember that πάροινος does not mean simply "drunken," but "impudent, arrogant in intoxication."[1] — μὴ πλήκτην] This word also may be taken in a narrower and a wider sense. Here, as in Tit. i. 7, it denotes the passionate man who is inclined to come to blows at once over anything. With these two ideas there are three placed in contrast, not, however, in exact correspondence, for in that case the reading of the *Rec.*, μὴ αἰσχροκερδῆ, would be indispensable, and for this reading there is too little testimony; but in such a way that the conduct denoted in the one case is opposed to that in the other. — ἀλλ' ἐπιεικῆ, ἄμαχον ἀφιλάργυρον] In Tit. iii. 2, as here, the first two expressions stand together. Ἄμαχος does not occur elsewhere in the N T. Ἐπιεικής does not mean "yielding," for it does not come from εἴκω, but from εἰκός (ἔοικα).—The nearest meaning is "beseeming." As used, however, it has mostly the sense of moderateness and gentleness (in Plutarch, *Pyrrh.* 23.—ἐπιεικῶς is used along with

---

[1] Comp. Aristophanes, *Acharnians*, 981, where the scholiast explains it μέθυσος καὶ ὑβριστής; see Pape on the word

πράως). Luther rightly: "*mild.*" Ἄμαχος is equivalent to peaceful; Luther: "not quarrelsome." — ἀφιλάργυρον (only here and in Heb. xiii. 5; φιλάργυρος, 2 Tim. iii. 2 and Luke xvi. 14; the substantive φιλαργυρία, 1 Tim. vi. 10) lays stress on a point of which no hint was given before It is joined with ἄμαχος, since avarice necessarily brings strife with it.

Ver. 4. In the second verse, the apostle touched on the subject of marriage-life; here, he directs how the bishop is to conduct himself in his own house. — τοῦ ἰδίου οἴκου καλῶς προϊστάμενον] Though ἴδιος is used at times in the N. T. instead of the simple possessive pronoun, it is here emphatic, in contrast with ἐκκλησία Θεοῦ, ver. 5. — οἶκος here, as elsewhere, denotes the entire household, including slaves. It is above all important that he should act properly in regard to the children; hence the apostle adds: τέκνα ἔχοντα ἐν ὑποταγῇ μετὰ πάσης σεμνότητος] From a comparison with the corresponding passage in Tit i. 6, it is clear that he is speaking here, not of the father's disposition, but of that of the children (in opposition to Hofmann). The ἔχοντα ἐν ὑποταγῇ corresponds in sense with μὴ . . ἀνυπότακτα in the other passage, and in construction with ἔχοντα . . . μὴ ἐν κατηγορίᾳ ἀσωτίας. The bishop is to preside over his house in such a way that the children shall not be wanting in submissiveness. The words μετὰ πάσης σεμνότητος are to be connected with what immediately precedes, and not with προϊστάμενον (Hofmann). If it be right to refer them to the fathers (Heydenrich, Matthies, van Oosterzee), ἔχειν must be explained as equivalent either to *tenere* (Matthies: "holding the children in obedience") or to κατέχειν (van Oosterzee). That, however, is arbitrary; besides, the parallel passage in Tit. i. 6, where ἀσωτία is the opposite of σεμνότης, is against it. Leo, Mack, de Wette, Wiesinger, are right therefore in referring the words to the children. The idea of σεμνότης does not forbid this reference, if only we avoid thinking of little children; comp., by way of contrast, the conduct of the children of the high priest Eli, in the O. T.

Ver. 5 in a parenthesis gives the reason why a bishop ought to know how to govern his house properly. — εἰ δέ τις τοῦ ἰδίου οἴκου προστῆναι οὐκ οἶδε] δέ shows that the confirmatory clause is adversative; the conclusion is made *a minori* ad majus. Bengel: plus est regere ecclesiam, quam familiam.[1] — πῶς ἐκκλησίας Θεοῦ ἐπιμελήσεται] The contrast here made becomes still more forcible when it is observed that in ver. 15 Paul calls the ἐκκλησία the οἶκος Θεοῦ. — ἐπιμελήσεται] The future here, as often with the Greeks, expresses the capability; see Bernhardy's *Syntax*, p. 377 The verb ἐπιμελέομαι has not only the more general meaning of "take care of something" (Luke x. 34, 35), but also more definitely, "fill an office, be overseer over something," in which sense it is used here. — For a right understanding of the connection of this verse with what precedes, it is to be observed that the first requisite for a successful superintendence is obedience (ὑποταγή) from the church towards its superintendent. It is the bishop's duty so to conduct himself that the members of the church may be obedient to him, not as servants to a master, but as children to a father, that they may show him obedience in love.

Ver. 6. Μὴ νεόφυτον] depending on δεῖ εἶναι in ver. 2, is attached to the previous accusatives, ver. 5 being a parenthesis. Νεόφυτος is rightly explained by Chrysostom: οὐ τὸν νεώτερον ἐνταῦθα λέγει, ἀλλὰ τὸν νεοκατήχητον; comp 1 Cor. iii. 6, 7 Heinrichs is wrong if he thinks that, on account of what follows, the explanation rejected by Chrysostom is really the right one; for the rapid promotion to the episcopate of one newly admitted into the church, might easily have consequences to be dreaded by the apostle. — The reason why a "novice" (Luther) should not be bishop is given in the words that follow: ἵνα μὴ τυφωθεὶς εἰς κρίμα ἐμπέσῃ τοῦ διαβόλου. **Τυφωθείς**: "*lest he being beclouded with conceit (of foolish pride).*" The verb (which occurs only here and in vi 4 and 2 Tim. iii. 4) comes from τῦφος, which in the figurative sense especially denotes darkness, as beclouding man's mind so that he does not know himself, so that the consciousness of his own weakness is hidden from him; in 2 Tim. iii. 4 it is appropriately joined with μηδὲν ἐπιστάμενος (comp. Athenaeus, vi. 238d). **Τυφωθείς** describes the conduct of the νεόφυτος which brings on him the κρίμα τοῦ διαβόλου. — εἰς κρίμα ἐμπέσῃ τοῦ διαβόλου] Nearly all expositors take ὁ διάβολος here and in

---

[1] Theodoret ὁ τὰ σμικρὰ οἰκονομεῖν οὐκ εἰδώς, πῶς δύναται τῶν κρειττόνων καὶ θείων πιστευθῆναι τὴν ἐπιμέλειαν.

ver. 7 to be the devil. Some, again, explain it as "the libellous fellow" (Mosheim, Wegscheider, Hofmann, Luther: "the slanderer"). Against this latter view, however, there are three decisive arguments—(1) According to the constant usage of the N T., the substantive ὁ διάβολος always denotes the devil (it is otherwise in the LXX., but only in Esth. vii. 4, viii. 1).[1] (2) The singular has the definite article, which seems to mark out one definite individual, for the collective use of the singular can always be inferred from the context (as in Matt. xii. 35; Rom. xiv. 1; 1 Pet. iv. 18; Jas. ii. 6; this, indeed, is less the case in Jas. v. 6); besides, here the idea of "libeller" is too indefinite for the train of thought, hence Hofmann is forced to define it arbitrarily: "whoever makes it his business to speak evil *of Christianity.*" (3) If, in the expression ἡ τοῦ διαβόλου παγίς, at 2 Tim. ii. 26, τοῦ διαβόλου cannot mean anything else than the devil, it is arbitrary to render it otherwise when used in the same expression at ver. 7.— κρίμα is not equivalent to "charge, accusation" (Matthies), but "*the judgment,*" especially "the judgment of *condemnation.*"— τοῦ διαβόλου is mostly (even by Wiesinger and van Oosterzee) taken to be the *genitivus objecti* (comp. especially Rev. xvii. 1), equivalent to "the judgment which is executed on the devil" (van Oosterzee), because κρίνειν is not the devil's business; Bengel: diabolus potest opprobrium inferre (ver. 7), judicium inferre non potest, non enim judicat, sed judicatur.[2] But the notion that the devil is delivered to condemnation because of self-conceit, cannot be scripturally proved. For this reason, and also because τοῦ διαβόλου in ver 7 is manifestly the subjective genitive, it is preferable to take it in the same way here (so, too, Plitt).[3] Of course the κρίμα of the devil cannot mean a trial which the devil holds, but the judgment which

---

[1] Paul uses the word only here and in ver. 7 ; 2 Tim. ii 26 , Eph. iv. 17, vi. 11 In 2 Tim. ii 26 and in Eph. vi 11, even Hofmann takes it to be the devil ; but, on the other hand, both here and in Eph iv. 17 he takes it to be the human slanderer.

[2] It is out of place to appeal to 2 Pet. ii. 4 and Jude 6 (Wiesinger), since in these passages mention is made, not of the judgment which will be passed on the devil, but of the judgment which will be passed on a number of wicked angels.

[3] Had the apostle been thinking of the judgment which will be passed on the devil (Matt. xxv. 41 ; Rev. xx. 40 [14, 15]), he would have expressed himself more clearly, with something like this ἵνα μὴ κρινῆται σὺν τῷ διαβόλῳ.

serves to give him foundation for accusing man with God (comp. the name for the devil, κατήγωρ, in Rev. xii. 10).[1]

Ver. 7. Δεῖ δὲ καὶ μαρτυρίαν καλὴν ἔχειν ἀπὸ τῶν ἔξωθεν] Δεῖ δέ (which does not present something opposed to ver. 6) adds a *new* requirement to those already given in vv. 2–6, a requirement needed for the sake of those who are not Christians. Thus δεῖ here becomes connected with the δεῖ in ver. 2. — μαρτυρία occurs in the Pauline Epistles only here and in Tit. i. 13. — ἀπὸ τῶν ἔξωθεν] οἱ ἔξωθεν (for which Paul commonly uses οἱ ἔξω) are those outside the church, ἀπό is equivalent not to "among," but to "*from;*" the testimony comes from those who are not Christians. In the choice of a bishop, care is to be taken that he is a man who has led an irreproachable life even in the eyes of those who are not Christians. The reason is added just as in ver. 6 : ἵνα μὴ εἰς ὀνειδισμὸν ἐμπέσῃ καὶ παγίδα τοῦ διαβόλου] ὀνειδισμόν may be taken absolutely (Wiesinger, Plitt), or joined with τοῦ διαβ. (van Oosterzee). The former view is supported by the fact that ἐμπέσῃ separates ὀνειδ. from παγίδα ; the latter, by the fact that the preposition is not repeated before παγίδα. The passage in vv. 14, 15, when compared with this, supports the former view, which is further established as correct by the consideration that we cannot well suppose ὀνειδίζειν to be an act of the devil. Since ὀνειδισμός is not defined more precisely, it must be taken as quite general in meaning. — καὶ παγίδα τοῦ διαβόλου] the same expression in 2 Tim. ii. 26; in 1 Tim. vi 9 it stands without τοῦ διαβ., and there, too, it is joined with πειρασμός (elsewhere only in Rom. xi. 9, which follows Ps. lxix. 23). It is a figurative name for the lying in wait of the devil, who is represented as a hunter. The idea of its association with ὀνειδισμός is this, that the disgrace incurred by one who has not a good testimony from the non-Christians, is used by the devil as a snare, not only to tempt him, but also to seduce him into apostasy from the gospel.[2]

Ver. 8. From this to ver. 13 we have instructions regarding

---

[1] Hofmann asserts that it is irrational to speak of a judgment which the devil pronounces ; but we may ask, on the other hand, whether it is not irrational to speak of a devil *without* judgment.

[2] In explaining τοῦ διαβόλου, Hofmann explains ἐμπέσῃ (εἰς) παγ. τ. διαβ. to

the deacons. —διακόνους ὡσαύτως σεμνούς κ.τ λ] The deacons, as at first instituted in the church at Jerusalem, were originally almoners of the poor (Acts vi. 1–6). They are mentioned again only in Phil i. 1. In Rom. xvi. 1, Paul calls Phoebe a διακόνος of the church at Cenchrea. There are some other passages which allude to the diaconate—Rom. xii. 7 ; 1 Cor. xii. 28 (ἀντιλήψεις) ; 1 Pet. iv. 11. It is known that this office in the church was afterwards not confined to its original object, but there is nothing to indicate how far it was developed in the apostolic age. Many of the duties assigned to the deacons in later times, can only be arbitrarily connected with the office in the apostolic age. Only it is to be observed that both here and in Phil. i 1, the deacons are named *after* the bishops. — ὡσαύτως] marks here, as in ii. 9, the transition to ordinances in regard to another class of persons, indicating at the same time their similarity to those preceding — σεμνούς] The accusative is dependent on δεῖ εἶναι, which is to be supplied ; regarding the idea contained in the word, see ii. 2 — μὴ διλόγους] the word δίλογος only here. In Prov. xi. 13, LXX ; in Ecclus v. 9, 14, vi. 1, xxviii 13, we have the similar word : δίγλωσσος [1] (comp. also δίψυχος in Jas. iv. 8) ; Theophylact : ἄλλα φρονοῦντες καὶ ἄλλα λέγοντες, καὶ ἄλλα τούτοις καὶ ἄλλα ἐκείνοις. — μὴ οἴνῳ πολλῷ προσέχοντας] προσέχειν here, as in iv. 13 and Heb. vii 13 . " *be addicted to ;* " Tit. ii. 3 . μὴ οἴνῳ πολλῷ δεδουλωμένας. — μὴ αἰσχροκερδεῖς] only here and in Tit. i. 7 , comp. 1 Pet v. 2 : ἐπισκοποῦντες . . . μηδὲ αἰσχροκερδῶς, ἀλλὰ προθύμως ; and Tit. ii. 11, where it is said of the heretics that they by unseemly doctrine destroy houses αἰσχροῦ κέρδους χάριν. These passages show that we are not to think here of gain from " dishonourable dealing " (Luther, Theodoret : ἐκ πραγμάτων αἰσχρῶν καὶ λίαν ἀτόπων), but rather of using the spiritual office for a material advantage (comp. vi. 5).

Ver. 9 Ἔχοντας τὸ μυστήριον τῆς πίστεως ἐν καθαρᾷ συνειδήσει] The emphasis is not on ἔχοντας, as if it meant

mean, that the slanderer tries to ensnare such a one in *the* sense of "showing him as an evidence of the state of morality in an association which selects such a man as its head " (¹).

[1] Theogn. v. 91 . ὃς μιῇ γλώσσῃ δίχ᾽ ἔχει.

"holding fast," but on ἐν καθαρᾷ συνειδήσει (Wiesinger). — τὸ μυστήριον τῆς πίστεως] This collocation occurs nowhere else. Πίστις is not the doctrine of faith (Heumann), but subjective faith (de Wette). Μυστήριον is the subject-matter of faith, i.e. the divine truth, which is a secret not only in so far as it was hidden from the world until it was revealed at the appointed time (Rom. xvi. 25) and remains hidden to every man till the knowledge of it is wrought in him by the Spirit of God (1 Cor. ii. 7–10, 14), but also in so far as it is even to the believer ὑπερβαλλοῦσα τῆς γνώσεως (Wiesinger). The expression is synonymous with that in ver. 16 . τὸ τῆς εὐσεβείας μυστήριον. — ἐν καθαρᾷ συνειδήσει] Comp. i 5, 19. The clause is to be joined closely with ἔχοντας, and is to be understood neither specially of occupying the office, nor quite generally of the virtuous life, or "the moral disposition" (Hofmann), but of purity and uprightness in regard to the mystery of the faith. It stands in contrast with the impurity of the heretics, who had their conscience stained by the mingling of truth with errors; comp. iv. 2.

Ver. 10 Καὶ οὗτοι δὲ δοκιμαζέσθωσαν πρῶτον] The particles καὶ ... δέ mean *and also*, καί being purely copulative , δέ, however, opposing and emphasizing[1] something new. Since this new thing, which is necessarily emphatic, always stands between καί and δέ, οὗτοι, as van Oosterzee has rightly seen, must be opposed to those before named, i.e to the presbyters; it is to be explained: " and *these* too, i.e. not only the presbyters, but also the deacons, are first to be proved." It is wrong, therefore, to make δοκιμαζέσθωσαν emphatic, and to explain οὗτοι without reference to those before named (" and these are further to be proved"), as was done in the former editions of this commentary.[2] Had he wished to say that, the apostle could not but have written καὶ δοκιμαζέσθωσαν δὲ οὗτοι; comp. John viii. 16. It is true that nothing has been said hitherto about an examination in regard to the office of presbyter; but, of course, such an examination must have

---

[1] Comp Meyer on John vi. 51 , Hartung, *Lehre von den Partik. d. gr Spr* I. pp 181 ff ; Buttmann, p 312

[2] Wiesinger, too, seems to take it in this way " These, however, also are first to be proved, then they may serve "

preceded the election. The examination for the office of deacon would certainly refer to the life and stedfastness in the faith. He does not say who was to undertake the examination, but it is natural to suppose that it was to be undertaken by those who elected. At the first institution of the diaconate the *election* was made by the church, the installation to the office by the apostles. It is not known how it was managed later in the apostolic age. Heydenreich makes the examination too formal when he says: "They are to be examined first by Timothy, with the aid of the presbytery; the votes of the members of the church are to be taken concerning his worthiness," etc On the other hand, the force of δοκιμαζέσθωσαν must not be weakened by such explanations as: "Paul wishes only those to be made διάκονοι regarding whom a definite opinion had already been formed in the church" (so in the second edition of this commentary); or: "it is the moral testing which naturally took place when they lived for some time under the eyes of the church and its leader;" or· "it is in substance the same thing as μὴ νεόφυτον, used regarding the choice of presbyters" (Hofmann) — It is quite wrong, with Luther ("and these are first to be tried") and others, to understand the words as if they meant that candidates were first to be tried in the affairs of the diaconate. — εἶτα διακονείτωσαν, ἀνέγκλητοι ὄντες] The participle expresses the condition under which they are to be admitted to the office of deacon Διακονεῖν, as applied definitely to the office of deacon, occurs only here, at ver 14, and in 1 Pet iv 11.

Ver 11. Γυναῖκας ὡσαύτως σεμνὰς κ τ.λ.] No further hint is given as to what women he is here speaking of; only it is to be observed that these instructions regarding them are inserted amongst the rules for the diaconate, since ver. 12 continues to speak of the latter. They must therefore, at all events, be regarded as women who stand in close relation to the deacons — either the wives of the deacons or the deaconesses. Mack's supposition, that they are the wives of the deacons *and of the bishops*, is quite arbitrary. The second view is found as early as in Chrysostom (γυναῖκας διακόνους φησί), Theophylact, Oecumenius, Grotius, and others; de

Wette, Wiesinger, and Hofmann also think it correct. The principal grounds for it are—(1) the word ὡσαύτως, which indicates that the apostle here passes (see ver. 8) to a new class of ecclesiastical persons (Wiesinger); and (2) the fact that the instructions given in this whole section are rather directions for election than exhortations to the persons named. On the other hand, the omisson of αὐτῶν (de Wette, Wiesinger) and the expression πιστὰς ἐν πᾶσιν, usually understood, as de Wette wrongly thinks, of conjugal fidelity, are of no weight. — Against this view, however, there are two circumstances which should be considered, viz., that the instruction regarding the deaconesses is inserted among those given to the deacons, and also that the apostle calls them quite generally γυναῖκες, instead of using the definite αἱ διάκονοι (comp. Rom. xvi 1). This makes it probable that by the γυναῖκες we should understand the deacons' wives (so, too, Plitt). The reason of the special exhortation would then be, not, as Heydenreich says, that even the domestic life of the deacons should be considered, but that the office of the deacons, consisting in the care of the poor and the sick, was of a kind in which their wives had to lend a helping hand. Hence we can explain why the wives of the bishops are not specially mentioned.[1] — μὴ διαβόλους] διάβολος, as an adjective: "slanderous," occurs only in the Pastoral Epistles, here and at 2 Tim iii. 3, Tit. ii. 3 — νηφαλίους] is not equivalent to μὴ οἴνῳ πόλλῳ προσεχούσας, ver 8 ; it is to be taken in the same sense as in ver. 2 (in opposition to Wiesinger, van Oosterzee). — πιστὰς ἐν πᾶσιν] " faithful in all things ;" ἐν πᾶσιν forbids us to limit the command of fidelity to any one sphere ; it is not merely faithfulness at home nor in the duties of the church that is meant.

Ver 12. The apostle returns to the deacons, and gives regarding their domestic life the same instructions as he gave in vv. 2–4 in regard to the bishops.

Ver. 13. To these instructions he adds in this verse a reason : οἱ γὰρ καλῶς διακονήσαντες (διακονεῖν is here and in ver. 10 used in the official sense) βαθμὸν ἑαυτοῖς καλὸν περι-

---

[1] Van Oosterzee's view is arbitrary, that *those* deacons' wives are meant who at the same time held the office of deaconess.

ποιοῦνται.¹ The word βαθμός, which occurs only here, denotes, like *gradus*, in the figurative sense, a degree of honour. As to what is to be understood by this, expositors are not agreed; but we may reject at once all explanations in which a comparative is put in place of the positive καλόν. This objection applies to the view that βαθμός denotes here the higher ecclesiastical office, the office of bishop (Jerome: "bonum hic pro gradu majori posuit; sunt enim minores [diaconi]," Bengel: "gradum ab humilitate diaconiae ad majora munera, in ecclesia. Qui in minore gradu fidelis est, ad majora promovetur," so, too, Theophylact, Erasmus, Beza, Grotius, Heumann, Heydenreich, Baur, Plitt, and others), which view, moreover, presupposes a regulation of rank altogether foreign to the apostolic age. The same objection applies to the view that βαθμὸς καλός is a higher stage of the life of faith, *i e.* an increase in Christian perfection. The expositors who hold by the positive καλός, interpret the idea, some of the future, others of the present life. The *former* understand by it " a higher stage of blessedness;" so Theodoret (τὸν τίμιον τοῦτον βαθμὸν ἐν τῷ μέλλοντι λήψονται βίῳ), Flatt, and others , the *latter* explain the expression as applying to "respect in the church;" so Calvin, Planck, Wegscheider, Leo, Matthies, and others — Heinrich, de Wette, and Wiesinger agree with the view of the former, only modifying it to mean not a stage of holiness, but "the expectancy of it." This modification is, however, unwarrantable, since the idea of "expectancy or claim" is imported. βαθμός means a stage; it cannot at the same time mean the claim to a stage; and if βαθμός must mean the claim to something, then there is nothing to indicate what the claim refers to — The decision between the two interpretations depends on the explanation of the words that follow: καὶ πολλὴν παρρησίαν ἐν πίστει τῇ ἐν Χριστῷ Ἰησοῦ] παρρησία means, in the first place, candour in speech; then more generally, bold courage in action, synonymous with ἄδεια

---

¹ Hofmann thinks that ver 13 is connected only with ver 12; because a man might fill the office of deacon well, though he lacked the qualities named in vv 8-10, but not if his house were badly managed. But that is not the case. Those qualities, not less than the one given in ver. 12, are the necessary conditions for filling the office of deacon well.

(Hesychius); and lastly, firm confidence in something; thus in reference to men, 2 Cor vii. 4 (πολλή μοι παρρησία πρὸς ὑμᾶς), or to God, viz. the confidence which the Christian in faith has in the saving grace of God; so in the Epistle to the Hebrews and in the First Epistle of John.[1] If βαθμός is to be referred to future blessedness, then παρρησία here, as in 1 John iii. 21, Heb. iv. 16, is confidence toward God. But in 1 John iii. 21 we have πρὸς τὸν Θεόν along with παρρησία, and in Heb. iv. 16 μετὰ παρρησίας is added to define more precisely the clause: προσερχώμεθα τῷ θρόνῳ τῆς χάριτος; as to the parallel passage in vi. 19, to which de Wette likewise appeals, the reference to the future life is distinctly expressed by the words εἰς τὸ μέλλον. Of all this there is nothing here; there is nothing, either here or with καλὸν βαθμόν, to direct us to the future life, nothing to indicate that with παρρησία we should supply πρὸς τὸν Θεόν, or the like. Hence it is more natural to refer these ideas to the sphere in which the διακονεῖν takes place, and to understand by βαθμός, respect in the church;[2] by παρρησία, confidence in their official labours These two things stand in closest relation to one another, since only *he* can possess right confidence in his office who is open to no just reproach, who is honoured for conducting himself well in the matters with which his office is concerned. Wiesinger, against this view, maintains that "the aorist (διακονήσαντες) makes the βαθμὸν ἑαυτ. καλ. περιπ appear to be the *final result* of the official labour;"[3] but if that were the case, the present περιποιοῦνται should not have been used, but the perfect; for the acquisition does not take place *after* the official labour, but during it — Certainly the aorist is somewhat strange; but it may mean that the βαθμὸς κ.τ.λ. is always the result of good service.[4] — The verb περι-

---

[1] Regarding Luther's translation of παρρησία by "joyfulness," see my *Comment. on the Epistles of John*, 3d ed , on 1 John iv. 17

[2] Van Oosterzee's opinion is manifestly wrong, that βαθμός is "a beautiful stage of the spiritual life, and also of eternal blessedness "

[3] The other grounds apply only to the exposition of Matthies, who understands by βαθμὸς καλός "the influential post;" by παρρησία, "the free play of thought and speech, a wide open field of spiritual activity." In this he certainly exceeds the meaning which may be assigned to these words

[4] Hofmann's explanation of βαθμός and παρρησία agrees in substance with that

ποιεῖσθαι, in the N. T. only here and in Acts xx. 28, has even in classical writers the meaning "gain for oneself." The dative ἑαυτοῖς is added to show clearly that he is speaking of the gain to the deacons themselves, and not to the congregation — ἐν πίστει τῇ ἐν Χριστῷ 'Ιησοῦ] is not to be joined with βαθμόν and παρρησίαν (van Oosterzee), but only with παρρησίαν[1] It is not the sphere in which, nor the object in regard to which, there is παρρησία (Heumann: "the boldness to teach the Christian faith even in public;" Wegscheider: "free activity for Christianity, or a greater sphere for the spread of Christianity"); but it denotes the παρρησία as Christian, as rooted in Christian faith The construction of πίστις with ἐν following it, is found also in 2 Tim. iii 15; Gal. iii. 26; Eph. i. 15, Col. i. 4 (only that in these passages there is no article before ἐν, while there is one before πίστις; on the other hand, comp. Acts xx 21, xxvi. 18). This construction may be explained to mean that Christ is the object of faith already apprehended; the believer not only has Christ before him, but he lives in communion with Him.

Vv. 14, 15. The apostle has come here to a resting-point, since he has brought to an end his instructions regarding some of the chief points to be noticed in the affairs of the church; but, before passing to any new matter, he casts a glance back on the instructions he has given, and tells what was the occasion of his giving them — ταῦτά σοι γράφω] Bengel's explanation: "ταῦτα, i.e. totam epistolam," in which Hofmann agrees,[2] is so far right, that ταῦτα refers rather to the instructions that precede (from ii 1 onward). — ἐλπίζων ἐλθεῖν πρός σε τάχιον] ἐλπίζων does not give the real ("hoping," Matthies), but the adversative ground (Leo. Part ἐλπίζων per καίπερ seu similem

given here. He is wrong, however, in asserting that the deacons do not acquire both *during*, but only after their tenure of office If the latter were the case, the means by which it takes place would not be given

[1] Hofmann, indeed, holds even this connection of ideas to be unsuitable, but we do not see why the παρρησία may not be marked as Christian, as rooted in faith in Christ To connect it with what follows, would be to suppose that the apostle lays emphasis on a point, which to Timothy would be self-evident

[2] Hofmann's assertion, that the reference of ταῦτα to what precedes is forbidden by the present γράφω (for which we should have had ἔγραφα), is contradicted by 1 Cor. iv 14, xiv. 37, 2 Cor. xiii. 10; Gal. i. 20; also by 1 John ii. 1

particulam esse resolvendum, nexus orationis docet; so, too, Wiesinger, van Oosterzee, Plitt). The real ground is given by the following ἵνα. Hofmann asserts, but does not prove, that this view does not accord with the following δέ. Hofmann finds that ἐλπίζων only expresses an accompaniment of the act of writing, and that it was added "lest Timothy should infer from the sending of an epistle that the apostle meant to leave him for some time in Ephesus;" but in this he imports a motive of which the context furnishes no hint. — τάχιον (comp. on this form, Winer, p. 67 [E T. p. 81]; Buttmann, p. 24) is here taken by most expositors as a pure positive "soon;" the comparative sense (according to Winer, pp 227 f. [E. T. p 304]), though in the background, has not wholly disappeared. "sooner" (not "than the arrival of this letter," or "than thou wilt have need of these instructions," Winer) "than is or was to be expected."—In spite of this hope, the apostle's arrival might possibly be longer delayed, and this possibility had induced him to impart his instructions by writing, lest Timothy should be without them. — ἐὰν δὲ βραδύνω (the verb only here and at 2 Pet. iii 9), ἵνα εἰδῇς πῶς δεῖ ἐν οἴκῳ Θεοῦ ἀναστρέφεσθαι] πῶς δεῖ ἀναστρέφεσθαι refers not so much to the Christian life in general, as to behaviour in church life, viz. in divine service and in church arrangements. This limitation is clearly indicated by the connection with what precedes, the ταῦτα referring us back (in opposition to Hofmann). Its subject is either Timothy, in which case σέ is to be supplied (Luther: "how thou shouldst walk," so, too, Wiesinger), or no definite subject should be supplied. "how one should walk."[1] Both explanations are possible in language and in fact; but the second may be preferred, because Paul

[1] The impersonal δεῖ is usually joined with the accusative and infinitive, the infinitive denoting the thing, the accusative the person who must do the action expressed by the verb. More frequently the person is not named, but is easily supplied from the context, as e g in Matt xxiii. 23, where ὑμᾶς, in Luke xii. 12, where again ὑμᾶς, and in Luke xv 32, where σέ is to be supplied Hofmann is therefore wrong in asserting that there is no linguistic justification for supplying σέ here, where εἰδῇς precedes Sometimes, however, δεῖ refers to no particular person, so John iv. 20 ὅπου προσκυνεῖν δεῖ, Acts v. 29 πειθαρχεῖν δεῖ Θιῷ, xv 5: δεῖ περιτέμνειν αὐτούς; Tit. 1. 11: οὓς δεῖ ἐπιστομίζειν; the δεῖ in that case corresponds to the English "one must." It is arbitrary, with Hofmann, to supply τινά here, and understand by it one who "has to govern a house of God."

in the preceding part (to which ταῦτα refers) did not say what Timothy was to do, but what arrangements were to prevail in the church; Hofmann thinks differently, as he understands ταῦτα of the whole epistle. The expression οἶκος Θεοῦ denotes properly the temple at Jerusalem (Matt. xxi. 13), then also the O. T. people as the church in which God had His dwelling (Heb. iii. 2, 5); in Christian usage it is the N. T. people in whom the dwelling of God has been fully realized; Heb iii. 6 (Heb. x. 21); 1 Pet. iv. 17; synonymous with it are the expressions: κατοικητήριον Θεοῦ, Eph. ii. 22; ναὸς Θεοῦ, 1 Cor. iii. 16; 2 Cor vi. 16.—To elucidate the symbolic expression, Paul adds. ἥτις ἐστὶν ἐκκλησία Θεοῦ ζῶντος] The pronoun ἥτις (= " seeing it ") makes the explanatory sentence emphatic, by indicating why there should be such behaviour in the house of God as Paul had prescribed (which Hofmann denies); and the reason is not simply that it is an ἐκκλησία, *i.e.* a church, and as such has necessarily certain definite ordinances, but still more definitely because it is a church of God, of the *living* God, who as such esteems highly His ordinances in His church.—There follow in simple apposition the words: στύλος καὶ ἑδραίωμα τῆς ἀληθείας] These words are in apposition to ἐκκλησία Θ. ζ, and as such are rightly explained by the older[1] and most of recent commentators (Luther, Melanchthon, Calvin, Beza, Mack, Matthies, de Wette, Wiesinger, Hofmann, now, too, by van Oosterzee, 3d ed.[2]). Some Protestant commentators, however, influenced by their polemic against the Catholic idea of the church, have taken these words as the beginning of the following sentence (first, in the edition of the N. T. at Basel, 1540, 1545 ; later, Bengel, Mosheim, Heydenreich, Flatt, formerly also van Oosterzee). The reasons against this construction are—(1) That the new thought would be taken up in a very abrupt and sudden manner, while by connecting it with the previous words, the train of thought is suitable and natural; (2) That " grammatically

---

[1] Theodore of M rightly says. ἐκκλησίας οὐ τοὺς οἴκους λέγει τοὺς εὐκτηρίους κατὰ τὴν τῶν πολλῶν συνήθειαν, ἀλλὰ τῶν πιστῶν τὸν σύλλογον, ὅθεν καὶ στύλον αὐτὴν καὶ ἑδραίωμα τ. ἀλ. ἐκάλεσεν, ὡς ἂν ἐν αὐτῇ τῆς ἀληθείας τὴν σύστασιν ἐχούσης.

[2] Van Oosterzee is, however, inclined to conjecture that "there is here a corruption of the text which cannot now be restored with certainty."

the third defining term, simply adjectival, ὁμολ. μέλα, cannot well be placed in co-ordination with two predicates like στύλος and ἑδραίωμα" (Wiesinger, following Schleiermacher); and (3) That, whereas τὸ τῆς εὐσεβείας μυστήριον is nothing else than the ἀλήθεια, this construction would make the former designate the latter as στύλος καὶ ἑδρ., which would clearly be unsuitable. There is manifestly nothing to be said for the opinion of some commentators,[1] that by στ κ ἑδρ. we are to understand Timothy.[2] — στύλος in the figurative sense occurs only here and at Gal ii. 9, Rev. iii. 12 The οἶκος Θεοῦ is called στύλος τῆς ἀληθείας, inasmuch as the pillar supports and bears the roof resting on it (see Meyer on Gal. ii. 9), but not "inasmuch as it serves to elevate something and make it manifest" (Hofmann). The same idea is expressed by the second word ἑδραίωμα, the base, foundation (similarly θεμέλιος, 2 Tim. ii. 19), a word which is only used here in the N T. The thought that the divine truth is supported and borne by the church, has nothing startling when we remember that the church, as the οἶκος Θεοῦ, has the Spirit of God, which is the Spirit of truth; the Spirit of truth, therefore, is its indwelling, all-penetrating principle of life, by which it stands in closest communion with its head.[3] But if the church is set up to be the preserver of divine truth, it is all the more important that all should be well-ordered in it These words stand, therefore, in close connection with what precedes, but, at the same time, they make the transition to what follows, where the apostle in a few brief characteristics gives the nature of the truth, that he may from this point return to his polemic against the heretics, and continue it further.

[1] Gregory of Nyssa (de Vita Mosis) οὐ μόνον Πέτρος καὶ Ἰάκωβος καὶ Ἰωάννης στῦλοι τῆς ἐκκλησίας εἰσι ... ὁ θεῖος ἀπόστολος καὶ τὸν Τιμόθεον στῦλον καλὸν ἐτεκτήνατο, ποιήσας αὐτὸν, καθὼς φησὶ τῇ ἰδίᾳ φωνῇ, στῦλον καὶ ἑδραίωμα τῆς ἐκκλησίας.
[2] Though Chrysostom construes rightly, he yet inverts the meaning of the sentence οὐχ ὡς ἐκεῖνος ὁ Ἰουδαϊκὸς οἶκος θ., τοῦτο γάρ ἐστι τὸ συνέχον τὴν πίστιν καὶ τὸ κήρυγμα· ἡ γὰρ ἀλήθειά ἐστι τῆς ἐκκλησίας καὶ στῦλος καὶ ἑδραίωμα
[3] Wiesinger rightly calls attention to the distinction which should be made between "the truth as it is in itself, and the truth as it is acknowledged in the world," and then says "in the former respect it needs no support, but bears itself, in the latter, it needs the church as its support, as its bearer and preserver." If the Catholic Church has drawn wrong conclusions from the apostle's words, it has itself to blame, and not the apostle.

Ver 16. Καὶ ὁμολογουμένως μέγα ἐστὶ τὸ τῆς εὐσεβείας μυστήριον] καί connects what follows with the preceding words, and in such a way as to emphasize the following predicate. — ὁμολογουμένως] which only occurs here, means neither " manifestly " (Luther), nor " according to the song of praise " (Mack), nor even " correspondingly " (Hofmann [1]); but: " as is acknowledged" (comp. 4 Macc. vi. 31, vii. 16, xvi. 1; Josephus, Antiq. i. 10. 2, ii. 9. 6). — μέγα] comp Eph. v. 32 (καὶ τὸ μυστήριον τοῦτο μέγα ἐστίν), has the sense of " important, significant." — The subject of the sentence τὸ τῆς εὐσεβείας μυστήριον, is a paraphrase of the ἀλήθεια in the preceding verse. It is so called by the apostle, because, as the substance of the Christian fear of God, or piety, it is hidden from the world: the sense is the same, therefore, as that of τὸ μυστήριον τῆς πίστεως in ver. 9 It is wrong to translate it, as Luther does: " the blessed secret," or to explain it: " the doctrine which leads to godliness." Wiesinger is incorrect in explaining it: " a secret accessible only to godliness;" and Hofmann in saying: " the truth which is of such a nature as to produce godliness where it finds acceptance." — The purport—i.e. the christological purport—is now given in the next clauses, Paul laying stress on it on account of the polemical tendency of the epistle against the heretics (chap. iv.), whose theology and Christology were in contradiction with the gospel. — As to the construction of these clauses, there would be no difficulty with the reading Θεός. If ὅ be read, it must relate to μυστήριον, which also might be the construction with ὅς. According to the Vulgate (sacramentum quod manifestatum est), the latter is the construction adopted by the Latin Fathers who understood Christ to be the μυστήριον,[2]— an interpretation quite unjustifiable and unsuitable to the general train of thought. Several expositors (Mangold, Hofmann, and others)

[1] Hofmann, without reason, takes objection to the sense given to the apostle's remark, that believers acknowledged the secret of godliness to be great. But if this thought is meaningless here, not less is the one he substitutes " to the greatness of the house of God corresponds the greatness of the mystery of piety."

[2] Even Buttmann is of this opinion, as he quotes this passage (μυστήριον, ὅς ἐφανερώθη) under the rule (p. 242), that the relative agrees with the natural gender of the preceding substantive.

assume the first clause: ὅς ... σαρκί, to be the subject, and the other five clauses to form the predicate; but "on account of the parallelism, that is not advisable" (Winer, p. 519 [E. T. p 736]). It is much more natural from their similar form to regard all six clauses as co-ordinate. Then the subject to which ὅς relates is not named; but, according to the purport of the various clauses, it can be none other than Christ. This curious omission may be thus accounted for; the sentence has been taken from a formula of confession, or better, from an old Christian hymn, as its metrical and euphonious character seems to indicate; comp. Rambach's *Anthologie christl. Gesange aus allen Jahrh. d Kirche*, I. 33, and Winer, p. 547 [E. T. p. 797]. This view is also adopted by Heydenreich, Mack, de Wette, Wiesinger, van Oosterzee, Plitt — The opinion of Matthies is untenable, that the apostle does not name Christ expressly, in order to maintain the character of τὸ μυστήριον (in the sense : Acknowledged great, etc,... he who is revealed, etc), and that this absolute use of the relative pronoun is found elsewhere in the N. T. In the passages quoted by him, Rom. ii. 23, 1 Cor. vii. 37, John i 46, iii. 34, 1 John i. 3, the pronoun has not the absolute meaning alleged by him. The first clause runs: ἐφανερώθη ἐν σαρκί] ἐφανερώθη is often used of Christ's appearance on earth, of His becoming man, 1 John i. 2, iii. 5; it presupposes a previous concealment,[1] and consequently the pre-existence of Christ as the eternal Logos. — 'Ἐν σαρκί] (comp. 1 John iv. 2 : ἐληλυθὼς ἐν σαρκί ; Rom. viii. 3 : ἐν ὁμοιώματι σαρκὸς ἁμαρτίας) denotes the human nature in which Christ appeared; John i. 14 : ὁ λόγος σὰρξ ἐγένετο. — With this first clause the second stands in contrast · ἐδικαιώθη ἐν πνεύματι] means (as in Matt. xi. 19 ; Luke vii. 35): to be shown to be such a one as He is in nature; here, therefore, the sense is: He was shown in His divine glory (as the Logos or eternal Son of God), which was veiled by the σάρξ. 'Ἐν πνεύματι is contrasted with ἐν σαρκί, the latter denoting the earthly, human manner of His appearing, the former the inner principle which formed the basis of His life. Though ἐν with πνεύματι has not entirely

---

[1] Hence the same word is used also of the resurrection and second coming of Christ.

lost its proper meaning, yet it shades off into the idea of the means used, in so far as the spirit revealed in Him was the means of showing His true nature.¹ It would be wrong to separate here the πνεῦμα from His person, and to understand by it the spirit proceeding from Him and imparted to His own; it is rather the living spiritual principle dwelling in Him and working out from Him (so, too, Plitt). — Chrysostom diverges from this exposition, and explains ἐδικαιώθη by: δόλον οὐκ ἐποίησεν, ὅπερ ὁ προφήτης λέγει· ὃς ἁμαρτίαν οὐκ ἐποίησε; and Bengel takes the meaning of the expression to be that Christ bore the sins of the world (peccata peccatorum tulit . . et justitiam aeternam sibi suisque asseruit); but both views import ideas which are here out of place. The expression ἐν πνεύματι has also found very varying interpretations. Instead of πνεῦμα being taken in its real sense, particular elements of it in the life of Christ, or particular modes of revealing the πνεῦμα, have been fixed upon, or πνεῦμα has been taken simply of the divine nature of Christ.² — ὤφθη ἀγγέλοις] The right meaning of this third clause also can only be got from a faithful consideration of the words. The word ὤφθη is in the N. T. frequently joined with the dative, Matt. xvii. 3; Luke i. 11; Acts vii. 2; 1 Cor. xv. 5–8; Heb. ix. 28, etc. In all these passages it is not the simple "was seen," but "was revealed" or "appeared;" it always presupposes the activity of the thing seen. — From the analogy of these passages, we must think here of Christ going to those to whom

¹ Baur is wrong in explaining ἐν πνεύματι "as spirit." This cannot be justified by exegesis, and hence Baur contents himself with the mere assertion that it is so.

² The older expositors take πνεῦμα to denote particularly Christ's miracles (Theodoret: ἀπεδείχθη διὰ τῶν θαυμάτων καὶ ἀπεφάνθη, ὅτι Θεὸς ἀληθὴς καὶ Θεοῦ υἱός). Others apply it to the Spirit imparted to Him in baptism, others, to the outpouring of the Spirit at Pentecost, others, to Christ's resurrection as the most glorious work of the Spirit (so Heydenreich in particular). Akin to this view is that of Hofmann, who says that πνεῦμα is "that which quickens, makes alive," and deduces from this "that spirit changed the existence of Christ in the flesh . . into something that had its nature from the Spirit," and explains ἰδικ. ἐν πν. as relating to the justification He received through His resurrection. All these explanations fall to the ground when it is observed that the context contains no reference to any such special fact. Glassius explains it thus: Justus declaratus est et filius Dei comprobatus in Spiritu i. e. per deitatem suam, cujus vi miracula fecit.

He became visible, so that all explanations which take ὤφθη merely as "was seen" are to be rejected — In the N. T. ἄγγελοι is especially applied to angels; in itself the word may also denote human messengers (comp. Jas. ii. 25). To take it here in this latter sense (which Hofmann does), as denoting the apostles to whom Christ appeared after His resurrection, is impossible, because nothing, not even the article, is used here to point to them in particular. If, then, ἄγγελοι can only mean angels, it is most natural to take ὤφθη ἀγγέλοις of the ascension, by which Christ — as the Glorified One—was made manifest to angels (so, too, Plitt). Still there is nothing here to lay stress on the ascension (as is done in the sixth clause); the point is, that He who was justified ἐν πνεύματι presented Himself to the angels in His glory. — Baur, indeed, in gnostic fashion interprets the passage of Christ as passing through the various series of aeons, but it is clear that the words neither demand nor even justify such a view. No less arbitrary is de Wette's opinion, that probably the ὠφθῆναι ἀγγέλοις relates to a supernatural scene differing from the ascension, and forming the antithesis to the descent into hell. — The very form of the expression shows that we are not to think of appearances of angels at various moments in the earthly life of Christ, as some expositors suppose. More noteworthy is an explanation given by Chrysostom and approved by some later expositors, especially by Matthies and Wiesinger. Chrysostom says · ὤφθη ἀγγέλοις· ὥστε καὶ ἄγγελοι μεθ᾽ ἡμῶν εἶδον τὸν υἱὸν τοῦ Θεοῦ, πρότερον οὐχ ὁρῶντες. Theodoret's expression is still more pointed : τὴν γὰρ ἀόρατον τῆς θεότητος φύσιν οὐδὲ ἐκεῖνοι ἑώρων, σαρκωθέντα δὲ ἐθεάσαντο. Matthies appeals to passages which he thinks are elucidated by the words, passages where Christ is said to have been manifested as . . head to all things in heaven and on earth, Eph. i. 20 ff, iii. 10, iv. 8 ff.; Col. i. 15 ff, ii. 10, 15 ; Heb. i 6 ff. But, though Christ's lordship over all is spoken of in such passages, it is not said that Christ was made manifest to the angels only by means of His incarnation. The only passage which might be quoted here is Eph. iii. 10, which, however, rather declares that to the angels the eternal decree of the divine love or of God's wisdom was to be made known διὰ τῆς ἐκκλησίας. But *such* cannot possibly be the meaning of ὤφθη ἀγγέλοις Wiesinger simply explains it: "the angels saw the σαρκωθέντα on earth;" but obviously the sentence is meant to express something which befell not men, but *angels* — ἐκηρύχθη ἐν ἔθνεσιν] for ἐκηρύχθη, comp. Phil. i. 15; and for ἐν ἔθνεσιν, Matt. xxviii. 19. There is no good reason for taking ἔθνη here as relating not to the nations in general, but, as Hofmann thinks, to the heathen exclusive of the Jews.[1] — ἐπιστεύθη ἐν κόσμῳ] ἐπιστεύθη is not, with some expositors, to be explained by ἐδικαιώθη: "He has been testified" (viz by the miracles of the apostles), or by "fidem sibi fecit" ("he gained belief for Himself"); it is to be taken in its proper meaning. The word κόσμος has the same general meaning as the preceding ἔθνη; van Oosterzee is wrong in thinking that it ought to be taken here in an ethical sense. — "Jesus is personally the subject-matter of preaching and of faith" (Hofmann). — ἀνελήφθη ἐν δόξῃ] Mark xvi. 19; Acts i 11 (Acts x. 16), where the same verb joined with εἰς οὐρανόν is used of Christ's ascension. This supports the opinion of most expositors, that the same fact is mentioned here. — ἐν δόξῃ] may be taken as an adverbial adjunct equivalent to ἐνδόξως (similarly 2 Cor. iii. 8; Col. iii. 4); but in that case the expression of this sixth clause would be quite out of keeping with the others. Wahl takes the expression per attractionem pro . ἀνελ. εἰς δόξαν καὶ ἐστὶν ἐν δόξῃ, which is the only right exposition.[2] The apostle did not write εἰς δόξαν, but ἐν δόξῃ, to show that Christ not only entered into glory, but abides for ever in it (so, too, Wiesinger, van Oosterzee). Still we cannot go so far as Matthies, who says that the result rather than the act of the transition is here mentioned; the expression with forcible brevity includes both points. De Wette's assertion, too, is quite arbitrary, that Paul is speaking here not of the historical ascension, but of a heavenly occurrence — In what relation now do these six clauses stand towards each other?—

---

[1] We cannot, in any case, see how "the sentence is emptied of its meaning" by regarding Israel as included in the idea of ἔθνη.

[2] Strange to say, Hofmann disputes this, on the ground that Jesus "was not received into glory, but into the celestial sphere" He appeals for this to Heb. i. 3, which is utterly from the point.

We cannot help seeing that there is a definite order in their succession. It is beyond doubt chronological, since the second clause does not relate to the outpouring of the Holy Spirit, and the last points more to Christ's life in glory than to the historical ascension. But, at the same time, we can recognise a close relation between the clauses. Matthies, de Wette, Wiesinger, and Hofmann have adopted three groups, each containing two clauses; but, though ἀγγέλοις and ἔθνεσιν are contrasted, still this arrangement would separate between the fourth and fifth clauses, whose connection Theodoret rightly points out. οὐκ ἐκηρύχθη μόνον, ἀλλὰ καὶ ἐπιστεύθη. Besides, in order to make the correspondence complete, ἐκηρύχθη ἐν ἔθνεσιν should have come before ὤφθη ἀγγέλοις. It is more correct, therefore, to divide the whole into two parts, each with three clauses, the two first in each case referring to what took place on earth, the third to what took place in heaven (so, too, Plitt[1]).

---

[1] Baur maintains that in these six clauses every two form a contrast, the one being more gnostic, the other more anti-gnostic. But in that case the author of the epistle would, in the second part, have very strangely given up the order observable in the first. Besides, of all the clauses, the third has by far the most resemblance to Gnosticism.

CHAPTER IV.

VER. 1. πλάνοις] For this, many cursives and Fathers have πλάνης, which, however, is only a correction, perhaps after 1 John iv. 6. —Ver 2. Instead of the form κεκαυτηριασμένων (*Rec.* Tisch), we should probably, after A L ℵ, read κεκαυστηριασμένων (Lachm. smaller ed, Buttm). — For ἰδίαν συνείδησιν, which is supported by the weightiest authorities, D* has (in Matthaei, E) συνείδησιν ἑαυτῶν. — Ver. 6. For Ἰησοῦ Χριστοῦ, so many important authorities (A D F G, many cursives, etc.) have Χριστοῦ Ἰησοῦ, that the latter must be held the right reading. — τῆς καλῆς διδασκαλίας] for which some cursives, etc., have τῇ καλῇ διδασκαλίᾳ, which may have arisen from a belief that these words are co-ordinate with τοῖς λόγοις. — For the *Rec* ᾗ παρηκολούθηκας (Tisch.), Lachm. smaller ed., and Buttm, following A 80, have adopted the gen ἧς παρηκ, an attraction seldom occurring, but not without examples; see Winer, p. 148 [E. T. p. 204] — Ver. 8. In ℵ the preposition πρός is wanting before ὀλίγον; possibly πρὸς ὀλίγον may have been formed on the analogy of the πρὸς πάντα. — For the *Rec.* ἐπαγγελίαν, which is found in the weightiest authorities, and is received by nearly all critics and editors, K ℵ, many cursives have the plural ἐπαγγελίας This is defended by Matthaei and Rinck as the original reading, but is disputed by Reiche (*Comment. crit.* I pp. 389 f.) It is at least possible that the singular found its way into the text as a correction — Ver 10 καὶ κοπιῶμεν, *Rec*, supported by F G K, most cursives, etc (Tisch 7); in A C D ℵ 17, 47, *al.*, Syr. Arr Copt. Arm Vulg. etc, καί is wanting, and is therefore omitted by Lachm Buttm. and Tisch. 8. Its genuineness is very doubtful. — Instead of the *Rec* ὀνειδιζόμεθα (supported by D L, most versions, Theodoret, etc, Tisch 7), A C F G K ℵ, *al.*, have the reading ἀγωνιζόμεθα, which has been adopted by Lachm. Buttm. Tisch 8. The authorities give a preference to the latter reading, yet it may have arisen from Col. i. 29. Reiche defends the *Rec.*; we cannot decide with certainty which is original; see further in the exposition of the verse. — Ver. 12. Between ἐν ἀγάπῃ and ἐν πίστει the *Rec.* has ἐν πνεύματι; rightly withdrawn from the text as not genuine by Griesb. Scholz, Lachm. Tisch, following the weightiest authorities (A C D F G 31, 47, 70, 71, *al.*, Syr. utr Erp. Copt. etc., Clemens,

Chrys. etc.); comp. Reiche (*Comment crit.* I. p. 392). — Ver. 15. For ἐν πᾶσιν, Lachm. Buttm and Tisch. rightly adopted πᾶσιν (*without* ἐν), after A C D F G ℵ 17, 31, *al.*, Syr. Erp. Copt. etc., Clem. Chrys. etc It is defended, too, by Reiche as the original reading; ἐν appears to have been inserted from the analogy of Rom. i. 19, 1 Cor. xi. 19.

Ver. 1. In the first five verses of this chapter, Paul speaks of the heretics, directing special attention in ver. 3 to one point in their doctrine. — τὸ δὲ πνεῦμα ῥητῶς λέγει] The δέ connects this verse with the beginning of iii. 16, and connects it by way of contrast. Τὸ πνεῦμα is the Holy Spirit, as the source of prophecy. To explain the expression by οἱ πνευματικοί (Heydenreich) is inaccurate. Paul goes back here to the fundamental basis of all prophecy. — ῥητῶς (ἅπαξ λεγ.) means: "*in express words*," and is used particularly with quotations [1] Heydenreich is inaccurate in explaining it as equivalent to σαφῶς, φανερῶς; Luther: "distinctly." The apostle, then, appeals here to a prophecy of the Spirit expressly worded. Such a prophecy of the future apostasy lay before him in many utterances, both of Christ and of others; besides, the Spirit declared them to the apostle himself.—Leo is wrong: animus mihi praesagit. — ὅτι ἐν ὑστέροις καιροῖς ἀποστήσονταί τινες τῆς πίστεως] We might readily take ὕστεροι καιροί here as equivalent to ἔσχατοι καιροί (comp 2 Tim. iii. 1 : ἔσχαται ἡμέραι; 1 Pet. i 5 : καιρὸς ἔσχατος; 2 Pet. iii. 3; Jude, ver 18; in Ignatius, *Ep ad Ephes.* c xi.: ἔσχατοι καιροί); but we must not overlook the difference between the two expressions. The former points simply to the future, the latter to the last time of the future, immediately preceding the completion of God's kingdom and the second coming of Christ (so, too, van Oosterzee, Hofmann). It is unsuitable to press καιρός here in the sense of "the fitting time," and to translate it with Matthies: "in the fitting time hereafter."—Τινές are not the heretics, but those who are led away from the faith by the heretics The apostasy belonged to the future, but the heresy to the present. Hofmann thinks differently, assigning

---

[1] [Huther must mean that ῥητῶς is ἅπαξ λεγ in the N. T , for it is found in Sext. Empir *adv. Log* i. 8 ὁ Ξενοφῶν ῥητῶς φησίν, also in Strabo, i. p. 4 B, and Polybius, ii 23 5.—Tr.]

the heresy also to the future, though the apostle's expression does not warrant this.[1] We must not, however, with Otto, infer that in the apostle's time the heretics were still outside the church.—ἀποστήσονται τῆς πίστεως] "This sentence forms the antithesis to what has preceded, iii. 15, 16" (Wiesinger); for the expression, comp. Luke viii. 13; Heb. iii. 12; Wisd. iii. 10; 1 Macc. i. 15, and other passages.—προσέχοντες] comp. 1. 4; the partic. tells how the apostasy is brought about.—πνεύμασι πλάνοις] the πνεύματα πλάνα are in contrast with the πνεῦμα in ver. 1; and the former are as little to be identified with the heretics, as the latter with the prophets (Wolf: spirituales seductores, i.e. doctores seducentes). The πνεύματα are rather the active spiritual powers hidden in the heretics, the tools and servants of the devil. As the truth is one, so also is its principle one: τὸ πνεῦμα τῆς ἀληθείας. Error on the other hand is manifold, and is supported by a plurality of spirits, who may, however, be regarded as a unity: τὸ πνεῦμα τῆς πλάνης, 1 John iv. 6. — These πνεύματα are called πλάνα, because they seduce man from the truth to falsehood; comp 2 John ver. 7.— καὶ διδασκαλίαις δαιμονίων] δαιμονίων is not the objective (Heydenreich: "doctrines regarding demons, a characteristic of Essene-gnostic heretics who spoke so much of the higher world of spirits, of aeons," etc.), but the subjective genitive (Wiesinger, van Oosterzee, Winer, p. 176 [E. T. p. 233]). The δαιμόνια are the source of the doctrines which are opposed to the truth, of the σοφία δαιμονιώδης (Jas iii. 15); comp. Col. ii. 22. It is wrong to suppose that the δαιμόνια are the heretics themselves As with πνεῦμα in ver. 1, Paul goes back here to the inner grounds; the διδασκαλίαι proceeding from these form the opposite of the διδασκαλία ἡ τοῦ σωτῆρος ἡμῶν Θεοῦ.[2]

Ver. 2. Ἐν ὑποκρίσει ψευδολόγων] Leo· "errarunt sine dubio, qui genitivos, qui sequuntur, ψευδολόγων, κεκαυτηριασ-

---

[1] Plitt is not wrong in observing that "the errors now described by the author were no longer matters purely of the future, they were already appearing"

[2] The expression δαιμόνια occurs often in the synoptic Gospels; in John only in the singular Paul has it only here and in 1 Cor x. Otto uses this last fact as a proof that the two epistles were contemporaneous, but he is wrong; the reference is different in the two cases, in the passage of 1 Cor. it is not the "gnostic" heresy that is spoken of.

μένων, κωλυόντων, lege appositionis, junctos esse dicebant cum voc. δαιμονίων;" but we must also reject Leo's opinion, that ἐν ὑποκρ. ψευδ. was added to the previous statement as a second characteristic of the heretics, meaning: eadem simulantes, quae simulare solent homines ψευδολόγοι, etc.; ψευδολ, κεκαυτηρ., κωλυόντων denote the heretics themselves, and not those whom they imitated. To regard the genitive ψευδολόγων as dependent on διδασκαλίαις, and ἐν ὑποκρίσει as defining more precisely the substantive following it (Estius. doctrinis, inquam, hominum in hypocrisi loquentium mendacium), would make a double difficulty of construction. Nor can Luther's translation be defended: "by means of such as are speakers of lies in hypocrisy." Ἐν ὑποκρίσει is either to be taken with ἀποστήσονται (so Bengel: Constr. cum deficient; hypocrisis ea, quae est falsiloquorum, illos auferet; τινες aliqui, illi, sunt seducti; falsiloqui, seductores; falsiloquorum, genitivus, unice pendet ab hypocrisi), or, still better, with προσέχοντες (Wiesinger, van Oosterzee, Plitt). The objection of Matthies, which agrees with Leo's explanation, that in that case we should have had instead of ἐν either διά or ἕνεκα with the article, is contradicted by the usage of the N. T. In the N. T. ἐν is not seldom used with the instrument, and in regard to the article there prevails a greater freedom of use than in classic Greek Hofmann strangely combines δαιμονίων ἐν ὑποκρίσει ψευδολόγων into one idea, explaining δαιμονίων to be an adjective with ψευδολόγων, and ἐν ὑποκρίσει also as a qualification of ψευδολόγων in the sense of "hypocritical."[1] — The hypocrisy of the heretics consisted in giving themselves, in obedience to a false spiritualism (see ver. 3), the appearance of a spiritually-inspired life. — The word ψευδολόγοι ("liars," Luther) occurs only here in the N. T. In sense it is equivalent to ψευδοδιδάσκαλος, 2 Pet. ii. 1, and ψευδοπροφήτης, 1 John iv. 1 (comp ματαιολόγοι, Tit. i. 10). — κεκαυτηριασμένων τὴν ἰδίαν συνείδησιν] On the grammatical structure, comp. vi. 5

---

[1] Hofmann opposes the view here put forward that ἐν ὑποκρίσει is to be taken with προσέχοντες, and makes the curious remark that ἐν "can only introduce that which is of use to me for doing something, not that which makes me do a thing only in so far as it is of use to another to determine me to do it' (¹).

(διεφθαρμένοι ἄνθρωποι τὸν νοῦν; the more precise definition is not infrequently added in the accusative, see Winer, p 215 [E. T. p. 287]), "*branded as to their conscience*" (Wahl: κεκαυτηριασμένην ἔχοντες τὴν ἰδ συνείδησιν). — It is to be noted that the καυτηριάζειν (cauterio notare) was not only done on slaves "ut facilius possent discerni" (Leo), but was also a form of punishment for marking criminals as such (comp. Meyer on Gal. vi. 17). As these bore the brand on their forehead,—that is the figurative expression,—so do the heretics bear it on their conscience, *i.e.* they bear in their conscience the knowledge of their guilt. Theophylact rightly: ἐπεὶ συνίσασιν ἑαυτοῖς ἀκαθαρσίαν πολλήν, διὰ τοῦτο τὸ συνειδὸς αὐτῶν ἀνεξαλείπτους ἔχει τοὺς καυτῆρας τοῦ ῥυπαροῦ βίου. Theodoret (followed by Heumann) wrongly understands the apostle's expression to denote moral deadness: νέκρωσις καὶ ἀποβολὴ πάσης αἰσθήσεως, ἐσχάτη ἀναλγησία· ὁ γὰρ τοῦ καυτῆρος τόπος νεκρωθεὶς τὴν προτέραν αἴσθησιν ἀποβάλλει. The apostle does not blame the heretics for having a conscience completely blunted, but for acting against their conscience; comp. Tit. iii. 11 : αὐτοκατάκριτος. — On ἰδίαν, de Wette remarks that it is not emphatic here; but it is not improbable that the apostle had some such side-thought in mind as Bengel suggests : dum aliis tamen urgent (so, too, Wiesinger).

Ver. 3. Further description of the heretics. — Κωλυόντων γαμεῖν] Since even the Essenes and Therapeutae made abstinence from marriage a necessary condition of a holy life, there is no ground whatever for supposing that this description proves the heretics to have been followers of the later Christian gnostics (especially of Marcion, according to Baur). — ἀπέχεσθαι βρωμάτων] similar construction in ii. 12, 1 Cor. xiv. 34; the infinitive is dependent on the κελευόντων implied in κωλυόντων (= κελευόντων μή), see Winer, p. 578 [E. T p 777], Buttmann, p. 343. Isidor of Pelusium unnecessarily corrects ἀπέχεσθαι into ἀντέχεσθαι In the Epistle to the Romans (chap. xiv.) the apostle speaks of weak brethren's anxiety in regard to the enjoyment of many meats, and the heretics combated in the Epistle to the Colossians are distinctly described as forbidding the enjoyment of certain meats ; but neither here nor in these passages is it said what kinds of meat were forbidden, nor why (comp. also Tit. i. 14, 15). It is, however, not improbable—if we follow the analogy of later gnostics—that animal food, and perhaps also wine (Col ii. 6 : ἐν βρώσει ἢ ἐν πόσει), are specially meant. There is no indication that the prohibition was founded on gnostic dualism (van Oosterzee); it is more probable that the false asceticism of the heretics was connected with the Mosaic distinction between clean and unclean (comp. Tit. i. 15); so also Wiesinger.[1]—In the Epistle to the Colossians (ii. 22) the apostle indicates the perversity of such a prohibition in a brief relative clause; and so also here. — ἃ ὁ Θεὸς ἔκτισεν εἰς μετάληψιν κ τ.λ.] Different answers have been given to the question why only the second, and not also the first error is refuted. It may have been that the heretics did not make abstinence from marriage, as they made abstinence from certain meats, a command laid on all. It may have been, too, "that the prohibition to marry stood in manifest contradiction with the divine order of creation, whereas the prohibition of certain meats might appear less objectionable because of its analogy with the prohibition in the law of Moses" (Hofmann) Besides, the apostle has already indicated in ii. 15 the opposition of the gospel to this prohibition to marry.—The word μετάληψις occurs only here, though in Acts xxvii. 33 we find μεταλαβεῖν τροφῆς.—The apostle does not content himself with saying that God made food to be enjoyed, but he shows at the same time how God meant it to be enjoyed, viz.: μετὰ εὐχαριστίας (comp. on this 1 Cor x. 31). He then limits the general thought by a special reference to believers: τοῖς πιστοῖς καὶ ἐπεγνωκόσι τὴν ἀλήθειαν, as those in whom the purpose of creation is fulfilled, solis filiis suis Deus totum mundum et quicquid in mundo est destinavit, qua ratione etiam vocantur mundi heredes (Calvin). The apostle's thought is distorted by adding "also" before τοῖς πιστοῖς, as is done by some expositors.—Heydenreich rightly says that the words are equivalent to ἵνα οἱ πιστοὶ καὶ οἱ ἐπεγνωκότες τὴν ἀληθ. μεταλαβῶσιν αὐτῶν μετὰ

---

[1] Hofmann, with no good reason, declares, on the other hand, that attention is directed here to the Essenes and Therapeutae, and to the weak Christians mentioned in the Epistle to the Romans, as well as to the heretics at Colosse.

εὐχαριστίας. Hofmann unjustifiably takes exception to this, and—in spite of ὅτι beginning a new sentence—seeks to connect τοῖς πιστοῖς not with what goes before, but with what follows (¹). The added words: τοῖς πιστοῖς κ τ.λ., show most clearly the perverse conduct of the heretics in forbidding the enjoyment, and to believers of all people. Πιστοί are "believers," and not "those convinced that enjoyment is permitted to them;" ἐπεγν. τ. ἀλήθ also does not denote a special class of the πιστῶν. "the Christians who have come to the true gnosis" (as Heydenreich thinks probable), but the πιστοί themselves, as those who, in contrast to the heretics, have recognised the truth, ι e the divine truth Καί is epexegetical; comp. ii. 4.

Ver. 4. "Ὅτι πᾶν κτίσμα Θεοῦ καλόν] This verse gives the ground of the preceding thought, which Hofmann denies. Bengel wrongly takes it to be in apposition to ἀλήθειαν. — κτίσμα, which does not occur elsewhere in Paul, means here of course the creatures of God destined for nourishment. On the principle here expressed, comp. Rom xiv. 14: οὐδὲν κοινὸν δι' αὐτοῦ, and ver. 20: πάντα καθαρά; Acts x. 15. ἃ ὁ Θεὸς ἐκαθάρισε, σὺ μὴ κοίνου — καὶ οὐδὲν ἀπόβλητον] comp. Iliad, iii. 65: οὗτοι ἀπόβλητ' ἐστὶ θεῶν ἐρικυδέα δῶρα, and the scholiast's remark. ἀπόβλητα· ἀποβολῆς ἄξια· τὰ ὑπὸ θεῶν, φησί, διδόμενα δῶρα οὐκ ἔστι μὲν ἀρνήσασθαι Here the thought stands in contrast with the idea of defilement caused by partaking of certain meats. Going back to the μετὰ εὐχαριστίας in ver 3, the apostle defines it more precisely, though not by mentioning an accessory point merely: μετὰ εὐχαριστίας λαμβανόμενον (Eph. v. 20 εὐχαριστοῦντες πάντοτε ὑπὲρ πάντων), because God wishes His gifts to be enjoyed with thankful heart, and the purpose of creation is therefore fulfilled only by him who partakes with thankfulness.

Ver. 5 serves to elucidate the thought expressed in ver. 4, that every meat *taken with thanksgiving* is good, and not to be rejected — Ἁγιάζεται γὰρ διὰ λόγου Θεοῦ καὶ ἐντεύξεως] ἁγιάζειν is not "declare to be clean and permissible," but "make something holy." In itself the meat is not something holy, for, as a purely material thing, it can be called neither holy nor unholy (so also van Oosterzee). It is less suitable to say, with Wiesinger, that "the κτίσις being burdened with a curse, is subject to ματαιότης and the δουλεία τῆς φθορᾶς;" but it is made holy for those who enjoy it by the λόγος Θεοῦ. Wahl and Leo take Θεοῦ to be the objective genitive, and interpret it as "oratio ad Deum facta," which makes the expression synonymous with ἔντευξις following it; but λόγος Θεοῦ never occurs in this sense. Other expositors have supposed that reference is made to some particular passage of the Scriptures, either to Gen. i. 31 or Acts x. 15; but de Wette rightly remarks that the words in that case go quite beyond ver. 4, and touch on the question whether certain meats are clean or unclean. For the same reason, λόγος Θεοῦ cannot mean generally "the expressions of the divine doctrine, the principles of Christianity" (Heydenreich). Since the expression points back to μετὰ εὐχαριστίας in ver. 4, and is closely connected with ἔντευξις, it can only mean the word of God occurring in the prayer of thanksgiving (de Wette, Wiesinger, van Oosterzee), either in this sense, that the word of thanks itself is called the Word of God, inasmuch as it is the expression of God's indwelling Spirit, or because the prayer is supposed to consist of the words of Scripture.[1]— Regarding ἔντευξις, see ii. 1.

Ver 6 After describing the heretics, the apostle turns again to Timothy, exhorting him, in the first place, with special regard to the matters last under discussion, and then more generally in regard to the duties of his office. — ταῦτα ὑποτιθέμενος τοῖς ἀδελφοῖς] ταῦτα does not, as Heydenreich supposes, pass over all intermediate matter and go back to the christological doctrines expressed in iii. 16. It is more correct, with Hofmann, to refer it to the whole section from iii. 16 to iv. 5 (so Chrysostom); but possibly also Paul had in view only the prohibitions of the heretics (Wiesinger; van Oosterzee doubtfully). — ὑποτίθεσθαι (the middle only here, the act. in Rom. xvi 4), properly: "put under the hand or foot," may

[1] In the *Apostolic Constitutions*, vii. 49, there stands the following grace before meat εὐλογητὸς εἶ, Κύριε, ὁ τρέφων με ἐκ νεότητός μου, ὁ διδοὺς τροφὴν πάσῃ σαρκί, πλήρωσον χαρᾶς καὶ εὐφροσύνης τὰς καρδίας ἡμῶν, ἵνα πάντοτε πᾶσαν αὐτάρκειαν ἔχοντες, περισσεύωμεν εἰς πᾶν ἔργον ἀγαθὸν ἐν Χρ Ἰησοῦ, τῷ Κυρίῳ ἡμῶν, δι' οὗ σοὶ δόξα, τιμὴ καὶ κράτος εἰς τοὺς αἰῶνας, ἀμήν.

also mean "instruct" (Josephus, *Antiq.* i. 14), as much as 'advise" or "command" (Josephus, *Bell. Jud.* ii. 8. 7), here it stands more in the latter sense; Luther. " point out."— Hofmann wrongly explains it as equivalent to "take as a theme," and—against the natural structure of the sentence— connects it with what follows, though in this way it becomes tolerably superfluous. — καλὸς ἔσῃ διάκονος Χριστοῦ Ἰησοῦ] Paul here uses διάκονος, inasmuch as Timothy was formally appointed to serve in the work of Christ, it has the same meaning as " so wilt thou well occupy the office committed to thee (διακονία, 2 Tim. iv. 5)." To this is attached the participial clause: ἐντρεφόμενος τοῖς λόγοις τῆς πίστεως κτλ] The present participle does not stand for the perfect participle, but brings out how Timothy is to behave at all times, in order to fulfil his commission as a καλὸς διάκονος Ἰ. Xp. It declares that he is to be one who makes the words of faith his nourishment. It is inaccurate, therefore, to translate ἐντρεφόμενος by innutritus (Bengel[1]), or "reared" (Luther). As to the meaning of the word ἐντρέφεσθαι (in N. T. a ἅπαξ λεγ), see Philo, *Leg. ad Caj.* · ἐνετράφης τοῖς ἱεροῖς γράμμασιν, and Plato, *Leg.* vii. 798a · οἷς γὰρ ἂν ἐντραφῶσι νόμοις. — The λόγοι τῆς πίστεως are the words in which faith expresses itself. The added words: καὶ τῆς καλῆς διδασκαλίας (see i. 10), make the contrast with the heretics more decided, and the further clause: ᾗ (ἧς) παρηκολούθηκας, shows that Timothy had hitherto been faithful to pure doctrine. This latter perfect stands in apt contrast with the present participle ἐντρεφόμενος. The original meaning of the verb: "follow near any one," furnishes naturally for the present context the meaning: "*which thou hast faithfully followed*, to which thou hast remained faithful." The translation: "according to which thou hast formed thyself," is inaccurate; the word occurs in the N. T. only here and in 2 Tim. iii. 10, as well as in Luke i. 3 and Mark xvi. 17.

---

[1] Bengel, however, did not overlook the signification of the present altogether, since he explains thus Praesens cum respectu praeteriti, innutritus, nutrimentum perpetuum. Chrysostom remarks τὸ διηνεκὲς τῆς εἰς τὰ τοιαῦτα προσοχῆς δηλῶν Winer says. "ἐντρεφόμενος shows that the λόγοι τῆς πίστεως are to Timothy a permanent means of nourishment and culture."

Ver. 7. The exhortation to Timothy in the previous verse, that he should continue faithful to sound doctrine, is followed by an injunction to keep from heresy. — τοὺς δὲ βεβήλους καὶ γραώδεις μύθους παραιτοῦ] παραιτοῦ· τὴν τελείαν ἀποφυγὴν αἰνίττεται, Chrysostom; "have nothing to do with" Here, as in i. 4, the apostle calls the heresies μῦθοι, in reference to the fictions they contained; but at the same time he describes them more precisely by the adjectives βέβηλοι and γραώδεις. On the former, comp. i. 9 (Luther "unspiritual") It is in contrast with ὅσιος, and would be manifestly too strong, if the μῦθοι were only "things which bear no moral fruit," which "have an innocent aspect," and only "*possibly* lead to apostasy" (against Wiesinger).[1] Γραώδης (occurring only here) is equivalent to "old-wifish" (Luther), *i e*. antiquated; comp. 2 Tim. ii 23. Otto regards "the μῦθοι γραώδεις on the *formal* side as myths, such as are told *to children* by old fathers;" but the passages quoted by him from Plato (*Republic*, i. 350 E; ii. 377 C, and 378 D) do not support his opinion. These merely say that nurses, mothers, and more generally old wives, are to tell myths to the children, from which we can infer neither that γραώδεις refers merely to the *form* of the story, nor that Paul had any thought of a reference to children.—The apostle's exhortation does not touch so much on Timothy's teaching as on his own personal conduct; but correctness of conduct is all the more necessary that it is a condition of the right fulfilment of his διακονία. — γύμναζε δὲ σεαυτὸν πρὸς εὐσέβειαν] After telling Timothy what he is not to do, viz. that he is not to give himself up to the μύθοις βεβήλοις, he tells him now what —in contrast to these things—he is to do. The δέ indicates not only the transition to a new thought (Hofmann), but also the contrast to what has preceded. The figurative expression γυμνάζειν is used also in classic Greek of every straining exercise. This meaning is to be maintained here; Theodoret: γυμνασίας ἄρα χρεία καὶ πόνων διηνεκῶν· ὁ γὰρ γυμναζόμενος

---

[1] Hofmann is right in saying that βίβηλος does not pi operly mean "wicked" or "godless," but "unholy" He, however, overlooks the fact that it denotes not simply the negation, but also the opposite of what is holy. He is wrong, therefore, in maintaining: "the apostle cannot, however, truly describe in this way the doctrines of devilish liars."

καὶ ἀγῶνος μὴ ὄντος ἀγωνίζεται ἱδρῶτος ἄχρι — πρός indicat finem, ad quem illa γυμνασία vergat (Leo); this goal is εὐσέβεια, i.e. Christian piety rooted in faith. Comp. on this verse, 2 Tim. ii 22, 23.

Ver. 8. The reason for the previous exhortation is given by contrasting the σωματικὴ γυμνασία with the γυμνασία πρὸς εὐσέβειαν. — ἡ γὰρ σωματικὴ γυμνασία πρὸς ὀλίγον ἐστὶν ὠφέλιμος] Regarding the meaning of σωματ γυμν., there are two opinions which need no refutation. the one is that it means the ceremonial law (Braun, *Selecta sacra*, i 10, § 156), the other is that of Chrysostom, who understands by it disputation with the heretics[1] It is a question whether Paul makes use of the word with or without reference to the heretics. Many expositors (of the older, Ambrosius, Thomas; of the more recent, Calvin, Grotius; also Heydenreich, Leo, Matthies) adopt the former view, and explain the σωματικὴ γυμνασία to mean the practice prevailing among the heretics of abstaining from marriage and from certain meats. The connection of ideas is against this view, since in the words immediately preceding he was not speaking of rules of abstinence, but of the myths of the heretics; the sense is also against it, for Paul could not possible say of the heretics' mode of life, which before he had called devilish, that it was πρὸς ὀλίγον ὠφέλιμος κ.τ λ. Wiesinger thinks the apostle had in mind, not that degenerate form of asceticism which was to appear in the future, as he described in ver. 3, but "the phenomena of the present," viz an asceticism to which even Timothy (v. 23) had some inclination. But since, in Wiesinger's opinion, even this asceticism is to be regarded as an *error*, we cannot well refer to it the words πρὸς ὀλίγον ἐστὶν ὠφέλιμος. — Hofmann understands the σωματικὴ γυμνασία to be a discipline such as the apostle practised on himself in abstaining from things permitted; not, however, as if the self-denial were anything in itself, but only lest he should be hindered by the needs of the body from attaining the goal. For this Hofmann quotes 1 Cor. ix. 27. But the discipline which Paul practised on himself was by no means

---

[1] Chrysost. μηδὲ εἰς γυμνασίαν ποτὲ καταθῇς σιαυτόν, διαλεγόμενος πρὸς ἐκείνους· οὐ γάρ ἐστι πρὸς τοὺς διεστραμμένους μαχόμενον ὀνῆσαι τί ποτέ.

a purely bodily one; it was rather a γυμνασία πρὸς εὐσέβειαν, since the faithful fulfilment of official duty formed part of the εὐσέβεια. The expression is therefore to be explained simply from itself, and we must understand by it the exercise of the body in general, as Theodoret, Pelagius, Wolf, and others (of those more recent, Mack, de Wette, and van Oosterzee) have rightly explained it.—The reason why Paul here speaks of bodily exercise is contained in the previous exhortation : γύμναζε σὲ πρὸς εὐσέβειαν. This he wishes to make emphatic by contrasting with it the γυμνάζειν practised so carefully among the Greeks, though only πρὸς ὀλίγον ὠφέλιμον. The connection of ideas is by no means, as de Wette thinks, a mere "lexical allusion," nor is the idea itself superfluous. — πρὸς ὀλίγον is in Jas. IV 14 used of time : "for a short time" In this sense many have taken it here ; but the contrasted πρὸς πάντα is against this It is inaccurate also to regard, as Heumann does, πρὸς ὀλίγον as equivalent to ὀλίγῳ (Luther: "of little use"); it means "for little." Paul does not mean to say that the σωμ. γυμνασία is of *no* use, but that its use extends to little, only to some relations of the present, earthly life.[1] It is different with that to which Timothy is exhorted : ἡ δὲ εὐσέβεια πρὸς πάντα ὠφέλιμός ἐστιν] A more exact contrast would have been presented by ἡ δὲ γυμνασία ἡ πρὸς εὐσέβειαν ; but Paul could here speak at once of the use of εὐσέβεια in order to strengthen the previous exhortation. Πρὸς πάντα is here opposed to πρὸς ὀλίγον. The general reference thus given must not be arbitrarily limited. There is nothing, no active occupation, no condition, no human relation, on which the εὐσέβεια does not exercise an influence for good. — ἐπαγγελίαν ἔχουσα ζωῆς τῆς νῦν καὶ τῆς μελλούσης] This participial clause gives a reason for the words immediately preceding, and confirms them. De Wette, and following him Wiesinger, explain (by appealing to passages such as Ex. xx. 12 ;

---

[1] If ὀλίγον (without πρός), the reading of א, is correct, then the meaning is that which Luther has expressed. Still ὀλίγον might be taken also as a milder expression for the absolute negation : of *little* use, *i.e.* properly speaking, of *no* use, viz. for the calling of a Christian. But even this view does not justify the interpretation of γυμνασία which we have rejected above.

Deut. iv. 40; Matt. vi. 33; Eph. vi. 2, and others) ζωὴ ἡ νῦν as equivalent to "a long and happy life." But ζωή with ἡ νῦν cannot have a meaning different from that which it has with ἡ μέλλουσα. It is incorrect also to understand by ζωή "eternal life, life in the full and true sense of the word" (Hofmann),[1] for it is arbitrary to maintain that τῆς νῦν καὶ τῆς μελλούσης was added to ζωῆς only as an after-thought. This contrast forbids us to understand ζωή as anything else than simply "life;" ζωὴ ἡ νῦν is the present, ζωὴ ἡ μέλλουσα is the future life which follows the earthly. The genitive is to be taken as a *more remote* objective genitive,— "promise for the present and the future life" (so, too, van Oosterzee and Plitt). The *thing promised* is not indeed named, but it can be easily supplied.

Ver. 9 serves to strengthen the expression immediately preceding (not the thought in iii. 16, against Heinrichs), whereas in i. 15 (comp. also iii. 1) the same words refer to what follows. The γάρ in ver. 10 prevents us from connecting them with what comes next. It is no less unsuitable to refer them, as Hofmann does, to the ὅτι following, and to regard εἰς τοῦτο . . . as a parenthesis. This connection is opposed not only by the harshness of the construction, but also by the consideration that, as a matter of fact, the conduct of the Christian, viz. ἠλπικέναι κ.τ.λ., needed for Timothy no such confirmation as is given in these words.[2]

Ver. 10. Εἰς τοῦτο γὰρ κοπιῶμεν καὶ ὀνειδιζόμεθα κ.τ λ.] The particle γάρ shows that this verse is to serve as a reason or confirmation of the preceding thought that godliness is profitable for all things, having promise of this and the future life. Εἰς τοῦτο is by expositors either referred directly to this thought (de Wette, van Oosterzee), or is joined with the ὅτι following (Wiesinger); in the latter case the ἠλπίκαμεν points only to the thought in ver. 8. The former construction deserves the preference, not only because it is more

---

[1] It is clear that ζωή is not the "*blessed life*" (Matthies), since εὐσέβεια itself denotes the blessed life

[2] This difficulty is concealed in Hofmann by laying the emphasis on Θεῷ ζῶντι, so that πιστὸς ὁ λόγος κ.τ.λ. is to refer to the thought that God is a living God.

natural to refer the τοῦτο to the thought of ver. 8 so purposely confirmed by ver. 9 ; and also because εἰς τοῦτο cannot be taken as equivalent to διὰ τοῦτο (by which Theodoret paraphrases it), *id circo* (Beza). Εἰς always points to a goal (and not to the reason of something). Ἠλπικέναι, however, as an already existing condition, cannot be regarded as the goal to which the κοπιᾶν is directed, hence Luther's translation: "to this end we labour also . . . that we . . . have hoped," cannot be justified. The meaning therefore is: In regard to this, that godliness has promise, viz in order that this promise may be fulfilled in us, we labour.—With the *Rec.* καὶ κοπιῶμεν καὶ ὀνειδιζόμεθα, καὶ . . . καί is either equivalent to "both . . . and," or the first καί is equivalent to "yea also," and the second καί is simply "and " In the former case the two ideas κοπιᾶν and ὀνειδίζεσθαι are more widely separated, in the latter, they are more closely connected. The second view seems to be more natural. There is very weighty authority for the reading: κοπιῶμεν καὶ ἀγωνιζόμεθα, which also gives a thoroughly appropriate meaning ; but still the *Rec*, for which, too, almost all expositors (de Wette, Wiesinger, Reiche, van Oosterzee, Hofmann, and others) have decided, might be preferred. The change of ὀνειδιζόμεθα into ἀγωνιζόμεθα may be easily explained from the following facts, that in Col. i. 29 κοπιᾶν is joined with ἀγωνίζεσθαι, that ὀνειδίζειν does not occur elsewhere in Paul (except at Rom xv. 3 in an O. T. quotation), that the passive ὀνειδιζόμεθα does not seem suitable, whereas ἀγωνιζόμεθα agrees well with the figure in ver. 8. On the other hand, the change of ἀγωνιζόμεθα into ὀνειδιζόμεθα is scarcely explicable. The plural κοπιῶμεν is not to be limited to the apostle, or to him and Timothy ; it expresses the general Christian consciousness. The verb, often joined with another verb which has in it the idea of active exertion (1 Cor. iv. 12, Eph. iv. 28; Col. i. 29), does not denote simple labour, but labour with trouble and suffering: "to toil and moil" (Heydenreich); καὶ ὀνειδιζόμεθα again points to the reproach which the Christian bears from the world. Ὀνειδιζόμεθα is a "concise expression for we endure to be slandered" (Wiesinger). — ὅτι ἠλπίκαμεν ἐπὶ Θεῷ ζῶντι]

If εἰς τοῦτο refers to what precedes, ὅτι is equivalent to "because," the meaning in that case is: in regard to the promise given to εὐσέβεια, we take trouble and reproach upon ourselves, because we have set our hope on the living God, and are certain, therefore, that that promise does not remain unfulfilled. Ὅτι refers to both the preceding verbs, and does not merely stand "in close connection with the latter," as van Oosterzee without reason thinks. The perfect ἠλπίκαμεν as here: 1 Cor. xv. 19, 2 Cor. i. 10.—God is here called the *living* God, inasmuch as He fulfils what He has promised. — Ἐλπίζειν is construed with ἐπί and the dative, because the living God is regarded as the ground on which the hope rests. The construction is only found here at vi. 17, and at Rom. xv. 12 in an O. T. quotation. Elsewhere ἐλπίζειν is construed with ἐν, or εἰς, or ἐπί and the accusative —The relative clause ὅς ἐστι σωτὴρ πάντων ἀνθρώπων, μάλιστα πιστῶν serves as a seal of the hope grounded in God. Since God is the σωτήρ, this hope, too, cannot be vain; de Wette is wrong, therefore, in asserting that this clause is "out of all keeping." —The first words are explained by ii. 4: ὃς πάντας ἀνθρώπους θέλει σωθῆναι. By μάλιστα πιστῶν it is indicated that the will of God unto salvation is realized only in the case of believers. Μάλιστα does not stand here "unsuitably" (de Wette); it rather gives suitable expression to the thought that God is and continues to be the σωτήρ for all, whether they desire σωτηρία or not; but in the proper and special sense the σωτηρία is only for believers who really desire it.

Ver. 11. Παράγγελλε ταῦτα καὶ δίδασκε] Timothy is to proclaim to the community that which Paul has enjoined to him. Ταῦτα refers not only to what is in ver. 10 (according to Hofmann: "to God's living power and willingness to help"), but to everything that has been said previously in regard to εὐσέβεια. The two verbs παραγγέλλειν and διδάσκειν tell how he is to proclaim these things. They are not distinguished from each other as referring, the one to private, the other to public instruction, nor as expressing, the one, generally public proclamation, the other, more especially exact instruction, explanation, information (Matthies); but παραγγέλλειν, which in the N. T. has constantly the sense of "command," indicates that Timothy is to hold up these things (ταῦτα) to the community as the standard of their conduct.

Ver. 12. From this verse on to the end of the chapter, Paul instructs Timothy how he is to behave towards the community that his παραγγέλλειν καὶ διδάσκειν (ver 11) may not be in vain. — μηδείς σου τῆς νεότητος καταφρονείτω] σου is dependent on τῆς νεότητος, which is the object of καταφρον. Wahl, on the contrary (followed by Leo and Matthies), construes σου directly with καταφρ., and takes τῆς νεότ as a genitive defining the substantive more precisely (= μηδεὶς διὰ τὴν νεότητα καταφρονήσῃ σου, Chrysostom), so that καταφρ. here (like κατηγορεῖν) would be connected with a double genitive (comp. Buttmann, p. 143). This construction, however, is more forced than the former, and καταφρ. occurs nowhere else with it.—According to the form of the sentence, the command is directed to the community, but in sense to Timothy. Timothy is not to permit the authority entrusted to him as representative of the apostle, to be limited on account of his youth: "*permit no one to despise thy youth.*" The ἀλλά, however, attached to this injunction shows that he is to effect this especially by his Christian conduct, most expositors find here *only* this last thought.—That he may retain respect, he is to make himself an example to all: ἀλλὰ τύπος γίνου τῶν πιστῶν. A comma is not unsuitably placed after πιστῶν, giving the clause greater independence, and making the qualifications that follow: ἐν λόγῳ κ τ λ, more emphatic. On the exhortation τύπος γίνου, comp. besides Tit ii. 7, Phil. iii 17: 2 Thess. iii. 9; 1 Pet. v. 3. Γίνου does not mean "*become,*" as if Timothy had not been so hitherto, but "*be.*" The next five words: ἐν λόγῳ κ τ λ., tell wherein Timothy is to be an example to believers. We cannot but observe that there is a certain order in the succession of the words. First we have ἐν λόγῳ and ἐν ἀναστροφῇ. Λόγος includes every kind of speaking (not merely *doctrine*), *i e.* teaching, exhorting, warning, comforting, etc., both in public assemblies and in private intercourse. Ἀναστροφή is the life as embodied in deeds. Word and life are the two forms of revealing the inner hidden disposition. To this inner life we are directed by the next words: ἐν ἀγάπῃ, ἐν πίστει, which denote the powers that give motion to the Christian life. The last word: ἐν ἁγνείᾳ, gives, finally, the nature of the life that is rooted in faith and love. The word does not denote here specially chastity in the relation of sex, but generally "purity of moral behaviour" (Hofmann); comp. ἁγνός, v. 22; 2 Cor vii. 11; Jas. iii. 17; ἁγνότης, 2 Cor. vi. 6; ἁγνίζειν, Jas iv. 8; 1 Pet. i. 22; 1 John iii. 3.

Ver. 13. "Ἕως ἔρχομαι] comp. iii. 14. De Wette says in explanation: "so long as thou in my absence dost preside over the church at Ephesus." This does not agree with the circumstances, inasmuch as Timothy had not been installed as the regular superintendent of the church. That was an office held more by presbyters. — πρόσεχε (1. 4, iii. 8, iv. 1) "curam et studium nava;" de Wette. "*wait*." — τῇ ἀναγνώσει, τῇ παρακλήσει, τῇ διδασκαλίᾳ] Bengel rightly says. "lectioni Scripturae sacrae in ecclesia; huic adjunguntur duo praecipua genera, adhortatio, quae ad agendum et doctrina, quae ad cognoscendum pertinet." — ἀνάγνωσις in Acts xiii. 15, 2 Cor. iii 14, is used of the reading of the law and the prophets in the synagogue, this custom was continued· in Christian congregations.—The two expressions παράκλησις and διδασκαλία are found elsewhere in connection with one another (Rom. xii. 7, 8; comp. also παράγγελλε καὶ δίδασκε above). Chrysostom is wrong in his explanation: παράκλησις· πρὸς ἀλλήλους, διδασκαλία· πρὸς πάντας. With as little ground do others understand by διδασκ. private instruction, and by παράκλ. public preaching; or also by the former, instruction for catechumens, and by the latter, instruction for the church.[1]

Ver. 14. Μὴ ἀμέλει τοῦ ἐν σοὶ χαρίσματος] Timothy is not to let the χάρισμα lie unused; he is to apply it diligently and faithfully to the purpose for which it was imparted to him. This exhortation does not imply blame, nor does that given in 2 Tim. i. 6.—The word χάρισμα may be applied to every gift of God bestowed on man by God's χάρις. In the N. T. it denotes both generally the new spiritual life wrought in the believer by the Holy Spirit, and also specially every

---

[1] Van Oosterzee's remark is also wrong· "The former was necessary for individuals in special circumstances, the latter for all every day," because all need continually both the διδασκαλία as well as the παράκλησις.

faculty imparted for special Christian work (ἱκανότης, comp. 2 Cor. iii. 5). Here, where he is speaking of Timothy's official work, it can only mean the faculty given him for the office (not simply "the gift of teaching," as Hofmann thinks), in regard both to the κυβέρνησις and specially to the παράκλησις and διδασκαλία (not, however, as Chrysostom explains it, the διδασκαλία itself) It is not to be taken as denoting the office itself; the ἐν σοί is against this, and nowhere in the N. T. has the word this meaning.[1] — ὃ ἐδόθη σοι] not as Heinrichs says· *a me, Apostolo*, but, as a matter of course, by the Holy Spirit (1 Cor. xii 4). — διὰ προφητείας μετὰ ἐπιθέσεως τῶν χειρῶν τοῦ πρεσβυτερίου] διά is here "by means of," so that the προφητεία is to be regarded as the means through which the χάρισμα was given to Timothy (by the Holy Spirit). It is arbitrary to weaken this, the proper meaning of the preposition, as Beza does when he explains it: per prophetiam i. e ita jubente per os prophetarum spiritu sancto;[2] and as Otto also does, when he finds here the thought that the ordination was *occasioned* by the προφητεία. Though Hofmann in his *Schriftbeweis* (II. 2, pp. 278 f.) had explained it: "The word of prophecy pointed out Timothy as the one to be appointed the apostle's colleague," he now says : "διὰ προφητείας does not mean *by means of* prophecy, but *in consequence of* prophecies" This latter explanation, however, agrees with the one which he disputes, since the expression "in consequence of" gives not merely the relation of time, but also the relation of cause. We must reject even the

---

[1] Otto grants, indeed, that χάρισμα never stands exactly for office, but thinks that χάρισμα may be used as a *predicate* of the idea, office, which is certainly right. Otto, however, does not wish to take χάρισμα here as the office generally speaking, but (distinguishing in the office—(1) the rights of office , (2) the occupations of office) as the *rights of office* "A position of power working out from within " To ἐν he assigns the meaning "resting upon some one ," but, whatever Otto may say against it, the ἀναζωπυρεῖν (2 Tim i 6) does not accord with that idea. So long as any one holds the office, the *rights of office* remain to him undiminished; for these he not in the person, but in the office, in the person only as holding the office. For such a meaning of ἐν, Otto has produced some passages from classic Greek, but none from the N T.

[2] Beza goes still farther wrong when he continues "Potest tamen etiam sic accipi, ut idem valeat εἰς προφητείαν, i. e. ad prophetandum ; vel ἐν προφητίᾳ, ita ut quod sit hoc donum exprimat apostolus "

qualification of the meaning which Matthies demands : " The fundamental meaning of the preposition διά, which may be shortly defined as means, may be so modified in many cases as to give the manner in which something is done, or the intermediating form under which something comes into life " We must reject this, because, as de Wette rightly remarks, there would otherwise be no indication of a relation of cause. Besides, such passages as Acts viii. 17, 18, ix 17, xix. 6, 2 Tim. i. 6, prove that we must keep by the proper meaning of διά. The προφητεία is mentioned as the means, but in close connection with ἐπίθεσις τῶν χειρῶν. Προφητεία (1. 18) is not equivalent to "foretelling," but is more generally the word proceeding immediately from the Holy Spirit—whether the word of promise, or of exhortation, or of prayer. This word was spoken at the time (μετά) when the presbytery laid their hands on Timothy and appointed him to his ministry. Μετὰ ἐπιθέσεως τ. χ. is to be taken in close connection with διὰ προφητείας ; the laying on of hands is to be regarded as part of the means , comp 2 Tim. 1 6.[1] Otto wrongly says · " The laying on of hands is not a coefficient of the ordination, but an act connected with the ceremony of ordination ; the χάρισμα was imparted to Timothy *along with* the laying on of hands, not by *means of* the laying on of hands." Wherein, then, did the ceremony of ordination consist ? It is curious that Hofmann, influenced by 2 Tim. i 6, says regarding μετά, that " it was of course the *apostle's* business to impart the gift to Timothy by laying on of hands," but then grants that " the presbytery of Timothy's home-church took part in the laying on of hands," without telling us what then signified the presbytery's laying on of hands. The hands were imposed by the presbytery, but Paul does not say who uttered the προφητεία Leo remarks : " adfuerunt fortassis, quum manus imponebantur Timotheo, prophetae Christiani, qui praesagiebant faustissima quaevis, et dignum eum fore dicebant ecclesiae doctorem " (similarly Wiesinger, van Oosterzee, and others). It is, however, most probable to assume that

---

[1] De Wette rightly "The προφ is only named as a part of the whole act of consecration by which the χαρ was imparted, and the preposition διά is not to be referred in strictness only to προφ , but also to the next words."

they who uttered the προφητεία were the same as they who laid their hands on Timothy,[1] so that we cannot think here of prophets, in the narrower sense of the word, as present at the ordination.—The ἐπίθεσις τῶν χειρῶν is well known as a symbolic action of the early Christians; it was the symbol and means not only of imparting the Holy Spirit in general (Acts viii. 17, xix. 6, Heb. vi. 2), but also of bestowing the inward equipment for a special Christian ministry (Acts vi. 6, xiii. 3; comp. also Acts xiv. 23). By the presbytery, we must understand the college of presbyters belonging to the church in which the hands were imposed. What church this was, we are not told. Ecclesiastical tradition, followed by Mack, makes it the church at Ephesus, Matthies, Leo, de Wette, Wiesinger, and others think it more probable that the ordination took place at Lystra, where Paul assumed Timothy as his companion, and that the ordination was held for this very purpose.[2] To this latter view we must object, that there is no passage in the N T. to prove that the reception into the number of the colleagues of the apostles was made with such a solemn ceremony. It is more natural to suppose that such a reception took a freer form, and that a regular ordination was only held after a more independent position had been assigned to the colleague, a position not merely of carrying out certain instructions, but of representing the apostle in a more complete way, viz. in a particular church, such as Timothy now held. Perhaps, therefore, this ordination of Timothy had taken place when Paul on his departure for Macedonia left Timothy behind him in Ephesus as his substitute (i. 3); still it is also possible that it had been done on some earlier occasion"—It is strange that in 2 Tim. i. 6

---

[1] Bengel is wrong "Constr prophetiam presbyterii, nam manus imposuit Paulus Timotheo, impositio manus propiie fit per unam personam et quidem digniorem, prophetia vero fiebat etiam per aequales, per plures"

[2] So also Hofmann, in whose opinion the "precedent" here alluded to (which, however, he is not willing to recognise as an ordination) must have taken place in Timothy's "home-church."

[3] Otto, in accordance with his whole view, places Timothy's ordination in the last period of Paul's three years at Ephesus. The reasons by which he seeks to establish this period as the one most exactly corresponding in Timothy's life, are anything but sufficient.

the laying on of hands is mentioned only as the act of the *apostle*. Paul might certainly be speaking there of some other occasion than here, for the consecration by laying on of hands might be imparted on different occasions *to the same man*. It is more probable, however, that he is speaking of the same occasion in both passages, and "that Paul imposed hands along with the elders, but as the first" (de Wette).— It is further to be remarked that the word πρεσβυτέριον occurs elsewhere in the N. T. only as a name for the Jewish Sanhedrim (Luke xxii. 66 ; Acts xxii. 5), and that it is used here only of the college of the Christian presbyters of a church.

Ver. 15. In order that Timothy may rightly lay to heart the exhortations just given, Paul continues : ταῦτα μελέτα, ἐν τούτοις ἴσθι] ταῦτα referendum ad omnia ea, quae a ver 12, usque ad ver 14, praeceperat Paulus Timotheo, Leo. — μελετᾶν occurs elsewhere in the N. T. only at Mark xiii. 11 and Acts iv. 25, where it means "think, consider, reflect on something," equivalent to meditari. The more original meaning, however, is " exercere, carry on something with care ;" this is to be maintained here, where it is a matter of putting recommendations into practice. De Wette : "let this be thy care." — ἐν τούτοις ἴσθι] added to strengthen the preceding words ; it is equivalent in meaning to the Latin omnis (totus) in hoc sis (Hor. *Ep* i 1, 11, quid verum atque decens curo . . . et omnis in hoc sum). — ἵνα σου ἡ προκοπὴ φανερὰ ᾖ πᾶσιν] With προκοπή (only elsewhere in Phil. i. 12, 15), "progress," not ' progressiveness " (Hofmann), we may either supply " in filling thy office " (Heydenreich , de Wette · to the perfection of the God-man, 2 Tim. iii. 17), or more generally, "in the Christian life." The purpose of this lay in the fact that Timothy was to be a τύπος τῶν πιστῶν.

Ver 16. Cumulat sane h. l Paulus adhortationes, unde ejus amorem in Timotheum et in Christianos Timotheo subditos intelligas, Leo — ἔπεχε σεαυτῷ] "*take heed to thyself,*" refers to ver. 12 , καὶ τῇ διδασκαλίᾳ refers to ver. 13. Heinrichs wrongly combines the two together as an hendiadys ("pro σεαυτῷ ut possis tradere bonam διδασκαλίαν ") On the other hand, however, we must not understand the διδασκαλία to mean the doctrine of others (Heydenreich. take heed, that nothing is neglected in the instruction of Christians by the teachers placed under thy oversight) — ἐπίμενε αὐτοῖς] αὐτοῖς is not masculine, as Grotius and Bengel think, the one understanding it of the Ephesians, the other of the audientes. It is neuter, and as such it is to be referred not only to what immediately preceded (= "in this attention to thyself and to the doctrine"), but, glancing back to τούτοις, ταῦτα in ver 15 (Wiesinger), it is to be referred also to all the precepts from ver. 12 onward. Hofmann is wrong in connecting τῇ διδασκαλίᾳ with ἐπίμενε, and explaining αὐτοῖς as the dativus commodi, for, on the one hand, no subject precedes to which αὐτοῖς could be referred, and, on the other, there is nothing to show that αὐτοῖς is the dat. commodi. — The exhortations close with words confirming them: τοῦτο γὰρ ποιῶν] "if thou doest this" (regarding the form of the clause, comp. ver. 6); καὶ σεαυτὸν σώσεις καὶ τοὺς ἀκούοντάς σου] Without reason, de Wette thinks that σώσεις has in Timothy's case a different meaning from that which it has in the case of others; that in his case it is to be understood of the *higher* (¹) σωτηρία, in theirs simply of the σωτηρία. Σώζειν means originally "save," but in the N T. it has in connection with Christian doctrine not only a negative, but also a positive meaning. Hence we cannot, with Mack, take it here as signifying merely, protecting from heresy and its effects. Luther translates it rightly: "thou shalt make blessed," etc —*i e* thou shalt further thine own salvation as well as the salvation of those who hear thee, *i.e.* of the church assigned to thee.

CHAPTER V.

VER. 4. μανθανέτωσαν] The reading μανθανέτω, which is found in some cursives, 3, 35, and many others, as well as in Vulg Clar. Ambr. Aug. Ambrosiast. Pel., is to be regarded as a correction, τὶς χήρα being supposed to be the subject of the verb. As to the correctness of this supposition, see the exposition — ἀπόδεκτον] The words καλὸν καί, which precede in the *Rec*, are rightly omitted from the text by Griesb, who follows all uncials, very many cursives, versions, etc ; they are beyond doubt taken from ii. 3 — Ver. 5. Instead of ἐπὶ τὸν Θεόν, ℵ and some other authorities have the reading ἐπὶ κύριον. — Ver. 8. τῶν οἰκείων] The article is wanting in A D* F G ℵ; probably not genuine; Lachm. Buttm. Tisch. 8 omitted it. — For the active προνοεῖ (Tisch. 7), D* F G K ℵ, *al.*, have the middle προνοεῖται (Tisch. 8), which, however, may be a correction after Rom. xii. 17; in 2 Cor. viii. 21 the reading is doubtful — Ver. 10. ἐτεκνοτρόφησεν] The reading ἐτεκνοφόρεσεν in F G, gr. is strange, since the word occurs nowhere else. — Ver. 11. For καταστρηνιάσωσι (*Rec.* Lachm. ed maj, Tisch. 7, following C D K L ℵ, most others), A F G 31 have the reading καταστρηνιάσουσιν (Lachm. ed. min., Buttm. Tisch. 7). The infrequency of the construction of ὅταν with the indic. pres., which occurs only a few times in the N. T (compare especially Rev. iv. 9), might be an argument for the originality of the latter reading; but most authorities are against it. — Ver. 14 Before νεωτέρας there stands in D* and some cursives the article τάς; some other cursives, as well as Slav. Chrys. Theodor. etc., have χήρας after νεωτέρας; clearly an explanatory correction. — Ver. 15. It is doubtful whether τινες was originally placed *before* or *after* ἐξετράπησαν. For the former position (*Rec.* Tisch. 8) we have the authority of ℵ C D K L P, *al.*; for the latter (Lachm. Buttm. Tisch. 7), that of A F G, *al.* — Ver. 16. The *Rec.* πιστὸς ἢ πιστή is found in D K L, nearly all cursives, some versions, and in Ath. *contra Arr.* Tisch. 7 retained the *Rec.*; on the other hand, Lachm. Buttm. Tisch. 8 omitted πιστὸς ἤ. The expositors (also Reiche) have declared for the *Rec.* It is to be noted further, that in Vulg. ed. Ambros. Aug. Pel. the words ἢ πιστή are omitted, and also that in Boern. Vulg. ms. the translation *si quis fideles habet viduas* is found For further remarks, see the exposition of the verse. — Instead of ἐπαρκείτω (*Rec* Tisch. 7, following C D K L P, *al*), A F G ℵ have the middle ἐπαρκείσθω (Lachm. Buttm. Tisch. 8), which is indeed the original reading, the change being occasioned by the ἐπήρκεσεν in ver. 10, and the ἐπαρκέσῃ in ver. 16. — Ver 18. For βοῦν ἀλοῶντα οὐ φιμώσεις, Lachm. and Buttm, on the authority of A C P 37, 57, 73, 80, *al*, Copt. Arm. Vulg. Chrys. etc, read οὐ φιμώσεις βοῦν ἀλοῶντα, which, however, might be a correction after 1 Cor. ix 9. Tisch. has the common reading. — Ver. 20 After τοὺς, Lachm. and Buttm, on the authority of A D* Clar. Theoph Ambros Jerome, read δέ, which in F G, Boern. Vulg. ms. is found after ἁμαρτάνοντας. This variety in the position of δέ makes it suspicious in any case. — Ver. 21. Χριστοῦ Ἰησοῦ (Scholz, Lachm. Buttm. Tisch. Reiche, etc.), instead of the usual reading κυρίου Ἰησοῦ Χριστοῦ Against κυρίου we have the testimony of A D* F G 17, 31, *al*., Copt. Sahid Aeth. Clem Basil. etc, and for Χριστοῦ Ἰησοῦ we have that of A D* G 17, 31, 73, *al*, versions, even the Sahidic and Fathers. — For πρόσκλισιν (*Rec*, with the authority of F G K, many others, It. Vulg. etc.) it is too rash, with Lachm. and Buttm, on the authority of A D L 10, 31, *al*, Ath Bas. etc., to read πρόσκλησιν; because, notwithstanding the testimony of the oldest MSS, the sense almost imperatively demands πρόσκλισιν. This is a case where Tisch.'s words (see the article "Bibeltext des N. T" in Herzog's *Real-Encyklopädie*, II pp 183 f) apply· "In spite of the great preference to be given to our oldest Greek MSS, we must not overlook the fact that sometimes those opposed to them, and centuries later, have at the same time the authority of much older versions and Fathers." Tisch. retained the *Rec*; he explains (*lc* p 164) πρόσκλησιν as an itacism occasioned by the dictation of the text; similarly Reiche on the passage. — Ver. 23 *Rec* στόμαχόν σου (Tisch 7, after D F G K L, *al*); the σου is wanting in A D* P ℵ (Lachm. Buttm. Tisch. 8); in any case, the later addition is easier to explain than the omission — Ver. 25. After ὡσαύτως, Lachm, on the authority of A F G g, inserted δέ; it is possible that δέ was struck out by a copyist on the analogy of ii 9. — τὰ καλὰ ἔργα] Instead of this reading, A D F G ℵ 37, 116, *al*, Vulg. Clar Boern Theophyl Aug. Ambros. Pelag. are decisive for τὰ ἔργα τὰ καλά (Lachm Buttm Tisch.). — Instead of the *Rec* ἐστι after πρόδηλα, there stands in D F G P 17, 67* 93, *al*., εἰσιν, in A ℵ 67* it is omitted (Lachm. Buttm. Tisch.) — δύναται] Lachm. Buttm and Tisch read the plur. δύνανται, on the authority of A D ℵ 17, 44, 67, 71, *al*., plur. edd. Theodoret.

Vv. 1, 2. Directions regarding Timothy's behaviour towards elder and younger church-members of both sexes. — πρεσβυτέρῳ μὴ ἐπιπλήξῃς] Chrysostom rightly remarks: ἄρα τὸ ἀξίωμα νῦν φησίν; οὐκ οἶμαι· ἀλλὰ περὶ παντὸς γεγηρακότος. Otherwise we could not but take νεώτεροι as equivalent to διάκονοι, and understand by νεώτεραι the deaconesses, which, however, would be arbitrary There is, besides, no ground for Mack's opinion, that the οἱ νεώτεροι mentioned in Acts v. 6 (ver. 10: οἱ νεανίσκοι) were "church servants." By far the greater number of expositors rightly agree with Chrysostom. — ἐπιπλήσσειν] only occurring here, properly "strike upon," then "scold, make violent reproaches." The opposite: Gal. vi. 1, καταρτίζειν ἐν πνεύματι πραότητος. It is presupposed in this and the next exhortations that the church-members named had been guilty of some transgression or other. — ἀλλὰ παρακάλει ὡς πατέρα κ.τλ] It is not to be forgotten that Timothy was still a νέος. As such he is in his office to deal in childlike respect with the elder men and women, if they had rendered themselves liable to his correction. — νεωτέρους ὡς ἀδελφούς] supply only παρακάλει; still Bengel is right in meaning when he remarks on μὴ ἐπιπλήξῃς: hoc pertinet etiam ad ea, quae sequuntur. By ὡς ἀδελφούς and ὡς ἀδελφάς it is implied that Timothy was not to exalt himself over those who were of the same age as himself or younger, but that he was to deal with them in brotherly love as his equals. — The addition ἐν πάσῃ ἁγνείᾳ, which follows ὡς ἀδελφάς, may grammatically be referred to all the members; but Chrysostom[1] and most expositors since, connect it closely with the words immediately preceding. Rightly; since, even when taken in the more general sense of "purity of morals" (iv. 12), it cannot rightly be referred to the preceding relations; but it is very appropriate to the last, all the more if it be taken in the more special sense of "modesty, chastity."[2]

---

[1] Chrysostom μὴ μοί, φησὶ, τὴν τῆς μίξεως μόνον εἴπῃς ἁμαρτίαν, ἀλλὰ μηδὲ ὑποψίαν, φησὶ, ὁῶς ἐπ ἰδὴ γὰρ αἱ πρὸς τὰς νεωτέρας γινόμεναι ὁμιλίαι δυσκόλως διαφεύγουσιν ὑποψίαν, δεῖ δὲ γίνεσθαι παρὰ τοῦ ἐπισκόπου καὶ τοῦτο, διὰ τοῦτο ἐν πάσῃ ἁγνείᾳ προστίθησι. —On the words ὡς ἀδελφάς, Bengel briefly and aptly says hic respectus egregie adjuvat castitatem.

[2] Comp. Athenagoras, Leg pro Christ p. 36. καθ' ἡλικίαν τοὺς μὲν υἱοὺς καὶ

Ver. 3. From this to ver. 16 we have instructions regarding the widows of the church. — χήρας τίμα] Theodoret, Theophylact, Pelagius, and most recent expositors, among others, de Wette and Wiesinger, refer τίμα to the support of the widows by money. De Wette explains τίμα directly as "care for them, support them," adding, "he is speaking of support from the church-purse." Wiesinger, on the other hand, remarks: "We do not say that τιμάω means 'support' exactly, but it means an honouring which was to manifest itself in supporting them." In proof of this view, appeal is made to the passages in Acts vi. 1, xxviii. 10; Matt xv. 4–6; but wrongly. In the two last passages the meaning "support with money" can only arbitrarily be given to τιμᾶν (see Meyer on Acts xxviii. 10); and though the widows were supported by the church, as we learn from Acts vi. 1 (comp. also Ignatius, *ad Polycarp* chap. iv; Justin Martyr, *Apolog.* i 67), we cannot from that draw any inference as to the meaning of τιμᾶν. But even the context does not necessitate us to specialize the meaning. Granted that all that follows referred only to money-support to be given to the widows, why should not these special exhortations be introduced by one of a more general nature? Besides, the support mentioned being the business of the church, and not of Timothy alone, the apostle—according to the analogy of καταλεγέσθω (ver. 9)—would not have written τίμα, but χῆραι τιμάσθωσαν. Hence, with several old and some recent commentators, such as Matthies, van Oosterzee, Plitt, Hofmann, we should retain the usual meaning of τιμᾶν. Their support by the church is simply a consequence and proof of the τιμᾶν. — τὰς ὄντως χήρας] is added to define more precisely what widows Paul was thinking of, viz. those who are widows in the true and proper sense of the word (Luther: right widows). Ὄντως is used as an adjective only here in the N. T. (Plato, *Phaedr.* 260a: τὰ ὄντως ἀγαθά). What kind of widows are meant thereby, we are to infer from what follows.

Vv. 4–8. There are two opposing views regarding the explanation of this section. (1) The view upheld by the

θυγατέρας νοοῦμεν, τοὺς δὲ ἀδελφοὺς ἔχομεν καὶ ἀδελφάς· καὶ τῆς προβεβηκόσι τὴν τῶν πατέρων καὶ μητέρων τιμὴν ἀπονέμομεν.

majority of recent commentators, de Wette, Wiesinger, van Oosterzee, Plitt, which is as follows. Paul is giving Timothy instructions to support the "*real*" widows. From these he distinguishes (ver. 4 being in contrast with ver. 3) the widow who has children or grandchildren, because they are able and ought to care for her. With μανθανέτωσαν we should supply as subject τέκνα ἢ ἔκγονα, and we should understand by τὸν ἴδιον οἶκον and τοῖς προγόνοις the widowed mother or grandmother. Ver. 5 contrasts again with ver. 4; καὶ μεμονωμένη explains the signification of ἡ ὄντως χήρα. The predicate ἤλπικε κ.τ λ. denotes the life-work which the "right," *i.e.* the forsaken, widow has to fulfil, her fulfilment of it being a necessary condition of receiving support. Ver. 6 declares negatively what conduct the apostle expects from an ὄντως χήρα, and to such conduct Timothy (ver. 7) is to exhort them. At ver. 8, Paul returns to ver 4, τις referring to the widows' relations, and τῶν ἰδίων καὶ μάλιστα [τῶν] οἰκείων to the widows themselves.—(2) The view upheld by most older and some recent commentators, especially Matthies and Hofmann, which is as follows After enjoining on Timothy to honour the "real" widows, Paul first directs the widows who have children or grandchildren (still uncared for), to show these all loving care, and thereby recompense the love shown to themselves by their parents. The subject of μανθανέτωσαν is τις χήρα (as a collective idea); τὸν ἴδιον οἶκον are the children or grandchildren, and οἱ πρόγονοι the dead parents of the widow Ver. 5 describes the "real" widow as one who in her loneliness leads a life pious and consecrated to God; and as a contrast to this we have the picture of a wanton widow in ver. 6. In ver. 8, again (ver. 4), widows who have relations needing their care are again reminded of the duty of this care.[1]—Each of these views has its difficulties Against the *second* view, the supporters of the first maintain the following points:—(1) that as ver. 4 is in contrast with ver 3, and ver. 5 in contrast again with ver. 4 (δέ), the χήρα spoken of in ver. 4 cannot be regarded as belonging to the ὄντως χήραις, and (2) that as εὐσεβεῖν (ver. 4) applies more naturally to the

---

[1] Hofmann, however, takes these verses (5–8) in a different way from that in which they are here interpreted by most expositors, see farther on.

conduct of children towards their mother (or grandmother) than *vice versa*, and as the thought: the widow is by her care for her children to make recompense for the care shown to herself by her parents, is "somewhat far-fetched" (de Wette), the ὄντως χήρα can only mean the widow with no relations for whom it is her duty to care.—But the *first* view has also its difficulties. If we adopt it, we find it strange that the apostle should not have written simply αὐτήν for τὸν ἴδιον οἶκον, and αὐτῇ for τοῖς προγόνοις, all the more that οἱ πρόγονοι is a name for "progenitors." Further, πρῶτον, which Wiesinger translates inaccurately by "before all," does not get its full force. It is arbitrary to understand by τέκνα ἢ ἔκγονα, *grown-up* children, especially as the expression τέκνα ἔχειν makes the children appear dependent on the mother (comp. iii. 4; Tit. i. 6). De Wette says regarding ver 5: The author would have more clearly said: "Remind a true and forsaken widow to whom thou dost give support, that it falls upon her to show an example of confidence in God and of continual prayer," but we can hardly think that the apostle would have expressed *this* thought in such an uncertain way. Even the three repetitions of the same thought in vv. 4, 8, and 16, is at least very strange. Finally, the idea of money-support, on which this view lays all stress, is purely imported. These difficulties are too considerable for us to regard the *first* view as right in spite of them [1]—De Wette and Wiesinger are certainly right in regarding ver. 4 as contrasted with ver 3, and ver. 5 with ver. 4, as well as in thinking that the word μεμονωμένη sets forth the apostle's mark of the ὄντως χήρα; but they are not justified in inferring that in ver. 4 he is speaking of a widow with relations who can take care of her. Why, in that case, should the apostle in ver. 5 have said regarding the ὄντως χήρα, that she was to προσμένειν ταῖς δεήσεσι καὶ ταῖς προσευχαῖς, and to do so νυκτὸς καὶ ἡμέρας, for all this is in no way opposed to what is said in ver. 4? The

---

[1] Van Oosterzee, in agreeing with the *first* view, thinks it puzzling that this commentary gives the preference to the second. But he does not by this furnish anything towards the solution of the question, all the less that he has neglected to enter in any way upon the difficulties surrounding the view he adopts.

προσμένειν leads us to suppose that the apostle was thinking of a widow who had not to care for relations.—The right view will accordingly be this. After exhorting Timothy to honour the "real" widows (see on ver. 3), Paul distinguishes from these ὄντως χήραις, in the first place, the one who is *not forsaken*, but has children or grandchildren (not grown up); and he lays it on her as a duty not to neglect them. Then he describes the conduct of the "*real*" or *forsaken* widow, who has therefore no ἴδιον οἶκον, showing what beseems her in her position in life as a Christian widow; so that he is contrasting the widow who works diligently for her own, and the lone widow who continues day and night in prayer. As opposed to the latter (or even to both), he mentions in ver. 6 the χήρα σπαταλῶσα, who is, however, to be considered as dead, because her conduct is in entire contradiction with her widowed state. Then there is a natural transition to the exhortation in ver. 7, which gives the apostle an opportunity for uttering, in ver. 8, a general maxim in order to impress once more on the widow with relations to care for, the exhortation in ver. 4. — Ver. 4. τέκνα ἢ ἔκγονα] ἔκγονα here (in connection with τέκνα) means the "grandchildren" (τέκνα τέκνων, Hesychius).[1] In classical usage, ὁ ἔκγονος is usually the son (ἡ ἔκγονος, the daughter), but also the grandson, τὰ ἔκγονα denotes properly posterity (comp. Wisd. xl. 15, xliv. 11, xlv. 13, xlvii. 22; synonymous with τὸ σπέρμα). — μανθανέτωσαν] The subject for this verb *might* be taken from the object in the protasis, but the formation of the sentence is more correct, if we take the subject of the protasis (τις χήρα) to be the subject here also. Τις χήρα is then a collective idea, and takes the plural. Winer, too (p. 586 [E T. p 787]), supports this opinion. — πρῶτον] viz, before they give themselves up to the care of the church for them, with special reference to what follows: χήρα καταλεγέσθω, ver. 9, or better perhaps: "before she makes work for herself outside the house" (Hofmann). — τὸν ἴδιον οἶκον εὐσεβεῖν] The term οἶκον likewise shows that he is speaking not of the things

[1] Luther translates it "Neffen" (nephew), which in Old German usage has the meaning "descendant, grandchild;" comp. Gen. xxi. 23, Job xviii. 19; Isa. xiv. 22.

which the children are to do for their widowed mother (or grandmother), but of the things which the widows as mothers are to do for the children ; because the mother or grandmother does not necessarily belong to the οἶκος of a grown-up son or grandson, whereas the children not grown up necessarily belong to the οἶκος of the widowed mother. The meaning therefore is: they are not to forsake their house, *i e.* their children or grandchildren The term εὐσεβεῖν is used to show that the house is a temple to whose service they are to devote themselves. Matthies inaccurately translates : " practise piety in regard to one's own house." Οἶκον is not the accusative of reference, but purely an objective accusative, comp. Acts xvii. 23, and Meyer on the passage. " To honour one's house " is therefore equivalent to serving it with pious heart ; [1] Luther's translation: " rule divinely," is not to the point. — καὶ ἀμοιβὰς ἀποδιδόναι τοῖς προγόνοις] According to the context, the meaning is this : the widows by the εὐσεβεῖν of their house, *i.e.* by their pious care for their children and grandchildren, are to recompense the love shown to themselves by their parents. Chrysostom : ἀπῆλθον ἐκεῖνοι (οἱ πρόγονοι)· οὐκ ἠδυνήθης αὐτοῖς ἀποδοῦναι τὴν ἀμοιβὴν· ἐν τοῖς ἐκγόνοις ἀμειβοῦ· ἀποδίδου τὸ ὀφείλημα διὰ τῶν παίδων. Though this thought is peculiar, it is neither *ingenuous* (de Wette) nor *far-fetched* (Wiesinger). — ἀμοιβή, in the N. T. ἅπαξ λεγόμ ; ἀμοιβ. ἀποδιδόναι, Euripides, *Orestes*, 467. — οἱ πρόγονοι, in contrast with the previous τὰ ἔκγονα : the progenitors; in the N. T. only here and 2 Tim. i. 3. It would be against usage to understand by it the (widowed) mother or grandmother who is still alive. — τοῦτο γάρ ἐστι ἀπόδεκτον κ τ.λ] comp. ii. 3.

Ver. 5 defines more precisely what widows the apostle specially exhorts Timothy to "honour."—ἡ δὲ ὄντως χήρα καὶ μεμονωμένη] καὶ μεμονωμένη is an epexegetical addition, defining ἡ ὄντως χήρα as one with no relatives who take care of her, or of whom she takes care. — ἤλπικεν ἐπὶ τὸν Θεόν]

---

[1] It is certainly correct that εὐσεβεῖν is used properly of conduct towards God, and then of conduct towards parents and persons of higher position , but it is not restricted to such use. In Euripides, *Alcestis*, 1151, it is used, *e g* , of ξένοι Hofmann well says : "If a widow turns her back on the house of her dead husband and of her relations, she neglects her nearest duty, and sins against the holiness of family ties."

The distinction between ἐλπικέναι ἐπί with the dative (iv. 10) and ἐλπικ. ἐπί with accusative, is that in the former case the object furnishes the ground on which the hope rests; in the latter, the goal towards which it is directed. — καὶ προσμένει (strengthened form of μένει; τῇ προσευχῇ προσκαρτερεῖν, Rom. xii. 12; Col. iv. 2) ταῖς δεήσεσι κ. ταῖς προσευχαῖς (comp. ii. 1) νυκτὸς κ. ἡμέρας (1 Thess ii. 9). With this we may compare what Luke (ii. 37) says of Anna the prophetess. Jerome (*Ep. ad Gerontiam*): quibus deus spes est, et omne opus oratio. Matthies rightly remarks: "The idea of the genuine widow is explained not abstractly, but in concrete form, in actual realization, for which reason we have the indicative used instead of the imperative or optative, as if a single representative of the whole class were described in living, personal form." Hofmann will not allow this natural explanation to stand, because "the predicate which names a moral behaviour does not accord with a subject denoting an outward state." Taking ἢ δέ as a relative pronoun, he connects it with ἤλπικεν ἐπὶ Θ., and regards καὶ προσμενεῖ (for προσμένει) as the apodosis, ὄντως χήρα καὶ μεμονωμένη forming an affix to ἢ δέ. Apart from the objection that the meaning advanced by Hofmann would have been expressed much more naturally by ἡ δὲ ὄντως χήρα κ. μεμ., ἢ ἤλπικεν ἐπὶ Θεὸν, καὶ προσμενεῖ, the meaning would be far from appropriate here. Besides, it gives no characteristic mark of the widow, for the hope which results in continual prayer is not peculiar to widows. Hofmann in his polemics does not observe that, in the apostle's presupposition, she whose outward condition is more definitely described is a believing widow. When this is observed, we cannot deny the appropriateness of the reference (in Wiesinger) to 1 Cor. vii. 32 ff.

Ver. 6. Ἡ δὲ σπαταλῶσα] The opposite of the ὄντως χήρα who has dedicated her life to piety. Σπαταλᾶν, "revel, be wanton," occurs elsewhere only in Jas. v. 5 (Wisd. xxi. 15). There is nothing to show that the apostle was here thinking of the squandering of the support received. — ζῶσα τέθνηκε] These words have been taken as exhorting Timothy to consider the wanton widow as dead, and not to support her; but this takes away all point from the words. The right meaning is obtained by comparing such passages as Eph. iv. 18, Rev. iii. 1, and others similar. While the widow who conducts herself as a widow should, lives in God, the wanton widow leads a life given up to the desires of the world, a life only in appearance, the very opposite of the true life. Theophylact: κἂν δοκεῖ ζῆν κατὰ τὴν αἰσθητὴν, τέθνηκε κατὰ πνεῦμα.

Ver. 7. After describing briefly the conduct of the two classes of widows, the apostle continues: καὶ ταῦτα παράγγελλε] ταῦτα refers to what was said regarding widows Timothy is, by way of exhortation, to announce to the church, therefore to the widows, what the apostle has written to him; παράγγελλε, comp. iv. 11. — ἵνα ἀνεπίληπτοι ὦσιν] ἵνα here gives the purpose (at 2 Thess. iii. 12 it stands after παραγγέλλειν κ παρακαλεῖν in a different sense). The subject of the clause is not the dependants (τέκνα καὶ ἔκγονα, ver 4) of the widows, much less they along with the widows (Heydenreich), or men and women (Grotius), but the widows spoken of in the preceding verses.

Ver. 8 Εἰ δέ τις τῶν ἰδίων καὶ μάλιστα [τῶν] οἰκείων οὐ προνοεῖ] "*But if any one does not take care for his relatives, and especially for those of his household;*" τις is here quite general in meaning, and this generality must in the first place be maintained — τῶν ἰδίων and [τῶν] οἰκείων are not neuters, but masculines. In the N. T., as a rule, οἱ ἴδιοι are those in close fellowship and community with another. For instance, in John xiii. 1 the relation of Christ to His disciples is thus named. Οἱ ἴδιοι is here wider in meaning than οἱ οἰκεῖοι, which is "those properly of the household." Hofmann thinks that, if the reading without the article be adopted, μάλιστα does not belong to the verb, but to οἰκείων = οἰκειοτάτων. It is well known that in classic Greek the superlative is sometimes expressed by μάλιστα before the positive. But this usage is never found in the N. T.; and besides, here, where οἰκεῖος refers to τὸν ἴδιον οἶκον (ver. 4), and is therefore equivalent to "member of the household or family," the superlative οἰκειότατος is meaningless. To paraphrase it into "nearest kinsman of all" is purely arbitrary. At any rate, the article is by no means necessary before οἰκείων, since

the ἴδιοι and the οἰκεῖοι belong to one class; the intervening μάλιστα makes no difference, although it lays special emphasis on the latter. — τὴν πίστιν ἤρνηται] inasmuch as he does not do that to which faith, if it be a living faith, incites him; fides enim non tollit officia naturalia, sed perficit et firmat, Bengel. — καὶ ἔστιν ἀπίστου χείρων] Ἄπιστος here is not (as at 2 Cor. iv. 4; Tit. i. 15) "an enemy of Christ," but "one who is not a Christian," one who as such is incited by natural law to love his own children (comp Matt. v. 46, 47).
—Calvin says on this: quod duabus de causis verum est, nam quo plus quisque in cognitione Dei profecit, eo minus habet excusationis; . . . deinde hoc genus officii est, quod natura ipsa dictat, sunt enim στοργαὶ φυσικαί.—The reference of this general thought varies according to the various interpretations of ver. 4. If τέκνα καὶ ἔκγονα be taken there as the subject of μανθανέτωσαν, then it refers to the relation of these to the widowed mother or grandmother; if the proper subject be αἱ χῆραι, it refers naturally to the conduct of the widows. There is nothing to show that the apostle here was thinking of the mutual relation between the widows and their dependants (Matthies) Still less correct is it, with Hofmann, to wrench ver. 8 away from ver 4, and to understand by τις "*the father of a family*," "who at his death leaves wife and child unprovided for, when he might well have provided for them." Such a sudden transition from what hitherto has been the subject of discussion would be exceedingly strange; nor is there any hint of it given by the verb προνοεῖν, which denotes care in general terms, not "care for those left behind at death." Paul has hitherto been speaking of the conduct of widows, and only to that same subject can this verse be referred.

Vv. 9 ff. From this point the apostle takes up a special class of widows, viz. those who had been placed by the church on a formal list, and who accordingly possessed a certain position of honour in the church. From ver. 16 it is to be inferred that it was the duty of the church to care for them so long as they lived, while from ver. 10 it appears that they had to perform for the church certain labours of love suited to them. The various views regarding them have already been given in the Introduction, § 5 ; each has its special difficulties. Still Mosheim's view is the most probable,[1] only what the apostle says of these widows does not justify us in transplanting into the apostolic age the ecclesiastical institution of the χῆραι (πρεσβύτεραι, πρεσβύτιδες) in the same form as it had at a later date. We have here only the tendencies from which the institution was gradually developed. Though the apostle takes it for granted that the church takes care of these widows, we cannot conclude that, as the older expositors assume,[2] he means by the καταλεγέσθω their reception into the number of the widows to be supported by the church. Poor widows, like poor persons generally, would surely be supported by the church without being placed in the special class of the χῆραι here meant — Vv. 9, 10. χήρα καταλεγέσθω] καταλέγειν (ἄπ. λεγ in N. T), properly "select," then "*place upon a list*," used especially of the citizens chosen for service in war; comp Aristophanes, *Acharn.* 1629, *Lysist.* 14. 6. χήρα is not the subject, but the predicate ; Winer, p 549 [E T p 738] · "*as widow let her be registered* (enrolled) who is not under sixty" (so, too, Wiesinger, Hofmann). The common translation is : "let a widow be chosen" (so de Wette, van Oosterzee, Plitt). — μὴ ἔλαττον ἐτῶν ἑξήκοντα γεγονυῖα] Leo and some others connect γεγονυῖα with what follows (Vulgate · quae fuerit unius viri uxor ; so Luther) A comparison with iii. 2 shows that this is incorrect; besides, the construction itself demands the connection with what precedes. The genitive does not depend on γεγονυῖα (as Luke ii. 42 : ὅτι ἐγένετο ἐτῶν δώδεκα), but on ἔλαττον, and is equivalent to ἢ ἔτη ἑξήκοντα (comp Demosthenes, *in Timocrat.* p 481 : γέγονα οὐκ ἔλαττον ἢ τριάκοντα ἔτη) — ἑνὸς ἀνδρὸς γυνή, after the explanation given at iii. 2 of the corresponding expression . μιᾶς γυναικὸς ἀνήρ, denotes

---

[1] With his view de Wette and Wiesinger agree , also Hofmann in substance. Even van Oosterzee refers us to Mosheim , but he wrongly identifies the widows here mentioned with the deaconesses, whereas Mosheim clearly distinguishes between them.

[2] Chrysostom in his commentary explains this passage as meaning, receiving in order to care for. In his *Hom* 31, *in div N T. loc* , however, he interprets it of receiving into an ecclesiastical office, saying καθάπερ εἰσὶ παρθένων χοροὶ, οὕτω καὶ χηρῶν τὸ παλαιὸν ἦσαν χοροὶ, καὶ οὐκ ἐξῆν αὐταῖς ἁπλῶς εἰς τὰς χήρας ἐγγράφεσθαι.

the widow who has lived in sexual intercourse with no one but her lawfully wedded husband. — ἐν ἔργοις καλοῖς μαρτυρουμένη] μαρτυρεῖν in the N. T. has often the meaning. give one a good testimony; hence the passive is: *possess a good testimony* (μαρτυρίαν καλὴν ἔχειν, iii. 7). 'Εν here (as elsewhere in connection with verbs of similar meaning, see Wahl, *s v. ἐν H. a*) gives the ground (of the good testimony); comp. Heb xi. 2, for which in Heb. xi. 39 we have διά. — The ἔργα καλά (comp. ver. 25, vi. 18, and other passages in the Pastoral Epistles) are not only works of benevolence, although to these chief attention is directed, but generally "*good works*." — εἰ ἐτεκνοτρόφησεν] εἰ cannot be joined immediately with καταλεγέσθω, since the sense forbids us to consider this and the following clauses as co-ordinate with what precedes. It is rather attached to the ἐν ἔργ καλ. μαρτυρουμένη, not, however, in such a way (as Heydenreich thinks) as to stand for ὅτε (which is also not the case in Acts xxvi. 22, 23), but in such a way as to distribute the preceding idea into its single parts, and connect them with it in free fashion, "*if namely*." Luther. "and who has a testimony of good works, as she has brought up children." — On ἐτεκνοτρόφησεν (ἅπ. λεγ) Theodoret remarks · οὐ θρέψαι μόνον ἀπαιτεῖ, ἀλλὰ καὶ τὸ εὐσεβῶς θρέψαι Wrong; the verb, not "rear" (van Oosterzee), but "nurse" (Luther), refers to the attention of love, as do the verbs that follow, compare Acts xxii. 3. ἀνατεθραμμένος distinguished from πεπαιδευμένος. There is no reason for thinking here of strange children, since it may rightly be called a καλὸν ἔργον, if a mother does not entrust the rearing of her children to others, but takes care of them herself (in opposition to Leo and Wiesinger), the apostle is not thinking of the distinction between strange children and one's own. Heydenreich, de Wette, and others think that Paul bases this exhortation on the ground that the τεκνοτροφία was part of the official duties of a χήρα, and that she must have practised them before; but they are wrong, because in that case we could not but consider the ξενοδοχεῖν κ.τ λ as also the special duties of such widows. — εἰ ἐξενοδόχησεν] comp. iii. 2, Tit. i. 8 (φιλόξενος), Rom. xii 13, Heb xiii. 2. The word ξενοδοχεῖν (Euripides, *Alc.* 555) is in the N. T. ἅπαξ λεγ — εἰ ἁγίων πόδας ἔνιψεν] comp. John xiii. 5 ff.; also Luke vii. 44. Wahl: pedum lotio (apud Judaeos) opus erat servile eademque apud eos in primis humanitatis officiis hospiti praestandis ponebatur. The feet-washing is meant literally, and not merely as "a symbolic expression for the manifestations of self-denying love" (first ed.); although Paul might at the same time be thinking of other services of lowly love. Theophylact: εἰ τὰς ἐσχάτας ὑπηρεσίας τοῖς ἁγίοις ἀνεπαισχύντως ἐξετέλεσε. — The ἅγιοι are not merely the ξένοι (in opposition to Wiesinger), but the Christians in general who came into the house as guests. — εἰ θλιβομένοις ἐπήρκεσεν] Bengel arbitrarily limits the meaning of θλιβόμενοι, wishing to interpret it only of the poor; it is to be taken more generally as equivalent to "*those in distress.*" Ἐπαρκεῖν in the N. T. only here and at ver. 16. — After naming several works of love in detail, the apostle adds more generally, in order to exhaust the ἐν ἐργ. καλ. μαρτυρεῖσθαι: εἰ παντὶ ἔργῳ ἀγαθῷ ἐπηκολούθησε[1] Hence we must not here think of works of benevolence only, but take πᾶν ἔργον in its entire meaning — ἐπακολουθεῖν (in the N. T. only here at ver. 24, at Mark xvi. 20, where it is absolute, and at 1 Pet. ii. 21, where it is joined with τοῖς ἴχνεσι) is mostly referred to persons, but we cannot therefore, with Schleiermacher, supply here αὐτοῖς, *i.e.* θλιβομένοις.[2] It stands here in the same sense as διώκειν, vi. 11; 1 Thess v. 15, Heb. xii. 14. Luther: "who has followed every good work."[3]

Ver. 11. Νεωτέρας δὲ χήρας παραιτοῦ] νεωτέρας is not here strictly comparative in reference to ver. 9 (Wiesinger: "widows under sixty years"); it is rather a positive, as in

---

[1] This Hofmann wrongly disputes, wishing to lay the emphasis not on παντὶ ἔργ ἀγαθ., but on ἐπηκολούθησι "if there was any good to be done, *she was to follow after it with all diligence*, she was to make it her business."

[2] Bengel gives a peculiar reference to the word, which cannot be justified, saying antistitum et virorum est bonis operibus praeire Tit. iii. 8, 14, mulierum, subsequi, adjuvando pro sua parte.

[3] Hofmann is indeed not wrong in contending against the view that ver. 15 points to the services which the widows here mentioned are to perform for the church. He says that this verse only tells that "she must have fulfilled the duties of a mother and a Christian housewife." But the enumeration of all these duties indicates that as a church-widow she must be practised in the exercise of many services of love

vv. 1, 2 (so, too, van Oosterzee). — παραιτοῦ] in opposition to καταλεγέσθω, ver. 9 (and in opposition to τίμα in ver. 3); yet in such a way that, according to the analogy of the passages, iv. 7, 2 Tim. ii. 23, Tit. iii. 10, Heb. xii. 25, it denotes not only that they are to be omitted from the καταλέγεσθαι, but also that they are to be avoided personally. Luther: "the young widows, however, get rid of."[1] The reason for this injunction is given by the apostle in the next words: ὅταν γὰρ καταστρηνιάσωσι τοῦ Χριστοῦ γαμεῖν θέλουσιν] The meaning of the verb is variously given by expositors. Several take it as equivalent to "be voluptuous, lust after," and so refer it to sexual relation, appealing to Rom. xviii. 9, where στρηνιᾷν is used along with πορνεύειν. But this collocation does not prove that the verbs are related in sense, all the less that in the passage πορνεύειν is not used literally. Even in Rev. xviii. 3, στρῆνος has not the meaning of sexual desire, but more generally of "wantonness." There is no justification, therefore, for de Wette's translation: "to feel sexual desire," and that of Jerome (Ep. 123, al 11, ad Agerochiam al. Gerontiam): quae fornicatae sunt. Others maintain here the more general meaning of the word luxuriari (Wiesinger; van Oosterzee also translates: "if they have become luxurious," but explains it of voluptuous desire, of the pruritus libidinosus). Since the word στρῆνος also occurs in the sense of violent desire for something (Lycophr. 438, see Pape, 5, s v.), Plitt explains στρηνιᾷν as equivalent to "go in pursuit of the satisfaction of one's desires," but without saying what desires are here meant. In Pape, the word is explained as equivalent to "be insolent" (στρῆνος = "insolence"), so, too, in Stephanus (καταστρηνιάω = insolentius et lascivius me gero adversum); similarly Theophylact. καθυπερηφανεύεσθαι It

---

[1] Baur at an earlier period (Die Sog. Pastoralbriefe, p. 47) construed νεώτεραι χῆραι grammatically together, and only—very arbitrarily, it is true—maintained that these χῆραι are distinguished from those in ver. 9 by being only virgins (and not ὄντως χῆραι) bearing the name of χῆραι. Later (Paulus, d Ap. J Chr. p. 497) he expressed the opinion that νεωτέρας and χήρας are not to be taken together, that the one is the subject rather, the other the predicate, and that the words accordingly have the sense· "Younger persons of the female sex do not receive into the list of the χῆραι" This only adds to the arbitrariness of the historian, the arbitrariness of the exegete.

will be most correct to adhere to the meaning "be luxurious." In all these various explanations the prefix κατα is taken in the sense of hostile opposition, and the genitive τοῦ Χριστοῦ regarded as the object to which those widows are opposed by their στρηνιᾶν. This reference of κατα is in entire accordance with Greek usage; comp in the N. T. the words: καταδυναστεύω, κατακαυχάομαι, καταναρκάω, κατασοφίζομαι. Hofmann's explanation completely diverges from these: "After such widows have let the Saviour have their whole desire, after they have delighted in Him, they wish to marry." For this interpretation of καταστρηνιᾶν Χριστοῦ, Hofmann appeals to Ps xxxvii. 4, where the Hebrew הִתְעַנַּג עַל־יְהוָֹה ("rejoice in God, delight in God") is translated in the LXX. by καταστρυφᾶν τοῦ κυρίου But to this there are three objections—(1) This interpretation of καταστρυφᾶν in a good sense is quite singular in nature, (2) καταστρυφᾶν cannot without proof be considered identical with καταστρηνιᾶν; and (3) ὅταν is explained simply by "after that," whereas it properly means. "*in case that, so soon as.*" Ὅταν may indeed be sometimes rendered by "after that;" but whereas the latter only expresses the relation of time, ὅταν is only used in such cases of an inner relation. In the present case it shows that the θέλειν γαμεῖν is something which has its ground or presupposed condition in the καταστρηνιᾶν of the widows But how can it be imagined that delight in the Lord gives any ground whatever for the desire of marriage? — Besides, the whole context compels us to take καταστρ. in a bad sense.[1] — γαμεῖν θέλουσιν] We must not overlook the fact that Paul does not say simply γαμοῦσιν; he wishes here to bring out the direction in which their thoughts turn If a widow received the honourable distinction of καταλέγεσθαι, she had to recognise it as her duty to devote her life henceforth to her office, to her works of love for the church. These she

[1] Even earlier expositors rejected the strange opinion which Heydenreich adopts, that "στρηνιᾶν in its root-signification and origin παρὰ τῷ στεριῖν καὶ ἀποσπᾶν τὰς ἡνίας means, cast off the reins, be or become unbridled."—Quite as wrong is the inversion of thought which Heinrichs takes up, saying clarius mentem expressisset Ap. inverso ordine ὅταν γὰρ γαμεῖν θέλωσιν, καταστρηνιῶσι τοῦ Χριστοῦ; for γαμεῖν θέλουσιν is a consequence of the καταστρηνιᾶν, not vice versâ.

must regard as her life-vocation. But in young widows the worldly desire was roused only too easily, so that they put aside their life-vocation, and sought only their own satisfaction in forming a new marriage, thereby withdrawing themselves from the work for the church. Their thoughts were therefore turned to something else than the things to which their position in the church directed them.[1]

Ver. 12. Ἔχουσαι κρίμα, ὅτι] Almost all expositors take ὅτι as introducing the object, so that what follows describes the κρίμα which the widows have to suffer There is variance only in the more precise definition of κρίμα, whether it is to be understood as the judgment of God (Wiesinger, van Oosterzee), or the judgment of men (Wegscheider: "they draw blame on themselves;" Plitt · "they meet with reproof"), or the judgment of their own conscience (so in this commentary; comp. iv. 2 : κεκαυτηριασμένοι τὴν ἰδίαν συνείδησιν). Hofmann takes ὅτι as "because," as there is no article with κρίμα: "they are liable to condemnation," but this makes the meaning of κρίμα ἔχειν too vague. Since the use of the article in the N. T. is so wavering, it is difficult to come to a definite conclusion. Plitt's explanation may be taken as the most natural. — ὅτι τὴν πρώτην πίστιν ἠθέτησαν] τὴν πίστιν ἀθετεῖν in Polybius (who often uses ἀθετεῖν by itself) is "fidem fallere, break a pledge." This meaning has rightly been maintained here by most. So Chrysostom : παρέβησαν τὰς συνθήκας; Augustine on Ps. lxxv.· primam fidem irritam fecerunt; voverunt et non reddiderunt. We cannot infer from this expression that any formal oath not to marry again was demanded when they were received into the number of church-widows; but it certainly does follow that the reception pledged the widows to devote their lives only to the service of the Lord. To this pledge they were unfaithful so soon as they began the behaviour described in ver. 11. It is out of place here to appeal to such passages in the Fathers as testify that in later times the *deaconesses* had to vow that

---

[1] It is to be noted that Paul does not speak of the θέλειν γαμεῖν on the part of the widows as necessarily a καταστρηνιᾶν τοῦ Χριστοῦ. He is not uttering any general principle; he is dealing only with the actual circumstances which were occurring among the widows under discussion.

they would not marry. Πρώτην does not stand for πρότεραν, but is used by the apostle because the vow (tacit or expressed) to serve the Lord was taken at the *beginning* of their new position in life. Calvin wrongly takes the πρώτη πίστις as the fides in *baptismo* data, referring the unfaithfulness to the desire to marry, which is defined more precisely by ὅταν καταστρηνιάσωσι τ. Χρ.

Ver. 13. "Ἅμα δὲ καὶ ἀργαὶ μανθάνουσι περιερχόμεναι τὰς οἰκίας] By far the greater number of expositors connect μανθάνουσι immediately with περιερχόμεναι, "they learn to run about in houses" (Luther; so, too, de Wette, Wiesinger, van Oosterzee). But μανθάνειν with the partic. does not mean *learn;* it is "*observe, perceive, remark;*" μανθάνειν, in the sense of *learn* ("accustom oneself"), has always the infinitive (comp. ver. 4) Leo therefore takes it here as "be wont to;" but this sense only occurs in the preterite Winer (pp. 325 f. [E. T p 436]) thinks it probable that ἀργαὶ μανθάνουσι are to be taken together, "*they learn idleness*" (or "they learn to be lazy," so in the second edition of this commentary; so, too, Hofmann). It is in favour of this construction that the chief emphasis is laid on ἀργαί; but no passage can be found confirming it.[1] Besides, the position of ἀργαί shows that it belongs to the subject. Bengel had taken refuge in supplying something explaining it: discunt quae domos obeundo discuntur, i. e. statum familiarum curiose explorant. Buttmann (pp. 260 f) agrees with this explanation, only that he regards the supplied words. statum, etc., as too arbitrary and sweeping; he observes: "what they learn περιερχόμεναι τ. οἰκ. is sufficiently indicated, not indeed grammatically, but in sense, by ἀργαί, φλυαροί, περίεργοι, λαλοῦσαι τὰ μὴ δέοντα." But if, as Buttmann thinks, we are to assume here an anacolouthon, it would be more natural to find the hint of what is to be supplied in the περιερχόμεναι τ οἰκ, so that the meaning would be: they learn περιερχόμεναι this very περιέρχεσθαι.

[1] Winer, indeed, quotes two passages, one from Plato, *Euthyd.* 276b · οἱ ἀμαθεῖς ἄρα σοφοὶ μανθάνουσι, and the other from Dio Chi 55 558 ὁ Σωκρά-ης ὅτι μὲν ταῖς ὧν ἐμάνθανι λιθοξόος τὴν τοῦ πατρὸς τέχνην, ἀκηκόαμεν Buttmann remarks on the first, that the addition σοφοί (which is quite meaningless) is rejected on MS. authority, and on the other that it is of quite a different nature. In both cases he is clearly right.

— On the construction περιερχόμεναι τὰς οἰκίας, comp. Matt. iv. 23 : περιῆγεν ὅλην τὴν Γαλιλαίαν. — οὐ μόνον δὲ ἀργαὶ, ἀλλὰ καὶ φλύαροι κ.τ.λ] φλύαροι, " talkative " (Luther), only occurs here ; the verb φλυαρέω in 3 John 10. Theophylact : περιοδεύουσαι τὰς οἰκίας, οὐδὲν ἀλλ' ἢ τὰ ταύτης εἰς ἐκείνην φέρουσι, καὶ τὰ ἐκείνης εἰς ταύτην. Calvin : ex otio nascebatur curiositas, quae ipsa garrulitatis est mater. — καὶ περίεργοι, " inquisitive," Luther (likewise ἄπ. λεγ ; but in 2 Thess. iii 11 : μηδὲν ἐργαζομένους, ἀλλὰ περιεργαζομένους), forms a peculiar contrast to the preceding ἀργαί ; Chrysostom ὁ γὰρ τὰ ἑαυτοῦ μὴ μεριμνῶν τὰ ἑτέρου μεριμνήσει πάντως — λαλοῦσαι τὰ μὴ δέοντα] added to define further what precedes. — In these two verses Paul sets forth the danger of receiving young widows into the class of church-widows. It is not improbable that there were definite instances, and these caused the apostle to speak in this general way.

Ver. 14. Positive instructions regarding young widows. — βούλομαι οὖν] βούλομαι does not express a wish merely (de Wette. " I hold it to be advisable, desirable "), but a definite command ; comp. ii. 8. — οὖν shows that this thought is a deduction from the one previous ; Leo : quae quum ita sint — νεωτέρας, sc. χήρας, not the virgins, as Baur thinks. — γαμεῖν] used also in 1 Cor. vii. 39 of the re-marriage of widows — τεκνογονεῖν (ἄπ. λεγ., the substantive in ii. 15) does not include, according to the notion peculiar to himself, the rearing of children (van Oosterzee). The apostle mentions single points; every one can supply the appropriate details for himself. Leo rightly says that the idea of rearing children is included rather in the next word. — οἰκοδεσποτεῖν (ἄπ. λεγ , the substantive often occurs in the N. T.) denotes properly the work of the husband, and is equivalent to τοῦ οἴκου προΐστασθαι, iii. 4, 12 ; here it is used of the wife, who necessarily has her share in ruling the household. — μηδεμίαν ἀφορμὴν διδόναι τῷ ἀντικειμένῳ λοιδορίας χάριν] The last words: λοιδορίας χάριν, are not to be taken with βούλομαι (Mack: " I will . . . for the sake of the reproach which would otherwise be cast upon the church;" the meaning is obviously the reverse of this, so soon as these words are placed in thought after γαμεῖν, since χάριν never loses the sense of "for the sake of"), nor with τῷ ἀντικειμένῳ (Leo: "inimico ad calumniandum parato"). They are to be connected with ἀφορμὴν διδόναι, but not in such a way as to form a supplement to that phrase (de Wette, with the remark that this is indeed a strange construction; also Wiesinger); the supplement should have been in the genitive, see 2 Cor. v. 12. In short, λοιδορ χαρ. only defines ἀφορμὴν διδόναι more precisely. A definite object is not to be supplied (Leo: occasionem sc. ipsas seducendi praebere, so, too, van Oosterzee, and in this commentary), but the interpretation is: "*they are to afford the enemy no opportunity for slandering,*" i.e. they are to abstain from everything which the enemy may use for slandering the church (not merely the widows); so, too, Hofmann on the whole. By the ἀντικείμενος is meant either the devil (so most of the older commentators,[1] also Leo and Matthies; van Oosterzee uncertain) or the human enemy, the Jew and Gentile (so de Wette, Wiesinger, Plitt, Hofmann). Hofmann is wrong, however, in asserting that τοῦ σατανᾶ in ver. 15 is decisive against the first explanation, for αὐτοῦ would have been used.—De Wette joins the last part of the clause to what precedes, in such a way as to supply: "and in this way." But there is no hint of this limitation. If we add it simply to what precedes, it is more natural to refer it to the whole conduct of the widows

Ver. 15. Reason for the injunction given: ἤδη γάρ τινες ἐξετράπησαν ὀπίσω τοῦ σατανᾶ.—τινές, viz. "widows;" ἐξετράπησαν κ.τ.λ.; comp. i. 6; ὀπίσω, comp. Acts v. 37, xx. 30: they have turned away, viz. from the Christian path of life, and have followed Satan This does not necessarily mean a formal apostasy from Christianity, or a connection with the heretics, it may also mean yielding oneself up to an un-Christian, carnal life (Wiesinger). This arose from their not living in accordance with the rule laid down by the apostle.—On ἤδη, Bengel rightly remarks: particula provocandi ad experientiam. De Wette is quite unjustified in asserting that Paul could not yet have had such an experience.

---

[1] Comp. *Constit. Apost.* III. 2 νεωτέραις (χήραις) δὲ μετὰ τὴν τοῦ πρώτου τελευτὴν συγκεχωρήσθω καὶ ὁ δεύτερος, ἵνα μὴ εἰς κρίμα τοῦ διαβόλου ἐπίσωσι, καὶ παγίδας πολλὰς, καὶ ἐπιθυμίας νοήτους.

Ver 16. According to Heydenreich, Leo, de Wette, Wiesinger, van Oosterzee, and other expositors, this verse is *in substance* a repetition of what was already said in vv. 4 and 8; but if a right view of those verses be taken, there is not so much repetition. — Hofmann wishes to separate ver. 16 from what precedes it, as he separates ver. 8 from the preceding words: "If in ver. 16 the apostle comes to speak of the case in which the support of a widow is not to fall a burden on the church, this has no reference to the honouring of widows." There is as little ground for the one separation as for the other; for it is not to be supposed that καταλέγεσθαι in ver. 9 does not refer to the church's support. — εἴ τις πιστὸς ἢ πιστὴ ἔχει χήρας] so runs the *Rec.* (Tisch. 7) But the weightiest MSS. have the reading εἴ τις πιστὴ ἔχει χήρας (Tisch. 8), which is decidedly to be preferred. The other is only a pointless correction, arising from the idea that the husband should be named along with the wife, and without considering that ἤ is by no means suitable to the mention of both together, and that τὶς πιστή must in any case be a Christian *spouse*. The reason why the wife and not the husband is named is, that on her was laid the duty of caring for the widows belonging to the house. The ἔχειν expresses the close connection of the widows with the particular family, a connection which may most naturally be supposed to be one of kin.[1] Erasmus translates it · si qua mater habet filiam viduam; and de Wette, too, supposes that by widow here we are to understand the daughter, niece, etc., not the mother, aunt, etc. This limitation, however, is not contained in the expression itself. Had Paul thought of the relationship in this definite way, he would have expressed himself accordingly. — καὶ μὴ βαρείσθω ἡ ἐκκλησία] let not a charge or burden be laid on the church by undertaking the support of such widows. (The verb belongs to later Greek for the common βαρύνειν; only the form βεβάρημαι is Attic; comp. Butt-

---

[1] Hofmann thinks that "here the case is supposed of a Christian woman having widows in her house who, for a long or short period, are serviceable, helpful to her." But, as a matter of course, such widows receive hire from those in whose service they work, and their support can therefore not be laid as a burden on the church.

mann, *Ausf. Gr.* II. p. 88.) — The next words give the reason: ἵνα ταῖς ὄντως χήραις κ τ.λ. — On the train of thought in this section dealing with widows, Matthies rightly says. " Complaints are made from the most various quarters regarding difficulties and inequalities, regarding want of order and clearness, regarding repetition and confusion in this section ; but all this is, for the most part, founded on presuppositions which have no basis in fact." We cannot but see that the train of thought is simple and natural, so soon as we observe that the chief point in the apostle's mind in this section is the injunction regarding the καταλέγεσθαι of the widows, and that in ver 4 he is not speaking as in ver. 16 of widows to be cared for, but of those who have to care for the children or grandchildren belonging to them.

Ver. 17. In this and the following verses Paul instructs Timothy as to his behaviour towards the presbyters.[1] — οἱ καλῶς προεστῶτες πρεσβύτεροι διπλῆς τιμῆς ἀξιούσθωσιν] On καλῶς προεστῶτες, comp. iii. 4. The contrast to the elders "who superintend well," is formed by οἱ ἁμαρτάνοντες, ver. 20, not merely, as van Oosterzee thinks, "those who distinguish themselves *less* in their office ;" καλῶς does not denote a special distinction, but conduct worthy of the office. —Chrysostom explained τιμή by θεραπεία καὶ τῶν ἀναγκαίων χορηγία ; de Wette translates it directly by "*reward*" True, τιμή does occur in classic use in the sense of " present, reward " ; but the context by no means demands that meaning here (in opposition to de Wette). We must keep here to the general meaning of τιμή, "honour,"—as in vi. 1 (comp. also τιμᾶν, ver. 3),—although we may grant that the apostle was thinking particularly of the honour which the church was bound to show to their elders by presenting them with the means necessary for their support. It is quite erroneous to interpret τιμή of a maintenance definitely fixed. The adjective διπλῆς is taken by most expositors in the wider

---

[1] Strange to say, Hofmann asserts that in ver 17 πρισβύτιροι are not the presbyters, but "the men of advanced years, from whom the superintendents were chosen, and out of these the apostle exalts those who occupy this office worthily." Only in ver. 19 does he think that πρισβύτιρος is used in the official sense.

sense, but though in the use of διπλόος it is not necessary to urge an accurate measure, still it is never equivalent to πλείων. It is certainly wrong to refer (see de Wette on the passage) the διπλῆς here to the heavenly and earthly honour (Ambrosius), or to the distinction between respect and reward (Matthies), or to the double portion of the first-born (Grotius), or to the double portion which, according to the *Const. Apost.* ii. 28, the presbyter received in the oblations (Heydenreich and Baur); all these references are arbitrary. The double honour here is that which comes to the presbyter on account of his office (not, as Hofmann thinks, on account of his age[1]), and that which he obtains by filling his office well — μάλιστα οἱ κοπιῶντες ἐν λογῷ καὶ διδασκαλίᾳ] On κοπιῶντες, comp. iv. 10. Wiesinger says rightly: "we need not seek any special emphasis in κοπιῶντες: those who toil and moil in opposition to those who do not; κοπιάω is used, as elsewhere, of the teacher's arduous vocation." — The preposition ἐν denotes that λόγος κ. δ. is the sphere in which the work takes place (van Oosterzee). — λόγῳ καὶ διδασκαλίᾳ is not to be taken as an hendiadys. Λόγος is more general, διδασκαλία more special. Special stress is laid here on the latter, because activity in teaching was of special importance as a bulwark against heresies. This addition does not prove that at the time when this epistle was composed there was a clear distinction between ruling and teaching presbyters (in opposition to de Wette and Baur). The apostle might quite well have used the same expressions, although the individual superintendents laboured according to their gifts and free determination, not according to fixed rules.

Ver. 18 furnishes the reason for the instruction given in ver. 16, a reason which attaches itself to the idea of κοπιῶντες. — λέγει γὰρ ἡ γραφή βοῦν ἀλοῶντα οὐ φιμώσεις] This expression is found in Deut. xxv. 4. φιμόω, though often used figuratively in the N. T., stands here in its literal meaning. The whole passage, however, is taken figuratively, just as at 1 Cor. ix. 9, where Paul handles it at greater length. Even Philo says (*De Sacrif.*). οὐ γὰρ ὑπὲρ τῶν ἀλόγων ὁ νόμος, ἀλλ' ὑπὲρ τῶν νοῦν καὶ λόγον ἐχόντων. — To these words of

[1] It might even be a younger man who filled the office of a presbyter.

Scripture the apostle further adds: καὶ ἄξιος ὁ ἐργάτης τοῦ μισθοῦ αὐτοῦ] These words are not quoted from the O. T., for the passages to which attention has been directed at Lev. xix. 13 and Deut. xxiv. 14 run differently; but they are found in the N. T. at Luke x. 7 (similarly Matt. x. 10). Hence Baur and Plitt maintain that they are quoted from Luke. — The λέγει ἡ γραφή does not, however, compel us so to refer the words; the apostle simply adds to the words of Scripture a proverb (Christ, too, in the passage quoted seems to use the phrase as proverbial). So Calvin, also Wiesinger, van Oosterzee, Hofmann. — The two sentences, according to the apostle's meaning, express the same thought; hence it is not improbable that the second was added as an interpretation of the first.

Ver. 19. The apostle now defines the proper conduct on Timothy's part towards the presbyters who do not superintend the church καλῶς, but expose themselves to blame, thereby doing hurt to their official influence. — Κατὰ πρεσβυτέρου κατηγορίαν μὴ παραδέχου] Chrysostom wrongly remarks on πρεσβυτέρου. οὐχὶ τὸ ἀξίωμα, ἀλλὰ τὴν ἡλικίαν. Timothy is not to receive an accusation (κατηγορια, Luke vi. 7; John xviii 29) in order to decide regarding it, ἐκτὸς εἰ μὴ ἐπὶ δύο ἢ τριῶν μαρτύρων. On the pleonasm, ἐκτὸς εἰ μή, see Lobeck, *ad Phryn.* p. 459; comp. 1 Cor. xiv 5, xv. 2. Paul is here referring manifestly to the Mosaic law, Deut. xix. 15 (LXX: ἐπὶ στόματος δύο μαρτύρων καὶ ἐπὶ στόματος τριῶν μαρτύρων στήσεται πᾶν ῥῆμα); comp. Deut xvii. 6 (ἐπὶ δυσὶ μάρτυσιν ἢ ἐπὶ τρισὶ μάρτυσι) It is a question whether he does so in the sense—corresponding with the law—of ordaining that Timothy is only to receive an accusation against a presbyter when supported by the testimony of two or three witnesses (so de Wette,[1] Wiesinger, van Oosterzee, and in general most expositors); or whether here, as in Matt. xviii. 16, there is only a somewhat general reference to the law, and it is merely said that Timothy is to receive the accusation only when brought before him in presence of two

[1] De Wette's question, whether Timothy was not to observe this precept of justice in the case of accusations against others, is not to the point. Timothy was not appointed judge over all matters of private dispute

or three witnesses[1] (so Hofmann; comp, too, Winer, p. 351 [E. T. p. 469]; Buttmann, p. 289; ἐπὶ μαρτύρων occurs also in the classics in the sense of " before witnesses ") As he is not speaking here of a decision, but only of the *reception* of an accusation (in order that a decision may be made), and as the construction also is irregular, the second view may be adopted as the more probable one (different in the third edition of this commentary). Reference to the law is made in the N. T. also at Matt. xviii. 16, 2 Cor. xiii. 1, and Heb. x. 28; comp., too, John viii. 17.

Ver. 20 contains a further instruction regarding his conduct toward the presbyters — τοὺς ἁμαρτάνοντας] does not refer to the members of the church in general (de Wette, Wiesinger), but to the presbyters (van Oosterzee, Plitt, Hofmann),—those presbyters who, in their official work or general walk, do not conduct themselves in a manner worthy of their office. In such cases it does not matter whether a charge against them is brought before Timothy or not [2] — ἐνώπιον πάντων ἔλεγχε] The most natural reference of πάντες also is to the presbyters. It would clearly be too much to expect that Timothy should punish *all* sinners before the whole church (comp. Matt. xviii. 15-17); that would be unsuitable, even in the case of presbyters who had sinned. On ἐλέγχειν, " censure," comp. Luke iii 19, Tit. i. 13, ii 15 — "ἵνα καὶ οἱ λοιποὶ φόβον ἔχωσι] "οἱ λοιποί may be only the rest of the same class to which the ἁμαρτάνοντες belong," Hofmann.

Ver. 21. The apostle concludes the section, on the proper conduct towards the presbyters, with a solemn adjuration to observe the precepts given. — διαμαρτύρομαι ἐνώπιον τοῦ Θεοῦ καὶ Χριστοῦ Ἰησοῦ καὶ τῶν ἐκλεκτῶν ἀγγέλων] In the N. T. the verb διαμαρτύρεσθαι means " testify " (so Acts viii. 25, x. 42, xviii. 5, etc.) and " *adjure*," and in the latter sense often serves to strengthen an exhortation (Luke xvi. 28; Acts ii. 40, 1 Thess. iv. 6; 2 Tim. ii. 14, etc.); so, too, here. The addi-

---

[1] The suitability of such a precept is manifest when we consider the position which Timothy had to take up towards the presbyters; comp on this Hofmann.

[2] Neither the present (ἁμαρτάνοντας) nor the lack of δέ disproves this view The aorist (ἁμαρτήσαντας) would have pointed to some earlier incident, and δέ would be necessary only if the apostle had had clearly in mind the contrast to the καλῶς προιστῶντες πρεσβύτεροι mentioned in ver 17

tion καὶ τῶν ἐκλεκτῶν ἀγγέλων is explained from the idea that the throne of God is surrounded by angels as His servants. The reference to the last judgment is wrong, as in Bengel (with whom Wiesinger and van Oosterzee agree): repraesentat Timotheo judicium extremum, in quo Deus revelabitur et Christus cum angelis coram conspicietur. Paul is appealing, not to something future, but to something *present* — The ἐκλεκτῶν cannot be taken as a genitive dependent on τῶν ἀγγέλων (= "before the angels of the elect, *i.e.* believers," so Hofmann); ἐκλεκτῶν, as its position between the article and the substantive shows, is an adjective belonging to ἀγγέλων.[1] It does not distinguish *higher* angels from *lower*,[2] nor the *good* from the *bad*, nor the guardian angels of Timothy and the Ephesian church (Mosheim) from all others, nor the angels in general from earthly beings, it is to be taken simply as an epitheton ornans. The angels as such are ἐκλεκτοὶ Θεοῦ, whom God has chosen as the objects of His love; comp. 1 Pet ii. 4, where ἐκλεκτός is synonymous with ἔντιμος. Wiesinger rightly remarks that ἐκλεκτοί is to be taken as a general epithet of all angels, like ἅγιοι ἀγγ, ἄγγ φωτός, and the like. It is added in order to give greater solemnity to the form of adjuration. Comp. with it the form in Josephus, where (*Bell. Jud.* ii. 16. 14) in Agrippa's address to the Jews we have: μαρτύρομαι δι' ἐγὼ μὲν ὑμῶν τὰ ἅγια καὶ τοὺς ἱεροὺς ἀγγέλους τοῦ Θεοῦ. — ἵνα ταῦτα φυλάξῃς] ταῦτα does not refer to "everything that has been said to Timothy regarding his conduct towards each class" (Hofmann), but to what was said in vv. 17–20 regarding the presbyters. The solemn adjuration is due to the importance which the office of presbyter had for the church.

---

[1] Cases occur in which the genitive of a substantive is governed by a substantive likewise in the genitive (e g 2 Cor. iv 4), cases, too, in which the dependent genitive precedes the substantive governing it (e g Rom xi 13), but none in which the genitive of a substantive—in form adjectival—governed by a substantive in the genitive, stands between it and the article belonging to it.

[2] Baur explains the expression from the gnostic idea of angels who stand in special connection with the Redeemer. Irenaeus, 1 4 5 οἱ ἡλιωκότες αὐτοῦ (τοῦ Σωτῆρος) ἄγγελοι, vii 1 οἱ περὶ τὸν Σωτῆρα ἄγγελοι, iv 5. οἱ ἄγγελοι οἱ μετ' αὐτοῦ οἱ δορυφόροι. — But apart from other reasons, the expression here used is much too indefinite to be referred to that idea. Van Oosterzee takes ἐκλεκτοί to denote the *highest* orders of angels, but does not prove that the word is used in such a way.

De Wette, Wiesinger, van Oosterzee refer it only to ver. 20 ; but this is contradicted by the close connection of the verse with what precedes. — Χωρὶς προκρίματος, μηδὲν κ.τ.λ] πρόκριμα, "*prejudice*," in a favourable as well as an unfavourable sense Several expositors take it here in an unfavourable sense, so that the next words : μηδὲν ποιῶν κατὰ πρόσκλισιν, form a contrast to χωρὶς προκρίματος (so in this commentary). But as there is nothing to indicate a contrast, it is better to take the second member as defining the first more precisely : '*without prejudice, doing nothing by favour*." — Hofmann translates πρόκριμα by "preference" (so Leo); but Wiesinger has already remarked that this meaning cannot be proved. If πρόκλησιν were to be taken as the original reading, it would have to be explained as Theophylact explains it. προσκαλεῖταί σε τὸ ἐν μέρος εἰς τὸ βοηθεῖν αὐτῷ μὴ τοίνυν ποιήσῃς κατὰ τὴν ἐκείνου πρόσκλησιν, which nevertheless is still an artificial interpretation.[1]

Ver. 22. The exhortation in this verse: χεῖρας ταχέως μηδενὶ ἐπιτίθει, is not defined further. In the N. T. the laying on of hands is mentioned on various occasions; thus specially in healing the sick (whether by Christ or His disciples), in bestowing the divine blessing (Matt. xix 13, 15), in imparting the Holy Spirit (Acts viii 17), in appointing to a definite ecclesiastical office (Acts vi. 6), in setting apart for special church work (Acts xiii. 3). It has been thought that Paul has here in mind the laying on of hands which was done at the readmission of excommunicated persons (de Wette, Wiesinger); but there is no trace in the N. T. of the existence of this custom in apostolic times. It is more natural to refer it to the ordination, whether of a presbyter or deacon (besides the older expositors, Mosheim, Otto, van Oosterzee,[2] Plitt, and others); but in that case ver. 22 should have come before ver. 21. Hofmann thinks that it is used

---

[1] Reiche is wrong in saying Huther et Matthies, quin lectionem hanc (πρόσκλησιν) absurdam Lachmanni auctoritate sequantur, *parum abesse* videntur. The reading πρόσκλισιν is distinctly enough preferred by Matthies, as well as in this commentary, in spite of the weight allowed to the important authorities that testify for the other reading

[2] Van Oosterzee wrongly thinks that vv 24, 25, are in favour of this explanation , there is in them no hint of any reference to ordination

of the appointment to a church office; but of this there is no hint in the context. It will be most correct to take the exhortation quite generally, so that the meaning is, Timothy is to lay hands ταχέως, *i.e.* " in over-hasty fashion," on no one—whatever the occasion may be. The reason why not, is given in the next words μηδὲ κοινώνει ἁμαρτίαις ἀλλοτρίαις. The ἀλλοτρίαι ἁμαρτίαι are not, as Hofmann thinks, the sins of those who are hasty in the laying on of hands, but the sins of those on whom hands are too hastily laid. He who thoughtlessly lays hands on the unworthy, thereby declaring them worthy of the divine blessing, makes himself a sharer in their sins. Against this Timothy is to guard; he is rather to observe what Paul expresses by saying. σεαυτὸν ἁγνὸν τήρει. This exhortation is in itself quite general, but it stands here in close relation to the foregoing warning. Timothy is to keep himself pure (ἁγνός as in iv. 12, not in the special meaning "chaste"), particularly in not making himself a partaker of others' sins by laying hands on them too hastily This reference, declared by van Oosterzee to be the only one possible, is wrongly denied by de Wette and Wiesinger. Heinrichs and others err in regarding the apostle's exhortation as "a prohibition against intercourse with wicked men."

Ver. 23. Μηκέτι ὑδροπότει κ.τ.λ.] Of course the apostle does not mean to forbid Timothy to drink water at all, but only urges him not to avoid wine altogether. ὑδροποτεῖν does not exactly mean "drink water," but: "*be a water-drinker*," and is only used of a man who makes water his special and exclusive drink; see Winer, p. 464 [E. T. p. 624] The reason of Timothy's abstinence from wine is not that he, after the fashion of the Essenes, regarded its enjoyment as something not permitted to him, nor that he subjected himself to an asceticism wrong in nature (Wiesinger); but that, in his zeal for moderation (which is a part of the ἁγνεία), and in order to set an example against excess, he avoided wine, whereby, however, he might appear to favour a false asceticism (so, too, van Oosterzee) If this be kept in view, we cannot overlook the connection of the verse with what precedes De Wette rightly remarks (following Estius, Grotius, and others) that this exhortation contains a limitation of the previous exhortation, and at the same time a contrast to exaggerated asceticism As a reason for Timothy's enjoying some wine, Paul adduces his sickliness It does not, however, follow, as Matthies thinks, that the apostle made this exhortation *only* out of concern for Timothy's health. Had that been the case, we cannot but hold, with Schleiermacher, that the apostle here descends to particulars which strangely interrupt the train of thought, since ver. 24 is clearly attached again to ver. 22.

Ver 24. This and the following verse, in close relation to one another, as ὡσαύτως shows, express a truth quite general, which the context defines more precisely — τινῶν ἀνθρώπων αἱ ἁμαρτίαι πρόδηλοί εἰσι] πρόδηλος does not mean "formerly manifest" (Calvin, Beza, Leo, Mack, Matthies, and others), but "manifest before all eyes" (Chrysostom, Theodoret, de Wette, Wiesinger, Hofmann, and others). Comp Heb vii. 14 (see Delitzsch, comment. on the passage); Judith viii 29 ; 2 Macc. iii 17, xiv. 39 ; so also in the classics (comp. the Latin propalam).—προάγουσαι εἰς κρίσιν is here, as often, intransitive (opp. ἀκολουθεῖν, comp Matt. xxi 9), equivalent to "*precede.*" According to the sense, we must supply as the dative of more precise definition : "those who have committed the sins." — εἰς κρίσιν, equivalent to "to judgment" The meaning therefore is : some men are in such a condition that their sins are not only made manifest by the κρίσις, but they are already notorious beforehand , they precede to judgment those who have practised them, and thus show in anticipation the result of the judgment. — The next clause forms the contrast to this thought : τισὶ δὲ καὶ ἐπακολουθοῦσιν] ἐπακολουθεῖν corresponds to the προάγειν, and ἄδηλοι naturally suggests itself in contrast with πρόδηλοι The meaning is : Some men are in such a condition that—in regard to the κρίσις—their sins follow them, i e. that their sins are only made manifest by their coming to judgment , the judgment alone makes their sins manifest. — Mack imports arbitrary references by his interpretation : " they follow *hard on their heels, so that they cannot remain unknown, except to those hasty and careless* in observing." — De Wette is right in his explanation : "with some they are only known afterwards," but he is wrong in his additional remark: "when they have gone on a longer or shorter distance;" on this point there is clearly nothing said here.—As the verse has the appearance of an aphorism, κρίσις is to be taken quite generally, but since the apostle utters this general sentence in reference to ver. 22, it is to warn Timothy that he is to lay hands on no man rashly, etc, without a κρίσις, i e without subjecting him to a judgment whereby sins, usually hidden, may become manifest.—As there is no good ground for interpreting ver. 22 of ordination, it is wrong to take κρίσις here as identical with δοκιμάζειν, iii 10. For de Wette's explanation also· "the ecclesiastical decision of the moral censor," there is no sufficient ground. There is as little ground for the opinion of some expositors (Wiesinger, van Oosterzee, Hofmann) who interpret the κρίσις of the judgment of God, and find the thought expressed that in the divine judgment all sins alike, whether manifest before or hidden, shall come to light Wiesinger further assumes that thereby the exhortation to Timothy to beware of others' sins as of *his own*, is strengthened But, on the one hand, it is arbitrary to supply Θεοῦ with κρίσις,[1] on the other hand, the apostle is not discussing various sins, but the sins of various men. Further, it is wrong to obscure the meaning of ἐπακολουθοῦσιν, and to put in its place the thought, "they are hidden." Besides, we cannot see how the thought thus taken could serve Timothy as a standard for his conduct, for *those* sins which are only made manifest by the last judgment must remain hidden to Timothy, in which case he could not be reproved for laying hands on those who had committed such sins.[2] To the opinion that Paul wished to strengthen his exhortation to Timothy by alluding to the last judgment there is this objection, that the only reason for drawing a distinction between manifest and hidden sins, would have been a suspicion on Paul's part that Timothy was guilty of

---

[1] It is certainly correct to say that κρίσις, even without Θεοῦ, sometimes in the N. T. denotes the judgment of God, but this only takes place when the context gives clear indication of it, as in Jas. ii 13, which is not the case here

[2] This objection does not affect Hofmann's interpretation, for he—unjustifiably —separates vv 24, 25 from what precedes, and wishes to regard them as introductory to what follows.

secret sins But how could he have such a suspicion, and how can this interpretation agree with τινῶν ἀνθρώπων and τισὶ δέ?—The κρίσις here mentioned is therefore not the divine judgment, but a trial which Timothy must hold, lest the thing of which he is warned in ver 22 should happen (so, too, Plitt).

Ver. 25 supplements ver 24, the distinction between manifest and hidden being applied to good works. — ὡσαύτως καὶ τὰ ἔργα τὰ καλὰ πρόδηλα] It may be supposed from what precedes that τινῶν ἀνθρώπων is to be supplied here. But it is improbable that Paul was thinking definitely of this, otherwise the clause following would have received another form. Hofmann maintains that the *Rec.* πρόδηλά ἐστιν is the original reading, taking the words ὡσαύτως . . καλά as a complete clause, and explaining πρόδηλά ἐστιν by · "there are manifest (ones)" This purely arbitrary view needs no refutation. The assertion that the apostle could not say that the good works were manifest, is contradicted by the addition of the necessary restriction in the next words. — καὶ τὰ ἄλλως ἔχοντα is not to be referred to καλά, but to πρόδηλα. the good works with which it is different, *i.e.* which are not πρόδηλα — κρυβῆναι οὐ δύνανται] "can, however, not remain continually hidden;" they will likewise become manifest on a careful κρίσις. Ver. 24 was a warning against showing favour too hastily; this verse is a warning against condemning too hastily.

218   THE FIRST EPISTLE TO TIMOTHY.

CHAPTER VI.

VER. 1. The reading δούλου (F G) is to be regarded as a correction; so, too, with the reading δουλείας (73, Sahid.). — Ver. 2. In ℵ the words ὅτι ἀδελφοί εἰσιν are omitted, probably through an oversight. Instead of the curious ἐυεργεσίας here, F G, gr. 46, and some other cursives have the reading εὐσεβείας; 45 has ἐργασίας — Ver. 3. Instead of προσέρχεται (Rec with the support of nearly all MSS., Lachm. Buttm. Tisch. 7), ℵ has the reading προσέχεται (in Latin: acquiescit), which Tisch 8 adopted This form occurs nowhere else in the N. T. — Ver. 4. Tisch. 7 read ἔρεις, after D F G L, etc , Tisch. 8, on the contrary, ἔρις (Rec. with the support of A K ℵ, etc , so, too, Lachm. Buttm.). It can hardly be decided which is the original reading, the meaning is substantially the same in either case; possibly the singular was changed into the plural on account of the other plurals. — Ver. 5. Instead of the Rec. παραδιατριβαί, Griesb rightly adopted διαπαρατριβαί, on the weightiest authority: A D F G ℵ, al , 10, 17, 23, etc , Clem Basil. Chrys. etc. In one MS. διαπαραδιατριβαί is found, others have διατριβαί, others, παρατριβαί, and one δι' ἃ παρατριβαί, which Reiche approves. — The words ἀφίστασο ἀπὸ τῶν τοιούτων are, according to A D* F G ℵ 17, 67** 93, al , Copt. Sahid. Aeth Vulg It, probably to be considered an addition not genuine, although they are found in K L, nearly all cursives, and the Fathers, Ambros Pel. Chrys. etc , Griesb. marked them as very much to be suspected; Lachm Buttm Tisch. omitted them; Reiche, on the other hand, defended them as genuine. — Ver. 7. δῆλον] is wanting in several of the weightiest authorities, in particular A F G ℵ 17, Copt. Sahid Aeth etc., on which account it was also struck out by Lachm Buttm Tisch 8. But as it is almost indispensable for the sense, its omission may perhaps be only an oversight, unless ὅτι, as Buttm p 308, thinks, be elliptical for δῆλον ὅτι. — Ver 8 Instead of διατροφάς, D F G and several cursives have the common singular form διατροφήν; and instead of ἀρκεσθησόμεθα, there is found in 30, 117, 219, al , Vulg Chrys. etc., the form ἀρκεσθησώμεθα ; see on this, Winer, p 72 [E T. p. 89]. — Ver. 9. After παγίδα, D* F G, several cursives, Fathers, and versions have τοῦ διαβόλου, which, however, is to be regarded as an insertion from iii. 7 — Ver. 11. Lachm. Buttm. Tisch 8, omitted the article τοῦ before Θεοῦ; it is wanting in A ℵ 17. — In ℵ the word εὐσέβειαν is wanting — πραότητα] This reading stands only in later MSS, A F G ℵ 71, Ignat. Petr. Alex. Ephr. Hesych. have πραυπάθειαν, which is therefore rightly adopted by Scholz, Lachm Buttm. Tisch. — Ver. 12. εἰς ἥν] The Rec is εἰς ἥν καί The καί was rightly omitted by Griesb, on the authority of all uncials. many cursives, Syr. Arr. Copt. etc, Chrys. Theodor. etc. — Ver 13. The σοι after παραγγέλλω (Rec. supported by the most important authorities, Lachm. Buttm. Tisch. 7) was omitted by Tisch. 8, on the authority of F G 17, etc.; so, too, with the article τοῦ before Θεοῦ, after ℵ, though it stands in nearly all authorities Instead of ζωοποιοῦντος (Rec K L ℵ, al.), A D F G 17, etc., Ath Cyr. etc. have ζωογονοῦντος, which deserves preference as the more unusual word   Lachm Buttm. and Tisch adopted it into the text; Reiche, on the other hand, defends the Rec., especially on the ground that Paul uses the word ζωοποιεῖν continually of the futura hominum mortuorum ad vitam restitutio, quacum rerum universarum instauratio conjuncta erit. — Ver. 17 ἐν τῷ νῦν αἰῶνι] is changed in D E, Syr Copt. Sahid. Vulg. etc. into τοῦ νῦν αἰῶνος For αἰῶνι, ℵ has καιρῷ, and for ὑψηλοφρονεῖν, ὑψηλὰ φρονεῖν, which Tisch. 8 adopted — ἐν τῷ Θεῷ] For the preposition ἐν (Rec. D*** K L, Tisch. 7, Reiche), A D* F G ℵ, several cursives, etc, have ἐπί (Lachm. Buttm Tisch 8). This reading seems, however, to have arisen from a correction in order to make this clause symmetrical with the one previous. The article τῷ (Rec A D*** E K L, etc , Lachm Buttm. Tisch. 7) is wanting in D* F G ℵ, al (Tisch 8). — τῷ ζῶντι] omitted by Lachm. and Tisch, after A G 17, 23, 47, al., many versions, is to be regarded as not genuine It may have been inserted from a recollection of iv 10 — πάντα πλουσίως] adopted by Griesb. Scholz, Tisch for πλουσίως πάντα, after D E 17, 44, 46, al., Syr Arr. Copt.Vulg etc ,Basil.Chrys. Theodoret, etc. Lachm. and Buttm read, on the authority of A 17, 37, 57, al , τὰ πάντα πλουσίως, which might deserve preference as the more difficult reading. — Ver. 19 The Rec. αἰωνίου is manifestly a correction of the original ὄντως (in A D* E F G ℵ 17, 23, 31, 57, al., Syr. utr. Erp. Copt. etc , Constitut Clem. Orig Basil. etc), which Griesb rightly received into the text. — Ver. 20. παραθήκην] rightly adopted by Griesb. for παρακαταθήκην, on the authority of A D E F G ℵ 31, 37, 44, al , Sahid. Syr Clem Ignat al ; comp 2 Tim i. 12, 14. The reading καινοφωνίας (for κενοφ), in F G 73, It Vulg. (profanas vocum novitates) and the

Latin Fathers, is an oversight arising from the similarity of αι and ε in sound. — Ver. 22. ἡ χάρις μετὰ σοῦ] For σοῦ, Lachm. Buttm Tisch. 8, after A F G 17, al., adopted μεθ' ὑμῶν, perhaps a correction from 2 Tim. iv. 22 and Tit iii. 15. Tisch. 7 had the *Rec.* σοῦ, after D E K L, most cursives, several versions, etc. — The *Rec.* ἀμήν at the end (after D** K L) is to be regarded as not genuine, on the authority of A D* F G א, etc.

Vv. 1, 2. Precept regarding the conduct of Christian slaves. — ὅσοι εἰσὶν ὑπὸ ζυγὸν δοῦλοι] δοῦλοι is added to explain εἰσὶν ὑπὸ ζ. Paul does not say simply ὅσοι εἰσὶν δοῦλοι, because he wishes to mark the oppressive circumstances of the condition of a slave. ζυγός is not used elsewhere in the N. T. of the yoke of slavery (in Herodotus. δούλιον ζυγόν) The expression is not to be limited to those slaves who were oppressed more than usual by their masters, as Heydenreich thinks, quoting 1 Pet. ii. 18. It is clear from the clause ἵνα κτλ, as well as from the contrast in ver. 2, that Paul is thinking here of the slaves who had heathen masters. — τοὺς ἰδίους δεσπότας] ἰδίους is so far emphatic, that it directs attention to the circumstance of the personal relation more than would be done by the usual pronoun. — πάσης τιμῆς (*i.e.* of all honour which is due to them as masters) ἀξίους ἡγείσθωσιν (f. ἀξιοῦν, v. 17), comp. the exhortations in Tit ii. 9 ; Eph. vi. 5–8, Col. iii. 22–25 ; 1 Pet. ii. 18. — In confirmation, Paul adds ἵνα μὴ τὸ ὄνομα κτ.λ.; comp. Tit. ii. 10. The meaning is correctly given by Chrysostom : ὁ ἄπιστος ἂν μὲν ἴδῃ τοὺς δούλους διὰ τὴν πίστιν αὐθάδως προφερομένους, βλασφημήσει πολλάκις ὡς στάσιν ἐμποιοῦν τὸ δόγμα· ὅταν δὲ ἴδῃ πειθομένους, μᾶλλον πεισθήσεται, μᾶλλον προσέξει τοῖς λεγομένοις — τὸ ὄνομα τοῦ Θεοῦ] comp. Rom. ii. 24. — ἡ διδασκαλία] the gospel, as the doctrine prevailing among Christians. — Ver 2. οἱ δὲ πιστοὺς ἔχοντες δεσπότας] The adversative δέ shows that the apostle is here speaking of other slaves than in ver. 1, viz, as he himself says, of those whose masters are πιστοί, not keeping their slaves as ὑπὸ ζυγόν, but treating them kindly and gently because of their πίστις. This last point is, indeed, not formally expressed here, but it is presupposed in μὴ καταφρονείτωσαν. — πιστούς is either to be joined with δεσπότας as an adjective, or to be taken as a substantive, δεσπότας defining it more precisely: " who have believers as masters." The order of the words might give the preference to the latter view. — μὴ καταφρονείτωσαν] καταφρονεῖν denotes here conduct towards masters in which the honour due to them is not given. — ὅτι ἀδελφοί εἰσιν] These words are not the ground of the previous exhortation, they are the ground on which the δοῦλοι might be led to think their masters of little worth; not the slaves, but the masters, form the subject (de Wette, Wiesinger, van Oosterzee, and others) — ἀλλὰ μᾶλλον δουλευέτωσαν] μᾶλλον, equivalent to " all the more." — ὅτι πιστοί εἰσι καὶ ἀγαπητοί, οἱ κ.τ.λ] With ἀγαπητοί we must supply Θεοῦ (Rom. i. 7; comp. Rom xi. 28): " beloved of God;" this is supported by the close connection with πιστοί. — The subject is formed not by the slaves (Wetstein: intelligo non de dominis, sed de servis, qui dant operam, ut dominis beneficiant et bene de iis mereantur), still less by both slaves and masters (Matthies), but by the masters only. The only possible construction is this, that οἱ . . . ἀντιλαμβανόμενοι forms the subject, πιστοὶ . . ἀγαπητοί the predicate; for the article shows that the words οἱ τῆς κ.τ λ do not give a more precise definition of what precedes. Most recent expositors (de Wette, Wiesinger, van Oosterzee, Plitt, also hitherto in this commentary) understand by ἡ εὐεργεσία the kindness which the slaves show to their masters by faithful service, and explain ἀντιλαμβάνεσθαι as equivalent to " receive, accept;" but this explanation cannot be justified by usage.[1] In the N. T the word occurs only in Luke i 54 and Acts xx. 35, in the sense of "accept of some one." This sense it has also in classic Greek, when it refers to persons; in reference to things, it means : " carry on something eagerly," also: " make oneself master of a thing." Hofmann accordingly

---

[1] De Wette wrongly seeks to justify this meaning by saying that ἀντιλαμβάνεσθαι also means. " perceive with the senses," and that in Porphyrius, De Abstin. i 46, it means. μήτε ἐσθίων πλειόνων ἡδονῶν ἀντιλήψεται Though the Vulg. translates it : " qui beneficii participes sunt," and Luther " and are partakers of the benefit," the word is taken in a sense foreign to it The same is true of Heydenreich's explanation " συγκοινωνοὶ τῆς χάριτος " (Phil. i. 7), wherein he also arbitrarily takes ἐνέργεια as equivalent to χάρις.

is not incorrect in translating: "devote themselves to kindness, making it their business." If we keep strictly to this meaning, as indeed we must, then the words οἱ τ. εὐεργ. ἀντιλαμβανόμενοι apply to the Christian masters in regard to their conduct towards their slaves, so that the meaning of the exhortation is: "*Serve* (your masters) *all the more, that they, devoting themselves to kindness towards you, are believers and beloved* (of God)." So rightly Theophylact: οἱ τῆς εὐεργεσίας ἀντιλαμβανόμενοι, τουτέστι: οἱ δεσπόται οἱ φροντίζοντες τοῦ εὐεργετεῖν τοὺς δούλους, so, too, Chrysostom, Grotius, Wegscheider, Leo, and others. De Wette, against this explanation, maintains that "it makes the predicate 'believing' somewhat superfluous, because the masters, being kindly towards their slaves, are already showing their Christian faith in action." He is wrong, for, on the one hand, εὐεργεσία towards slaves might be true even of heathen; and, on the other, Paul wishes to insist on the Christian belief of the masters as a motive for careful and faithful service. Hofmann is wrong in thinking that καὶ ... ἀντιλαμβ does not depend on ὅτι, but forms an independent clause in this sense, that the slaves who serve their masters willingly in distributing their alms, are beloved (viz. by their fellow-Christians). This view is opposed not only by the καί (for to what previous sentence is it to be attached?), but also by this, that whereas the ἀντιλαμβανόμενοι are the slaves, τῶν δεσπότων is arbitrarily supplied with εὐεργεσίας. — The apostle concludes the exhortations given in regard to the slaves with the words: ταῦτα δίδασκε καὶ παρακάλει, which Lachm. Buttm. and Tisch wrongly refer to what follows, comp iv 11, v. 7; the right construction is given by de Wette, Wiesinger, van Oosterzee, and others.

Vv. 3–5. Description of the heretics. — εἴ τις ἑτεροδιδασκαλεῖ] On ἑτεροδιδασκαλεῖν, comp i. 3, εἴ τις often occurs in the epistle for ὅστις or the like; comp iii. 5, v. 8; the thought is given in its most comprehensive form. — καὶ μὴ προσέρχεται κ.τ.λ.] defines ἑτεροδιδασκαλεῖν more exactly, characterizing it as opposed to the pure doctrine of the gospel, as a preaching therefore of heresy (not merely "of a doctrine which has not the quality of being pious" (!), Hofmann). — προσέρχεσθαι is used of mental agreement, and is equivalent to "agree with" (de Wette, Wiesinger, van Oosterzee); comp. Philo, *de Gigantt.* p. 289. μηδενὶ προσέρχεσθαι γνώμῃ τῶν εἰρημένων. On ὑγιαίνουσι λόγοις, comp. i. 10. Hofmann arbitrarily explains the word by. "devote oneself to a thing; employ one's pains on it." If προσέχεται is the correct reading, then it is to be explained: "and does not *hold fast* by sound words." The genitive τοῦ κυρίου ἡμ. 'Ι. Χρ. gives the source from which the λόγοι proceed. Καὶ τῇ κατ' εὐσέβειαν διδασκαλίᾳ] an epexegetic addition to what preceded. The expression is not, with Leo and Wiesinger, to be explained by: doctrina ad pietatem ducens; κατά rather expresses the relation of correspondence, suitability (van Oosterzee). By εὐσέβεια is meant Christian piety. — Ver. 4. τετύφωται] comp. iii. 6 [1] With this word begins the apodosis, which Wegscheider, Mack, and others find expressed only in ἀφίστασο ἀπὸ τ. τοιούτων, which words we can hardly consider genuine. μηδὲν ἐπιστάμενος (comp. i. 7), the participle is not to be resolved into "although," all the more that τετύφωται conveys a suggestion of dumbness. Their knowledge, on which they presume, is limited to fables, and does not penetrate into the truth. — ἀλλὰ νοσῶν περὶ ζητήσεις καὶ λογομαχίας] νοσῶν, in contrast with ὑγιαίνουσι λόγοις in ver. 3. — Περὶ ζητήσεις κ.τ.λ. gives the sickness of which he is ill (comp. Plato, *Phaedr.* p 288 : ὁ νοσῶν περὶ λόγων ἀκοήν; Winer, p. 379 [E. T. p. 506]). Luther, not clear: "diseased *in* questions," Stier, correct: "diseased *with*." — On ζητήσεις, comp. i. 4 ; the addition of λογομαχίαι denotes more exactly the nature of the ζητήσεις. Calvin: λογομαχίας nominat contentiosas disputationes de verbis magis, quam de rebus, vel (ut vulgo loquuntur) sine materia aut subjecto. The word (occurring only in later Greek) is ἅπ. λεγ., the verb λογομαχεῖν, 2 Tim. ii. 14. — Hitherto he has described the "condition of soul among the ἑτεροδιδασκαλοῦντες" (Wiesinger); the consequences of their ζητ. and λογομ., particularly the destructive

---

[1] Hofmann thinks that τιτύφωται does not here, as in iii. 6, contain the idea of darkness, since "Paul means to express regarding the schismatics an opinion, not in regard to their moral, but in regard to their spiritual condition." This opinion is contradicted by the fact that in what follows νοσῶν κ. τ. λ. manifestly denotes a moral fault.

tendencies, are given in what follows ἐξ ὧν γίνεται κ.τ λ.] φθόνος, ἔρις,[1] βλασφημίαι, form a climax. βλασφημίαι and ὑπόνοιαι πονηραί are wrongly understood by Chrysostom of conduct towards God. On the latter expression, equivalent to "wicked suspicion" (Luther), see Wisd. iii 24; the word is ἅπ. λεγ in the N. T. Hofmann wishes to separate πονηραί from ὑπόνοιαι, and to connect it with the next word, "because ὑπονοεῖν in itself means suspecting evil." But, on the one hand, ὑπονοεῖν has often the simple meaning "conjecture" (e g Acts xiii. 25; also in classic Greek); and, on the other hand, "the suspicion of something evil," and "the evil, wicked suspicion," are by no means identical things. — Ver. 5. διαπαρατριβαί] This word and παραδιατριβαί (according to the usual reading) are not equivalent, as Heydenreich thinks; see Winer, p 96 [E. T. p. 126]. The distinction between παρατριβή and διατριβή is to be maintained. Διατριβή means, in regard to time. "its consumption, pastime, occupation;" with the prefix παρα there is added the idea of idle, useless, so that παραδιατριβή denotes the useless occupation of time. The word παρατριβή (only in later Greek) means: "wrangling, dispute,," δια serves to intensify the meaning, hence διαπαρατριβή is equivalent to "*continuous* or *violent wrangling*" (de Wette). Luther translated it: "scholastic disputes." As the idea of strife has been given already by ἔρις, we might be inclined to consider the *Rec.* to be the original reading, were the evidence for it not too weak. The same may be said of the reading διατριβαί, which Hofmann, without sufficient ground, maintains to be "what was originally written" At any rate, the idea "continual wrangling" is not so identical with that of "strife" (ἔρις) as to prevent them from being used together.[2] Reiche paraphrases the reading δι' ἃ παρατριβαί as equivalent to per quae, nempe vitia morbosque animi vs 4, exoriuntur rixae et certamina, etc.; but δι' ἃ is not equivalent to *per* quae, and the previous ἐξ ὧν is against

---

[1] Clemens Al. *Stromata*, vii. p. 759 ὑπὸ δοξοσοφίας ἐπηρμένοι ἐρίζοντες πιλοῦσι.

[2] Oecumenius explains the expression ἀπὸ μεταφορᾶς τῶν ψωραλέων προβάτων, and Chrysostom says likewise καθάπερ τὰ ψωραλία τῶν προβάτων παρατριβόμενα νόσου καὶ τὰ ὑγιαίνοντα ἐμπίμπλησιν, οὕτω καὶ οὗτοι οἱ πονηροὶ ἄνδρες.—The meaning "provocations" (Mack), and this other "wicked and hurtful meetings or clubs" (Heinrichs), can be assigned neither to παραδια-ριβαί nor to διαπαρατριβαί.

this construction. — διεφθαρμένων ἀνθρώπων τὸν νοῦν] Regarding this accus., see Winer, p. 205 [E. T. p. 287]; comp. 2 Tim. iii. 8 (Xenophon, *De Exped. Cyri,* iv. 259 : διεφθαρμένοι τοὺς ὀφθαλμούς): "*whose understanding is destroyed.*" — καὶ ἀπεστερημένων τῆς ἀληθείας] "*who have been robbed of the truth.*" This and the previous participial clauses indicate that formerly the heretics had their understanding sound, and were in possession of the truth, but that they had lost both these jewels, according to iv. 1, by the influence of demons. It should never have been denied that they who are thus described were actual heretics. — The next clause adds another peculiar characteristic, which proves the διεφθαρμένων κ.τ λ.: νομιζόντων πορισμὸν εἶναι τὴν εὐσέβειαν] πορισμός (only here and at ver. 6 ; comp. Ecclus. xiii. 19, xiv. 2) is equivalent to "*means of gain,*" *i.e.* a business bringing gain ; Luther : " trade." — Wegscheider wrongly explains εὐσέβεια as equivalent to ἡ κατ' εὐσέβειαν διδασκαλία. The idea is to be kept in its proper meaning ; although that which the heretics made to appear εὐσέβεια was not εὐσέβεια, but only the appearance of it (2 Tim. iii. 5 : μόρφωσιν εὐσεβείας), by means of which they sought to make earthly gain (Tit. i. 11). — As to the construction, it seems most natural to make the substantive at the beginning of the verse dependent on ἐξ ὧν γίνεται, ver. 4, along with the substantives before it Hofmann, on the contrary, thinks it curious, " that besides the bad things already mentioned, there should also be named those with whom they occur ;" and he wishes rather to regard πονηραὶ διατριβαί (which he reads) as in apposition to ζητήσεις καὶ λογομαχίας, just as in Jas. iii. 8, where the nominative stands in apposition to the previous accusative as a kind of exclamation. This construction is possible, but it is by no means necessary, and from the structure of the sentence not even probable. — The last remark furnishes the apostle with an opportunity for a digression on Christian contentment.[1]

Ver. 6. Ἔστι δὲ κ.τ.λ.] Calvin: eleganter et non sine ironica correctione in contrarium sensum eadem verba retorquet.

---

[1] Hofmann's opinion, that the deductions following are not occasioned by the conduct of the heretics, but by Timothy's conduct, are not warranted by the exhortation in ver. 11 : ταῦτα φεῦγε.

The *meaning* is: piety is certainly a πορισμός, but in another and higher sense than the heretics suppose; ἔστι is opposed to νομιζόντων (ver. 5), Wiesinger — πορισμὸς μέγας κ.τ.λ.] πορισμός has here the same meaning as before; Luther wrongly says: "it is, however, a great gain, one that is blessed," etc. — ἡ εὐσέβεια μετὰ αὐταρκείας] "*Piety when united with contentment*," which certainly belongs of necessity to true piety. The gain of which the apostle is here thinking is not the heavenly, eternal blessings (Theodoret: τὴν γὰρ αἰώνιον ἡμῖν πορίζει ζωήν; Calvin, Heydenreich, Matthies, and others), but the gain to which we are directed in the next verses, 7–10. Several expositors hold the gain to be the αὐταρκεία itself (so Chrysostom, Bengel: nam affert αὐταρκείαν; de Wette, and others[1]); but this reference is not indicated in the added words · μετὰ αὐταρκείας. On αὐτάρκεια, comp. Phil. iv. 11: ἐγὼ ἔμαθον ἐν οἷς εἰμι αὐτάρκης εἶναι.

Ver. 7 begins the confirmation of the principle that godliness with contentment is a great πορισμός. The apostle here places two clauses together, each of which contains a well-known and undoubted truth: "*We brought nothing into the world,*" and "*We can take nothing out of it.*" (The same two thoughts are found elsewhere in collocation; so Job i. 21; Eccles. v. 14; also in the profane writers, *e.g.* Seneca, *Ep* 102: non licet plus efferre, quam intuleris. For the second thought, comp Job xxvii. 19; Ps. xlix. 12.) The question is only, in what relation do they stand to one another? According to the common view, the first thought serves to confirm the second: "As we brought nothing in, it is manifest that we will take nothing out." Against this, Hofmann maintains that the second thought is in no way a consequence of the first. He therefore takes δῆλον ὅτι as an adverbial: "clearly," standing at the end of the sentence, but belonging to both clauses; and he explains: "Clearly we have brought nothing in, and can also take nothing out." He is certainly right that the first does not strictly prove the second; but then the apostle did not intend that it should; he simply placed the two sentences

---

[1] Van Oosterzee: "In one short, compressed sentence, the apostle expresses two chief ideas, that true piety of itself makes content, and that by doing so it brings great gain."

together, the second corresponding to the first in such a way as to be confirmed by it in popular opinion. Hence it is not right to connect—contrary to the order of the words— δῆλον ὅτι with the first sentence. As to the lack of δῆλον before ὅτι (see the critical remarks), de Wette observes: " that in popular logic the consequence is often quoted with ὅτι as the reason, *e g.* Homer, *Il.* xvi. 35, *Od.* xxii. 36." This, however, is not to the point here ; in the two passages quoted, ὅτι simply denotes the logical ground of knowledge.

Ver. 8. Ἔχοντες δέ] De Wette thinks that for δέ we should have had οὖν. This is certainly right, still the bearing of this verse on the previous one would have been different from what it is now. The apostle used δέ because he had in mind the contrast to those striving after earthly gain. — διατροφὰς καὶ σκεπάσματα] The same collocation in *Sextus Empiricus*, Book ix. 1 , the two expressions only occur here in the N. T. (διατροφή, 1 Macc. vi. 49) Σκέπασμα, the covering, hence both clothing and dwelling Here it is to be taken in the former sense; de Wette, Wiesinger, van Oosterzee, and others include both senses in it; but it is more than improbable that one word should be used to denote two different objects. Chrysostom : τοιαῦτα ἀμφιέννυσθαι, ἃ σκεπάσαι μόνον ἡμᾶς ὀφείλει καὶ περιστεῖλαι τὴν γύμνωσιν. In food and clothing the necessary wants of life are also elsewhere summed up; comp. Matt vi. 25 ; Jas. ii. 15; Gen. xxviii. 20. — τούτοις ἀρκεσθησόμεθα] "*we will be content with them.*" Hofmann's explanation is wrong: "so will we *have enough* of them." The passive ἀρκεῖσθαι occurs as a personal verb only in the sense of "*be content with;*" comp. Luke iii. 14; Heb. xiii. 5; 3 John 10; 2 Macc. v. 16; 4 Macc. vi. 22 ; so, too, continually in profane writers, comp. Pape, *s.v.* — The future is here taken imperatively by several expositors. It is well known that the imperative is often expressed by the future, but there is no passage which exactly corresponds with this (comp. Buttmann, p. 221). It is better, therefore, to take the future here in the sense of sure expectation (so de Wette, Wiesinger, van Oosterzee, Plitt; comp. Winer, p. 296 [E. T. p. 396]).

Ver. 9. Οἱ δὲ βουλόμενοι πλουτεῖν] δέ expresses opposition

to what immediately preceded. πλουτεῖν is properly not "become rich," but "*be rich.*" — ἐμπίπτουσιν (cf. iii. 7) εἰς πειρασμὸν καὶ παγίδα] De Wette explains it inaccurately: "to whom enticing opportunities present themselves for unrighteous gain." In ἐμπίπτειν is contained the indication of the power which the πειρασμός ("the temptation to enrich oneself unrighteously") exercises over them. — By παγίδα, the πειρασμός is defined to be a power fettering and taking prisoner. — καὶ ἐπιθυμίας πολλὰς ἀνοήτους καὶ βλαβεράς] This is the consequence immediately connected with what precedes: by falling into πειρασμός, they fall into *many* foolish and hurtful lusts, *i.e.* these lusts are not only excited in them, but gain power over them. Thus the seductive power of the πειρασμός can be recognised in the ἐπιθυμίαις. These are also ἀνόητοι, because instead of the gain which was expected to come from satisfying them, they bring hurt only. — αἵτινες (explanatory: "such as") βυθίζουσι εἰς ὄλεθρον καὶ ἀπώλειαν] βυθίζειν; in the literal sense at Luke v. 7; 2 Macc xii. 4.—Destruction is likewise the deep into which they are plunged by their desires. The expression is strengthened by bringing together the two synonymous ideas. There is no ground for van Oosterzee's conjecture that ὄλεθρος denotes the destruction of the body, ἀπώλεια the destruction of the soul. De Wette incorrectly explains the words of "moral ruin," against which Wiesinger justly observes: "they are in that already." ὄλεθρος stands here as in 1 Thess. v. 3, 2 Thess. i. 9 (ὄλεθρος αἰώνιος); ἀπώλεια, as in Phil. i. 28 (opp. ἡ σωτηρία), iii. 19, and other passages.—There is no good ground (with Olshausen in Wiesinger) for understanding ὄλεθρος exclusively of temporal destruction.

Ver. 10 gives a reason for the thought in ver. 9. — ῥίζα γὰρ πάντων τῶν κακῶν ἐστὶν ἡ φιλαργυρία] It is to be observed that Paul does not mean to say, whence all κακά whatever proceed, but what proceeds from φιλαργυρία. Hence there is no article with ῥίζα. Hence, too, de Wette's correcting remark, that ambition, too, may entirely destroy man, does not affect the author of the epistle. — By τὰ κακά may be understood both physical and moral evils (wickedness); here the latter idea is uppermost (otherwise in Polycarp, *Ep.* 4:

ἀρχὴ πάντων χαλεπῶν φιλαργυρία). Φιλαργυρία only here in the N. T. (Jer. viii. 10, LXX). — ἧς τινὲς ὀρεγόμενοι] ὀρέγεσθαι does not mean deditum esse, but it is to be acknowledged that the manner of connection is not exact, since φιλαργυρία, as de Wette rightly says, is itself an ὄρεξις. Hofmann's interpretation is artificial. He makes ὀρέγεσθαι denote here "the grasping of a man after something out of his way," and "the thing after which he reaches sideways is said to be the plant which afterwards proves to be to him a root of all evils," so that ἧς does not refer to φιλαργυρία, but to ῥίζα πάντων τῶν κακῶν. — ἀπεπλανήθησαν ἀπὸ τῆς πίστεως] The reason of this is the inner connection between faith and blessedness. The denial of the one necessarily implies the denial of the other. The aorist passive has a neuter sense; Luther rightly: "have gone astray from the faith" The compound only here and at Mark xiii. 22; the ἀπό added serves to intensify the meaning. — καὶ ἑαυτοὺς περιέπειραν ὀδύναις πολλαῖς] περιπείρειν ἀπ. λεγ. "pierce through," not "sting all round, wound in every part" (Matthies). The ὀδύναι πολλαί, here regarded as a sword with which they have pierced themselves through, are not the outward pains which they have drawn on themselves by avarice, but the stings of conscience ("the precursors of the future ἀπώλεια," Wiesinger) which they have prepared for themselves by apostasy from the faith. To this his own experience the apostle here directs attention, that he may thereby present more vividly the destructiveness of the φιλαργυρία.

Ver. 11. The apostle again turns to Timothy, exhorting him to a faithful fulfilment of his Christian and evangelical vocation — σὺ δέ] opposed to τινές, ver. 10. — ὦ ἄνθρωπε [τοῦ] Θεοῦ] The expression may be taken in a more general or a more special sense; so, too, in 2 Pet i. 21. It does not, however, follow "that Paul thus names Timothy here because of his evangelic office;" the exhortations following rather show that the apostle was thinking of Timothy's position as a Christian; comp. 2 Tim. iii. 17. — ταῦτα φεῦγε] ταῦτα refers to the φιλαργυρία and that which is connected with it (de Wette, Wiesinger, and others); not to everything that has been said in vv. 3–10, because "vv. 17 ff. show that the author is keeping in view the subject of riches," de Wette. φεύγειν vitare; comp. 2 Tim. ii. 22; 1 Cor. vi. 18. Hofmann wrongly deduces from this exhortation that Timothy had some inclination to φιλαργυρία; one might as well deduce from the next exhortation that Timothy had no inclination to δικαιοσύνη κ.τ.λ. It is to be observed that it is not said φεῦγε ἀπό or ἐκ τούτων; comp., besides, the passages quoted. — δίωκε δὲ τὴν δικαιοσύνην] διώκειν here as in Deut. xvi. 20, LXX.; Rom. xii. 13, and other passages of the N. T. (neque exteris scriptoribus infrequens est haec hujus verbi notio; see Xenophon, *Cyropaedia*, viii. 1. 39; Thucydides, ii. 63; Leo). Paul names six Christian virtues which Timothy is to cultivate, the six being arranged in pairs The two most general in meaning are placed first: δικαιοσύνην (righteousness) and εὐσέβειαν (comp. Tit. ii. 12). Then follow πίστιν (not "faithfulness or conscientiousness," but "faith") and ἀγάπην as the ground principle of the Christian life. Last come ὑπομόνην and πραυπάθειαν (ἅπ. λεγ., Philo, *de Abrah.* p. 379), which denote the Christian conduct proper in regard to the hostility of the world against the gospel, the former being opposed to submission, the latter to exasperation

Ver. 12. *Ἀγωνίζου τὸν καλὸν ἀγῶνα τῆς πίστεως*] Here, as in i. 18 (τὴν καλὴν στρατείαν), we must not overlook the definite article. The struggle to which Timothy is summoned is the struggle (comp. 1 Cor. ix 25) of the faith appointed to Christians; on this comp. 2 Tim. iv. 7. — ἐπιλαβοῦ τῆς αἰωνίου ζωῆς] ἐπιλαμβάνειν (comp. 1 Cor. ix. 24 and Phil. iii. 12, where the apostle uses the expressions λαμβάνειν and καταλαμβάνειν) denotes the actual grasping, αἰώνιος ζωή being regarded as the βραβεῖον; not, however, according to Winer's remark (p. 293 [E. T. p. 392]), "as result of the struggle, but as object of the striving." It is not improbable that Paul is here speaking figuratively. It is different, however, with the next words: εἰς ἣν ἐκλήθης, by which eternal life is pointed out as the goal of Timothy's vocation; comp. 1 Pet. v. 10. — καὶ ὡμολόγησας τὴν καλὴν ὁμολογίαν] Heinrichs incorrectly takes καί for καὶ γάρ: "for thou hast also." Commonly this clause is made to depend still on εἰς ἥν (Leo: εἰς ἥν pertinet non solum ad ἐκλήθης, sed etiam ad ὡμολόγησας). De Wette, on the contrary (Wiesinger and van Oosterzee agree with him), rightly regards it as simply co-ordinate with εἰς ἣν ἐκλήθης. So, too, Hofmann: "the relative clause, as is not seldom the case in Greek, passes into a clause independent of the relative." Still the two clauses must be taken as standing in close connection; Timothy's καλὴ ὁμολογία is the answer which he gave to the κλῆσις proclaimed to him (so, too, Hofmann). — τὴν καλὴν ὁμολογίαν] In this phrase, too, expositors have not observed the definite article. Paul does not say that Timothy confessed a confession good "in its contents and in the enthusiasm of its utterance," de Wette; but that he confessed *the* good confession, *i e* the definite confession of Christ to which the disciples of the Lord are appointed. Hence it is quite wrong to think of ὁμολογία as a vow or the like; that contradicts the constant usage of the N. T.; comp. 2 Cor. ix. 13; Heb. iii. 1, 4, 14, x. 23. — Paul is clearly referring here to a definite fact in Timothy's life, but what it was he does not say. Chrysostom says. ἀναμιμνήσκει τῆς κατηχήσεως αὐτόν, and thinks therefore of the confession of Timothy at his baptism. Others, on account of ver. 13, understand it of a confession which Timothy had confessed during a persecution. According to most, Paul is here thinking of the same act as that to which iv. 14 refers. Since in this whole section, vv. 11–16, there is nothing to direct the attention to Timothy's official position, and since the ὁμολογία is closely joined with the ἐκλήθης, the view first given is to be considered the right one (Hofmann).

Vv. 13, 14. Παραγγέλλω σοι] Matthies regards τὴν καλὴν ὁμολογίαν as the subject belonging to this, but against this construction there is both the meaning of the verb and the τηρῆσαί σε following.[1] Leo justly says: quo magis ad finem vergit epistola, eo gravior existit apostoli oratio. To give his exhortation greater force, Paul adds to παραγγέλλω (comp. i. 3) the words of adjuration: ἐνώπιον τοῦ Θεοῦ κ.τ.λ. — *Τοῦ ζωογονοῦντος τὰ πάντα*] ζωογονεῖν in the classic usage, equivalent to "bring forth alive, make alive," serves in the

---

[1] The objections made by Matthies against the correct construction are only founded on this, that he considers the definite article τήν to be unsuitable before καλὴν ὁμολογίαν.

LXX. for translating the Piel and Hiphil of חָיָה in the double signification: "maintain in life," Ex. i. 17; Judg. viii. 19, and other passages; and "make alive," 1 Sam. ii. 6 (comp. 2 Kings v. 7). In the N. T. it occurs here and at Luke xvii. 33, Acts vii. 19, in the sense of "maintain in life." When connected with τὰ πάντα, ζωογ. is not to be understood specially of the *resurrection* (de Wette, van Oosterzee), but either "*of God's might that upholds everything*" (Wiesinger, Hofmann), or, still better, of "*His power that quickens everything*" (Plitt), in the same sense as it is said of God in Neh. ix. 6: σὺ ζωοποιεῖς τὰ πάντα. God is therefore mentioned here as the source of life for the universe (τὰ πάντα), there being a special reference to ver. 12: ἐπιλαβοῦ τῆς αἰωνίου ζωῆς. — Καὶ Χρ. Ἰησ. τοῦ μαρτυρήσαντος ἐπὶ Ποντίου Πιλάτου τὴν καλὴν ὁμολογίαν] τὴν κ. ὁμολογίαν is not dependent on παραγγέλλω (Matthies: "I make known to thee . . . the good confession"), but on μαρτυρήσαντος. It is open to question, however, whether the καλὴ ὁμολογία is the confession of the Christian which Timothy too has made (Wiesinger, Plitt, Hofmann), or the confession which Christ made (Leo, van Oosterzee). In the former case, μαρτυρεῖν is much the same as "testify, *i.e.* confirm, declare for truth;" in the latter it is kindred in meaning with ὁμολογεῖν. Wiesinger asserts that μαρτυρεῖν never has the latter meaning, but unjustly; because in John v. 32 we have μαρτυρίαν μαρτυρεῖν, and in John iii. 11 we have ὃ οἴδαμεν λαλοῦμεν καὶ ὃ ἑωράκαμεν μαρτυροῦμεν (1 John i. 2; Rev. i. 2). On the contrary, there is no passage to be found where μαρτυρεῖν with the accus. means so much as "confirm the truth of an utterance by a testimony in regard to it."[1] The first view, therefore, is to be rejected as contrary to usage. Besides, the confession made by Jesus, and Timothy's confession mentioned in ver. 12, are not in contents different from one another. De Wette thinks that μαρτυρεῖν "is used

[1] Had Paul wished to express the thought that Christ had confirmed, by word or deed, the truth of the Christian confession, he would have written the dative τῇ καλῇ ὁμολογίᾳ — The expression μαρτυρίαν μαρτυρεῖν, also occurring in classic Greek, does not mean: "confirm the truth of a testimony," but simply "testify, *i.e.* make a testimony" — The old expositors justly directed attention to Matt. xxvii. 11 and John xviii. 26 f. in regard to ἡ καλὴ ὁμολογία.

here in the well-known ecclesiastical signification, consequently that Christ is represented as the first martyr," and that the meaning is: " Christ confirmed the confession of the truth by His suffering and death." This is not only against the usage of the N. T., but fails also by generalizing in an arbitrary way the idea of ἡ καλὴ ὁμολογία — If ἡ κ ὁμολ. is the confession which Christ witnessed of Himself, ἐπὶ Ποντ. Πιλ. cannot mean: "under Pontius Pilate " (de Wette), but only: "*before* Pontius Pilate." Ἐπί stands here as in Matt xxviii. 14, Acts xxv. 9, xxvi. 2, and other passages. — As the words added with τοῦ Θεοῦ point back to τῆς αἰων. ζωῆς, so do those added here with Χρ. Ἰησ. point back to καὶ ὡμολόγησας κ τ λ. — τηρῆσαί σε τὴν ἐντολὴν ἄσπιλον, ἀνεπίληπτον] These words, depending on παραγγέλλω, give the purpose of Paul's exhortation to Timothy. Τηρεῖν, joined with ἐντολή in many passages of the N T., means "keep, observe,' as in chap. v 22 (de Wette and most expositors; Wiesinger differs). — Τὴν ἐντολήν is not a single moral or official law given specially to Timothy; it is synonymous with ἡ παραγγελία in i. 5 (so, too, Hofmann), pointing out the law of the gospel as the divine standard, according to which the Christian has to regulate his life [1] — ἄσπιλον and ἀνεπίληπτον must, from their position, be referred to ἐντολήν (with de Wette, van Oosterzee, Plitt, Hofmann, and others), and not to σε, as Leo, Matthies, Wiesinger, and most suppose.[2] Expositors take ἄσπιλον and ἀνεπίληπτον as two co-ordinate adjectives, so that for the sense καί has to be supplied between them (so hitherto in this commentary). This, however, is against usage; καί is dropped only when more than two attributes are reckoned, comp. *e g*. iii. 2 ff, or when the one adjective forms *one* idea with the substantive, so that the other adjective defines the compound idea more precisely (comp. *e.g.* 1 Cor. x. 4; see Winer, pp 488 f. [E. T. p. 659]). It is more correct, therefore, to connect ἄσπιλον closely with

---

[1] The special reference to ver. 12 (van Oosterzee) is arbitrary. Still it might perhaps be said that Paul sums up in τὴν ἐντολήν the commands which he gave to Timothy in vv. 11, 12. In this command, however, there is also contained the sum of the whole Christian law.

[2] Wiesinger thinks that ἄσπ. and ἀνεπίλ. denote the *result* of τηρῆσαι τὴν ἐντολήν. But how can this be justified grammatically?

ἐντολή, and to take ἀνεπίληπτον in such a way that it declares how Timothy is to keep this ἐντολὴ ἄσπιλος: he is to keep the commandment which is in itself spotless, and to keep it so as to expose it to no blame.—μέχρι τῆς ἐπιφανείας τ. κυρίου ἡμ. Ἰησ. Χρ.] ἡ ἐπιφάνεια is the second coming of Christ. The word occurs outside of the Pastoral Epistles only in 2 Thess. ii. 18 (2 Tim. iv. 1, 8; Tit. ii. 13; in 2 Tim. i. 10, it is used to denote Christ's first coming in the flesh). For the second coming we usually have ἀποκάλυψις (1 Cor. i. 7) or παρουσία. The word ἐπιφάνεια brings into prominence the element of visibility in the παρουσία; comp. 2 Thess. ii. 8 (Wiesinger). Chrysostom's explanation is wrong: μέχρι τῆς σῆς τελευτῆς.— Bengel: fideles in praxi sua proponebant sibi diem Christi, ut appropinquantem, nos solemus nobis horam mortis proponere.

Vv 15, 16. The apostle concludes with a doxology, which is attached to the previous words by means of the relative clause ἦν . . . δείξει κ.τ.λ. — ἦν καιροῖς ἰδίοις δείξει] On καιροῖς ἰδ., comp. ii. 6; Tit. i. 3, also Gal. vi 9. — δείξει] Bengel: ostendi dicitur, quod jam ante erat, Acts iii. 20. The verb does not mean "effect," nor is it, with Heydenreich, to be translated. "which He will show *in its majesty*, will cause to follow and present *in visible glory*," but simply: "*which He will make visible, cause to appear*." The expression is used by the apostle in reference to Christ's present hiddenness. The hope of the near return of Christ did not lead the apostle to fix arbitrarily the hour when that would take place. —Instead of the simple Θεός, there follows, as subject to δείξει, a series of designations for God, by which Paul represents God as the blessed, the only potentate, the immortal, the invisible— in *one* word, the absolute (comp. with this i. 17). This he does not simply for the purpose "of giving to his words a more solemn conclusion" (de Wette), but to satisfy the inward impulse of naming the chief features of the idea of God as rooted in the Christian consciousness—specially in opposition to the fictions of the heretics (according to Wiesinger, "in antithetic reference to the striving after earthly riches, rebuked in the preceding verses"). — ὁ μακάριος] comp. i. 11; μακάριος is to be taken as an adjective, as is clear from the omission of the article before μόνος. — Καὶ μόνος δυνάστης]

To God alone as the Almighty is the predicate δυνάστης due in the absolute sense; hence the addition of μόνος. The supreme power contained in δυνάστης (comp. 2 Macc. xii. 15, 3 Macc. v. 51) is made still more prominent by the next words: ὁ βασιλεὺς τῶν βασιλευόντων κ.τ.λ.; comp. i. 17; Rev. xvii. 14; Deut. x 17; Ps. cxxxvi. 3. — Ver. 16. ὁ μόνος ἔχων ἀθανασίαν] comp. i. 17. 'Αθανασία is synonymous with ἀφθαρσία, 1 Cor. xv 53; Justin Martyr (*Quaest. et Respons. ad Orthod.* 61): μόνος ἔχων τὴν ἀθανασίαν λέγεται ὁ Θεός, ὅτι οὐκ ἐκ θελήματος ἄλλου ταύτην ἔχει, καθάπερ οἱ λοιποὶ πάντες ἀθάνατοι, ἀλλ' ἐκ τῆς οἰκείας οὐσίας. — φῶς οἰκῶν ἀπρόσιτον] This idea that God, who is Himself called light (1 John i. 5), dwells in light, is found nowhere else in the N. T.; but we may compare with it Ps. civ. 2; Ezek. i. 26 ff. Chrysostom remarks on this: οὐκοῦν καὶ τόπῳ ἐμπεριείληπται; ἄπαγε οὐχ ἵνα τοῦτο νοήσωμεν, ἀλλ' ἵνα τὸ ἀκατάληπτον τῆς θείας φύσεως παραστήσῃ, φῶς αὐτὸν οἰκεῖν εἶπεν ἀπρόσιτον, οὕτω θεολογήσας, ὡς ἦν αὐτῷ δυνατόν. — The verb οἰκεῖν is found only here in the N. T. with an accusative, the construction is often found in the classics, also 2 Macc. v. 17, vi. 2. — ἀπρόσιτος is ἅπ. λεγ in Holy Scripture. This participial clause does not serve as a reason for the one previous (Hofmann: "*by* dwelling in light unapproachable"), but adds to it a new definition of the divine nature. — To the idea that God is surrounded by an unapproachable majesty of light, there is attached the corresponding thought: ὃν εἶδεν οὐδεὶς ἀνθρώπων, οὐδὲ ἰδεῖν δύναται; on which comp. John i. 18; 1 John iv. 12; Matt. xi. 27. The following two sentences may serve as explanation: Theophilus (*ad Autol* p. 71): τὸ εἶδος τοῦ Θεοῦ . . μὴ δυνάμενον ὀφθαλμοῖς σαρκίνοις ὁραθῆναι; and Dionysius Areop (*De Divin. Nom.* ch. i. p. 376, I. ed. Corder): πάσαις διανοίαις ἀδιανόητόν ἐστι τὸ ὑπὲρ διάνοιαν ἕν.[1] — ᾧ τιμὴ καὶ κράτος αἰώνιον] comp. i. 17

---

[1] There is no good ground for deriving, with Hofmann, all these names for God from His relations "to other potentates who meet with trouble, whom death does not permit to abide, who are not unapproachable and invisible." And there is as little ground for saying that this doxology was added, because the apostle intended to describe "God who will grant to see the appearance of

Ver. 17. The apostle might have stopped at ver 16; but, glancing back to vv. 9 ff., he adds another injunction in regard to the rich.[1] — τοῖς πλουσίοις ἐν τῷ νῦν αἰῶνι] Chrysostom: εἰσὶ γὰρ καὶ ἄλλοι πλούσιοι ἐν τῷ μέλλοντι. Still we cannot press the contrast so far as to make the earthly riches necessarily exclude the heavenly (wealth in God, Luke xii. 21). — παράγγελλε μὴ ὑψηλοφρονεῖν] ὑψηλοφρονεῖν only here and at Rom. xi. 20 (Rom. xii. 16: τὰ ὑψηλὰ φρονεῖν): "exalt themselves haughtily over others because of their possessions." — μηδὲ ἠλπικέναι ἐπὶ πλούτου ἀδηλότητι] ἀδηλότης (ἄπ. λεγ.), from ἄδηλος, which is equivalent to "not manifest, hidden," is properly "hiddenness," then "uncertainty." The word indicates that it is uncertain whether or not riches continue to him who possesses them (comp. 1 Cor. ix. 26: ἀδήλως). Instead of the substantive, we might have had the adjective: ἐπὶ τῷ πλούτῳ τῷ ἀδήλῳ (Luther: "on uncertain riches"); still the form of expression here makes the idea of uncertainty more prominent (see Winer, p. 221 [E. T. p. 296]), and that is all the more appropriate here that it points out more forcibly the folly of the hope. Hofmann explains ἀδηλότης unsuitably by "hiddenness," in the sense of "the rich man having put his riches safely away," as if riches would be put safely away by being hidden. — ἀλλ' ἐν τῷ Θεῷ] The construction of ἐλπίζειν with ἐν is in the N. T. the more uncommon one, but comp. Eph. i. 12; 1 Cor. xv. 19. —The truth that all hope must rest on God is confirmed by adding the words: τῷ παρέχοντι ἡμῖν τὰ πάντα (i.e. all that we possess) πλουσίως εἰς ἀπόλαυσιν] εἰς ἀπόλαυσιν (comp. iv. 3: εἰς μετάληψιν) is not added by way of opposition to a wrong abstinence, but in opposition to the ὑψηλοφρονεῖν and ἠλπικέναι ἐπὶ πλούτῳ. The apostle means to say that God does not give us earthly blessings that we may possess them and be proud over them, but that we may enjoy them,— according to His will,—and therefore use them rightly.

Jesus as judge with reward or punishment, to describe Him as a potentate who is infinitely more and higher than all earthly kings and lords," and did so because Timothy "was in danger of injuring his position as a Christian, and his calling as a teacher *for the sake of gain*" (!).

[1] "There Paul had spoken of the dangers of those who *wish* to become rich; now he turns to those who *are* rich" (van Oosterzee).

Ver. 18. The negative ideas of the previous verse are followed by four positive, joined two and two. — ἀγαθοεργεῖν, πλουτεῖν ἐν ἔργοις καλοῖς] These ideas are synonymous, the second, however, being stronger than the first It is not probable that we are to think only of the practice of benevolence; that is brought out in the next two expressions. On ἀγαθοεργεῖν, comp. Acts xiv. 17, where, however, the *Rec.* has ἀγαθοποιῶν; the word ἀγαθοποιεῖν in Num. x. 32, LXX.; 1 Macc xi 33. — πλουτεῖν ἐν ἔργ ἀγ. hints at τοῖς πλουσίοις ἐν τ. νῦν αἰῶνι (Wiesinger). — εὐμεταδότους εἶναι, κοινωνικούς] The two expressions occur only here in the N. T.: μεταδίδωμι is, however, used specially of giving to the poor in Luke iii. 11; Rom. xii. 8; Eph. iv. 28. Some expositors wrongly find in κοινωνικούς an express contrast to ὑψηλοφρονεῖν; Chrysostom : = ὁμιλητικοί, προσηνεῖς. It stands here like κοινωνεῖν, Gal. vi. 6, κοινωνία (joined with εὐποιία), Heb. xiii. 16.

Ver. 19. Ἀποθησαυρίζοντας ἑαυτοῖς θεμέλιον καλόν] The participle tells what the rich desire by the conduct already mentioned; it is not to be exchanged with the infinitive. Ἀποθησ. and θεμέλιον are not exactly suitable to one another. This, however, is not to be corrected by conjecturing (with Clericus) κειμήλιον or (with Lamb, Bos) θέμα λίαν καλόν, nor by explaining θεμέλιον as equivalent to θέμα (Tob. iv. 9, Leo: "and gather for themselves a good fund for the future"), nor even by taking ἀποθησ. as absolute and θεμέλιον as in apposition. Wolf: ita ... ut divites thesauros sibi ipsis colligere jubeantur, qui sint fundamento alicui olim inservituri, Luther: "gather treasures, to themselves a good ground for the future." — ἀποθησαυρίζειν] "lay something aside for the purpose of preserving, and therefore collect." It is unnecessary to give the word here the more general signification of "acquire." The apostle's thought is, that the rich, by giving away their θησαυρούς in sympathetic love, are gathering for themselves a treasure, and are also laying a good foundation on which their future salvation is built. — εἰς τὸ μέλλον is not to be connected with καλόν, but with the verb: "for the future." — ἵνα ἐπιλάβωνται τῆς ὄντως ζωῆς] ἵνα does not express the consequence, "so that," but the purpose, "in order that" 'Επιλάβωνται, comp. ver. 12, de Wette, rightly: "in order that they (at the same time planting their feet on this basis) may seize," τῆς ὄντως ζωῆς, comp. v. 3.

Vv. 20, 21. Final exhortation and benediction to Timothy. The apostle begins fervently and impressively with: ὦ Τιμόθεε (Matthies). — τὴν παραθήκην φύλαξον] comp. 2 Tim. i. 12, 14, παραθήκη is a "possession entrusted;" Paul does not say what kind of possession. Even in these parallel passages a more precise definition is not given, except that at ver. 12 he denotes by μου that it is entrusted to him, and in ver. 14 adds the adjective καλήν. In any case there is meant by it here a gift entrusted to Timothy by God, which gift he is to preserve (φύλαξον) from every hurt. As the apostle puts its preservation (φυλάσσειν) in close connection with the ἐκτρέπεσθαι of the heretics, we may understand by it either Timothy's διακονία (de Wette, Otto), or the gospel, "sound doctrine" (Wiesinger, van Oosterzee, Hofmann)—As the chief purpose of the epistle is to instruct Timothy regarding his conduct in the ministry committed to him, it seems right to understand by παραθήκη a possession entrusted, not to all Christians, but to Timothy in particular. Thus—in spite of the absence of σου—the first view deserves the preference, all the more that in the other passages quoted this meaning of the word is the most suitable. The next word, ἐκτρεπόμενος, shows that Timothy would injure his office by entering upon the βέβηλοι κενοφωνίαι. Plitt arbitrarily takes παραθήκη as equivalent to "eternal life." — ἐκτρεπόμενος τὰς βεβήλους κενοφωνίας] ἐκτρέπεσθαι, properly: "turn away from anything;" then with the accusative (as in 2 Tim. iii. 5: ἀποτρέπεσθαι): "avoid," synonymous with παραιτεῖσθαι. — κενοφωνία] synonymous with ματαιολογία, i. 6 ; comp. 2 Tim. ii. 16 : "*empty talk without anything in it.*"—This talk is still more precisely defined by the next words : καὶ ἀντιθέσεις τῆς ψευδωνύμου γνώσεως] It is to be observed that ἀντιθέσεις is closely connected with the previous κενοφωνίας, the article τάς belonging to both words and the genitive τῆς ψευδ. γνώσεως referring to both alike. Hence ἀντιθέσεις must here express some thought corresponding with κενοφωνίας. It is not therefore advisable to understand by it in general terms "the statutes of the heretics against the gospel" (Matthies, Wiesinger), or "the controversial theses of the heretics directed against the gospel" (so before in this commentary [1]); it is much more correct to understand it of the theses which the heretics sought to maintain against one another (Hofmann). Thus understood, the word corresponds to λογομαχίαι in ver. 4 It is possible that these had the character of *dialectic* proofs (Conybeare and Howson, quoted in van Oosterzee), but the word itself does not show this. Baur's assertion is purely arbitrary, that the contrariae oppositiones are here meant which Marcion exerted himself to establish between the law and the gospel. — τῆς ψευδωνύμου γνώσεως] The expression is easily explained by the fact that the heretics boasted of possessing a knowledge, a φιλοσοφία (Col. ii. 8), in which there was a more perfect science of divine things than that presented by the gospel — Paul was also acquainted with a γνῶσις, which, however, was rooted in faith, and was effected by the πνεῦμα Χριστοῦ But the γνῶσις of the heretics did not deserve this name, and hence Paul called it ψευδώνυμος (occurring only here in the N. T.), on which Chrysostom aptly remarks . ὅταν γὰρ πίστις μὴ εἶ, γνῶσις οὐκ ἔστιν. Baur, without just ground, seeks to draw from the use of this word a proof for his hypothesis that the epistle was composed at the date of the heresy of Marcion. — Ver. 21 ἥν τινες ἐπαγγελλόμενοι] ἐπαγγέλεσθαι stands here in the same sense as in ii 10 , Luther inexactly · "which some allege" — περὶ τὴν πίστιν ἠστόχησαν] The same construction in 2 Tim ii. 18 , with the genitive, i. 6 The ἐπαγγέλεσθαι τὴν ψευδ. γν includes (comp. i. 6) the ἀστοχεῖν περὶ τ. πίστιν, "erring in regard to the faith." This Wiesinger wrongly denies, with the remark that "the apostle did not consider the mere occupation with such things to be apostasy, but only a possible occasion for apostasy.[2] Ἐπαγγ manifestly denotes more than merely

---

[1] Against these explanations there is also the relative clause ἥν κ τ λ attached to γνώσεως, since, of course, the followers of a γνῶσις containing anti-evangelic doctrines had departed from the faith

[2] Hofmann, coinciding with Wiesinger's view, says · "The occupation with that which claimed, but did not deserve, the name of science, brought them unawares on the wrong track ," but the "unawares" is purely imported into the verse.

being occupied with a thing. By τινες here, as in i. 3, 6 (vi. 3), we must understand the heretics.

Ver. 22. The benediction, as in the other Pauline Epistles. If ὑμῶν is the right reading, we can only infer from it that Paul intends the benediction for the whole church, not that he addresses the epistle to the whole church along with Timothy.

Παύλου ἡ πρὸς Τιμόθεον ἐπιστολη δευτέρα.

A, *al.* have the shorter superscription: πρὸς Τιμόθεον β'; so, too, D E F G, but with ἄρχεται preceding.

CHAPTER I.

Ver. 1. Tisch, on the authority of D E F G K P ℵ, *al*, several versions, and Fathers, adopted Χριστοῦ 'Ιησοῦ instead of the *Rec.* 'Ιησοῦ Χριστοῦ (A L, pl. etc., Lachm. and Buttm.). For the singular ἐπαγγελίαν, ℵ has the plural ἐπαγγελίας. — Ver. 3. To τῷ Θεῷ there is added μου in D* E 17, Sahid. Vulg. ed. Sixtin. Demidor Clar. Germ Or Ambrosiast. etc. Imitation of Rom. i 8. — Ver 4 The reading ἐπιποθῷ (G, Boern. utrumq. Chrys.) seems only to have arisen from an endeavour to simplify the structure of the sentence. — Ver. 5. For λαμβάνων (*Rec.* with D E K L, *al.*, Chrys. Theodoret, etc.), Lachm. Buttm. Tisch read λαβών, on the authority of A C F G 17, 31. This latter deserves preference as the more difficult reading, all the more that it is preceded by the present ἐπιποθῶν. — Instead of Λωίδι, some MSS. have Λωΐδι, others Λωΐδη, and one Λαΐδι; still the *Rec.* is too strongly supported to leave doubts of its correctness. For Εὐνίκη, several cursives have Εὐνείκη. — Ver. 7. δειλίας] The reading δουλείας (in 238, Aeth. Didym Chrys.) has clearly arisen from Rom. viii. 15 — Ver. 11. ἐθνῶν (Tisch. 8 omits) may possibly have been inserted on the analogy of 1 Tim. ii. 7; but since it is wanting only in A ℵ, and some cursives, it is safer to regard it as the original reading, all the more that it is necessary for the meaning — Ver. 12. In ℵ, καί is wanting before ταῦτα; all other MSS, however, support its genuineness. — For παρακαταθήκην (*Rec*), we must read here and at ver. 14, παραθήκην, just as in 1 Tim. vi. 20. — The μου that follows is wanting in D* E and some cursives, it was probably omitted because in those two other passages no pronoun stands with the word. — Ver. 15. The mode of writing the name Φύγελλος varies very much; the best supported is Φύγελος, which Lachm. and Tisch. adopted. — For 'Ερμογένης, Tisch. has adopted 'Ερμογένης, with the remark: testatur antiquissimus accentuum testis D*** etc. — Ver. 16. For ἐπησχύνθη (Rec), all uncials, except K, several cursives, also Basil. Oec. Theodoret, have ἐπαισχύνθη (Lachm. Buttm. Tisch.); comp. Winer, p. 70 [E T. p. 86]. — Ver. 17. Tisch. 7 retained the Rec. σπουδαιότερον, with D*** E K L, al. Lachm. and Tisch. 8 adopted σπουδαίως, on the authority of C D* F G ℵ, al ; Buttm. read σπουδαιοτέρος, on the authority of A. This last reading seems to be only a correction of the Rec. Which of the two others is the original one, cannot be decided. The positive may be considered a correction of the comparative; but, on the other hand, the latter is more usual with Paul than the former, which occurs with him only in Tit. iii. 13. Besides, the comparative is often found in Paul where we might expect the positive (comp. 1 Tim iii 14)

Vv. 1, 2. Διὰ θελήματος] comp. on 1 Tim. i. 1. — The words of this address are peculiar : κατ' ἐπαγγελίαν ζωῆς τῆς ἐν Χριστῷ Ἰησοῦ; they are not to be joined with θελήματος, nor with the following Τιμοθέῳ, but with ἀπόστολος κ.τ.λ. Ἐπαγγελία in the N. T. constantly means " *the promise;* " it is incorrect to translate it here by " preaching;" comp. 1 Tim. iv. 8. Its object is the ζωή, the blessed life which " exists objectively, and is presented in Christ " (Wiesinger). The preposition κατά shows that Paul's apostleship stands in connection with this promise. Matthies defines this connection more precisely by saying that κατά denotes the *harmony* between the plan of salvation, of which that ἐπαγγελία is the chief element, and the apostleship. But it is more natural, and more in accordance with the passage in Tit. i. 2, to explain it, as does Theodoret, followed by de Wette and Wiesinger: ἀπόστολόν με προεβάλετο ὁ Θεὸς, ὥστε με τὴν ἐπαγγελθεῖσαν αἰώνιον ζωὴν τοῖς ἀνθρώποις κηρύξαι, so that κατά directs attention to the purpose; see Winer, p. 376 [E. T. p. 502]. Otto contends that κατά means " for the purpose," and that κηρύξαι should be supplied. He explains it more generally : " in the matter of, in regard to," with the remark : " Paul means to say that his apostolic office ... in its entire work is *defined* by that promise." This explanation, however, comes back substantially to the former one, since the work of the apostolic office is specially the κηρύσσειν.

Hofmann explains κατά as equivalent to "in consequence of," in the sense, viz., that the promise of life forms the presupposition of Paul's apostleship; but for this there is no support in usage; besides, it is self-evident that without that promise of life there would be no apostleship. — Ver. 2. Τιμοθέῳ ἀγαπητῷ τέκνῳ] ἀγαπητῷ, in distinction from γνησίῳ, 1 Tim. i. 2 and Tit. i. 4, does not indicate a greater confidence, nor even blame, as if Timothy, by showing a want of courageous faith, no longer deserved the name (Mack).

Ver. 3. Χάριν ἔχω τῷ Θεῷ] As in several other epistles, Paul begins here with a thanksgiving to God,—only he usually says εὐχαριστῶ or εὐλογητὸς ὁ Θεός. The expression is only in 1 Tim. i. 12 (elsewhere in the N. T. Luke xvii. 9; Heb. xii. 28). To τῷ Θεῷ there is next attached the relative clause: ᾧ λατρεύω ἀπὸ προγόνων ἐν καθαρᾷ συνειδήσει, which is added because the apostle wishes to remind Timothy of his πρόγονοι, viz. his grandmother and mother,—not to bring into prominence a relationship *different* from the apostle's own (Hofmann), but one *corresponding* with his own. — ἀπὸ προγόνων is not equivalent to ἀπὸ βρέφους, iii. 15; it means that the apostle serves God "in the manner handed down by his progenitors, as they had done" (Buttmann, p. 277), or that the service of the πρόγονοι, *i.e.* not the ancestors of the Jewish people (Heydenreich and others), but the progenitors of the apostle himself (so most expositors), is continued in him, and denotes therefore "the continuity of the true honouring of God by Judaism" (de Wette). Otto says that the expression is not to be referred to the education (Flatt) or disposition (Winer, p. 349 [E. T. p 465]; van Oosterzee, Wiesinger), but to the ancestral mode of worship; but, in reply, it is to be observed, that on account of ἐν καθαρᾷ συνειδήσει the reference to disposition is by no means to be considered as excluded.[1] The apostle, by his conversion to Christianity, did not interrupt his connection with the λατρεύειν of his ancestors, because it was a necessary condition of the new faith to honour the God of revelation whom the Jews served. This utterance regarding the apostle himself,

---

[1] Had the apostle not been conscious that his ancestors had served God ἐν καθ. συνειδ., he would not have expressed himself as he does here.

and particularly the words ἐν καθαρᾷ συνειδ., are not in contradiction with 1 Tim. i. 13 and similar passages, since the apostle, even while he was zealous for the law, served the God of his fathers ἐν καθ. συνειδ., as little then as afterwards falsifying the revealed word with arbitrary fictions, which was done by the heretics; comp. Acts xxiii. 1, xxiv. 14 ff. Hofmann is wrong in breaking up the inner relation of these words, referring λατρεύω only to ἀπὸ προγόνων, and not also ἐν καθ. συνειδήσει, which he refers only to the apostle. This he does, although the structure of the sentence is most decidedly against such a distribution of the references. — On ἐν καθ. συνειδ., comp. 1 Tim. i. 5.[1] — ὡς ἀδιάλειπτον κ.τ.λ.] ὡς does not give the reason of thanksgiving, as Chrysostom explains it: εὐχαριστῶ τῷ Θεῷ, ὅτι μέμνημαί σου, φησὶν, οὕτω σὲ φιλῶ, and as Luther translates: "that I," etc. Against this there is not only the word ὡς, but also the sense. The apostle, in his giving of thanks to God, often indeed recalls his μνεία of those to whom he writes (Rom. i. 9; Phil. i. 3; 1 Thess. i. 2; Philem. 4), but he never points them out as the ground of his thanksgiving. Otto, while granting that there are objections to it, wishes to take ὡς as the same as ὅτι, and to regard it as a particle of the *reason*, equivalent to ὅτι οὕτως, which, however, cannot be justified from usage.[2] Just as little should we take ὡς adverbially with ἀδιαλ. Mack: "I thank God, etc.

[1] Otto rightly: "With Paul συνείδησις is purely the self-consciousness of the subject. The consciousness is pure, when it is conscious of no impure strivings. Impurity appears whenever any one, under the pretence of serving God, follows after his own selfish purposes" There is no ground for Hofmann's assertion, that the καθ. συνείδησις is only "a conscience free from consciousness of guilt, such as only that man can have who is conscious of the forgiveness of his sins."

[2] The particle ὡς does sometimes occur in classic Greek in such a way that it is resolvable into ὅτι οὕτως, but, as is shown in the very nature of the word, only *in cases when* the sentence beginning with ὡς expresses something *surprising*, something *exciting astonishment*, in particular, therefore, after the verb θαυμάζω. It follows, as Pape says, *s.v*., that "in such cases we may translate it with the simple *how*." That such is the case, is proved by all the quotations brought together by Otto (p. 301) from the Greek classics. It is therefore *entirely erroneous* for Otto to say quite generally that "it is in the manner of genuine Greek to contract the causal ὅτι with the following οὕτως into the adverbial pronoun ὡς" Only if the ἀδιάλειπτον ἔχω τὴν περὶ σοῦ μνείαν occurred to the apostle as something *strange*, *astonishing*, could ὡς be explained here by ὅτι οὕτως.—Besides, it is inaccurate for Otto to ascribe to ὡς a causal signification, and then call the clause beginning with it an objective clause.

... I keep right continually," etc. — A subordinate clause begins with ὡς, which, however, does not mean: "since, quippe, siquidem" (Heydenreich, Flatt, Matthies: "in so far"), "so often" (Calvin: "quoties tui recordor in precibus meis, id autem facio continenter, simul etiam de te gratias ago"), but expresses the parallel relation of the subordinate clause to the principal one, and should be translated by "as" (Wiesinger, van Oosterzee); in Gal. vi. 10, ὡς has a very similar meaning. The sense accordingly is: "*I thank God, as I am continually mindful of thee in my prayers*," so that already in the subordinate clause it is indicated that the thanksgiving to God refers to Timothy. In Rom. i. 9, ὡς stands in quite another connection, which makes de Wette's objection all the less justifiable, that here it has been taken from that passage. — ἀδιάλειπτον ἔχω τὴν περί σου μνείαν] De Wette arbitrarily maintains that Paul would have said: ἀδιαλείπτως μνείαν σου ποιοῦμαι. Though Paul does so express himself in Rom. i. 9 (and similarly Eph i. 16), it does not, however, follow that he might not use another form of expression in another epistle, especially since the connection of μνείαν with ἔχειν is by no means unusual with him; comp. 1 Thess. iii. 6. — ἀδιάλειπτον stands first for emphasis. There is nothing strange here in μνεία being joined with περί, since μνᾶσθαι takes that construction even in the classics; comp. Herod. i. 36, Plato, *Lach.* p. 181 A; Xenophon, *Cyrop.* i. 6. 12, so, too, with μνημονεύειν, Heb. xi. 22. — ἐν ταῖς δεήσεσί μου νυκτὸς καὶ ἡμέρας] ταῖς is not to be supplied before νυκτός, since the last words are not to be taken with δεήσεσι, but either with ἀδιαλ. ἔχω κ.τ.λ. (Wiesinger, van Oosterzee) or with what follows (Matthies, Plitt, Hofmann). The first construction is preferable, because the chief emphasis is laid on the preceding thought, the ἐπιποθῶν being made subsidiary; besides, the apostle had no particular reason for directing attention to the uninterrupted duration *of his longing* for Timothy as the source of his unceasing prayer. The assertion, that νυκτὸς καὶ ἡμέρας is superfluous on account of the previous ἀδιάλειπτον, is not to the point; comp. Acts xxvi. 7, where the same words are added with ἐν ἐκτενείᾳ.

Ver. 4. As in Rom. i. 11, Phil. i. 8, and other passages,

Paul also expresses here his longing to see the person to whom the epistle is addressed. The participle ἐπιποθῶν is subordinate to the previous ἔχω; to it, in turn, the next participle μεμνημένος is subordinated. The longing for Timothy causes him to be continually remembered in the apostle's prayers, and the remembrance is nourished by thinking of his tears. — σου τῶν δακρύων] By these are meant—as the verb μεμνημένος shows—not tears which "Timothy shed" when at a distance from the apostle (Wiesinger), and of which he knew only through a letter (which Timothy therefore "shed by letter," Hofmann); but the tears of which he himself had been witness, the tears which Timothy shed probably on his departure from him (van Oosterzee, Plitt). These were, to the apostle, a proof of Timothy's love to him, and produced in him the desire of seeing Timothy again, that he might thereby be filled with joy. In this connection of the clauses with one another, the apostle has not yet given the object of thanks appropriate to the χάριν ἔχω, he does not do so till ver. 5.[1] — According to Hofmann, the reason of the thanks is already given in the participial clause μεμνημένος. But the idea that Paul thanks God for Timothy's tears, is out of all analogy with the other epistles of the apostle. Even the ἵνα χαρᾶς πληρωθῶ is against this view, for the apostle could not possibly say that he remembers Timothy's tears in order that he may be filled with joy.

Ver. 5. Ὑπόμνησιν λαβὼν τῆς κ.τ.λ.] This participial clause is to be taken neither with μεμνημένος nor with ἐπιποθῶν (de Wette, Leo); the sense forbids us to subordinate it to one of these ideas, and the want of the copula καί to co-ordinate it with them. Otto joins it with ἵνα χαρᾶς πληρωθῶ: "that I may be filled with joy, as I (sc. by thy personal presence in Rome) receive a renewal of my remembrance of thy unfeigned faith." Against this construction,

[1] Against this view it cannot be maintained that it makes a subordinate participle μεμνημένος depend on the subordinate participle ἐπιποθῶν, for that is not in itself impossible, nor can it be said "that the insertion of a clause μεμνημένος between ἰδεῖν σε and ἵνα is intolerable," since the chief stress is not on μεμνημένος, but on ἐπιποθῶν κ τ λ. Further, it cannot provoke objection that Timothy's tears nourished in the apostle the longing to see him again, since these were a proof of his love—and of his faith.

however, there are the following reasons :—(1) That to supply "by thy presence" is not only arbitrary, but does not suit with the idea ὑπόμνησιν λαμβάνειν, since the impression made on us by anything before the eyes cannot be described as reminding us of that thing. (2) That, if the remembrance of Timothy's constancy in the faith is so unceasing with the apostle that he thanks God for it, it is quite inconceivable how he could still wish to receive a ὑπόμνησις of it (3) That we see ourselves forced by it to prefer the reading λαμβάνων (which Tisch. adopted) to λαβών. — The only remaining course is to connect ὑπομν. λαβ. with χάριν ἔχω τῷ Θεῷ (so Wiesinger, Plitt, and others). It does stand at some distance from it, but that cannot be considered a good reason against the construction The construction in Phil. i. 3-5 is similar. Nor can we make objection that " Paul according to this view would not thank God because Timothy stands in such faith, but because he has been brought to his recollection" (Hofmann), for the participial clause does not give the reason of the thanksgiving directly, but only hints at it. It is the same here as at Eph. i. 15 and Col. i. 3, where, too, the subject of thanksgiving is not the ἀκούειν, but that which the apostle had heard. — ὑπόμνησιν λαβών is not equivalent to "recordans, as I remember" (de Wette: " retaining the remembrance"), for ὑπόμνησις in the N. T. (comp. 2 Pet i. 13, iii. 1; also Ecclus. xvi 11; 2 Macc. vi. 17) has an *active* signification; it is equivalent, therefore, to "since I have received remembrance," *i.e.* "since I have been reminded" (Wiesinger, van Oosterzee, Hofmann). It is not said what had reminded the apostle of Timothy's faith. Bengel supposes that it was *externa quaedam occasio*, or a *nuntius a Timotheo;* Wiesinger, that it was Onesimus. But it suits better with the context to regard the tears just mentioned as causing the recollection, inasmuch as they were to the apostle a proof of his unfeigned faith. It is unnecessary to derive the ὑπόμνησις from some inner working of the apostle's soul (so formerly in this commentary), there is no hint of any such thing. The present λαμβάνων is not against this interpretation, since these tears came so vividly before the apostle's soul that he was thereby reminded more and more of

Timothy's faith. — τῆς ἐν σοὶ ἀνυποκρίτου πίστεως] see 1 Tim. i. 5; this, now, is the subject of the thanksgiving. — As Paul is conscious that the God whom he serves was the God also of his ancestors, he can remind Timothy of the fact that the faith which dwells in him was before the possession of his grandmother and mother.[1]— ἥτις ἐνῴκησε πρῶτον] ἐνοικεῖν as in ver. 14; Rom. viii. 11; 2 Cor vi. 16. The word is chosen here "to denote faith on its objective side as a possession coming from God" (Wiesinger), and it declares that "it has not become a merely transient feeling, but an abiding principle of life dwelling in them" (van Oosterzee). — πρῶτον is not, with Luther, to be translated by "before," but to be taken in its proper meaning, in reference to the πρόγονοι of Timothy. The point brought out is, that Timothy was not the first of his family to be a believer, but we cannot press the point so far as to suppose that a distinction is drawn between the apostle whose ancestors served God as Jews, while Timothy's ancestors were heathen (so Hofmann). — ἐν τῇ μάμμῃ σου κ τ λ.] Regarding μάμμη, see Wahl on the passage. —This grandmother of Timothy is not mentioned elsewhere. Of the mother, it is said in Acts xvi. 1 ff that she was a γυνὴ Ἰουδαία πιστή; her name is given only here. The mention of the two is not to be regarded as a superfluous—or even surprising—afterthought. Paul might repose in Timothy all the greater confidence, that he, brought up by a pious mother, had before him her example and that of his grandmother. — This confidence the apostle expresses still more definitely in the next words: πέπεισμαι δὲ, ὅτι καὶ ἐν σοί, with which Heydenreich wrongly supplies ἐνοικήσει instead of ἐνοικεῖ.

Ver. 6. Δι' ἣν αἰτίαν ἀναμιμνήσκω σε κ.τ.λ.] This verse

---

[1] Since Timothy's ἀνυπόκριτος πίστις is Christian faith, faith in Jesus Christ, it is manifestly wrong to regard the πίστις of the grandmother and mother as only faith in the O. T. promise (Otto); the relative ἥτις shows that the two are identical. From Paul's ascription to himself of a λατρεύειν ἀπὸ προγόνων, we cannot infer, with Otto, that the "matter of faith on the part of Timothy's πρόγονοι cannot be taken *further* than on the part of the apostle's πρόγονοι." The apostle does not at all boast of the πίστις of his ancestors, but says merely that he serves *the same* God as they had served. Timothy's faith could only mean something to him, if it was not only faith in the promise, but also faith in Him who had appeared according to the promise.

contains the chief thought of the whole chapter. By δι' ἥν αἰτίαν (a formula which occurs in Paul only here, at ver. 12, and at Tit. i. 13 ; αἰτία not at all in the other Pauline epistles), the apostle connects his exhortation with the previous πέπεισμαι κ.τ.λ, since his conviction of Timothy's faith was the occasion of his giving the exhortation. There is no ground for the objection raised by Otto against this connection of thought, that αἰτία " never expresses anything but the external objective occasion ;" he is no less wrong in wishing to refer δι' ἥν αἰτίαν not to ἀναμιμνήσκω, but to ἀναζωπυρεῖν. In that case the apostle would have written δι' ἥν αἰτίαν ἀναζωπύρει κ τ λ (as Otto explains the expression). The verb ἀναμιμνήσκειν, properly, " remind of something," contains in itself the idea of exhorting; the apostle finely interprets the word so as to make Timothy appear himself conscious of the duty which was urged on him, ὑπομιμνήσκειν is often used exactly in this way. — ἀναζωπυρεῖν τὸ χάρισμα τοῦ Θεοῦ] ἀναζωπυρεῖν : ἅπ. λεγ · "fan into life again ;" comp. Jamblichus, *De Vit. Pyth*. chap. xvi.· ἀνεζωπύρει τὸ θεῖον ἐν αὐτῇ. By χάρισμα τ. Θ is meant here, as in 1 Tim. iv. 14, the fitness (ἱκανότης) bestowed by God on Timothy for discharging the ἔργον εὐαγγελιστοῦ (iv. 5), which fitness includes both the capacity and also (though Hofmann denies this) zeal and spirit for official labours The context shows that the courage of a Christian martyr is here specially meant. This παρρησία is not the work of man, but the gift of God's grace to man. It can only be kept alive unceasingly by the labour of man. Chrysostom : δεῖ σου προθυμίας πρὸς τὸ χάρισμα τοῦ Θεοῦ· . . . ἐν ἡμῖν γάρ ἐστι καὶ σβέσαι, καὶ ἀνάψαι τοῦτο ὑπὸ μὲν γὰρ ῥαθυμίας καὶ ἀκηδίας σβέννυται, ὑπὸ δὲ νήψεως καὶ προσοχῆς διεγείρεται. Bengel is not incorrect in remarking on this exhortation : videtur Timotheus, Paulo diu carens, nonnihil remisisse ; certe nunc ad majora stimulatur. His former zeal seems to have been weakened, particularly by the apostle's suffering (ver. 8), so that it needed to be quickened again.[1] Otto here, too, understands by χάρισμα, the "*right*

---

[1] It has been already remarked (Introd. § 3, p. 27) that Otto is not justified in accusing Timothy of having almost laid down his office through anxiety and timidity. It is a part of this accusation that Otto here finds it said that

of office;" but this does not accord with the verb ἀναζωπυρεῖν, since the *right* did not need to be revived However Timothy might conduct himself in regard to the right imparted to him, it remained always the same; if he did not exercise it as he should have done, he *himself* or *his activity* needed the ἀναζωπυρεῖν, but not the *right* which had been delivered to him with the office.[1] On the next words: ὅ ἐστιν ἐν σοὶ διὰ τῆς ἐπιθέσεως τῶν χειρῶν μου, comp. 1 Tim. iv. 14. There can be no reason for doubting that the same act is meant in both passages. As to the difficulty that, whereas in the former passage it was the presbytery, here it is Paul who is said to have imposed hands, see the remark on that passage. The reason for this lies both in the character of the epistle, "which has for its foundation and in part for its subject the personal relation between the apostle and Timothy," as well as in Paul's exhortation to Timothy in ver. 8, "to make the gift an effective agent for him through whom the gift was received" (Wiesinger).

Ver 7 The exhortation in ver 6, Paul confirms by pointing to the spirit which God has given to His own people: οὐ γὰρ ἔδωκεν ἡμῖν ὁ Θεὸς πνεῦμα δειλίας] By ἡμῖν, Otto understands not Christians in general, but the apostle and Timothy in particular as office-bearers. The context, however, does not demand such special reference, since the apostle, in order to confirm his exhortation to Timothy, might very well appeal to a fact which had been experienced by Christians in general as well as by himself. Besides, the ἡμᾶς in ver 9 is against Otto's view. Πνεῦμα here is *either*—(1) the objective spirit of God, the Holy Spirit (Bengel, Heydenreich, Otto), of whom it is first said negatively that it is not a spirit of δειλία, i.e. not

"Timothy was to resume the duties delivered to him by the apostolic laying on of hands"—The meaning of ἀναζωπυρεῖν is mistaken by van Oosterzee and Plitt, if they think that we cannot infer from it that there had been an actual decrease of Timothy's official zeal

[1] Otto contends, that "along with the office, when the hands were laid on him, Timothy received the understanding, the personal gifts for filling it" Against this it is to be remarked—(1) That the natural talents are not bestowed along with the office, but the conscious and intentional concentration and employment of them in the office, otherwise the receiver of the office is only a dead machine in it, and (2) that the apostle, in laying on hands, acted as the instrument of the Holy Spirit; and of this Timothy was also aware

a spirit producing δειλία in man, and then positively that it is a spirit of δύναμις κ.τ λ., *i.e.* a spirit imparting δύναμις to man; *or* (2) πνεῦμα is the subjective condition of man, the spiritual life wrought in him by the Spirit of God (Mack, Matthies, Leo, similarly, too, Hofmann[1]), which is then described more precisely as a spirit, not of δειλία, but of δύναμις κ.τ.λ. The context in which the similar passage in Romans stands, and especially the passage corresponding to this in Gal. iv. 6, make the first view preferable. — δειλία denotes timidity in the struggle for the kingdom of God; comp. John xiv. 27 ; Rev. xxi. 7, 8.—The ideas δύναμις, ἀγάπη, and σωφρονισμός are closely related to each other. That the Christian, as a warrior of God, may rightly wage the warfare to which he is appointed, he needs first δύναμις, *i.e.* power, not only to withstand the attacks of the world, but also to gain an increasing victory over the world. He has need next of ἀγάπη, which never suffers him to lose sight of the goal of the struggle, *i.e.* the salvation of his brethren, and urges him to labour towards it with all self-denial. Lastly, he has need of σωφρονισμός. While Chrysostom and Theophylact leave it uncertain whether this word is to be taken intransitively, reflectively, or transitively (Theophylact . ἢ ἵνα σώφρονες ὦμεν· . . . ἢ ἵνα σωφρονισμὸν ἔχωμεν τὸ πνεῦμα, κἄν τις πειρασμὸς ἡμῖν ἐπιγένηται, πρὸς σωφρονισμὸν τοῦτον δεχώμεθα ἢ ἵνα καὶ ἄλλοις ὦμεν σωφρονισταί), later expositors (Hofmann too "discretion") have taken it as synonymous with σωφροσύνη (thus Augustine, *ad Bonif.* iv. chap. 5 : continentia ; Vulgate . sobrietas , Beza : sanitas animi ; Leo . temperantia) , de Wette, Wiesinger, van Oosterzee, Plitt make it reflective, "*self-control*" (properly, therefore, "the σωφρόνισις directed towards oneself"). Neither explanation, however, can be justified by usage. Etymology and usage are decidedly in favour of the *transitive* meaning, which therefore must be maintained, with Otto, unless we attribute to the apostle a mistake in the use of the word. In itself the Holy Spirit might be called πνεῦμα σωφρονισμοῦ in *the other* sense, since

---

[1] Hofmann, to a certain extent, combines the two, saying · "The spirit which we have received is, looking to its source, the Spirit of God , but, looking to what we become through it, it becomes in us the spirit of our life thus created."

the σωφρονίζειν is His characteristic, He practises it; but, as the preceding genitives denote effects, and not qualities, of the spirit, the genitive σωφρονισμοῦ would stand to πνεῦμα in a relation differing from that of the other genitives. The Holy Spirit can therefore receive such a designation here, only in so far as He produces the σωφρονίζειν (comp. Tit. ii. 4) in the Christian, i.e. impels him not to remain inactive when others go wrong, but to correct them that they may desist. Thus taken, the idea of σωφρονισμός appropriately includes that of ἀγάπη, part of which is to be active in amending the unhappy circumstances of the church,—here all the more appropriately because the thought which is true of all Christians is specially applied here to Timothy.[1]

Ver. 8. Μὴ οὖν (deduction from what has preceded: since God has given us the spirit of δύναμις κ.τ.λ., then, etc.) ἐπαισχυνθῇς τὸ μαρτύριον τοῦ κυρίου ἡμῶν] On the construction, comp. Rom i 16: οὐ ἐπαισχύνομαι τὸ εὐαγγέλιον. — μαρτύριον, like μαρτυρεῖν in 1 Tim. iii. 16, does not denote the martyrdom of Christ, nor even specially the testimony regarding the martyr-death of Christ (Chrysostom: μὴ αἰσχύνου, ὅτι τὸν ἐσταυρωμένον κηρύσσεις), but more generally the testimony regarding Christ, which certainly includes the other special meaning. Κυρίου is not the subjective genitive (Wahl. testimonium quod dixit Jesus de rebus divinis quas audivit a Patre, Hofmann: "the truth of salvation witnessed by Christ"[2]), but the objective (de Wette, Wiesinger)—The connection between this and the preceding thought is brought out by Bengel's words: timorem pudor comitatur; victo timore, fugit pudor malus. — μηδὲ ἐμὲ τὸν δέσμιον αὐτοῦ] Paul places himself in immediate connection with the gospel, as he was a prisoner because of his witness of Christ; and the reason of the special mention of himself lies in the summons to Timothy to come to him at Rome.[3]

---

[1] The explanation here given of σωφρονισμός is in substantial agreement with that proposed by Otto, except that Otto regards the σωφρονισμός as a work, *official* in kind.

[2] Hofmann for this explanation appeals wrongly to 1 Cor. i. 6, ii. 1; besides, μαρτύριον does not mean "truth of salvation," unless it is so defined.

[3] Wiesinger "Here the twofold contents of the epistle are set forth as the theme; for the contents of the epistle are simply the general duties laid on

Paul calls himself δέσμιος Χριστοῦ here and at Eph. iii 1, Philem. 9, because he bore his bonds for Christ's sake; or better, because "Christ (Christ's cause) had brought him into imprisonment and was keeping him there" (Winer, p. 178 [E. T. p. 236]; Meyer on Eph. iii. 1; Wiesinger). The expression in Philem. 13 : δεσμοὶ τοῦ εὐαγγελίου, forbids the explanation: "a prisoner belonging to Christ." Hofmann is inaccurate: "a prisoner whose bonds are part of his relation to Christ"—ἀλλὰ συγκακοπάθησον τῷ εὐαγγελίῳ] "*but suffer with* (sc. me) *for the gospel;*" the verb, occurring only here and perhaps at ii. 3 (the simple form at ii. 9, iv. 5, Jas. v. 13), is limited more precisely by the reference to the previous ἐμέ. Luther ("suffer with the gospel, as I do") refers the συν to the dative following; but against this there is the unsuitable collocation of person and thing. Chrysostom rightly says . συγκακοπάθησον, φησὶ, τῷ εὐαγγελίῳ, οὐχ ὡς τοῦ εὐαγγελίου κακοπαθοῦντος, ἀλλὰ τὸν μαθητὴν διεγείρων ὑπὲρ τοῦ εὐαγγελίου πάσχειν. The dative τῷ εὐαγγ. is to be taken as dativus commodi (Mack, Matthies, Wiesinger, van Oosterzee, Plitt, Hofmann), as in Phil. i. 27 : συναθλοῦντες τῇ πίστει τοῦ εὐαγγελίου; in Heb. xi. 25. συγκακουχεῖσθαι τῷ λαῷ, the dative has another meaning. — κατὰ δύναμιν Θεοῦ] These words do not belong, as Heinrichs thinks possible, to τῷ εὐαγγελίῳ, in the sense : doctrina cui inest δύναμις Θεοῦ, but to the preceding verb. The meaning, however, is not : " strengthened through God's aid " (Heydenreich), but κατά denotes the suitability : "in accordance with the power of God which is effectual in thee," or "which will not fail thee" (Hofmann). Δύναμις Θεοῦ is not here "the power produced by God," nor is it "God's *own* power" (Wiesinger), in the sense of an abstract idea apart from its actual working in the believer.

Ver. 9. In the series of participial and relative clauses which here follow each other in the Pauline manner, the apostle details the saving works of God's grace, not so much "to bring into prominence the δύναμις Θεοῦ" (Wiesinger), as to strengthen the exhortation in ver. 8. — τοῦ σώσαντος ἡμᾶς

Timothy as a preacher of the gospel, and the particular service of love which he was to render to the imprisoned apostle."

καὶ καλέσαντος κλήσει ἁγίᾳ] This thought is closely related to the one preceding, since the mention of the divine act of love serves to give strength in working and suffering for the gospel. — The καλεῖν is placed after the σώζειν, because the salvation of God, the σωτηρία, is imparted to man by God through the call. The thought is to be taken generally of all Christians, and not merely to be referred to Paul and Timothy, as several expositors think, at the same time explaining κλῆσις of the special call to the office of Christian teacher (Heydenreich). — Κλῆσις in the N. T. constantly denotes the call to partake in the kingdom of God, the call being made outwardly by the preaching of the gospel, inwardly by the influence of the spirit working through the word. Κλῆσις and καλεῖν are similarly joined in Eph. iv. 1. — The added ἁγία defines the κλῆσις more precisely in its nature, not in its working (de Wette, " hallowing ").—In order to denote the σώζειν [1] and καλεῖν as purely acts of God's grace, and thus set the love of God in clearer light, Paul adds the words. οὐ κατὰ τὰ ἔργα ἡμῶν, ἀλλὰ κ.τ.λ. The first clause is negative, declaring that our works were not the standard (κατά) of that divine activity (comp. Tit. iii. 5). The second clause is positive, setting forth the principle by which alone God has guided himself. De Wette is inaccurate in explaining κατά as giving the motive; that is not given by κατά, but by ἐξ, comp. Rom. ix. 11. The only rule for God in the work of redemption is God's ἰδία πρόθεσις; comp. on this Rom. viii. 28 f., Eph. i. 11; Tit. iii. 5: κατὰ τὸν αὐτοῦ ἔλεον. Ἴδιος is here emphatic, in order to show that this his purpose has its ground in himself alone.[2] — καὶ χάριν τὴν δοθεῖσαν ἡμῖν ἐν Χριστῷ Ἰησοῦ πρὸ χρόνων αἰωνίων] By this addition still greater emphasis is laid on the thought contained in the previous words, since the ἰδία πρόθεσις is called a χάρις which has been already given us in Christ πρὸ χρόνων αἰωνίων. It is natural to take πρὸ χρόν. αἰων. as identical with πρὸ τῶν αἰώνων, 1 Cor. ii. 7 (Eph. i. 4. πρὸ καταβολῆς

---

[1] De Wette's assertion, that with Paul God is never the Saviour, is contradicted by 1 Cor 1 21.
[2] Πρόθεσις, as Wiesinger rightly remarks, is not equivalent to "foreordination," but to "purpose," see Rom. 1 13, Eph 1 9, 11.

κόσμου), *i.e.* to regard it as a term for eternity, since the χρόνοι αἰώνιοι are the times beginning with the creation (so hitherto in this commentary). Heydenreich and others with this view explain διδόναι as equivalent to "destinare, appoint;" but as the word does not possess this meaning, it is better to adhere to the idea of *giving*, but in an *ideal* signification, "in so far as that which God resolves in eternity is already as good as realized in time" (de Wette). Ἐν Χριστῷ Ἰησοῦ, which is attached immediately to δοθεῖσαν, denotes Christ Jesus as the mediator through whom grace is imparted to us, but in such a way that Christ's mediatorship is regarded as one provided by God before time was.[1] But the expression πρὸ χρόν αἰων. may be otherwise taken. In Tit. i. 2, it clearly has a weaker signification, viz. "from time immemorial" (similarly Luke i. 70 . ἀπ' αἰῶνος). If the expression be taken in that way here, δοθεῖσαν may be explained in the sense that to us the χάρις is already given in the promise (Tit. i. 2 also refers to God's promise); so Hofmann. In that case, however, ἐν Χριστῷ Ἰησοῦ is not to be taken in the sense of mediation, which does not agree with the addition of Ἰησοῦ to Χριστῷ, but as Hofmann explains it : "τὴν δοθ. ἡμ. ἐν Χριστῷ Ἰησοῦ denotes that the grace given us was given that Christ Jesus might be given us; He, however, has been given us from the beginning of time, when God promised the Saviour who was to appear in the person of Jesus." This view (especially on account of Tit i. 2) might be preferred to the one previously mentioned. As contrasted with κατὰ τὰ ἔργα ἡμῶν, stress is to be laid on πρὸ χρόνων αἰωνίων. If the imparting of the grace is eternal (resting on the eternal counsel of God), it is all the less dependent on the works of man.

Ver. 10. Φανερωθεῖσαν δὲ νῦν] These words form a contrast with τὴν δοθεῖσαν . . . πρὸ χρόν. αἰων., the grace being con-

---

[1] Hofmann, in his *Schriftbew* I. p. 232, puts forward the explanation · "It is the eternal conduct of God the Father to the Son, in which and with which there is given to us who are in Christ the grace of God eternally;" but he has since withdrawn it.—Wiesinger remarks that the πρόθεσις is not to be understood of a purpose in reference to *individuals*, but of the purpose in reference to the *world*, and that every position of the *individual* is grounded on this eternal grace presented to the *world* in Christ ; but this limitation is in no way indicated by the context

cealed which was bestowed on Christians in Christ *before* the ages. It is to be observed that the idea of the φανέρωσις does not refer here to the decree, but to the grace of God; Heydenreich is therefore inaccurate in saying that "the φανεροῦν here denotes the execution of the divine decree which was made from eternity, and has now come forth from its concealment." The means by which the φανέρωσις of the divine grace has been made, the apostle calls the ἐπιφάνεια τοῦ σωτῆρος ἡμῶν Χριστοῦ Ἰησοῦ. Ἐπιφάνεια is used only here to denote the appearance of Christ in the flesh. As a matter of course (so, too, van Oosterzee, Plitt, and others), it denotes not only the birth of Christ, but also His whole presence on the earth up to His ascension. There is added τοῦ σωτῆρος ἡμῶν in reference to τοῦ σώσαντος ἡμᾶς, ver. 9, in order to make it clear that the grace eternally given to us was made manifest by the appearance of Christ Jesus, because He appeared as our σωτήρ (see on 1 Tim. i. 1). The means by which He showed Himself to be this, and by which He revealed that grace, are told us in the two participial clauses: καταργήσαντος μὲν τὸν θάνατον, φωτίσαντος δὲ ζωὴν καὶ ἀφθαρσίαν διὰ τοῦ εὐαγγελίου. — καταργεῖν, properly, "make ineffectual," means here, as in 1 Cor xv. 26, Heb. ii. 14, "*bring to nought.*" Θάνατος is death, as the power to which man is, for his sins, made subject, both for time and for eternity. It is not the "prince of the realm of the dead," as Heydenreich thinks (also in Heb. ii. 14 there is a distinction between θάνατος and διάβολος) Still less to the point is the hypothesis of de Wette, that the καταργεῖν τὸν θάνατον is spoken "with subjective reference to the power of death over the mind, or the fear of death;" the discussion here is not of subjective states of feeling, but of objective powers. The question whether θάνατος means here physical or eternal death, may be answered in this way, that the apostle regards the two as one in their inner relation to one another.[1] The second clause: φωτίσαντος δὲ κ.τ.λ., corresponds with the first: καταργ. κ τ.λ. Φωτίζειν has usually the intransitive significa-

[1] Wiesinger "Death as the power to which the whole man, both body and soul, has fallen a prey in consequence of sin, and which makes the bodily death the precursor of death eternal."

tion: "shine," Rev. xxii. 5 ; but it occurs also as transitive, both in the literal and derivative sense, Rev. xxi. 23, John i. 9. In 1 Cor. iv. 5, it is synonymous with φανεροῦν: "bring to light from concealment;" so, too, in Ecclus. xxiv. 30, and in this sense it is used here. The expression is all the more pointed that θάνατος is "a power of darkness" (Wiesinger); comp. Luke i. 79. — Heydenreich's explanation: "Christ raised the hope of immortality to fullest certainty," weakens the apostle's meaning ζωή denotes the blessed life of the children of God, which is further described as eternal, ever-during, by the epexegetical καὶ ἀφθαρσία (Wiesinger). This life was originally hid in God, but Christ brought it to light out of concealment, and brought it διὰ τοῦ εὐαγγελίου. These added words are to be referred only to the second clause, for the annihilation of death was not effected by the gospel, but by Christ's death and resurrection —On the other hand, the revelation of life was made by the preaching of the gospel, inasmuch as Christ thereby places before us the ζωὴ καὶ ἀφθαρσία as the inheritance assigned us in Him — It is incorrect, with Wiesinger, to separate διὰ τοῦ εὐαγγελίου from the nearest verb to which it is thoroughly suited if taken in a natural sense, and to connect it with the more distant φανερωθεῖσαν, the means of which, moreover, is already given in διὰ τῆς ἐπιφανείας. Plitt wrongly thinks that the construction here is somewhat careless, and that διὰ τ εὐαγγ. is to be co-ordinated with διὰ τῆς ἐπιφανείας, giving a still more precise definition to φανερωθεῖσαν.

Ver. 11. Εἰς ὃ ἐτέθην κ.τ λ] With these words the apostle turns to his office and his suffering in his office, in correspondence with μηδὲ ἐμὲ τ δέσμ. αὐτοῦ, ver. 8. The relative ὅ does not refer to the thoughts expressed in the previous verses, but to εὐαγγελίου: "for which," i.e. in order to preach it. Comp. the parallel passages in 1 Tim. ii. 7.

Ver. 12. Δι᾽ ἣν αἰτίαν (see on ver. 6) refers to what immediately precedes: "therefore, because I am appointed apostle." — καὶ ταῦτα πάσχω] goes back to ver. 8. Καὶ expresses the relation corresponding to what was said in ver. 11. — ἀλλ᾽ οὐκ ἐπαισχύνομαι] viz. of the sufferings; said in reference to μὴ οὖν ἐπαισχυνθῇς in ver. 8. Imprisonment is to me not a disgrace, but a καύχημα: comp Rom. v. 3; Col. i. 24. The apostle thereby declares that his suffering does not prevent him from preaching the μαρτύριον τοῦ κυρίου (ver. 8) as a κῆρυξ κ τ.λ. The reason is given in the next words: οἶδα γὰρ ᾧ πεπίστευκα. Heydenreich inaccurately: "I know Him on whom I have trusted," de Wette rightly: "I know on whom I have set my trust"—This is defined more precisely by. καὶ πέπεισμαι, ὅτι δυνατός ἐστι κ τ.λ, which words are closely connected with those previous, in the sense: I know, that He in whom I trust is mighty, etc. — The confidence that God can keep His παραθήκη, is the reason of his οὐκ ἐπαισχύνεσθαι. With οἶδα ... καὶ πέπεισμαι, comp. Rom. xiv. 14; with ὅτι δυν. ἐστι, comp. Rom. xi. 23, xiv. 4; 2 Cor ix. 8. — On the meaning of τὴν παραθήκην (Rec. παρακαταθήκην) μου, expositors have spoken very arbitrarily. Theodoret says: παρακαταθήκην, ἢ τὴν πίστιν φησὶ καὶ τὸ κήρυγμα, ἢ τοὺς πιστοὺς, οὓς παρέθετο αὐτῷ ὁ Χριστὸς ἢ οὓς αὐτὸς παρέθετο τῷ κυρίῳ, ἢ παρακαταθήκην λέγει τὴν ἀντιμισθίαν — The same substantive occurs again at ver. 13; so, too, at 1 Tim. vi. 20.—It is hardly possible to imagine that Paul in ver. 14 should have meant something else by παραθήκη than he means here; all the less that he connects the same verb with it in both passages. Though here we have μου, and God is the subject, still the supposition is not thereby justified.[1] The genitive μου may either be subjective or objective. In the former case, ἡ παραθ. μου is something which Paul has entrusted or commended to

---

[1] Wiesinger adduces three counter-reasons—(1) in ver. 14 φυλάσσειν is represented as Timothy's business, here as God's; (2) in ver. 14 παραθήκη refers to the doctrine, here it is represented as a personal possession; (3) in ver. 14 he is discussing the right behaviour for Timothy, here the confidence in the right behaviour. But against the *first* reason, it is to be observed that φυλάσσειν of every gift of grace is the business both of God and of the man to whom it is entrusted, in ver. 11 it is expressly said, διὰ πνεύματος ἁγίου. Against the *second* reason, it may be urged that to interpret παραθήκη of doctrine in ver. 14 is at least doubtful; but even if it were correct, still the gospel, too, might be regarded as something given personally to the apostle; comp. 1 Tim i. 11. τὸ εὐαγγέλιον ... ὃ ἐπιστεύθην ἐγώ; Rom. ii. 16 τὸ εὐαγγέλιόν μου. Against the *third* reason, it may be said that no one can really keep the blessing entrusted to him without having confidence that God keeps it for him, and no one can have this confidence without himself preserving the blessing (διὰ πν ἁγίου).

God; in the latter, something which God has entrusted to Paul, or laid aside for him (a deposit destined for him). With the former view Hofmann understands by παραθήκη the apostle's *soul* which he has commended to God, but there is nothing in the context to indicate this. Hofmann appeals to Ps. xxxi 6; but against this it is to be observed that nothing can justify him in supplying the idea of "*soul*" with the simple word παραθήκη —With the latter view of the genitive, Wiesinger understands by it the ζωὴ καὶ ἀφθαρσία (iv. 8. ὁ δικαιοσύνης στέφανος) already mentioned; so, too, Plitt, van Oosterzee, too, agrees with this view, though he, without good grounds, explains μου as a subjective genitive. Against this interpretation there is the fact that with the sentence εἰς ὃ ἐτέθην the apostle's thought has already turned from the ζωὴ καὶ ἀφθαρσία to his διακονία. The following interpretation suits best with the context. for what other reason could there be for the apostle's οὐκ ἐπαισχύνομαι than the confidence that God would keep the διακονία in which, or for whose sake, he had to suffer, would keep it so that it would not be injured by his suffering.—It is less suitable to understand by the παραθήκη the gospel, because the μου, pointing to something entrusted to the apostle personally, does not agree with this. By adding εἰς ἐκείνην τὴν ἡμέραν, the apostle sets forth that the παραθήκη is not only kept "*till* that day" (Heydenreich, Wiesinger, Otto [1]), but "*for* that day," i e. that it may be then manifested in its uninjured splendour. The phrase ἐκείνη ἡ ἡμέρα is equivalent to ἡ ἡμέρα τοῦ Χριστοῦ, "the day of Christ's second coming"; it is found also in ver. 18, iv. 8, 2 Thess. i. 10, and more frequently in the Gospels. On the meaning of the preposition εἰς, comp. Meyer on Phil. i. 10.

Ver. 13. Exhortation to Timothy. — ὑποτύπωσιν ἔχε ὑγιαι-

[1] Otto wrongly uses this passage to support his assertion that in this epistle "there is no trace to be found of forebodings and expectations of death." He says. "If Paul has confidence in the Lord, that he can maintain for him the παραθήκη till the παρουσία, he must also have hoped that his official work would not be interrupted by his bodily death, since the apostle in it does not in any way express the hope that God would *maintain for him* his official work till the day of Christ " The "*for him*" is arbitrarily imported, and φυλάσσειν does not mean "*maintain*."

νόντων λόγων, ὧν κ.τ.λ.] For ὑποτύπωσις here, as in 1 Tim. i. 16, "*type*" is to be retained. There is no reason for explaining the word here by "sketch" (Flatt), or docendi forma et ratio (Beza), or a written sketch given by the apostle to Timothy (Herder). Timothy is to carry with him the words he had heard from Paul as a *type*, *i.e.* in order to direct his ministry according to it. Luther translates ὑποτύπωσις by "pattern" (so, too, de Wette, Wiesinger, and others), but the reference thus given is not in the words themselves. The verb ἔχειν stands here in the sense of κατέχειν. Bengel rightly: vult Paulus ea, quae Timotheus semel audierat, semper animo ejus observari et impressa manere. It is incorrect, with Hofmann, to take ὑποτ. ὑγιαιν. λόγων as the predicate of the object, and to assume accordingly that it is a contracted form for ὑποτύπωσιν ἔχε ὑγιαινόντων λόγων τὴν ὑποτύπωσιν τῶν λόγων ὧν κ.τ.λ. Such a contraction is inconceivable, nor does Hofmann give any instance to prove its possibility. The words ἐν τῇ πίστει καὶ ἀγάπῃ τῇ κ.τ.λ, which are neither to be joined with ἤκουσας, nor, with Hofmann, referred to what follows, show that the ἔχειν does not take place externally, but is an effort of memory. 'Εν is not equivalent to "with" (Heydenreich); the πίστις and ἀγάπη are rather regarded as the vessel, in which Timothy is to keep that type. The added words: τῇ ἐν Χριστῷ 'Ιησοῦ, which go only with ἀγάπῃ (de Wette, Wiesinger, Hofmann), mark the Christian character of the love which Paul desires from Timothy: "the love grounded in Jesus Christ;" comp. 1 Tim. i. 14. On the expression λογ. ὑγ., comp. 1 Tim. i. 10. The article is wanting, "because this expression had become quite current (like νόμος and others) with the author" (de Wette, Wiesinger).

— Why this exhortation, as de Wette thinks, gives Timothy a low place, we cannot understand; every appearance of such a thing disappears when it is remembered that the apostle, grey-headed and near his end, is speaking to his pupil and colleague after enduring painful experience of the unfaithfulness of others, to which unfaithfulness he returns afterwards. — Even de Wette wrongly asserts that this verse has no connection with the one preceding; for Paul has been speaking of himself and of the gospel entrusted to him, with the desire that Timothy should always keep in mind his example.

Ver. 14. The exhortation in this verse is most closely connected with that in ver. 13, for παραθήκη here, as in ver. 12, is the ministry of the gospel. — τὴν καλὴν παραθήκην φύλαξον] ἡ καλὴ παραθήκη is, like ἡ καλὴ διδασκαλία, 1 Tim. iv. 6 ; ὁ καλὸς ἀγὼν κ.τ λ., to be taken in a general objective sense. There is no sufficient reason for interpreting παραθήκη otherwise than in ver. 12—whether, with Wiesinger and Hofmann, as equivalent to " the sound doctrine," or, with van Oosterzee, as equivalent to τὸ χάρισμα. Since all that the apostle has enjoined on Timothy from ver. 6 onward has special reference to the discharge of his office, we may surely understand παραθήκη to have the same meaning here as in ver. 12 ; besides, as already remarked, it is not conceivable that Paul, in two sentences so closely connected, should have used the same word with different meanings. It need not excite wonder that in ver. 12 Paul looks to God for the preservation of the παραθήκη, while here he lays it on Timothy as a duty; God's working does not exclude the activity of man. Φυλάσσειν here, as in ver. 12, is : " *to keep from harm uninjured,*" and from the tendency of the whole epistle it is clear that this exhortation referred to the heresy which perverted the gospel. — διὰ πνεύματος ἁγίου] Chrysostom : οὐ γὰρ ἐστὶν ἀνθρωπίνης ψυχῆς οὐδὲ δυνάμεως, τοσαῦτα ἐμπιστευθέντα ἀρκέσαι πρὸς τὴν φυλακήν. Timothy is not to employ any human means for preserving the παραθήκη; the only means is to be the Holy Spirit, *i e.* he is to let the Spirit work in him free and unconfined, and only do that to which the Spirit impels him. The Spirit, however, is not something distant from him, as is shown by the words : τοῦ ἐνοικοῦντος ἐν ἡμῖν. On ἐνοικοῦντος, comp. ver. 5. 'Εν ἡμῖν denotes the Spirit as the *one* principle of the new life, working in *all* believers. 'Ημῖν, here as in ver. 6, must not be referred simply to Paul and Timothy ; nor is it to be overlooked that Paul does not say ἐν σοί.

Ver. 15. The apostle reminds Timothy of those who had deserted him. This is done to incite Timothy to come to Rome with the greater speed, and also not to be ashamed of

Paul, the prisoner of Christ, as the others had been (ver. 8). — οἶδας τοῦτο] expresses not the probability merely (as Matthies says), but the certainty that he knows. — ὅτι ἀπεστράφησάν με] The aorist passive has here the force of the middle voice; for the same construction, comp. Tit i 14; Heb. xii 25; see Wahl on the passage, and Buttmann, p. 166. The word does not denote the departure of any one, but is equivalent to aversari, properly, "turn one's countenance away from any one," and so "throw off inwardly the acquaintance of any one" (so in the N. T., in the LXX., the Apocrypha of the O. T., and the classical writers; comp. Otto, p. 283). Without reason, de Wette denies that it has this meaning here. There is therefore in the verb no ground for the common opinion that the πάντες οἱ ἐν τῇ 'Ασίᾳ had been with Paul in Rome, and had again returned to Asia (Matthies, de Wette, Wiesinger). Nor is there more ground in the term used for the subject; πάντες οἱ ἐν τῇ 'Ασίᾳ are "all who are in (proconsular) Asia;" but, as a matter of course, that cannot mean all the Christians there. Perhaps Paul was thinking only of his colleagues who were then residing in Asia (Otto), but in that case he would surely have designated them more precisely. It is possible that the construction has its explanation in the addition ὧν ἐστιν Φύγελλος καὶ Ἑρμογένης, viz.. "all the Asiatics, to whom belong Phygellus and Hermogenes." In any case, these two are named because they were the most conspicuous in their unfaithfulness to the apostle Paul gives no hint of it, and we can hardly think it probable that they were heretics, and that the other Asiatics had also fallen away from the truth (Otto).

Vv. 16–18. With these unfaithful Asiatics, Paul contrasts the faithfulness of Onesiphorus, probably that he might place an example before Timothy. — δῴη ἔλεος ὁ κύριος τῷ 'Ονησιφόρου οἴκῳ] διδόναι ἔλεος does not occur elsewhere in the N. T. Regarding the form δῴη, proper to later Greek, see Buttmann, *Ausfuhrl. Gramm.* § 107, Rem 9, Winer, pp. 75 f. [E T p. 94]. By ὁ κύριος we must understand Christ, according to the usage of the N. T. Onesiphorus is named only here and at iv. 19. Many expositors (also Hofmann) think that his household only is in both passages mentioned, because he was no longer in life. This opinion is confirmed by the way in which mercy is wished for him in ver. 18 (de Wette). — Paul expressed such a wish because of the love that had been shown him; ὅτι πολλάκις με ἀνέψυξε] ἀναψύχειν, properly, " cool," then " refresh, enliven " (*Od.* iv. 568 : ἦτορ), occurring only here in the N. T. (more frequently in the LXX.; ἀνάψυξις, Acts iii. 19), is not to be derived from ψυχή (Beza), but from ψύχω. De Wette, without ground, thinks that a bodily refreshment of meat and drink only is meant, it should rather be referred more generally to all proofs of love on the part of Onesiphorus. These were all the more precious to the apostle that they were given to him in his imprisonment, and proved that Onesiphorus was not ashamed of his bonds (vv. 8, 12); this is expressed in the words that follow. On ἄλυσιν, comp. Eph. vi. 20. — Ver. 17. ἀλλά] in opposition to the preceding οὐκ. — γενόμενος ἐν 'Ρώμῃ] (comp. Matt. xxvi. 6 ; Acts xiii 5). It is not said what moved him to journey to Rome; it is mere conjecture to suppose that it was business matters. — σπουδαιότερον (*Rec.* Tisch. 8 : σπουδαίως) ἐζήτησέ με] The comparative is the right reading, and is to be explained by referring to τ. ἄλυσίν μου οὐκ ἐπαισχύνθη, " *all the more eagerly*" (Wiesinger, Hofmann). — The ζητεῖν stands in sharp contrast with ἀπεστράφησάν με, ver. 15 — The addition of καὶ εὗρε brings out that Onesiphorus had sought him till he found him. — Paul at first wished mercy only to the house of Onesiphorus; he now does the same to Onesiphorus himself. — Ver. 18. Matthies, Wiesinger, Hofmann think that εὑρεῖν ἔλεος is a play on words with the preceding εὗρε, but this is at least doubtful. — The repetition of κύριος is striking: ὁ κύριος... παρὰ κυρίου. We can hardly take these to refer to two different subjects (according to de Wette, the first being God, the second Christ; according to Wiesinger and Hofmann, the very opposite). — ὁ κύριος here is in any case Christ, as in ver. 16, iv. 18 (certainly not: " the world-ruling, divine principle," Matthies) The apostle in what follows might simply have said εὑρεῖν ἔλεος ἐν ἐκ. τ. ἡμέρᾳ; but in his mental vision of the judgment, seeing Christ as judge, he writes down παρὰ κυρίου just as it occurs to him, without being anxious to remember that he had begun with δῴη αὐτῷ ὁ κύριος.[1] The phrase εὑρίσκειν ἔλεος παρά with genitive does not occur elsewhere; only in the Song of the Three Children, ver. 14, have we εὑρεῖν ἔλεος; in 2 John 3 : ἔσται... ἔλεος ... παρὰ Θεοῦ. As to the expression, we should compare especially Heb. iv. 16 : ἵνα λάβωμεν ἔλεος καὶ χάριν εὕρωμεν (εὑρίσκ. χάριν, Luke i. 30; Acts vii. 46, and often in the LXX. and the Apocrypha of the O. T.). On ἐν ἐκείνῃ τῇ ἡμέρᾳ, comp. ver. 12. This wish the apostle utters not only because of the love Onesiphorus had shown him in Rome, but also because of what he had done in Ephesus, of which, however, he does not wish here to speak further, as it is well known to Timothy. — καὶ ὅσα ἐν Ἐφέσῳ διηκόνησε] Heydenreich, Hofmann,[2] and some others supply μοί, others τοῖς ἁγίοις, both are unnecessary. Even without supplying anything, we can of course understand that he is speaking of services rendered in the church. On the other hand, there is nothing to indicate that Onesiphorus was actually a διάκονος of the church. — βέλτιον σὺ γινώσκεις] The adverb βέλτιον only here; the comparative does not simply stand for the positive, see Winer, pp. 227 f. [E. T. p. 304]. There is a comparison implied here: "than I could tell thee," or the like.[3]

---

[1] Van Oosterzee. "An inartistic form of expression, in which the second κύριος may be taken for the reflective pronoun."

[2] Hofmann supposes that those services are meant which Onesiphorus, after his return from Rome to Ephesus, rendered to the apostle for the purpose of disarming the charges that had brought him into prison. This, however, is a mere conjecture.

[3] Otto supposes that Onesiphorus was the first to seek Paul out in his imprisonment, and that he brought the news spoken of from Ephesus; but these are conjectures which can hardly be called probable, as there is no ground on which to rest them.

CHAPTER II.

VER. 3 In place of σὺ οὖν κακοπάθησον, we should read συγκακο-πάθησον, which is supported by the weightiest authorities, and adopted by Lachm Buttm Tisch. It is found in A C* D* E* F G ℵ 17, 31, *al*, Vulg. It Aug. Ambrosiast. Pel. Gildas The *Rec* is found apart from K L only in the altered text of C D E, and especially in the Greek Fathers, for which reason Reiche regards it as the original reading. Probably the beginning of ver. 1 gave occasion to the alteration, which was also recommended by the lack of any word to which the prefixed preposition refers. Even the occurrence in some MSS. of the reading συνστρατιώτης for στρατιώτης is a proof that συγκακοπ is original.[1] — For Ἰησοῦ Χριστοῦ we should read Χριστοῦ Ἰησοῦ, following the weightiest authorities. — Ver. 4 The words τῷ Θεῷ added to στρατευόμενος in some MSS., etc., have arisen from a misapprehension; the apostle is speaking not of God's foes, but of foes in general — Ver. 6. The reading πρότερον in ℵ for πρῶτον seems to be a mere correction. — Ver. 7. ἃ λέγω] Lachm. Buttm Tisch. rightly read ὃ λέγω, after A C F G, 17, *al*, Chrys., ἃ is a correction, in order to bring out a reference to the three previous sentences. — δώσει] for δώῃ, after A C* D E F G ℵ 17, *al.*, Copt. Arm. etc., Ambrosiast Pel. etc., δώῃ is explained from i. 17, 18. — Ver. 12. For ἀρνούμεθα we find in A C several cursives, translations, and Fathers, the future ἀρνησόμεθα, which Lachm. Buttm and Tisch adopted ; the presents (ὑπομένομεν ; ἀπιστοῦμεν) seem to be in favour of our adopting the present here ; but the very same reason might have suggested the alteration of the future into the present. — Ver. 13. After ἀρνήσασθαι we should read γάρ, according to the weightiest authorities, and this Griesb. adopted into the text. — Ver. 14. τοῦ κυρίου] Instead of this, C F G ℵ 37, *al.*, Copt. Arm. etc, Chrys Theoph. etc., have τοῦ Θεοῦ (Tisch 8); but τοῦ κυρίου is

---

[1] To Reiche's remark Quomodo in unius Codicis D lectione συνστρατιώτης lectionis συγκακοπ. praesidium sit, non video, it may be replied that the scribe was probably induced by the previous συγκακ. to prefix συν also before the word στρατιώτης.

the original reading, the correction may be explained from 1 Tim v 21, 2 Tim iv. 1. — Instead of the infinite λογομαχεῖν (C*** D E F G K L ℵ, the cursives, several versions, etc., Tisch), we find λογομάχει in A C* Aeth. Vulg. etc. (Lachm. Buttm). According to the former reading, the verb λογομ is dependent on διαμαρτυρόμενος; according to the latter, διαμαρτ is connected with what precedes, and λογομάχει begins a new imperative clause. For the decision on the point, see the explanation of the verse — Eἰς οὐδέν] A C, 17, al, have ἐπ' οὐδέν (Lachm Buttm. Tisch.); F G ℵ (first hand), Vulg It Ambrosiast Pelag etc, ἐπ' οὐδενὶ γάρ. Of these various readings, least can be said for ἐπ' οὐδενὶ γάρ; it seems to have arisen from an endeavour to form these words in the same way as those that follow; even the γάρ is only an insertion by way of explanation. Of the two others, ἐπ' οὐδέν is to be preferred as the less usual form, εἰς οὐδέν occurs elsewhere in the N. T, and εὔχρηστος, especially in iv. 11, is construed with εἰς. — Ver. 19 ℵ has πάντας before τοὺς ὄντας, probably a later addition. — κυρίου for Χριστοῦ was rightly adopted by Griesb — Ver 21 ἡγιασμένον, εὔχρηστον, instead of ἡγιασμ. καὶ εὔχρ, after A C** D* E* F G, etc. — Ver. 22. Between μετά and τῶν there is found πάντων (Lachm. Buttm.) in A C F G 17, 23, al, Aeth. Slav. etc, Chrys. Theodoret, etc., F G further omit the article τῶν. Since πάντες stands in the same expression at Rom. xi 12, 1 Cor i 2, it seems to have been inserted from these passages Tisch. omits πάντων, on the authority of D E K L, al, Vulg. Copt Syr. etc. — Ver. 25 For δῷ, Lachm. Buttm. and Tisch. rightly read δώῃ, after A C D* F G ℵ (first hand), 31, al., Ephr. Chrys ms Isidor.

Ver. 1. After interrupting his exhortations by an allusion to the unfaithful Asiatics and to the faithful Onesiphorus, Paul with σύ resumes his exhortations to Timothy, at the same time connecting them by οὖν with those already given. In the first place, he now appeals to him: ἐνδυναμοῦ ἐν τῇ χάριτι τῇ ἐν Χρ 'Ιησ] ἐνδυναμοῦσθαι does not mean: " feel oneself strong," nor . " depend on something " (Heydenreich); but: " become strong, grow strong " (see Eph. vi. 10). The active voice is found in iv. 17 and 1 Tim. i. 12. As the apostle sees the end of his labours draw nearer, he is the more anxious that Timothy, for whom he has the warmest paternal love (τέκνον μου), should become a stronger and bolder champion for the Lord. — ἐν τῇ χάριτι] may either be a completion of the idea of ἐνδυναμοῦ (Wiesinger), or define it more precisely (van Oosterzee, Plitt, Hofmann). The second view is the correct one: Timothy is to become strong by the χάρις ἡ ἐν Χρ., that he may be capable of discharging faithfully the office entrusted to him; comp. the passage in Eph. vi 10. — ἡ χάρις ἡ ἐν Χρ. 'I.] is not the office of teacher (Calovius and others), nor is it equivalent to χάρισμα, i 6; on the other hand, it is not " the life imparted by divine grace," nor " the redemption" of the Christian (Wiesinger); it is objectively the grace dwelling in Christ, the grace of Jesus Christ, or better: " the grace obtained for us in the person of Christ" (Hofmann). — ἐν is explained by Chrysostom and others as equivalent to διά; this is not incorrect, only that ἐν indicates a more internal relation than διά. The believer lives *in* the grace which is in Christ; the strengthening to which Timothy is exhorted can only be effected by his abiding in this grace.

Ver. 2. While ver 3 corresponds with the first verse, ver. 2 seems to contain a thought foreign to this connection. But as the contest to which Paul is exhorting Timothy, consists substantially in the undaunted preaching of the pure gospel and in the rejection of all heresy, it was natural for him to exhort Timothy to see that others were armed with the word for which he was to strive. The true warrior must care also for his companions in the fight. — καὶ ἃ ἤκουσας παρ' ἐμοῦ] (comp i. 13 · διὰ πολλῶν μαρτύρων) These words belong immediately to ἤκουσας, Heydenreich is wrong in supplying μαρτυρούμενα or βεβαιούμενα. According to Clemens Alexandrinus, *Hypotyp* 1. 7, Oecumenius, Grotius, and others, μάρτυρες is equivalent to νόμος καὶ προφηταί, for which there is as little justification as for the opinion that the other apostles are meant. The preposition διά is explained by Winer, p. 354 [E. T. p. 473]: "intervenientibus multis testibus, with *intervention, i.e.* here in presence of many witnesses " (so, too, the more recent expositors). Right; but διά is not equivalent to ἐνώπιον (1 Tim. vi. 12). Διά intimates that the witnesses were present to confirm the apostle's word, or, as Wiesinger says, " that their presence was an integral element of that act to which the apostle is alluding." — According to Matthies, van Oosterzee, Hofmann, the apostle is thinking here of his public discourses on doctrine; but the whole character of the expression, particularly also the otherwise superfluous addition of διὰ πολλῶν μαρτύρων, make it more probable that the words refer to a definite fact, the fact spoken of in 1 Tim. iv. 14; 2 Tim. i. 6 (Wiesinger). In that case, the μάρτυρες are the presbyters and other members of the church who were present at Timothy's ordination. Mack rightly directs attention to 1 Tim. iv. 14; but he is wrong in explaining διὰ μαρτ. by διὰ προφητείας, " in consequence of many testimonies" — ταῦτα παράθου πιστοῖς ἀνθρώποις] Heydenreich: "this doctrine commit to faithful keeping and further communication as a legacy, as a precious jewel" (comp. Herod. ix. 45: παραθήκην ὑμῖν τὰ ἔπεα τάδε τίθεμαι); but the expression ἃ ἤκουσας does not refer so much to the whole of evangelic doctrine as to the instructions given to Timothy for the discharge of his office. — πιστοῖς ἀνθρώποις] not " believing," but " faithful, trustworthy " men. — οἵτινες ἱκανοὶ ἔσονται καὶ ἑτέρους διδάξαι] Heydenreich thinks that this denotes a second quality of those to be instructed by Timothy, a quality in addition to their " honest sense," viz their capacity for teaching; but οἵτινες, which, as contrasted with the simple relative pronoun, refers to a subject undefined, but in various ways definable (see Ellendt, *Lex. Soph.* II. p. 387), points back to πιστοῖς, so that the meaning is: " who as such," etc. The future ἔσονται does not stand in the same sense as the present, but denotes their capacity as one depending on the tradition to be imparted to them (" as the consequence of the παρατίθεσθαι," Wiesinger). The καί before ἑτέρους is not to be overlooked; " others too," *i.e.* " others in turn " Who are the ἕτεροι? According to the common presupposition, with which van Oosterzee also agrees, the ἕτεροι are the church, or more generally the hearers of the preaching of the gospel. But in this view the καί, which does not belong to ἑτέρους διδάξαι (Hofmann), but to ἑτέρους, is inexplicable; it is more probable that Paul means other πιστοὶ ἄνθρωποι (de Wette, Wiesinger). Paul gathered round him pupils to whom he gave instructions in regard to their office; they, too, are to do the same; those chosen by them the same in their turn, etc, that in the church there may abide a stock of apostolic men who will see to the propagation of pure doctrine. — The words διὰ πολλῶν μαρτύρων show that there is no thought of a secret doctrine; nor is he speaking of the regular employment of teachers who, in the absence of Timothy, are to take his place in the church at Ephesus, "ne sine episcopo vaga oberret ecclesia" (Heinrichs). Ver. 3. Συγκακοπάθησον] Timothy is not to shun a community of suffering with the apostle, i. 8, 12, 16. — ὡς καλὸς στρατιώτης Ἰησοῦ Χριστοῦ] στρατιώτης stands elsewhere in the N. T. only in its proper sense, but, as is well known, the kindred words στρατεία, στρατεύεσθαι, are often used of the Christian life. Here, however, the apostle is speaking not generally of Timothy's work as a Christian, but more specially of his work in the office committed to him, viz. of his struggle against the opponents of evangelic truth and the toils connected therewith.

Ver. 4. " Hoc versu commendatur τό abstine ; accedit versu seq. τό sustine " (Bengel). — οὐδεὶς στρατευόμενος] alludes to στρατιώτης : " no one serving as a soldier" (de Wette); comp. 1 Tim. i. 18. — ἐμπλέκεται ταῖς τοῦ βίου πραγματείαις [1]] ἐμπλέκεσθαι elsewhere only in 2 Pet. ii. 20. — πραγματεῖαι] occurs only here in the N. T. (the verb πραγματεύεσθαι, Luke xix. 13), αἱ τοῦ βίου πραγμ are the occupations which form means of livelihood; Heydenreich : " the occupations of the working class as opposed to those of the soldier class." — From these the στρατευόμενος abstains ἵνα τῷ στρατολογήσαντι ἀρέσῃ] στρατολογήσας (only here), from στρατολογεῖν. "gather an army, raise troops," is a term for a general. — Only that soldier who gives himself up entirely to military service, and does not permit himself to be distracted by other things, only he fulfils the general's will. The application to the στρατιώτης Ἰησ. Χρ. is self-evident; *he*, too, is to devote himself entirely to *his* service, and not to involve himself in other matters which might hinder him in his proper calling. The literal interpretation, according to which the apostle or preacher should take no

---

[1] Ambros. *de Offic* i 1 · is, qui imperatori militat, a susceptionibus litium, actu negotiorum forensium, venditione mercium prohibetur humanis legibus. — Athan *Dict et Interpr. Parab. S Ev.* qu. 119 : εἰ γὰρ ἐπιγείῳ βασιλεῖ ὁ μέλλων στρατεύεσθαι οὐκ ἀρέσει, ἐὰν μὴ ἀφήσῃ πάσας τὰς τοῦ βίου φροντίδας, πόσῳ μᾶλλον μέλλων στρατευθῆναι τῷ ἐπουρανίῳ βασιλεῖ ,

concern whatever in civil affairs, is contradicted by Paul's own example, according to the precept here given, he is to avoid them only when they are a hindrance to the duties of his office.

Ver 5 A new thought is added, that the contender who wishes to be crowned must contend νομίμως. — ἐὰν δὲ καὶ ἀθλῇ τις] καί connects this thought with what precedes · "if one, too, does not permit himself to be kept from the struggle by other occupations;"[1] but the figure here is different from that we had in ver. 4, ἀθλεῖν (ἄπ. λεγ in the N. T) denoting the contest in running, to which the Christian calling is often compared; comp iv. 7, 8, 1 Cor. ix. 24, 25. — οὐ στεφανοῦται, ἐὰν μὴ νομίμως ἀθλήσῃ] The runner, in order to gain the prize, must in the contest adhere to its definite rules. Theodoret: καὶ ἡ ἀθλητικὴ νόμους ἔχει τινὰς, καθ' οὓς προσήκει τοὺς ἀθλητὰς ἀγωνίζεσθαι· ὁ δὲ παρὰ τούτους παλαίων, τῶν στεφάνων διαμαρτάνει. In this, too, according to 1 Cor. ix. 25, ἐγκρατεύεσθαι should be observed ; comp Galen, *Comm in Hippocr.* i 15· οἱ γυμνασταὶ καὶ οἱ νομίμως ἀθλοῦντες ἐπὶ μὲν τοῦ ἀρίστου τὸν ἄρτον μόνον ἐσθίουσι, ἐπὶ δὲ τοῦ δείπνου τὸ κρέας. The word νομίμως occurs only here and in 1 Tim. i. 8. — The thought contained in it is this, that Timothy, in order to share in the reward, must conduct himself in his evangelic warfare according to the laws of his evangelic office.

Ver. 6. To the two foregoing sentences Paul adds still another, expressed figuratively: τὸν κοπιῶντα γεωργὸν δεῖ πρῶτον κ.τ.λ. Many expositors assume that there is here an inversion of phrase, and explain the words as equivalent to τὸν γεωργόν, κοπιῶντα πρῶτον, δεῖ τῶν καρπῶν μεταλ., or as Wahl and Winer (in the earlier editions of his *Grammar*) put it, τὸν γεωργὸν, τὸν θέλοντα τῶν καρπῶν μεταλ, δεῖ πρῶτον κοπιᾷν, so that πρῶτον is attached to κοπιᾷν in meaning, and the sentence contains an exhortation ; Beza : necesse est agricolam, ut fructus percipiat, prius laborare. Heinrichs, on the other hand, remarks: nihil attinet, mutare quidquam, aut transponere, dummodo πρῶτον cum Grotio adverbialiter pro *ita demum* dictum putemus, emphasinque ponamus in τὸν κοπιῶντα. But this explanation of πρῶτον cannot be justi-

---

[1] Hofmann denies this connection of thought, maintaining wrongly that καί could only have this meaning if the apostle had continued to use the same figure.

fied. Matthies, de Wette, and others reject the supposition of any inversion, and explain πρῶτον as "first before all others," so that the meaning would be: "as the husbandman first enjoys the fruits of the field, so, too, has the servant of the gospel a notable reward to expect for his work" (de Wette); but this thought diverges entirely from that contained in vv. 4, 5, and neglects, besides, the emphasis laid on κοπιῶντα. — It is accordingly to be explained: Not every one, but *that* husbandman who toils hard at his work, is first to enjoy the fruits; Wiesinger: "the working farmer has the right of first enjoying the fruits, not he who does not work; therefore, if thou dost wish to enjoy the fruits, work." So, too, van Oosterzee. Hofmann, against this explanation, upholds the meaning of δεῖ, which does not express what *ought to* happen, but what *must* happen, in so far as it lies in the nature of things. Δεῖ certainly has this meaning of necessity (not that of duty); but if κοπιῶντα be regarded as furnishing the condition under which the husbandman tilling the ground must, before all others, be partaker of the fruits of the ground tilled, then δεῖ in the former explanation presents no difficulty; in this case it cannot be said, with Hofmann, that the πρῶτον is meaningless. It is to be observed that κοπιῶντα does not contrast the husbandman who works with the husbandman who does *not* work, but the husbandman who works hard with the husbandman who carries on his work *lazily*. — Hofmann, in interpreting the sentence as declaring that Timothy must bear everything, whether good or bad, that arises from his work, departs from the figure, which clearly does not say that the husbandman must content himself alike with good fruit and with weeds, but rather that in the nature of things the husbandman should before all others enjoy the fruit for which he has laboured. It is incorrect, with Theodoret and Oecumenius, to understand πρῶτον of the preference over the pupil which is the teacher's due; or to find in the words of the apostle the thought that the teacher must appropriate to himself the fruits of the spirit which he wishes to impart to others. Even Chrysostom rightly rejected the opinion,[1] that here the

---

[1] This opinion is also brought forward by Otto, who refers all three sentences to anxiety regarding bodily wants, as if Timothy had become careless in his

apostle is speaking of the bodily support due to the teacher; but he himself gives the words a wrong subsidiary sense when he thinks that Paul wishes to console Timothy regarding the preference shown in the reward.

Ver. 7. As he has been expressing his exhortations in figurative gnomes, Paul thus continues: νόει, ὃ λέγω] which does not refer immediately to the thoughts expressed, as Heydenreich, Matthies, and others think, but to the form of expression. It does not mean, therefore: "lay these exhortations to heart," but: "mark or understand what I say" (de Wette); comp. Matt. xxiv. 15; Eph. iii. 4, 20, so, too, Hofmann, only that he for no sufficient reason refers the words merely to the last sentence. Plitt is of opinion that the apostle is intending thereby to give a quite general warning against misconceptions; but this would be an arbitrary disturbance of the connection of ideas. — To this exhortation Paul confidently adds that God will not fail to bestow on Timothy understanding in this and all other points, γάρ here, as elsewhere, is a particle of explanation. — ἐν πᾶσι belongs to this verse, and not, as Sam. Battier thinks, to the following one

Ver 8 Μνημόνευε Ἰησοῦν Χριστόν] μνημονεύειν is usually followed by the genitive; but the accusative is found both here and at 1 Thess. ii. 9. Timothy is to remember Jesus Christ, that he may gain the proper strength for discharging his official duties—to remember especially His resurrection, in which He triumphed over sufferings and death, and in which is contained for the believer the seal of his victory,[1] hence Paul adds: ἐγηγερμένον ἐκ νεκρῶν, "as one who rose from the dead." — The added asyndeton: ἐκ σπέρματος Δαβίδ, does not denote the humiliation, but the Messianic dignity of

---

office through fear of suffering want in it. This, however, is a reproof which cannot be justified. Van Oosterzee rightly says. It is undoubtedly a Pauline principle that the teacher has a right to suitable support from the church; but this is not the principle taught *here*.

[1] Hofmann wrongly maintains that "the remembrance of Jesus Christ was not to be a pledge to Timothy of his victory over all he had to encounter for Christ's sake, but only to make him willing to endure." Such willingness could only have come to him from the conviction that the victory of Christ was a pledge of victory to the believer.

Christ[1] The antithetical relation between the two clauses is here the same as in Rom. i. 3, 4 (ἐκ σπ. Δαβίδ ... ἐξ ἀναστάσεως νεκρῶν), where it is distinctly marked by κατὰ σάρκα .. κατὰ πνεῦμα. Hofmann incorrectly makes both ἐκ σπέρμ. Δ. and ἐκ νεκρῶν depend on ἐγηγερμένον; in that case the verb would have to be taken in two different senses; besides, ἐκ τ. σπέρμ. is nowhere found in connection with ἐγείρεσθαι. There is nothing to indicate (Wiesinger) that ἐκ σπέρμ Δαβίδ is an antithesis "to the docetic error of the heretics" (van Oosterzee). Heydenreich rightly rejected the secondary references which many expositors give to these words, such as: that they indicate a similarity between the vicissitudes of Christ's life and those of David; or that they are to serve as a proof of the certainty of Christ's resurrection (Michaelis); or that they denote the whole state of Christ's humiliation (Mosheim), and so on. — The added words: κατὰ τὸ εὐαγγέλιόν μου, may be referred either to μνημόνευε κ.τ.λ. (Hofmann), or to the attributes of 'Ιησ. Χριστόν. The latter reference is the more probable one; Paul, as a rule, does not use the formula κατὰ τὸ εὐαγγ to denote the rule for the believer's conduct, but to confirm a truth he has expressed (comp. Rom. ii. 16, xvi 25; 1 Tim i. 11). To refer it only to ἐκ σπέρμ. Δ. is arbitrary. Still more arbitrary is Jerome's opinion, that Paul by τὸ εὐαγγ μου means the gospel of Luke (Baur).

Ver. 9. In this verse Paul again, as before, points to his own example, in order to encourage Timothy to the συγκακοπαθεῖν τῷ εὐαγγελίῳ, i. 8, ii. 3. — ἐν ᾧ] according to Paul's manner, refers to εὐαγγέλιον immediately preceding, and not to the more distant 'Ιησοῦν Χριστόν. The preposition ἐν is not equivalent to διά, Col. iv. 3 (Heydenreich). Matthies presses the original signification too far when he gives the interpretation: "the gospel is, as it were, the ground and soil in which his present lot is rooted." Beza rightly gives the meaning thus: cujus annuntiandi munere defungens; de

[1] Hofmann (Schriftbew. II. 1, pp. 113 f.) "Timothy being disinclined to suffer for the gospel's sake, the apostle reminds him that through death Jesus attained to the heavenly glory, to which He had a right through His descent from the line of David." — Van Oosterzee incorrectly assumes that ἐκ σπέρμ Δ. simply denotes the *human* origin of Jesus. The apostle clearly goes beyond this in mentioning David by name.

Wette says: "in preaching which." Comp Phil. iv. 3; 1 Thess. iii. 2. Hofmann incorrectly explains ἐν by "in consequence of," which ἐν never does mean, not even in 1 Tim. i. 18 — κακοπαθῶ] is an allusion to ver. 3. — μέχρι δεσμῶν] comp. Phil. ii. 8: μέχρι θανάτου. — Ὡς κακοῦργος directs attention to the criminal aspect of Paul's bonds, and thereby strengthens the κακοπαθῶ μέχρι δεσμῶν.[1] The word κακοῦργος occurs only here and in Luke's gospel; it is synonymous with κακοποιός, 1 Pet. iv. 14. — ἀλλ' ὁ λόγος τοῦ Θεοῦ οὐ δέδεται] Chrysostom explains it: δεσμοῦνται μὲν αἱ χεῖρες, ἀλλ' οὐχ ἡ γλῶττα; comp. Phil. i. 12. The meaning according to this would be: "the bonds do not, however, hinder me from freely preaching the gospel." But this limitation is not contained in the words themselves; they have rather the more general meaning · "though I (to whom the gospel is entrusted) am bound, the gospel itself is not thereby fettered, but goes freely forth into the world and works unfettered" (2 Thess. iii. 1: ὁ λόγος τοῦ κυρίου τρέχει). This is the very reason of the apostle's joy in his bonds, that Christ is preached; comp. Phil. i. 18. This connection of ideas does not, however, compel us to take διὰ τοῦτο with these words (Hofmann). If so connected, διὰ τοῦτο would rather appear to be a modification added loosely; besides, Paul never places it at the end of a sentence. — Some have wrongly understood by ὁ λόγ. τ. Θ. here, the divine promises, and have taken οὐ δέδεται to mean that these do not remain unfulfilled.

Ver. 10. Διὰ τοῦτο] Bengel: "quia me vincto evangelium currit." Heydenreich wrongly refers it at the same time to the reward to which ver. 8 alludes The knowledge that the gospel is unfettered in its influence enables Paul to endure all things for the sake of the ἐκλεκτοί. Διὰ τοῦτο cannot be referred to what follows (Wiesinger), because of the διὰ τοὺς ἐκλεκτούς; it would be another thing if ἵνα κ.τ.λ. were joined immediately with ὑπομένω; but even in that case the "abrupt transition" would still be an objection. — πάντα ὑπομένω] ὑπομένειν does not denote suffering pure and simple, but the willing, stedfast endurance of it — By adding to πάντα

[1] Otto, opposed to Wieseler, rightly remarks that these words do not justify any inference as to an increase in the severity of his imprisonment.

ὑπομένω the words διὰ τοὺς ἐκλεκτούς, explained by the succeeding clause, Paul declares that he patiently endured everything for the sake of the ἐκλεκτοί, because he knows that the gospel is not bound—is not made ineffectual—by his bonds. Were it otherwise, were the gospel hindered in its influence by his suffering, then he would not endure for the sake of the ἐκλεκτοί. Hofmann has no grounds, therefore, for thinking that the connection of διὰ τοῦτο with the sentence following it would give an impossible sense. It is wrong to supply καί before διὰ τ. ἐκλ. (Heydenreich), as if these words furnished an additional reason to that contained in διὰ τοῦτο.
— οἱ ἐκλεκτοί] This name is given to believers, inasmuch as the deepest ground of their faith is the free choice of God (1. 9). Heydenreich leaves it indefinite whether " Christians already converted" are meant here, or "those elected to be future confessors of Christianity ," so, too, Matthies ; de Wette, on the other hand, understands only the latter, whereas Grotius and Flatt think only of the former. The words themselves do not prove that Paul had any such distinction in mind ; καὶ αὐτοί does not necessarily imply a contrast with present believers (de Wette), but may be quite well used in relation to the apostle himself, who was conscious of the σωτηρία attained in Christ (Wiesinger, van Oosterzee). Comp. especially Col. i. 24, where the apostle places his suffering in relation to the ἐκκλησία, as the σῶμα τοῦ Χριστοῦ, of which the ἐκλεκτοί are members.[1] In how far the apostle bears his afflictions διὰ τοὺς ἐκλ., is told by the words : ἵνα καὶ αὐτοὶ σωτηρίας τύχωσι τῆς ἐν Χρ. Ἰησοῦ. The question how the apostle might expect this result from his πάντα ὑπομένειν, cannot be answered by saying, with Heinrichs: "as he hoped to be freed from his sufferings ," the result was to be effected not by a release, but by the patient endurance of the suffering, inasmuch as this bore testimony to the genuineness and strength of his faith, not, as van Oosterzee thinks, because the apostle stedfastly continued to preach. The apostle's suffer-

---

[1] Hofmann rightly remarks "The apostle names those towards whom he has to fulfil his calling, for the elect's sake, because this designation denotes the heaviness of his responsibility, if he did not help those destined for salvation to that for which God ordained them "

ing for the gospel was itself a preaching of the gospel. We must, of course, reject the notion that Paul regarded his sufferings as making atonement for sin, like those of Christ. — The addition μετὰ δόξης αἰωνίου points to the future completion of the salvation. It directs special attention to an element contained in the σωτηρία, and does not contrast the positive with the negative conception (Heydenreich).

Vv. 11–13. In order to arouse the courage of faith, Paul has been directing attention to the resurrection of Christ and to His own example; he now proceeds, in a series of short antithetical clauses, to set forth the relation between our conduct here and our condition hereafter. This he introduces with the words πιστὸς ὁ λόγος. The γάρ following seems, indeed, to make the words a confirmation of the thought previously expressed, as in 1 Tim. iv. 9 (Chrysostom, Oecumenius, Theophylact, Flatt, de Wette, Wiesinger, Plitt); but Paul only uses this formula to confirm a *general* thought. There is, however, no general thought in the preceding words, where Paul is speaking only of his own personal circumstances. Hence the formula must, as in 1 Tim i. 15, iii. 1, be referred here to what follows, and γάρ explained by "namely" (so, too, van Oosterzee). — We cannot say for certain whether the sentences following are really strophes from a Christian hymn (Munter, *Ueber die alteste christliche Poesie*, p. 29, and Paulus, *Memorabilia*, i. 109) or not; still it is not improbable that they are, all the more that the same may be said of 1 Tim. iii. 16. The first sentence runs: εἰ συναπεθάνομεν, καὶ συζήσομεν] σύν refers to Christ, expressing fellowship, and not merely similarity. De Wette points us to Rom. vi. 8 for an explanation of the thought; but the context shows that he is not speaking here of spiritual dying, the dying of the old man, which is the negative element of regeneration (against van Oosterzee), but of the actual (not merely *ideal*) dying with Christ. In other words, he is speaking of sharing in the same sufferings which Christ endured (so also Hofmann), and whose highest point is to undergo death. The meaning therefore is: "if we in the faith of Christ are slain for His sake;" comp. Phil. iii. 10; also Rom. viii. 17; Matt. v. 11; John xv. 20, and other passages. The aorist συναπεθάνομεν is either to be taken: "if we have entered into the fellowship of His death," or it denotes the actual termination: "if we are dead with Him, we shall also live with Him." — συζήσομεν, corresponding to συναπεθάνομεν, is not used of the present life in faith, but of the future participation in Christ's glorified life (so, too, Hofmann); comp. 1 Thess. v. 10. — Ver. 12. The second sentence runs: εἰ ὑπομένομεν, καὶ συμβασιλεύσομεν] This sentence corresponds with the previous one in both members; comp. Rom. viii. 17, where συμπάσχειν and συνδοξασθῶμεν are opposed to one another. On συμβασ., comp. Rom. v. 17 (ἐν ζωῇ βασιλεύσουσι); it denotes participation in the reign of the glorified Messiah.[1] Like death and life, so are enduring and reigning placed in contrast. — The third sentence is a contrast with the two preceding: εἰ ἀρνησόμεθα, sc. Χριστόν] comp. Matt. x. 33; 2 Pet. ii. 1, Jude 4; used here specially of the verbal denial of Christ, made through fear of suffering. κἀκεῖνος ἀρνήσεται ἡμᾶς: "he will not recognise us as His own," the result of which will be that we remain in a state without grace and without blessing. The meaning of this sentence is confirmed by ver. 13. — εἰ ἀπιστοῦμεν, ἐκεῖνος πιστὸς μένει] ἀπιστεῖν does not mean here: "not believe, be unbelieving"[2] (Mark xvi 11, 16; Acts xxviii. 24), but—in correspondence with ἀρνεῖσθαι—"be unfaithful," which certainly implies lack of that genuine faith from which the faithful confession cannot be separated. In Rom. iii. 3 also, unbelief and unfaithfulness go together, since the people of Israel, to whom the λόγια Θεοῦ were given, showed themselves unfaithful to God by rejecting the promised Messiah, and this after God had chosen them for His people. — ἐκεῖνος πιστὸς μένει] πιστός can only mean "faithful." The faithfulness of the Lord is shown in the realization of His decree—both in acknowledging and in rejecting; the context preceding shows

---

[1] The συζῆν begins for the believer immediately after his death (Phil. i 23; comp also Luke xxiii. 43); the συμβασιλεύειν not till after Christ's παρουσία; comp. Hofmann.

[2] Such is the explanation of Chrysostom, who gives Christ's resurrection as the subject of unbelief εἰ ἀπιστοῦμεν, ὅτι ἀνέστη, οὐδὲν ἀπὸ τούτου βλάπτεται ἐκεῖνος, and assigns to ἀρνήσασθαι γὰρ ἑαυτ. οὐ δύν. the strange signification of οὐκ ἔχει φύσιν μὴ εἶναι.

that the latter reference predominates. — The next words confirm this truth: ἀρνήσασθαι γὰρ ἑαυτὸν οὐ δύναται, which declare the ἀπιστία of the Lord to be an impossibility, since it involves a contradiction of Himself, of His nature.

Ver. 14. In this verse the apostle goes on to set before Timothy how he is to conduct himself in regard to the heresy appearing in the church. — ταῦτα ὑπομίμνησκε] ταῦτα refers to the thoughts just expressed and introduced by the formula πιστὸς ὁ λόγος; of these thoughts Timothy is to remind the church, not future teachers in particular (Heydenreich). The apostle says ὑπομιμνήσκειν, because these thoughts were known to the church; comp. 2 Pet. i. 12 (οὐκ ἀμελήσω . . . ὑμᾶς ὑπομιμνήσκειν . . . καίπερ εἰδότας). — διαμαρτυρόμενος ἐνώπιον τοῦ κυρίου] iv. 1; 1 Tim. v. 21. With the reading λογομάχει (see the critical remarks) these words belong to what precedes, a new section beginning with μὴ λογομάχει; on the other hand, with the *Rec.* μὴ λογομαχεῖν, the infinitive depends on διαμαρτ. Hofmann wishes to take the *Rec.* imperatively; but to give an imperative force to an infinitive standing among several imperatives, would be something unheard of. — It can hardly be decided which is the right reading. De Wette and Wiesinger have declared themselves for the *Rec.*, because " the verb διαμαρτ. is commonly used by Paul for introducing exhortations, and is not in keeping with the weak appeal ταῦτα ὑπομίμνησκε." These reasons, however, are not sufficient, since διαμαρτ. may quite as well be connected with what precedes as with what follows, although it does not occur elsewhere in the N. T. in such a connection; and ταῦτα ὑπομ. is not used by the apostle in so weak a sense that he could not strengthen it by such a form of adjuration. Nor can it be maintained that the exhortation μὴ λογομάχει is unsuitable for Timothy, since there is again at ver. 16 an exhortation quite similar in nature; comp. also ver. 23. There is more force in Reiche's observation: supervacaneum . . . fuisset, Timotheo, uno quasi halitu bis fere idem imperare, μὴ λογομάχει, and ver. 16, τὰς δὲ . . . κενοφωνίας περιΐστασο; but, on the other hand, μὴ λογομάχει is a suitable addition to the exhortation: ταῦτα ὑπομίμνησκε. On the whole, seeing that the transition from the one exhortation to the other is somewhat abrupt, and that the authorities are mostly on the side of the *Rec*, this reading should be preferred. — On the conception of λογομαχεῖν, comp 1 Tim. vi. 4. — εἰς [ἐπ'] οὐδὲν χρήσιμον] Regarding this appended clause in apposition, see Winer, p. 497 [E. T. p. 669]. χρήσιμος is a word which only occurs here; in Tit. iii 9 the ζητήσεις of the heretics are called ἀνωφελεῖς καὶ μάταιοι. — ἐπὶ καταστροφῇ τῶν ἀκουόντων] "*which is useful for nothing, (serving rather) to the perversion of the hearers;*" Chrysostom: οὐ μόνον οὐδὲν ἐκ τούτου κέρδος, ἀλλὰ καὶ βλάβη πολλή.[1] — καταστροφή (opposed to τῇ οἰκοδομῇ) here and in 2 Pet. ii 16, where it has its proper meaning; it is synonymous with καθαίρεσις in 2 Cor. xiii 10. Ἐπί here does not express the aim (Gal v. 13; Eph. ii. 10), but the result (Wiesinger). Xenophon, *Memor.* ii. 19 : ἐπὶ βλάβῃ.

Ver. 15. Continuation of the exhortation to Timothy — σπούδασον σεαυτὸν δόκιμον παραστῆσαι τῷ Θεῷ] σπουδάζειν expresses the eager striving, as in Eph. iv. 3, 1 Thess. ii. 17, etc., and has a suggestion of making haste, iv. 9, 21; Tit. iii 12. — δόκιμον, equivalent to probatus, *tried*, is absolute, and should not be taken with ἐργάτην (Luther, Mack). A more precise limitation is given in the next words : παραστῆσαι τῷ Θεῷ; comp Rom. vi. 13, 16, and other passages in the Pauline epistles; here it has the additional meaning: " for the service of." Hofmann gives an unsuitable construction by joining τῷ Θεῷ—in spite of παραστῆσαι—with δόκιμον (= " approved by one "), separating ἐργάτην ἀνεπαίσχυντον from one another, and connecting ἐργάτην with δόκιμον, so that ἀνεπαίσχυντον forms a second predicate to ἐργάτην, ὀρθοτομοῦντα κ.τ.λ being added as a third. All this not only assigns to δόκιμος a meaning which it never has in the N. T. (not even in Rom xiv. 18 ; comp. Meyer on the passage), but separates παραστῆσαι from the τῷ Θεῷ standing next to it, although Paul almost never uses the word without adding a dative of the person (comp. in particular, Rom. vi. 13, xii. 1,

---

[1] The harm of λογομαχιῖν consists not so much in this, "that its tendency with those who listen to it is to make the Christian doctrine seem uncertain, since it produces such contention" (Hofmann), as in this, that those who give ear to it are led away from the fundamental principles of Christianity.

1 Cor. viii. 8 ; 2 Cor. xi. 2 ; Eph. v. 27). — ἐργάτην ἀνεπαίσχυντον] ἐργάτης specially de opere rustico ; used, besides, of the work in the field of God's kingdom (2 Cor. xi. 13 ; Phil. iii. 2). — ἀνεπαίσχυντος ; in the N. T. a ἅπαξ λεγ., and in classic Greek used only in Sp as an adverb with the signification : "immodestly, shamelessly." It is synonymous with ἀναίσχυντος, which in classic Greek is used only in a bad sense : "one who is not ashamed when he ought to be." It cannot, of course, have this meaning here. The most reliable interpretation is to keep by the fundamental meaning of the word taken in a good sense : "who is not ashamed, because he has nothing to be ashamed of." Bengel. cui tua ipsius conscientia nullum pudorem incutiat ; de Wette, Wiesinger, van Oosterzee, Plitt translate it simply : "who has nothing to be ashamed of" Hofmann arbitrarily explains it as equivalent to : "of whom God is not ashamed," a meaning suitable to the context only if δόκιμος be taken in the sense he maintains. The next words make the definition still more precise : ὀρθοτομοῦντα τὸν λόγον τῆς ἀληθείας] ὀρθοτομεῖν, ἅπαξ λεγ, is rightly explained by most as recte tractare (which is the actual translation of the Vulgate); but there is very great variety in the derivation of the notion. Melanchthon, Beza, and others derive the expression ab illa legali victimarum sectione ac distributione Lev. i. 6 ; Vitringa, from the business τοῦ οἰκονόμου, cui competat panem cibosque frangere, distribuere filiis familias ; Pricaeus, a lapicidis ; Lamb. Bos, from the ploughers, qui arantes τέμνειν τὴν γῆν, σχίζειν et ἐπισχίζειν ἀρούρας dicuntur, yet in such a way that is committed to those qui rectas vias insistunt. De Wette (Wiesinger agreeing with him) maintains the latter ; recte secare viam, λόγον being put for ὁδόν. Certainly τέμνειν is often joined with ὁδός, κέλευθος ; but it does not follow that in ὀρθοτομεῖν by itself there is contained a reference to the way[1] As little

---

[1] De Wette, indeed, appeals to LXX Prov. iii. 6, xi. 5, but in these passages ὁδόν appears, and the verb, like the ישר, has the transitive signification "make straight, smooth." — Nor does the passage in Eurip *Rhes* v. 422 · εὐθεῖαν λόγων τέμνων κίλινθον, justify de Wette's explanation. The possibility of substituting λόγον for ὁδόν is not proved simply by remarking that "the word is a way" We certainly do speak of "walking in the path of the divine word, of virtue," etc., but not of "walking in the divine word, in virtue."

can we say that any other of the references is contained in it The word in itself means: "cut rightly," or, according to Pape: "cut straight, in straight direction;" then, the notion of τέμνειν falling into the background, as is often the case with καινοτομεῖν, it has the more general signification: "deal rightly with something so as not to falsify it."[1] — Hofmann's explanation is curious: "cut straight through the word of truth, i.e. cut it, so that it is a straight cut, passing into the heart of it, whereas a slanting cut would not reach the inner part of the word of God, but only touch the outwork" This explanation—apart from other reasons—is refuted by the fact that ὀρθοτομεῖν has not the signification: "cut through the middle point." The Gloss. ordinar. explains it: secundum competentiam singulorum, ut: altis spiritualia, lac distribuere parvulis, so that Paul is directing Timothy to preach the word according to his hearers' capacity of understanding. This is the meaning also according to Luther's translation: "who rightly parts the word of truth;" but the thought is entirely foreign to the context.[2] — Chrysostom explains it by τέμνειν τὰ νόθα καὶ τὰ τοιαῦτα ἐκκόπτειν; so, too, Oecumenius; but this is unsuitable, for there is nothing false in the λόγος τῆς ἀληθ., and therefore nothing to be separated from it. — The expositors are quite wrong who refer the expression to a life in accordance with God's word = κατὰ τὸ εὐαγγέλιον ὀρθότατα βιοῦν. — The right interpretation makes it the simple opposite of καπηλεύειν τὸν λόγον τοῦ Θεοῦ, 2 Cor. ii. 17.[3]

Ver. 16. Τὰς δὲ βεβήλους κενοφωνίας (comp. 1 Tim. vi. 20) περιΐστασο] "avoid" (comp. Tit. iii. 9, synonymous with ἐκτρέπεσθαι, 1 Tim. vi. 20); properly: "go out of the

---

[1] Perhaps the expression may be explained in this way, that the imparting of the λόγος τῆς ἀληθείας makes it necessary to part it, since only a part of it can be delivered each time; it therefore amounts to saying that this parting is to be done rightly, so that the λόγος τῆς ἀληθείας may receive no injury.

[2] In Beza's explanation. nihil praetermittere, quod dicendum sit, nil adjicere de suo, nil mutilare, discerpere, torquere, deinde diligenter spectare, quid ferat auditorum captus, the first part alone is to the point

[3] In the Fathers the word ὀρθοτομία is sometimes found synonymous with ὀρθοδοξία. Clemens Alex Stromata, vii p. 762 τὴν ἀποστολικὴν ἐκκλησιαστικὴν σώζων ὀρθοτομίαν τῶν δογμάτων; but this usage took its rise from the above passage.

way." Beza is wrong: cohibe, i. e. observa et velut obside, nempe ne in ecclesiam irrepant. — The reason for the exhortation follows in the next words: ἐπὶ πλεῖον γὰρ προκόψουσιν ἀσεβείας] προκόπτειν here is intransitive (comp. iii. 9, 13), and ἀσεβείας is the genitive depending on ἐπὶ πλεῖον,[1] not the accusative, as if προκ. had here the transitive meaning "to further." The subject is formed by the heretics whom the apostle has in mind, not the κενοφωνίαι, as ὁ λόγος αὐτῶν shows. Hence Luther's translation is incorrect: "it (evil talking) helps much to ungodly character;" besides, it puts the present for the future. Bengel: Futurum, proprie; est enim praedictio, ut ἕξει, ver. 17; comp. iii 3 ff, 6. Hofmann wishes a distinction to be made between those who deal in βεβ. κενοφωνίαι and those to whose number Hymenaeus and Philetus belong; and according to him, the subject should be taken from the ὧν ἐστι κ.τ λ, so as to mean the followers of these two heretics. We cannot, however, understand why Paul should not have included among the βεβ κενοφωνίαις the heresy that the resurrection had already taken place, unless this expression be greatly weakened, as Hofmann indeed does, to favour his view of the heresy at Ephesus (see Introduction, § 4). In any case, it is a mistake to take the subject for προκόψουσιν only from what follows, since such subject does not present itself naturally; and there is least ground of all for supposing that it must be οἱ περὶ Ὑμέναιον καὶ Φιλητόν. — The γάρ, which refers only to the sentence immediately preceding, makes the increasing godlessness of the heretics the reason why Timothy should not meddle further with the κενοφωνίαι, but simply oppose to them the word of truth.

Ver. 17. The increase of the ἀσέβεια is closely connected with the further spread of the heresy. On this point the apostle says: καὶ ὁ λόγος αὐτῶν ὡς γάγγραινα νομὴν ἕξει] γάγγραινα, an eating ulcer, like cancer, called in Galen the cold burn (σφάκελος); νομὴν ἔχειν = νέμειν (Acts iv. 17: ἐπὶ πλεῖον διανέμεσθαι), "eat into the flesh, spread;" comp. Polybius (ed. 2, Tauchnitz), i. 4, viii. 5: ἡ τοῦ πυρὸς νομή is

---

[1] In Diod. Sicul there occurs. ἐπὶ πλεῖον κακίας προβαίνειν; see Bengel on the passage.

equivalent to the spreading of fire; i. 81, 6, used of an ulcer (Pape, *s.v. νομή*). — Jerome, *Ep. ad Galat.*: doctrina perversa, ab uno incipiens, vix duos aut tres primum in exordio auditores reperit, sed paulatim cancer serpit in corpore. The body on which the gangrene is found, and in which it spreads ever wider, is the church. He is therefore speaking here not so much of the *intensive* increase of the evil (Mack, Wiesinger) in those attacked by it, as of its *extensive* diffusion (so most expositors), thinking, at the same time, of the ever deepening mark which it is making on the inner life of the church. Chrysostom rightly says: τὸ πᾶν λυμαίνεται; but his further explanation is not apposite: ἐνταῦθα τὸ ἀδιόρθωτον αὐτῶν δηλοῖ, for the apostle does not say here that the heretics are beyond amendment. — Of these heretics Paul mentions two: Hymenaeus and Philetus, of whom nothing further is known, except that the former is possibly the same as the one named in 1 Tim. i. 20 (see on that passage).

Ver. 18. More precise description of the heretics, in the first place generally, as men who "*have erred in regard to the truth*" (de Wette) —περὶ τὴν ἀλήθειαν ἠστόχησαν] see 1 Tim. i. 6, vi. 21. The chief point in their heresy is given thus: λέγοντες τὴν ἀνάστασιν ἤδη γεγονέναι — Both Irenaeus and Tertullian mention Gnostics, who denied the resurrection in its literal sense.[1] There is no ground for Baur's assertion, that there is allusion here to Marcion. The passage in 1 Cor. xv. 12 proves that the doctrine of the resurrection of the dead had even in the apostolic age become a stumbling-block to many in the church. — The denial of these heretics was closely related to views which made a false contrast between flesh and spirit. — They had already exercised an injurious influence on others, as the next words declare. καὶ ἀνατρέπουσι τὴν τινῶν πίστιν] not: "whereby they make many err in their persuasion," πίστιν is the Christian faith which includes the certainty of the future resurrection, and ἀνατρέπειν (see Tit. i. 11) means "*evertere, destroy.*"

---

[1] Comp Tertullian, *De Resurr.* chap. XIX. resurrectionem mortuorum distorquent asseverantes ipsam etiam mortem spiritualiter intelligendam . . . resurrectionem eam vindicandam, qua quis addita veritate redanimatus et revivifactus Deo, ignorantiae morte decussa, velut de sepulcro veteris hominis eruperit.

Ver. 19. As a contrast to the unsettling action of the heretics, we have ὁ μέντοι στερεὸς θεμέλιος τοῦ Θεοῦ ἔστηκεν] θεμέλιος (properly an adjective, supply λίθος) is originally the foundation-stone of a building, if that signification be retained here, the building can only mean the church of Christ. The question then arises, what is its foundation-stone? and to this various answers have been given. Ambrosius understands it to be God's promises; Bengel, the fides Dei immota; Heinrichs, the Christian religion; Ernesti, the doctrine of the resurrection (ver. 18); Calvin, the election of grace. All this is arbitrary. The θεμέλιος must be something which, according to the next verse, can also be regarded as οἰκία, viz. as Heydenreich says: ἐκκλησια τεθεμελιωμένη ὑπὸ Θεοῦ (similarly de Wette and Wiesinger). Paul, however, calls it θεμέλιος, not because that word denotes a building, which is not the case, but because the church, as it was originally set by God in the world, only forms the foundation of the building which is to be perfected gradually (so, too, van Oosterzee). Chrysostom's explanation is inapposite: αἱ στερεαὶ ψυχαὶ ἑστήκασι πεπηγυίαι καὶ ἀκίνητοι; for Paul is not thinking here of individual believers, but of the church of which they are members. Possibly the θεμέλιος does not mean anything definite, and the apostle "merely intends to say that the church is firmly founded" (Hofmann); but that is not probable, especially as the attribute στερεός and the verb ἔστηκεν point to a definite, concrete conception in the apostle's mind. — στερεός and ἔστηκεν form a contrast to ἀνατρέπουσι. Though the faith of some may be destroyed, the foundation of God, i.e. which God has laid, still stands firm, unwavering. — The mark of this is given in the next words: ἔχων τὴν σφραγῖδα ταύτην] σφραγίς, "the seal," is partly a means of keeping safe, partly a sign of relevancy, partly a form of declaration whereby a document or the like is proved to be valid. Here it is the inscription [1] on the θεμέλιος, according to Wiesinger, "as a guarantee that the ἐκκλησία ὑπὸ τοῦ Θεοῦ τεθεμελιωμένη has an existence not to be shaken;" or, better still, as

---

[1] The figure is founded on the custom of placing inscriptions on the doorposts as well as on the foundation-stones; comp. Deut. vi. 9, xi. 20; Rev. xxi. 14.

God's testimony to the peculiar nature of the structure (similarly Hofmann: "because through it God so acknowledges the structure as to declare of what nature He means it to be when thus founded"), van Oosterzee combines the two interpretations. — Paul mentions two inscriptions. The first, with allusion to Num. xvi. 5 (the LXX. puts וַיֵּדַע for וַיֹּדַע), is ἔγνω κύριος τοὺς ὄντας αὐτοῦ. Haec sententia . . . a parte Dei (Wolf). — ἔγνω] Bengel: *novit amanter, nec nosse desinit, sed perpetuo servat suos*: a word of comfort for the believers exposed to the destroying influence of the heretics in the church. The other inscription (with which we may compare Num. xvi. 26 ; Isa. lii. 11) runs : ἀποστήτω ἀπὸ ἀδικίας πᾶς ὁ ὀνομάζων τὸ ὄνομα κυρίου] Haec sententia . . . a parte hominum (Wolf). Ἀδικία is the sum total of everything opposed to God, including heresy. — ὀνομάζειν τὸ ὄν. τ. κυρ., according to Wahl, is equivalent to קָרָא בְּשֵׁם יְהֹוָה, nomen Dei invocare. This is incorrect; it corresponds rather to the phrase : ἐπικαλεῖσθαι τὸ ὄνομ. κυρίου (τὸν κύριον, ver. 22). Bengel correctly says: quisquis nominat nomen Christi, ut domini sui. — This second inscription is an exhortation to believers to abstain from all unrighteousness notwithstanding the seductive influence of the heretics. — Heydenreich: two truths must likewise characterize the indestructible temple of God, the church, and these denote the comfort and hope, but also the duty and reponsibility of the true worshippers of Jesus.[1]

Ver. 20. To the church as the θεμέλιος τοῦ Θεοῦ only those belong whom the Lord acknowledges as His, and who abstain from every kind of ἀδικία. This thought is contained in ver. 19. But there were also in the church ἄδικοι, opposing the gospel by word and deed. This strange fact Paul now explains by a figure : ἐν μεγάλῃ δὲ οἰκίᾳ] The Greek expositors understand by οἰκία "the world," to which Calvin rightly objects: ac contextus quidem huc potius nos ducit, ut

---

[1] Chrysostom understands θεμέλιος of individual believers, and is therefore compelled to give this thought an incorrect reference : πόθεν δηλοὶ εἰσίν, ἀπὸ τοῦ τὰ γράμματα ταῦτα ἔχειν ἐπὶ τῶν πραγμάτων, ἀπὸ τοῦ γνωρίζεσθαι ὑπὸ τοῦ Θεοῦ καὶ μὴ συμπαραπόλλυσθαι, ἀπὸ τοῦ ἀφιστάναι ἀπὸ ἀδικίας, ταῦτα τὰ γνωρίσματα τοῦ θεμελίου.

de ecclesia intelligamus; neque enim de extraneis disputat Paulus, sed de ipsa Dei familia. It is different with the similar passage in Rom. ix. 21 ff.— οὐκ ἔστι μόνον σκεύη χρυσᾶ καὶ ἀργυρᾶ, ἀλλὰ καὶ ξύλινα καὶ ὀστράκινα] By the *former* articles are meant the worthy, genuine members of the church; by the *latter*, those not genuine (not: those less good, Estius, Mosheim, and others): "each class, however, contains degrees within itself, comp. Matt. xiii. 23." (Wiesinger). The apostle's distinction is given more precisely in the next words, which cannot be referred alike to each of the two classes named, but express the same antithesis: καὶ ἃ μὲν εἰς τιμήν, viz. the σκεύη χρ. κ. ἀργ., ἃ δὲ εἰς ἀτιμίαν, viz. the σκεύη ξυλ. κ. ὀστράκ. To this Hofmann objects, that the material of the vessels does not determine their purpose and use, and that the second clause, therefore, does not correspond with the first; "the first antithesis rather declares that in the house of God there are members of rich gifts and spiritual attainments, and members whose gifts are few and who spiritually are of no consideration." But in this way there is manifestly imported an antithesis of which there is no hint in the context. It is indeed true that vessels even of wood and clay may be applied to honourable uses; but undue pressure is laid on the apostle's words when they are interpreted in accordance with such a possibility — εἰς τιμήν and εἰς ἀτιμίαν do not refer to the house, nor to their possessor, on whom they bring honour or shame (Matthies), but to the vessels themselves (de Wette, Wiesinger, van Oosterzee). To some honour is given, to others shame, *i.e.* in the various uses to which they are applied by their possessors. The insertion of ἑτοιμασμένα would give an unsuitable thought, see Meyer and de Wette on Rom. ix. 21.

Ver. 21. Without explaining the figure, the apostle carries it on, but in such a way as to show to the members of the church how each one may become a vessel to honour.— ἐὰν οὖν τις ἐκκαθάρῃ ἑαυτὸν ἀπὸ τούτων] ἐκκαθαίρειν, according to classic Greek (also 1 Cor. v. 7), is an intensive form of καθαίρειν (N. T. καθαρίζειν). Chrysostom rightly says: οὐκ εἶπε· καθάρῃ, ἀλλ' ἐκκαθάρῃ, τουτέστι, παντελῶς καθάρῃ. The opinion (formerly expressed in this commentary) was incorrect, that ἐκ only foreshadows the ἀπὸ τούτων. The translation is inaccurate " if one keeps himself pure " (Heydenreich, equivalent to καθαρὸν, ἁγνὸν ἑαυτὸν τηρεῖν); Luther rightly : "purifies himself." The word indicates the departure from impure companionship; comp. ver. 19, ἀποστήτω, and 1 Tim. vi. 5 (according to *Rec.*), ἀφίστασο ἀπὸ τῶν τοιούτων.[1] Wiesinger makes the construction pregnant. "separate oneself from these by self-purification;" it is more correct, however, to regard the separation itself as the purification. — ἀπὸ τούτων] cannot according to the context be taken as a collective neuter: "from such things," ἀπὸ τῶν εἰρημένων, ἡγοῦν ἀδικίας, ἀτιμίας, or even ἀπὸ τῶν βεβήλων κενοφωνιῶν, ver. 16, it refers rather to ἃ δὲ εἰς ἀτιμίαν. Luther: "from such people," comp. the passage quoted, 1 Tim. vi. 5. Hofmann is altogether mistaken in his curious idea that ἀπὸ τούτων means "from that time forward," and is to be connected with what follows. This reference is nowhere in the N. T. expressed by ἀπὸ τούτων (comp. Matt. xxvi. 29 . ἀπ' ἄρτι), besides, this more precise definition of ἔσται is quite superfluous, whereas ἐκκαθάρῃ ἑαυτόν without more precise definition is too general. — ἔσται σκεῦος εἰς τιμὴν, ἡγιασμένον] Lachmann has wrongly deleted the comma between τιμ. and ἡγιασμ. Εἰς does not depend on ἡγ., but σκ. εἰς τιμ. forms here, like ἃ μὲν εἰς τιμήν in ver. 20, *one* idea to which various attributes, ἡγιασμένον being the first, are added in order to describe the nature of such a σκ. εἰς τιμ. — ἡγιασμένον] is not = σκεῦος ἐκλογῆς, Acts ix. 15 (Heydenreich), but: "*sanctified*," as belonging to the Lord. Εὔχρηστον = "*good for using;*" τῷ δεσπότῃ, "*the master of the house;*" εἰς πᾶν ἔργον ἀγαθὸν ἠτοιμασμένον (comp. Rev. ix. 7), "*prepared for every good work.*" While all expositors join τῷ δεσπότῃ with εὔχρηστον, Hofmann prefers to refer it to what follows, without giving any reason for so doing. Elsewhere in the N. T. εὔχρηστος occurs only in con-

---

[1] Bengel remarks: Activum cum pronomine reciproco indicat liberrimam facultatem fidelium.—Beza seeks, on the other hand, to save the doctrine of predestination · Volumus et efficimus, sed per eum qui gratis et in solidum efficit in nobis bonam et efficacem voluntatem, tum quod ad διάθεσιν, tum quod ad ἐνέργειαν attinet.

nection with the dative of more precise definition (iv. 11; Philem. 11).

Ver. 22. Timothy is exhorted to Christian behaviour; it is impossible to overlook the connection with what precedes. — τὰς δὲ νεωτερικὰς ἐπιθυμίας] νεωτερικαί is ἅπ. λεγ., juveniles, quibus juvenes indulgent, not cupiditates rerum novarum. Chrysostom and Theophylact rightly remark that the meaning is not to be limited too closely to πορνεία. Theodoret: τρυφὴν, γέλωτος ἀμετρίαν, δόξαν κενὴν καὶ τὰ τούτοις προσόμοια. Hofmann supposes that the desires are meant which are found in younger members in contrast with those advanced in years, e g. the desire for brilliant gifts and offices; but neither the context nor the expression supports his interpretation. This reference is rather a pure importation into the text, and is adopted by Hofmann that it may agree with his erroneous view of ver. 20; it is opposed, finally, by the δίωκε δικαιοσύνην κ.τ λ. — δίωκε δὲ δικαιοσύνην κ τ λ.] very similar to 1 Tim. vi. 11. — εἰρήνην, "i e. inner fellowship and harmony" (de Wette). — μετά should not be construed with δίωκε, but with εἰρήνην; comp. Heb. xii. 14. — μετὰ πάντων τ. ἐπικαλουμένων τὸν κύριον] This expression occurs somewhat frequently as a name for Christians; comp. Acts ii. 21, ix 14; Rom. x. 12. The passage in 1 Cor. i. 2 shows that Christ is meant by κύριος. — ἐκ καθαρᾶς καρδίας] belonging not to δίωκε but to ἐπικαλουμένων, stands here in special contrast to the heretics who did also call Christ their Lord, but not from a pure heart. Chrysostom's remark · μετὰ τῶν ἄλλων οὐ χρὴ πρᾷον εἶναι, goes too far, since in ver. 25 there is an express appeal for πρᾳότης towards the ἀντιδιατιθέμενοι; still the believer can only keep peace with those who call on the Lord out of a pure heart, the others he must oppose. Εἰρήνη is mentioned last, because the apostle is thinking of it specially; comp. the next verses.

Ver. 23 is in contrast (δέ) with ver. 22. As in 1 Tim. i 4, vi. 4, ζητήσεις are brought forward as the characteristic of heresy. Paul calls them μωραὶ καὶ ἀπαίδευτοι] μωραί, Tit. iii. 9. — ἀπαίδευτοι, properly, "uninstructed;" in N. T. ἅπ. λεγ.; more frequently found in LXX. and Apocrypha, but only in reference to persons. It is synonymous with μωρός

(בכלי); even here, where it refers to things, it is synonymous with μωρός (= ineptus). There is no just ground for Hofmann's supposition, that it is to be derived here not from παιδεύεσθαι, but from παιδεύειν, and hence that it means "unsuited for educating spiritually" (Mosheim, Heydenreich, Mack, Matthies). — On παραιτοῦ, comp. 1 Tim. iv. 7, v. 11. — εἰδώς does not give the reason why Timothy should follow the exhortation (equivalent to "since, or because, you know "); it forms part of the exhortation in the sense: "as you know (consider);" comp. Tit. iii. 11 ; 1 Cor. xv. 58 ; Col iii. 24, iv. 1. — ὅτι γεννῶσι μάχας] μάχαι, Jas. iv. 1, synonymous with πόλεμοι; opposed to εἰρήνη, ver. 22.

Vv. 24–26. In regard to the last thoughts, Paul gives a sketch of the conduct which beseems the δοῦλος κυρίου. Δοῦλος κυρίου is here, as often, one who has been charged with the office of preaching the gospel. — Οὐ δεῖ μάχεσθαι] Luther is inaccurate: "must not be disputatious;" it does not denote so much the disposition as the act, and is in close relation with the preceding μάχας, it furnishes the reason, therefore, why he should not devote himself to foolish investigations, which only give rise to contentions. — ἀλλ' ἤπιον εἶναι πρὸς πάντας] ἤπιος, here and at 1 Thess. ii. 7, " *amiable, friendly;* " properly, "addressing in a friendly manner," it forms a pointed antithesis to μάχεσθαι. — διδακτικόν (1 Tim. iii. 2). Hoc non solum soliditatem et facilitatem in docendo, sed vel maxime patientiam et assiduitatem significat, Bengel. According to the context here, the word expresses not only the ability, but also the willingness to teach. — ἀνεξίκακον] ἅπ. λεγ (ἀνεξικακία, Ecclus. ii. 19, kindred in meaning with ἐπιείκεια), denotes the opposite of irritability: "*patient, submissive*" in regard to contradiction (perhaps slanderous). — Ver. 25. ἐν πραότητι is wrongly joined by Luther with ἀνεξίκακον: "who can endure the wicked with gentleness;" it belongs rather to what follows, and describes the manner of παιδεύειν — παιδεύειν is here equivalent not to erudire, but to corripere. Luther: "punish," set right, see 1 Tim. i. 20. — τοὺς ἀντιδιατιθεμένους] ἅπ. λεγ., synonymous with ἀντιλέγοντες, Tit. i. 9, and denoting all opposed to the word of truth preached by the δοῦλος κυρίου. The context

PASTORAL EPISTLES. T

compels us to interpret it not as "the unbelievers" (Hofmann), but specially the heretics. The name, however, is not given to them because they are "weak in faith" (Wiesinger). Luther's translation is too strong: "contumacious;" comp. with this passage Tit. i 9, 13 The rule here laid down is not in contradiction with the ἔλεγχε αὐτοὺς ἀποτόμως, Tit i. 13, not because the ἀντιδιατιθέμενοι here are different from the ἀντιλέγοντες of Tit i 9, as Hofmann maintains, but because even with the ἐλέγχειν ἀποτόμως there should also be the ἐν πραότητι παιδεύειν. The purpose which should guide the servant of the Lord in his conduct towards the ἀντιδιατιθέμενοι is given in the next words. — μήποτε δώῃ αὐτοῖς ὁ Θεὸς μετάνοιαν] μήποτε, "whether it may not be," is joined with the conjunctive and the optative; comp. Buttmann, p. 220. The μετάνοια is here supposed to be necessary because the ground of opposition is ἀδικία; μετάνοια is the change of thought which is necessary εἰς ἐπίγνωσιν ἀληθείας. — Ver. 26. καὶ ἀνανήψωσιν ἐκ τῆς τοῦ διαβόλου παγίδος] In the verb ἀνανήφειν, the ἀνα may express motion from beneath, as in other verbs thus compounded (e.g. ἀναζέω), so that it is equivalent to "become sober," i e. "come up out of the stupefaction which holds them down" (Hofmann[1]); but the usual meaning of the word in classic Greek is, however, "become sober again." If the word has this meaning here, then the ἀντιδιατιθέμενοι must be the heretics. The error into which they had fallen is to be compared with the intoxication which beclouds men's wits; the verb is ἅπ. λεγ. In 1 Cor xv. 34 we have ἐκνήφειν — The figure παγίς is certainly not in harmony with this verb; but a collocation of various figurative expressions is not infrequent; here it is more easy to justify it, as an intermediate thought like καὶ ῥυσθῶσιν (Heydenreich) may be at once supplied. The collocation may indeed be altogether avoided, if, with Michaelis and Hofmann, we connect ἐκ τῆς ... παγίδος with ἐζωγρημένοι following; but against this there is the signification of this word, which does not mean being saved, but being taken captive. — ἐζωγρημένοι ὑπ' αὐτοῦ εἰς τὸ ἐκείνου θέλημα] ζωγρεῖν has here the same

---

[1] Hofmann appeals to ἀναζῆν, Rom. vii. 9, for this signification; but comp. Meyer on that passage.

meaning as in Luke v. 10 "*catch*," the notion "alive" being allowed to fall into the background It is questionable whether the devil or the δοῦλος κυρίου (ver. 24) is to be regarded as the ζωγρῶν. Several expositors, Wetstein, Bengel, Mack, Wiesinger, Hofmann, and others, have declared themselves in favour of the second view. But against this there is the perfect, since the ἀνανήφειν does not take place until they *have been caught* by the δοῦλος Θεοῦ,[1] besides, the meaning thus obtained would be open to the reproach of being too artificial[2]—With the *first* view (Matthies, de Wette, van Oosterzee, Plitt) ἐζωγρημένοι may be joined in a natural sense with the preceding παγίδος; Luther is therefore right: "by whom they are caught at his will." The last words · εἰς . . θέλημα, are by Beza joined with ἀνανήψωσιν. ad illius, nempe Dei, voluntatem, videlicet praestandam, hunc enim locum sic esse accipiendum mihi videtur utriusque illius relativi pronominis (αὐτοῦ . . . ἐκείνου) proprietas et ipsa constructio postulare. But ἐκείνου may very easily refer to the same subject as αὐτοῦ; see the passage cited by de Wette, Plato, *Cratylus*, p 430 E: δεῖξαι αὐτῷ, ἂν μὲν τύχῃ, ἐκείνου εἰκόνα, comp. also Kuhner, § 629, A 3.—As with Beza's interpretation, ἐζωγρ. ὑπ. αὐτοῦ, "would be made too bare" (de Wette), the additional clause under discussion is to be joined with ἐζωγρημένοι, as indeed it ought to be, according to its position. — Aretius takes the correct view of ἐζωγρ., but wrongly explains the words εἰς κ.τ.λ. as equivalent to "according to *God's* will, *i.e.* so long as God pleases" Heinrichs, too, though he refers ἐκείνου rightly, wrongly says it is equivalent to ex suo arbitrio, pro suo lubitu Εἰς stands here rather as in 2 Cor. x. 5; the θέλημα τοῦ διαβόλου is regarded "as a local sphere" into which they have been taken; see Meyer on the passage quoted.

---

[1] Hofmann does not acknowledge the validity of the objection "The perfect partic express nothing else than a condition abiding thenceforward," but this "thenceforward" is quite unsuitable here, for in the connection of ἐζωγρημένοι with ἀνανήψωσι that perfect does not show the position into which they enter only by ἀνανήφειν—and which remains thenceforward, but to the position in which they were when the ἀνανήφειν took place

[2] This is valid also against Theophylact's explanation. ἐν πλάνῃ νήχονται· ἀλλὰ ζωγρηθέντες ὑπὸ Θεοῦ . . . ἀνανήψωσιν ἀπὸ τῶν ὑδάτων τῆς πλάνης.

CHAPTER III.

VER. 1. γίνωσκε] For this, Lachm. and Buttm., on the authority of A F G 238, *al*, Aeth. Boern Aug, adopted γινώσκετε. Tisch., on the authority of C D E K L ℵ, most cursives, versions, etc, retained the *Rec*, of which reading nearly all expositors, even Reiche, have declared themselves to be in favour. Still the plur. might be the original reading, since there was no occasion for changing the sing. into the plur. — Ver. 2. ℵ omits οἱ before ἄνθρωποι, a mere alteration, because the art. seemed to present a difficulty in meaning — Ver. 3. ℵ omits ἄστοργοι. — Ver. 6. αἰχμαλωτίζοντες, for αἰχμαλωτεύοντες, was adopted even by Griesb, on the authority of A C D* E F G ℵ, many cursives, versions, and Fathers. — Before γυναικάρια the *Rec.* has the art. τά, which, however, was deleted by Griesb., on the authority of A C D E F G ℵ, etc — Ver. 8 The two names are differently written by some MSS., for Ἰανῆς, C* has Ἰωάννης, Vulg. Cypr. etc. have *Jamnes*, for Ἰαμβρῆς, F G, Vulg. It, many Fathers, also the Talmudists, have Μαμβρῆς. Matthaei thinks that this change was made arbitrarily by Origen, who had a fashion of altering proper names, partim propter ineptas allegorias, partim propter ineptas etymologias suas — Ver 9. The reading in A, διάνοια for ἄνοια, must be regarded as an arbitrary alteration. — Ver 10. παρηκολούθηκας] *Rec*. Tisch. 7; for this, A C F G ℵ 17, *al*., have the aorist παρηκολούθησας, which was adopted by Lachm. and Tisch. 8; F and G have the simple ἠκολούθησας. The perf seems to be a correction made after the analogy of 1 Tim. iv. 6. — Instead of the difficult τῇ ἀγωγῇ, there is found in D* gr. τῇ ἀγάπῃ, a manifest correction. — Ver. 11. For ἐγένετο, Lachm. and Buttm. read ἐγένοντο, after A 38, *al.*; but there is not sufficient testimony to establish its genuineness. — Ver. 12. Tisch. 7: εὐσεβῶς ζῆν, *Rec* supported by a large majority of authorities; on the other hand, Tisch. 8: ζῆν εὐσεβῶς (Lachm. Buttm.), after A P ℵ, etc. — Ver. 14. τίνος] The reading τίνων, which has the testimony of A C F G 17, 71, *al*., Slav. It. Ambrosiast, and was adopted by Lachm. Buttm. Tisch., deserves to be preferred to the usual τίνος, for this reason, that the latter may easily be explained to have arisen from thinking here of Paul only. De Wette is undecided, but Reiche is in favour of the *Rec.* — Ver. 15. The art. τὰ before ἱερά is placed in brackets by Lachm. and omitted by Tisch. 8; it is wanting in C** D* F G ℵ. — Ver. 16 As καί seems to disturb the construction, it is omitted in several versions and Fathers, Origen even has once: θεόπνευστος οὖσα, ὠφέλιμός ἐστι — For ἔλεγχον, Lachm. Buttm. and Tisch. adopted ἐλεγμόν, on the authority of A C F G ℵ, 31, 71, 80, *al.*

Ver. 1. Consequent on the previous exhortations we have a foreshadowing of the evil state of things in the future. — τοῦτο δὲ γίνωσκε] Even if the plural γινώσκετε be the correct reading, it does not follow that the epistle was directed to others beside Timothy; when an exhortation is general in nature, there is nothing strange in an extension of the point of view. — ὅτι ἐν ἐσχάταις ἡμέραις] comp. 1 Tim. iv. 1; Grotius wrongly translates. posthac. It denotes a definite period, not, however (as in Acts ii. 17; Heb. i. 1), the present, the time between the appearance of Christ in the flesh and His second coming to judgment (Heydenreich), nor the time in which the errors shall come to an end (Mack), but the time immediately preceding Christ's παρουσία, in which time, according to apostolic prophecy, the might of the wicked one shall be fully revealed in order to be completely overcome; comp. 2 Pet. iii. 3; Jude 18. — ἐνστήσονται] ἐνίστημι, as an intransitive verb, has the sense of "be near at hand," but in such a way that it passes over into the sense of "be present;" thus in Rom. viii. 38, 1 Cor. iii. 22, ἐνεστῶτα and μέλλοντα stand in sharp antithesis as "things present" and "things future." Bengel therefore is correct: aderunt. The same is the case with the Latin instare; hence there is no ground for finding fault with the Vulg. "instabunt" (de Wette), since in the future something future was denoted. Luther is not quite exact: "will come." — καιροὶ χαλεποί] de Wette: "critical times;" καιρός is not simply the time, but the state of things at the time. — The next verses show in what way these καιροί will show themselves to be χαλεποί.

Vv. 2–5. Ἔσονται γὰρ οἱ ἄνθρωποι] The article οἱ is not to be overlooked. Luther is inaccurate: there will be men,

Nouveau Test. à Mons · il y aura des hommes. The article points to the generality, but, as Matthies rightly observes, not exactly " all without exception, rather taking the average, as a general rule." — Bengel : majore gradu et numero tales, quam unquam, *in ecclesia*. — Mack is incorrect: " the people of whom I am speaking." — φίλαυτοι (ἄπ. λεγ) It may be explained from Arist. *ad Nicom*. ix. 8 : τοὺς φιλαύτους ἐν αἰσχρῷ ἀποκάλουσι. Heinrichs, on the analogy of 1 Cor. x 24, says. ζητῶν τὰ ἑαυτοῦ, μὴ τὰ τοῦ ἑτέρου. — φιλάργυροι] only elsewhere in Luke xvi 14 ; the substantive occurs in 1 Tim. vi. 10 — ἀλάζονες, ὑπερήφανοι] Rom. i. 30; the first expresses boastfulness without intending contempt for others, the second, pride and haughtiness with contempt for others, see Meyer on that passage. Hofmann's explanation of ἀλάζων is not appropriate · " he who attributes to himself an honour which is not his " — βλάσφημοι] " slanderous;" not quite " blasphemous " (Matthies) In 1 Tim. i. 13 a definite reference to divine things is given by the context — γονεῦσιν ἀπειθεῖς] Rom. i. 30. — ἀχάριστοι] elsewhere only in Luke vi 35 (Ecclus. xvi. 29 ; Wisd. xxix. 17). — ἀνόσιοι] 1 Tim. i. 9. Beza : quibus nullum jus est nec fas. — Ver. 3. ἄστοργοι] Rom i. 31, especially of the natural affection between parents and children : caritate a natura ipsa nobis insita orbati, Heinrichs. — ἄσπονδοι] Rom. i 31 ; both those who make no covenant (Luther : " irreconcilable ") and those who do not keep a covenant made, " covenant-breaking " Hofmann says · " one who is destitute of moral sense of justice ;" but that does not give the reference peculiar to the word. — διάβολοι] 1 Tim. iii. 11 — ἀκρατεῖς (ἄπ. λεγ), " having no control over one's passions ;" 1 Cor. vii. 5 : ἀκρασία ; the opposite is ἐγκρατής, Tit. i. 8. — ἀνήμεροι] (ἄπ. λεγ.). Oecumenius makes it equivalent to ὠμοί, ἀπάνθρωποι ; synonymous with ἀνελεήμονες, Rom i. 31. — ἀφιλάγαθοι (ἄπ. λεγ), the opposite · φιλάγαθοι, Tit. i. 8. Theophylact · ἐχθροὶ παντὸς ἀγαθοῦ Luther wrongly : " unkindly." — Ver. 4. προδόται] Luke vi. 16 , Acts vii. 52 ; here: " men among whom there is no fidelity " (Wiesinger). — προπετεῖς] (Acts xix. 36), qui praecipites sunt in agendo (Bengel), " foolhardy." Hofmann's is too weak : " inconsiderate." — τετυφωμένοι] 1 Tim. iii. 6, vi. 4, "puffed up," not merely "made stupid" (Hofmann). — φιλήδονοι μᾶλλον ἢ φιλόθεοι (both words ἅπ. λεγ Philo, de Agricult. : φιλήδονον καὶ φιλοπαθὴ μᾶλλον ἢ φιλάρετον καὶ φιλόθεον ἐργάζεσθαι); such paronomasia are often found in the N. T. ; see Wilke's *Hermeneutik*, vol. II. p. 346 : " rather hunting after pleasure than seeking after God."[1] — Ver. 5. ἔχοντες μόρφωσιν εὐσεβείας] μόρφωσις, Rom ii. 20, in a different meaning from here ; see Meyer on that passage. We must not, like Beza, understand it to be vera forma et effigies pietatis, sicut in lege proponitur ; it rather denotes *the external form* in general. But as Paul contrasts it here with δύναμις, it acquires the signification of mere *appearance* in distinction from true nature. — τὴν δὲ δύναμιν αὐτῆς ἠρνημένοι] δύναμις in contrast with μόρφωσις. "the living, powerful nature of genuine blessedness" (Heydenreich). — ἠρνημένοι] 1 Tim. v. 8 ; Tit. i. 16, ii. 12 : "they show that they do not possess the δύναμις, and do not wish to possess it." — This ends the enumeration of the characteristics which Paul uses to describe the men in the last times — Rom i. 30, 31 is similar to this passage ; Wiesinger (following Olshausen) aptly remarks : " it is a new heathendom under a Christian name which the apostle is here describing." — A definite connection between the ideas cannot be established,[2] but in both passages kindred ideas are placed together. Thus the two first are compounded with φίλος, then follow three expressions denoting arrogance ; to γονεῦσιν ἀπαθεῖς there is added ἀχάριστοι, this word begins a longer series of words beginning with ἀ privative, and the series is interrupted by διάβολοι, the next expressions : προδόται, προπετεῖς, seem to form a paronomasia ; to προ-

---

[1] Theod. v Mopsu.· φίλαυτοί εἰσιν οἱ πάντα πρὸς τὴν ἑαυτῶν ὠφέλειαν ποιοῦντες, ἀλαζόνες καυχώμενοι ἔχειν ὃ μὴ ἔχουσιν, ὑπ.ρήφανοι μεγάλα φρονοῦντες ἐπὶ τοῖς οὖσιν, βλάσφημοι κατηγορίαις χαίροντες, ἀνόσιοι ἐπιμέλειαν τοῦ δικαίου μὴ ποιούμενοι, ἄστοργοι περὶ οὐδένα σχέσιν ἔχοντες, ἄσπονδοι οὐ βέβαιοι περὶ τὰς φιλίας, οὐδὲ ἀληθεῖς περὶ ἃ συντίθενται, διάβολοι ταῦτά τε ἐκεῖ, ἐκεῖνα ἐνταῦθα λέγοντες ἐπὶ τῷ κατεργάζεσθαι μάχην, ἀκρατεῖς ἥττους τῶν παθῶν, ἀνήμεροι οὐδεμιᾶς χρηστότητος ἐπιμιλούμενοι, τετυφωμένοι μεγάλα φρονοῦντες ἐπὶ τοῖς μὴ προσοῦσι

[2] Hofmann does indeed seek to establish an order in accordance with definite points of view, but he does not accomplish this without much ingenuity and many inaccurate interpretations.

πετεῖς there is added the kindred notion τετυφωμένοι; some more general notions close the list. But this very confusion brings out more vividly the varied manifestations of the evil one. It is to be observed, however, that the list begins with φίλαυτοι, that accordingly only such qualities are enumerated as have their root in φιλαυτία, and that hypocrisy is the last mentioned, as the means by which the selfish man seeks to conceal his selfishness by a show of piety. — Heydenreich wrongly tries to establish in the particular expressions a special reference to the peculiar nature of the heretics. — As the closing word, Paul adds the exhortation: καὶ τούτους ἀποτρέπου] ἀποτρέπου, ἅπ. λεγ (1 Tim. vi. 20. ἐκτρέπεσθαι), is kindred in meaning with παραιτοῦ, ii. 23: "from these things turn away, these things avoid." — This exhortation shows that Paul in single phenomena of the day already recognised the approach of the καιροὶ χαλεποί which were to come fully in the future.

Ver. 6. In this verse the apostle passes on to definite facts in the present. We cannot but see that he is thinking of the heretics on whose ἀσέβεια he lays stress also in other passages; comp. ver. 8 (ii. 16). Hofmann says that "Paul was thinking of people who wished to be considered, and pretended to be, on good terms with Timothy;" but there is no hint of this in the context. By similarity of disposition they belong already to the number of the godless men of the future; hence Paul says. ἐκ τούτων γάρ εἰσιν] γάρ gives the reason of the previous exhortation, as the apostle means to declare that men such as he has described already exist. — οἱ ἐνδύνοντες εἰς τὰς οἰκίας] ἐνδύνειν here, "*enter, press into*," with a suggestion of secrecy; Luther: "who slip into houses here and there;" Bengel: irrepentes clanculum; in this sense the word is ἅπαξ λεγ.[1] The form of expression οἱ ἐνδύνοντες shows that this ἐνδύνειν is a characteristic of those of whom the apostle is speaking. — The purpose of this secret entering is given in the next words: καὶ αἰχμαλωτίζοντες γυναικάρια κ.τ.λ.] αἰχμαλωτίζειν, a verb belonging to later Greek: "make a prisoner of war;" it denotes here, getting complete

---

[1] Chrysost. εἶδες, τὸ ἀναίσχυντον πῶς ἐδήλωσε διὰ τοῦ εἰπεῖν, ἐνδύνοντες· τὸ ἄτιμον, τὴν ἀπάτην, τὴν κολακείαν.

possession of; the word is thoroughly apposite for describing the conduct of the founders of heretical sects [1]— γυναικάρια] ἄπ. λεγ, the diminutive with a suggestion of contempt; "the contemptuous epithet indicates their weakness and proneness to temptation" (van Oosterzee). — The nature of these γυναικάρια is described in the following three participial clauses: σεσωρευμένα ἁμαρτίαις] σωρεύειν (Rom xii. 20), "gather, heap up," corresponds to the Latin cumulare. "cumulatae peccatis." — ἀγόμενα ἐπιθυμίαις ποικίλαις (Rom. viii. 14: Gal. v. 18, ἄγεσθαι πνεύματι). Luther is inaccurate: "who go on with manifold lusts" Their internal motive and spring of action are their manifold lusts; Chrysostom: τί ἐστι ποικίλαις, ἐνταῦθα πολλὰ ἠνίξατο, τὴν τρυφὴν, τὴν ἀσχημοσύνην, τὴν λαγνείαν. Comp. Tit. iii. 3. — Ver 7. πάντοτε μανθάνοντα] Bengel adds the adverb: curiose. The incentive of their μανθάνειν was not the search after truth, but mere desire for entertainment, a longing for intellectual pastime (comp. the description of the Athenians, Acts xvii. 21), this longing makes them the prey of teachers who promise new wisdom. Hence it goes on: καὶ μηδέποτε εἰς ἐπίγνωσιν ἀληθείας ἐλθεῖν δυνάμενα] μηδέποτε is ἄπ λεγ.; δυνάμενα is emphatic; they *cannot* attain to the truth, because the necessary conditions do not exist in their inner life. Chrysostom: ἐπειδὴ ἑαυτὰς κατέχωσαν ταῖς ἐπιθυμίαις ἐκείναις καὶ τοῖς ἁμαρτήμασιν, ἐπωρώθη αὐτῶν ἡ διάνοια —Mosheim thinks that the three participial clauses describe the three different classes of the γυναικάρια: (1) sinners, (2) seekers after happiness, (3) devotees; they rather denote various traits in the same persons, and "the very union of such traits is characteristic" (de Wette).—It is no matter of surprise that the heretics, to win more followers, turned their attentions to the fair sex; that has been done by heretics in all ages. It is a charge brought specially against the Gnostics by various writers. Irenaeus, i. 13. 3, says of Marcus the Valentinian Gnostic: μάλιστα περὶ γυναῖκας ἀσχολεῖται; and Epiphanius, *Haer.* xxvi, expressly upbraids the Gnostics with ἐμπαίζειν τοῖς γυναικαρίοις and with ἀπατᾶν τὸ αὐτοῖς πειθόμενον γυναικεῖον

---

[1] The word occurs in Ignatius (*Ep. ad Philadelph* chap. ii.) in the same sense as here πολλοὶ λύκοι ἀξιόπιστοι ἡδονῇ κακῇ αἰχμαλωτίζουσι τοὺς θεοδρόμους.

γένος;[1] see Baur, p. 36. This, however, cannot be taken as a proof of the later composition of the epistle, all the less that many expressions in the descriptions of the Fathers show that they had this description in their thoughts.

Ver. 8. Further description of the heretics: ὃν τρόπον δὲ Ἰαννῆς καὶ Ἰαμβρῆς ἀντέστησαν Μωυσεῖ] Paul here compares the heretics to the Egyptian Magi who are mentioned in Ex. vii. but not named. Origen (*Tract.* 35 *in Matt.*) thinks that the apostle extracted them from a liber secretus which bore the title "Jamnes et Mambres." That is, however, doubtful; Theodoret's supposition is more probable: τὰ μέντοι τούτων ὀνόματα οὐκ ἐκ τῆς θείας γραφῆς μεμάθηκεν ὁ θεῖος ἀπόστολος, ἀλλ' ἐκ τῆς ἀγράφου τῶν Ἰουδαίων διδασκαλίας. The names were a part of Jewish tradition from which they passed into the Talmudic and other Jewish writings; see Targum Jonathan, Ex. vii. 11, xxii. 22. Even the Pythagorean Numenius in the second century mentioned them, as Origen (*Contra Celsum*, iv.) and Eusebius (*Praep. Evangel.* ix. chap. 8) inform us. "According to Jewish tradition, they are said to have been the sons of Balaam, and at first the teachers of Moses, but afterwards his chief opponents, and to have perished at last with the Egyptian army in the Red Sea," see Heydenreich and Wetstein on this passage.—The correlation of ὃν τρόπον . . . οὕτω does not necessarily place emphasis on the similarity of the *manner* of the act, but often only on the similarity of the act itself (comp. Matt. xxiii. 37; Acts vii. 28). Possibly, therefore, the heretics are compared with these sorcerers only because they both withstood the truth (so Plitt).— Possibly, also, it is because the resemblance lay in the heretics preaching the same thing as Timothy, just as the sorcerers did the same thing as Moses, the heretics and the sorcerers having the

---

[1] The passage, quoted by Mack from Jerome (*Ep. ad Ctesiphontem*), is very descriptive: Simon Magus haeresin condidit adjutus auxilio Helenae meretricis; Nicolaus Antiochenus omnium immunditiarum conditor choros duxit foemineos; Marcion quoque Romam praemisit mulierem ad majorem lasciviam; Apelles Philemonem comitem habuit; Montanus Priscam et Maximillam primum auro corrupit, deinde haeresi polluit, Arius ut orbem deciperet, sororem principis ante decepit Donatus Lucillae opibus adjutus est; Elpidium caecum Agape caeca duxit, Prisciliano juncta fuit Galla.

same purpose of striving against the truth (so Hofmann). Still the mention of the sorcerers at all is strange; hence we may suppose that the heretics by some more characteristic trait suggested the resemblance to the apostle's mind, and that this trait was their use of magic arts, to which there is allusion made also in γόητες, ver. 13 (de Wette, Wiesinger, van Oosterzee [1]). The δέ not only marks the transition to a new thought, but also introduces something in contrast to what preceded: what they did they did with an appearance of piety, but in truth they were opposing the truth. — κατεφθαρμένοι τὸν νοῦν] The verb καταφθείρω (ἅπ. λεγ; in 2 Pet. ii. 12 it is the reading of the *Rec.*, but there is more testimony for the simple verb) is synonymous with διαφθείρω, 1 Tim. vi. 5. — ἀδόκιμοι περὶ τὴν πίστιν] Luther's translation: "incapable of believing," is inaccurate; nor is Beza's explanation suitable rejectanei, i e. falsae et adulterinae doctrinae doctores, quos oporteat ab omnibus rejici. Ἀδόκιμος is one who does not stand proof, and in connection with περὶ τὴν πίστιν one who does not stand proof in regard to faith · "not standing proof in respect of faith" (Matthies, de Wette); comp. 1 Tim. i. 19. The description here given of the heretics is the same as in 1 Tim. vi. 5 : διεφθαρμένοι τὸν νοῦν καὶ ἀπεστερημένοι τῆς ἀληθείας.

Ver. 9. A ground of comfort. — ἀλλ' οὐ προκόψουσιν ἐπὶ πλεῖον] This appears to stand in contradiction with ver 13 and ii 16, 17. Bengel remarks: non proficient amplius: non ita, ut alios seducant; quamquam ipsi et eorum similes proficient in pejus ver. 13 Saepe malitia, quum late non potest, profundius proficit This, however, is not a satisfactory explanation, since νομὴν ἕξει, ii. 17, and πλανῶντες, ver. 13, point to the increasing extent of the heresy. Chrysostom, however, says rightly: κἂν πρότερον ἀνθήσῃ τὰ τῆς πλάνης, εἰς τέλος οὐ διαμένει. The contradiction exists only when the apostle's words are wrongly pressed so as to contain a denial of *every* further extension of the heresy. For the present their influence is extending; but later it will come to

---

[1] Van Oosterzee here makes an apposite allusion to Simon Magus, to Elymas, to the itinerating devil-exorcisers among the Jews, and to the magic arts practised from time immemorial at Ephesus, comp. Acts xix. 19.

an end; this does not contradict the apostle's prophecy in vv. 1-5, since Paul does not say that the demoralization of men will be brought about by the heretics of whom he is thinking here. Hofmann sees no apparent contradiction, as he supposes that Paul in the passages mentioned is not speaking of the same people; but in this he is wrong, since both the context and the expression show that those mentioned in ver. 13 are the same as those in vv. 6-9.— The apostle confirms the thought expressed by adding the words · ἡ γὰρ ἄνοια αὐτῶν ἔκδηλος ἔσται πᾶσιν] The ἄνοια (= "want of judgment, senselessness") of the heretics does not refer so much to their doctrines opposed to the truth, as to their conduct described in ver. 6. — ἔκδηλος (ἅπ. λεγ.) . . . ὡς καὶ ἡ ἐκείνων ἐγένετο] "as they were put to shame before Moses," Ex. viii 18 f, ix. 11 (de Wette).

Vv. 10, 11 As a contrast to the heresy, the apostle now describes Timothy's former conduct, for the purpose of inciting him to show a like fidelity still. — σὺ δὲ παρηκολούθησας] The verb denotes neither that he was an actual witness (Chrysostom. τούτων σὺ μάρτυς, so, too, Theophylact, Oecumenius, Erasmus, and others,—this exposition is unsuitable, since these events, ver. 11, in the apostle's life had taken place before Timothy's conversion), nor even that the knowledge was gained through others (Luther · "thou hast come to know"). Παρακολουθεῖν means "follow," either theoretically, as in Luke i. 3 ("of intellectual following after, by which the knowledge of a thing is gained," Meyer on the passage), or practically, as in 1 Tim. iv. 6. Here it can only have the latter meaning. Here, however, as in 1 Tim. iv. 6, it is not equivalent to imitari, follow as a *pattern* (de Wette), for that does not agree with διωγμοῖς (ver. 11), but the apostle's διδασκαλία, ἀγωγή κ.τ λ. are regarded as guides by which Timothy is to steer his course through life (so also van Oosterzee, Hofmann, Otto[1]). Wiesinger explains it: "thou hast let thyself be moved by my διδασκαλία κτλ to *join*

---

[1] Otto "παρακολουθεῖν is to be taken in its most literal sense, not comprobari, amplecti, or even imitari, but *follow after* Timothy of his own accord not only *followed after* his doctrine, but also his sufferings, for that these lay in the path of an apostle was shown clearly enough by events in Antioch, Iconium, and

thyself to me." But this explanation unjustifiably limits the παρακολουθεῖν to "the act by which Timothy first joined himself to the apostle;" further, this notion of joining himself is imported; and finally, it would seem superfluous to enumerate the particular points if they are only to be understood as motives for Timothy's joining himself to the apostle. — The aorist says that Timothy followed the apostle before; there is no indication whether he did so later. This earlier period was, of course, the time when he was the apostle's συνεργός The perfect would have meant that Timothy continued to do so. — μου τῇ διδασκαλίᾳ] comp. 1 Tim. iv. 6 — τῇ ἀγωγῇ] With this and the following words μου is to be supplied. Mack wrongly says that μου is not to be supplied, and that ἀγωγή and the terms following do not refer to Paul, but to Timothy. "thou hast followed my doctrine in behaviour," etc. Apart from the unnatural construction, this view is decidedly opposed by ver. 11, for it is quite untenable to suppose that Timothy in the places named suffered persecution just as Paul did. — ἀγωγή (ἅπ. λεγ.) in classic Greek is both transitive, "the guidance," and intransitive, "mode of life," ratio vivendi The latter meaning (see Esth. ii. 20) should here be retained, the word cannot of itself mean guidance of *the church*, as some interpret it. Luther says well: "my manner." — τῇ προθέσει] cf. Acts xi. 23, "the purpose on which the mode of life is founded." — τῇ πίστει] not "fidelity in office," nor "conscientiousness," but "faith." — τῇ μακροθυμίᾳ κτλ] The difference between μακροθυμία and ὑπομονή is, that the former is applied to one who is not irritated, the latter to one who is not discouraged. — Ver. 11. τοῖς διωγμοῖς, τοῖς παθήμασιν] The transition to these is formed by ὑπομονή. The idea of διωγμοῖς is expanded by adding παθήμασιν. The apostle is thinking specially of his persecutions, and his reason is that Timothy shrank to a certain extent from suffering; comp. i. 6–8. — οἷά μοι ἐγένοντο (ἐγένετο)] οἷα is distinguished from the relative ἅ, inasmuch as it points to the nature of the

---

Lystra. Hence, however, he is not to be surprised if he finds on his way the very thing he had willingly followed after."—Hofmann explains it : "Timothy as scholar followed that in which Paul had preceded him as teacher, so that Christianity taught him what Christianity was."

παθήματα; ἅ would have limited παθήμασιν to what the apostle had to endure in Antioch, etc.; but οἷα indicates that he means by παθήμασιν all sufferings of the same nature as those endured in Antioch, etc. This is the case also with οἵους farther on. The sufferings endured in Antioch, etc., are mentioned because they took place at the time when Timothy was adopted by Paul as his colleague.—In the next words: οἵους διωγμοὺς ὑπήνεγκα, the verb is emphatic; it was important, when directing Timothy to the example given him, to remind him that the persecutions had been borne undauntedly—and then that the Lord had granted rescue from them all; hence he continues: καὶ ἐκ πάντων με ἐρύσατο ὁ κύριος. Erasmus, Flatt, Mack, Heydenreich unnecessarily take the sentence: οἵους . . . ὑπήνεγκα, as a touching appeal; Hofmann, both this sentence and the preceding one. οἷά μοι ἐγένετο κ.τ λ. This would only be an unsuitable interruption of the quiet train of thought.[1] — ὑποφέρειν denotes persevering, stedfast endurance, 1 Cor. x. 13, 1 Pet ii. 17. — καὶ ἐκ πάντων με κ.τ.λ.] Chrysostom· ἀμφότερα παρακλήσεως, ὅτι καὶ ἐγὼ προθυμίαν παρειχόμην γενναίαν, καὶ οὐκ ἐγκατελείφθην He mentions his sufferings, and his rescue from them, that he may encourage Timothy to be ready to suffer for Christ's sake. It is to be observed that με ἐρύσατο refers not only to rescue from bodily danger, but also to rescue from the danger of being unfaithful to his calling, so that out of his sufferings he had issued without hurt to body *or soul;* comp. iv. 17.

Ver. 12. The principle here laid down is intended, like the mention of Timothy's conduct in ver 11, to incite Timothy to willing endurance of suffering — καὶ πάντες δέ] καὶ . . . δέ, see 1 Tim. iii. 10. — οἱ θέλοντες] is here emphatic: "they whose thoughts are thus directed." — ζῆν εὐσεβῶς] the adverb

---

[1] Hofmann maintains that if the sentences beginning with οἷα and οἵους were to be relative sentences, the apostle would have written τοῖς διωγμοῖς, οἵους ὑπήνιγκα, τοῖς παθήμασιν, οἷά μοι ἐγίνετο; but this would make too wide a separation between the cognate ideas διωγμοῖς and παθήμασιν, and the second sentence οἷα κ.τ.λ, would be only a weak appendage. — The objection, that the relative sentence with διωγμοῖς is quite superfluous, is quite removed if the emphasis be placed on ὑπήνιγκα Nor can it be said that "διωγμούς is unskilfully introduced," since this introduction was necessary, if the apostle wished to express his thought in a relative clause.

εὐσεβῶς only here and in Tit. ii. 12. — ἐν Χριστῷ 'Ιησοῦ] denotes the pious life as Christian in its nature; but it is to be observed that, according to the apostolic view, true εὐσέβεια is possible only in communion with Christ. Bengel: extra Jesum Christum nulla pietas Hofmann unsuitably remarks that the emphasis should not be on ἐν Χρ. 'Ιησ., but on εὐσεβῶς, for ζῆν εὐσεβῶς ἐν Χρ. 'Ιησ. forms only *one* idea: that of the Christian life of piety. — διωχθήσονται] expresses the certainty: Christian piety cannot continue without persecution, because the world is hostile to the kingdom of God; comp. John xv. 19, 20; Matt. x. 22, 38, and other passages. Wiesinger rightly remarks: "Not to comfort himself does the apostle say this, but to show that his experience was a universal one, as something necessarily bound up with εὐσεβῶς ζῆν," and, it should be added, to give encouragement to Timothy.

Ver. 13. Matthies (with whom Wiesinger agrees) thus states the connection between this and the preceding verses: " Quite different is it with evil men, who, instead of suffering for the truth, proceed always farther in their wickedness;" but there is no real opposition in the two thoughts thus opposed.[1] The apostle here continues the description of the heretics which was interrupted at ver. 10, in contrast with οἱ θέλοντες εὐσεβῶς ζῆν, he calls them πονηροὶ ἄνθρωποι καὶ γόητες, and says of them, προκόπτειν ἐπὶ τὸ χεῖρον, which is all the more suitable that it was the very reason why persecution was threatening the honest disciples of Christ, and with them Timothy — πονηροὶ δὲ ἄνθρωποι] As the article is wanting, the thought is quite general, but καὶ γόητες clearly shows that the heretics mentioned above are specially meant (in opposition to Hofmann). Paul gives this name to the heretics, with reference to ver. 8, where he compared them to the Egyptian *sorcerers*. The word γόης is ἅπ. λεγ (γοητεία, 2 Macc. xii. 24); it is equivalent to μάγος, Acts xiii. 6, 8 (comp., too, Acts viii. 9, 11). Hofmann generalizes the idea to that of a *traitor;* but this is all the more arbitrary, that the expression is undoubtedly an allusion to ver. 8. — προκόψουσιν

---

[1] Wiesinger argues, on the other hand, that "suffering for the sake of holiness, and advance in wickedness with outward success," do form a contrast, but the idea "with outward success" is entirely imported.

ἐπὶ τὸ χεῖρον] denotes a greater degree of wickedness, while ver. 9 refers to the increase in the extent of its influence — How this increase of wickedness comes to pass, is told by the words πλανῶντες καὶ πλανώμενοι. Bengel and Heydenreich make πλανῶντες and γόητες, πλανώμενοι and πονηροί parallel to each other; for this, however, there is no ground. Even the meaning of πλανώμενοι is against the parallel, for it is neither transitive : "leading astray" (Matthies), nor middle : qui se seducendos permittunt (Bengel), nor even intransitive · "going astray" (Hofmann), it is purely passive : "being led astray" (Luther), or otherwise it would have been put first. He who leads others astray is himself led astray.

Ver. 14. To the good testimony given to] Timothy by Paul in ver. 10, there is added the exhortation to stand stedfast in the truth. — σὺ δέ] said in opposition to the heretics. — μένε ἐν οἷς ἔμαθες] μένε, see 1 Tim. ii. 15 ; John viii 31. — ἐν οἷς is equivalent to ἐν τούτοις, ἅ. —"Εμαθες] comp. ii. 2. — καί] (sc. ἅ ; not ἐν οἷς, as Heydenreich suggests) ἐπιστώθης] not = quae tibi concredita sunt (Beza, Luther. "and is entrusted to thee "); for πιστόω does not mean " entrust to," but confirmare. It is rightly interpreted by the Greek expositors, with whom also de Wette and Wiesinger agree ; Theophylact: μετὰ πληροφορίας ἔμαθες , properly, "of which thou hast been assured," i e. of which thou hast been convinced for certain ,[1] it serves to give "more force to ἔμαθες " (Wiesinger), by declaring that Timothy was also convinced of the truth of what he learnt (so, too, van Oosterzee, Plitt, Hofmann). — To strengthen the exhortation, Paul reminds Timothy of those from whom he learnt the truths of the gospel : εἰδὼς παρὰ τίνων ἔμαθες] εἰδώς, see ii. 23. — παρὰ τίνων] With the usual reading παρὰ τίνος, which Hofmann prefers, τίνος is not, as some think, Christ, but the apostle as teacher ; but still it would be strange for Paul not to name himself directly and without periphrasis, as he usually does when speaking of himself ; comp. ii. 2. If τίνων be the correct reading, then

---

[1] In classic Greek πιστόω occurs specially in connection with ὅρκῳ; thus Thucydides, iv. 88 : καὶ πιστώσαντες αὐτὸν τοῖς ὅρκοις, i.e. "after they had made sure of him by oath "="after they had made him swear." Comp. also Hom. Od. l. 21. 218 : also 2 Macc. vii. 24, xii. 25.

these teachers cannot be the πολλοὶ μάρτυρες mentioned in ii. 2 (Matthies), nor Paul and Barnabas (according to Acts xvi. 1 comp with xiv. 6 ff., Grotius); but only, as is shown by ἀπὸ βρέφους following, the grandmother and mother of Timothy, whose faith the apostle expressly mentions, i. 5 (so, too, van Oosterzee and Plitt). — Timothy had already been instructed in the truth of the gospel before Paul met with him, nay, even before this instruction he had been carefully made acquainted with the holy Scriptures. This very fact, that from childhood he had been under the influence of divine truth and been nourished by the bread of life, was to be an incentive to him to adhere faithfully to this word of truth.

Ver. 15. Καὶ ὅτι] Most expositors, including Wiesinger, Plitt, and Hofmann (*Schriftbew* I. pp. 675 f., and so also in his commentary), assume that εἰδώς and ὅτι . . . οἶδας are co-ordinate sentences giving the reason why. In justification of this irregular construction, Bengel directs us to John ii. 24, 25; Acts xxii. 29; but wrongly.[1] — Beza, on the other hand, gives the right construction by making καὶ ὅτι dependent on εἰδώς. sciens a quo didiceris, teque a puero sacras literas novisse. This, too, de Wette (van Oosterzee agreeing with him) adopts, correctly remarking that εἰδώς usually denotes not only knowledge, but also reflection. — ἀπὸ βρέφους τὰ ἱερὰ γράμματα οἶδας] ἀπὸ βρέφους, Mark ix. 21: παιδιόθεν. Chrysostom: ἐκ πρώτης ἡλικίας; comp. *Antip. Th* 32: ἐκ βρέφεος ᾿Απὸ βρέφους stands first because it is emphatic; it points back to παρὰ τίνων ἔμαθες. In order that he may continue in what he has learned, Timothy is to remember his teacher, and also that he has known the holy Scriptures from childhood. — τὰ ἱερὰ γράμματα] This name for the O. T. only occurs here; in John vii. 15 without ἱερά; the more usual name is αἱ γραφαί, with and without ἅγιαι. De Wette's conjecture is quite arbitrary, that the author of the epistle was also thinking here

[1] Hofmann, in regarding the appeal to Acts xxii. 29 as appropriate, overlooks the difference of construction in the two passages. In Acts xxii. 29, two sentences beginning with ὅτι are dependent on ἐπιγνούς, whereas here the first independent sentence would be expressed by a participle (εἰδώς instead of ὅτι οἶδας), to which a sentence beginning with ὅτι is made co-ordinate. This irregularity of construction is manifestly not removed by Hofmann's remark, that the first sentence gives an additional fact, the second furnishes a reason

of some writings of the N T. — τὰ δυνάμενά σε σοφίσαι εἰς σωτηρίαν] τὰ δυνάμενα is present and not preterite ("quae poterant," Bengel); it tells us of a permanent characteristic of the O. T. (de Wette, Wiesinger). Σοφίζειν is equivalent to sapientem reddere; to explain the word as synonymous with διδάσκειν is inaccurate. When joined with εἰς σωτηρίαν it is usually taken in the sense: "teach the way to holiness;" but, as Paul adds διὰ πίστεως κ.τ.λ, which cannot be joined immediately with σωτηρίαν (= τὴν διὰ σωτηρ.), but belongs to σοφίσαι, that interpretation is here unsuitable; he who has faith is already on the way to σωτηρία, or rather is in possession of the σωτηρία. We must therefore adhere to the full signification of σωφίζειν; so that he is speaking here not of the first instruction in salvation, but of the ever deepening knowledge of it, how that furthers the σωτηρία (so, too, Wiesinger, van Oosterzee, Plitt) — διὰ πίστεως τῆς ἐν Χρ. Ἰησοῦ] comp. 1 Tim iii. 13. Wiesinger rightly remarks that these words are not to be taken as giving the means immanent in the Scriptures, but "contain the necessary condition attached to the use of the O. T." (de Wette). Hofmann asserts that σοφ. εἰς σωτηρίαν only denotes an instruction, "giving complete acquaintance with salvation;" for "in order that Timothy might *remain* in what he had learnt, it was only necessary for the Scripture to teach what he knew" But what any one already knows does not require still to be taught to him; and instruction leading on to knowledge ever more complete, does not hinder him from abiding in what he has already learnt. According to Hofmann, διὰ πίστεως is to be joined with σωτηρίαν, because—as he strangely enough asserts—"instruction by means of faith is a chimera" (!).

Ver. 16. Reason given for the last thought — πᾶσα γραφὴ θεόπνευστος καὶ ὠφέλιμος πρὸς κ τ.λ.] πᾶσα γραφή, not: "the whole of Scripture" (Beza: tota scriptura, i e. Canon Hebraeorum), but "every Scripture;" or, still better, "all Scripture." — θεόπνευστος] ἅπ λεγ.; the explanation of this word, which also in classic Greek is applied to seers and poets, is specially aided by the passage in 2 Pet i. 21: ὑπὸ πνεύματος ἁγίου φερόμενοι ἐλάλησαν οἱ ἅγιοι Θεοῦ ἄνθρωποι. — In various old versions (Syr. Vulg.; so also in Clement, Origen, Tertullian, etc.) καί is wanting; and Luther did not express it in his translation; in that case θεόπν. is clearly an attribute belonging to the subject; Luther: "all Scripture inspired by God is." With the correct reading, however, θεόπν. may be a predicate; so Bengel: est haec pars non subjecti (quam enim scripturam dicat Paulus, per se patet), sed praedicati, so, too, Matthies, de Wette, Wiesinger, van Oosterzee, and others. Other expositors, again, such as Grotius, Rosenmüller, Heinrichs, Plitt, Hofmann, take θεόπνευστος as an attribute of the subject, even with this reading, and explain καί as " also." This construction is the right one. On the one hand, it is ungrammatical to explain πᾶσα γραφή by "the whole of Scripture." Wiesinger argues against this by appealing to Eph. ii. 21 and to Heb. iii. 3, see Meyer on the one passage and Delitzsch on the other, where, too, Lunemann translates: "every house."[1] Wiesinger argues also that γραφή is regarded as a proper name, which he tries to prove by 2 Pet. i. 20 and John vii. 15; but, though a substantive is used once without an article, it does not follow that it has the signification of a proper name (on John vii. 15, comp. Meyer). On the other hand, this sentence does not properly give a reason for the preceding thought (Wiesinger), but rather confirms it, and hence there was no reason for directing attention to the fact that the *whole* of Scripture is θεόπνευστος. There was no doubt on that point (viz. that the *whole* of Scripture and not a part of it was inspired by God), but on the point whether the Scriptures as θεόπνευστοι are *also* (καί serves to confirm) ὠφέλιμοι. There is no ground for asserting that, with this view, there could not have been an ellipse of ἐστιν (Wiesinger). — πρὸς διδασκαλίαν κ.τ.λ.] Heydenreich thinks that the apostle is not speaking here of the profitableness of Scripture in general and for all Christians, but of its utility to teachers of religion. So also Hofmann: "The sentence does not say of what service Holy Scripture is to him who reads it, but what use can be made of it by him who teaches." This view, however, is wrong; neither in ver. 14 nor ver. 15 is there anything said regarding Timothy's work in teaching; the apostle does

---

[1] Not less inappropriate is van Oosterzee's appeal to Eph iii. 15 (comp. Meyer on the passage, and Winer, pp. 105 f. [E. T. pp. 137 f.]) and to 1 Pet. i. 15.

not pass on to this point till the next chapter, ver. 17 notwithstanding. — πρὸς διδασκ.; Holy Scripture is profitable for teaching by advancing us in knowledge; πρὸς ἔλεγχον (or ἐλεγμόν), by convincing us of sin and rebuking us on account of sin. Theodoret: ἐλέγχει γὰρ ἡμῶν τὸν παράνομον βίον. Chrysostom understands it only of the conviction of error; so, too, Bengel: convincit etiam in errore et praejudicio versantes; Heydenreich, too, refers it, like διδασκαλία, only to what is theoretical. Ἐλέγχειν certainly does occur in this sense, Tit. i. 9, 13, but it is more frequently used of what is practical, 1 Tim. v. 20; Tit. ii. 15. — πρὸς ἐπανόρθωσιν] by working amendment in us. Theodoret: παρακαλεῖ καὶ τοὺς παρατραπέντας ἐπανελθεῖν εἰς τὴν εὐθεῖαν ὁδόν; — ἐπανορθ. (ἅπ. λεγ) is synonymous with νουθεσία, 1 Cor. x. 11. — πρὸς παιδείαν τὴν ἐν δικαιοσύνῃ] by advancing us in the further development of the Christian life. Luther is not wrong in translating παιδεία by "correction," inasmuch as in N. T. usage it is applied to the education which not only developes the existing good, but also counteracts existing evil. δικαιοσύνη: "the Christian life of piety."— Theodoret: ἐκπαιδεύει ἡμᾶς τὰ εἴδη τῆς ἀρετῆς. — There is an obvious climax in the series of these thoughts.

Ver. 17. Ἵνα declares the purpose which Scripture is to serve. — ἄρτιος ᾖ ὁ τοῦ Θεοῦ ἄνθρωπος] ἄρτιος (literally, "adapted") is a ἅπ. λεγ., equivalent to τέλειος, Col. i 28, "perfect;" according to Hofmann: "in suitable condition," which, however, agrees with the notion of perfection. — ὁ τοῦ Θεοῦ ἄνθρωπος] is mostly understood by expositors to denote those entrusted with the office of evangelist, and is referred specially to Timothy. The latter point is clearly wrong, since ver. 16 is general in sense; the apostle speaks here not of Timothy only, but of every one who is an ἄνθρ. τ. Θεοῦ. Even although Timothy is so named in 1 Tim. vi. 11 with reference to his office, it does not follow that here, where the thought is quite general, it is a name for the office; every believing Christian by his relation to God (van Oosterzee: "he who by the Holy Spirit is born of God and is related to God") may receive the same name. — πρὸς πᾶν ἔργον ἀγαθὸν ἐξηρτισμένος] a more precise definition of ἄρτιος. — πᾶν ἔργ.

ἀγ is also, for the most part, understood to have an official reference. Bengel: genera talium operum enumerantur ver. 16; nam homo Dei debet docere, convincere, corrigere, instituere iv. 2. But this is wrong; it is rather to be taken quite generally (Wiesinger, van Oosterzee; de Wette differs). Ver. 16 does not tell for what purpose Scripture may be used with others, but what is its influence on one who occupies himself with it; and though iv. 2 does deal with Timothy's official work, that does not prove that πᾶν ἔργ. ἀγ. is only to be limited to this special thought. — ἐξηρτισμένος] *equipped*, Luther: "skilled." — The same word occurs in Acts xxi. 5, but in another connection (see Meyer on the passage); corresponding to it we find κατηρτισμένος in Luke vi. 40 and other passages.

CHAPTER IV.

VER. 1. διαμαρτύρομαι] The words οὖν ἐγώ following this in the *Rec.* were omitted from the text by Griesb., on the authority of A C D* E F G L ℵ 17, *al.*, Syr. Erp. Copt. etc. — The same is the case with the words τοῦ κυρίου, against which there is the testimony of A C D* F G ℵ 31, 37, *al.* — For κρίνειν the aorist κρῖναι is found in F G, several cursives, Theodoret, and Theoph.; this construction does occur sometimes in the N. T. (also in classic Greek), but there is not sufficient authority for it here. — κατὰ τὴν ἐπιφάνειαν] For κατά (*Rec.* after D*** E K L, etc), καί is the reading of A C D* F G ℵ 17, *al.*, Copt. Vulg. ms. It. Harl. etc. This reading, as it implies a change of construction in the verb, and even then makes the connection difficult, is of a kind which would easily give occasion for correction; the easiest correction was into κατά. Chrysostom in his commentary reads· ἐν τῇ ἐπιφανείᾳ Lachm Buttm. Tisch rightly adopted καί, which is approved also by Matthies, de Wette, Wiesinger, and van Oosterzee. Reiche, on the other hand, because of the difficulty of the reading καί, regards the *Rec.* as the original reading, while he connects κατά with μέλλοντας κρίνειν as a preposition of time. — Ver. 2. Tisch. 7 reads ἐπιτίμησον, παρακάλεσον, with the majority of the authorities; whereas Tisch. 8 reads παρακάλεσον, ἐπιτίμησον The placing of ἐπιτίμησον first may be a correction, because this word is related in meaning to the previous ἔλεγξον. — Ver 3. τὰς ἰδίας ἐπιθυμίας] adopted by Griesb. in place of τὰς ἐπιθυμίας τὰς ἰδίας, on the authority of A C D E F G ℵ 3, 37, *al.*, Arm. Vulg etc. — Ver. 6. Instead of τῆς ἐμῆς ἀναλύσεως, which is the *Rec.* supported by D E K L, *al.* (Tisch. 7), it is more correct, with Lachm. Buttm. and Tisch. 8, to read τῆς ἀναλύσεώς μου, on the authority of A C F G ℵ, *al.* — Ver 7. For τὸν ἀγῶνα τὸν καλόν (Tisch. 7), Lachm. Buttm. Tisch. 8, on the authority of A C F G ℵ, *al.*, adopted τὸν καλὸν ἀγῶνα, which is certainly in harmony with the usage of the Pastoral Epistles, but for that very reason may be a correction. — Ver. 10. For the *Rec.* ἐγκατέλιπεν (D* K ℵ, etc.), Tisch. 7 adopted the imperfect ἐγκατέλειπεν, on the authority of A C D** and *** E F G L, etc.; Tisch. 8 retained the *Rec*, which is supported by D* K ℵ, etc.

— In C ℵ, several cursives, and Fathers, Γαλίαν is found instead of the *Rec.* Γαλατίαν; Epiph. *Haer.* 57, dis. says : οὐ γὰρ ἐν Γαλατίᾳ, ὡς τίνες πλανηθέντες νομίζουσιν, ἀλλὰ ἐν τῇ Γαλίᾳ; of this reading Reiche says : est utique notatu digna ; . . . me cum Bengelio in hanc lectionem inclinare sentio. But the MSS. almost all support the *Rec.*; and it cannot be inferred from the name Κρήσκης (Crescens) that this man was sent more probably to Gaul, where Latin was in use, than to Galatia, where Greek was spoken (Reiche); it is too rash, therefore, to regard this as the original reading. Tisch 8, however, adopted it, whereas Tisch. 7 does not even mention it; Hofmann thinks it the correct reading. — Ver. 11. For ἄγε, Lachm. Buttm. and Tisch. 7 read the form ἄγαγε, which, however, does not seem to have sufficient testimony in A 31, 58, etc.; Tisch. 8 retained the *Rec.*, with the support of almost all authorities. — Ver 13 For φελόνην are found also the forms φαιλώνην, φαιλόνην, φελώνην ; but φελόνην is best supported While Tisch. 7 adopted the imperfect ἀπέλειπον, on the authority of A C F G, etc., Tisch. 8 read the aorist ἀπέλιπον (*Rec.*), on the authority of D E K ℵ, *al* ; so, too, Lachm. and Buttm. — Ver 14. ἀποδώσει] This is rightly read by Scholz, Lachm Buttm Tisch 8, on the authority of A C D* gr E F G ℵ 6, 17, *al.*, Copt. Arm. etc , Chrys. Theodoret, instead of ἀποδώῃ, which has the support of D*** E** K L, etc , Tisch. 7, Reiche — Ver 15 ἀνθέστηκε] Lachm. Buttm. Tisch. 8 rightly read ἀντέστη, on the authority of A C D* F G ℵ, *al.;* Tisch. 7 read ἀνθέστηκεν, on the authority of D*** E K L, etc. — Ver. 16 συμπαρεγένετο] Following A C F G ℵ 17, *al* , Lachm. Buttm. Tisch 8 adopted the simple παρεγένετο ; — no doubt the compound συμπαραγ. (Tisch. 7) occurs seldom in the N T., being found elsewhere only in Luke xxiii. 48; but it seems nevertheless to be a correction made on account of μοι. Here, too, the readings vary between the imperfect ἐγκατέλειπον (*Rec.*) and the aorist ἐγκατέλιπον , Tisch. 7 has the former, Tisch. 8 the latter , comp vv. 10 and 13. — Ver 17. Instead of the singular ἀκούσῃ, Lachm. Buttm. and Tisch. rightly read the plural ἀκούσωσι, supported by A C D E F G ℵ 17, 39, *al* — Ver 18 Καί at the beginning of the verse was rightly omitted by Lachm. Buttm. and Tisch , on the authority of A C D* ℵ 31, *al.*, versions, Fathers , it was inserted to connect this verse with the preceding one. — Ver. 20. Μιλήτῳ] For this A has Μηλωτῷ, and Arab. Μελίτῃ. — Ver. 22. For the *Rec.* ὁ κύριος Ἰησοῦς Χριστός (C D E K L), Lachm. and Buttm have ὁ κύριος Ἰησοῦς (A 31), Tisch. only ὁ κύριος (F G 17, etc.). Lachmann's reading should perhaps have the preference, as it is the one most open to correction. — ἀμήν was omitted by Griesb. as a later addition.

Vv. 1, 2 Exhortation to faithful performance of official duty, enforced by the introductory formula: διαμαρτύρομαι ἐνώπιον τοῦ Θεοῦ κ.τ.λ.] comp. ii. 14; 1 Tim. v. 21. — τοῦ μέλλοντος κρίνειν ζ. κ. νεκρ.] Theophylact rightly expounds it: ζῶντας καὶ νεκροὺς λέγει τοὺς ἤδη ἀπελθόντας, καὶ τοὺς τότε καταλειφθησομένους ζῶντας; comp. 1 Thess. iv. 16, 17; 1 Cor. xv 51, 52. Christ is called judge of the dead and the living, also in Acts x. 42; 1 Pet. iv. 5; it is quite wrong to suppose that the *spiritually* dead and living are meant. The allusion to the last judgment gives special strength to the exhortation. — καὶ τὴν ἐπιφάνειαν αὐτοῦ] Most expositors adopt κατά, the usual reading, as the correct one, and then take it as a preposition of time (Matt. xxvii. 15; Acts xiii. 27; Heb. iii. 8), belonging to κρίνειν. With the correct reading, τὴν ἐπιφ κ.τ.λ. depends on διαμαρτύρομαι as the accusative of the oath (so, too, van Oosterzee and Plitt). It is, however, to be noted that in the N. T. διαμαρτύρεσθαι does not mean "swear" by itself, but only in connection with ἐνώπιον τοῦ Θεοῦ (only in the Pastoral Epistles), and therefore only in this connection does it, like other verbs of swearing, govern the accusative, as Hofmann rightly remarks. Hence it follows that καί does not connect ἐπιφάνειαν with the previous ἐνώπιον, but belongs to the following καί. "both . . . and" (Hofmann). De Wette, appealing to Deut. iv. 26, incorrectly expounds it: "I call his appearance, etc., to witness;" present things may be summoned as witnesses, but not future events like the ἐπιφάνεια of Christ. — The Vulg. has: per adventum, without καί: probably a translation of κατά, which is taken as κατά with the genitive, Matt. xxvi. 63. —ἐπιφάνεια, see 1 Tim. vi. 14. — καὶ τὴν βασιλείαν αὐτοῦ] Several expositors join the two expressions as an hendiadys (Bengel: ἐπιφάνεια est revelatio et exhortus regni) = τὴν ἐπιφ. τῆς βασιλείας αὐτοῦ; but the αὐτοῦ with ἐπιφ. is against this. The two things are considered separately (Wiesinger: "the repetition of αὐτοῦ is rhetorical; each element is intended to be taken independently, and considered in its full significance"); the βασιλεία αὐτοῦ is the regnum gloriae which begins with the return of Christ. — The reason for adding these words lies in the κρίνειν ζ. κ. ν.; Paul says he has Christ's second coming and kingdom in his thoughts, that he may give greater importance to his exhortation. — Ver. 2. κήρυξον τὸν λόγον] In 1 Tim. v. 21, διαμ. is followed by ἵνα with the conjunctive, but here we have the simple imperative, which makes the appeal all the more urgent (Wiesinger) — τὸν λόγον, sc. τοῦ Θεοῦ] This more precise definition is wanting here, because the emphasis lies chiefly on the verb, Paul indicating to Timothy the work to be done. — ἐπίστηθι εὐκαίρως ἀκαίρως] Most expositors join these words closely with κήρυξον in sense. Heydenreich: ἐπίστηθι, sc. τῷ κηρύσσειν. Theodoret: οὐχ ἁπλῶς καὶ ὡς ἔτυχεν αὐτὸν κηρύττειν παρεγγυᾷ, ἀλλὰ πάντα καιρὸν ἐπιτήδειον πρὸς τοῦτο νομίζειν. Vulg.: "insta;" Luther: "persist," so also van Oosterzee, similarly Wiesinger, who, in harmony with ἐπίμενε αὐτοῖς, 1 Tim. iv. 16, expounds it: "keep one's attention or activity directed to a thing." But this is not the usual meaning of the verb; it means rather "*step towards* or *draw near*" (Hofmann is less precise: "approach, appear"), comp. Luke ii. 8, 38, and other passages. The word is defined more precisely by κήρυξον τὸν λόγον: draw near with the preaching of the word. Who are the persons to whom Timothy is to draw near, may easily be supplied from the context, viz to those to whom he has to preach the word. It is incorrect to think only of the whole church (Bretschneider: accede ad coetus christianos, so also de Wette), or only of the individual members (so before in this commentary). Plitt is correct: "draw near (to men), viz. with the word." — εὐκαίρως ἀκαίρως [1]] Chrysostom: μὴ καιρὸν ἔχε ὡρισμένον, ἀεὶ σοὶ καιρὸς ἔστω. The further definition given by Chrysostom: κἂν ἐν τοῖς κινδύνοις, κἂν ἐν δεσμωτηρίῳ ᾖς κ.τ.λ., or by Theodoret: καὶ ἐν δεσμωτηρίῳ, καὶ πλοίῳ καὶ παρακειμένης τραπέζης, and others similar by other expositors, are wrong, since we ought to think here not so much of the circumstances in which Timothy (or more generally the preacher of the word) may be, but of the circumstances of the hearers: "whether the time seems to thee seasonable or unseasonable for it" (de Wette,

---

[1] Similar collocations without any particle of union or separation are not found in the N. T., but occur in Greek and Latin classics; see Bengel on this passage. Nicetas Choniates. παιδαγωγῷ ἐμβριθεῖ ἔοικὼς, εὐκαίρως ἀκαίρως ἐπίπληττιν. Julian: ἐπορεύετο ἐπὶ τὰς τῶν φίλων οἰκίας ἄκλητος κεκλημένος. Virgil· digna indigna pati.

Wiesinger, van Oosterzee). Hofmann is wrong: "whether he comes seasonably or not to those whom he approaches with the word;" for there was no need to tell Timothy that the preacher was not bound to inquire into his hearers' opinion and act accordingly. For the truth, the occasion is always seasonable. He who desires to wait until the occasion seem completely favourable for his work, will never find it. This is particularly true of the exercise of the evangelic office. — Note, finally, Beza's remark: nempe quod ad carnis prudentiam pertinet; nam alioqui requiritur sanctae prudentiae spiritus, captans occasiones ad aedificationem opportunas. — ἔλεγξον] should be restricted neither to heresies nor to moral transgressions, it includes blame of everything blameworthy. — ἐπιτίμησον] stronger than ἔλεγξον: "blame with decided manifestation of dislike;" often in the Gospels, also in Jude 9. — παρακάλεσον] Blame and exhortation should be joined in order to cause edification; blame by itself embitters, exhortation by itself is ineffectual. — ἐν πάσῃ μακροθυμίᾳ καὶ διδαχῇ] An appendix to παρακάλεσον, or, according to the reading of Tisch. 8, to ἐπιτίμησον, with which, however, it seems less appropriate. On μακροθυμία, comp. iii. 10. — διδαχῇ] The exhortation is to be of a kind that will instruct; the purpose, as Heydenreich aptly remarks, is not to produce momentary emotion and violent tumult of feeling Διδαχή is instruction, and is not equivalent to studium alios vera docendi. It is wrong, too, to make it an hendiadys, as if it were ἐν πάσῃ διδαχῆς μακροθυμίᾳ — Note the connection of this verse with iii 16. The preacher of the divine word has not to perform the work of teaching, of reproving, etc., without placing himself under the teaching, the reproof, etc, of the divine word.

Vv. 3, 4. Ground of the previous exhortation, ἔσται γὰρ καιρὸς, ὅτε] see ii. 16, 17, iii. 1 ff. — The ἔσται shows that he is speaking not of the present (Heinrichs), but of the future; comp. iii. 1; 1 Tim. iv. 1. — τῆς ὑγιαινούσης διδασκαλίας] see 1 Tim. i. 10. — οὐκ ἀνέξονται] comp. Acts xviii. 14; 2 Cor. xi. 4. De Wette: "find intolerable, because not consistent with their desires." — ἀλλὰ κατὰ τὰς ἰδίας ἐπιθυμίας] "according to wilful, selfish lusts;" the accent is on ἰδίας—a contrast to obedience under the divine will. —

ἑαυτοῖς ἐπισωρεύσουσι διδασκάλους] ἐπισωρεύειν (ἅπ λεγ, the simple form in iii. 6), "heap up, procure in abundance." Heydenreich's conjecture is groundless, that the word here has the suggestion of: they will set him up *for a burden* to themselves (Luther: "burden themselves") for their own hurt; on the other hand, Chrysostom is right: τὸ ἀδιάκριτον πλῆθος διὰ τοῦ· ἐπισωρεύσουσι, ἐδήλωσε. We cannot but see that the word here is meant to indicate the contemptible part of their conduct. The ἐπι does not compel us to follow Hofmann in his exposition: "in addition to those who represent sound doctrine;" what follows rather shows that they turn away from all such — The reason is given in the words: κνηθόμενοι τὴν ἀκοήν. Κνήθω (ἅπ. λεγ.), tickle, cause to itch; κνηθόμενοι τὴν ἀκοήν, "be tickled in the ear," i.e. feel a tickling in the ear (τὴν ἀκοήν being the accusative of more precise definition). This tickling is usually taken to mean a pleasant sensation,[1] so Hesychius: ζητοῦντες τὶ ἀκοῦσαι καθ᾽ ἡδονήν, and almost all expositors. But this view, before adopted in this commentary, is opposed by the fact that ζητοῦντες is purely imported. The present participle cannot mean: "that they *wish* to feel a tickling in the ear, but only that they do feel it." Hofmann is therefore right in explaining this tickling of the ear to mean the desire of hearing something different from what they had heard before, "because they feel a tickling in the ear, they procure for themselves teachers after their own lusts." — Ver. 4. καὶ ἀπὸ μὲν τῆς ἀλ. κ τ.λ.] τῆς ἀληθείας = τῆς ὑγ. διδασκαλίας — ἐπὶ δὲ τοὺς μύθους] see 1 Tim. i. 4. — ἐκτραπήσονται] see 1 Tim. i. 6.

Ver. 5. A general exhortation summing up the particulars already mentioned. — σὺ δέ] see iii. 10. — νῆφε ἐν πᾶσι] νήφειν, synonymous with γρηγορεῖν, 1 Thess. v. 6, and σωφρονεῖν, 1 Pet. iv. 7, opposite of "be intoxicated;" it denotes the clear prudence in thought and action which it is all the more necessary for Timothy to show, because there is impending what the apostle in vv. 3, 4 has described. — ἐν πᾶσι] "in all parts." — κακοπάθησον] see i. 8, ii. 3. — ἔργον ποίησον εὐαγγελιστοῦ] According to Eph. iv. 11, there were special

---

[1] Plutarch (*De Superst.* p. 167): μουσικὴν ἀνθρώποις οὐ τρυφῆς ἕνεκα καὶ κνήσεως ὤτων δοθῆναι.

evangelists, who were distinct both from the apostles and from the pastors and teachers. Theodoret characterizes them in the well-known words: περιιόντες ἐκήρυττον. They did not belong to a particular church like the ποιμένες, but travelled about like the apostles, preaching the Gospel to the Jews or heathen. They could lay no claim to authority in their office, since, as Otto rightly remarks (comp. too, Hofmann, *Schriftbew.* II. 2, pp. 272 f.), they laboured not in consequence of an office committed to them, but by means of a χάρισμα imparted to them, as did also the προφῆται. It is incorrect to identify them with the assistant apostles. Philip was an evangelist (Acts xxi. 8), but not an assistant apostle. Timothy, Titus, and others were assistant apostles, and as *such*, evangelists only in the same sense in which the apostles themselves were evangelists; standing in closer relation to the apostles, they were their συνέργοι in all official duties, and all they did belonged to their διακονία (so, too, Plitt).[1] As the εὐαγγελίζεσθαι was Timothy's chief vocation (as with the Apostle Paul, 1 Cor. i. 17), the apostle exhorts him: ἔργον ποίησον εὐαγγελιστοῦ, adding the further exhortation: τὴν διακονίαν σου πληροφόρησον. This latter is not to be taken as a mere repetition of the preceding one, or as "only laying emphasis on the same thought by the use of πληροφόρησον" (Wiesinger), since, as the whole of the first epistle testifies, his διακονία included more than the εὐαγγελίζεσθαι (which Hofmann wrongly denies[2]). — πληροφορεῖν] synonymous here with πληροῦν, which is even the reading of

---

[1] Wiesinger is wrong in thinking that Timothy's office was only that of an evangelist, and therefore quite the same as Philip had, and that his labours beyond that in Ephesus did not belong to his διακονία. It is certain that his labours were done on the special commission of Paul; but it is incorrect to suppose that Paul commissioned him to do anything beyond his office — Otto's remark on the relation of the evangelists to the assistant apostles agrees in substance with what has been said above, only it might be more than doubtful that their preaching, as he thinks, was confined to an *account of Christ's words and works*, that they were therefore only "heralds of the gospel *history* "— Otto rightly says that the assistant apostles "represented the apostle in the entire range of his work."

[2] Hofmann, without reason, supposes that at the time when Paul wrote this epistle, and even before, Timothy was no longer an assistant to Paul in the apostleship. There is no hint of this anywhere; on the contrary, the contents of the second epistle are decidedly against the supposition.

some MSS. Luther rightly: "execute;" see Col. iv. 17; Acts xii. 25. Though πληροφορεῖν in this sense is ἅπ. λεγ., still it is well employed "to indicate the full measure of activity, in which not the least point may fail" (van Oosterzee). Beza's exposition is too ingenious: ministerii tui plenam fidem facito, i.e. veris argumentis comproba te germanum esse dei ministrum.

Ver. 6. Paul points to his approaching death in order to strengthen his exhortation to Timothy to fulfil his duties faithfully. As he himself cannot any longer contend against the increasing disorder, Timothy must be all the more careful to prove himself faithful. — ἐγὼ γὰρ ἤδη σπένδομαι] ἐγώ is emphatic by position, being in contrast with σύ, ver. 5. — ἤδη] not "soon," but "already;" it denotes present time; his sufferings form already the beginning of the σπένδεσθαι. — σπένδομαι] Wahl wrongly takes the verb here in the middle voice: sanguinem meum libo, i. e. vires et vitam impendo. But it is impossible thus to supply the object; the verb is passive. It does not, however, stand for κατασπένδομαι: "I am besprinkled," i.e. I am consecrated for the sacrificial death (Heydenreich and others); the proper meaning is to be retained: "*I am made a libation, poured out as drink-offering*" (de Wette, Wiesinger, van Oosterzee, Hofmann). The meaning is, dropping the figure, already is my blood shed; comp. Phil. ii. 17. De Wette maintains that the form of expression is incorrect without ἐπὶ τῇ θυσίᾳ κ.τ.λ.; but why, it is difficult to see. Heinrichs wrongly lets the idea of sacrifice drop out of the word, and explains it quite generally as effundere, i.e. viribus defici, "my end is already near, it is all over with me." Luther translates it inexactly, but rightly enough in meaning: "I am already offered." — Paul does not use θύομαι, but σπένδομαι, not because he means to declare that he is *fully and completely* offered for God's cause (Oecumenius: τῆς μὲν θυσίας μέρος τὶ μόνον Θεῷ εἰς θυμίαμα ἀφιεροῦτο· ἡ δὲ σπονδὴ ἅπασα αὐτῷ ἀφιέρωται), but because the shedding of blood is analogous to the pouring out of the drink-offering; and as the libation formed the conclusion of the sacrifice, the apostle's martyrdom closed his apostolic service, which to him was the same as a service of sacrifice (Rom. x. 16; Phil. ii. 17). — The idea contained in the figurative expression that his death was near, is again expressed by Paul in the next words: καὶ ὁ καιρὸς τῆς ἀναλύσεώς μου ἐφέστηκε] The verb ἀναλύειν means "unloose what was tied," so that ἀνάλυσις might be equivalent to "unloosing," dissolutio (Vulgate, Matthies); but it is more correct to return to the usage by which in nautical language ἀναλύειν with or without ἄγκυραν means "weigh anchor, depart," or even of an army, "strike tents, set out on the march." Hence ἀνάλυσις is equivalent to "departure, setting out," and ought to be explained as the departure from this life; see Phil. i. 23.[1] Elsner and Wolf think that there is here a special reference to rising from table, and that the word is used in very close connection with σπένδομαι: moris olim erat, ut, qui de conviviis discederent, diis libarent; discedentes autem dicebantur ἀναλύοντες et libantes (Wolf), and that Paul means to say: se ex hac vita molestiisque exsatiatum abiturum, libato non vino, sed sanguine suo (Elsner). But, on the one hand, the allusion to σπένδομαι is not to heathen, but to Jewish ritual; and, on the other hand, there is no hint of the figure of a feast. Not less arbitrary is Beza's explanation, that ἀνάλυσις refers specially to the departure from battle. — ἐφέστηκε] "is near at hand;" Luther incorrectly: "is ready."

REMARK—According to the exposition which has been given here, and which, in substance, is generally accepted, this passage decidedly contradicts the hypothesis that Paul wrote this epistle at the beginning of the imprisonment mentioned by Luke. Otto, therefore, to favour this hypothesis, finds himself compelled to give σπένδομαι another signification. This he tries to obtain from a searching consideration of the passage in Phil. ii. 17. He tries to prove that the apostle in that passage could only have used σπένδομαι in the sense of "devotion to his missionary labours." His proof is based on the assertion— apparently to the point, but in reality erroneous—that when the particles εἰ καί are joined together, "the καί resumes the statement made under εἰ the conditional particle, at the same

---

[1] Otto objects, that in Phil. 1 23 ἀναλῦσαι does not of itself mean the departure from the flesh, but only when connected with the co-ordinate σὺν Χριστῷ εἶναι But his objection is made still less forcible by the fact that this meaning of the word is clearly indicated, not only by the preceding σπένδομαι, but also by vv. 7, 8.

time *marking it as an actual fact.*" This assertion is apparently to the point, since εἰ καί is used often where an *actual* fact is under discussion; and in this way, *e g*, the passage at 2 Cor. iv 16 may be explained: "if our outward man is destroyed,—*and it is actually being destroyed,*—then," etc. But the assertion is erroneous, because εἰ καί is also used in passages where no actual fact is under discussion. This, *e g*, is the case in the passage 1 Cor. vii. 21, where, clearly, the explanation cannot be given: "if thou canst become free—*and thou canst indeed become free.*" Otto has quite overlooked the fact that εἰ καί with the indicative cannot be different from the simple εἰ with the indicative, and this does not *declare* the fact to be actual, but only *supposes* it to be actual, whether actual or not, the fact *may* be actual, but it may quite as well not be actual, comp. 1 Cor. xv. 12, 13, where both cases stand close to one another. Hence it is not the case that σπένδεσθαι must denote something which, as the apostle said it of himself, did *actually* take place; it cannot therefore be understood to mean the apostle's martyrdom, because, according to Phil. i. 25, he was expecting to be freed from imprisonment, but must mean simply the cessation of his missionary labours.—As for the evidence by which Otto seeks to obtain this meaning for σπένδεσθαι, it must be held erroneous, since there is no justification whatever for the assertions on which it rests—viz. (1) that by the ἐγώ contained in σπένδομαι (standing here in opposition to σύ) the apostle meant his "apostolic labours;" and (2) that in Acts xxiii. 11, by the word of the Lord "Rome was appointed to the apostle as the goal of his apostolic calling, beyond which he was not to preach the gospel." Though it may be said that "the apostle's *ego* lived and wrought only in one thing, and that, to preach the gospel to the heathen," it by no means follows that when he is speaking of *himself*, he does not mean *himself*, his person, but his apostolic calling. And though, according to Phil. i 25, 26, the apostle expects to continue his labours after the Roman imprisonment, it is a pure fiction to suppose that these labours were to be episcopal rather than apostolic.[1]—As a result of this interpretation of σπένδομαι, Otto cannot understand ἀνάλυσις to mean the departure from this life; it is quite consistent for him, therefore, to say: " ἀνάλυσις can only be the discessus, abitus from the place in which Paul then was, this place being the τέρμα of his apostolic career." This exposition presupposes an erroneous view of Acts xxiii. 11,

---

[1] Weiss (*Stud. u. Krit.* 1861, p 588) rightly says· "If it be said to the apostle that he is to testify also in Rome, there is not the slightest hint that he is to advance with his preaching *only so far as Rome.*"

and its unsuitability becomes all the clearer when Otto continues: "when the messenger has come to his destination, and executed his commission, he must return to him by whom he was sent; Paul was sent by Christ, to Christ he must return; this is what the apostle says: the time of my return home is near, for I am at the goal, and have discharged my commission." And then Otto still thinks that the apostle might with this cherish the expectation of being able to labour among the Philippians *for a longer period*, since ἐφέστηκεν does not mean "is near," but simply "is impending" (!). Finally, there is nowhere the slightest trace that the apostle thought at any time before his death of ceasing to be the apostle of the Lord.

Ver. 7. In the prospect of his approaching end, Paul expresses the consciousness of having been faithful in the career appointed to him, and the hope of the heavenly reward. —There is no ground whatever for de Wette's assertion, that this expression is opposed to Christian humility. — τὸν καλὸν ἀγῶνα ἠγώνισμαι] Luther inaccurately: "I have fought a good fight." The definite article must not be overlooked; see 1 Tim. vi. 12. The perfect ἠγώνισμαι shows that the apostle now stood at the end of the fight to which he was called as the apostle of the Lord,[1] and that he had fought through it faithfully.—Baur, quite arbitrarily, is of opinion that Phil. i. 30 was here made use of; as little was the passage at Phil. iii. 12 ff. used (de Wette). — τὸν δρόμον τετέλεκα] The same thought is expressed by the more definite figure of a *race*. The point chiefly brought out is that the apostle, after continuing it without stopping, now stands at the goal. Compare with this passage Acts xx. 24; the same figure is used also in 1 Cor. ix. 24, and is indicated in Phil. iii. 12 ff. — τὴν πίστιν τετήρηκα] "*I have kept the faith,*" viz. against all inducements to deny it. Heydenreich wrongly takes this expression also as a figurative one, and expounds πίστις to mean fidelity in observing the laws of battle and rules of the race; comp. against this, 1 Tim. vi. 12. — τὸν καλὸν ἀγῶνα τῆς πίστεως] Bengel: res bis per metaphoram expressa nunc tertio loco exprimitur proprie.

---

[1] Hofmann wrongly maintains that the apostle is not speaking here of his labours in the calling of an apostle, but generally of his Christian calling. The context clearly points to the former.

Ver. 8. Λοιπόν] Wahl interprets it by ἤδη (jam, already), but this meaning is very doubtful. Other expositors take it to be equivalent to τὸ λοιπόν: "for the future;" Heydenreich: "one day, after course and fight are finished." But the present ἀπόκειται is against this; it cannot be "future in sense" (Hofmann), for the signification of the word forbids it. Beza's interpretation suits the context best: "in reliquum;" and with this de Wette and Wiesinger agree. At the end of his life-course, when he has faithfully played out his part, there remains nothing more for the apostle—than to receive the reward which is already prepared for him. — ἀπόκειταί μοι] comp. Col. i. 5 (see my Commentary, p. 57). — ὁ τῆς δικαιοσύνης στέφανος] Continuation of the figure from ver. 7. — ὁ στέφανος is used for the prize of victory in 1 Cor. ix. 25. The genitive τῆς δικαιοσύνης, like τῆς ζωῆς in Jas. i. 12, Rev. ii. 10, and τῆς δόξης in 1 Pet. v. 4, may be taken most naturally as the genitivus appositionis, and δικαιοσύνη as the perfect state, granted at the judgment to the believer by the sentence that justifies him (so, too, van Oosterzee). Δικαιοσύνη does not denote the act of justifying so much as the state of justification.—Two other interpretations are found in Heinrichs: στεφ δικαιοσ., *i.e.* corona, vel quae δικαίως dabitur ei, qui ea dignus est, a δικαίῳ κριτῇ ("the crown of just recompense," Heydenreich, Matthies, and others, but δικαιοσύνη never means recompense), vel quae mihi ob δικαιοσύνην debetur. This last interpretation is found in Chrysostom: δικαιοσύνην ἐνταῦθα τὴν καθόλου φησὶν ἀρετήν; also in de Wette, Wiesinger, Plitt. It is indeed possible, but improbable, because in that case we would not be told of what the crown of victory consists. Besides, the analogy of the passages quoted is against this interpretation.[1]—It is manifestly quite out of place to understand δικαιοσύνη here, as Calovius and Mosheim do, of the imputed righteousness of Christ. — ὃν ἀποδώσει (often used to denote the divine recompense on the day of

[1] Hofmann disputes the interpretation given above, because "Life, glory is a blessing, whereas righteousness is a condition which is rewarded;" but righteousness, taken as it is taken here, is a blessing. On the other hand, Hofmann disputes Wiesinger's interpretation, at the same time giving one of his own which is far from clear: "he who obtains the στέφανος adjudged to him, is thereby acknowledged to be a righteous man."

judgment, Matt. xvi. 27; Rom. ii. 6) μοι ὁ κύριος (*ie* Christ) ἐν ἐκείνῃ τῇ ἡμέρᾳ, ὁ δίκαιος κριτής (see ver. 1), in apposition to ὁ κύριος. There is nothing strange in laying stress on the *righteousness* of the judge, since that forms the main element in the divine judgment. God's χάρις does not take away His δικαιοσύνη, and the gospel does not deny, but confirms, the truth that for the believer the judgment will take place κατὰ τὰ ἔργα αὐτοῦ, or κατὰ τὴν πρᾶξιν αὐτοῦ. To this truth Paul often directs attention, not only for exhortation, but also for comfort; see 2 Thess. i. 5.[1]—While Paul expresses for himself the hope of the reward of victory, he knows that he is not claiming something special for himself alone. Hence he adds: οὐ μόνον δὲ ἐμοί (*sc.* ἀποδώσει κ.τ.λ.), ἀλλὰ καὶ πᾶσι τοῖς ἠγαπηκόσι] the perfect in the sense of the present: "who have fixed their love on," *i.e.* "who love" (comp. Winer, p. 256 [E. T. p. 341]). But if we proceed from the standpoint of ἀποδώσει, the perfect may also be understood to mean: "to those who in this mortal life have longed for the appearing of the Lord" (Hofmann). — τὴν ἐπιφάνειαν αὐτοῦ] is not to be understood of the first appearance of the Lord in the flesh, i. 10, but, according to the context, and in harmony with ver. 1, of the second coming. The verb ἠγαπηκόσι is not opposed to this, for it is used elsewhere to denote the desire for something future; see 1 Pet. iii. 10. Matthies: "to all who in love for Him wait longingly for His second coming."

Ver. 9. From this verse to the end we have detached commissions and items of news. "This forms the second chief section of the epistle. The apostle, with his usual habit of keeping the more personal matter for the end, places it after the exhortations given to Timothy about his office"

---

[1] De Wette is wrong in his assertion, that this passage is incompatible with Paul's view of grace, and that from a subjective standpoint God's righteousness can only be feared if we are rightly humble and have knowledge of self. If it is not denied that in the Pauline passages, Rom ii. 5 ff., 2 Thess i. 5, a reward is expected from God's righteousness, we cannot see why Paul could not possibly have claimed it for himself. Was the consciousness of his fidelity in the service of the Lord, which, moreover, he expresses elsewhere, altogether incompatible with his utterance of humility in Phil. iii. 12?—The contrast of objective and subjective point of view—to which contrast de Wette makes appeal—does not exist for the Christian consciousness.

(Wiesinger). — σπούδασον ἐλθεῖν πρός με ταχέως] Here the apostle's wish that Timothy should come to him, hinted already in i. 3, 8, is distinctly expressed. Even if it were the proximate cause of his writing, it is arbitrary to regard this as the chief purpose of the epistle, as de Wette does.[1]— The apostle wished him to come, because those who had assisted him hitherto had left him.

Ver. 10. Δημᾶς γάρ με ἐγκατέλιπεν] ἐγκαταλείπειν is equivalent to "leave in the lurch." It is wrong to interpret this either of a departure from the place merely, or of an entire apostasy from the gospel. Demas is mentioned also in Col. iv. 14 and Philem. 24 as a σύνεργος of the apostle. — ἀγαπήσας τὸν νῦν αἰῶνα] The reason why Demas had left him; ἀγαπήσας, not "having fixed his love on" (Matthies), but "because he loved." — τὸν νῦν αἰῶνα] the present world, as opposed to the future, *i.e.* the earthly, visible blessings of life. In the desire for these things, Demas had left the apostle and gone to Thessalonica, καὶ ἐπορεύθη εἰς Θεσσαλονίκην, perhaps "for the sake of trade," as some conjecture, or because it was his native place. Chrysostom : τῆς ἀνέσεως ἐρασθείς, τοῦ ἀκινδύνου καὶ τοῦ ἀσφαλοῦς, μᾶλλον εἵλετο οἴκοι τρυφᾶν, ἢ μετ᾽ ἐμοῦ ταλαιπωρεῖσθαι καὶ συνδιαφέρειν μοι τοὺς παρόντας κινδύνους. — Κρήσκης εἰς Γαλατίαν, sc. ἐπορεύθη, but without ἀγαπήσας τὸν νῦν αἰῶνα. Crescens is mentioned only here. Nothing further is known of him, nor do we know why he had set out for Galatia, and Titus for Dalmatia. The verb ἐπορεύθη is against the suggestion of Matthies, that they had been sent thither by Paul.[2]

Ver. 11. Λουκᾶς ἐστὶ μόνος μετ᾽ ἐμοῦ] There is no reason for doubting that this Luke was the apostle's well-known assistant. He accompanied Paul on his second missionary journey from Troas, Acts xvi. 10, then on his third journey, Acts xx. 5–xxi. 18. He was with Paul both in his imprisonment at Caesarea and in the first imprisonment at Rome,

---

[1] Hofmann's remark is purely hypothetical, that σπούδασον κ.τ.λ. is not an invitation, but refers to Timothy's willingness to come, which he had expressed to Paul in a letter.

[2] Hofmann, taking Γαλίαν to be the original reading, supposes that Crescens and Titus had left the apostle in order to work for the gospel in places to which Paul himself had not come.

Acts xxvii.; Col. iv. 14; Philem. 24. — Μάρκον ἀναλαβὼν ἄγαγε (or common reading: ἄγε) μετὰ σεαυτοῦ] Mark, too, is the young apostle with whom we are acquainted from the Book of Acts. According to Col. iv. 10, Philem. 13, he was likewise with Paul in his first Roman imprisonment; ἀναλαβών, see Acts xx. 14. It is not known where Mark was at this time. The reason why Paul wished to have him is given in the words. ἔστι γάρ μοι εὔχρηστος εἰς διακονίαν] εὔχρηστος, ii. 21. Διακονία here is to be understood of the apostolic office[1] (according to Wiesinger: "of Mark's personal services, but certainly in the apostle's vocation").

Ver. 12. Τύχικον δὲ ἀπέστειλα εἰς Ἔφεσον] Tychicus was in Greece with Paul on the third missionary journey, and preceded him to Troas, Acts xx. 4, 5. According to Col. iv. 7 and Eph. vi. 21, Paul sent him from Rome to Asia Minor. Otto thinks that this was the occasion mentioned here, and tries to prove it particularly by an interpretation of the passages quoted from the Epistles to the Colossians and the Ephesians. There are, however, well-founded objections to his theory. The facts are such, the two occasions on which he was sent can obviously not be identical. — εἰς Ἔφεσον] Paul here mentions Ephesus as the place to which he had sent Tychicus; but we cannot infer from this, as Theodoret and de Wette infer, that Timothy had not at that time lived in Ephesus.—The reason why he was sent is not given. Possibly it was to convey this epistle (Wieseler); but not probably, for in such a case Paul would have certainly written πρὸς σέ (Tit. iii. 12; Wiesinger).

Ver. 13. Timothy is commissioned to bring with him certain belongings. The first named is τὸν φελόνην. On the various spellings of this word, see the Greek lexicons. Regarding the meaning, Chrysostom said: φελόνην ἐνταῦθα τὸ ἱμάτιον λέγει· τινὲς δέ φασι τὸ γλωσσόκομον, ἔνθα τὰ

---

[1] What Otto (pp. 257 ff.) on this passage adduces regarding the relation of Mark to Paul are groundless suppositions. It is a purely arbitrary assumption that Mark, after abstaining for some time from work among the heathen, had again offered his services to Paul through Timothy. And it is equally an assumption to say, that from the words εὔχρηστος κ.τ.λ. it would appear that Mark could not have hitherto given Paul his services, because in that case Paul would not have "censured him regarding his usefulness for the ministry" (!).

βιβλία ἔκειτο; and the most recent expositors are still at variance. Matthies takes it in the second meaning: "*cloak-bag*, covering for books," because it is improbable that Paul should have left his *travelling cloak* behind him. De Wette adopts the first meaning, for the reason given by Bengel: theca non seorsum a libris appellaretur. This is the more probable view; there is little force in the objection, that we cannot see what use Paul would have for the mantle when he was expecting death so soon. — ὃν ἀπέλιπον ἐν Τρωάδι παρὰ Κάρπῳ] From this it is clear that Paul had been in Troas before he came to Rome, but the time is not stated. In any case, it is very improbable (see Introd. p. 25) that this sojourn was the one mentioned in Acts xx. 6. He did not, however, touch at Troas on his voyage from Caesarea to Rome — Carpus is mentioned only here — καὶ τὰ βιβλία, μάλιστα τὰς μεμβράνας] Since Paul says nothing further about them, it is idle conjecture to define more precisely the contents of the books written on papyrus, and of the more valuable rolls of parchment.

Vv. 14, 15. Warning against a certain Alexander. Ἀλέξανδρος ὁ χαλκεύς] see on 1 Tim. i. 20. — πολλά μοι κακὰ ἐνεδείξατο] The words point to a personal injury which he had inflicted on the apostle. This must, however, be added to an attitude of opposition to his words, as is shown in the words: λίαν γὰρ ἀντέστη τοῖς ἡμετέροις λόγοις] It is doubtful where this was done, and where Alexander was at the time of the composition of this epistle. Further, the warning · ὃν καὶ σὺ φυλάσσου, may refer both " to Timothy's presence in Ephesus and to his future stay in Rome " (de Wette) Wiesinger conjectures that this Alexander, a native of Ephesus, had come from there to Rome to give testimony against the apostle (at his πρώτη ἀπολογία, ver. 16), and had afterwards returned to Ephesus.[1] This conjecture obtains some probability from the fact that in the very next verse

[1] Hofmann supposes that this Alexander was the same as the one mentioned in Acts xix., and that he had given testimony against the apostle in Ephesus The opinion is manifestly too far-fetched, that Luke would not have mentioned him in the Acts, if the Roman Theophilus, for whom in the first place he wrote the Acts, "had not known Alexander from some other source, in the manner in which we make acquaintance with him in the passage before us."

Paul speaks of the ἀπολογία; but this fact cannot be regarded as making the matter certain. The words preceding this warning, if we read ἀποδώσει αὐτῷ ὁ κύριος κατὰ τὰ ἔργα αὐτοῦ, present no difficulty. Even with the reading ἀποδώῃ they cannot form a reason for reproaching the apostle with a desire for vengeance; Christian love does not extinguish the feeling of justice; besides, the apostle does not speak the words because of the personal injury, but because of Alexander's hostility to the truth. Justin (*quaest*. 125, *ad Orthod*.) says of these words: πρέπουσα ἀνδρὶ ἀποστόλῳ μὴ ἐκδικοῦντι ἑαυτὸν, ἀλλὰ διδόντι τόπον τῇ ὀργῇ; comp. Rom. xii. 19; 1 Pet. ii. 23

Vv. 16, 17. Information regarding the apostle's present condition, ἐν τῇ πρώτῃ μου ἀπολογίᾳ] ἀπολογία: the public appearance before the court; comp. Phil. i. 7. Ἐν τῇ πρώτῃ shows that there was a second appearance in order to bring the case to an end. On the time when the first trial took place, see the Introduction, where, too, there is a discussion of Otto's hypothesis, that it means the proceedings before Festus, as recounted in Acts xxv. 6–12. — οὐδείς μοι παρεγένετο] "no one stood on my side, was present with me," viz as *patronus*[1] (defender). It is the negative expression of the thought which in the next words is given positively: ἀλλὰ πάντες με ἐγκατέλιπον As to the reason why they had left the apostle, Theodoret says rightly: οὐ κακοηθείας ἦν, ἀλλὰ δειλίας ἡ ὑποχώρησις. — However much this want of evangelic spirit may have pained the apostle, he says no word in anger: μὴ αὐτοῖς λογισθείη: "may it not be reckoned to them, but pardoned." — Ver 17. ὁ δὲ κύριός μοι παρέστη] said in sharp antithesis to the previous thought The presence of the Lord manifested itself to the apostle in the courage which he had to testify freely and openly regarding Him; hence καὶ ἐνεδυνάμωσέ με] Chrysostom: παρρησίαν ἐχαρίσατο; comp. 1 Tim. i. 12; Phil. iv. 13. According to Otto, this expres-

---

[1] Wolf: verb. συμπαραγίνεσθαι indicat patronos et amicos, qui alios, ad causam dicendam vocatos, nunc praesentia sua, nunc etiam oratione adjuvare solebant. Graeci dicunt nunc παραγίνεσθαι, nunc παριῖναι, nunc συμπαριῖναι. — See further, in Rein, *Röm. Privatrecht*, p. 425, Schomann, *Attisch. Recht*, p. 708.

sion means simply that the Lord "maintained the apostle's cause against his accusers," which is clearly an unjustifiable paraphrase of the word, as the apostle is speaking not of *his cause*, but of *himself*. Even if ἐνεδυνάμωσε be used in a forensic sense, its signification cannot be altered; it applies to the strengthening which enabled the apostle so to speak as to ward off sentence against him. The purpose of this strengthening was: ἵνα δι' ἐμοῦ τὸ κήρυγμα πληροφορηθῇ] According to the meaning suitable to the word πληροφορεῖν in Rom. iv. 21, xiv. 5, Beza translates: "ut per me praeconio evangelii fides fieret." Heydenreich, too, thinks that πληροφ. refers to the confirmation of the gospel or testimony to it, either through the proofs delivered by Paul or through the joy he exhibited. But it is safer to take πληροφ. in the same sense here as in ver. 5, some of the MSS. even reading πληρωθῇ for πληροφορηθῇ. It is, however, inaccurate to take the expression in the sense of: "that I might be enabled to preach the gospel" (de Wette). In this interpretation full force is not given to πληροφορεῖν. These words must be taken in very close connection with καὶ ἀκούσῃ πάντα τὰ ἔθνη, and referred to the apostle's being called to preach the gospel to the heathen. The κήρυγμα, sc. τοῦ εὐαγγελίου, was *fulfilled* by Paul, inasmuch as it was done openly before all people (Wieseler, Wiesinger) in the metropolis of the world (was delivered before the corona populi, before the court). Hofmann, regarding this interpretation of the apostle's words as forced, understands ἵνα κ.τ.λ. in this way: "If courage and strength had failed the apostle before the heathen tribunal of the metropolis of the world ... his confident belief that the heathen world was called to become the church of Christ would have been shattered." But the words δι' ἐμοῦ ... πληροφορηθῇ distinctly say that the preaching had been carried out by the apostle himself, and not simply that the preaching to be done by others would not be hindered by him, *i.e.* by his conduct. — The ἵνα was fulfilled by the apostle's speech in the πρώτη ἀπολογία. Otto, on the contrary, asserts that the first ἀπολογία and the preaching in Rome took place at different times, and that ἵνα refers to what was to be done afterwards in Rome by the apostle. This is wrong, since in that case ἵνα ought not to stand *before*, but *after* ἐρρύσθην. — καὶ ἐρρύσθην ἐκ στόματος λέοντος] second proof of the help and presence of the Lord. — στόμα λέοντος has been very variously explained. The expression is not to be taken literally (Mosheim), but figuratively, and is to be referred to the punishment of being thrown to the lions. — Chrysostom and many after him take Nero to be the λέων; Pearson again takes Helius Ceasareanus, since Nero at the time had departed for Greece. Wahl thinks λέων a metaphor for tyrannus crudelis, while Wolf explains it to be omnis illa hostium caterva, quorum conatus in prima apologia tunc facta eluserit.[1] All these interpretations are inappropriate. In the first place, the metaphor is not in λέων alone, but in στόμα λέοντος (so, too, van Oosterzee, Hofmann); and, secondly, this expression can hardly be referred simply to the danger that threatened the apostle from men, but also to the danger prepared for him by the might of Satan, which was opposed to Christ. Hence the interpretation "*deadly danger*" (so de Wette, Wiesinger, van Oosterzee) is not sufficient.[2] Paul escaped from the danger impending over him, unhurt in body and soul (see on iii. 11), escaped as a conqueror in the eyes of the Lord, and hence he says: ἐρρύσθην ἐκ στόματος λέοντος.

Ver. 18. In the assured confidence of faith, the apostle adds to ἐρρύσθην the word of hope: ῥύσεταί με ὁ κύριος ἀπὸ παντὸς ἔργου πονηροῦ, for he knows that the Lord—even if it be through death (ver. 6)—will bring him into His kingdom. ἔργον πονηρόν is not equivalent to evil, as Luther translates it and Matthies explains it: "from every evil circumstance." Taken in this sense, the thought would be quite irreconcilable with the apostle's conviction in ver. 6. Besides, in the N. T. πονηρόν never refers to merely external affliction; it denotes rather what is morally evil. Still it cannot here mean the evil work which the apostle might do

---

[1] Otto adopts an explanation to suit his opinion that this ἀπολογία took place in Caesarea before Festus: "Judaism was the lion that panted for the apostle's blood," and from it the apostle was delivered when he appealed to the emperor, and Festus received the appeal.

[2] Hofmann "His danger was a greater one, to lose . . . before the tribunal his courage in confessing Christ. That he had escaped it, he owes thanks to God's help."

(Chrysostom: πᾶν ἁμάρτημα; Grotius: liberabit me, ne quid agam Christiano, ne quid Apostolo indignum; de Wette "from all evil work which I might do through want of stedfastness, through apostasy, and the like;" so, too, Beza, Heydenreich, and others). It must be interpreted of the wicked works of the enemies of the divine word; only with this view is the verb ῥύσεται appropriate, especially when combined with σώσει (Wiesinger, van Oosterzee, Hofmann). The apostle was still exposed to the attacks of the evil one, but he expresses the hope that the Lord would save him from them, so that they would do him no harm. Not, indeed, that he would not suffer the martyrdom he expected, but that through this he would come into the heavenly kingdom of the Lord, where there was prepared for him στέφανος τῆς δικαιοσύνης (ver. 8). — καὶ σώσει εἰς τὴν βασιλείαν αὐτοῦ τὴν ἐπουράνιον] σώσει εἰς is a pregnant construction: he will save me and bring me into = σώζων ἄξει μὲ εἰς (Heydenreich).—The expression ἡ βασιλεία ἡ ἐπουράνιος does not occur elsewhere in the N. T; but the idea is thoroughly apostolic and Pauline. For though Paul often calls Christ's kingdom a future one, Christ is also present to him as βασιλεὺς ἐν τοῖς ἐπουρανίοις, whose βασιλεία, therefore, is also a present one.[1] The context points to this meaning here. In Phil. i. 23, Paul expresses the longing to come to Christ *through death;* here he expresses the hope that the Lord would remove him into His kingdom ἐκ παντὸς ἔργου πονηροῦ.—As a suitable and natural utterance of awakened feeling, there follows a doxology which in this place cannot surprise us, though commonly his doxologies refer to God and not to Christ specially.[2]

Ver. 19. Paul sends greetings to Prisca and Aquila—Paul had become acquainted with them in Corinth (Acts xviii. 2), from which they accompanied him to Syria (ver. 18). When Paul wrote the Epistle to the Romans they were in Rome (Rom. xvi. 13), but they were in Corinth at the time of his

---

[1] There is nothing to indicate that the apostle is here alluding to the heavenly kingdom of the Lord, "in contrast with the *earthly dominion of the present*" (Hofmann).

[2] In Rom. xvi. 27, ix. 5, Heb. xiii. 21, the reference is at the very least doubtful.

writing the First Epistle to the Corinthians (1 Cor. xvi. 19). — καὶ τὸν 'Ονησιφόρου οἶκον, see on i. 16.

Ver. 20. Ἔραστος ἔμεινεν ἐν Κορίνθῳ] While on his third journey, the apostle sent forward a certain Erastus from Ephesus to Macedonia along with Timothy (Acts xix. 22). It can hardly be doubted that it is the same man who is mentioned here. It is more uncertain if the one alluded to in Rom. xvi. 23 is also the same (as Otto thinks); still it does favour the identity that the latter dwelt in *Corinth* as ὁ οἰκόνομος τῆς πόλεως, and that the Erastus here mentioned remained in *Corinth*. Meyer, however (see on Rom. xvi. 23), and Wiesinger think it improbable. Hofmann holds that the Erastus mentioned in Acts xix. 22, and the city chamberlain in Rom. xvi. 23, are two different men, and that the one mentioned here is identical with the latter. — ἔμεινε] *i.e.* "he remained in Corinth, viz. when I left it;" the tense favours this view. Paul notices the fact because he thought that Timothy believed that Erastus had left Corinth with the apostle. Hug explains it: "Erastus, whom I expected in Rome, remained behind in Corinth;" but this would suit better with the perfect Besides, there is nothing to indicate such an expectation — Τρόφιμον δὲ ἀπέλιπον ἐν Μιλήτῳ ἀσθενοῦντα] Trophimus, an Asiatic, accompanied Paul on his third journey, and went before him from Greece to Troas (Acts xx. 4). His presence in Jerusalem was the occasion of the tumult against Paul (Acts xxi. 29).—From this passage it would appear that Trophimus had wished to accompany the apostle on his journey, but had been left behind at Miletus sick. The apostle cannot have been in Miletus with Trophimus before the first imprisonment in Rome; hence the expositors who deny that Paul was twice imprisoned in Rome, and admit the genuineness of the epistle, are driven to great straits in interpreting this passage. Thus Hug, Hemsen, and Kling hold ἀπέλιπον to be the third person plural. Wieseler does not give the proper force to ἀπέλιπον, which— as de Wette rightly remarks—presupposes that they had been previously together in Miletus. Regarding the views of Wieseler and Otto, comp. Introduction, § 3, pp. 19, 20. It is altogether arbitrary to read ἐν Μελίτῃ, or to suppose that

Miletus in Crete is meant—The reason for speaking about Erastus and Trophimus appears in ver 21; comp. vv. 9, 10. He did not mention them in ver. 10, because "there he was speaking only of those who had already been with him in Rome and had left him" (Wiesinger). Hofmann thinks that Paul mentions them in reply to a question from Timothy regarding the two who might serve as witnesses for his defence; but this is mere conjecture, for which no good grounds can be given.[1]

Ver. 21. Σπούδασον πρὸ χειμῶνος ἐλθεῖν] see ver. 9, ταχέως. Even if πρὸ χειμῶνος is to be connected with ταχέως, it does not follow that the epistle was written just before winter; comp. Introd. § 3. Χειμών may indeed mean the "winter-storm" (Wieseler), but it is more natural here to understand it of the season of the year (Wiesinger). Timothy is to come to the apostle before winter, that the winter might not prevent him from coming soon.—Finally, Paul sent greetings from Eubulus, Pudens, Linus, and Claudia, who are mentioned only here, and from all the Christians in Rome These are named specially, not as the apostle's σύνεργοι, but probably because they were personally acquainted with Timothy. Linus is probably the one whom the Fathers name as the first bishop of Rome.

Ver. 22. Benediction This is peculiar in its nature. Only at the end of the First Epistle to the Corinthians do we find, as here, a double benediction, and there it runs differently. For ὁ κύριος . . . and ἡ χάρις . . . the form elsewhere is always ἡ χάρις τοῦ κυρίου. — μετὰ τοῦ πνεύματός σου] comp. Gal. vi. 18; Philem. 25. — ἡ χάρις μεθ' ὑμῶν] comp. 1 Tim. vi. 22.

---

[1] Hofmann regards them as suitable witnesses for the defence, assuming that the charge against the apostle rested on this, that his preaching of the gospel was contrary to the constitution of the state. Erastus was present in Corinth on the occasion mentioned in Acts xviii 12, and Trophimus when Paul was made a prisoner at Jerusalem. Both might therefore testify that Paul was not to blame for these tumults.

Παύλου τοῦ ἀποστόλου ἡ πρὸς Τίτον ἐπιστολή.

In A, *al.* the inscription begins with ἄρχεται; in D E F G it runs simply πρὸς Τίτον.

CHAPTER I.

Ver. 1. For Ἰησοῦ Χριστοῦ, Buttm. and Tisch. 7, following A, *al*, adopted Χριστοῦ Ἰησοῦ; but the majority of the most important MSS. (D** E F G H J K L ℵ) support the *Rec.* (Lachm. Tisch 8). — Ver. 4. χάρις καὶ εἰρήνη] So Scholz, Tisch., following C* D E F G J ℵ 73, *al.*, Syr. Copt. Chrys. Aug. *al.*—Lachm. and Buttm. retained the usual reading: χάρις, ἔλεος, εἰρήνη; it is found in A C** K L, etc, but seems nevertheless to be a correction from the analogy of 1 Tim i. 2; 2 Tim. i. 2.—Tittmann's reading: χάρις, ἔλεος, καὶ εἰρήνη, is quite arbitrary. — Matthaei: ἔλεος nullus meorum omittit, nec ex quinque iis, quos postea consului. Reiche decided for the reading of Tisch. — καὶ κυρίου Ἰησοῦ Χριστοῦ] For this Lachm. Buttm Tisch. read καὶ Χριστοῦ Ἰησοῦ, on the authority of A C D* *al*, Vulg. Copt. Arm. Theodoret, etc. — Ver. 5. So far as internal evidence goes, we cannot decide whether the *Rec.* κατέλιπον or the reading ἀπέλιπον (Lachm. Tisch.) is the original one; both may be corrections, the latter on the analogy of 2 Tim. iv. 20, the former on the analogy of Acts xviii. 19, xxiv. 27. Hofmann prefers καταλείπειν, because it means: "leaving some one behind in going away;" but the simple verb is in no way unsuitable in the passage. The external evidence (A C D* F G, *al.*, Or. Basil. ms.) is in favour of ἀπέλιπον. It is uncertain, too, whether the aor. ἀπέλιπον (*Rec.* supported by D E K ℵ, *al.*, Lachm. Buttm. Tisch. 8) or the imperf. ἀπέλειπον (A C F G J L, *al*, Tisch. 7) is the original reading. Hofmann prefers the imperf. "because it was part of the purpose for which Paul at that time left Titus behind;" but this would not prevent the apostle from writing the aor.—The authorities waver between the middle ἐπιδιορθώσῃ (*Rec.* Tisch.) and the act. ἐπιδιορθώσῃς (Scholz, Lachm. Buttm).

CHAP. I. 1.   333

Since in classic Greek the middle is more current than the active, it may be supposed that the middle was a correction. It can hardly be supposed that the copyists did not know the middle form (Hofmann). — Ver. 10 In A C J ℵ, many cursives, etc., καί is wanting between πολλοί and ἀνυπότακτοι, for which reason it was omitted by Lachm. and Tisch. 8. Tisch. 7 retained it, on the authority of D E F G K L, several cursives, etc. The καί was perhaps added to be in accordance with classical usage.—In several MSS. (F G 67* 73, al), as well as in some versions, Oecum. Hilar., a καί was inserted after ἀνυπότακτοι. — Ver 15. The μέν following πάντα in the *Rec.* is to be deleted, on the authority of A C D* E* F G ℵ 17, al., Vulg It. Or. Tert. etc.—For μεμιασμένοις, μεμιαμμένοις is found in A C K L ℵ, many cursives, etc, and was adopted by Lachm. Buttm and Tisch. (see Winer, p. 84 [E. T. p. 108]). D* has μεμιανμένοις

Ver. 1. Παῦλος δοῦλος Θεοῦ] This designation, which indicates generally the official position (Wiesinger: " δοῦλος Θεοῦ here in the same sense as in Acts xvi. 17, Rev. i. 1, xv. 3, etc., not as in 1 Pet. ii. 16, Rev. vii. 3," etc.), is not usually found in the inscriptions of the Pauline Epistles. In the Epistle of James we have. Θεοῦ καὶ κυρίου 'Ι. Χρ. δοῦλος, and in writing to the Romans and Philippians Paul says δοῦλος 'Ι. Χρ. — ἀπόστολος δὲ 'Ι. Χρ.] δέ indicates here not so much a contrast (as Mack thinks) as a further definition (Matthies : a more distinct description); comp. Jude 1. With this double designation comp Rom. i. 1 : δοῦλος 'Ι. Χρ., κλητὸς ἀπόστολος. — κατὰ πίστιν ἐκλεκτῶν Θεοῦ] κατά is explained by Matthies to mean: "according to faith, so that the apostleship is described in its normal state, in its evangelic character," but it is altogether opposed to the apostolic spirit to make appeal on behalf of the apostleship to its harmony with the faith of the elect. Κατά rather expresses here the general relation of reference to something: "in regard to faith;" the more precise definition must be supplied. This, however, can be nothing else than that which in Rom. i 5 is expressed by εἰς (εἰς ὑπακοὴν πίστεως ἐν πᾶσι τ. ἔθνεσιν). It is on account of the πίστις ἐκλ. Θεοῦ that he is a δοῦλ. Θεοῦ and ἀπόστ. Χρ., and to this his office is related, see 2 Tim. i. 1. This general relation is limited too precisely by the common exposition: "for *producing* faith," etc.[1] Hofmann thinks the apostle uses κατὰ πιστ. ἐκλ. to describe faith as that which is presupposed in his apostleship, as that without which he would not be an apostle; but, on the one hand, we should in that case have had μου; and, on the other hand, κατά does not express a presupposition or condition. — The expression ἐκλεκτοὶ Θεοῦ is taken by de Wette in a proleptic sense, to mean those who, by the free counsel of God, are predestinated to faith; and κατὰ πίστιν ἐκλ. Θ., according to him, declares the faith of these elect to be the aim of the apostolic office. Wiesinger, on the contrary, thinks the expression ἐκλεκτοὶ Θεοῦ quite abstract, leaving it uncertain "whether the κλῆσις has already taken place in their case or not," but he agrees with de Wette in taking the ἐκλεκτοί to be the object of the apostolic labours, so that the meaning is: in order to produce or further faith in the elect. But in the N. T. the expression ἐκλεκτοὶ Θεοῦ is always used of those who have already become believers, never of those who have not yet received the κλῆσις. Since it cannot be said that the purpose of the apostolic office is to produce faith in the ἐκλεκτοί (Plitt: "that the elect may believe"), who as such already possess faith, nor that it is to further their faith, πίστις ἐκλεκτῶν must be taken as *one* thought, the genitive serving to define more precisely the faith to which Paul's apostolic office is dedicated. We have therefore here a contrast between the *true* faith and the false πίστις, of which the heretics boasted. — καὶ ἐπίγνωσιν ἀληθείας τῆς κατ' εὐσέβειαν] In genuine faith the knowledge of the truth is a substantial element; and Paul here lays stress on this element to point the contrast with the heretics. The ἐπίγνωσις is the subjective aspect, as the ἀλήθεια is the objective. — τῆς κατ' εὐσέβειαν serves to define ἀλήθεια more precisely, as Chrysostom says: ἐστὶ γὰρ ἀλήθεια πραγμάτων, ἀλλ' οὐ κατ' εὐσέβειαν, οἷον τὸ εἰδέναι τὰ γεωργικά, τὸ εἰδέναι τέχνας,

---

[1] There is no doubt that in classic Greek κατά sometimes denotes the aim of exertion; see Kuhner, § 607. — Herod. ii. 152: κατὰ τὴν ληΐην ἐκπλώσαντις. Thucydides, vi. 31: κατὰ θέαν ἧκιν. Odyssey, iii. 106: ἤ τι κατὰ πρῆξιν . . . ἀλάλησθι, κατὰ ληΐδα. But the relation here is quite different, being active. Κατὰ πίστιν would therefore mean "in order to believe," which would give no sense.

ἀληθῶς ἐστὶν εἰδέναι· ἀλλ' αὕτη κατ' εὐσέβειαν ἡ ἀλήθεια. De Wette, Wiesinger, van Oosterzee, Plitt interpret ἡ κατ' εὐσέβειαν: "leading to holiness," thus, indeed, naming a right element in truth, but one rather indicated than expressed by κατά; it is merely said that here a truth is under discussion which is in nature akin to εὐσέβεια. Hofmann translates it "piously," asserting that κατ' εὐσέβειαν without the article stands for an adjective; but had Paul used the clause as an adjective, he would certainly have written: τῆς κατ' εὐσέβειαν ἀληθείας (as in Rom. ix. 11: ἡ κατ' ἐκλογὴν πρόθεσις). Besides, the translation "piously" is not sufficiently clear.

Ver. 2. Ἐπ' ἐλπίδι ζωῆς αἰωνίου] ἐπ' ἐλπίδι, "in hope" (comp. Rom. iv. 18, viii 21; 1 Cor. ix. 10). It is not to be taken with ἐπίγνωσις ἀληθείας ("the knowledge of the truth which gives hope of an eternal life," Heydenreich, but with hesitation; Wiesinger: "it is a knowledge whose content is that ἀλήθεια, and whose ground and condition is the hope of eternal life, by which hope it is supported and guided"), nor is it to be taken with εὐσέβεια ("a holiness the possessor of which is justified in hoping for eternal life," which Heydenreich likewise considers possible), nor with τῆς κατ' εὐσέβειαν (Matthies: "truth and holiness in their inner relationship are founded evangelically on the hope of eternal life"), nor even with the two ideas closely connected: πίστιν and ἐπίγνωσιν ἀλ. (so Plitt. "the πίστις and the ἐπίγνωσις rest on the ἐλπίς"); but it is to be joined with ἀπόστολος κ.τ.λ. Paul by this declares that the ἐλπὶς ζωῆς αἰωνίου is the basis on which he stands as an ἀπόστολος Ἰησοῦ Χριστοῦ κατὰ πίστιν κ.τ.λ.[1] Van Oosterzee. "Paul in ver. 4 says he fulfils his task with or in hope of eternal life" (so, too, Hofmann). — The believer, it is true, possesses the ζωὴ αἰώνιος in the present; but its perfection will only be granted to him in the future (comp. Col. iii. 3, 4); here it is to be considered as a future blessing, which is indicated by ἐπ' ἐλπίδι. — ἣν ἐπηγγείλατο ὁ ἀψευδὴς Θεὸς πρὸ χρόνων αἰωνίων] ἥν relates to

---

[1] If ἐπ' ἐλπίδι be in this way connected with ἀπόστολος κ.τ λ., the objection of Wiesinger is overcome, viz. that in connecting it with ἀπόστολος there should be a δὲ or something similar to indicate the co-ordinate position of ἐπί and κατά.

ζωῆς αἰωνίου, and not, as some expositors (Flatt, Mack, and others) think, to ἀλήθεια.—ἐπηγγείλατο, viz. διὰ τῶν προφητῶν, comp. Rom. i. 2. — ὁ ἀψευδὴς Θεός] This epithet occurs only here; ἀψευδής is equivalent to πιστός, ἀληθής in regard to the divine promises, comp. Heb. vi. 18 : ἀδύνατον ψεύσασθαι Θεόν; 1 Cor. i. 9 ; Rom. iii. 4.— πρὸ χρόνων αἰωνίων here is not equivalent in meaning to πρὸ καταβολῆς κόσμου or similar expressions ; for in that case ἐπηγγείλατο must have meant promittere decrevit, or the like, as Chrysostom expounds it : ἄνωθεν ταῦτα προώριστο, which is impossible. It is equivalent to ἀπ᾿ αἰῶνος, Luke i. 70 : "before eternity, i.e before the earliest times " (Wiesinger, van Oosterzee, Plitt, Hofmann), comp. 2 Tim. i. 9. Calvin rightly says: hic, quia de promissione tractat, non omnia saecula comprehendit, ut nos adducat extra mundi creationem, sed docet, multa saecula praeteriisse, ex quo salus fuit promissa. De Wette rightly remarks that apparently the opposite is declared in μυστήριον χρόνοις αἰωνίοις σεσιγημένον, Rom. xvi. 25.

Ver. 3. Ἐφανέρωσε δὲ καιροῖς ἰδίοις τὸν λόγον αὐτοῦ] ἐφανέρωσε forms an antithesis to ἐπηγγείλατο. True, the promise is a revelation, but only a revelation in which the point under consideration still remains hidden. The object of ἐφανέρωσε is not the same as that to which ἐπηγγ. relates, viz ἥν, i.e. τὴν ζωὴν αἰώνιον; Beza: quam promiserat Deus . . . manifestam autem fecit . . . The object is τὸν λόγον αὐτοῦ, which is not to be taken as in apposition to ἥν (or as Heinrichs even thinks, to ἐλπίδα ζωῆς), though it is strange that ἐφαν. should begin a new sentence. This is one of the cases where—as Buttmann, p. 328, remarks—a relative sentence passes almost imperceptibly into a principal sentence, without such continuation changing the actual principal sentence into one subordinate. — τὸν λόγον αὐτοῦ] is, of course, not a name for Christ (scholiasts in Matthaei), but the gospel, which contains the ἀποκάλυψις μυστηρίου, Rom. xvi. 26, or, as is said here, τῆς ζωῆς αἰωνίου.[1] — καιροῖς ἰδίοις]

[1] Wiesinger rightly. "Any one can see why the apostle changes its object, or rather its name , eternal life is in its appearance still something future, revealed only as λόγος. Hence, too, it is plain that the ζωὴ αἰώνιος is here to be regarded as the content of this λόγος in specie."

comp. 1 Tim. ii. 6. How this φανέρωσις of the divine word took place, is told in the next words: ἐν κηρύγματι ὃ ἐπιστεύθην ἐγώ] κήρυγμα (see 2 Tim. iv. 17) is not quite "the general preaching of the gospel by the apostles" (Matthies, Wiesinger), the thought being limited by the words following; κήρυγμα is to be taken as forming one thought with what follows: " the preaching entrusted to me." Paul had some reason for describing *his* preaching as the means by which this revelation was made, since *he* recognised the depth of the divine decree as no other apostle had recognised it, and by him it was proclaimed " to all peoples" (see 2 Tim. iv 17). — ὃ ἐπιστεύθην ἐγώ] see 1 Cor. ix. 17 ; Gal. ii. 7 ; 1 Thess. ii. 4 ; 1 Tim. i. 11 — To define and emphasize the thought that the κήρυγμα was not according to his own pleasure, Paul adds: κατ' ἐπιταγὴν τοῦ σωτῆρος ἡμῶν Θεοῦ] comp. 1 Tim. i. 1. Hofmann construes differently, connecting together κατὰ πίστιν and ἐπ' ἐλπίδι as well as ἐν κηρύγματι, and then joining κατ' ἐπιταγήν immediately with ἀπόστολος. But this construction not only makes τὸν λόγον αὐτοῦ (which, according to Hofmann, is in apposition to ἥν) quite superfluous, but separates ideas closely attached to each other, κήρυγμα and λόγος, ἐπιστεύθην and κατ' ἐπιταγήν

Ver. 4 Τίτῳ γνησίῳ τέκνῳ κατὰ κοινὴν πίστιν] On γνησίῳ τέκνῳ, see 1 Tim. i. 2. Κατὰ κοινὴν πίστιν gives the point of view from which Titus can be considered the genuine son of the apostle. Beza : *i e.* fidei respectu quae quidem et Paulo patri et Tito filio communis erat. There is nothing to indicate that in using κοινήν Paul was thinking of an original difference between them, he being a Jewish Christian, Titus a Gentile Christian. — χάρις [ἔλεος], εἰρήνη κ.τ λ.] see on 1 Tim. i. 2. — The designation appended to Χριστοῦ, viz τοῦ σωτῆρος ἡμῶν, is peculiar to this epistle.

Ver. 5. The epistle begins by the apostle reminding Titus of the commission already given him by word of mouth. — τούτου χάριν ἀπέλιπόν σε ἐν Κρήτῃ] Regarding the time when this happened, see the Introduction ; as to the reading, see the critical remarks. — ἵνα τὰ λείποντα ἐπιδιορθώσῃς] τὰ λείποντα : quae ego per temporis brevitatem non potui coram expedire (Bengel). — ἐπιδιορθώσῃς] The preposition ἐπί does not serve here to strengthen the meaning (= omni cura corrigere, Wahl), but conveys the notion of something additional: "*still further bring into order.*" — τὰ λείποντα] means "that which is wanting," *i.e.* here that which was wanting for the complete organization of the church. The apostle himself had already done something, but in many respects the churches were not organized as they ought to be; presbyters had still to be appointed to gather single believers into a firmly-established church. This Titus was now to do,[1] as the next words say: καὶ καταστήσῃς κατὰ πόλιν πρεσβυτέρους. — κατὰ πόλιν] For the expression, comp. Luke viii. 1; Acts xv. 21, xx. 23; and for the fact, Acts xiv. 23. Baur wrongly assumes that each πόλις was to receive only *one* presbyter, see Meyer on Acts xiv. 23. — ὡς ἐγώ σοι διεταξάμην] "relates both to the fact and to the manner of it, the latter being set forth more fully in mentioning the qualities of those to be chosen" (de Wette). Hofmann, without sufficient ground, wishes πρεσβυτέρους to be regarded not as the object proper, but as something predicated of the object, which object is found by the words εἴ τις κ.τ.λ. This view is refuted by the addition of κατὰ πόλιν.[2]

Ver. 6. Εἴ τις ἐστίν] This form is not, as Heinrichs and Heydenreich think, selected to express a doubt whether such men could be found among the corrupt Cretans The meaning is rather: "*only such an one as.*" — ἀνέγκλητος] see 1 Tim. iii. 10; ἀνεπίληπτος is used in 1 Tim. iii. 2. The objection which de Wette raises on the ground that Titus is in the first place to have regard to external blamelessness, has been proved by Wiesinger to have no foundation whatever. — μιᾶς γυν. ἀνήρ] see 1 Tim iii 2. — τέκνα ἔχων πιστά] comp. 1 Tim. iii. 4, 5; πιστά, in contrast to those that were not Christian, or were Christian only in name. — μὴ ἐν κατηγορίᾳ ἀσωτίας] "qui non sunt obnoxii crimini luxus" (Wolf);

---

[1] Theod v. Mops ὁ γὰρ τῆς εὐσεβείας λόγος παρεδίδοτο πᾶσι παρ' αὐτοῦ, ἐλείπετο δὲ οἰκονομῆσαι τὰ κατὰ τοὺς πεπιστευκότας καὶ εἰς ἁρμονίαν αὐτοὺς καταστῆσαι ταῖς ἐκκλησιαστικαῖς διατυπώσεσι.

[2] Hofmann rightly remarks, that (according to the apostle's injunction) "Titus was to appoint the superintendents according to his own choice, and was not to cause them to be elected by the Christians who were still to be organized into a community."

ἀσωτία is a debauched, sensual mode of life (1 Pet. iv. 4; Eph. v. 18). Chrysostom: οὐκ εἶπε μὴ ἁπλῶς ἄσωτος, ἀλλὰ μηδὲ διαβολὴν ἔχειν τοιαύτην, μηδὲ πονηρᾶς εἶναι δόξης. — ἢ ἀνυπότακτα] see 1 Tim. iii. 5. Comp. the picture of the sons of Eli in 1 Sam. ii. 12 ff. As the bishop is to be an example to the church, his own house must be well conducted.

Ver 7. Δεῖ γάρ] The statements of ver. 6 are now confirmed by alluding to the higher moral necessity; "δεῖ is the emphatic word" (Wiesinger). — τὸν ἐπίσκ. ἀνέγκλητον εἶναι] ἀνέγκλ. is resumed from ver. 6, that the thought may be further developed. It is to be noted that the name ἐπίσκοπος appears here; it is given to the presbyter as superintendent of the church. As such "he must not be liable to any reproach, if he is to guide the church" (Wiesinger). — ὡς Θεοῦ οἰκόνομον] is added to give the reason for that higher necessity of the ἀνέγκλ εἶναι; Heydenreich wrongly turns it to mean simply that he must know how to superintend his house well. — ὡς = "as," i.e. "since he is." — Θεοῦ οἰκόνομος is the bishop in so far as there is committed to him by God authority in the ἐκκλησία as the οἶκος Θεοῦ (1 Tim. iii. 15). Mack is not wrong in proving from this expression that the ἐπίσκοποι are not merely "ministers and plenipotentiaries of the church." Even if they are elected by the church, they bear their office as divine, not exercising it according to the changing pleasure of those by whom they are elected, but according to the will of God. — μὴ αὐθάδη] occurs only here and in 2 Pet. ii. 10. It is compounded of αὐτός and ἀδέω, and synonymous with αὐτάρεσκος (2 Tim. iii. 2: φίλαυτος), "who in everything behaves arrogantly and regardlessly as seems good in his own eyes;" Luther: "wilful." — μὴ ὀργίλον] ἅπ. λεγ. "passionate," οἱ ὀργίλοι ταχέως ὀργίζονται. — μὴ πάροινον] see 1 Tim. iii. 3. — μὴ πλήκτην] see also 1 Tim. iii. 3. — μὴ αἰσχροκερδῆ] see 1 Tim. iii. 8; perhaps with special reference to the opportunities which the bishop had in his office of acquiring gain. — These five negative qualifications are opposed to arrogance, anger, and avarice; several positive qualifications follow.

Ver. 8. Ἀλλὰ φιλόξενον] see 1 Tim. iii. 2. — φιλάγαθον] ἅπ. λεγ. (the opposite in 2 Tim. iii. 3), loving either the good or what is good. Chrysostom is inaccurate: τὰ αὐτοῦ πάντα τοῖς δεομένοις προϊέμενος; and Luther: "kindly." — σώφρονα] see 1 Tim. iii. 2. — δίκαιον, ὅσιον] These two ideas are frequently placed together; comp. 1 Thess. ii. 10; Eph. iv. 24; Plato (Gorg. 507 B) thus distinguishes between them: καὶ μὴν περὶ μὲν ἀνθρώπους τὰ προσήκοντα πράττων δίκαι' ἂν πράττοι, περὶ δὲ θεοὺς ὅσια. — δίκαιος is one who does no wrong to his neighbour; ὅσιος is one who keeps himself free from that which stains him in the eyes of God; synonymous with ἄκακος, ἀμίαντος, Heb. vii. 26. — ἐγκρατῆ] ἅπ. λεγ., Chrysostom: τὸν πάθους κρατοῦντα, τὸν καὶ γλώττης, καὶ χειρὸς, καὶ ὀφθαλμῶν ἀκολάστων· τοῦτο γὰρ ἐστὶν ἐγκράτεια, τῷ μηδενὶ ὑποσύρεσθαι πάθει. There is no ground for limiting the word to the relation of the sexes; besides, ἐγκράτεια and ἐγκρατεύεσθαι in the N. T. hardly convey anything more than the general idea of self-control. The three last qualifications are closely related to each other, describing the conduct of the man towards his neighbour, towards God, towards himself; comp. ii. 12. — The positive qualifications in this verse are not *direct* antitheses to the negative qualifications in the preceding verse; still there is a certain antithesis of cognate ideas. This is the case with μὴ αὐθάδη and φιλόξενον, φιλάγαθον; with μὴ ὀργίλον, μὴ πάροινον, μὴ πλήκτην, and σώφρονα; μὴ αἰσχροκερδῆ and δίκαιον, ὅσιον, ἐγκρατῆ. Still these epithets, though corresponding to one another, are not quite the same in the extent of their application.

Ver. 9. To these requisites, somewhat general in nature, Paul adds another with special bearing on the official duties of a bishop: ἀντεχόμενον τοῦ κατὰ τὴν διδαχὴν πιστοῦ λόγου] The exposition given by most of the compound idea τοῦ ... λόγου is inaccurate and confused. Heydenreich divides the expression into two parts: (1) ὁ πιστὸς λόγος, "the true doctrine of the gospel;" and (2) ὁ λόγος κατὰ τὴν διδαχήν, "the doctrine in which the bishop is instructed," and gives the following translation: "holding firmly, as instructed, by the word which is certain (to reliable doctrine)." But manifestly this translation arbitrarily inverts the meaning. The words κατὰ τὴν διδαχήν are not dependent on πιστοῦ, but on λόγου, defined by πιστοῦ, so that τοῦ κ. τ. διδ. πιστοῦ λόγ. is equivalent to τοῦ πιστοῦ λόγου, τοῦ κατὰ τὴν διδαχήν. Ὁ πιστὸς λόγος does not occur elsewhere in our epistles, but there is no doubt that Paul means thereby the pure, wholesome word (λόγοι ὑγιαίνοντες, 1 Tim. vi. 3 ; οἱ λόγοι τῆς πίστεως, 1 Tim. iv. 6) of the gospel, in contrast to the false doctrine of the heretics. He uses the epithet πιστός because it is not treacherous, it can be relied on : "*the sure, reliable word.*" This sure word is defined more precisely by κατὰ τὴν διδαχήν] διδαχή is not active (Luther : "that which can teach"), but means, as it often does in the N. T., "*doctrine.*" Here it denotes "the Christian doctrine," which is none other than that preached by Christ Himself and by His apostles ; so Matthies, Wiesinger, Plitt, Hofmann. It is less appropriate to explain διδαχή to be " the instruction imparted " (so van Oosterzee, and formerly in this commentary);[1] comp. 1 Tim. iv. 6 ; 2 Thess. ii. 15. — ἀντέχεσθαι (in Matt. vi. 24, synonymous with ἀγαπᾶν, opposed to καταφρονεῖν ; used in a similar sense, 1 Thess. v. 14) occurs often in Polybius (see Raphelius on the passage) in the sense of : adhaerere, studiosum esse (ἀντέχεσθαι τῆς ἀληθείας). Here, too, it has this meaning, as in Phil. ii. 16 : ἐπέχειν ; 2 Thess. ii. 15 : κρατεῖν, "*adhere to.*" Luther : " he holds by the word." — Heydenreich rightly remarks that this does not indicate the zeal the teacher was to show in speaking of divine doctrine, but his own internal adherence, etc — ἵνα κ.τ.λ.] This adherence to the word is necessary for the bishop that he may discharge the duties of his office. It is further defined more precisely in two ways: ἵνα δυνατὸς ᾖ καὶ . . . καί : " both . . . and." The first is : παρακαλεῖν ἐν τῇ διδασκαλίᾳ τῇ ὑγιαινούσῃ, which refers to believers. παρακαλεῖν] *encourage, exhort ;* viz. to remain in the way on which they have entered, and to advance ever further in it, ἐν being here instrumental: " through, by means of." Matthies is incorrect : " to edify in sound doctrine ;" comp. 1 Thess. iv. 18 — ἡ διδασκ. ἡ ὑγιαιν.] see 1 Tim. i. 10. — The second is : τοὺς ἀντιλέγοντας ἐλέγχειν] " By correction and reproof to

---

[1] Several expositors cite, in explanation of this expression, the passage from Polyb. p. 815 · οἱ κατὰ τὴν παράκλησιν λόγοι, and according to this ὁ κατὰ τὴν διδαχὴν λόγος would be the word whose content is doctrine. But the attribute πιστός makes this explanation unsuitable.

refute those who contradict" (viz. the pure doctrine of the gospel), by which are meant the heretics. — Even in classic Greek, the two conceptions "refute" and "reprove" are sometimes combined in ἐλέγχειν; see Pape, s v. — This verse leads on to further description of the heretics.

Ver. 10. Εἰσὶ γάρ] γάρ shows that this verse serves to explain the preceding words. — πολλοὶ [καὶ] ἀνυπότακτοι] If καί be read, the phrase should be explained by the usage common in Greek of joining πολλοί with an adjective following it (see Matthiae, § 444, 4, p. 830), and ἀνυπότακτοι taken as an adjective. If καί be omitted, ἀνυπότακτοι may be taken as a substantive. The heretics are so named because they set themselves in opposition to the gospel and refuse obedience to it; the word is found also in 1 Tim. i. 9; Tit. i. 6. — The heretics are further styled ματαιόλογοι] see 1 Tim. i. 6, and φρεναπάται (ἄπ. λεγ.; the verb in Gal. vi. 3), "*misleaders*," almost synonymous with γόητες, 2 Tim iii. 13. — μάλιστα οἱ ἐκ περιτομῆς] A name for the Jewish-Christians, as in Gal. ii. 12. — μάλιστα indicates that the preachers of heresy in Crete were chiefly Jewish Christians, but that they had also found followers among the Gentile Christians. These appended words do not compel us to take ἀνυπότακτοι as the predicate, and the Christians of Crete as the unexpressed subject of εἰσίν (in opposition to Hofmann). Of course Paul by εἰσὶν γὰρ κ τ λ. means to say that Crete is the place where such chatterers are to be found.

Ver. 11. Οὓς δεῖ ἐπιστομίζειν] goes back to the end of ver. 9. — ἐπιστομίζειν (ἄπ λεγ.) is from ἐπιστόμιον, which denotes both the bridle-bit and the muzzle, and is equivalent either to freno compescere, coercere (synonymous with τοὺς χαλινοὺς εἰς τὰ στόματα βάλλειν, Jas. iii. 3), or to os obturare (= φιμοῦν, Matt. xxii. 34). The latter signification is more usual (see Elsner, p. 332): "put to silence." Theophylact: ἐλέγχειν σφοδρῶς, ὥστε ἀποκλείειν αὐτοῖς τὰ στόματα. — οἵτινες (= quippe qui, and giving the reason for οὓς δεῖ) ὅλους οἴκους ἀνατρέπουσι] The chief emphasis is laid on ὅλους: not merely individuals, but also whole families are misled by them into unbelief. — Ἀνατρέπειν] see 2 Tim. ii. 18; "the figure is here used in keeping with οἴκους" (Wiesinger). —

διδάσκοντες ἃ μὴ δεῖ] " teaching what should not be taught;" this shows the means by which they exercise so destructive an influence; ἃ μὴ δεῖ, equivalent to τὰ μὴ δέοντα, 1 Tim. v. 13.[1] — This refers to ματαιόλογοι, just as ἀνατρέπουσι does to φρεναπάται. — The purpose is briefly set forth by αἰσχροῦ κέρδους χάριν. The disgrace of their gain consists in the means they employ for acquiring it. The apostle adds these words to point out the selfish conduct of the heretics, who work only for their own profit.

Ver. 12 Paul quotes the saying of a Cretan poet as a testimony regarding the Cretans. — εἰπέ τις ἐξ αὐτῶν ἴδιος αὐτῶν προφήτης] ἐξ αὐτῶν is by most expositors referred to the preceding πολλοί or to οἱ ἐκ περιτομῆς; but such a reference is unsuitable; the apostle is rather thinking of Cretans in general. — The ἴδιος αὐτῶν declares still more strongly that the saying proceeds from a Cretan and not from a stranger, see Winer, p 139 [E. T. p. 192]. — προφήτης] According to Chrysostom, Theophylact, Epiphanius, Jerome, it is Epimenides who is meant. This Epimenides was a contemporary of the seven wise men, and by some was even reckoned as one of them in place of Periander; he was born in the sixth century B C. The saying quoted by Paul, which forms a complete hexameter, is said to have been in his lost work περὶ χρησμῶν. Theodoret, on the other hand, ascribes the saying to Callimachus, who, however, was a Cyrenian in the third century B.C.; besides, it is only the first words that occur in his *Hymn. ad Jov* ver. 8. Epiphanius and Jerome think that Callimachus took the words from Epimenides Paul does not call Epimenides a προφήτης because poets and philosophers were often called prophets in ancient times, but because the saying of Epimenides described beforehand the character of the Cretans as it was in the apostle's time Still it is to be noted that this very Epimenides was famed among the Greeks for his gift of wisdom, so that even Cicero (*De*

---

[1] The distinction between ἃ μὴ δεῖ and ἃ οὐ δεῖ is rightly given by Winer, p 448 [E. T. p 603]. The former expresses as a moral conception what the latter denotes objectively. We cannot, however, go as far as Hofmann, who says: "μή indicates that they who thus teach are conscious they ought not to do so, and teach in this way nevertheless."

Divinat. xviii.) places him among those vaticinantes per furorem. Comp. Diogenes Laertius, *Vita Philos.* p. 81, ed. Henr. Steph. — Κρῆτες ἀεὶ ψεῦσται] Chrysostom refers these words chiefly to the pretence of the Cretans that Jupiter lay buried among them; to this, at any rate, the verse of Callimachus refers;[1] but the Cretans in ancient times were notorious for falsehood, so that, according to Hesychius, κρητίζειν is synonymous with ψεύδεσθαι καὶ ἀπατᾶν; for proofs of this, see in Wetstein. — κακὰ θηρία] denoting their wild, unruly character; some expositors refer this name specially to the greed of the Cretans, as Polybius, book vi., specially mentions their αἰσχροκερδία καὶ πλεονεξία; but it is more than improbable that Epimenides had this meaning in his words. — γαστέρες ἀργαί] synonymous with Phil. iii. 19. ὧν ὁ Θεὸς ἡ κοιλία (comp. Rom. xvi. 18, 2 Pet. ii. 13, 14); this denotes the Cretans as men given to sensuality. Plato, too (*De Legg.* i.), reproaches them with lust and immodesty. — The apostle's purpose in quoting this saying of Epimenides is indicated in the next verse. The national character of the Cretans was such that they were easily persuaded to listen to the heretics, and hence it was all the more necessary to oppose the latter firmly.

Ver. 13. In confirmation of the verse quoted, Paul says: ἡ μαρτυρία αὕτη ἐστὶν ἀληθής, and attaches to it an exhortation to Titus.[2] Bertholdt, without reason, holds this verse to be a later interpolation. — δι' ἣν αἰτίαν] see 2 Tim. i. 6. Chrysostom: διὰ τοῦτο· ἐπειδὴ ἦθος αὐτοῖς ἐστιν ἰταμὸν καὶ δολερὸν καὶ ἀκόλαστον; it refers to the picture of the Cretan

---

[1] This verse runs·

Κρῆτες ἀεὶ ψεῦσται.   καὶ γὰρ τάφον, ὦ ἄνα, σεῖο
Κρῆτες ἐτεκτήναντο·   σὺ δὲ οὐ θάνες ἐστὶ γὰρ ἀεί.

[2] De Wette thinks this confirmation by Paul himself hard and unjust, since the gospel had been received in Crete in such a way that several churches were formed in a short time. But in spite of the character here described, there might still be many individuals ready to receive the gospel; and yet because of that peculiarity there was ground for anxiety lest they should be easily misled into unfaithfulness. De Wette is also wrong in thinking that the expression regarding the Cretans in vv. 12 f. does not harmonize with the apostle's prudence in teaching —But how bitterly Luther expresses himself regarding the Germans, calling them, *e.g.*, animals and mad beasts! Was Luther on that account deficient in prudence in his teaching?

character given in the testimony. — ἔλεγχε αὐτοὺς ἀποτόμως] ἔλεγχε, as in ver. 9; "the apostle here drops all reference to the bishops to be appointed, and assigns to Titus himself the duty of applying a remedy" (Wiesinger). — αὐτούς] not so much the heretics as the Cretans, who were exposed to their misleading influence. These latter needed the ἐλέγχειν, because they were not resisting the heretics as they ought, but (as οἵτινες ὅλους οἴκους ἀνατρέπουσι shows) were yielding to them easily. — ἀποτόμως] "sharply, strictly;" elsewhere only in 2 Cor. xiii. 10; the substantive ἀποτομία in Rom. xi. 22. — ἵνα ὑγιαίνωσιν ἐν τῇ πίστει] "that they may be sound in the faith" De Wette takes this as the immediate contents of the ἐλέγχειν, just as ἵνα occurs with παρακαλεῖν, but without good grounds. 'Ἐν here is not instrumental (Heinrichs. per religionem), but πίστις is the subject in which they are to be sound.

Ver. 14. One especial requisite for the ὑγιαίνειν ἐν τῇ πίστει is given by Paul in the participial clause: μὴ προσέχοντες Ἰουδαϊκοῖς μύθοις καὶ ἐντολαῖς κ.τ.λ.] προσέχοντες, see 1 Tim. i. 4, iv. 1. Here, as in the epistles to Timothy, the heresies are called μῦθοι, from the theories they contained; see on 1 Tim. i. 4. Here, however, they are further defined by the epithet Ἰουδαϊκοί, as they were peculiar to Jewish speculation, though their substance was derived from Gentile modes of thought. The description, too, in the First Epistle to Timothy shows that to the speculative part of the heresy there was added a legal element founded on an arbitrary interpretation of the Mosaic law. The ἐντολαί of the heretics are here called ἐντολαὶ ἀνθρώπων ἀποστρεφομένων τὴν ἀλήθειαν: "commands of men which depart from the truth," because they were founded not on Christianity, but on the arbitrary wills of men estranged from Christianity. These ἐντολαί consisted not so much of moral precepts, as of prohibitions of food and the like, see 1 Tim. iv. 3. Hofmann refers the adjective Ἰουδαϊκοῖς, and the defining words ἀνθρώπων κ.τ.λ., to both substantives,—a possible construction, but not necessary. His reasons are far from sufficient. — ἀποστρεφομένων] see 2 Tim. i. 15.

Ver. 15. The apostle, bearing in mind the prohibitions of

the heretics, opposes to them a general principle which shows their worthlessness. — πάντα καθαρὰ τοῖς καθαροῖς] πάντα quite generally: *all things in themselves,* with which a man may simply have to do, but not a man's actions, nor, as Heydenreich thinks, the errors of the heretics. The usual explanation which limits the bearing of the words to the arbitrary rules of the heretics regarding food and other things, is only so far right that Paul lays down his general principle with special reference to these rules; but πάντα itself should be taken quite generally. Even the exposition of Matthies: " all that falls into the sphere of the individual wants of life," places an unsuitable limitation on the meaning Chrysostom rightly: οὐδὲν ὁ Θεὸς ἀκάθαρτον ἐποίησεν — καθαρά as the predicate of πάντα is to be connected with it by supplying ἐστί: "*all is pure,*" viz. τοῖς καθαροῖς. Bengel: omnia externa iis, qui intus sunt mundi, munda sunt. Many expositors wrongly refer the conception of καθαροί to knowledge, as Jerome: qui sciunt omnem creaturam bonam esse, or as Beza: quibus notum est libertatis per Christum partae beneficium. It should rather be taken as referring to disposition: to those who have a pure heart everything is pure (not: " to them everything *passes* for pure"), *i.e.* as to the pure, things outside of them have no power to render them impure. From the same point of view we have in the *Testam XII. Patriarch. test. Benjam.* chap viii.: ὁ ἔχων διάνοιαν καθαρὰν ἐν ἀγάπῃ, οὐχ ὁρᾷ γυναῖκα εἰς πορνείαν· οὐ γὰρ ἔχει μιασμὸν ἐν τῇ καρδίᾳ. Kindred thoughts are found in Matt. xxiii 26; Luke xi. 41, comp. also the similar expression in Rom xiv 20. On καθαροῖς, van Oosterzee remarks " By nature no one is pure; those here called καθαροί are those who have purified their heart by faith, Acts xv. 9." This is right, except that Paul is not thinking here of the means by which the man becomes καθαρός; the indication of this point is given afterwards in ἀπίστοις. The apostle purposely makes the sentence very emphatic, because it was with the distinction between pure and impure that the heretics occupied themselves so much. — The contrast to the first sentence is given in the words: τοῖς δὲ μεμιαμμένοις καὶ ἀπίστοις οὐδὲν καθαρόν. Regarding the form μεμιαμμένος, see Winer, p 84 [E. T.

p. 108] [also Veitch, Irregular Greek Verbs, *s.v.*]. The verb forms a simple contrast with καθαροῖς, and stands here not in a Levitical (John xviii. 28), but in an ethical sense, as in Heb. xii. 15; Jude 8. Καὶ ἀπίστοις is not an epexegesis of μεμιαμμ., but adds a new point to it, viz. the attitude of the heretics towards the saving truths of the gospel. The two words do not denote two different classes of men, as the article τοῖς is only used once. To these impure men nothing is pure, *i.e.* every external thing serves only to awaken within them impure lust. — ἀλλὰ μεμίανται αὐτῶν καὶ ὁ νοῦς καὶ ἡ συνείδησις] This sentence expresses positively what οὐδὲν καθαρόν expressed negatively, at the same time furnishing the reason for the preceding thought. De Wette's opinion therefore is not correct, that "for ἀλλά there should properly have been γάρ, the author, however, makes moral *character* equivalent to moral *action*." The relation of the two sentences is pretty much the same as if, *e g*, we were to say: he is not rich, but his father has disinherited him. If Paul had used γάρ, the sentence would simply have furnished the reason for what preceded; ἀλλά, on the other hand, indicates the contrast. Still we must not conclude, with Hofmann, that the second sentence merely says the same thing as the first. It should be interpreted: "but to them everything is impure, because their νοῦς and their συνείδησις are defiled." — Νοῦς and συνείδησις do not here denote the inner nature of man on the two sides of knowledge and will (so Hofmann). Νοῦς is the spiritual faculty of man acting in both directions; in N. T. usage the reference to action prevails, νοῦς being equivalent to the practical reason. Συνείδησις, on the other hand, is the human consciousness connected with action, and expressing itself regarding the moral value of action, it corresponds to "conscience" (see on 1 Tim. 1. 3).[1] The two conceptions are distinguished from each other by καὶ ... καί,

---

[1] De Wette asserts, without reason, that συνείδησις is the "consciousness *that follows*," since the consciousness of the deed may precede as well as accompany and follow it —Wiesinger explains νοῦς inaccurately by . "the entire spiritual habitus" (van Oosterzee still more inaccurately by "the tendency of the man, the direction of his entire disposition"), but συνείδησις quite accurately by · "the moral consciousness of my thinking and action in their relation to the law."

and at the same time closely connected. By this, however, no special emphasis is laid on the second word (formerly in this commentary). In iii. 11 (αὐτοκατάκριτος) and 1 Tim. iv. 2, the apostle again says as much as that the conscience of the heretics was defiled. Though the thought contained in this verse is quite general in character, Paul wrote it with special reference to the heretics, and is therefore able to attach to it a further description of them.

Ver. 16. Θεὸν ὁμολογοῦσιν εἰδέναι] not: " they pretend" (Matthies), but " they loudly and publicly confess,"[1] that they know God. Paul leaves it undecided whether their confession is correct or not. He does not grant to them, as de Wette thinks, that " they have the theoretical knowledge of God, and in a practical aspect," nor does he deny this to them. His purpose here is to declare that, in spite of this their confession, their actions are of such a nature as to argue that they had no knowledge of God: τοῖς δὲ ἔργοις ἀρνοῦνται] ἀρνοῦνται, opposed to ὁμολογοῦσιν, see 1 Tim. v. 8; 2 Tim. iii. 5. Supply Θεὸν εἰδέναι (so, too, van Oosterzee, Hofmann). — βδελυκτοὶ ὄντες καὶ ἀπειθεῖς] βδελυκτός (ἅπ. λεγ), equivalent to abominabilis, detestable (comp. Luke xvi. 15); Luther: " whom God holds in abomination." — The word is joined with ἀκάθαρτος in Prov. xvii. 15, LXX. Paul does not apply this epithet to the heretics, because they were defiling themselves with actual worship of idols, which especially was regarded by the Jews as βδέλυγμα, but in order to describe their moral depravity. — καὶ ἀπειθεῖς] " and disobedient," synonymous with ἀνυπότακτοι in ver. 10; this indicates why they are βδελυκτοί. — καὶ πρὸς πᾶν ἔργον ἀγαθὸν ἀδόκιμοι] " the result of the preceding characteristics " (Wiesinger); ἀδόκιμος, as 2 Tim. iii. 8.

---

[1] Hofmann asserts that this explanation is contrary to the meaning of the word, and that ὁμολογεῖν here must be taken in its most general signification as = "declare, affirm;" but we cannot see why. It is to be noted that ὁμολογεῖν in the N. T. always indicates an utterance more or less emphatic, also Matt. vii 23 (comp. Meyer on the passage).

CHAPTER II.

VER. 3. ἐν καταστήματι] For this F G, without reason, have κατασχήματι. — Some MSS. (C H** *al*) have the reading ἱεροπρεπεῖ, Vulg.: in habitu sancto, which gives a good enough meaning, but must, however, be regarded as a mere correction; see Reiche on the passage. — μὴ οἴνῳ] A C ℵ 73, *al*, have the reading μηδέ for μή. — Ver 4. For the *Rec*. σωφρονίζωσιν, supported by C D E K L, σωφρονίζουσιν is read by A F G H ℵ, *al*. (Lachm Tisch). The conjunctive seems to be a correction, because the indicative contradicts the force of the ἵνα; but also in 1 Cor. iv. 6, Gal. iv. 17, it stands after ἵνα. In these passages, however, Meyer explains ἵνα as equivalent to *ubi*; comp. Winer, pp. 272 f. [E. T. p. 363], and Buttm. p. 202 As in later postapostolic times, the construction with the indic. was not unusual; σωφρονίζουσιν is possibly to be ascribed to a later copyist — Ver. 5. Instead of the word οἰκουρούς (*Rec*. supported by D*** H J K, the cursives, Fathers, and versions), which occurs frequently in classic Greek, A C D* E F G ℵ have the word οἰκουργούς (Lachm. Buttm. Tisch.), which is not used elsewhere. Matthies declares this to be a lectio vitiosa et inepta; so Reiche. De Wette thinks it an error in copying, as the word does not occur elsewhere. This certainly is possible, and yet it is strange that it should have such weighty testimony. Matthaei thinks that the scribae istorum sex codicum were so very barbari that the word οἰκουρός was unknown to them; but that is hardly conceivable. — Ver. 7. The *Rec*. ἀδιαφθορίαν (D*** E* L, *al*, Chrys.) is to be exchanged for the reading ἀφθορίαν (A C D* E* K ℵ, *al*., Lachm. Buttm. Tisch.), though Reiche seeks to prove from the meaning of two substantives not used elsewhere that the *Rec* should be preferred. As the adj. ἀδιάφθορος frequently occurs, and ἄφθορος but seldom, we may readily suppose that the *Rec*. was a correction in keeping with the more usual adjective. — After σεμνότητα, D** E, gr. 23, 44, and many other cursives, etc., have the word ἀφθαρσίαν; but the weightest authorities are against its genuineness, A C D* (E apud Mill) F G 47, *al*., Syr. Erp. Copt. Aeth. Vulg. It. etc. — Ver. 8 περὶ ἡμῶν] so Griesb. Scholz, Tisch., supported by C D E F G K L P ℵ

17, 23, al, many versions and Fathers. Lachm retained the common reading. — Both readings give a good sense, but the testimony assigns the preference to ἡμῶν. Matthies wrongly says that A C D E F G have the reading ὑμῶν — Ver. 9. Instead of ἰδίοις δεσπόταις (Tisch. 8, on the authority of C F G K L א), Lachm. (so, too, Tisch. 7) reads δεσπόταις ἰδίοις, on the authority of A D E 27, al., Vulg It Jerome, Ambrosiast al — Ver. 10. For μή, the correction μηδέ is found in D F G, al, 17. — πᾶσαν πίστιν] for πίστιν πᾶσαν (Tisch 7). This is read by Lachm. Buttm Tisch 8, on the authority of A C D E א 31, 37, al., Vulg Clar. Germ. Jerome, Ambrosiast. — After διδασκαλίαν Griesb inserted τήν, with the support of the weightiest authorities, A C D E F G I א, al., Chrys. Theodor. — Ver. 11. Instead of ἡ σωτήριος (Tisch. 7), σωτήριος, *without the article*, has been adopted by Lachm. Buttm. Tisch 8, on the authority of A* C* D א, Syr. utr The reading: τοῦ σωτῆρος ἡμῶν, found in F G, Copt. Aeth. al, must have arisen from ver. 10; still א has σωτῆρος. — Ver. 13. Tisch. 7 reads Ἰησοῦ Χριστοῦ, with the support of most MSS., on the other hand, Tisch. 8 reads Χριστοῦ Ἰησοῦ.

Ver. 1. Instructions to Timothy how he is to exhort the various members of families, down to ver 10. — σὺ δέ] see 2 Tim. iii. 10, iv. 5. A contrast with the heretics, not, however, as Chrysostom puts it: αὐτοί εἰσιν ἀκάθαρτοι· ἀλλὰ μὴ τούτων ἔνεκεν σιγήσῃς It is with regard to their unseemly doctrine that Paul says: σὺ δὲ λάλει ἃ πρέπει τῇ ὑγιαιν. διδασκαλίᾳ. In contrast with their μῦθοι and ἐντολαὶ ἀνθρώπων, Titus is to speak things in harmony with sound doctrine, by which are meant not so much the doctrines of the gospel themselves, as the commands founded on them, vv 3 ff. (Wiesinger) On τῇ ὑγ διδ., see i 9.
Ver. 2. The members of the family are distinguished according to age and sex. First, we have πρεσβύτας, which is not equivalent to πρεσβυτέρους, the official name, but denotes age simply: senes aetate; Philem. 9; Luke i. 18. — νηφαλίους εἶναι] The accusative does not depend on a word understood such as παρακάλει, but is an object accusative to the verb preceding λάλει ἃ πρέπει: "viz. that the old men be νηφάλιοι." — νηφαλίους] see 1 Tim. iii. 2. — σεμνούς] see 1 Tim ii. 2. — σώφρονας] i 8, 1 Tim. iii. 2. — ὑγιαίνοντας τῇ πίστει, τῇ ἀγάπῃ, τῇ ὑπομονῇ] On the use of the dative

here, for which in i. 13 there stands the preposition ἐν, see Winer, p. 204 [E. T. p. 272], it is to be explained as equivalent to "in respect of, in regard to."—Τo πίστις and ἀγάπη, the cardinal virtues of the Christian life, ὑπομονή (quasi utriusque condimentum, Calvin) is added, the stedfastness which no sufferings can shake. All three conceptions are found together also in 1 Thess. i. 3 (ἡ ὑπομονὴ τῆς ἐλπίδος); ὑπομ. and πίστις in 2 Thess. i. 4; ἀγ. καὶ ὑπομ., 2 Thess. iii. 5, comp. also 1 Tim. vi. 11; 2 Tim. iii 10.

Ver. 3. Πρεσβύτιδας ("the aged women" = πρεσβύτεραι in 1 Tim. v. 2) ὡσαύτως (see 1 Tim. ii. 9) ἐν καταστήματι ἱεροπρεπεῖς] κατάστημα is taken in too narrow a sense, only of the clothing (Oecumenius: τὰ περιβόλαια). It denotes the entire external deportment; Jerome: ut ipse earum incessus et motus, vultus, sermo, silentium, quandam decoris sacri praeferant dignitatem. Heydenreich, on the other hand, makes the conception too wide, when he includes under it the temper of mind. — ἱεροπρεπεῖς] (ἄπ. λεγ) is equivalent to καθὼς πρέπει ἁγίοις, Eph. v. 3, comp. also 1 Tim. ii. 10. Luther rightly. "that they behave themselves as becometh saints"— μὴ διαβόλους] see 1 Tim iii. 11.— μὴ οἴνῳ πολλῷ δεδουλωμένας is equivalent to μὴ οἴν. π. προσέχοντας in 1 Tim. iii. 8 — καλοδιδασκάλους] (ἄπ. λεγ) Beza: "honestatis magistrae; agitur hic de domestica disciplina;" but not so much by example as by exhortation and teaching, as appears from what follows.

Vv. 4, 5. "Ἵνα σωφρονίζωσι τὰς νέας κ.τ.λ] Since σωφρονίζειν must necessarily have an object, τὰς νέας κ.τ.λ should not, like πρεσβύτας νηφαλίους εἶναι, ver. 2, and πρεσβύτιδας, ver. 3, be joined with λάλει, ver. 1 (Hofmann), but with σωφρονίζουσιν, so that the exhortations given to the *young women* are to proceed from the older women.[1] — σωφρονίζειν]

---

[1] Of course there might be circumstances in which σωφρονίζειν could stand without an object, as e g παρακαλεῖν in 2 Tim. iv. 2 (to which Hofmann, appeals), but here a definite object was needed to tell to whom the σωφρον. of the older women had reference, it being impossible to assign it to them without some limitation. It is to be noted that in the passage—in which παρεκάλεσεν is joined with another transitive verb—the object is very easily supplied, and that in the N. T., when παρακαλεῖν is used, the more precise limitation is expressly given, or can be easily supplied from the context

(ἅπ. λεγ.) is properly "bring some one to σωφροσύνη," then "amend," viz. by punishment; it also occurs in the sense of "punish, chastise;" it is synonymous with νουθετεῖν.[1] According to Beza, it expresses opposition to the juvenilis lascivia et alia ejus aetatis ac sexus vitia. — The aim of the σωφρονίζειν is given in the next words: φιλάνδρους (ἅπ. λεγ.) εἶναι, φιλοτέκνους (ἅπ. λεγ.). These two ideas are suitably placed first, as pointing to the first and most obvious circumstances of the νέαι. — Ver. 5. σώφρονας ἁγνάς] The latter is to be taken here not in the general sense of "blameless," but in the more special sense of "chaste" (Wiesinger). — οἰκουρούς (*Rec*); Wahl rightly: "ex οἶκος et οὖρος custos: custos domus, de feminis, quae domi se continent neque περιέρχονται, 1 Tim. v. 13." Vulgate. domus curam habentes; Luther: "domestic." The word οἰκουργούς (read by Tischendorf, see critical remarks) does not occur elsewhere; if it be genuine, it must mean "*working in the house*" (Alford: "workers at home"), which, indeed, does not agree with the formation of the word. The word οἰκουργεῖν occurring in later Greek means: "make a house;" see Pape, *s v*. — Chrysostom: ἡ οἰκουρὸς γυνὴ καὶ σώφρων ἔσται· ἡ οἰκουρὸς καὶ οἰκονομική· οὔτε περὶ τρυφὴν, οὔτε περὶ ἐξόδους ἀκαίρους, οὔτε περὶ ἄλλων τῶν τοιούτων ἀσχοληθήσεται. — ἀγαθάς] is rightly taken by almost all as an independent epithet: "kindly." Some expositors, however, connect it with οἰκουρούς (so Theophylact, Oecumenius); but this is wrong, since οἰκουρούς is itself an adjective. Hofmann joins it with οἰκουργούς, and translates it "good housewives" (so Buttmann, in his edition of the N. T., has no comma between the two words), but where are the grounds for explaining οἰκουργούς to mean "*housewives*"? — ὑποτασσομένας τοῖς ἰδίοις ἀνδράσιν] On τοῖς ἰδίοις ἀνδρ., comp. 1 Cor. vii. 2. The thought that wives are to be subject to their husbands is often expressed in the N. T. in the same words, comp. Eph. v. 22; Col. iii. 18; 1 Pet. iii. 1. It is to be noted that the apostle adds this ὑποτασσομένας after using φιλάνδρους. The one thing does not put an end to the other; on the contrary, neither quality is of the right kind unless it

---

[1] Dio Cassius, lv. p. 650: διὰ τοὺς μὲν λόγοις νουθετεῖν, τοὺς δὲ ἀπειλαῖς σωφρονίζειν.

includes the other. How much weight was laid by the apostle on the ὑποτάσσεσθαι may be seen from the words: ἵνα μὴ ὁ λόγος τοῦ Θεοῦ βλασφημῆται, which are closely connected with ὑποτασσομένας κ.τ.λ.; comp. ver. 10, where the same thought is expressed positively, and 1 Tim. vi. 1. The apostolic preaching of freedom and equality in Christ might easily be applied in a fleshly sense for removing all natural subordination, and thus disgrace be brought on the word of God; hence the express warning. The remark of Chrysostom: εἰ συμβαίη γυναῖκα πιστὴν ἀπίστῳ συνοικοῦσαν, μὴ εἶναι ἐνάρετον, ἡ βλασφημία ἐπὶ τὸν Θεὸν διαβαίνειν εἴωθεν, is unsatisfactory, because the apostle's words are thereby arbitrarily restricted to a relation which is quite special.

Ver. 6. Τοὺς νεωτέρους] "*the younger men;*" not, as Matthies supposes, the younger members of the church, without distinction of sex [1] — ὡσαύτως] here, as in ver. 3, on account of the similarity of the exhortation. — παρακάλει σωφρονεῖν] equivalent to σώφρονας εἶναι, opposed to omnibus immoderatis affectibus (Beza). Hofmann: "The whole purport of the apostle's exhortations is included by the apostle in the one word σωφρονεῖν, which therefore contains everything in which the moral influence of Christianity may be displayed."

Vv. 7, 8. The exhortation by word is to be accompanied by the exhortation of example. — περὶ πάντα] does not belong to what precedes, but begins a new sentence, and is put first for emphasis. Πάντα is not masculine: "towards every one," but neuter. "in regard to all things, in all points." — σεαυτὸν παρεχόμενος τύπον καλῶν ἔργων] On the use of the middle παρέχεσθαι with the pronoun ἑαυτόν, "show himself," see Winer, p. 242 [E. T. p. 322] (comp. Xenophon, *Cyrop.* viii. 1. 39: παράδειγμα . . . τοιόνδε ἑαυτὸν παρείχετο). — τύπον, "type," is in the N. T. only found here with the genitive of the thing. — καλὰ ἔργα] 1 Tim. v. 10; an expres-

---

[1] Hofmann remarks that the transition to the younger men makes it clear "that he was to exhort the younger women also himself, and not merely by means of the older ones;" but in that case Paul would simply have written· τοὺς νεωτέρους σωφρονεῖν, and further, in that case it would have been more natural for him to mention the νεώτεροι first and then the νέαι.

sion often occurring in the Pastoral Epistles. — ἐν τῇ διδασ-καλίᾳ ἀφθορίαν] This and the following accusatives are dependent on παρεχόμενος; see Col. iv. 1. Luther inaccurately: "with unadulterated doctrine, with sobriety," etc.; Jerome: in doctrina, in integritate et castitate. — ἀφθορία, only in later Greek, is from ἄφθορος (in Artemidorus, ver. 95: de virginibus puerisque intactis et illibatis legitur; Reiche; Esth. ii. 2: κοράσια ἄφθορα καλὰ τῷ εἴδει), which is equivalent to "*chaste*," and therefore means "*unstained chastity*." Ἀδιαφθορία (*Rec.*) is of more general signification; it is also used of virgin chastity (Artac. 26, Diodorus Siculus, i. 59), but denotes in general soundness, also especially incorruptibility. Older as well as more recent expositors (Heydenreich, Mack, Wiesinger) refer the word here to the disposition: "purity of disposition;"[1] but it is more in accordance with the context to understand by it something immediately connected with the διδασκαλία, to which σεμνότητα also refers. Matthies, de Wette, and others refer it (as does Luther also) to the subject-matter of the doctrine; de Wette: "incorruptness in doctrine, i.e. unadulterated doctrine." But in that case it would mean the same thing as the following λόγον ὑγιῆ; there is no justification for Bengel's interpreting ἐν διδασκαλίᾳ to mean *public* addresses, and λόγον the talk of daily intercourse. According to its original meaning, ἀφθορία is most suitably taken to mean chastity in doctrine, which avoids everything not in harmony with its true subject and aim, and it has a special reference to the form (comp. 1 Cor. ii. 1, 3). So, too, van Oosterzee: "the form of the doctrine which Titus preaches is to be pure, chaste, free from everything that conflicts with the nature of the gospel." — σεμνότητα, on the other hand, denotes dignity in the style of delivery. Both these things, the ἀφθορία and the σεμνότης, were injured by the heretics in their λογομαχίαις.[2] — λόγον ὑγιῆ ἀκατάγνωστον (ἅπ. λεγ.) refers to the subject-matter of the doctrine: "*sound,*

---

[1] Reiche, who prefers the reading ἀδιαφθορίαν, agrees with the exposition of Erasmus: integritas animi nullis cupiditatibus corrupti, non ira non ambitione non avaritia.

[2] Hofmann wishes to refer both words to the subject-matter and form alike, and so, also, with λόγον ὑγιῆ; but we cannot see why in that case Paul does not specially name the latter.

unblameable word," in opposition to the corruptions made by the heretics.—The purpose is thus given : ἵνα ὁ ἐξ ἐναντίας ἐντραπῇ] ὁ ἐξ ἐναντίας (ἅπ. λεγ.), qui ex adverso est ; according to Chrysostom : ὁ διάβολος καὶ πᾶς ὁ ἐκείνῳ διακονούμενος ; but the next words are against this interpretation. According to ver. 5 and 1 Tim. vi. 1, it means the non-Christian opponent of the gospel, and not the Christian heretic (Heydenreich, Wiesinger). — ἐντραπῇ, "*be ashamed, take shame to oneself;*" 1 Cor. iv. 14 ; 2 Thess. iii. 14. The reason for the shame is contained in the words : μηδὲν ἔχων περὶ ἡμῶν (or ὑμῶν) λέγειν φαῦλον] "*having nothing wicked to say of us.*"—If περὶ ἡμῶν be the correct reading, it is not to be limited to Titus and Paul, but should be taken more generally. With the reading ὑμῶν, on the other hand, the apostle's words refer to Titus and the churches that follow his example.

Vv. 9, 10. Exhortation in regard to slaves. — δούλους ἰδίοις δεσπόταις (or δεσπόταις ἰδίοις) ὑποτάσσεσθαι] The construction shows that Paul is continuing the instructions which he gives to Timothy in regard to the various members of families, so that vv. 7 and 8 are parenthetical ; παρακάλει is to be supplied from ver. 6. Heydenreich and Matthies wrongly make this verse dependent on ver. 1. The harder the lot of the slaves, and the more unendurable this might appear to the Christian slave conscious of his Christian dignity, the more necessary was it to impress upon him the ὑποτάσσεσθαι. Even this is not sufficient, and so Paul further adds : ἐν πᾶσιν εὐαρέστους εἶναι. Ἐν πᾶσιν, equivalent to "*in all points*" (ver. 7 : περὶ πάντα ; Col iii. 20, 22 : κατὰ πάντα), is usually joined with εὐαρέστους εἶναι ; Hofmann, on the contrary, wishes to connect it with ὑποτάσσεσθαι. Both constructions are possible ; still the usual one is to be preferred, because the very position of the slaves made it a matter óf course that the ὑποτάσσεσθαι should be evinced in its full extent, whereas the same could not be said of εὐάρεστοι εἶναι, since that goes beyond the duty of ὑποτάσσεσθαι. The word εὐάρεστος occurs frequently in the Pauline Epistles, but only in speaking of the relation to God. The two first exhortations refer to general conduct ; to these the apostle adds two special points: μὴ ἀντιλέγοντας and μὴ νοσφιζομένους. Hofmann is wrong in saying that μὴ ἀντιλέγοντας is the antithesis of εὐαρέστους. The conduct of slaves, which is well-pleasing to masters, includes more than refraining from contradiction. Van Oosterzee says not incorrectly: "It is not contradiction in particular instances, but the habitus that is here indicated." Luther: "not contradicting." The verb νοσφίζεσθαι is found only here and in Acts v. 2, 3 : "*not pilfering, defrauding*."— The next words: ἀλλὰ πᾶσαν πίστιν ἐνδεικνυμένους ἀγαθήν (Luther · "but showing all good fidelity"), is in the first place opposed to μὴ νοσφιζομένους, but includes more than merely to abstain from defrauding (in opposition to Hofmann). As in ver. 5, so, too, here, where the maintenance of the natural duties of subordinates is under discussion, the apostle adds ἵνα τὴν διδασκαλίαν κ.τ.λ., except that the expression is now positive, whereas before it was negative; the thought is substantially the same. — ἡ διδασκαλία is equivalent to ὁ λόγος, τὸ εὐαγγέλιον. — τοῦ σωτῆρος ἡμ. Θεοῦ] see 1 Tim. i. 1 ; not, as some expositors (Calvin, Wolf) think, Christ, but God. — κοσμῶσιν] "*do honour to.*" — ἐν πᾶσιν] ver. 9, "*in all points*," not "with all, in the eyes of all" (Hofmann).—Chrysostom : οὐ γὰρ ἀπὸ δόγματος δόγματα, ἀλλ' ἀπὸ πραγμάτων καὶ βίου τὰ δόγματα κρίνουσιν οἱ Ἕλληνες· ἔστωσαν ἐν αὐτοῖς καὶ γυναῖκες καὶ δοῦλοι διδάσκαλοι διὰ τῆς οἰκείας ἀναστροφῆς.

Vv. 11–14. Foundation for the moral precepts given from the nature of Christianity: eximium ex evangelii medulla motivum inseritur (Bengel).—Chrysostom (πολλὴν παρὰ τῶν οἰκετῶν ἀπαιτήσας τὴν ἀρετήν, ἀπάγει καὶ τὴν αἰτίαν δικαίαν, δι' ἣν ὀφείλουσι τοιοῦτοι εἶναι οἱ οἰκέται) and others refer ver. 11 (γάρ) only to the exhortation to slaves which immediately precedes. It is more correct, however, to refer it to the whole sum of moral precepts, given from ver. 1 onwards (so, too, van Oosterzee, Plitt, Hofmann). — ἐπεφάνη γὰρ ἡ χάρις τοῦ Θεοῦ] ἐπεφάνη (see iii. 4) is used of the sun in Acts xxvii. 20. Possibly Paul is speaking here with this figure in mind (comp. Isa. ix. 2, lx. 1 ; Luke i. 79), as Heydenreich, Wiesinger, van Oosterzee suppose ; but possibly, also, the expression simply means that the χάρις τοῦ Θεοῦ, formerly hidden in God, has come forth from concealment and become manifest and visible. — ἡ χάρις τοῦ Θεοῦ] The old writers on dogma give to this expression, which denotes the absolute ground of the work of redemption, too special a reference to Christ's incarnation; Oecumenius: ἡ μετὰ σαρκὸς ἐπιδημία; Theodoret: τούτου χάριν ἐνηνθρώπησεν ὁ μονογενὴς τοῦ Θεοῦ υἱὸς, ἵνα κ.τ λ. It need hardly be said that he is speaking here not simply of a revelation of the divine grace *by teaching*, but also of its appearance *in act*, viz. in the act of redemption. — To define the χάρις more accurately, there is added: σωτήριος πᾶσιν ἀνθρώποις] not: "as bringing salvation" (de Wette, van Oosterzee). This would make σωτήριος here the main point, which from the context it cannot be; the main point is not given till παιδεύουσα. Σωτήριος is rather an adjective qualifying the substantive χάρις: "there appeared the grace bringing salvation to all men." With the *Rec.* ἡ σωτήριος this construction is beyond doubt. — πᾶσιν ἀνθρώποις] does not depend on ἐπεφάνη, but on σωτήριος. Matthies is not intelligible in regarding it as dependent on both.[1] — The emphasis laid on the universality of the salvation, as in 1 Tim. ii. 4 and other passages of the Pastoral Epistles, is purely Pauline.

Ver. 12. Παιδεύουσα ἡμᾶς, ἵνα κ τ.λ] On this the chief emphasis is laid. By παιδεύουσα the apostle makes it clear that "the grace of God has a paedagogic purpose" (Heydenreich). Here, as also elsewhere in the N. T., παιδεύειν does not simply mean "educate," but "educate by disciplinary correction." Hence Luther is not incorrect in translating: "and chastises us." This reference is to be noted here, as is shown by the next words: ἀρνησάμενοι κ.τ.λ. *Ἵνα* does not indicate the purpose here, but the object to be supplied, for παιδ. is not subjective, but objective; the sentence beginning with ἵνα might also have been expressed by the infinitive; comp. 1 Tim i. 20 ; not therefore "*in order that* we," but "*that* we." On this use of ἵνα, see Winer, pp. 314 ff.[2] [E. T. pp.

---

[1] Wiesinger translates: "for there appeared the grace of God which brings salvation to all men;" and on the construction of πᾶσιν ἀνθρώποις he afterwards says "according to the context, it can only be construed with σωτήριος."

[2] Wiesinger translates. "educating us, that we ... live holily," but thinks that ἵνα is to be retained in its proper signification as denoting the *aim* of the

420–426]. — ἀρνησάμενοι] see i. 16 : "denying," *i.e.* renouncing, abandoning. — τὴν ἀσέβειαν] is not equivalent to εἰδωλολατρείαν καὶ τὰ πονηρὰ δόγματα (Theophylact), but is the opposite of εὐσέβειαν: the behaviour of man, ungodly, estranged from God, of which idolatry is only one side. — καὶ τὰς κοσμικὰς ἐπιθυμίας] κοσμικός only here and in Heb. ix 1, but there in another connection. The κοσμ. ἐπιθυμίαι are not " desires or lusts referring to the earthly, transient world " (first edition of this commentary; so, too, Wiesinger), but " the lusts belonging to the κόσμος, *i.e.* to the world estranged from God," which, indeed, is the same thing (so, too, van Oosterzee). Kindred conceptions are found ἐπιθυμία σαρκός, Gal. v. 15 ; Eph. ii. 3 ; ἀνθρώπων ἐπιθυμίαι, 1 Pet. iv. 2. — σωφρόνως καὶ δικαίως καὶ εὐσεβῶς ζήσωμεν] see i. 8 (σώφρονα, δίκαιον, ὅσιον). This denotes the life of Christian morality in three directions. Immediately after ἐπιθυμίαι we have the opposing conception σωφρόνως, which expresses self-control. Δικαίως denotes generally right conduct such as the divine law demands, having special reference here, as in i. 8, to duty towards one's neighbour. Εὐσεβῶς (opposite of ἀσέβειαν) denotes holiness in thought and act.—Even the older expositors find in the collocation of these three ideas an expression for the whole sum of duties. Wolf: optime illi res instituunt, qui per τὸ εὐσεβῶς officia adversus Deum, per τὸ δικαίως officia adv. proximum, per τὸ σωφρόνως vero illa adv. hominem ipsum indicari existimant; still it might be doubtful whether Paul regarded the ideas as so sharply distinct from each other. — ἐν τῷ νῦν αἰῶνι] Paul adds this to remind Titus that for the Christian there is another and future life towards which his glance is directed even in this ;— still these words cannot be construed with προσδεχόμενοι.

Ver. 13. Προσδεχόμενοι τὴν μακαρίαν ἐλπίδα] The strange collocation of προσδεχ. and ἐλπίδα is found also in Acts xxiv. 15 : ἐλπίδα ἔχων . . . ἣν καὶ αὐτοὶ οὗτοι προσδέχονται ; so, too, in Gal. v. 5 : ἐλπίδα . . . ἀπεκδεχόμεθα. The reason of it is that ἐλπίς not only denotes actively the hope, but also

παίδευμα. In its proper signification, however, ἵνα does not give the *aim*, but the *purpose*. If it be taken in this sense here, we cannot but translate it "in order that."

passively the thing hoped for, the subject of the hope ; comp. Col. i. 5 : ἡ ἐλπὶς ἡ ἀποκειμένη ἐν τ. οὐρανοῖς ; comp, too, Rom. viii. 24. — μακαρίαν] Paul thus describes the ἐλπίδα in so far as the expectation of it blesses the believer. Wolf wrongly interprets ἡ μακ. ἐλπίς as equivalent to ἡ ἐλπιζομένη μακαριότης. — This ἐλπίς is further defined by the epexegesis : καὶ ἐπιφάνειαν τῆς δόξης τοῦ μεγάλου Θεοῦ καὶ σωτῆρος ἡμῶν Ἰ. Χριστοῦ] According to Hofmann, the adjective μακαρίαν as well as the genitive τῆς δόξης κ.τ λ. belongs to both substantives, to ἐλπίδα and to ἐπιφάνειαν, because, as he thinks, ἡ μακαρία ἐλπίς is not a conception complete in itself. But Rom. xv. 4 shows this to be wrong. The genitive could only be construed with the two substantives by giving it a different reference in each case. Hofmann, indeed, maintains that this presents no difficulty, as it occurs elsewhere ; but he is wrong in his appeal to Rom. xv. 4 (comp. Meyer on the passage) and to 1 Pet. i. 2 and 2 Pet. iii. 11 (comp my commentary on the passages).—Beyond doubt, the ἐπιφάνεια τῆς δόξης κ τ.λ. denotes Christ's second coming (1 Tim. vi. 14), it may, however, be asked whether μεγάλου Θεοῦ is an independent subject or an attribute of Ἰησ Χρ. The older expositors are of the latter opinion ; the orthodox even appealed to this passage against the Arians. Ambrosius, however, distinguishes here between Christus and Deus Pater.[1] Erasmus, too, says : simul cum Patre apparebit eadem gloria conspicuus Dominus ac Servator noster J. Chr.; and Bengel says of Θεοῦ simply : referri *potest* ad Christum. Among more recent expositors, Flatt, Mack, Matthies, Wiesinger, van Oosterzee, Hofmann, adopt the former view ; while de Wette, Plitt, Winer, pp. 123 f. [E. T. p 162], adopt the latter. Heydenreich leaves the question undecided.[2] It cannot be decided on purely grammatical grounds, for μεγ. Θεοῦ and σωτῆρος ἡμ. *may* be two attributes referring to Ἰησ Χριστοῦ ; still it

---

[1] The words of Ambrosius are hanc esse dicit beatam spem credentium, qui exspectant adventum gloriae magni Dei, quod revelari habet judice Christo, in quo Dei patris videbitur potestas et gloria, ut fidei suae praemium consequantur. Ad hoc enim redemit nos Christus, ut, puram vitam sectantes, repleti bonis operibus, regni Dei haeredes esse possimus

[2] Heydenreich wrongly supposes that δόξα here is the glory which God and Christ will give to believers.

may be also that σωτήρ. ἡμῶν 'Ιησ. Χρ. is a subject distinct from μεγ. Θεοῦ, even although only *one* article is used.[1] The question can only be answered by an appeal to N. T. usage, both for this passage and others like it: 2 Pet i. 1; Jude 4; 2 Thess. i. 12. In 2 Pet. i. 11, iii 18, the unity of the subject is beyond doubt. The following points may be urged in favour of distinguishing two subjects:—(1) In *no single* passage is Θεός connected directly with 'Ιησοῦς Χριστός as an attribute (see my commentary on 2 Pet. i. 1); *i.e.* there *never* occurs in the N. T. the simple construction ὁ Θεὸς ἡμῶν 'Ιησ. Χρ., or ὁ Θεὸς 'Ιησοῦς Χρ, or 'Ιησ. Χρ. ὁ Θεὸς ἡμῶν, whereas κύριος and σωτήρ are often enough construed in this way. (2) The collocation of God (Θεός) and Christus as two subjects is quite current, not only in the Pastoral Epistles (1 Tim. i. 1, 2, v. 21, vi. 13; 2 Tim. i. 2, iv. 1; Tit. i. 4), but also in all the epistles of the N. T., Pauline or not, *so much so*, that when in some few passages the turn of the expression is such as to make Θεός refer grammatically to Christ also, these passages have to be explained in accordance with the almost invariable meaning of the expression. (3) The addition of the adjective μεγάλου indicates that Θεοῦ is to be taken as an independent subject, especially when it is observed how Paul in the First Epistle to Timothy uses similar epithets to exalt God's glory; comp. 1 Tim. i. 17, iv. 10, vi. 15, 16, especially i. 11: ἡ δόξα τοῦ μακαρίου Θεοῦ. It is true the expression ὁ μέγας Θεός is not found in the N. T., except in the *Rec* of Rev. xix. 17, but it occurs frequently in the O. T.: Deut. vi. 21, x. 17;

---

[1] Hofmann wrongly asserts that because σωτῆρος ἡμῶν stands before 'Ιησοῦ Χριστοῦ, and with μιγάλου Θιοῦ under one and the same article, therefore ἡμῶν *must* belong to μιγάλου Θιοῦ as much as to σωτῆρος, and μιγάλου to σωτῆρος as much as to Θιοῦ, and both together to 'Ιησοῦ Χριστοῦ as predicate. There are instances enough of two distinct subjects standing under *one* article only, and we cannot see why these instances should not be quoted here. It cannot indeed be said that σωτῆρος ἡμῶν 'Ι. Χρ. needs no article; for, although σωτήρ as well as κύριος may be construed with 'Ι. Χρ. without the article, still there is no instance of κύριος ἡμῶν being without the article when construed with 'Ι. Χρ. But the article before μιγ Θιοῦ may, according to N T. usage, be also referred to σωτῆρος 'Ι. Χρ without making it necessary to assume a unity of subject; comp. Buttm. pp. 84 ff.; Winer, pp 118 ff [E T. p. 158] Hofmann is no less wrong in what he says regarding the *necessity* of the reference of μιγάλου and of ἡμῶν. Paul, indeed, might have written: τοῦ μιγ Θιοῦ καὶ 'Ιησ Χρ τοῦ σωτῆρος ὑμῶν, but he could also express the same thought in the way he has written it.

Neh. ix. 32; Dan. ii. 45, ix. 4.[1] — For the unity of the subject only one reason can be urged with any show of force, viz. that elsewhere the word ἐπιφάνεια is only used in reference to Christ; but Erasmus long ago pointed out that it does not stand here ἐπιφ. τοῦ Θεοῦ, but τῆς δόξης τοῦ Θεοῦ. Wiesinger, too, has to admit "that, according to passages like Matt. xvi. 27, Mark viii. 38, Christ appears in the glory of the Father and at the same time in His own glory (Matt. xxv. 31), and His appearance may therefore be called the appearance both of God's glory and of His own." Wiesinger, indeed, tries to weaken this admission by remarking that in reality it is Christ Himself who will appear ἐν δόξῃ τοῦ πάτρος, and not God, that therefore δόξα would be construed with the genitives in quite different relations, and that on grammatico-logical principles it must mean either ἐν σωτῆρι ἡμῶν Ἰησ. Χριστῷ, or, τοῦ σωτῆρος ἡμῶν ἐν τῇ δόξῃ τοῦ μεγάλου Θεοῦ (Matthies). But his remark is wrong Even if the subjects be distinct, the genitive τοῦ μεγ. Θεοῦ stands in the same relation to τῆς δόξης as does the genitive σωτῆρος ἡμ. Ἰ. Χρ. Nor is the form of expression necessary on which Matthies insists, because in the N. T. *God* and *Christ* are often enough connected simply by καί without marking their mutual relations. Wiesinger further remarks that no reason whatever can be found in the context for connecting Θεός here as well as Christ with the ἐπιφάνεια, but he has manifestly overlooked the relation of προσδεχόμενοι τὴν ἐπιφάνειαν τῆς δόξης τοῦ μεγ. Θεοῦ to ἐπεφάνη ἡ χάρις τοῦ Θεοῦ.[2] — Chrysostom rightly says: δύο δείκνυσιν ἐνταῦθα ἐπιφανείας· καὶ γάρ εἰσι δύο· ἡ μὲν πρότερα χάριτος, ἡ δὲ δευτέρα ἀνταποδόσεως. The χάρις of God has already appeared; the δόξα of God appears only at the day of completion, when Christ is made manifest in His δόξα, which is the δόξα of God.

---

[1] Usteri (*Paul. Lehrb* 5th ed p. 326) says "God the Father did not need the extolling epithet μέγας;" to which it may be replied: "Did Christ need such an epithet?"—If Hofmann be right in remarking that Christ is not ὁ Θεός, which is the subject-name of the Father, then it is very questionable that Paul would call Him ὁ μέγας Θεός.

[2] Van Oosterzee has advanced nothing new in support of the view disputed above. The appeal to 2 Pet. i 11 is of no use, unless it be proved in passages beyond dispute that Θεός, like κύριος, is joined with Ἰησοῦς Χριστός as an attribute.

Though not so directly as it would have been if the subjects were identical, this passage is still a testimony in favour of the truth of the doctrine of Christ's divinity.[1] — Matthies suggests that in the expression τοῦ μεγάλου Θεοῦ there is an allusion to the *great Zeus* worshipped in Crete, but that is more than improbable. — The genitive σωτῆρος is not dependent on ἐπιφάνειαν, but on τῆς δόξης. In 1 Pet. iv. 13 also Christ's second coming is called the revelation of His δόξα.

Ver. 14. The thought in this verse is very closely related to ver. 12 : παιδεύουσα ἡμᾶς, ἵνα κ.τ.λ., as it shows how far the appearance of the grace of God exhorts us to deny ἀσέβεια κ τ.λ. In construction, however, it is connected with σωτῆρος ἡμ 'Ι Χρ. — ὃς ἔδωκεν ἑαυτόν] comp. Gal. i. 4, equivalent to παρέδωκεν ἑαυτόν, Eph. v. 25. The conception of the *voluntary* submission to death is not contained in ἑαυτόν (Heydenreich) so much as in the whole expression. — ὑπὲρ ἡμῶν] is not equivalent to ἀντὶ ἡμῶν, but: "*for us, on our behalf;*" the notion of ἀντί, however, is not excluded (Matt. xx. 28). The purpose of this submission is given in the next words : ἵνα λυτρώσηται ἡμᾶς] λυτροῦσθαι : "set free by means of a ransom" In Luke xxiv. 21 (comp. too, 1 Macc iv. 11, and other passages in the Apocrypha) the reference to ransom falls quite into the background ; but in 1 Pet. i. 18, 19, where, as here, the redemption through Christ is spoken of, the τίμιον αἷμα of Christ is called the ransom. The same reference is indicated here by the previous ἔδωκεν ἑαυτόν, comp. 1 Tim. ii. 6. The middle form includes the reference which in the next clause is expressed by ἑαυτῷ. — ἀπὸ πάσης ἀνομίας] "from all unlawfulness." 'Ανομία is regarded as the power from which Christ has redeemed us ; it is opposed to σωφρόνως καὶ δικαίως καὶ εὐσεβῶς ζῆν : "the unrighteousness in which the law of God is unheeded." It is wrong to understand by ἀνομία " not only the sin, but also the punishment incurred by sin " (Heydenreich), or only the latter ; comp. Rom. vi. 19, 2 Cor. vi. 14, and especially 1 John iii. 4: ἡ ἁμαρτία ἐστὶν ἡ

---

[1] Calvin : Verum brevius et certius repellere licet Arianos, quia Paulus, de revelatione magni Dei locutus, mox Christum adjunxit, ut sciremus, in hujus persona fore illam gloriae revelationem, ac si diceret, ubi Christus apparuerit, tunc patefactum nobis iri divinae gloriae magnitudinem.

ἀνομία. — καὶ καθαρίσῃ ἑαυτῷ λαὸν περιούσιον] positive expression of the thought which was expressed negatively in the previous clause. De Wette and Wiesinger without reason supply ἡμᾶς as the object of καθαρίσῃ; the object is λαὸν περιούσιον. — περιούσιος (ἅπ. λεγ in N. T.). Chrysostom wrongly interprets it by ἐξελεγμένος, οὐδὲν ἔχων κοινὸν πρὸς τοὺς λοιπούς; Theodoret more correctly by οἰκεῖος; so, too, Beza: peculiaris, and Luther: "a people for a possession." The phrase λαὸς περιούσιος belongs to the O. T., and is a translation of the Hebrew עַם סְגֻלָּה, Ex. xix. 5; Deut. vii. 6, xiv. 2, xxvi. 18, LXX.; in the church of the N. T. the promise made to the people of Israel is fulfilled, comp. 1 Pet. ii. 9: λαὸς εἰς περιποίησιν. — ἑαυτῷ corresponds with λυτρώσηται ἀπό. The sentence is pregnantly expressed, and its meaning is: "that He by the purifying power of His death might acquire for Himself (ἑαυτῷ) a people for a possession." — The moral character of the λαὸς περιούσ. is declared by the words in apposition, ζηλωτὴν καλῶν ἔργων: accensum studio bonorum operum. — De Wette is inaccurate in saying that the apostle is speaking here not of reconciliation, but *only* of moral purification. Wiesinger rightly asks: "What else are we to understand by ἔδωκεν ἑαυτὸν ὑπὲρ ἡμῶν than the reconciling death?" But de Wette is so far right, that reconciliation is not made the chief point here, but rather, as often in the N. T., *e.g.* 1 Pet. i. 17, 18, the design is mentioned for which Christ suffered the death of reconciliation; comp. Luther's exposition of the second article of faith.

Ver. 15. Ταῦτα (viz. these moral precepts, see ver. 1, with the reasons given for them, vv. 11–14) λάλει καὶ παρακάλει καὶ ἔλεγχε] The distinction between these words is correctly given by Heydenreich. Λαλεῖν denotes simple teaching, παρακάλ. pressing exhortation, ἐλέγχ. solemn admonition to those who neglect these duties. "The theoretic, the paraenetic-practical, and the polemic aspects of the preaching of the gospel are combined" (Matthies). — μετὰ πάσης ἐπιταγῆς] According to 1 Cor. vii. 6, συγγνώμη is the opposite of ἐπιταγή; this clause therefore enjoins that Titus is not to leave it to the free choice of the church whether his exhortations shall be obeyed or not, but to deliver them as commands.

De Wette translates: "with all recommendation," which is right in sense; still ἐπιταγή is not properly recommendation but command, and it is therefore better to say, "*with entire full command*" — With this the final words are closely connected: μηδείς σου περιφρονείτω] περιφρονεῖν (ἅπ. λεγ); properly: "consider something on all sides;" then: "think beyond, despise," equivalent to καταφρονεῖν; comp. 1 Tim. iv. 12. Luther is right in sense: "let no man despise thee," viz. by not receiving thy teachings, exhortations, and admonitions as commands, and by thinking lightly of them. There is nothing to suggest that Titus is to conduct himself so that no one may be right in despising him.

CHAPTER III.

VER. 1. ἀρχαῖς καὶ ἐξουσίαις] In A C D* E* F G ℵ 17, 31, *al.*, Damasc. καί is wanting, and was therefore omitted by Lachm. Buttm. and Tisch. It can hardly be done without; but, as the καί is wanting also between the next two words, it seems to have been wanting here originally, and to have been inserted later. F G have a καί inserted between the verbs. — Ver. 2. For μηδένα, F G have μή ; but the former is supported alike by suitability to the context and by the weightiest testimony. — Instead of πραότητα (*Rec.*), Lachm. Buttm Tisch., on the authority of A C, etc , adopted here and elsewhere the form πραΰτητα. — ℵ has, instead of ἐνδεικνυμένους πραΰτητα, the reading ἐνδείκνυσθαι σπουδήν. — Ver. 5. ὧν] For this we should probably read ἅ, as is done by Lachm. and Tisch. 8, on the authority of A C* D* F G ℵ 17, *al.*, Clem. Cyr. The ὧν, which Tisch. 7 retained, seems to be a correction from the analogy of classic Greek. — For τὸν αὐτοῦ ἔλεον, Lachm. Buttm. and Tisch., on the authority of A D* E F G 31, *al.*, Clem. Max. *al*, read τὸ αὐτοῦ ἔλεος; D E F G Ambr. Aug. etc., put αὐτοῦ after ἔλεος. — Before λουτροῦ, Lachm and Buttm. put τοῦ, on the authority of A. — After ἀνακαινώσεως, D* E* F G, Ambr. Aug etc., have the reading διά, which is manifestly an interpretation. — Ver. 7. γενώμεθα] Lachm. Buttm. Tisch. rightly read γενηθῶμεν, on the authority of A C D* F G, 17, *al.*, Chrys. Ath — Ver. 8. τῷ Θεῷ] According to all uncials, the τῷ should be deleted ; so, too, with τά before καλά. — Ver. 9. For ἔρεις (Tisch. 7) there is found in D E F G ℵ the singular ἔριν (Tisch. 8), which is indeed the original reading altered on account of the plurals around it — Ver. 10. The *Rec.* μετὰ μίαν καὶ δευτέραν νουθεσίαν (Lachm. Buttm Tisch. 8) is supported by A C K L ℵ, all cursives, Vulg. etc. ; Tisch. 7 adopted instead of it: μετὰ μίαν νουθεσίαν καὶ δευτέραν, on the authority of D E F G, several Fathers, etc. Reiche rightly prefers the *Rec*. — Ver. 13. Tisch. 7 reads ʼΑπολλώ, while Tisch. 8 gives ʼΑπολλών ; some MSS have ʼΑπολλώνα. — While Tisch. 7, with the support of most authorities, read λείπῃ (so, too, Lachm. and Buttm.), Tisch. 8 adopted λίπῃ, on the authority of ℵ D* etc. — Ver. 15. In D** and D*** E F G H K L, *al.*, several versions, etc., the word ἀμήν forms the close; but it is wanting in A C D* 17, etc. Tisch. and Buttm. omitted it; Lachm. enclosed it in brackets.

Vv. 1, 2. Instructions to give exhortations regarding conduct towards the authorities and towards all men. — ὑπομίμνησκε αὐτούς] (see 2 Tim. ii. 14) presupposes that they are aware of the duties regarding which the exhortation is given. It is not so certain that Paul is alluding to definite precepts already expressed by him. — αὐτούς] viz. the members of the church. — ἀρχαῖς (καὶ) ἐξουσίαις ὑποτάσσεσθαι] ἀρχαὶ κ. ἐξουσίαι as a name for human authorities is used also in Luke xii. 11 (comp. too, Luke xx. 20; ἐξουσίαι alone, in Rom. xiii. 1). The two words are joined together in order to give fuller expression to the notion of authority. It cannot, however, be shown that the one denotes the higher, the other the lower authorities (Heydenreich). It is at least doubtful whether this inculcation of obedience to the authorities had its justification in the rebellious character of the Cretans nationally (Matthies and others). Similar precepts also occur in other epistles of the N. T.; and here the exhortation harmonizes with the injunctions given in chap. ii. The Christians needed the exhortation all the more that the authorities were heathen. — πειθαρχεῖν] here in its original signification: "*obey the superior.*" Its meaning in Acts xxvii. 21 is more general. The πειθαρχεῖν is the result and actual proof of the ὑποτάσσεσθαι. The want of καί does not prove, as de Wette thinks, that it does not belong to the datives ἀρχαῖς (κ.) ἐξ. Καί would have been out of place here, since the following words also are to be construed with that dative. — πρὸς πᾶν ἔργον ἀγαθὸν ἑτοίμους εἶναι] not to be taken generally, but in very close connection with ἀρχαῖς: "*for the authorities* prepared to every good work" (so, too, Wiesinger and van Oosterzee). The ἀγαθόν is not without significance, as it points to the limits within which they are to be ready to obey the will of the authorities. Theodoret: οὐδὲ γὰρ εἰς ἅπαντα δεῖ τοῖς ἄρχουσι πειθαρχεῖν, ἀλλὰ τὸν μὲν δασμὸν καὶ τὸν φόρον εἰσφέρειν, καὶ τὴν προσήκουσαν ἀπονέμειν τιμήν· εἰ δὲ δυσσεβεῖν κελεύσειεν, ἀντικρὺς ἀντιλέγειν; comp. Acts iv. 19. — Ver. 2. μηδένα βλασφημεῖν] The new object μηδένα shows that from this point he is no longer speaking of special duties towards superiors, but of general duties towards one's neighbour. Βλασφημεῖν is used specially in reference to what is higher, but it occurs also in the more general sense of "*revile.*" Theodoret: μηδένα ἀγορεύειν κακῶς. — ἀμάχους εἶναι, ἐπιεικεῖς] see 1 Tim. iii. 3; the first expresses negatively what the second expresses positively. — πᾶσαν ἐνδεικνυμένους (see ii. 10) πραΰτητα πρὸς πάντας ἀνθρώπους] Chrysostom: καὶ Ἰουδαίους καὶ Ἕλληνας, μοχθήρους κ. πονηρούς. — It is impossible not to see that the apostle is thinking specially of conduct towards those who are not Christian.

Ver. 3. ῏Ημεν γάρ] γάρ shows that the thought following it is to give a reason for the previous exhortation. But the reason does not lie in this verse taken by itself (Chrysostom: οὐκοῦν μηδενὶ ὀνειδίσῃς, φησὶ· τοιοῦτος γὰρ ἦς καὶ σύ; so, too, Hofmann), but in this verse when connected with the verse following. The meaning therefore is: As we were in the state in which they are now, but were rescued by the kindness of God, it becomes us to show kindness and gentleness towards those whom we were at one time like. ῏Ημεν stands first as emphatic; ποτέ, "at one time," viz. before we became believers. Wiesinger: "The contrast to ποτέ is given by ὅτε δέ in ver. 4; we have here the well-known contrast between ποτέ and νῦν; comp. Rom. xi. 30; Eph. ii. 2, 11, 13, v. 8; Col. i. 21, iii. 7, 8; they are the two hinges of the Pauline system." — καὶ ἡμεῖς] "*we too;*" ἡμεῖς includes all believing Christians. It is to be noted that even here Paul makes no distinction between Jewish and Gentile Christians (otherwise in Eph. ii. 3). — ἀνόητοι] is equivalent to ἐσκοτισμένοι τῇ διανοίᾳ, Eph. iv. 18; without understanding, viz. in reference to divine things; not simply: "blinded regarding our true destiny" (Matthies), or: "without knowing what is right" (Hofmann). Heinrichs refers this and πλανώμενοι to idol-worship, but the apostle is not speaking here of Gentile Christians alone. — ἀπειθεῖς] disobedient to divine law; Heydenreich wrongly refers it to the relations with the authorities. — πλανώμενοι (see 2 Tim. iii. 13) stands here not in a neuter, but in a passive sense: "led astray," proceeding on a wrong path, not merely "in regard to knowledge," but more generally. Wiesinger: "*sc.* ἀπὸ τῆς ἀληθείας, ἀλήθεια being regarded not as abstract truth, but as the sum total of moral good;" comp Jas. v. 19; Heb. v. 2. — δουλεύοντες ἐπιθυμίαις καὶ ἡδοναῖς ποικίλαις (see 2 Tim. iii. 6) ἡδοναί, as Jas. iv. 1, 3. He who follows his lusts is a slave to them, hence δουλεύοντες; see Rom. vi. 6, 12. Michaelis gives it too narrow a meaning by referring it to sins of lust. — ἐν κακίᾳ καὶ φθόνῳ διάγοντες] κακία is not "vileness," but "wickedness;" comp. Col. iii. 8; Eph. iv. 31; otherwise in 1 Cor. v. 8 and other passages, where it is synonymous with πονηρία. — διάγοντες] connected with βίον only here and in 1 Tim. ii 2. — στυγητοί (ἅπ. λεγ) is equivalent to μισητοί (Hesychius), "detested and detestable;" it is wanting in Luther's translation. — μισοῦντες ἀλλήλους] comp. Rom. i. 29.

Vv. 4–6. "Ὅτε δὲ ἡ χρηστότης καὶ ἡ φιλανθρωπία κτλ.] χρηστότης as a human quality; 2 Cor. vi. 6; Gal. v. 22, Col. iii. 12; used of God, Rom. ii. 4, xi 22 (often in the LXX); with special reference to God's redemptive work in Christ, Eph. ii. 7. — φιλανθρωπία] elsewhere only in Acts xxviii. 1 (2 Macc. vi. 22, xiv. 9) as a human quality. De Wette remarks on it. "unusual for the idea of χάρις." The reason why Paul makes use of the word here is contained in ver. 2, where he exhorts to πραΰτης πρὸς πάντας ἀνθρώπους. Χρηστότης corresponds in conception to πραΰτης (both words stand closely connected in Gal v. 22 and Col. iii. 12); and in allusion to πρὸς π. ἀνθρ., Paul adds φιλανθρωπία. The goodness and love of God to man, on which our salvation is based, should lead us to show benevolence and gentleness to all men. At the same time, the χρηστότης and φιλανθρωπία of God form a contrast with the conduct of men as it is described in ver. 3 in the words: ἐν κακίᾳ . . . μισοῦντες ἀλλήλους. Hofmann rightly remarks that as φιλανθρωπία has the article, it is made independent and emphatic by the side of the χρηστότης; it does not, however, follow from this that χρηστότης here denotes "the goodness of God in general towards His creatures." — ἐπεφάνη] just as in ii. 11. — τοῦ σωτῆρος ἡμῶς Θεοῦ] see 1 Tim. i. 1. — Ver. 5. The apodosis begins here and not at ἔλεος, so that the words οὐκ . . . ἔλεος modify ἔσωσεν; so more recent expositors, even Hofmann. —

οὐκ ἐξ ἔργων τῶν ἐν δικαιοσύνῃ ἃ ἐποιήσαμεν ἡμεῖς] On ἐξ, comp. Rom. iii. 20. Matthies wrongly: "not from works appearing in the form of righteousness which we accomplished, *i.e.* not from our works produced with the appearance of righteousness." Ἔργα τὰ ἐν δικαιοσύνῃ are rather: "*works which are done in righteousness*." Ἐν denotes the condition of life in which the works are accomplished (de Wette, Wiesinger). Δικαιοσύνη here is not justification (van Oosterzee: justitia coram Deo), but righteousness, *integrity;* so, too, Hofmann. — ἃ ἐποιήσαμεν ἡμεῖς] ἡμεῖς is added emphatically to make the contrast all the stronger (Wiesinger). Paul is not speaking of works which may have been done by us, but denies that we have done such works of righteousness. Bengel rightly: Negativa pertinet ad totum sermonem: non fueramus in justitia: non feceramus opera in justitia: non habebamus opera, per quae possemus salvari.[1]—The thought here expressed is not, as de Wette thinks, unsuitable to the context. In its negative form it rather serves to give emphasis to ἀλλὰ κατὰ (*by means of*) τὸ αὐτοῦ ἔλεος, and hence to the conception of the divine χρηστότης and φιλανθρωπία. Wiesinger: "The apostle even by the contrast of the οὐκ wishes to make it quite clearly understood that saving grace is quite free and undeserved."[2]—On κατὰ τὸ αὐτ. ἔλεος, comp. 1 Pet. i. 3. — ἔσωσεν ἡμᾶς] sc. ὁ Θεός. As ὅτε . . . ἐπεφάνη does not mean: "when or after it had appeared," but: "*when it appeared*," the saving is here represented as simultaneous with the appearance of the divine χρηστότης κ.τ λ, although διά refers ἔσωσεν to its application to individuals, which is different in time from the ὅτε κ τ.λ. above. But Paul could rightly put these two things together, because the goodness of God which appeared in Jesus Christ comes to perfection in the

---

[1] Similarly Theophylact. ἔσωσιν ἡμᾶς οὐκ ἐξ ἔργων, ὧν ἐποιήσαμεν, ἀντὶ τοῦ· οὔτε ἐποιήσαμεν ἔργα δικαιοσύνης, οὔτε ἐσώθημεν ἐκ τούτων, ἀλλὰ τὸ πᾶν ἡ ἀγαθότης αὐτοῦ ἐποίησε.

[2] Hofmann is not correct in analysing ἔργων τῶν ἐν δικαιοσύνῃ into two statements He says that ἐξ ἔργων is "in the first place to be conceived by itself," and that τῶν ἐν δικ further "denies that we have done what we should have done in order to deserve to be saved." He then maintains that the relative sentence belongs to τῶν ἐν δικαιοσύνῃ. But ἔργα τὰ ἐν δικαιοσύνῃ forms *one* conception, and on this the relative sentence depends.

saving of individuals by the λουτρὸν παλιγγενεσίας; the former is the efficient cause of the other. — ἡμᾶς is not to be referred to all mankind, but to believers. The means by which the saving is effected are set forth in the words: διὰ (τοῦ) λουτροῦ παλιγγενεσίας καὶ ἀνακαινώσεως πνεύματος ἁγίου] The expression : τὸ λουτρὸν παλιγγενεσίας, has been very arbitrarily interpreted by some expositors, some taking λουτρόν as a figurative name for the regeneratio itself, or for the predicatio evangelii, or for the Holy Spirit, or for the abundant imparting of the Spirit. From Eph. v. 26 it is clear that it can mean nothing else than baptism; comp. too, Heb. x. 23; 1 Cor. vi. 11; Acts xxii. 16. — παλιγγενεσία] occurs also in Matt. xix. 28, but in quite a different connection, viz. in reference to the renovation of things at Christ's second coming; comp. however, 1 Pet. i. 3, 23, ἀναγεννάω, and John iii. 3 ff., γεννηθῆναι ἄνωθεν. — According to the context, Paul calls baptism the bath of the new birth, not meaning that it pledges us to the new birth (" to complete the process of moral purification, of expiation and sanctification," Matthies), nor that it is a visible image of the new birth (de Wette), for neither in the one sense nor in the other could it be regarded as a means of saving (ἔσωσεν ἡμᾶς διά). Paul uses that name for it as the bath by means of which God *actually* brings about the new birth.[1] Comp. with this the apostle's expressions elsewhere regarding baptism, especially Rom. vi. 3 ff., Gal. iii. 27, Col. ii. 12, which all alike assign this real signification to baptism. — καὶ ἀνακαινώσεως πνεύματος ἁγίου] The genit. πν. ἁγ. is the genit. of the efficient cause: "the renewal wrought by the Holy Spirit" (de Wette, Wiesinger, van Oosterzee). This may be taken as the *continuing* influence of the Spirit working in the regenerated Christian, or as the single act of inward change by which the man became a καινὴ κτίσις (2 Cor. v. 17), a τέκνον

---

[1] It is certainly right to say that baptism carries with it a pledge to continue the process of purification, and that, from its outward form, it bears in itself a symbolic character; only these are not the reasons for which the apostle calls it the λουτρὸν παλιγγενεσίας —In the first edition of this commentary I remarked : "Baptism is regarded as the inner new birth manifesting itself in the external act of the bath " This is not apposite, since baptism is not the new birth itself, but the means for producing it.

Θεοῦ. Here the word is to be taken in the latter signification, as is clear from its connection with ἔσωσεν ἡμᾶς,[1] otherwise in Rom. xii. 2; Eph. iv. 22–24. According to some expositors, the genit. ἀνακαινώσεως is dependent on διά; Bengel: duae res commemorantur: lavacrum regenerationis, quae baptismi in Christum periphrasis et renovatio Spiritus sancti. According to others, it depends on λουτροῦ, and is co-ordinate with παλιγγενεσίας; Vulgate: per lavacrum regenerationis et renovationis (de Wette, Wiesinger). The latter is the right view, for "what else could ἀνακαίνωσις πν ἁγ. be than the new birth denoted by παλιγγενεσία?" (Wiesinger). In this way ἀνακ. πν. ἁγ is added epexegetically to the previous conception παλιγγενεσία, explaining it, but not adding any new force to it.[2] Heinrichs quite wrongly thinks that πν. ἁγ. here is the πν. hominis, ipsius, which (quatenus antea fuit ψυχικόν, σαρκικόν, ἐπίγειον) becomes holy by the ἀνακαίν. — Ver. 6. οὗ ἐξέχεεν ἐφ' ἡμᾶς πλουσίως] οὗ is not dependent on τοῦ λουτροῦ, but on πνεύματος ἁγίου. The genit. οὗ is in accordance with the common Greek usage. Heydenreich explains it wrongly by supposing ἐξ or ἀφ' to have been omitted: "from which he abundantly, of which he poured out an abundant measure." — ἐξέχεεν ἐφ' ἡμᾶς] an expression which has passed from the O. T. (Joel iii. 1, Zech xii. 10) into the N. T. It is used to describe the gift of the Holy Spirit; see Acts ii. 17, 33, x. 45. The rich abundance of this gift is indicated by πλουσίως[3]—ἐφ' ἡμᾶς] goes back to ἡμᾶς in ver. 5.

---

[1] These words, παλιγγενεσία and ἀνακαίνωσις, do not occur in classic Greek In the former word, which Hofmann translates awkwardly enough by "resurrection," the prefix πάλιν points to the former sinless condition of man, into which he is restored from his corruption Thus παλιγγενεσία, in Matt xix 28, corresponds in conception to ἀποκατάστασις. It is doubtful whether the same reference is adapted to ἀνακαίνωσις (which only occurs here and in Rom. xii. 2), the ἀνα does not make such reference necessary Expositors tacitly avoid this question; comp Cremer, Wörterb d neut. Grac

[2] Hofmann indeed disputes our remark that ἀνακαιν. τ. πν is added epexegetically to παλιγγ; because, as he says, παλιγγενεσία is "an incident of the resurrection," whereas ἀνακαίνωσις is "a work of the Holy Spirit." But is not this renewing work of the Holy Spirit an incident for him on whom it is wrought? He further maintains that it might be said: ἔσωσεν ἡμᾶς δι' ἀνακαινώσεως πνεύματος ἁγίου, but not ἔσωσεν ἡμᾶς διὰ παλιγγενεσίας; but this we cannot admit. The latter may be said quite as much as the former.

[3] It is ὁ Θεός here who imparts the Holy Spirit, whereas in Acts ii. 33 the gift

Christians are saved by God pouring upon them, at baptism, the Holy Spirit, which renews them. The apostle is not speaking here of the gift of the Spirit which was made at Pentecost, but of the gift made to individuals, and made after the outpouring at Pentecost. — διὰ 'Ιησ. Χρ. τοῦ σωτῆρος ἡμῶν] This does not belong to ἔσωσεν, which is already defined by διὰ τοῦ λουτροῦ κ.τ.λ. It goes with ἐξέχεεν, so that Christ here, as elsewhere in the N. T., is represented as the medium by which the Holy Spirit is sent.[1] In order to understand the train of thought properly, we must note that the outpouring of the Holy Spirit is not a consequence, but the substantial inward fact in baptism, which is the bath of the new birth.

REMARK.—The question why the apostle here speaks of baptism is rightly answered by Wiesinger in this way. Baptism, as the bath of the παλιγγενεσία, "is the basis on which rests all further growth in the life of the Spirit," inasmuch as by it the believer is removed from the εἶναι ἐν σαρκί into the εἶναι ἐν πνεύματι or ἐν Χριστῷ, i.e. into the condition in which it is possible for him to live no longer κατὰ σάρκα, but κατὰ πνεῦμα. On the other hand, the apostle does not mention *faith* here as a medium of the saving love of God, because he is looking away entirely from the *human* aspect of the matter, and considering only the *divine* work in the saving of men. Leaving *faith* out of consideration, baptism is to the apostle what he says of it here, viz. the means of the new birth or renewal by the Holy Spirit, and also, according to ver. 7, of the completion of the δικαιοῦσθαι; and baptism does not become this to him by means of faith. Hence the apostle's expression cannot be rectified conjecturally by supplying this point, viz. faith. It is true that in other passages of the N. T. πίστις denotes that which brings about the new birth, the receiving of the Holy Spirit, justification; and the one expression should not be neglected for the sake of the other. There is here a problem which it is the task of Biblical Theology and of Dogmatics to solve; here, however, as the passage before us presents no handle for the discussion, it can only be indicated without

---

is ascribed to Christ; see John xiv. 16 comp. with John xv. 26. The explanation of this is contained in the διά

[1] Matthies remarks, by adding the words διὰ 'Ι. Χρ, faith is at the same time assumed as the subjective condition; but the remark is out of place, as Paul is not in the least discussing subjective conditions.

solving it. This much only may be said, that according to these sayings of the Scriptures, man only becomes a τέλειος ἐν Χριστῷ when he is justified and regenerated both by baptism and by faith (the faith, viz , which is πίστις ἐξ ἀκοῆς, Rom. x. 17).

Ver. 7. *Ἵνα* declares the purpose, not the consequence. It is doubtful whether it belongs to ἐξέχεεν (Heydenreich, Wiesinger, van Oosterzee, Plitt, Hofmann) or to ἔσωσεν as defined by διὰ τοῦ λουτροῦ ... τοῦ σωτῆρος ἡμῶν (Bengel, de Wette, and others). The thought is substantially the same with both constructions, since the σωτηρία is necessarily brought about by the outpouring of the Spirit. Still the structure of the sentence is in favour of the reference to ἐξέχεεν. Wiesinger rightly considers the other view "to be unnecessarily harsh, ignoring the explanatory relation of vv. 6 and 7 to ver. 5, and depriving ἐξέχεεν of its necessary definition." — δικαιωθέντες] not " found righteous " (Matthies), still less " sanctified," but " justified," *i e.* " acquitted of the guilt, and with it, of the punishment." Hofmann rightly says that this justification means the same thing as in Rom. iii. 24 ; that it does not mean the change of our conduct towards God, but of our relations to Him.[1] — τῇ ἐκείνου χάριτι] does not belong to what follows, but to what precedes. Justification is an act of *grace*. Ἐκείνου does not refer to God as the subject of ἐξέχεεν (van Oosterzee, Plitt, and formerly in this commentary, but to Ἰησοῦ Χριστοῦ (Hofmann), according to the usage of the N. T., for which see Acts iii. 13 ; John vii. 45. Comp. Winer, p. 148 [E. T. p. 196]; Buttmann, p. 91. Heydenreich and Wiesinger are wrong in referring it to πνεύματος ; for, on the one hand, this would involve the wrong conception that justification is a work of the Spirit ; and, on the other hand, there is no mention in the N. T. of a χάρις τοῦ πνεύματος. — Τῇ

---

[1] The apostle says nothing here regarding the relation of justification to the ἀνακαίνωσις wrought by the Holy Spirit It is wrong at any rate to regard the latter as the ground of the former, so that God justifies man because he is renewed. Nor, on the other hand, can the renewing be regarded as a later consequence of the justification, in the sense that God imparts to man the Holy Spirit after man has been justified. The two things are very closely connected. Justification is to be regarded as the ground of renewing, while renewing is the actual completion of justification. God justifies man so as to renew him, to make him His child born of the Spirit.

χάριτι points us back to οὐκ ἐξ ἔργων; Chrysostom: πάλιν χάριτι, οὐκ ὀφειλῇ — κληρονόμοι γενηθῶμεν [γενώμεθα] κατ' ἐλπίδα ζωῆς αἰωνίου] κατ' ἐλπίδα cannot, as Heydenreich thinks probable, be construed with ζωῆς αἰωνίου as one conception, so as to be equivalent to ζωῆς αἰωνίου ἐλπιζομένης. On the other hand, it is also unsuitable to take κατ' ἐλπ. ζ. αἰων. together: "in accordance with the hope of eternal life" (Matthies), because in that case κληρ. would not be defined. Κατ' ἐλπίδα should rather be joined with κληρ. γενηθ, and then the genit. ζωῆς αἰωνίου belongs to the latter. Chrysostom has two interpretations: κατ' ἐλπίδα, τουτέστι· καθὼς ἠλπίσαμεν, οὕτως ἀπολαύσομεν, ἤ, ὅτι ἤδη καὶ κληρονόμοι ἐστέ. According to the former view, the words would have to be translated: "in order that we, in proportion to our hope (*i.e.* as we hope), may become heirs of eternal life;" according to the latter, it would be: "that we, according to hope, might become heirs of eternal life." The latter view is the correct one. The apostle is speaking not of the future, but of the present condition of believers. They *are* heirs of eternal life; but they are so in hope, not yet in actual possession; for ζωὴ αἰώνιος in its full meaning is something future, Rom. vi. 22, 23. — κατ' ἐλπίδα stands here as τῇ ἐλπίδι in Rom. viii. 24; see Meyer on the passage.[1]

Ver. 8. Πιστὸς ὁ λόγος] refers, as in 1 Tim. iv. 9, to what precedes, but not to the last sentence merely. So Chrysostom: ἐπειδὴ περὶ μελλόντων διαλέχθη καὶ οὔπω παρόντων, ἐπήγαγε τὸ ἀξιόπιστον. It refers to the entire thought expressed in vv. 4–7. — καὶ περὶ τούτων βούλομαί σε διαβεβαιοῦσθαι] Regarding the construction of the verb διαβεβ., see on 1 Tim. i. 7. Vulgate rightly: de his volo te confirmare; Wiesinger: "and on these points I wish you to be strongly assured;" Beza, on the contrary: haec volo te asseverare. De Wette also maintains that περὶ τούτων is the immediate object, but with-

---

[1] This passage, vv. 4–7, is substantially different from that in ii. 11–14. While in the latter the chief point is the paedagogic aim of the work of redemption, and the apostle accordingly is thinking how Christians are pledged to a holy life, in the former the chief point is the undeserved love of God made manifest in the work of redemption. Hence in this passage also much emphasis is laid on the idea of regeneration, which is granted to the Christian by the gift of the Holy Spirit.

out proving it — *ἵνα φροντίζωσι καλῶν ἔργων προΐστασθαι οἱ πεπιστευκότες* [*τῷ*] *Θεῷ*] In harmony with the train of thought in vv. 2, 3 ff., Paul here gives a practical purpose as his motive. The subject *οἱ πεπιστευκότες Θεῷ* are Christians generally; the designation is used because the Cretan Christians had before been heathen. Luther translates it rightly: "*those who have become believers in God;*" while Wiesinger is wrong in explaining it: "those who have put faith in God, *i.e.* in His gospel." The phrase *πιστεύειν Θεῷ* expresses the relation to God Himself, not merely to His word; comp. Acts xvi. 34. *Θεῷ* is used here as *τῷ κυρίῳ* often is, comp. Acts xviii. 8, xvi. 15; it is synonymous with *εἰς τὸν Θεόν*, John xiv. 1; comp. *πιστεύειν τῷ ὀνόματι 'Ι. Χρ.*, 1 John iii 23, and *π. εἰς τ. ὄν*, John i. 12. Hofmann is altogether mistaken in construing *Θεῷ* with what follows. If *Θεῷ* were to be opposed to *ἀνθρώποις*, the latter would have been put before *ὠφέλιμα*; besides, *ταῦτα* clearly forms the beginning of a new clause. — *φροντίζειν* (*ἅπ. λεγ*, often in the Apocrypha of the O. T., also in the LXX.), "reflect on something, take an interest in something," here, as often in the classics, with a suggestion of anxiety (comp. 1 Sam. ix. 5, LXX.). — *καλῶν ἔργων*] depends on *προΐστασθαι*; it is quite general, and should not be restricted to the services to be rendered to the church (Michaelis), nor to official duties [1] (Grotius), nor to deeds of charity (Chrysostom).—*προΐστασθαι* here and in ver. 14 is used in the same sense as when it is joined with *τέχνης* (Synesius, *Ep.* 2; Athenagoras, xiii. 612*a*), being equivalent to *exercere*, "carry on, practise an art;" properly, it is "present oneself before." The Vulgate translates it: bonis operibus praeesse, which, however, is obscure; Beza incorrectly: bene agendo praecedere, which he explains in a peculiar fashion by sanctae et rectae vitae antistites. Wolf thinks that *προΐστ.* denotes not only the studium, but also the patrocinium of good works; comp. Rom. xii. 17: *προνοεῖσθαι*

---

[1] Hofmann, too (*Schriftbew.* II. 2), restricts *καλ. ἔργ. προΐστ.* to "honest exertion," by which "each one may support himself and contribute to the needs of others, or to the purposes of Christian church-life." This interpretation, however, he seems to have given up, as he does not mention it in his commentary.

καλά — ταῦτά ἐστι [τὰ] καλὰ καὶ ὠφέλιμα τ. ἀνθρώποις] see 1 Tim. ii. 3. Ταῦτα does not refer to καλῶν ἔργων (Heinrichs, Wiesinger), for the apostle certainly did not need to say that καλὰ ἔργα are καλά for men; nor does it resume περὶ τούτων (de Wette, Hofmann). It should be referred either to φροντίζειν καλ. ἐργ. προΐστασθαι (Heydenreich, Matthies) or to διαβεβαιοῦσθαι. The latter reference might be preferred—as confirming the exhortation made to Timothy. On the reference of ταῦτα to *one* subject, see Winer, p. 153 [E. T. p. 201].

Ver. 9. Contrast to the last words. — μωρὰς δὲ ζητήσεις καὶ γενεαλογίας κ.τ.λ.] ζητήσεις, see 1 Tim. i. 4; connected with μωράς also in 2 Tim. ii. 23; καὶ γενεαλογίας, see i. 4; the latter refers to the contents, the former to the form. — καὶ ἔριν [ἔρεις] καὶ μάχας νομικάς] ἔρις, like the other words, serves to describe the behaviour of the heretics; it is not therefore ἔρεις τὰς πρὸς αἱρετικούς, as Chrysostom interprets it, but quarrels such as take place among the heretics. The μάχαι νομικαί are disputes about the law and the individual precepts of the law, see 1 Tim. i. 7 and Tit. i. 14. — Heydenreich wrongly refers the adjective νομικάς also to ἔρεις. Hofmann even refers it to all the preceding conceptions, arbitrarily explaining νομικαί of the contents of the Pentateuch, *i.e.* of the Thora; with him, therefore, the ζητήσεις νομικαί are "discussions in which all disputed questions in the Thora are taken up," and the γενεαλογίαι νομικαί are "investigations into the historical contents of the Thora."— περιΐστασο] see 2 Tim. ii. 16. — With these fables and quarrels that go on among the heretics Titus is to have nothing to do. — Εἰσὶ γὰρ ἀνωφελεῖς καὶ μάταιοι] contrast with ταῦτά ἐστι καλὰ κ.τ.λ. — μάταιος, like ὅσιος, 1 Tim. ii. 8, is used as an adjective of two terminations.

Vv. 10, 11. An injunction regarding behaviour towards the heretics. — Αἱρετικὸν ἄνθρωπον] αἱρετικός (ἅπ. λεγ) is not equivalent to contentiosus, but is, according to Calvin: quisquis sua protervia unitatem ecclesiae abrumpit, any one who causes departure from the pure sound doctrine of the gospel. With this Wiesinger agrees, only that he wishes to consider the divisions as not brought about by heresies, but by "eccentricities and perversities." The word αἱρέσεις is often used by Paul of ecclesiastical divisions, 1 Cor. xi. 19, Gal. v. 20. So, too, in 2 Pet. ii. 1, where it expressly refers to heresies. Comp. also Rom. xvi. 17 : παρακαλῶ ὑμᾶς σκοπεῖν τοὺς τὰς διχοστασίας καὶ τὰ σκάνδαλα παρὰ τὴν διδαχὴν ἣν ὑμεῖς ἐμάθετε ποιοῦντας καὶ ἐκκλίνατε ἀπ' αὐτῶν. — μετὰ μίαν καὶ δευτέραν νουθεσίαν παραιτοῦ] Vitringa (*De Vet. Synag.* iii. 1. 10) understands παραιτοῦ to mean the formal excommunication, and νουθεσία the excommunicatio privata, as these were appointed among the Jews for certain cases. But he is wrong; Paul is not speaking here of excommunication proper. Νουθεσία (1 Cor. x. 11; Eph. vi. 4) is equivalent to "*reprimand*," including both blame and exhortation. This is not to be employed once, but several times : " after one or two." — παραιτοῦ] 1 Tim. iv. 7. Bengel : monere desine, quid enim juvat ? laterem lavares. — Ver. 11. εἰδώς] see 2 Tim. ii. 23. — ὅτι ἐξέστραπται ὁ τοιοῦτος] " that such an one is perverse;" comp. Deut. xxxii. 20 : ὅτι γενεὰ ἐξεστραμμένη ἐστιν, דּוֹר תַּהְפֻּכֹת ; it shows the total perversion of thought and endeavour. Baur says arbitrarily and wrongly : " he has turned away from us, and departed out of the communion of believers." — καὶ ἁμαρτάνει ὢν αὐτοκατάκριτος] defines the preceding words more precisely. Ὢν αὐτοκατάκριτος is connected with ἁμαρτάνει, but not with ἐξέστραπται also (Hofmann). The perversity shows itself in the fact that he sins condemning himself. Αὐτοκατάκριτος is equivalent to κεκαυτηριασμένος τὴν ἰδίαν συνείδησιν, 1 Tim. iv. 2, qui suopte judicio est condemnatus. The meaning is : he sins with the consciousness of his guilt and of his own condemnation, so that there is no hope of his return.

Ver. 12. Invitation from the apostle to Titus to come to him at Nicopolis so soon as he had sent Artemas or Tychicus. Artemas is not mentioned elsewhere; regarding Tychicus, see 2 Tim. iv. 12. The object in sending them is not told. Had the apostle's purpose been that Artemas or Tychicus should continue the work begun by Titus, he would surely have given some hint of it, and not contented himself with the simple πρὸς σέ. It is more probable that the apostle wished to have Titus brought by one of them, as he could not yet determine the exact time when he was to come (Hofmann). Nicopolis is a name borne by several cities, one in Epirus, built by Augustus as a memorial of his victory at Actium; another built by Trajan in Thrace; and another in Cilicia. In the subscription of the epistle there stands: ἀπὸ Νικοπόλεως τῆς Μακεδονίας, which may mean either the city in Thrace or that in Epirus. It does not appear from his words that Paul wrote the epistle there; on the contrary, the ἐκεῖ rather shows that Paul himself was not there when he wrote the epistle. His purpose was to pass the winter there; comp. Introd. § 3.

Ver. 13. Ζηνᾶν τὸν νομικόν] Zenas is otherwise unknown. The epithet τὸν νομ. shows either that he had been formerly a Jew learned in the Scriptures, a γραμματεύς (Matt. xxii. 35, and other passages), or—as is more probable—that he was one skilled in law, a jurisconsultus (Strabo, 12, p. 539: ἐξηγηταὶ τῶν νόμων, καθάπερ οἱ παρὰ ʿΡωμαίοις νομικοί) — καὶ ʾΑπολλώ] He is known from Acts and 1 Corinthians; but it is not known when he went to Crete.[1] — σπουδαίως πρόπεμψον] "equip carefully for departure;" on προπέμπειν, comp. 3 John 6. Wiesinger translates σπουδαίως by "hastily," unsuitably, as the words ἵνα κ.τ λ. show. In σπουδαίως the prevailing conception is zeal; σπουδαίως ἔχειν is equivalent to "be zealous for a thing." Luther: "make ready with diligence." — ἵνα μηδὲν αὐτοῖς λείπῃ] Hofmann's opinion, that "this is an imperative sentence in itself," is all the more arbitrary that ἵνα manifestly refers to σπουδαίως; comp. besides what was said on 1 Tim. i. 3.

Ver. 14. Μανθανέτωσαν δὲ καὶ οἱ ἡμέτεροι] οἱ ἡμέτεροι are the Christian brethren in Crete, not, as Grotius thought, Zenas and Apollo. Καί stands with reference not merely to the Jews (Hofmann), but to non-Christians in general. As non-Christians provide for the needs of their own, so ought Christians, and not refrain through their anxiety for heavenly things. — καλῶν ἔργων προΐστασθαι] in the same general

---

[1] Hofmann suggests that Zenas and Apollo set out from the place where Paul was at the time of writing the epistle, in order to proceed by Crete to Alexandria, which was Apollo's native place, and that Paul gave them this epistle to Titus to serve them also as a letter of recommendation. These are mere conjectures, for which there is no foundation.

sense as in ver. 8, but the words following give the phrase a more special reference to works of benevolence; εἰς τὰς ἀναγκαίας χρείας, "*in regard to the necessary wants.*" — ἵνα μὴ ὦσιν ἄκαρποι] The subject is οἱ ἡμέτεροι. Hofmann construes the words εἰς τὰς ἀναγκαίας χρείας with the clause of purpose following them. He says that "the particle of purpose is placed after the emphatic part of the clause," a thing which *frequently* occurs in the N. T., and for this he appeals to Winer, p. 522 [E. T. p. 764]. In this he is entirely wrong. Such a construction seldom occurs, and of all the passages there quoted by Winer, that from 2 Cor. xii. 7 alone is to the point; the rest are of quite another kind. It is quite clear from what was said on ἵνα in 1 Tim. i. 3,[1] that such a construction is not to be admitted here. The exhortation in the passage does not refer simply to the present case of equipping Zenas and Apollo, which indeed occasioned it, but is in general terms, and is applicable to all cases where the necessary wants of others have to be considered (van Oosterzee).

Ver. 15. End. — ἀσπάζονταί σε οἱ μετ' ἐμοῦ πάντες] is not to be understood generally of believers, but of the apostle's fellow-workers. — ἄσπασαι τοὺς φιλοῦντας ἡμᾶς ἐν πίστει] φιλεῖν marks the inner, personal relation. The distinction between ἀγαπᾶν and φιλεῖν is plain from a comparison of John iii. 16, ἠγάπησεν ὁ Θεὸς τὸν κόσμον, with John xvi. 17, ὁ πατὴρ φιλεῖ ὑμᾶς; also Matt. x 37: Ἡμᾶς, *i.e.* the apostle. — Ἡ χάρις μετὰ πάντων ὑμῶν] "with you all," *i.e.* "with thee and all Cretan believers." The form of the benediction does not imply that Titus was to communicate the epistle to the churches in Crete.

[1] To say that with the common construction the clause of purpose is too general (Hofmann), is not to the point, since it can easily be defined from what precedes.

www.ingramcontent.com/pod-product-compliance
Lightning Source LLC
Chambersburg PA
CBHW061422300426
44114CB00014B/1491